# TOYO ITO
## 2002-2014

伊 東 豊 雄 の 建 築 ②

# Preface  Toyo Ito
## 序　伊東豊雄

「せんだいメディアテーク」が完成したころ、悪友たちから「お前もこれでやることがなくなったな」と言われた。ひとつの建築が誕生するには偶然の力が大きく働く。コンペティションに勝つことに始まって、良いクライアントや良い施工者に恵まれるなど、設計者の能力を超えたところで結果は良くも悪くもなる。だから悪友たちの言うとおり、これ以上の建築をつくる機会はもうないかもしれないと自分でも思っていた。

だが出来上がった「せんだい」自体が自分の背中を押してくれた。「こんなぶっ飛んだ建築でもみんな喜んでくれるんだよ」という励ましである。この励ましが「オレもやれるじゃん」という自信につながった。

ちょうどそんなころ、スペインやアジアの国からのオファーがきた。これらの国の人びとは、自らの夢を建築家に託してくれるように感じられた。だからわれわれのぶっ飛んだアイデアでも受け入れ、素直に喜んでくれた。その最たる例が「台中国立歌劇院」である。

3次元曲面の連続体から成るこのプロジェクトのアイデアは、ベルギーでの「ゲント市文化フォーラム・コンペティション応募案」で思いついたものである。建築の内部を縦横に貫くチューブ、というアイデアは「ゲント」では受け入れられなかったが、「台中」が受け入れてくれた。「ゲント」のコンペティションから数えれば

When I completed Sendai Mediatheque, good friends told me, "There is nothing left for you to do." Chance has a great deal to do with the creation of a building. In the case of Sendai, it began with winning the competition and being blessed with a good client and a good builder. Factors that are beyond the control of the architect determine the quality of a building, which is why I myself thought that, as my friends said, I might have no opportunities to improve on Sendai.

However, the completed Sendai project itself emboldened me. I was encouraged by the fact that even an unorthodox building such as that could give people delight. That encouragement gave me confidence.

It was at such a time that offers came from Spain and countries in Asia. People in those countries entrusted their dreams to the care of an architect. That was why they accepted and took sincere delight in our unorthodox ideas. The best example of that is National Taichung Theater.

The idea for this project--a continuous, three-dimensionally curved form--was originally conceived for a competition for Forum for Music, Dance and Visual Culture, Ghent, Belgium. Ghent did not accept the idea of tubes that penetrate the inside of a building vertically and horizontally, but Taichung did. It has taken 11 years since the Ghent competition and almost nine years in Taichung. Although we have experienced numerous setbacks in that time, the structure has at last been completed and the scaffolding on the outside removed to

11年、「台中」だけでも9年になろうとしている。この間何度も挫折を味わいながらも、ようやく構造体は完成し、外部の足場も外れて全貌が見え始めた。オープンの日も近いだろう。
「せんだい」がスタートした時には、この建築は果たして実現するだろうかという不安にとりつかれていたのだが、「台中」の難易度は「せんだい」より10倍くらい高いといってよいだろう。今度こそ、これ以上のチャレンジはないといえるかもしれない。
しかし、2011年は私にとって生涯忘れ難い年になった。「みんなの森 ぎふメディアコスモス」の実施が決まり、事務所創立40周年のパーティーを「座・高円寺」で行った直後に3.11東日本大震災が発生、時期を同じくして私塾がスタートし、夏には私自身の建築ミュージアムが瀬戸内海の大三島にオープンした。
被災地には現在も通いながら「みんなの家」をつくる活動を続けている。東北の被災地と大三島を訪れて現地の人びとと対話を繰り返しながら3年が過ぎた。そして私たちは、これまで都市にばかり目を向けて建築を考えていたことをいまさらのように痛感した。
経済優先ですべてが動く都市よりも過疎といわれている地域にこそ、生き生きと未来を見据えた人びとがいることに心を動かされた。日本の将来はこうした地域にこそあるのかもしれないと、いま思い始めている。

2014年8月1日

reveal it in its entirety. The opening is no doubt close at hand. When the Sendai project started, there were doubts that the building would ever be realized, but Taichung has been ten times more difficult. It can perhaps be said at last that there is truly no bigger challenge left.

However, 2011 was a year that I will never forget. Immediately after the implementation of the Minna no Mori Gifu Media Cosmos project was decided and a party marking the 40th anniversary of the office was held at ZA-KOENJI Public Theatre, the Great East Japan Earthquake struck. It was also around this time that ITO JUKU began and, in summer, an architectural museum of my work opened on Omishima, an island in the Inland Sea.

I continue activities to create "Home-for-All" while frequently visiting disaster-stricken areas even now. In the three years that have passed, I have been engaged in repeated talks with local people on visits to disaster-stricken areas in the Tohoku region and Omishima. I have been made painfully aware of how, up to now, we have focused almost exclusively on architecture in cities.

I have been deeply moved to discover that it is not in the cities where economics takes priority but in areas that suffer from depopulation that people look to the future with the greatest enthusiasm and energy. I have begun to believe that it is precisely on such areas that Japan's future will rest.

August 1, 2014

# Profile 略歴

**伊東豊雄（いとうとよお）**

1941年生まれ。65年東京大学工学部建築学科卒業。65〜69年菊竹清訓建築設計事務所勤務。71年アーバンロボット設立。79年伊東豊雄建築設計事務所に改称。主な作品に「シルバーハット」、「八代市立博物館」、「大館樹海ドーム」、「せんだいメディアテーク」、「多摩美術大学図書館（八王子キャパス）」、「2009高雄ワールドゲームズメインスタジアム」、「台湾大学社会科学部棟」など。現在、「みんなの森 ぎふメディアコスモス」、「台中国立歌劇院」などが進行中。日本建築学会賞作品賞、ヴェネチア・ビエンナーレ金獅子賞、王立英国建築家協会（RIBA）ロイヤルゴールドメダル、朝日賞、高松宮殿下記念世界文化賞、プリツカー建築賞など受賞。東日本大震災後、被災各地の復興活動に精力的に取り組んでおり、仮設住宅における住民の憩いの場として提案した「みんなの家」は、2014年9月までに11軒完成、現在も4件が進行中。その役割も、コミュニティの回復、子どもたちの遊び場、農業や漁業の再興を目指す人びとの拠点などに発展している。2011年に私塾「伊東建築塾」を設立。これからのまちや建築のあり方を考える場としてさまざまな活動を行っている。

## Toyo Ito: Architect

Born in 1941. Graduated from the Department of Architecture, Faculty of Engineering, University of Tokyo in 1965. Worked at Kikutake Architects from 1965 to 1969. Established his own office, Urbot, in 1971. In 1979, the office's name was changed to Toyo Ito & Associates, Architects. Ito's major works include Silver Hut, Yatsushiro Municipal Museum, Odate Jukai Dome, Sendai Mediatheque, Tama Art University Library (Hachioji campus), Main Stadium for the World Games 2009 in Kaohsiung, and National Taiwan University, College of Social Sciences. His current projects include Minna no Mori Gifu Media Cosmos (tentative title) and National Taichung Theater. He has received numerous awards including the Architecture Institute of Japan Award, Golden Lion at the Venice Biennale, Royal Gold Medal from the Royal Institute of British Architects, Asahi Prize, Praemium Imperiale in Honor of Prince Takamatsu, and the Pritzker Architecture Prize. After the Great East Japan Earthquake in 2011, Ito has been energetically dedicated to reconstruction activity in the stricken area. He initiated the "Home-for-All" project, a series of communal huts where victims of the disaster can gather and communicate with each other. As of September 2014, eleven of the huts were completed, and four more are currently underway. The project was developed to satisfy various purposes including revitalizing the community, providing children with a place to play, and serving as a base for those working to reactivate the agriculture and fishing industry. In 2011, Ito established a small private architectural school ITO JUKU (Initiative for Tomorrow's Opportunities in Architecture), which encourages participants to consider the future of cities and architecture.

# Contents 目次

002 序　伊東豊雄
Preface  Toyo Ito

006 略歴
Profile

010 「建築」の力
藤森照信×伊東豊雄
The Power of Architecture
Terunobu Fujimori and Toyo Ito

Collected Works 2002-2014

044 **6** 意匠と構造の融合
Integration of Design and Structure

045 伊東豊雄との対話　Conversation with Toyo Ito

054 ブルージュ・パヴィリオン
Brugge Pavilion ［2002］

062 サーペンタイン・ギャラリー・パヴィリオン 2002
Serpentine Gallery Pavilion 2002 ［2002］

072 まつもと市民芸術館
Matsumoto Performing Arts Centre ［2004］

092 TOD'S表参道ビル
TOD'S Omotesando Building ［2004］

102 福岡アイランドシティ中央公園中核施設
ぐりんぐりん
Island City Central Park
"GRIN GRIN" ［2005］

116 瞑想の森 市営斎場
Meiso no Mori
Municipal Funeral Hall ［2006］

128 **7** 分節と連続
Division and Continuity

129 伊東豊雄との対話　Conversation with Toyo Ito

140 多摩美術大学図書館（八王子キャンパス）
Tama Art University Library
(Hachioji campus) ［2007］

156 座・高円寺
ZA-KOENJI Public Theatre ［2008］

170 2009高雄ワールドゲームズ
メインスタジアム
The Main Stadium for the World Games 2009 in Kaohsiung ［2009］

184 トーレス・ポルタ・フィラ／
バルセロナ見本市グランビア会場拡張計画
TORRES PORTA FIRA ［2010］／
Extension for the Fair of Barcelona Gran Via Venue ［2003-］

200 今治市伊東豊雄建築ミュージアム
Toyo Ito Museum of Architecture, Imabari ［2011］

218 今治市岩田健母と子のミュージアム
Ken Iwata Mother and Child Museum,
Imabari City ［2011］

226 **8** 最新プロジェクト
Latest Projects

227 伊東豊雄との対話　Conversation with Toyo Ito

244 台湾大学社会科学部棟
National Taiwan University,
College of Social Sciences ［2013］

262 松山 台北文創ビル
Songshan Taipei New Horizon Building ［2013］

274 みんなの森 ぎふメディアコスモス（建設中）
Minna no Mori Gifu Media Cosmos
(under construction) (tentative title)

288 CapitaGreen（建設中）
CapitaGreen (under construction)

300 （仮称）川口市火葬施設・赤山歴史自然公園（計画中）
Crematorium and Akayama Historic Nature
Park in Kawaguchi (tentative title) (under development)

310 バロックミュージアム・プエブラ（計画中）
Barroco Museo Internacional (under development)

320 **9** みんなの家
Home-for-All

320 伊東豊雄との対話　Conversation with Toyo Ito

324 みんなの家
Home-for-All ［2011-］

338 **10** 台中国立歌劇院
National Taichung Theater

339 伊東豊雄との対話　Conversation with Toyo Ito

344 台中国立歌劇院（建設中）
National Taichung Theater
(under construction)

376 作品データ
Data on Works

383 伊東豊雄年表
Toyo Ito Chronology

390 スタッフリスト
Staff List

391 クレジット
Credits

1〜5は『伊東豊雄の建築1　1971–2001』に収録
1 to 5 are included in *Toyo Ito 1 (1971-2001)*

6〜10「伊東豊雄との対話」は現スタッフによる
伊東豊雄氏へのインタビュー
Conversation with Toyo Ito (6-10) is an interview
conducted by the current staff.

# 「建築」の力

## 藤森照信×伊東豊雄

### 構造に対する認識を変えたふたつのパヴィリオン——ブルージュ・パヴィリオン、サーペンタイン・ギャラリー・パヴィリオン2002

**藤森**── 1巻では「せんだいメディアテーク」(2001年)まで取り上げたので、きょうは「せんだい」以降について話をしていきたいと思います。「せんだい」以降、目覚めたこと、やってみようと思ったこと、あるいは新しいテーマとして明快になったものというと、どういうことになりますか。

**伊東**── ひとつは「構造」ですね。「せんだい」でスラブを薄くつくるために鉄板を使うことを佐々木睦朗さんが提案されて、ぜひやってみたいと思いました。あの工事は大変だろうなと思っていたのですが、あれを実現できたことで、さまざまな可能性があることに気がついた。鉄といっても、特に鉄板ですね。「せんだい」が初めてで、その後、「多摩美術大学図書館(八王子キャンパス)」(2007年)もコンクリートアーチの芯には鉄板が入っているし、「座・高円寺」(2008年)の外壁や屋根も鉄板とコンクリートの組み合わせですね。

**藤森**──「ブルージュ・パヴィリオン」(2002年)の小さなものとか「サーペンタイン・ギャラリー・パヴィリオン2002」(2002年)といったパヴィリオン系も、相当鉄を意識してやりました?

**伊東**── そうですね。「サーペンタイン」は鉄ですね。

**藤森**──「ブルージュ」も鉄?

**伊東**──「ブルージュ」はアルミで、新谷眞人さんに構造をみてもらいました。これはものすごくシンプルな、門型ラーメン構造ですが、大学の構造の授業で最初に習うのがこのラーメン構造です。門型の構造体でモーメントがコーナーと真ん中と足回りで大きくなると教えられるのですが、「ブルージュ」はそれを証明しているような構造体です。両サイドにアルミパネルを貼ったハニカムパネルを用意して、どこまで両サイドのパネルを剥いでいけるか……。

**藤森**── ハニカムだけでもつか。

**伊東**── そう。ハニカムだけでは弱いから、それを取り去っても、コーナーと足元と真ん中にアルミパネルを楕円形に残す、それが「ブルージュ」のデザインです。

**藤森**── なるほど。それは普通気づかないですね。これは伊東さんの好みの形でそうしたと思えてしまう。

**伊東**── これを僕らは2分の1のアルミのモデルで実験してみたんですよ。そうしたら両サイドのパネルがある時とない時では、まったく強度が違う。

**藤森**── 要するに製図板効果みたいなものですね。真ん中に弱いものがあって、両側に薄くて強いものを貼っている。モノコックなんですね。

**伊東**── その通りです。これはなかなか構造的に面白かったですよ。

**藤森**── 面白い。しかも初歩的構造ですね。「サーペンタイン」は?

**伊東**── これはセシル・バルモンドという構造家と一緒にやったものですが、彼は構造の合理性というよりは、正方形を回転させながら外接させていくアルゴリズムによって出来るパターンでこの構造体をつくるやり方ですね。だから、ランダムに見えるラインだけで構造体が出来上がってくるので、結構話題になりました。

面白かったのは、中に入ると、柱梁じゃないから、コーナーのラインが消えて、ドームの中にいるように見えるんですよ。

**藤森**── パースが複雑になって人間の目が追えず、その果てに囲まれているように見えるということですか。

**伊東**── そう、囲まれているような。だから、これは自分でもまったく予想していなかったのですが、箱の中にいるという感覚がなくなってしまう。

### 鉄板による新しい構造への挑戦

**藤森**── 構造で金属というのは、基本的にはラーメン構造に代表されるフレームですね。フレーム構造の鉄というのは、「せんだい」以前にもやっていました?

**伊東**──「八代市立博物館・未来の森ミュージアム」(1991年)(p.048)のあとの「八代広域消防本部庁舎」(1995年)は、かなり典型的なフレーム構造ですね。

**藤森**── 面として鉄というか金属を考えるようになったのは、「せんだい」以降?

**伊東**── そうですね。あそこで高橋工業という気仙沼の……

**藤森**── 石山修武さんが助けたり、泣かせたりしたところですね(笑)。

**伊東**── そうそう。あのおやじさんは、「せんだい」以降一躍有名

# The Power of Architecture

## Terunobu Fujimori and Toyo Ito

### Two Pavilions that Changed the Perception of Structure
[Brugge Pavilion, Serpentine Gallery Pavilion 2002]

**Fujimori** — Volume 1 dealt with your works up to and including Sendai Mediatheque (2001). Today, I'd like to turn to your works since then. What have you discovered or wanted to try, and what new themes have you taken up since Sendai Mediatheque?

**Ito** — One is structure. Mr. Mutsuro Sasaki proposed using steel plate in Sendai Mediatheque in order to make the slabs thinner, and I was all for using it. I thought that construction work would involve a lot of time and effort, but the fact that we were able to realize it made me see that it offered diverse possibilities. I'm talking particularly of steel plate. Sendai Mediatheque was the first time I used it. Since then, steel plate has been used in the core of the concrete arches in Tama Art University Library (Hachioji campus) (2007) and in combination with concrete for the exterior walls and roof of ZA-KOENJI Public Theatre (2008).

**Fujimori** — Did you design the pavilions you've done such as the small Brugge Pavilion (2002) and Serpentine Gallery Pavilion 2002 (2002) with steel uppermost in your mind?

**Ito** — Yes. Serpentine was steel.

**Fujimori** — Is Brugge steel as well?

**Ito** — Brugge is aluminum. Mr. Masato Araya was the structural designer. It is quite a simple rigid portal frame structure--the first thing one learns about in a structure course at university. One is taught that in a portal framed structure, the moment is greatest at the corners, the middle and the base of the supports, and Brugge was like a demonstration of that fact. Honeycomb panels faced with aluminum panels on both sides were provided, and the question was to what extent could the aluminum panels be removed…

**Fujimori** — And the structure still holds with just the honeycomb panels.

**Ito** — Yes. Honeycomb panels alone are weak, so aluminum panels in elliptical shapes were left at the corners, the base of the supports and the middle. That is the design of Brugge.

**Fujimori** — I see. That's not something one realizes ordinarily. One would suppose you used the forms you did for reasons of personal taste.

**Ito** — We experimented with a half-scale aluminum model. We found that the strength of the structure is entirely different when there are panels on both sides.

**Fujimori** — In short, the effect is the same as with a drawing board. The core is weak but faced on both sides with a strong material. It's a monocoque structure.

**Ito** — That's right. It was quite interesting structurally.

**Fujimori** — Interesting, and not only that, structurally rudimentary. What about Serpentine?

**Ito** — That was done together with the structural designer Mr. Cecil Balmond. He was interested, not so much in rationality of structure, as in creating a structure out of a pattern produced by an algorithm which circumscribed and rotated a square. The structure was much talked about because it was made up of lines that seem random.

What was interesting was that, inside, the corner lines disappeared because there were no columns and beams. It was like being inside a dome.

**Fujimori** — Do you mean the perspective becomes too complex for the human eye, and in the end the effect is one of being encircled?

**Ito** — Yes, like being encircled. It was totally unexpected, even for me. It didn't feel like being inside a box.

### The Challenge of Creating New Structures Using Steel Plate

**Fujimori** — Metal in structure usually means frame structures such as rigid-frame structures. Did you use steel in frame structures before Sendai Mediatheque?

**Ito** — Yatsushiro Fire Station (1995), which came after Yatsushiro Municipal Museum (1991) (p. 048), is a fairly typical frame structure.

**Fujimori** — Did you begin to consider steel, or rather metal, in planar form after Sendai Mediatheque?

**Ito** — Yes. There, a company called Takahashi Kogyo in Kesennuma…

**Fujimori** — Mr. Osamu Ishiyama from this company had both helped and shed tears for this project.

**Ito** — Yes. With Sendai Mediatheque, the man who heads the company suddenly became well-known, and other architects began to use steel plate as well. Since the Great East Japan Earthquake, he's worked really hard and been engaged in various

になって、他の建築家たちも鉄板を使うようになった。東日本大震災後はずいぶん頑張って、気仙沼でいろんな支援活動をやっていますね。

**藤森** —— 震災のあとすぐ、NHKの現地からのテレビで「再建します！」と宣言していましたね。

**伊東** —— そうそう、僕らもささやかな支援をしました。

**藤森** —— 「せんだい」以前で、金属の板の構造で誰か思い浮かぶ人はいますか。石山さんは幻庵からずっと金属の板をやっていますが、僕は石山さん以外に思い浮かばなくて……。

**伊東** —— どうでしょう。

**藤森** —— いないんですよね、少なくとも僕らが一般的に知っているような人では。世界的に見ても金属の板の構造って、僕が見たことがあるのは、エッフェルが鉄板の巨大な灯台をつくっている。これはフランスの植民地のニューカレドニアにあるアメデ島、"天国に一番近い島"といわれた所に、輸送の安全のためにつくったものですが、シェルだからすごくいいんですよ。ビス留めで。

日本では犬吠埼の灯台も、これは明治のものですが、霧笛を鳴らす小屋が、やっぱり鉄板なんです。だから、土木的世界では鉄板でというのはいくつかありますが、鉄板って暑さ寒さの問題があるから、そうめったに普通の建築では使えなくて……。

**伊東** —— そうですね。菊竹清訓さんが沖縄でつくった、浮かんでいるものがありますよ。

**藤森** —— でもあれは船ですよ。

**伊東** —— そう、まさしく船。そうでないと浮かないからね。

**藤森** —— 船は昔からありますからね。つまり、シェルとかいろんな構造は、僕らの世代より前の世代が全部やってしまっているんですよ。だから、われわれというか日本で言うと—— これは世界で言うのと同じだけれど、丹下健三・坪井善勝以降で新しい構造の表現って、石山、伊東の鉄板が最初になるんじゃないかな。

**伊東** —— うーん。

**藤森** —— 磯崎新さん、槇文彦さん、要するに丹下さんの弟子世代は、構造にそんなに力を入れなかった。むしろ造形のほうだったからね。

**伊東** —— そうだと思います。僕は「せんだい」で構造に目覚めましたから。それで構造でいろんなことができるなと思うようになった。

それと、ちょうど「せんだい」のころから、コンピューターのメモリー容量がべらぼうに大きくなったので、なんでもコンピューターで解析できるようになりましたね。どんなモデルを出しても、構造解析していけば、部分的に修正すればいけるということになってきた。それまでと構造解析がまったく違うやり方に

なったことが大きいですね。

だから「TOD'S表参道ビル」（2004年）もそうだし、それから「瞑想の森 市営斎場」（2006年）は典型的ですね。僕らが中のボリュームに合わせてモデルをつくると、構造家の佐々木さんがシミュレーションをかけていく。大体シミュレーションを60〜70回やるんですって。そうすると、何回やってもほぼ同じところに落ち着く。だから、こういうモデルだったらこの辺が一番バランスがいいだろうというところで決まる。

**藤森** —— コンピューターの計算力のおかげですね。

## 構造を忘れさせたポストモダン

**藤森** —— もうひとつ、ポストモダンが完全に構造を忘れさせたでしょう。

**伊東** —— そうですね。

**藤森** —— あれはもう、本当に構造と関係ない、珍しい形をやれ、みたいな時代でしたからね。

**伊東** —— 表層の。

**藤森** —— それもボリュームとサーフェイスという時の表層じゃなくて、悪く言うと、その辺の看板と同じレベルで……。

**伊東** —— そうですね。

**藤森** —— でも、幸いなことは、僕らの世代はああいうポストモダンをやらなかったでしょう。もうちょっと上の人たちですよ。磯崎さんぐらいから相田武文さんくらいでしょう。

**伊東** —— 僕もちょっとハマリかけたけどね（笑）。

**藤森** —— どれで？

**伊東** —— 「中央林間の家」（1979年）は一番それに近いかもしれない。切り妻の屋根で、ファサードは目地を装飾的にしたりしているから……。

**藤森** —— そう？　僕は頭に入っていないですね。

**伊東** —— それぐらいでいいんですよ（爆笑）。その時、「Dom-ino」という真四角な家を同時にやっていて、それが「シルバーハット」（1984年）に変わっていくので、「中央林間」でポストモダンに行きかけて、もうそれで終わり。

大江宏さんは、「中央林間」に結構興味をもったんですよ。

**藤森** —— われわれの兄貴の先生世代では、大江さんだけですよ。大江さんは角館[1]で民家を加えたりしていますが、丹下さんは「ポストモダンに出口はない」[2]と全面否定している。結局、丹下さんの言う通りでしたけどね。

**伊東** —— 確かに。

**藤森** —— でも、ポストモダンを何で僕らの世代は回避したんだろう。石山さんもそうだし、伊東さんもそうだし、山本理顕さんも

support activities in Kesennuma.

**Fujimori** — Immediately after the disaster, he declared on an NHK television broadcast from the area, "We will rebuild!"

**Ito** — Yes. We provided a bit of support for that as well.

**Fujimori** — Can you think of anyone who used metal plates structurally before Sendai Mediatheque? Mr. Ishiyama has used metal panels ever since GEN AN, but I can't think of anyone else…

**Ito** — I wonder.

**Fujimori** — There isn't anyone. At least not anyone we are all familiar with. Even if we look outside Japan, the only example of metal plate structure I've seen is an enormous lighthouse of steel plates by Eiffel. It's on Amédée Island--the so-called "island closest to Heaven" in the French colony of New Caledonia that was constructed to assure safety of transportation. It's a wonderful shell structure that's bolted together.

In Japan, the structure housing the foghorn at a lighthouse in Inubosaki is also made of steel plates, though it dates from the Meiji period. So there are a number of public projects with steel-plate structures. However, the problem of hot and cold one has to deal with when using steel plates makes it difficult to use in ordinary buildings…

**Ito** — Yes. There's also the floating structure that Mr. Kiyonori Kikutake designed in Okinawa.

**Fujimori** — But that's a ship.

**Ito** — Yes, exactly. It wouldn't float otherwise.

**Fujimori** — Ships of course have a long history. That is, the generation before ours had already done shells and various other structures. Thus, for us or Japan-though this is also true for the world as a whole-the work Mr. Ishiyama and you have done with steel plate may represent the first new expression of structure since the work of Kenzo Tange and Yoshikatsu Tsuboi.

**Ito** — Hmm.

**Fujimori** — Mr. Arata Isozaki and Mr. Fumihiko Maki, that is, the generation of architects who were disciples of Tange, didn't put all that much effort into structure. Instead, they were more focused on design.

**Ito** — I think that's correct. I became aware of "structure" with Sendai. And I began to feel that diverse things could be done with "structure."

In addition, the memory capacity of computers became huge right around the time of Sendai, making it possible to computer analyze anything. One could produce any sort of model; with structural analysis, it could be made to work with partial corrections. The fact that structural analysis became entirely different in approach was a major factor.

That was also true with TOD'S Omotesando Building (2004), and "Meiso no Mori" Municipal Funeral Hall (2006) is a representative example. We created a model corresponding to the interior volume, and the structural designer Mr. Sasaki ran simulations. Generally, simulations are run 60 to 70 times. No matter how many more simulations are run beyond that, the result is pretty much the same. We decided on a model that would produce the most balanced solution.

**Fujimori** — So it was thanks to the computing capacity of computers.

## Neglect of Structure Induced by Postmodern Architecture

**Fujimori** — One other thing. Postmodern architecture made architects forget completely about structure.

**Ito** — Yes.

**Fujimori** — It was truly a time of preoccupation with unusual forms that had nothing to do with structure.

**Ito** — An interest in surfaces.

**Fujimori** — And it wasn't even an interest in surfaces in the sense of volumes and surfaces. The works were no better than billboards…

**Ito** — Yes.

**Fujimori** — Fortunately, our generation didn't practice that sort of postmodern architecture. It was people slightly older than us, from around Mr. Takefumi Aida to Mr. Isozaki.

**Ito** — I nearly fell into that trap myself (laughs).

**Fujimori** — With what work?

**Ito** — House in Chuorinkan (1979) may have been the closest I came. I gave it a gabled roof and used the joints on the facade in an ornamental way…

**Fujimori** — Really? I missed that.

**Ito** — I'm glad you did (burst of laughter). I was doing a square house called Dom-ino at the same time, and that evolved into Silver Hut (1984). So, Chuorinkan was my only work that is at all like postmodern architecture.

Mr. Hiroshi Ohe was rather interested in Chuorinkan.

**Fujimori** — Of the generation of architects who taught us, it was only Ohe who did postmodern work. He did a house in Kakunodate[1]. Tange rejected the movement completely, declaring that "Postmodernism is a dead end."[2] It was ultimately just that.

**Ito** — That's for certain.

**Fujimori** — But how did our generation manage to avoid postmodern architecture? Mr. Ishiyama managed to avoid it, as did you, and Mr. Riken Yamamoto. Our generation on the whole did avoid it.

013

そうだし、僕らの世代は大体回避したでしょう。

**伊東** ── 基本的に僕らは「歴史」をちゃんと身に付けていなかったからでしょうかね。僕らの後の世代はずいぶん違うと思う。

**藤森** ──「歴史」の問題なんだ！　上の世代は、当然ながら磯崎さんたちは歴史を結構ちゃんと身に付けていますね。自分の造形的教養の、丹下さん世代からずっと流れてくるものを身に付けている。

**伊東** ── 隈研吾さんたちと僕らの違いは、それが結構あると思いますね。

**藤森** ── 面白い問題ですね。隈さんは説明する時に歴史の話が出る。歴史を踏まえた能舞台を若いうちからやっている。歴史の話をすると誰も文句を言えないというか、わりと素直に納得してくれるんですね。つまり、普通の施主に対して、現代建築って説明不能で、ほとんど物理学に近い。自分たちはここのこういうテーマでやっていると言っても、普通の人はついてこられないけれど、歴史を使うと伝わりやすい。

**伊東** ── 僕らの世代は、一番そこに目がいっていないですね。

**藤森** ── そう。僕だって、歴史の引用をしていると言われるとものすごく嫌だから、絶対茶室で畳と障子は使わない。

**伊東** ── いやあ、藤森さんが障子と畳を使っていないというのは、意外な気がしますね。みんな藤森さんは当たり前のように使っているように思い込んでいるけれど、そう言えばそうですね。

**藤森** ── というのは、歴史の引用の一番の問題は、見た人の理解がそこで停止するんですよ。たとえ、それまで考えられたことのないような茶室をつくったとしても、畳と障子があると、世界の人が見ると「ああ、日本」となって、そこで終わり。

**伊東** ── それは面白い話だなあ。僕は全然意識していなかったですね。

**藤森** ── 危ないのは畳と障子。竹も危ないんです。だから竹も使わない。竹を使う時は、茶室や数寄屋的でない形で使っています。台湾の巨大な竹とか。

　これには歴史的経験もあって、戦前にそういうことが起きたのは、ブルーノ・タウトなんです。タウトが建築と工芸に竹を使うでしょう。そうすると日本の当時の若い建築家や工業デザイナーは本当に嫌になる。シャルロット・ペリアンも竹を使う。剣持勇さんとかタウトの下にいた人は、「自分たちはモダンの先端を学びたいと思っているのに、何だこれは？」となってしまう。

**伊東** ── そうですね。

**藤森** ── 僕は歴史家だから、伊東さん以上にそこは敏感なわけですよ。

**伊東** ── それはそうですね。

**藤森** ── ポストモダンが危なかったのも、例えばポストモダン的にギリシアの柱を立てたとすると、大勢の人が立てましたが、「ああ、ギリシアの柱だな」とか「ヨーロッパだな」ということで、そこで止まってしまう。ポストモダンにはその危険を感じましたね。

　僕は、いままで隈さんのことは「歴史意識」の問題としてはとらえていなかったですね。

**伊東** ── 隈さんたちがつくり始めたころ、すでにこの世代は歴史に対する抵抗感が全然ないんだなと思っていましたね。僕らはそのころ、歴史を引用するなんていうのは、絶対嫌だと思っていたから。

**藤森** ── 倫理的に許せない（笑）。

**伊東** ── そう。石井和紘さんは変なことをいっぱいやっていましたが、あのぐらいコミカルにやれば別ですけどね。

**藤森** ── あそこまでやればね。石井さんのポストモダンの中でも格別だと思ったのは、唐破風を使った[3]でしょう。あの時代に、磯崎さんはつくばでギリシャ・ローマの引用をやっていますが[4]、唐破風とか鳥居はやらない。どれくらい危険かわかっているから。磯崎さんは賢いんですよ。だけど石井さんは唐破風を使ったからね。石井さんのデザインは変わってるけど、天才的な変さですよ。

**伊東** ── そうですね。ポストモダンという意味を一番ちゃんとやっていたかもしれない。

**藤森** ── ポストモダンの原理主義者で、やってはいけないところまでやったんですよ。われわれの世代は歴史と完全に切れていた。最も極端に切れていたのが石井さんで、歴史を完全に笑い飛ばすような使い方をした。

　僕は、歴史の影響を受けるのも嫌だけど、バカにすることは絶対できないからね。

**伊東** ── それはそうだな。

**藤森** ── 職業柄できない。自分の飯の種ですからね。石山さんだって、彼も歴史の研究室を出てますから、絶対にあそこまではやらないでしょう。

## 逆転の発想から生まれたプラン
### ──「まつもと市民芸術館」

**藤森** ──「まつもと市民芸術館」（2004年）は、まず、とても劇場には使えないはずの敷地をよくあそこまで……。特に邪魔もののフライタワーを正面側にもってきたのは、すごいと思いました。世界で最初でしょう。

**伊東** ── いままでの設計で、あれが一番難しい設計だったと思います。

**藤森** ── プランニングが難しいと、全部が難しくなりますからね。

**Ito** — Maybe it was because basically we hadn't learned history properly. The generation that came after us is, I think, quite different.

**Fujimori** — It's a problem of history! The older generation, people such as Mr. Isozaki of course, have a proper grasp of history. Since Mr. Tange's generation, knowledge of history has been a part of design education.

**Ito** — I think that is partly what makes us different from Mr. Kengo Kuma's generation.

**Fujimori** — It's an intriguing question. History comes up in Mr. Kuma's explanations of his works. When he was still young, he produced a design for a Noh stage that has its basis in history. When he talks about history, no one can raise any objections; he's rather persuasive. That is, contemporary architecture is impossible to explain to lay persons; it's practically like physics. Ordinary people aren't able to follow an architect's explanation of themes he or she is pursuing, but history is easy to communicate.

**Ito** — That's the area our generation has neglected the most.

**Fujimori** — Yes. I don't like being told that I'm using historical allusions either, so I make it a point to never use *tatami* or *shoji* in my tea houses.

**Ito** — It comes as something of a shock to hear you say that you don't use *shoji* or *tatami*. Everyone's under the impression that you use them as a matter of course, but now that I think about it, you don't.

**Fujimori** — The biggest problem with referencing history is that it stops people from seeking any further understanding. Even if I designed a tea house that no one had thought of before, if it were to have *tatami* and *shoji*, then people in the rest of the world will say, "Ah, Japan," and that will be that.

**Ito** — That's interesting. I wasn't conscious of that problem at all.

**Fujimori** — *Tatami* and *shoji* are dangerous. So is bamboo. That's why I don't use bamboo either, or if I do, I use it in a form that is not typical of tea houses or the *sukiya* style. For instance, I may use enormous bamboo from Taiwan. Unless I do that, people really do cease to think about the design.

There is historical precedent for that. Before World War II, that sort of thing happened with Bruno Taut. He used bamboo in buildings and craftwork. Young Japanese architects and industrial designers of the time really disliked that. Charlotte Perriand used bamboo as well. People such as Mr. Isamu Kenmochi who had chosen to study under Taut because they wanted to learn leading-edge modern design were perplexed.

**Ito** — Yes.

**Fujimori** — Being a historian, I'm more sensitive to that than you are.

**Ito** — That stands to reason.

**Fujimori** — What was dangerous about postmodern architecture was…if, for example, someone uses Greek columns in a postmodern way--and many people did--an observer would think, "Ah, Greek columns" or "This is Europe," and cogitate no further. That was the danger I sensed with postmodern architecture.

Up to now, I'd never considered Mr. Kuma in the context of the problem of historical awareness.

**Ito** — When Mr. Kuma and others began their practices, I realized that their generation had no misgivings at all regarding history. We ourselves were absolutely against referencing history.

**Fujimori** — We thought it was ethically unforgivable (laughs).

**Ito** — Mr. Kazuhiro Ishii was doing lots of strange things of course, but when they're done that comically, it's a different story.

**Fujimori** — When done to that extent, yes. I thought that, among Mr. Ishii's postmodern works, the one in which he used the undulating gable known as *karahafu*[3] was exceptional. At the time, Mr. Isozaki referenced Greek and Roman architecture at Tsukuba[4] but never used *karahafu* or *torii*. That's because he knew how dangerous that would be. Mr. Isozaki is clever. But Mr. Ishii used *karahafu*. Mr. Ishii's designs are a bit eccentric, but his is the eccentricity of genius.

**Ito** — Yes. He may have adhered more closely to the idea of postmodernism than anyone else.

**Fujimori** — He was a postmodern fundamentalist and went to extremes. Our generation had cut itself off completely from history. In a sense, Mr. Ishii cut himself off most completely. It was as if he were laughing at history.

I don't like being influenced by history, but I would never make fun of it either.

**Ito** — No, of course.

**Fujimori** — It wouldn't square with my professional temperament. History is how I've made my living. Mr. Ishiyama also has a university background in history, so I doubt he'd ever go that far either.

## A Plan Generated through Reversal [Matsumoto Performing Arts Centre]

**Fujimori** — First of all, it's a wonder that you managed to fit Matsumoto Performing Arts Centre (2004) on such a small site… I was particularly impressed that the flytower, which is always a nuisance, was located more toward the front of the building. That's the first time I've seen it done anywhere in the world.

**伊東** ── あの敷地の中にあれだけのボリュームを入れるのは、本当に大変でしたね。両サイドから斜線がかかっているし、アルプスの水が流れているから、絶対地下はだめだと言われていたし……。

**藤森** ── 地下もダメだったんだ。おそらく浮いてしまう。

**伊東** ── そう、1mも掘るとビュッと水が溢れ出てくる。

**藤森** ── それは写真を見ていても気づかないですね。普通は駐車場から機械まで、地下に収める。言われないとわからない。

**伊東** ── それで、地下をつくった人もコンペではいたような気がしますが、地下は絶対無理だと思っていた。

**藤森** ── 劇場に裏から入って、フライタワーを正面側にもってくるプランは、やっているうちに……？

**伊東** ── それは賭けだったんですよ。コンペでこんなことをやるのはどうせ僕らだけだろうと思っていましたから、このプランが拒否されたら最初に落ちるだろう。でも、もしこれが評価されたら、絶対これで勝つという、イチかバチかだった。

　なぜこういうことをやったかというと、この敷地でオーソドックスにいくとすると、敷地の一番奥（裏側）にご神木があるんですよ。

**藤森** ── 神社のご神木？

**伊東** ── "ご神木"と周りの人が呼んでいる、大きな木が何本もあるし、民家もある。そこに搬入口をもっていくと、大きいトラックが出入りするからその木をどうしても切らなきゃならないし、民家からはすごく嫌われる。そこで、客席とステージを逆転させ、フライタワーを中央部に置くと木も残せるし、民家への圧迫感も小さくなると。普通オペラ劇場はT型に4面ステージをつくらなくてはいけないでしょう。

**藤森** ── そう、3方向にバックをとらないといけない。

**伊東** ── それがどうしてもとれない。ところが、実施案のように片側に寄せた田の字型にしたら4面とれるので、調べてみたら同じものがドイツにひとつあったんですよ。

　それで、オペラの専門家に聞いてもらったら、それはあり得ると。いけますよという返事をもらったので、じゃあこれだ！　と思ってやりました。坂本一成さんが審査員で、すごく評価してくれた。

　ただ、市長は、「松本はお城だから、石積みと木だ」と言っていたので、これを見て唖然としたらしいですね（笑）。

**藤森** ── この敷地で石積みと木だったら、公園をつくるしかないね（笑）。

　そういう時の検討は自分で紙の上でいろいろやるんですか。

**伊東** ── 僕もやるし、大体チームでやっていますね。

　4〜5人のチームでアイデア出しをやって、みんながこれが一番面白いということになりました。

**藤森** ── 僕らの世代では、伊東さんはフリーハンドの曲線が美しく描ける、ほとんど唯一の人だと思っているんですよ。本人はそう思っていないようですが（笑）、この曲線を描く才能は、これまで「まつもと」のような変な敷地で発揮されたことがないでしょう。普通もう少し広々とした所できれいな線を描いている。一番わかりやすいのは「八代博物館」ですが、もし「まつもと」をきれいな線を描けない人が描いたら、絶望的な形になると思います。

**伊東** ── でもまあ、自分ではちょっとこの外形はあまりうまくいかなかったなと思っているのですよ。大体ほかのプロジェクトではみんなカーブを使う時に、断片で終わっている。ぐるぐるっと連続してしまうことはないわけですよ。

**藤森** ── 直線上に着地すると。

**伊東** ── そう。「下諏訪町立諏訪湖博物館・赤彦記念館」（1993年）でもそうなっている。切れた曲線の方がエレガントだと思っているんですが、「まつもと」ではとにかく閉じざるを得ないから、つながってしまいました。

**藤森** ── ナメクジ化してしまう（笑）。それは嫌なの？

**伊東** ── やっぱり後で、もうちょっとなんとかなったかなあ……という気はしていますね。この時は敷地に余裕がなくて自由に描ける状況になかったので、つなぎ合わせ、つなぎ合わせて……。

**藤森** ── でも、これは曲線以外では絶望的なことになりましたよ。

**伊東** ── そうかもしれない。

**藤森** ── まず、入って左手の敷地の大段差をどうやって乗り越えるかという問題があった。しかし入っていくと、曲線の力で平面の段差にぶつからずにすっと滑り込んじゃうんですよね。

**伊東** ── そう、その辺は良かったと思っていますね。

**藤森** ── もうひとつ思ったのは、オペラ座はじめネオ・バロック期の古典的舞台の力ですね。劇場の中を古典的なままやると昔の真似に過ぎないけど、そうならなかったのは色の力。見る前から「中はどうするんだろう。突然オペラ座が出てくるのもナンだなあ」と思っていたんですが、このグラデーションの色、これが効いていますね。

　おまけに、それも紫色という一歩間違うと危ない色ですよ（笑）。僕が伊東さんはとんでもない色を使う人だと思ったのは、前にも話したように「下諏訪」をご案内いただいた時ですが、やっぱり色も曲線と同じで、やれる人とやれない人がいるんですよ。

**伊東** ── グラデーションというのがすごく好きなんですよ。これは身体化されているかもしれない。何かものが溶けていくとか、だんだん位相が変わっていくとか、そういう緩やかな変化が好きですね。パシッと変わるのじゃなくて。

**Ito** — I think that was the most difficult design I've ever done.

**Fujimori** — If the planning is difficult, everything becomes difficult.

**Ito** — It was really hard work fitting that much volume onto the site. There was a need for a setback on both sides, plus we were told that putting things underground was out of the question because water from the Japanese Alps was flowing there…

**Fujimori** — So you couldn't use even the underground portion of the site. The whole thing would have probably floated if you had.

**Ito** — Yes. One only needs to dig a meter below ground level, and water will well up.

**Fujimori** — One doesn't realize that looking at photographs. Ordinarily, everything from the parking to the machine room is accommodated underground. It's not something one would be aware of unless one were told.

**Ito** — There might have been some participants in the competition who used the underground portion, but I thought doing that would be out of the question.

**Fujimori** — How did you arrive at the idea of entering from the back and locating the flytower toward the front?

**Ito** — It was a gamble. We were fairly certain we would be the only ones in the competition to do something like that. If such a plan was rejected, we would be the first to be eliminated from consideration. But we were confident we would win if the jurors saw the virtue of the plan. It was all or nothing.

The reason we did it like this is that, if we had done it in an orthodox fashion on this site…there are sacred trees at the far end (that is, the back) of the site.

**Fujimori** — The sacred trees of a shrine?

**Ito** — There are several large trees that people in the area refer to as "sacred trees." There are houses there as well. If we located the delivery entrance there, we'd have to cut down those trees to make way for the large trucks going in and out, and residents in those houses would also hate the disturbance. But If we flipped the auditorium and the stage and located the flytower in the middle, we'd be able to preserve the trees and make the building less out of scale with the houses. Ordinarily, with an opera house, one needs to create, in addition to the main stage, a stage to the rear and two stages on the sides, all arranged in a T-shape in plan.

**Fujimori** — Yes. One needs to have auxiliary stages in three directions.

**Ito** — We couldn't fit them in, as hard as we tried. But then we found out that we could fit in four stages if we arranged them into a quadripartite square in plan, the scheme that was eventually adopted. When we investigated, we found a precedent for it in Germany.

An opera expert we consulted said that the arrangement was possible. We thought, this is it. Mr. Kazunari Sakamoto was on the jury and thought quite highly of it.

The only thing is, the mayor had been saying that since Matsumoto is famous for its castle, the centre should be built with wood and stonework. He was apparently dumbfounded when he saw the scheme (laughs).

**Fujimori** — The only way to make use of stonework and wood on this site would be to turn it into a park (laughs).

When there are ideas to be studied, do you do that yourself on paper?

**Ito** — I do it too, but it's generally done by the team.

A team of four or five people came up with ideas, and everyone agreed this was the most interesting one.

**Fujimori** — I think you are practically the only member of our generation that is able to draw beautiful curves freehand. You do have this ability, though you may not think of it as such (laughs), but I don't suppose you've ever had an opportunity to demonstrate it on a site quite as oddly shaped as the one for Matsumoto. You usually draw beautiful lines when you have more space to work with. The most obvious example is Yatsushiro Municipal Museum. If someone who couldn't draw lines beautifully had drawn the plan for Matsumoto, if would probably have been a disaster.

**Ito** — But I myself don't feel the exterior form was entirely successful. Curves used on other projects are generally fragmentary. They aren't meandering, continuous curves.

**Fujimori** — The curve usually comes to rest against a straight line.

**Ito** — Yes. That's what happens in Shimosuwa Municipal Museum (1993) as well. I think a fragmentary curved line is more elegant. With Matsumoto, we had no choice but to close off the form, so we ended up with a continuous curved line.

**Fujimori** — It becomes slug-like in shape (laughs). You don't like that?

**Ito** — I look back on the project and wonder if I couldn't have done something about it. There was no space to spare on the site, so I wasn't able to draw as I wished. It was a matter of cutting and pasting together, cutting and pasting together…

**Fujimori** — But it would have been a hopeless mess had you used anything other than curves.

**Ito** — You may be right.

**Fujimori** — First, there was the problem of how to overcome the great difference in level on the left side of the site, but thanks to the power of the curve, one slides in without colliding into the difference in level in plan.

だから、中でも壁を立てないでできるだけ連続して、光の状況で変えていく。今日、見ていただいた「台中国立歌劇院」（建設中）もそうですね。「まつもと」のホールでも、舞台側はできるだけ黒いほうが集中できるし、客席の奥へいくほどに明るくなっていくと、舞台から役者が空間を見渡した時、華やかな感じになっている。そういうことでグラデーションをつくりたかったんですね。

一番最初に「長岡リリックホール」（1996年）をやった時も、コンサートホールのほうは下から上にいくにしたがってグラデーションで淡くなっていくようなことをやっていました。だから、「まつもと」でもそれをぜひやりたいなと思っていましたね。

## 身体化された言語が生み出す造形

**藤森** ─ 建築における身体化したものって、訓練では身体化しないんですよ。気づいた時にはもう遅いというか、直しようのないものですよ。子どものころ、育つ過程で水みたいに溜ってしまっている。伊東さんの場合、どの辺からきていると思いますか。

**伊東** ─ 何からきているのかねえ。自分でよく言っているのは、「言語」じゃないかなと思いますね。言語感覚。僕は大体曖昧にしか話せないんですよ。歯切れも悪いし、藤森さんみたいに流暢にいかないでしょう（笑）。ずるずるっとして、どこかで途切れて「かもしれないなあ……」みたいな感じ。そういうのが好きなんですよ。

**藤森** ─ そのわりに、キツイことを言うけどねえ（笑）。本人の目の前でこんなことを言っちゃいけないんじゃないかということを言ってきましたよ（笑）。

**伊東** ─ いやあ、それはボキャブラリーが少ないからですよ。昔、篠原一男さんが「英語でしゃべると、自分はボキャブラリーが少ないから、強い表現になってしまう」と言っていましたね。それと同じで、ぼかしながら言うのがうまくできないから、つい強い言葉になって、その後「かもしれないなあ……」みたいなことでごまかしておこうと思うんですよね。

**藤森** ─ なるほど。「言葉」ね。

**伊東** ─ 言葉というのは、僕は自分の空間感覚に効いているような気がする。だから、音楽を聴いていても、ドビュッシーのような、ああいう東洋的というか、ホワーッと消えていくのが好きですね。

**藤森** ─ にじんで、消えていくような。

**伊東** ─ そう、水墨画みたいな音楽ですね。

**藤森** ─ なるほど。その反動として、ちゃんとにじませる場がないような時は、一気にごろんと強い言葉が出てくると（笑）。

**伊東** ─ そういう曖昧な空間をつくっていると、もう少し明快なものをやりたくなって、やってみるんですよ。そうすると、すぐ「やっぱり合わないなあ」と思って、また元に戻る。その繰り返しですね。

**藤森** ─ バシッとやりたくなる時もありますか。

**伊東** ─ ある、ある。さっきの「ブルージュ」と「サーペンタイン」を比べても、「ブルージュ」のほうが僕の感性には合っているんですよ。ふわっとした感じが。

**藤森** ─ なるほど。「サーペンタイン」のバシッというのよりは。

**伊東** ─ そう。セシル・バルモンドと組んでやるのと新谷さんと組んでやるのでは、やっぱり向こうの人と組んだ時には、何か違うなあというのはありますね。

**藤森** ─ ヨーロッパの言葉ぐらい、輪郭の明瞭な言葉はないですからね。

**伊東** ─ そうですね。

**藤森** ─ ヨーロッパの建築がああいう明快なものになって、いつも曖昧さを残すことを嫌ったのは、ギリシャ以来の言葉の問題かもしれない。

**伊東** ─ それはあると思いますよ。

**藤森** ─ まず、言葉を使って感じを表現し、次に言葉による論理が出てくる。論理学によって裏付けされて、曖昧なことは許さないからね。曖昧なことは、頭が悪いというふうに思われるだけですから（笑）。

**伊東** ─ そう。だから、僕も英語が下手だから、アメリカなんかでレクチャーする時に、瀧口範子さんが通訳してくれて、僕が「こうかもしれないなあ……」みたいなニュアンスで言っていることがバシッと断定されると、一方で「これは違うんだけどぁ……」と思う半面（笑）、「よくぞ言ってくれた。この人はすごいなあ」みたいな気持ちになりますね。

日本語って、やっぱり曖昧ですよね。曖昧に、曖昧にするように仕向けていくから……。

**藤森** ─ そうですね。それと話し言葉に主語がないから、分かったような分からないうちに話がどんどん次にいく感じですね。

**伊東** ─ そうですね。それが身体化されている。

**藤森** ─ もしかしたら中国の建築があんなに固いのは、漢字のせいなのかなあ。

**伊東** ─ あると思いますよ、それは。日本には「かな」があったというのは大きいでしょうね。

**藤森** ─ そうですね。僕が台湾に初めて来た時にびっくりしたのは、子どもが読んでいる漫画は、吹き出しが全部昔の正式な漢字なんですよ（笑）。漢字しかないから当たり前なんだけどね。

確かに、人間がまず最初に意志的に覚えさせられるのって、形じゃないですね。親から最初に学ばされるのは文字なんですよ。

**Ito** — Yes, that part came out well, I thought.

**Fujimori** — One other thing that occurred to me was the power of classical stages from the Baroque Revival period such as the Opéra in Paris. If one designs the inside of the theater in the classical manner, it is nothing more than imitation. What makes this different was the power of color. Even before I saw it, I wondered how you would do the inside. It would have been questionable if, all of a sudden, the Opéra appeared. The gradation of color you used is effective.

Not only that, it is in purple, which is a quite tricky color (laughs). As I've already said, It was my visit to Shimosuwa that convinced me that you are someone who uses surprising colors. It's the same with colors as with curved lines-there are those who are able to use them and those who aren't.

**Ito** — I very much like gradations. It may be ingrained. I like gradual changes such as things dissolving or going through a change of phase, little by little, instead of abrupt changes.

That is also why, inside, I prefer to make spaces continuous and change in the condition of light instead of putting up walls. The same is true of National Taichung Theater (under construction) which you saw today. In the hall at Matsumoto, the stage side is made as black as possible to facilitate concentration, and it becomes lighter, the further one goes toward the far end of the seats. When an actor looks out over the space from the stage, there is a sense of splendor. I wanted to create gradations through such effects.

Even when I first designed Nagaoka Lyric Hall (1996), I made the concert hall gradually more pale from the bottom to the top. That is why I wanted to do that in Matsumoto as well.

## Design Generated by Ingrained Language

**Fujimori** — A thing in architecture that becomes ingrained doesn't become ingrained through training. By the time one realizes that it has become a part of oneself, it is too late; there's no way of correcting it. It collects like water during one's childhood development. Where do you think it comes from in your case?

**Ito** — I wonder. I often attribute it to language, to linguistic sensibility. On the whole I can speak only ambiguously. I am vague; I can't speak fluently like you (laughs). I equivocate and use words such as "maybe." I like things that are equivocal.

**Fujimori** — For someone who likes to equivocate, you have a sharp tongue (laughs). You've said things that oughtn't to be said in the presence of the person in question (laughs).

**Ito** — That is because my vocabulary is limited. Mr. Kazuo Shinohara once said, "When I speak in English, I become harsher because of my limited vocabulary." It's the same for me. I speak forcefully because I'm not skilled at being evasive. That's why I try to soften the impact by adding "maybe."

**Fujimori** — I see. Language.

**Ito** — I feel that language has an effect on my own spatial sensibility. That's also why, when I'm listening to music, I like pieces such as works by Debussy--works that might be considered Oriental in character-that fade away light as air.

**Fujimori** — That becomes blurred and fade away.

**Ito** — Yes, music that is like an ink wash painting.

**Fujimori** — I see. And as an occasional reaction to that, when there is no opportunity to obfuscate, you blurt out forceful comments (laughs).

**Ito** — When I am creating ambiguous spaces like these, I am sometimes seized by a desire to be slightly more clear-cut and act accordingly. But when I do, I immediately realize I am not comfortable with it and go back to what I've been doing. This process of action and reaction is repeated time and again.

**Fujimori** — There are times when you want to be unambiguous?

**Ito** — Oh, yes. Of the two pavilions mentioned earlier, Brugge and Serpentine, the former suits my sensibility more. It has a buoyant quality.

**Fujimori** — I see. More so than the sharp-edged Serpentine.

**Ito** — Yes. Working with someone from outside Japan such as Mr. Cecil Balmond is somehow different from working with a fellow Japanese like Mr. Masato Araya.

**Fujimori** — European languages are very clear-cut.

**Ito** — Yes.

**Fujimori** — The reason European architecture became so lucid, the reason any ambiguity is abhorred, may be a question of language since the Greeks.

**Ito** — That probably is a factor.

**Fujimori** — First, language is used to express feelings; next, language produces logic. Logic is used to substantiate; it does not permit ambiguity. Ambiguity is dismissed as merely faulty thinking (laughs).

**Ito** — Yes. When I lecture in the United States, Ms. Noriko Takiguchi interprets for me because of my poor English speaking skills. When she turns an equivocal comment I have made into a decisive statement, I both worry that it is not quite what I meant to say (laughs) and am glad that she put it so forcefully.

Japanese is undoubtedly ambiguous. We are prompted to make things ambiguous…

**Fujimori** — Yes. And since there is no subject in spoken Japanese, conversation can progress without total comprehension on the part of either party of what is being

読み書きそろばんといっても、まず字が書けて読めなきゃいけない。あれが意外とわれわれの造形の基をつくっている。
伊東 ── すごく大きいと思いますね。
藤森 ── しかも、われわれ日本の子どもは、まずひらがなを覚えて、それから漢字を覚える。そういうのもあるのかなあ……。
伊東 ── 僕は大学を出た後、そのころはみんなハーバードに行くとかMITに行くとか言っていましたが、今にして思うと、アメリカに行かなくて良かったと思います。まあ、大学を出てから行っても、そんなに言語空間って変わらないとは思うけれど、高校ぐらいで行くと、完璧に変わってしまいますね。
藤森 ── 発想が変わるからね。
伊東 ── そうですね。性格まで変わるし。
藤森 ── 言語と建築の話は、初めて聞きました。おまけに、言語の形、文字という形と建築という形には共通性がある。
　確かに、言われてみたら、「まつもと」はひらがなの建築の代表ですよ。
伊東 ── （笑いながら）確かに。
藤森 ── こうやって見ると、平面は「心」の字のひらがな的崩しに……（笑）。
伊東 ── 「まつもと」は、内部では光の入ってくる所と暗い所で、リズムをつくりたいと考えていましたね。そういう密度が違うというのも関係しているかもしれない。

## イコンとしての構造体
### ──「TOD'S表参道ビル」

藤森 ── 「TOD'S表参道ビル」（2004年）はどうですか。
伊東 ── 「TOD'S」は、「サーペンタイン」は仮設ですぐ壊されたから、ああいうものを何か恒久的なものでやりたいなと思っていた時に、チャンスがきました。「TOD'S」は商業ビルだし、ファサードぐらいしかやることはないので、表参道のような場所で、鉄骨造にガラスのカーテンウォールの建物とはまったく違う何かをつくりたいと思いました。
藤森 ── それで打ち放し。
伊東 ── 敷地条件が悪かったので、小さくても周りに対抗できるような強いものをやるためには、とにかく打ち放しで強い表現にしたかった。なので、ファサードが構造体になるようにスタディしていましたね。そのころ、平田晃久君が「TOD'S」を担当していて、彼のアイデアは素晴らしかったです。
　最初にクライアントに持って行った時、水玉みたいにポツポツ丸い穴が開いている案とこれと2つ持って行って、「こっちをやりたいんですよ」と言ったら、しばらく黙ってしまった（笑）。

藤森 ── ポツポツをやりたかったんだ（笑）。
伊東 ── 超ワンマンの、ディエゴ・デッラ・ヴァッレさんという、イタリアでは気鋭の若手実業家で、自家用機で日本まで来るような人ですが、絶句していた。でもまあ、その日のうちに気に入ってくれて、じゃあこれでやれと言われましたけどね。
藤森 ── 社会に対しての説明の時に、木の形と言ったでしょう。あれは本気で言っていました？
伊東 ── そうです。平田君が木のパターンのスタディをやっていたから。
　「サーペンタイン」はアルゴリズムでやっていましたが、「TOD'S」は試行錯誤で枝ぶりを1本1本広げたり狭めたりしながら……。
藤森 ── 本当の自然の形を「建築」に置き換えることは絶対に不可能だから、やらないほうがいいという思いがあって、それで違和感があったんですよ。そういうことはあまり気にならなかった？
伊東 ── むしろ僕は、商業建築だから、何かイコンを感じさせたほうがいいなと思ったんです。そこしかない。中身はなんにもないわけだから。
　それで、ファサードだけ見ていたらそんなに木に見えるわけでもないんですが、6面すべてを同じパターンにして、内部からの見え方とか、さまざまな印象を組み合わせた時に、ファサードはけやきの木をシルエットにしたんだということが伝わってシンボルになると。商業建築としてはかなりうまくいったと思っています。
　敷地がL型に曲がっていて、すごく間口も狭いし……。隣地と接している面も同じようにつくったのですが、その建物が最近取り壊され、建て替えられている時だけ、きれいに見えましたね。

## 曲線と直線、自由曲面と水平面
### ──「福岡アイランドシティ中央公園中核施設ぐりんぐりん」、「瞑想の森 市営斎場」

藤森 ── 次は「福岡アイランドシティ中央公園中核施設ぐりんぐりん」（2005年）。
伊東 ── これは藤森さんにさんざん言われましたからね（笑）。
藤森 ── 植物って勝手に伸びちゃうから、本気でメンテしない限り大変ですよ。本気でメンテすれば大丈夫ですが、行政はあまりメンテにはお金を注がないのと、もうひとつは、スラブのヘリの厚さがなんとも……。
伊東 ── グリッドに分割するのですがモジュールが粗かったんですね。これはアルゴリズムじゃないから、グリッドに分割して

spoken.

**Ito** — Yes. That becomes ingrained.

**Fujimori** — Perhaps *kanji* is the reason Chinese architecture is so inflexible.

**Ito** — That probably plays a part. I think the presence of *kana* in Japanese played a major role.

**Fujimori** — Yes. When I first came to Taiwan, I was amazed to see the balloons in comics read by children all written in old, formal *kanji* (laughs). Of course, that's only to be expected because they only have *kanji*.

Humans certainly do not learn forms first. They are taught letters or characters by their parents. One can't learn reading, writing and arithmetic unless one is able to read and write letters or characters. That forms the foundation for design to a surprising degree.

**Ito** — I think it has a major influence.

**Fujimori** — What is more, children in Japan learn *hiragana* first, and then *kanji*. I wonder if that has an effect…

**Ito** — When I graduated from university, everyone was talking about going to places such as Harvard and MIT. Looking back, I am glad I did not go to the United States then. Of course, one's linguistic space may not change that much if one goes after graduating from university, but it changes completely if one goes, say, around high school.

**Fujimori** — One's character changes.

**Ito** — Yes. Even one's character will change.

**Fujimori** — This is the first time I've heard you talk about language and architecture. In addition, the shapes of letters or characters and architectural shapes have things in common.

Now that you mention it, Matsumoto is a typical work of *hiragana* architecture.

**Ito** — (Laughing) That is true.

**Fujimori** — Looked at with that in mind, the plan suggests the word *kokoro* written in cursive script…(laughs).

**Ito** — Inside Matsumoto, I wanted to create rhythm through the arrangement of places into which light is introduced and dark places. Differences in that sort of density may also be related to language.

## Structure as Icon
### [TOD'S Omotesando Building]

**Fujimori** — What about TOD'S?

**Ito** — Serpentine was a temporary structure and soon dismantled, so I was hoping to do something similar that was permanent. Then the chance to design TOD'S came along. TOD'S is a commercial building, and about the only thing we were able to do was the facade. For a place as distinctive as Omotesando I wanted to design something that was definitely not a steel-frame building with a glass curtain wall.

**Fujimori** — So you decided on an exposed concrete building.

**Ito** — I wanted something that was assertive despite the small size of the building because the site conditions were unfavorable. I wanted to use exposed concrete to create a powerful impression. We made studies that made the facade a part of the structure. Akihisa Hirata was the staff member in charge of TOD'S at the time, and he had a brilliant idea.

When we first took our design to the client, we took two schemes, this and another scheme in which round holes resembling large dots were punched into the wall. I said that I wanted to do the former, and the client was dumbstruck (laughs).

**Fujimori** — He wanted to go with the round holes (laughs).

**Ito** — Mr. Diego Della Valle, a young, dynamic businessman from Italy who runs the company by himself-the sort of businessman who travels to Japan in his own jet-was at a loss for words. Even so, that day, he approved the design.

**Fujimori** — You said it was a tree-form when you explained it to the public. Was that really what you were thinking?

**Ito** — Yes. Hirata was studying tree patterns.

We used an algorithm to design Serpentine, but with TOD'S, we designed the way the "branches" were arranged, one by one, through trial and error, spreading them out or bringing them closer together…

**Fujimori** — It struck me as incongruous. I thought translating an actual natural form into architecture was never going to work and ought not to be attempted. You never felt that way?

**Ito** — I felt something iconic was needed because it was a commercial building. Because that was all there was to it. There was nothing on the inside.

The facade by itself does not suggest a tree that much. However, the pattern was repeated on all six sides, and is combined with other impressions one gets including the way the facade looks from inside. As a result, it is communicated to the visitor that the facade is the silhouette of a zelkova tree; it becomes a symbol. I thought it worked rather well as a commercial building.

The site is L-shaped, and the frontage is quite narrow…

The same pattern was repeated on the side facing an adjacent building. That building was recently demolished, and the elevation was beautifully revealed, at least while new construction was going on.

つくったんですよ。そうすると、グリッドが粗かったので、あまりきれいなカーブにならなかったんですね。端部であんなカクカクするとは思いませんでした。

藤森 ── 難しいと思いました？

伊東 ── でも、型枠と配筋の時は本当にきれいで、ほれぼれしていたのですが、コンクリートを打ったら「なあんだ、こんなになっちゃったか」と落胆した（笑）。

藤森 ── 伊東さんでも自然が相手だと失敗するんだなと思って、ちょっと安心しましたね（笑）。

伊東 ── もうひとつは、恣意的なカーブだけでやっているから、そこに1枚でも水平のラインがあれば。スラブが1枚でもいいからスーッと空間を横断しているとか。

藤森 ── なるほど。自由曲線の座標に当たるような直線がない。

伊東 ── そう、なんにも建築的なものがなかったので、それもちょっとまずかったなと思いますね。その反省によってつくったのが「瞑想の森 市営斎場」（2006年）です。

藤森 ── いまの話、先ほど平面でフリーハンド的に曲線でやる時も、どこかで直線に当たりたいと言われましたが、立面においてもそうだったんですね。どこかで水平面に当たりたいと。

伊東 ── そうですね。

藤森 ── 絶対音感と同じように、伊東さんには"絶対水平感"がある。それにいかないと落ち着けない。すべての自由の線も最後は水平面にパッと着く。「せんだい」の時の床面に感じましたね。

　絶対水平感はおそらく、諏訪湖由来だろうと僕は思っているんですが、色はどこからきているのか、まだわからないんです。

伊東 ── 色は、前巻でも話したように全然自信がなくて、いろいろな色を使ってみるんですけどね。

藤森 ── 自信がなくてやっているの!?

伊東 ── そうです。今日も「台中国立歌劇院」の現場を歩きながら、どうしようと思って色はまだ悩んでいます。

藤森 ── 「台中国立歌劇院」の場合は「色」は効きますね。形がないというか、不連続でふにょ〜っとしているから。おまけに打ち放しが消えてしまうから、あとは「色」ですね。

伊東 ── そうなんですよね。

藤森 ── 話を戻しますが、そうすると「瞑想の森」は「ぐりんぐりん」のリベンジかな。見に行くと、絶対水平の上に、薄い物質がふわっと浮いて漂っているのがわかりますね。

　僕が設計がらみで初めて行政に連れて行かれたのが、この「瞑想の森」なんです。いま多治見市の博物館をやっていて、「先生の屋根の参考になるものがあるので、見に行きましょう」と言われて、どこに連れて行かれるのかと思ったら、「瞑想の森」だった（笑）。

伊東 ── へえー。

藤森 ── カーブした屋根が僕の参考になるかなと思って連れてってくれた……（笑）。それと構造もこのくらいまでは出来ますよということでした。

伊東 ── これは型枠の時は本当にきれいだった。だから内部も打ち放しのままでただ吹き付けだけにしてあります。

藤森 ── すごいね、これは。

伊東 ── 「台湾大学社会科学部棟」（2013年）の図書館はFRPで型枠をつくりましたが、「瞑想の森」は合板、普通のベニヤですからね。これは型枠の大きさもよくやったなあと思います。

藤森 ── きれいな建物だなぁ。見事なものですよ。屋上に上ると、やっぱりおお！　と思いましたね。

伊東 ── 上りました？

藤森 ── そう。屋根を見せるために連れて行かれたからね（笑）。でも私がやっている多治見の博物館のカーブした屋根はもっと武骨になります。

## 21世紀のアーチ
── 「多摩美術大学図書館」

伊東 ── 「多摩美術大学図書館（八王子キャンパス）」（2007年）は、「瞑想の森」と全然違うように見えますが、実は同じような柱で最初はスタディしていたんですよ。そうしたら、半分冗談みたいだけれども、模型を作る時に省略形で十字形になったんですね。

藤森 ── 省略形だったの！

伊東 ── そう。「瞑想の森」のような柱を作るのが大変だから省略形で作ったら、これでいこうということになって、それが最後はアーチになりました。

藤森 ── 開口部のアーチ状の曲線というのは、やっぱり何度も描いて……？

伊東 ── いや、それは僕はそんなにこだわっていなかったですね。これは中山英之君が担当して、これは何アーチというのかな、こういう曲線を半分に割って接線をずっと連ねていくナントカ曲線というのがあるんですよ。

藤森 ── アーチは、ローマ以来の歴史があって難しいんですよ。おまけにこれはスパンが少しずつ変わる。中山君がその辺はスタディしたということですが、内部はきれいだねえ。

伊東 ── これはまた佐々木さんが頑張って、鉄板を入れようと言い出しまして、真ん中は鉄板のアーチで出来ている。

藤森 ── 中に鉄筋の代わりに、鉄板が入っているんだ！

伊東 ── そう。この壁はわずか20cmなんですが、鉄板でまずア

## Curves and Straight Lines, Freely Curving Plane and Horizontal Plane
[Island City Central Park "GRIN GRIN"; Meiso no Mori Municipal Funeral Hall]

**Fujimori** — Next we come to Island City Central Park "GRIN GRIN" (2005).

**Ito** — This is something you criticized me mercilessly for (laughs).

**Fujimori** — Plants will continue to grow on their own, so they can cause a lot of trouble unless they are maintained in earnest. They are all right if maintained properly, but local governments don't invest too much money in maintenance. One other thing, the thickness of the edge of the slab is quite...

**Ito** — The building was divided into a grid, but the module was too large. This was not based on an algorithm but divided into a grid instead. The grid was too large, and as a result, we did not get neat curves. I did not think the edge would be so thick.

**Fujimori** — Did you think it was difficult?

**Ito** — The formwork and the reinforcements were beautifully arranged-I was quite taken by it. However, once the concrete was cast, I was disappointed by how it turned out (laughs).

**Fujimori** — I am somewhat reassured that even you can fail when you must deal with nature (laughs).

**Ito** — One other thing. It is all made up of arbitrary curves. If only there had been even one horizontal line, if even one slab had cut across the space.

**Fujimori** — I see. There is no straight line that might serve as a datum for the free curves.

**Ito** — Yes. I thought the absence of anything architectural was also a mistake. I kept that in mind when designing Meiso no Mori Municipal Funeral Hall.

**Fujimori** — Earlier, you said that when you use a freehand curve in plan, you want it to come to rest somewhere against a straight line. So what you are saying now is that it also applies to a curve in elevation, that you want it to come to rest somewhere on a horizontal plane.

**Ito** — Yes.

**Fujimori** — You have something similar to absolute pitch, an absolute ability to recognize the horizontal. You aren't comfortable unless you revert to it. All freely drawn lines ultimately come to rest on a horizontal plane. One felt that with the floor surfaces in Sendai.

I think your absolute ability to recognize the horizontal comes from Lake Suwa. I am still not sure where your sense of colors comes from.

**Ito** — As I said in the first volume, I am not confident at all about colors. I try all sorts of colors.

**Fujimori** — You aren't confident?

**Ito** — I'm not. Today, as we were walking around the construction site for National Taichung Theater, I was still worrying about what to do about the colors.

**Fujimori** — Colors will be effective for National Taichung Theater because there is no form, or rather, it is discontinuous and squishy. Also, the exposed concrete finish will disappear, so that only colors will be left.

**Ito** — Yes.

**Fujimori** — To go back to what was said earlier, is "Meiso no Mori" a demonstration that you've learned from the mistakes made in "GRIN GRIN"? When one visits "Meiso no Mori," one finds a thin material floating over the absolute horizontal plane.

People from the local government for which I am designing Tajimi Municipal Museum took me to see "Meiso no Mori". They told me looking at it might be helpful in connection with the design of the roof for my building. I was wondering where they were taking me, and it turned out to be "Meiso no Mori" (laughs).

**Ito** — Ah.

**Fujimori** — They took me there because they thought seeing a curved roof might prove helpful…(laughs). They also said they were capable of building a structure of that sort.

**Ito** — This was truly beautiful when the formwork was still in place. The interior was therefore also given an exposed concrete finish, with just a coating sprayed on.

**Fujimori** — This is really something.

**Ito** — I used FRP forms for the library at National Taiwan University, College of Social Sciences (2013), but at "Meiso no Mori," it was done with ordinary plywood. I was impressed by the size of the forms as well.

**Fujimori** — This is a beautiful building. It is splendid. When I ascended to the roof, I thought, wow.

**Ito** — You went on the roof?

**Fujimori** — Yes. After all, they'd taken me there to look at the roof (laughs). But the curved roof for Tajimi Municipal Museum, which I am working on, will be cruder.

## 21st-Century Arches
[Tama Art University Library (Hachioji campus)]

**Ito** — Tama Art University Library (Hachioji campus) (2007) may seem entirely different from "Meiso no Mori," but at first we made studies with similar columns. I am not making this up.

ーチを真ん中に組んで、その両サイドにコンクリートを打っているから、結構難しいことをやっているんですよ。そうすると耐火被覆も兼ねられるし、しっかり壁も維持できる。

これは鹿島建設がよくやったなあ。すごい施工の技術ですね。

**藤森** ── 確かに。これは技術的には大変ですよ。

**伊東** ── しかもこれは床が1階はスロープになっているから、その足元が結構難しいんですよ。全部角度が1本1本違っている上に、斜めにそれが突き刺さっているから。

**藤森** ── あとで直せないからね。

**伊東** ── そう。この施工は大変でしたね。日本のゼネコンは、そういう点ではすごい。だから、こんなことを言うと怒られるけれど、つまらない建築の精度を上げることにエネルギーを注いでいるのを見ると、もったいないなあと思いますよ（笑）。

## あえて閉じる
── 「座・高円寺」

**藤森** ── 「座・高円寺」（2008年）は、これは毎日中央線の上から見てますが、見えるとほっとする。

**伊東** ── あの場所は中央線があるし環七もあって、音がすごいし、空気も悪い。だから、絶対にこれは閉じないと成り立たないなと思って、ほかのコンペティターはみんなもっと地上部分を多くしていましたが、これは3分の2は地下です。だから、地上の3分の1はできるだけ低くして、芝居小屋みたいにしようと考えました。

そのためには、どうしても2つの300人収容のホールを重ねなくてはならない。それがまた勝負どころというか、普通そんなことをやると音が響くから、そのスタディを永田音響設計とずいぶんやりましたね。永田音響が完全に浮かせればいいだろうと言うので、地下のホールを浮き床にして躯体から切り離しました。ほとんど問題はないですね。

これは杉並区が演劇のためだけに同じ規模のホールを2つ企画したわけですよ。コンサートホールと劇場の組み合わせはよくありますが、これはどちらも演劇のためのホールで、ひとつはプロ仕様でいろんなことができる。もうひとつは区民用。これはすごく良かったですね。しかも、佐藤信さんが審査員でもありかつ芸術監督であったから、一貫して設計の初期から関わってくれたので、スムーズにいったと思います。

**藤森** ── このテント風の屋根と色は、なかなか出来ることじゃないと思いました。

**伊東** ── 色は、こういう周りが建て込んだ場所では、「これは白じゃないよね。白だったら浮いてしまうね」と思って、黒くしたんですよ。ところが、イワン・バーンという写真家が新宿まで入るような航空写真を撮ったら、「座・高円寺」だけが黒くて、ほかはほとんど白っぽい建物ばかりだったので、驚きました。まちの中の建物ってほとんどが白いんだなと思ってね。

**藤森** ── 僕もそれは気づいてなかった。白でやると、浮くどころか、埋没してしまうわけですね。

**伊東** ── そうなんですね。かえって沈んでしまう。

普通、公共建築だったらみんな開く、開くと言いますが、今回はあえて閉じるんだというコンセプトでコンペに提案して、それが成功しましたね。

このテントは芝居小屋のイメージなので、窓は絶対に四角い窓を開けたらダメだと思っていました。「窓がなくて、こんなに閉じていいのか？」とも言われましたが、絶対これで正解だったと思っている。

**藤森** ── そうですね。テントに四角い窓を開けたら変な感じです。

## 外部に開かれたスタジアム
── 「2009高雄ワールドゲームズメインスタジアム」

**伊東** ── 「2009高雄ワールドゲームズメインスタジアム」（2009年）は、台湾で最初の建物ですね。

**藤森** ── コンペ？

**伊東** ── これは設計・施工のコンペだったから、互助營造から誘われて、竹中工務店と3者でチームを組んでやったものです。2008年に北京でオリンピックがありましたね。あれに対抗して、2009年にワールドゲームをやるからということでスタジアムをつくったんです。施工はすごくいいですよ。

**藤森** ── 施工も大変だ。

**伊東** ── 全部屋根の鉄骨はスパイラルを描いているので太陽光パネルはすべてねじれています。それで、これも構造的にはやや曖昧。僕らはスパイラルをもっと徹底してやりたかったのですが……。

**藤森** ── こういう、曖昧でしかもちゃんとした形は、ほかの人では難しい。

**伊東** ── （笑いながら）まあ、ぐにゃぐにゃしていますね。そう言われれば。

**藤森** ── これも地面が大事なんですね。これがピシッとしていないとダメ（笑）。

**伊東** ── そうですね。このプロジェクトがあったために、台湾で次から次へと仕事がくるようになりました。この間、久しぶりに行ってみたら、すごくきれいに使ってくれていましたね。

When we were building the model, we used cruciform columns as approximations of what we intended.

**Fujimori** — They were approximations!

**Ito** — Yes. Making columns like those used in "Meiso no Mori" for the model was a lot of trouble, so we used these to merely suggest what they would be like. We then decided to go with those cruciform columns. Finally, they became arches.

**Fujimori** — Did you draw the curves of those arches over and over again…?

**Ito** — No. I was not that particular about them. Hideyuki Nakayama was in charge of them. I don't recall what these arches are called, but there is a curve made from these curves that are halved and joined at their tangents.

**Fujimori** — Arches have a long history that go back to the days of the Roman Empire and are difficult to do. Not only that, these arches all have slightly different spans. You say Hideyuki Nakayama studied this aspect of the design. The interior is beautiful.

**Ito** — Mr. Sasaki worked hard on this project as well. He suggested putting in steel plates. So there are arches of steel plate in the middle of the concrete arches.

**Fujimori** — Instead of steel reinforcement bars, there are steel plates inside!

**Ito** — Yes. This wall is only 20 cm thick. First, steel plates were arranged in the middle in form of an arch, then concrete was cast on both sides. So it was fairly difficult work. This also serves as fire protection and facilitates the maintenance of the walls.

Kajima Corporation did an excellent job. Their construction technology is superb.

**Fujimori** — That is for sure. This is technically quite difficult.

**Ito** — Not only that, the first floor is sloped, so the bottom portions of the arches were rather difficult to construct. They are not only all at different angles, they stick into the floor at a diagonal.

**Fujimori** — There is no way of correcting a mistake afterwards.

**Ito** — Yes. This construction work was difficult. General contractors in Japan are superb in that regard. They might take offense at this, but when I see them expending all that effort to improve precision on uninteresting buildings, I think, what a waste (laughs).

## Deliberate Enclosure
## [ZA-KOENJI Public Theatre]

**Fujimori** — I see ZA-KOENJI everyday from the Chuo Line and feel a sense of relief when I do.

**Ito** — That place is near the Chuo Line and the Number 7 Ring Road. It is noisy and the air is bad. I therefore thought that the only way one could have a theater there was to enclose it completely. The other participants in the competition all located a lot more of the facility aboveground, but I placed two-thirds of it underground. I made the one-third that was above ground as low as possible to suggest a small-scale theater.

To do that required stacking the two 300-seat halls, one on top of the other. That was the crucial decision. Ordinarily, doing that results in reverberations, so we made many studies of this arrangement together with Nagata Acoustics. Nagata Acoustics told us it should be all right if they were made to float completely, so we gave the underground hall a floating floor and isolated it from the building frame. There have been virtually no problems.

It was Suginami Ward's plan to have two halls of the same size, both for dramatic performances. A concert hall is often combined with a theater, but here both halls are for dramatic performances. One has professional specifications; many different things can be done with it. The other is to be used by the public. This is a terrific arrangement. Mr. Makoto Sato was on the jury and also the artistic director for the facility. He was therefore involved in the design from the start. I think it went quite smoothly.

**Fujimori** — Achieving this tent-like roof and the color must have been fairly difficult.

**Ito** — This is in a built-up area, and we thought making it white would produce a disconnection between it and the environment. That's why we made it black. However, when a photographer named Iwan Baan took aerial photographs of it that showed the city all the way to Shinjuku, ZA-KOENJI was the only thing that was black. Almost every other building was whitish. We were amazed. I thought, buildings in the city were almost all white.

**Fujimori** — I hadn't realized that a white building is more likely to disappear.

**Ito** — Yes. It doesn't stand out but instead blends in.

Ordinarily, everyone says that a public building ought to be made open, but this time we went ahead and proposed closing off the building. I think that accounted in part for our success in the competition.

This is imagined as a theater tent, so I thought having rectangular windows in it would be a mistake. I have been asked if I have second thoughts about making it windowless, but I am convinced this was the right solution.

**Fujimori** — Yes. Rectangular windows in a tent would have been incongruous.

## チューブ状の表現による高層ビル
——「トーレス・ポルタ・フィラ／バルセロナ見本市・グランヴィア会場拡張計画」

**藤森** ——「トーレス・ポルタ・フィラ／バルセロナ見本市・グランヴィア会場拡張計画」(2010年／2003年-)はスペインの建物だっけ。

**伊東** —— これは2002年からで、まだ続いていますが、最後の会議場のコンプレックスが経済状況の悪化で止まってしまって、恐らくもう打ち止めでしょう。それでエントランスホールや4つの展示パヴィリオンをやりました。

**藤森** —— 伊東さんが平気でキツイことを言う例のひとつで、原広司さんの大阪の梅田ビルについて、「超高層は上と下を変えたってダメだ。新しい超高層をやるとしたら、基準階を変えろ」と言ったんですよ。

**伊東** —— いやあ、そんなこと言いましたかね(笑)。

**藤森** —— 大体超高層って、基準階を積み上げるから経済的に成り立っているんですよ。基準階を変えていったら、オフィスビルは大変なことになる(笑)。

**伊東** —— そんなエラそうなことを言ったとしても、結局、基準階は基準階ですね。誰がやっても(笑)。

**藤森** —— 超高層は、今では世界中でやるけれど、結構無茶なやり方をしているものがありますね。でも、これは基準階を基準階的にやらないにもかかわらず、なんとなく一体感がある。

**伊東** —— スペインなんか、ヨーロッパでは最もやりやすいと思いますが、ヨーロッパでは、建築に対する固定観念があるからなかなか自由になれないですね。それに比べるとアジアはやりやすい気がします。

この間、初めてインドのル・コルビュジエを見に行ったんですよ。チャンディーガルとかアーメダバードに。そうしたら、ル・コルビュジエがヨーロッパにいる時より、いいんですよね。解放感があって、ああ、こんなに違うんだ！　と思いました。ロンシャンと同じころにチャンディーガルをやっているのに、やっぱりヨーロッパでやっているのと違う。

**藤森** —— 伝統の抑圧がある。

**伊東** —— そう。まあ、気候のせいもあるでしょうけれど……。だから、ヨーロッパにはそういう無言のプレッシャーというのがありますね。

**藤森** —— 文化の抑圧ね。ヨーロッパの人たちは、「建築」を最も文化の中の大事なもののひとつとしていますが、建築的原則は守る。

**伊東** —— そうですね。だからその分、建築家というのはちゃんと世の中に位置付けられている。日本の建築家は、そういう点ではまったく大事にされていないけれど、逆に自由度はあるというか、精神的にもすごく解放されているなと思いますね。日本の建築家が結構評価されるのは、そういうこともあるのかもしれない。

**藤森** —— わりと自由にやれる。

**伊東** —— そう。向こうの人はやっぱりどこかで"闘わなくてはならない"という気持ちが強いから、いつも逆にとらわれるのかもしれませんね。

## 3つの立体を組み合わせたミュージアム
——「今治市伊東豊雄建築ミュージアム」

**藤森** ——「今治市伊東豊雄建築ミュージアム」(2011年)のような幾何学、結晶体的なものはめずらしいですね。これもプロジェクトで見たことがあります。

**伊東** ——「オスロ市ダイクマン中央図書館 コンペティション応募案」(2009年)(p.137)ですね。いつも図書館は「せんだい」のように連続する空間ばかりやってきたから、今度は家がたくさん連なって、まちになっているような、小さな単位の連続体で図書館をやってみたいと思ったのです。

ちょうど「オスロ」で敷地を見に行った時、12月で雪の中に、夕方ぽつぽつ灯がついていて、車の中から「この家は何をしているんだろう……」と思いを馳せながら見ていたものだから、家がずっとつながっているまち、つまり集落のように形の異なる小さな単位の空間が次々に現れて書斎で本を読んでいるような図書館をやってみたいと思ったのですね。

コンペではそんなこちらの意図はまったく無視されて、あっさり落とされたので口惜しくて、どこかでこれをもう一回やってやろうと思っていたので大三島で小さなミュージアムとして実現したのです。

**藤森** —— これも鉄板構造。わりと素直な鉄板ですね。

**伊東** —— そうですね。スケールが小さいから。

当初は地形が盛り上がったような、波打つ地形のような屋根のスタディをしていて、最後にこうなった。ここは敷地より上に道路が通っているので、道路から建物を見ると、背後に海があり、その奥に陽が沈むので、建物がシルエットで見えるのです。

**藤森** —— 逆光で。

**伊東** —— ええ、逆光で。それで、キリッとした形がいいという訳で、いつもと逆に外形から決まったような印象がありましたね。だから、船のマストのような最上部はなくてもよかったんですが、絶対欲しかった(笑)。

## A Stadium Open to the Outside
[The Main Stadium for the World Games 2009 in Kaohsiung]

**Ito** — The Main Stadium for the World Games 2009 in Kaohsiung (2009) was my first building in Taiwan.

**Fujimori** — Was it a competition?

**Ito** — This was a design-construction competition. Fu Tsu Construction Co., Ltd. extended an invitation and formed a team with Takenaka Corporation and my office. The 2008 Olympics were held in Beijing, and the 2009 World Games was going to be held in Taiwan as a rival event. This was built as its venue. The construction is extremely well executed.

**Fujimori** — Construction work must have been difficult on this as well.

**Ito** — The steel frame for the entire roof is arranged in a spiral, and the solar panels are all twisted.

As a result, this too is structurally somewhat ambiguous. We wanted to create a more thorough spiral…

**Fujimori** — Others would find it difficult to design a form of this sort, one that is ambiguous yet neat.

**Ito** — (Laughing) As you say, it is indeterminate.

**Fujimori** — Here too the ground is important. The design would not work unless the ground was done exactly right (laughs).

**Ito** — Yes. Thanks to this project, I began to get one job after another in Taiwan. I revisited it for the first time in quite a while recently, and it was extremely well maintained.

## Tube-Like High-Rise Building
[TORRES PORTA FIRA / Extension for the Fair of Barcelona Gran Via Venue]

**Fujimori** — TORRES PORTA FIRA / Extension for the Fair of Barcelona Gran Via Venue (2010 / 2003-) is a project in Spain?

**Ito** — The project began in 2002 and is still going on. Work on the final conference hall complex has been suspended because of the worsening economic conditions and will probably be cancelled. So I ended up doing the entrance hall and four exhibition pavilions.

**Fujimori** — An example of a harsh comment you have nonchalantly made is the time you said, in connection with the Umeda Sky Building in Osaka by Mr. Hiroshi Hara, that there was no point in changing just the top and bottom of a super high-rise building. To create a new type of super high-rise building, one had to change the typical floor.

**Ito** — Did I say that (laughs).

**Fujimori** — A super high-rise building makes economic sense because one is stacking typical floors one on top of the next. If one changed the typical floor--that is, if one had differently arranged floors, office buildings would make no economic sense (laughs).

**Ito** — I may have talked big, but in the end, there is no changing the typical floor, is there? No matter who designs it (laughs).

**Fujimori** — Super high-rise buildings are constructed all over the world today, and there are some that have been designed in illogical ways. But this, despite the fact that the typical floor has not been designed in a typical floor-like way, somehow has a unified feeling.

**Ito** — I think Spain is the easiest country in Europe to work in, but generally in Europe it is difficult to work freely because they have fixed ideas about architecture. Compared with Europe, Asia is much easier to work in.

I recently went to see Le Corbusier's work in India for the first time--Chandigarh and Ahmedabad. I found his work there much better than those in Europe. They feel free and relaxed. I thought, how different it is. Chandigarh was done around the same time as Ronchamp, but it is still different from his work in Europe.

**Fujimori** — Tradition acts as a constraint.

**Ito** — Yes. Of course, the climate is probably also a factor… So in Europe, there is this sort of unspoken pressure.

**Fujimori** — Constraints imposed by culture. Europeans consider architecture to be one of the most important forms of culture, but they are careful to abide by architectural principles.

**Ito** — Yes. So to that extent, architects have a position in society. Architects in Japan, in that regard, are not treated with any respect, but conversely, they enjoy freedom--they are quite free psychologically as well. That may account in part for the fairly high regard in which Japanese architects are held in the architectural world.

**Fujimori** — We are able to design fairly freely.

**Ito** — Yes. Architects in Europe feel that ultimately they have to fight to achieve anything, and that may work against them.

## A Museum Made by Combining Three Solids
[Toyo Ito Museum of Architecture, Imabari]

**Fujimori** — A geometrical, crystalline work such as Toyo Ito Museum of Architecture, Imabari (2011) is quite rare. I saw this too in the project stage.

**Ito** — That was the Competition of the New Deichman Main Library (2009) (p. 137). Up to now I have designed libraries only as continuous spaces, as in Sendai. This time, I wanted to design a library as a sequence of small units, like a community made up of many houses.

## まん幕のイメージから生まれたミュージアム
―「今治市岩田健母と子のミュージアム」

**伊東** ― この「今治市岩田健母と子のミュージアム」（2011年）は「伊東ミュージアム」をつくっている最中に大三島に出来たものですが、岩田健さんという90歳になられる彫刻家のミュージアムです。
　大三島は不思議な魅力をもった島で、来た人はみんなこの島を気に入ってしまうんです。

**藤森** ― 海賊の聖地ですけどね。

**伊東** ― そう、大山祇神社がありますね。あそこの境内に入ると空気が変わります。僕も「最後はこの島に移り住んでもいい」と思っているぐらい。

**藤森** ― 大昔から人を惹き付けるものがあったんだろうね。

**伊東** ― そう。この島は"瀬戸内海のへそ"と言われていますが、僕の東京の塾生がこの島へ行って、島の人と話したりなんかしているうちにこの島をみんな好きになる。それでこの島のプロジェクトをやりたいと言って、いま自主的に塾生が行って、バス停をつくったり、島の人から頼まれて、隣の大島に御影石を彫っている石屋のおじさんたちと石のカフェをつくったり、空き家の修復をやろうとしている。
　この島に移住した塾生もいます。ミュージアムをつくった彫刻家の岩田健さんもこの島を訪れたら気に入ってしまったのです。
　もともと岩田さんは川口の人です。川口の駅前、商店街に岩田さんの彫刻がありますが、川口でなくてこの島に寄付したいと言って、自身の彫刻ばかりでなく、1億ぐらいのお金を投じてこのミュージアムをつくったのです。これはコンクリートで壁を囲った彫刻の庭園です。

**藤森** ― これもきれいな打ち放しですね。

**伊東** ― そうですね。大成建設がやっているから。日本のゼネコンの技術力はすごいなあ。

## 非均質さを生み出すアルゴリズム
―「台湾大学社会科学部棟」

**伊東** ―「台湾大学社会科学部棟」（2013年）は、特命で仕事がきました。

**藤森** ― 図書館のほうは建築をやっている人たちから見ると、フランク・ロイド・ライトのジョンソン・ワックス社によく似ている。

**伊東** ― それはよく言われましたね。

**藤森** ― それは別に意識していたわけではない？

**伊東** ― まったく意識していたわけではないのですが、ハスの花のようなスパイラルを描く幾何学形を組み合わせて柱の位置と屋根の形態をパターン化したのです。そうすると柱が密に立つ所と疎な場所があって、場所の違いを感じられると考えたのです。

**藤森** ― 研究室棟はいかがですか。

**伊東** ― 上は研究室で、下にいくにしたがって教室になって、吹き抜けている所が会議場です。これは大学だから、空調の費用をできるだけ抑えられるように、通風のことを随分考えました。これはかなりうまくいきましたね。

**藤森** ― ベランダみたいに出たのは、日除けを……？

**伊東** ― そうですね。日差しがすごく強いので。

**藤森** ― このタイプは、伊東さんのでは初めて見ましたね。

**伊東** ― 東雲で集合住宅をやった時[5]、サッシュを奥に入れて構造体のグリッドを表現しています。このような奥行きの深い陰影のはっきりしたファサードをつくるのは有効だと思います。

**藤森** ― なるほど。集合住宅のイメージ。

**伊東** ― そうですね。

**藤森** ― 研究室が一つひとつ入っているのが、道路側から見た時は、学生寮かと思いました。ただ、学生寮にしてはあまり学生の生活がうかがえないから……。

**伊東** ― まだ使ってはいませんね。家具がいまようやく入ったところで、6月から引っ越しが始まって、図書館にも本が入って、今年の9月にオープン予定ですね。
図書館は藤江和子さんに本棚や家具をお願いしたのですが、竹の家具でつくられまして、これはきれいに出来たなあ。箱細工をつくっている職人がつくってくれたので、ものすごくディテールがきれいですね。

**藤森** ― 水平にスーッと抜けていくのは、上手だねえ。

**伊東** ―（笑いながら）やっぱり水平が好きなんでしょうね。垂直は同じことの繰り返しになるから……。

## 都市的スケールの中にヒューマンスケールを組み込む
―「松山 台北文創ビル」

**藤森** ― もうひとつが「松山 台北文創ビル」（2013年）ですが、見た時にびっくりしましたね。床面積では、伊東さんの中では最大じゃないですか。

**伊東** ― そうですね。

**藤森** ― さすがにあの大きさになると、しかも打ち放しになると、能力を超えてしまうような感じがした（笑）。

**伊東** ― どういう意味？（笑）

When I went to Oslo to see the site for the competition, it was an evening in December and snowing. There were lights on here and there, and from inside the car I wondered what was happening in this house and that house. I wanted to design a library that was like a community made up of houses, where a succession of small spatial units of different forms would appear and where reading would be like reading in one's study.

My intention was completely disregarded in the competition and my proposal was flatly rejected. That bothered me, and I swore I would use the scheme somewhere once more. That was how this small museum on Omishima came about.

**Fujimori** — This too is a steel-plate structure. A fairly straightforward use of steel plate.

**Ito** — Yes, because the building is small in size.

At first, we studied a roof that was like the ground swelling or heaving upward, but in the end it became this. There is a road that overlooks the site. When one looks at the building from that road, one sees the sea in the background, and the sun sets in the sea on the far horizon. The building appears in silhouette.

**Fujimori** — It is backlit.

**Ito** — Yes, it is backlit. It was felt, therefore, that the building ought to have a clear-cut form. It was a reversal of our usual process of design, in that we decided on the exterior form first. Though a mast-like form on top was not necessary, I had to have it (laughs).

## A Museum Imagined as *Manmaku*
[Ken Iwata Mother and Child Museum, Imabari City]

**Ito** — Ken Iwata Mother and Child Museum, Imabari City (2011), was built on Omishima when we were doing the Ito Museum. It is a museum dedicated to the work of a 90-year old sculptor named Mr. Ken Iwata.

Omishima is a strangely attractive island. Visitors all fall in love with this island.

**Fujimori** — It is sacred land for pirates.

**Ito** — Yes. Oyamazumi Shrine is located there. The atmosphere is different inside the precinct. I would not mind living out my life on this island either.

**Fujimori** — There must be something that has drawn people there from way back in the past.

**Ito** — Yes. The island is called "the navel of the Inland Sea." Students at my school in Tokyo go to this island and talk with people of the island; they all fall in love with it. They said they wanted to do projects on the island, and now the students go there on their own to do things such as create bus stops, create a stone café together with a stone mason who carves granite on Oshima, a nearby island, and repair unoccupied houses.

There is even a student who has moved to the island. The sculptor Mr. Ken Iwata who created the museum is another person who visited the island and fell in love with it.

Mr. Iwata is originally from Kawaguchi. There is a sculpture by him in the shopping district in front of Kawaguchi Station, but he wanted to make a donation, not to Kawaguchi, but to this island. He not only donated sculptures but invested about a hundred million yen to create this museum.

This is a sculpture garden surrounded by a concrete wall.

**Fujimori** — This has a beautiful exposed concrete finish too.

**Ito** — Yes. That's because it was built by Taisei Corporation. The technical ability of general contractors in Japan is amazing.

## An Algorithm That Generates Nonuniformity
[National Taiwan University, College of Social Sciences]

**Ito** — I was asked to design National Taiwan University, College of Social Sciences (2013).

**Fujimori** — To an architect, the library closely resembles the Johnson Wax Headquarters by Frank Lloyd Wright.

**Ito** — I am often told that.

**Fujimori** — You did not deliberately design this with that in mind?

**Ito** — Not at all. We created a pattern for the locations of the columns and the configuration of the roof by combining geometrical forms that are like lotus flowers, arranged in a spiral. This resulted in places where columns were concentrated and places where columns were sparse. We thought this would enable people to recognize differences of place.

**Fujimori** — How is the research building?

**Ito** — The research rooms are on top, and these become classrooms on the lower floors. The large space is a conference hall. We undertook many studies of ventilation because we wanted to keep air conditioning costs as low as possible, this being a university. It worked out fairly well.

**Fujimori** — The veranda-like projections are sunshades…?

**Ito** — Yes. The sun is quite strong.

**Fujimori** — This is the first time I have seen this type of sunshade in your work.

**Ito** — When I designed multi-unit housing in Shinonome[5], I recessed the window frames and expressed the structural grid. I think a facade like this with deep recesses and clearly-defined areas of shade and shadow is effective.

**Fujimori** — I see. This is in the image of a multi-unit housing

藤森 ── やっぱりコンクリートの巨大な塊という感じになる。それは色を変えてみたり、いろいろ努力しておられるんですが、やっぱりあの大きさを作品としてコントロールするのは大変だなと思いました。

伊東 ── そうですね。でも、この隣にはいま台北ドームをつくっているし、大きなホテルがタワーで建ちつつあって、そういうボリュームと対抗できるように、あまり分節しないほうがいいと思ったんですね。しかも高速道路が通っているから、それに対して壁をつくったほうがいいとも思って、それであえてワンボリュームにまとめています。

藤森 ── 施工は良かったですね。尖った壁の角がピンと立っていて、補修の跡がなかったから、おお、ちゃんと打った！ と思いました。

伊東 ── あれも鹿島建設だったから。山本理顕さんがいま台湾でやっているらしくて、これを見にきて、「台湾でもこんなに打ち放しがきれいにできるんだ！」と感心してくれましたよ（笑）。

藤森 ── 屋上庭園もいいですね。これといい、波状にした屋根の屋上階もいい。問題は基準階ですよ（笑）。普通はこれを基準階とは言わないけれど。

伊東 ── 巨大な壁をつくらなくてはならない一方で、広場を挟んで低層の古い煙草工場と向かい合うから、これを段々にステップアップしていくようにしたのです。

藤森 ── これもグラデーションですね。

伊東 ── そうなんですよ。

藤森 ── なるほど。地形のグラデーション。それは効いていましたね。

## 五感に訴える
── 「台中国立歌劇院」

藤森 ── いよいよ「台中国立歌劇院」ですが、びっくりしました。僕は、変な言い方だけれど、日本近代の二大巨匠である、村野藤吾さんと丹下さんに見せてあげたかった。ふたりはきっと喜ばれると思いましたね。

伊東 ── それはすごいね（笑）。

藤森 ── 本当にすごいですよ。ただ、さっき言われた最後の仕上げ、色の問題はあるけれども、安心していますので（笑）。

　久しぶりにびっくりした。現代の建築はビルバオ・グッゲンハイム美術館以降、構造と関係なくどんどん自由に形をつくる。北京オリンピックはどれもそれです。

伊東 ── そうですね。

藤森 ── 構造的にはただのラーメンなのに、形はしたい放題というのは、やっぱりおかしい。構造をちゃんと表現するのが20世紀建築の大原則ですから、「台中国立歌劇院」は、それを守りながら、20世紀建築にはなかった味わいを特に内部で出している。
　でも、これは中を歩いてみないと分からないですね。

伊東 ── そうですね。

藤森 ── 意外だったのは、模型で見た時は迷路になっていると思ったんですが、全然違う。1階は、完全に自分がどの方向へ行けばいいか分かる。ほとんど流体が流れるようになっていて、明かりもあるから、どっちへ行けばいいか見当がつくし、間違ってもすぐ引き返せるでしょう。だから建築として、プランニングがよく出来ているのに、一方、歩き始めると迷路的な面白さもある。

伊東 ── おそらく、それは一番最初の単純で規則的なパターンから始まって、それを変形して今のような形になっていったのでルールが一応あるんです。逆にこの形をどんどん整形化していったら単純な元のパターンに戻るので。そういう意味で、わりとわかりやすくなっているのかもしれない。何らかの秩序をつくるということは改めて必要なことだと思いました。

藤森 ── だから空間が認識しやすい。

伊東 ── 構造的にも、ずれながらチューブが交互になっているような規則性があるので、無理をして壁を入れている部分もありますが、基本的な構造システムはグリッド状の空間として成立しています。

藤森 ── それと、「せんだい」で縦に開いている穴が横にも開いている。その感じはすごい。縦だけでも大変なのに。でも、歩いてみると、素直なプランでもある。
　迷ってもすぐ戻れるというか、要するにひと目で全体がわかるので、外が見えているせいもあるけれど、あっちに行ってダメだったらこっちに戻ればいいと。模型では全然わからなかった。

伊東 ── そうですね。あとは、内部で赤と青に塗装された2本のシャフトがあちこちから見えるので、さらに認識度が上がると思います。

藤森 ── 図面を見ていると上下の階の関係を理解するのが絶望的になるんですよ。でも歩いてみると、流体が斜面に応じて流れていくような素直さがあるね。

藤森 ── これは鉄筋コンクリート造というかコンクリート鉄筋造ですが（笑）、20世紀建築のコンクリート造形のピークは、ひとつはロンシャンの礼拝堂で、もうひとつは丹下さんで、柱梁の広島平和記念資料館など。これはそのどれでもない。初めてコンクリートでやりながら、構造がちゃんと表現されているということで、嬉しかったんです。
　伊東さんは、20世紀建築を内側からちゃんと超えたんだと思

project.

**Ito** — Yes.

**Fujimori** — When I saw from the street how the research rooms were arranged, I thought it was a student dormitory. Only, for a dormitory I could not see much sign of student life...

**Ito** — It is not yet in use. The furniture has at last been installed. In June, moving will start, the library will be stocked with books. Opening is expected to take place in September this year.

I asked Ms. Kazuko Fujie to design the bookshelves and furniture for the library. The pieces of furniture are made of bamboo. They are beautifully done. They were produced by craftsmen who ordinarily created intricately assembled boxes of wood, so the details are quite beautiful.

**Fujimori** — The way it is extended horizontally is well done.

**Ito** — (Laughing) I suppose I do love horizontals. Verticals end up being repetitions of the same thing...

## Incorporating Human Scale in Urban Scale
[Songshan Taipei New Horizon Building]

**Fujimori** — Then there is Songshan Taipei New Horizon Building (2013). I was astonished when I saw it. It must be the biggest thing you have done in total floor area.

**Ito** — Yes.

**Fujimori** — As might be expected, when a building is that big, and moreover is in exposed concrete, it goes beyond anyone's capability (laughs).

**Ito** — What do you mean (laughs)?

**Fujimori** — It can't help but seem like a huge mass of concrete. A great deal of effort has been made, changing colors and all that, but I think controlling a work of that size is still difficult.

**Ito** — Yes. But Taipei Dome is now being built next to it, and a large hotel tower is under construction. I felt that in order to stand up to those other buildings, this ought not to be articulated too much. Not only that, I felt a wall was needed against an expressway that passes by. That's why I went out of my way to consolidate the volume.

**Fujimori** — The construction work is excellent. The sharp corner of a wall that I saw was neatly executed. There were no signs that it had been mended afterwards, so I thought, aah, the concrete was properly cast.

**Ito** — That too was done by Kajima Corporation. Mr. Riken Yamamoto is doing work in Taiwan right now and came to look at this. He was impressed that exposed concrete could be done so beautifully in Taiwan (laughs).

**Fujimori** — The roof garden is nice too. I also like the wave-like roof of the penthouse. The problem is the typical floor (laughs). Although normally this wouldn't be called a typical floor.

**Ito** — On the one hand, I had to create an enormous wall, but on the other hand, the building faces an old, low-rise cigarette factory across a square, so on that side, the building was designed to gradually step up.

**Fujimori** — Gradations again.

**Ito** — That's right.

**Fujimori** — I see. Topographical gradation. That was effective.

## Appealing to All the Senses
[National Taichung Theater]

**Fujimori** — At last, we come to National Taichung Theater. I was amazed. This may seem like an odd way of putting it, but I think the two great masters of modern Japanese architecture-Mr. Togo Murano and Mr. Kenzo Tange-would have loved it.

**Ito** — That is high praise (laughs).

**Fujimori** — It's truly impressive. Only, as I said earlier, there is the question of the final finishes and colors, but I am confident it will be a success (laughs).

This is the most amazing building I've seen in quite a while. Since Guggenheim Museum Bilbao, contemporary architecture has increasingly adopted free forms that have no relationship to structure. That was true of all the buildings at the Beijing Olympics.

**Ito** — Yes.

**Fujimori** — Doing whatever one pleases with forms, even though the structures are simply rigid frames, is questionable. The proper expression of structure was the great principle of twentieth-century architecture, so National Taichung Theater is in accordance with that principle but is not like twentieth-century architecture in character, especially inside.

But of course we won't know that for certain until we have walked inside it.

**Ito** — Yes.

**Fujimori** — What was unexpected was that-when I saw the model, I thought it was a maze-but it is entirely different. On the first floor, one knows exactly in which direction to go. It is almost like the flow of liquid. There is also light so one understands which way one ought to go, and should one make a mistake, one can immediately retrace one's steps. So that, though it has been well planned as a building, for someone walking around in it, it has an interesting maze-like quality as well.

**Ito** — We began with a simple pattern that was like a rule to be followed, and then variations on that were developed to arrive at the present form. So that, up to a point, there is a rule. Conversely, were we to progressively emend this form, we

いました。
**伊東** ── 内側から？
**藤森** ── 僕の設計は、20世紀建築の外でやってるから、20世紀建築のグラウンドの中の芝生の上で遊んでいるようなものですが（笑）、伊東さんはグラウンドをちゃんと走りながら超えていったんだと思いました。だから、丹下さんと村野さんに見てもらえたらと思ったんです。
　だけどまあ、構造体の中身を見ると、とんでもないものですね（笑）。
**伊東** ── 去年の秋ぐらいに見ていただくともっと驚いたと思いますが、本当にもう鉄筋の塊で、手が鉄筋の間に入らないぐらいでしたから、あれでよくコンクリートを打ったなあと思う。あの鉄筋の塊を見て、うちのスタッフも絶望的な気持ちになりましたからね。
**藤森** ── 伊東事務所と建設業者が死力を尽くした、と感じましたね。
**伊東** ── それもずっとケンカしながらですからね。役所とは書類の山で……（笑）。
**藤森** ── それは現場事務所に積み上げられた書類箱の異様な山を見ればよくわかりますよ（笑）。
**伊東** ── 要するに3年ぐらい工期を越えているわけですね。あと1年では追いつかないと思うので、そうすると倍ぐらいの工期になるから、膨大なペナルティをかけられるらしい……。
**藤森** ── かける気でいるの？
**伊東** ── すぐ近くに市庁舎をつくっているのですが、それも工期が延びて、いま裁判になっているんですよ。「だから裁判は免れないぞ」と言われている（笑）。市長は「そんなことはやめろ」と言っていますが……。
**藤森** ── でも、出来上がったら、あれはそんなこと言うような人はいないですよ。台湾の中では隔絶していい建築だし、北京があのオリンピックで見せつけた、思いつきを技術とお金で無理やり実現させたようなものじゃないから、そこは必ず人びとに伝わると思いますよ。
**伊東** ── でも、予断は許されないので、建設業者と僕らはお互いに、裁判に備えて膨大な書類を用意しているのです（笑）。
**藤森** ── お互いに！（笑）
**伊東** ── そう。あの麗明營造という建設会社も、ここまでよくやったなと思いますが、当初は図面が描けないから、日本のゼネコンのようには施工図を描かないんですよね。
**藤森** ── 台湾では施工図は、設計者が描くものだと聞きましたよ。
**伊東** ── そうなんです。
**藤森** ── それも設計のうちだと。言われてみればそうだけどね（笑）。
**伊東** ── それで、足場をどう立てるかすら彼らは描けないから、構造屋さんと僕らで足場の図面まで描くわけ。そうすると、どんどんコストアップになるとか、それを「変更だ」と言うのです。それで「とんでもない。おまえらが図面を描かないから、おれたちがこんなことまで面倒みてやっているんだぞ」というような闘いを延々と続けてきましたが、去年ぐらいからかなり彼らもスムーズになってきて、この1年間で非常に顔が明るくなってきたねえ（笑）。
**藤森** ── ようやく、ですか。
**伊東** ── ようやく。それでこの間、上棟式が行われた時には、市長はもちろん市議会議員やゼネコンの連中も僕らも、みんな抱き合って喜んだ。
**藤森** ── じゃあ大丈夫ですよ。議員が大丈夫だったら。一番うるさいのは議員だから。
**伊東** ── ところが、上棟式をやっているのに、議員もいっさい中に入れてもらえないんですよ。危険だからと言って（笑）。外から眺めて、外で上棟式をやりましたが、市長もまだ一度も中に入ってないんですよ。
**藤森** ── へえー。でも、あれを外から見て理解するのは、難しいですよ。
**伊東** ── 難しいよね。
**藤森** ── そうすると、皆さん中を見るともう大感動だと思いますね。それでペナルティ問題は解決ですよ（笑）。
**伊東** ── 今年の11月末にとりあえず大ホールだけオープンしたいということで、エントランスホール、2階のホワイエ、そして大ホール周りは一応完成する予定です。ファサードの足場も夏には外れる予定です。

## 死力を尽くす

**伊東** ── 僕らも8年間、いま9年目に入って、ほかの設計料を全部注ぎ込んでいるような状況になってしまっていますね。毎週3〜4人が台中に通い、向こうに5人ぐらい常駐して、その中には台湾の女性と結婚した者もいます（笑）。
**藤森** ── 建設費は予定の何倍ぐらいかかったの？
**伊東** ── お金は、当初のレベルからほとんど変わっていない。
**藤森** ── シドニーオペラハウスは6倍か7倍ですよ。それを市民の寄付でまかなった。
**伊東** ── 市が認めた変更分は多少アップしても、ほとんど基本的には当初の予算通りですよ。だからゼネコンは「大赤字だ」と言っている。確かに儲からないとは思いますが、それでもあれを

would eventually arrive back at the simple, original pattern. In that sense, it may be easy to comprehend. I was reminded once more that creating some sort of order is necessary.

**Fujimori** — That is why the space is easy to understand.

**Ito** — There is structural regularity as well, in that the tubes are alternately displaced. Though there are places where walls have been forcibly introduced, the basic structural system works as a gridded space.

**Fujimori** — In addition, the holes that were opened in the vertical direction at Sendai have been opened horizontally here as well. That is amazing. It is difficult enough creating them in the vertical direction. Nevertheless, when one is walking, the plan is straightforward as well.

One can immediately retrace one's steps if one gets lost, that is, because one understands the whole at a glance, and also because the outside is visible, one can go back this way if that way turns out to be a mistake. I could not understand that at all from just the model.

**Ito** — Yes. Then, the fact that two shafts inside, painted red and blue, are visible from many different vantage points also improves one's orientation.

**Fujimori** — The relationship between upper and lower floors is impossible to understand from just the drawings. But walking through it seems straightforward; it is like the way a liquid will flow in response to a slope.

**Fujimori** — This is reinforced concrete construction or concrete steel-reinforcement construction (laughs), but concrete design in twentieth-century architecture has reached the park by Le Corbusier at Ronchamp and by Mr. Tange in his column-and-beam designs such as Hiroshima Peace Center. This belongs to neither camp. I was happy to see the structure properly expressed in your first work in concrete.

I believe you have succeeded in surpassing twentieth-century architecture on its own terms.

**Ito** — On its own terms?

**Fujimori** — My own work is done outside the framework of twentieth-century architecture. It is a bit like playing on the grass in the middle of the tracks that represents twentieth-century architecture (laughs). You, on the other hand, are running properly on the tracks and have passed it. That is why I wished Mr. Tange and Mr. Murano were alive to see this.

Nonetheless, the content of the structure is unbelievable (laughs).

**Ito** — You would have been even more astonished had you seen it in autumn last year. It was really just a mass of steel reinforcements. One could barely slip a hand between reinforcement bars, there were so tightly packed. It was amazing that the concrete was poured properly. My staff felt it was impossible when they first saw the mass of reinforcements.

**Fujimori** — Your office and the builder must have worked frantically.

**Ito** — And they did so while fighting all the time. There were heaps of official documents that had to be prepared…(laughs).

**Fujimori** — I understand. I saw the unusually high stacks of documents in the site office (laughs).

**Ito** — Construction is about three years behind schedule. We won't catch up for another year, which means the construction period will be twice as long as planned. A huge penalty would be imposed…

**Fujimori** — Are they likely to impose it?

**Ito** — The city hall is being built nearby, and construction on that is also behind schedule. That case is now in court. So we are told we cannot avoid being taken to court (laughs). Though the mayor is against it…

**Fujimori** — But when the building is completed, no one will say anything of the sort. It is one of the best buildings in Taiwan. People will certainly understand that it is nothing like the buildings constructed for the Beijing Olympics, projects where casually conceived ideas managed to get built willy-nilly through technology and money.

**Ito** — But there is no telling what will happen, so we and the builder are preparing an enormous number of documents just in case the matter does go to court (laughs).

**Fujimori** — Against each other! (laughs)

**Ito** — Yes. Lee Ming Construction Co., Ltd. has done a good job up to now, but at first it could not produce drawings as Japanese general contractors are able to do.

**Fujimori** — I understand that in Taiwan, the architects produce the construction drawings.

**Ito** — Yes.

**Fujimori** — They are considered a part of design. Which they are, when one thinks about it (laughs).

**Ito** — Since they can't even draw how the scaffolding ought to be erected, we and the structural designer produced the drawings. Then, they complain that costs keep increasing, or that it constitutes "a change in the design." We reply that that is nonsense. We are going through all this trouble and looking out for you because you can't produce drawings. So we were engaged in this continuous quarrel for a long time. They have become more polished since last year or so and been extremely cheerful in the past year (laughs).

**Fujimori** — At last?

**Ito** — At last. And at the recent topping-out ceremony, all of us,

やっていると、周りのマンションとかホテルから仕事がかなりきているらしい。

**藤森** ── それで経済的に回っているんだ。じゃあ、経済的に損しているのは伊東さんのところだけじゃないですか（笑）。

**伊東** ── そう。ローカルの設計事務所も大変だけれど……。

**藤森** ── いやあ、久しぶりに"死力を尽くした"建築を見ましたね。

**伊東** ── 僕らも理性を超えたところでものが出来ていくような体験をしましたね。いま思えば、「せんだい」は、日本のゼネコンがやってくれたこともありますが、まだかなり余裕があったような気がする。今回は本当に最後までこれは危ないと思っていましたね。

**藤森** ── もともと建築というのは、国を傾けてつくるようなものだったんですよ。昔は国がつぶれたり、暗殺されたりするから（笑）。

**伊東** ── 国はつぶれてもいいけれど、オレたちは殺されたくない（笑）。

**藤森** ── ピラミッド以来の、"死力を尽くして人工物をつくる"という建築の特性。戦争的性格。「せんだい」の時は、"死力を尽くしている"までの感じではなかった。

「台中国立歌劇院」は、鉄筋を見ると、これは全員が死力を尽くさなければできないとわかる。鉄の梁に名前が書いてあったでしょう。"死力を尽くした"後の勝利のしるし。

**伊東** ── そうですね。

## アジアの魅力

**伊東** ── でもいまの日本では、ああいうことはあり得ないでしょう。

**藤森** ── どういう意味で？

**伊東** ── 台湾ではなんだかんだと毎日文句を言いながらも許している役所があるわけですよ。そういうことが日本ではあり得ないし、議会だって許さないだろうし、選挙があったら市長は落選するだろうけれども、台湾ではこんなに工期が遅れてもマスコミもたたかないからね。

**藤森** ── なるほど。そこは何かあるんでしょうね。

**伊東** ── 何かに期待しているところが国全体にあって、こういうことができるんだろうなあ。そういう意味では、いまアジアだけがそういうことができる状況なんでしょうね。

**藤森** ── なるほどね。無理してもつくるという勢いがある。

**伊東** ── ええ。インドのル・コルビュジエを見て、そう思いましたね。

**藤森** ── 無理をしてもつくっていると。

**伊東** ── そう。

**藤森** ── 無理をしてつくらなくなった最初の国がアメリカだと、二川幸夫さんが言ってましたね。ローレンス・ハルプリンとかああいう人たちがいた時は、不動産屋として立派なものをつくりたいという気持ちがあったけれども、金融が不動産に手を付けるようになると、まったく計算だけだから、いまはほとんどアメリカが話題にならないでしょう。人も作品も。

**伊東** ── そう。建築家も育たなくなっていますね。

**藤森** ── ハーバードに今、知っている建築家います？

**伊東** ── あそこのモーセン・モスタファヴィさんという学部長は、日本でグラデュエートスクールのスタジオをやってくれと言われて、2年前12人の学生を預かりましたが、すごく喜んでくれてまた来年やってくれと言われている。一人ひとりの学生を相手にしたら、日本人の学生より優秀な学生も結構いるのですが、アメリカの社会では大らかな建築は成り立たないでしょうね。

考えてみると、ヨーロッパの中では、スペインが僕は一番自由だと思って、スペインにオフィスもつくっています。いまメキシコでもひとつミュージアムをやっていますが、いつも制度から解放されるような場所を求めているのでしょうね。

**藤森** ── みんな周縁です。

**伊東** ── そう、そういう所が僕は相性がいい……。

日本の中でも、川口のように東京に近い所は、公共としては初めてですよ。九州とか東北とか、東京から遠い所でようやく仕事ができていて、海外でもアメリカのプロジェクトはひとつもありません。ヨーロッパもラテンの国でないとできない。

今度台湾で「台中国立歌劇院」のような仕事が実現可能になったのは、かなり偶発的だと思うんですが……。

**藤森** ── 僕だって、極小建築ですが、主要な施主は台湾なんですよ。

**伊東** ── そうですね。やっぱり、それを楽しむとか喜ぶ余裕があるというか……。

**藤森** ── 建築に何かを求めているんですよ。

**伊東** ── その通りですね。

**藤森** ── 何で僕に茶室を頼んだんだと聞いたら、アイデンティティをつくらなきゃいけない時期にきていると言うんですね。台湾の場合、古くは中国、次に日本が入って、戦後はアメリカが入って、いまはグローバル化で世界ともいろいろ交流が始まっているのに、自分たちのアイデンティティが見つからないという問題意識が強くある。

僕が呼ばれたのも、台湾の人は世界で一番中国茶の好きな人たちだから、お茶を中心にアイデンティティをつくりたいということです。日本は、利休のおかげで茶を核とした一文化をつくり

the mayor of course, the city assembly members, the builder and we all hugged each other and celebrated.

**Fujimori** — Then there is no problem. If the assembly members are satisfied. They tend to complain the most.

**Ito** — But, even though it was a topping-out ceremony, the assembly members were not allowed inside either. They were told that it was dangerous (laughs). We looked at the building from outside. The ceremony was conducted outside. The mayor has not yet stepped inside even once.

**Fujimori** — Ah. But the building is difficult to understand from outside.

**Ito** — It is difficult.

**Fujimori** — If that is the case, everyone will be really excited when they see the inside. The problem of a penalty will be solved (laughs).

**Ito** — They want to open just the large hall for the time being, at the end of November this year, so the entrance hall, the second-floor foyer, and the area around the large hall are to be completed, up to a point. The scaffolding on the facade is expected to be removed in summer as well.

## An All-Out Effort

**Ito** — We have been pouring design fees from our other jobs into this project for the last eight, nine years. Three or four persons go to Taichung every week, five persons are stationed over there, and recently one of them even married a taiwanese woman (laughs).

**Fujimori** — How much has the construction cost increased over the initial estimate?

**Ito** — The cost has not changed that much from the initial amount.

**Fujimori** — The increase was six- or seven-fold for the Sydney Opera House. That was covered by public donations.

**Ito** — Though cost for changes that the city approved has increased slightly, basically we have hewed to the initial estimate. The general contractor is therefore saying it is operating at a great loss. Certainly the project is unlikely to be profitable in itself, but it seems to generate jobs for condominiums and hotels nearby.

**Fujimori** — That is balancing things out financially. So the only one that is suffering a loss is your office (laughs).

**Ito** — Yes. The local architectural office that is collaborating with us is also in a difficult situation…

**Fujimori** — This is the first building I have seen in a long time of which an architect has poured every last ounce of his or her energy.

**Ito** — To us it was as if this thing was being built in a place no longer governed by reason. Looking back, I feel we still had energy to spare at Sendai, though in part that was because there were things the Japanese general contractor did for us. This time, however, the outcome was in doubt until the very end.

**Fujimori** — Architecture was originally something that a country would empty its treasury to build. Long ago, countries would collapse, people would be assassinated (laughs).

**Ito** — I don't mind a country collapsing, but I don't want us getting killed (laughs).

**Fujimori** — It has been in the nature of architecture since the Pyramids to pour every last ounce of resource to create an artifact. It is not unlike war. Sendai was not an all-out effort in that sense.

The steel reinforcements at National Taichung Theater make it obvious the building would never have been constructed had not everyone poured every last ounce of his or her energy and resource into it. People wrote their names on steel bars. They were signs of victory after an all-out "war."

**Ito** — Yes.

## The Attraction of Asia

**Ito** — Such a thing would not be possible in Japan today.

**Fujimori** — In what sense?

**Ito** — In Taiwan, government offices may complain about this and that every day but are still tolerant. Such a thing would not be possible in Japan, and assemblies are not likely to tolerate such a thing. If there were to be an election, the mayor would be defeated, but in Taiwan, even when a project is behind schedule to this extent, even the media refrains from criticism.

**Fujimori** — I see. There must be something behind this phenomenon.

**Ito** — The entire country is excited that something is about to happen. They are looking forward to this thing. In that sense, Asia may be the only place where this sort of work can be done.

**Fujimori** — I see. There is energy--people push themselves to the limit to make things.

**Ito** — Yes. That was my feeling when I saw Le Corbusier's work in India.

**Fujimori** — Making things even if it means pushing themselves to the limit.

**Ito** — Yes.

**Fujimori** — Mr. Yukio Futagawa said the United States was the first country to stop pushing itself to get things built. When people such as Lawrence Halprin were active, there was a desire even on the part of developers to create excellent things.

上げている。そういうのをやりたいけれども、日本式茶室はやりたくない。お茶の原型は中国だという誇りがあるから。

**伊東** —— なるほど。

**藤森** —— 中国大陸の茶の文化的伝統はみんな消えたわけです。文化大革命とその前の毛沢東の革命で、お茶をたしなむような人たちは殺されるか香港と台湾に逃げちゃった。香港と台湾にはお茶の文化が残っていますから、それを基に自分たちのアイデンティティをつくりたい。ただ日本的では困るというので人を探していたら、僕が茶室という名で変なものをつくっていることが分かって、呼ばれた。

台中の人たちもアイデンティティを求めているんだと思うんですね。

**伊東** —— そうですね。

**藤森** —— アイデンティティといった場合、建築は誰でもなんとなく分かるんですよ。建築の専門家にしか分からないところもありますが、しかし日本の場合だと大体障子と畳と竹があったら、ちょっと見ただけで誰でも日本的だと分かる。建築は、基本的には「常識」の延長にある。しかも、昔につくったものより今のもののほうがいいとは言えないわけですね。昔だっていいものはいっぱいある。そういう領域はそんなにないんですよ。それが本来の建築の力だと思いますが、それを台湾の人たちは求めているんじゃないかと、思っています。

## これからのプロジェクト

**藤森** —— 建設中・計画中のものが挙がっていますが、それぞれテーマを……。

**伊東** —— 「みんなの森 ぎふメディアコスモス」(建設中)は、ちょうど震災の1カ月前にニンベの最終審査があって、これは国内では久しぶりに面白いコンペで、「せんだい」とほとんどプログラムが同じでした。著名建築家がみんな応募したから熾烈な争いでした。

**藤森** —— 大御所から若い連中まで、応募したんだ。

**伊東** —— そう。僕らの案は低層で、いまかなり気合いの入っているプロジェクトです。空気の流れをテーマに消費エネルギーを従来の半分にしようとしています。90m×80mの大平面の上に木造の屋根が架かるのですが、フローリングに使うぐらいの薄い板を3方向のレイヤーにして、それでシェル状の波打つ屋根をつくっている。アラップの金田充弘さんとやっていますが、いまモックアップが出来つつあって、今年の5〜6月で屋根が架かる予定で、年内には出来上がるはずです。

「台中国立歌劇院」に比べたら、はるかに理性的につくっていて(笑)、工期も1年半ぐらいですね。

「CapitaGreen」(建設中)は、超高層で、高さ245mです。

**藤森** —— どこにつくるんですか。

**伊東** —— シンガポール。あそこには丹下さんと黒川紀章さんの300m級のタワーが2本ありますが、そのすぐ近くですね。シンガポールでは都市計画局が中心部では高さまで指定するので250mと決められました。

これはオフィスビルですね。ただ、これもファサードの半分を緑にして、しかも屋上部分にスカイフォレストという森をつくるというので、また藤森さんに笑われるかもしれない(笑)。まあ、シンガポールは緑がすくすくと育ちますから。

**藤森** —— ますます悪い(笑)。

**伊東** —— でも、250mものタワーで、しかも民間のクライアントが、ファサードの半分を緑にしてもよくメンテナンスのことを言わないなと思って、感心します。緑あふれるタワーはシンボルになるからいいんだと。

**藤森** —— 日本だったらレンタブル比がなんだかんだで、こっちが消耗してしまう。

**伊東** —— レンタブル比は結構うるさいんですが、緑のテラスをつくることに関しては、ほとんど問題になりませんでしたね。これも年内に出来ます。

「(仮称)川口市火葬施設・赤山歴史自然公園」(計画中)は、市長が「瞑想の森」を見て、気に入ってくれて依頼されました。「瞑想の森」の3倍ぐらい面積があるんですが、いま実施設計が終わったところです。これも大きな公園の中にありますね。

「バロック・ミュージアム・プエブラ」(計画中)はメキシコのプエブラというまちでやっています。

**藤森** —— あのド派手なメキシカンバロックの?

**伊東** —— そう、スペイン人はメキシコを征服した後、ピラミッドを壊してその上に教会をつくるのですが、その時に布教のために現地のインディアンを使ってプリミティブな装飾にあふれた教会を建てるのです。あれをもっと世界に広めたいので、それをPRするためにミュージアムをつくるということで……。僕はこの装飾が結構好きで……。

**藤森** —— 意外だねえ(笑)。

**伊東** —— プエブラには3回ぐらい見に行ったんですよ。そうしたら「プロジェクトに興味があるか」と言われました(笑)。それでいま設計が終わって、これから着工するところです。

**藤森** —— ああいうガチャガチャしたものをやるわけにいかないでしょう?

**伊東** —— いやいや、もっと端正なものですね。アメリカのバークレーでチャレンジしていた曲面壁の組み合わせのミュージアム

When financial considerations become paramount in real estate dealings, then it becomes simply a matter of cold calculation. Nothing in the United States is discussed or worthy of discussion any more, neither architects nor works of architecture.

**Ito** — Yes. Architects of note no longer develop there.

**Fujimori** — Are there architects you are familiar with at Harvard now?

**Ito** — Mr. Mohsen Mostafavi, who is dean, wanted me to take charge of a Graduate School of Design studio in Japan. I accepted twelve students two years ago, and he was quite pleased and has told me he wants to do that again next year. Many of the students, individually, are as good as or better than Japanese students, but a broad-minded approach to architecture is not possible in American society.

**Ito** — I believe Spain is the freest country in Europe and I personally maintain an office there. I am also designing a museum now in Mexico. I am always seeking places that are free of institutional constraints.

**Fujimori** — They are all countries on the fringes.

**Ito** — Places like that suit me…

In Japan, my work in Kawaguchi is the first public project I have done so close to Tokyo. It was in places far from Tokyo such as Kyushu and Tohoku that I was at last able to work in the public sector, and I have still done no project in the United States. In Europe, my only works have been in Latin countries.

It was mostly by accident that I was able to get jobs such as National Taichung Theater in Taiwan…

**Fujimori** — My works abroad are quite small in size but mostly in Taiwan too.

**Ito** — Yes. There is enough freedom here that one is able to enjoy one's work…

**Fujimori** — They are looking for something from architecture.

**Ito** — Exactly.

**Fujimori** — When I asked why they wanted me to design a tea house, they told me it was because it was time to establish an identity. In the case of Taiwan, it was under the sway of China first, then Japan, and since the war, it has been under the influence of the United States. Now, globalization has initiated communication with different parts of the world, but they feel very strongly that they have not yet discovered their own identity.

The reason I was invited, they say, is that they want to create an identity centered on tea, because the people of Taiwan are the most avid drinkers of Chinese tea in the world. Thanks to Rikyu, Japan has developed a culture around tea. They want to do something like that but they don't want a Japanese-style tea house. That is because they take pride in the fact that China provided the original model for the culture of tea.

**Ito** — I see.

**Fujimori** — The cultural tradition of tea has completely died in continental China. The Cultural Revolution and Mao Zedong's revolution before that killed or drove off to Hong Kong and Taiwan people who were versed in tea. The culture of tea survives in Hong Kong and Taiwan, and it is on the basis of that that they want to create their own identity. But anything that is Japanese would be a problem. When they went searching, they discovered that I was creating odd works I called tea houses. That is how I came to be invited.

I think the people of Taichung are also seeking their own identity.

**Ito** — Yes.

**Fujimori** — Everyone somehow understands what identity is about as far as architecture is concerned. There are of course aspects of architecture that are understood only by architectural experts, but in the case of Japan, for example, everyone immediately understands that a work is Japanese if it has *shoji*, *tatami* and bamboo. Architecture is basically an extension of common sense or common knowledge. Not only that, something that is contemporary in architecture is by no means regarded as superior to something that is old. There were also lots of good things in the past. There are not many areas of human endeavor that are like that. I think that is the essential power of architecture, and I believe that is what the people of Taiwan are seeking.

## On-Going Projects

**Fujimori** — Many projects under construction or under-development stages are included in this volume. What is the theme of each?

**Ito** — Minna no Mori Gifu Media Cosmos (tentative title, under construction) is the result of a competition which had its final screening just a month before the Great East Japan Earthquake. It was the first interesting domestic competition in quite a while, and the program was practically the same as that of Sendai. All the well-known architects entered, so it was a fierce competition.

**Fujimori** — Architects from the young to the established entered the event.

**Ito** — Yes. Right now we are fairly fired up about this project, which is a low-rise scheme. The theme is the flow of air; we are trying to halve the conventional consumption of energy. A wooden roof is built over a large plan measuring 90 meters by 80 meters. Boards of the thickness of flooring are being layered

に再度チャレンジしています。

## 建築の豊かさを求める

**藤森** ── 伊東さんは昔、「晩年はもっと豊かな建築をつくりたい」と言ったことがありますね。あれは誰を意識して言ったの？

**伊東** ── それはもう、圧倒的にル・コルビュジエですよ。

**藤森** ── それはいいほうでしょう。よくないほうは、誰を意識したの？（笑）

**伊東** ── いやあ、日本の建築家って、ル・コルビュジエのような人が少ないでしょう。

**藤森** ── 丹下さんまでは、とにかく構造合理主義が徹底してあって、国立代々木競技場でピークに達する。今度の「台中国立歌劇院」は、おそらく日本における構造合理主義の、丹下さんの代々木に続く21世紀のピークだと思うんです。ところが、丹下さんの国立代々木競技場には明らかに伝統が感じられた。誰が見ても感じで分かるでしょう。だけど伊東さんの「台中国立歌劇院」は、それがないんですよね。

**伊東** ──（笑いながら）確かにね。

**藤森** ──「台中国立歌劇院」はどこにもつながらないから、僕はうんと無理して言えば、伊東さんのお父さんが大事にした李朝の焼きものかなと思って（笑）、李朝の壺につながると言えばつながるかなと思っていましたが、きょう実際に見たら、全然そういうものじゃない。

**伊東** ── でもコンペティションのインタビューで、この建物に愛称を付けるとすれば何ですかと聞かれ、とっさに思いついたのが「壺中居」という言葉でした。

**藤森** ── 今度の作品で、伊東さんの言われた「最後は豊かな建築をつくって締めにしたい」という夢が実現したなと思った。21世紀になって世界で生まれた建築の中の最高作でしょう。うれしかった。

**伊東** ── やっぱり、僕らは社会に対してものを言うといっても、建築を通して言うしかないですからねえ。

**藤森** ── そう。武器は「建築」以外にないんだから。

## 「建築」の力を再認識した「みんなの家」

**藤森** ── 最後に「みんなの家」（2011年〜）はどうですか。

**伊東** ──「みんなの家」を妹島和世さんや山本理顕さんとやってきて11件出来て、まだ何件かいま進行中ではありますが、これをやることで、建築家って何をやらなくてはならないかがよくわかったような気がしますね。

ひとつは、今度の「台中国立歌劇院」も互いに悪態をつきながらも、それでも一緒にやったという喜びがありますから、持続できたと思うので、そういう喜びを日本でももっともっと味わいたい。藤森さんはまさしくそれをやり続けているわけですからね。

**藤森** ── それだけだからね（笑）。

**伊東** ── いや、それだけで十分なんですよ。だから、もっと公共とも一体になってやるやり方はあり得るのにと思っていますね。

**藤森** ── 建築本来の、「建築」にしかない力です。

**伊東** ── そう。藤森さんに「まつもと」で文章を書いてもらった[6]時に、あのころから「建築って美しさより楽しさだ」と書きました。「みんなの家」をやっていて、楽しさを超えて、もっと力というか、元気を人に与えられるものだと思うようになって、それをやることが自分自身も豊かになるだろうなと思いますね。

そういう建築をやるには、まだまだ自分を捨てなくてはと思う。色気がすぐ出てしまって……（笑）。

**藤森** ── それは仕方ない。

**伊東** ── それは「みんなの家」をやって、ずいぶん感じましたね。そういう意味では、無駄ではないどころか、すごく良かったなと思っています。

**藤森** ──「みんなの家」は、「建築」の本当の原型ですね。それと21世紀建築の最先端と、両方を伊東さんはやっているわけですよ。

**伊東** ── そうですね。「みんなの家」は、ある種のユートピア的状況なんですよ。こんなことを言うと関わった人たちには悪いけれど、こういう時に人間って一番良くなるなあと思って……。

**藤森** ── 本当に心だけが残ってるような状況でしょう。建物はみんな津波で流されてしまっていて……。

**伊東** ── 僕らもそういう気持ちになっているし、役所との関わりがないから何も言われることもない。こういう状況でいつも建築が出来たらいいなあと、すごく思いますね。陸前高田で藤本壮介さん、平田晃久さん、乾久美子さんの3人で「みんなの家」をやった時は、まだ彼らは建築に対して色気があるんですよ。どんな状況でも。

**藤森** ── 自分を出したい。

僕の経験からいくと、自作のうち、心に残る作とそうでないものとが自分で分かる。僕の場合は高過庵がよく出来ていて、いま見ると自分がつくったという感じがしないんですよ。何かほかの人がつくったような、不思議な感じで見ている。「なんか面白いものが出来たな」みたいな。そういう抜けるものがあるんです。

**伊東** ── 抜けると同時に、自分を超えていくものがあるんですよね。

**藤森** ── そうそう。何か違うものがつくってくれたような。

n three directions to create an undulating shell roof. We are doing this with Mr. Mitsuhiro Kanada of Arup. A mock up is now being built, and the roof is scheduled to be constructed in May to June of this year. The project should be completed this year. Compared to National Taichung Theater, it is far more rational (laughs), and the construction period too is only about a year and a half.

**Ito** — CapitaGreen (under construction) is a super high-rise building 245 meters high.

**Fujimori** — Where will it be built?

**Ito** — Singapore. There are two towers in the 300-meter range there, one by Mr. Tange and the other by Mr. Kurokawa, and this will be right near them. The city planning bureau in Singapore, which determines even the heights of buildings in the central district, decided on a height of 250 meters.

This is an office building. You may laugh at this, but half the facade will be green, and, not only that, a so-called "sky forest" will be created on the roof (laughs). Greenery thrives in Singapore.

**Fujimori** — Worse and worse (laughs).

**Ito** — But this is a 250-meter tower. Not only that, I am impressed that the private-sector client has not complained about the cost of maintenance, even though we made half the facade green. The client says that is okay because a building full of greenery will become a symbol.

**Fujimori** — If this were in Japan, the architect would be exhausted fielding complaints about the ratio of rentable space.

**Ito** — The client is particular about the ratio of rentable space but has not made much of a fuss about creating green terraces. This project too will be completed this year.

**Ito** — We were commissioned to design Crematorium and Akayama Historic Nature Park in Kawaguchi (tentative title, under development) after the mayor saw "Meiso no Mori" and liked it. It is about three times the area of "Meiso no Mori." The final design was just completed. This too is inside a large park.

We are now doing a project called Barroco Museo Internacional (under development) in a place called Puebla in Mexico.

**Fujimori** — The place known for its extremely colorful Mexican Baroque?

**Ito** — Yes. After conquering Mexico, the Spaniards destroyed pyramids and built churches over them. In order to propagate Christianity, they built churches full of primitive ornamentation using the indigenous population as a labor force. The museum is intended to make that more widely known to the rest of the world…I sort of like this ornamentation…

**Fujimori** — That is unexpected (laughs).

**Ito** — I visited Puebla about three times to look at the buildings and was asked if I had interest in the project (laughs). The design is now finished, and construction work is about to begin.

**Fujimori** — You aren't going to do something covered in ornamentation, are you?

**Ito** — No, it will be more restrained. I once tried designing a museum with a combination of curved walls for Berkeley, California, and now I am taking up that challenge once more.

## In Pursuit of Richly Imaginative Buildings

**Fujimori** — You once said that in old age, you would like to create richly imaginative buildings. Who did you have in mind when you said that?

**Ito** — Le Corbusier of course.

**Fujimori** — As a positive example. Who did you have in mind as a negative example (laughs)?

**Ito** — There are not many people like Le Corbusier among Japanese architects.

**Fujimori** — Mr. Tange was a structural rationalist, through and through, and reached his peak with Yoyogi National Gymnasium. National Taichung Theatre is likely to be the peak of structural rationalism in the twenty-first century in Japan. But one clearly senses tradition in Mr. Tange's Yoyogi National Gymnasium. Everyone senses it. But there isn't that quality in your National Taichung Theatre.

**Ito** — (Laughing) That's for certain.

**Fujimori** — Since National Taichung Theater has no obvious connection to anything, I thought, if one bent over backwards, a connection might be found with the Joseon-Dynasty porcelain your father treasured (laughs). A connection with Joseon-Dynasty jars might be discovered. But today, when I looked the architecture, it was not like the jars.

**Ito** — But in the interview for the competition, when I was asked what nickname I might give this building, the word that immediately came to mind was "Kochukyo." (The title of a story in the *Hanshu* (Book of Han) about a man who discovers inside a jar a world different from everyday life).

**Fujimori** — With this work, I believe you have realized your declared ambition to create a richly imaginative building and thereby round off your professional career. This is the best work of architecture completed anywhere in the twentieth century so far. I am happy for you.

**Ito** — The only way we can say something regarding society is through architecture.

**Fujimori** — Yes. The only weapon we can wield is architecture.

**伊東** ── 確かにそうですね。

**藤森** ── そういうことは、日本の人だけが思うことかもしれない。

**伊東** ── そうかもしれないねえ。近代的自我をもっていたら、絶対そう思わないですね。

**藤森** ── そう。近代的自我は、日本人にとっては近代的自我だけれど、ヨーロッパの人にとっては、伝統的自我ですから。

**伊東** ── なるほど。

## 「建築」の力

**藤森** ── 僕はいま、台湾で空飛ぶ家という別荘をつくっているんですが、これは3、4人の女の人たちが注文主で、要求は「この世と少し離れたものをつくってほしい。そこに骨を埋めるから」というものなんですよ。

　先ほど被災地はユートピア的状況と言われましたが、そういうこの世のしがらみから離れた状況とか、この世ではないものをつくってくれとか、建築って不思議なものだなと思うんです。この世のもの、石とか木とか鉄で建築をつくってそこで寝泊まりするものから、この世でないものまで連続しているし、大昔から現代までずっと続いていて、昔のものもいまのものも同じようにいい。機械だと昔のものはどうしようもないですからね。

　だから、21世紀では「建築」のような存在はほとんどないと思いますよ。情報化とかIT機器とか、ああいうものにはそういう力はないから。建築は、なんとも不思議な魅力をもったものですね。

**伊東** ── それはいい話ですね。

1.「角館伝承館（現・角館樺細工伝承館）」（1978年）
2.『新建築』1983年9月号　篠原一男との対談「ポストモダンに出口はあるか？」
3.「直島町役場」（1983年）
4.「つくばセンタービル」（1983年）
5.「東雲キャナルコートCODAN2街区」（2003年）
6.『新建築』2004年7月号

## An Awareness of the Power of Architecture Reawakened by "Home-for-All"

**Fujimori** — Finally, how is "Home-for-All" project (2011-) doing?

**Ito** — I have been doing "Home-for-All" together with other architects including Ms. Kazuyo Sejima and Mr. Riken Yamamoto. There are now ten "Home-for-All" completed and a few are still underway. Doing this has made me realize what it is architects must do.

First, those of us involved in National Taichung Theater have badmouthed each other, but we have been able to continue because there is joy in working together. I would like to experience that a lot more in Japan. You yourself have continued to experience that joy.

**Fujimori** — That is the only thing I get out of it (laughs).

**Ito** — That is all that is needed. I believe therefore that working more closely together to do public projects is possible.

**Fujimori** — That is the essential and unique power of architecture.

**Ito** — Yes. You wrote in connection with Matsumoto[6] that "architecture is more about delight than beauty." Being involved in "Home-for-All," I have come to believe that it goes beyond delight. It is more about giving people power or energy. Being able to do that makes oneself richer as well.

I believe I must make even greater efforts at self-effacement in order to create such buildings. I am easily tempted by ambition… (laughs).

**Fujimori** — That can't be helped.

**Ito** — That has been impressed on me, doing "Home-for-All." In that sense, the project was not at all a waste of time and effort but a very good thing to have done.

**Fujimori** — "Home-for-All" is a true architectural archetype. You are thus doing both that and leading-edge works of twenty-first century architecture.

**Ito** — Yes. "Home-for-All" is being created under utopian conditions. I hope people who have been involved will forgive me for saying so, but I think an occasion such as this brings out the best in people…

**Fujimori** — People have truly been left with nothing but their lives. All buildings were washed away by the tsunami…

**Ito** — We approach the project in a similar spirit, and since we have nothing to do with the bureaucracy, we don't have officials telling us this or that. I truly wish we could practice architecture under such circumstances all the time. I was involved in "Home-for-All" in Rikuzentakata with Ms. Kumiko Inui, Mr. Sou Fujimoto and Mr. Akihisa Hirata and those three still have architectural ambitions. No matter the circumstances.

**Fujimori** — They want to express themselves.

Based on my own experience, I would say an architect understands which of his or her works are keepers and which are not. In my case, Takasugi-an seems to me well done. Looking at it now, it does not feel as if I'd designed it. It feels strange, as if I were looking at a work someone else had done. What an interesting thing, I think to myself. I'm at one removed from the work.

**Ito** — There is a sense of remoteness or separation, and at the same time a sense of having transcended oneself.

**Fujimori** — Yes. It's as if someone else had done it.

**Ito** — That is certainly the case.

**Fujimori** — That may be something only a Japanese would feel.

**Ito** — That may be. Someone with a modern sense of self would never feel that way.

**Fujimori** — Yes. What constitutes a modern sense of self to a Japanese is a traditional sense of self to a European.

**Ito** — I see.

## The Power of Architecture

**Fujimori** — I am currently designing a weekend house in Taiwan called Soratobu House (Flying House). The clients are three or four women, and their wish is for a place that is slightly removed from this world, because they plan to spend their last days there.

You said earlier that conditions were utopian in disaster-stricken areas. To design under conditions where ties to this world have been broken, or to be asked to design a place that is not of this world--architecture is strange, is it not? It can mean everything from buildings made from materials of this world such as stone, wood and steel where one can take shelter for the night to places that are not of this world. It has continued to exist since ancient times, and things from the past can be just as good as things built today. Machines from the past, in contrast, are completely useless today.

I do not believe there is anything else that is at all like architecture in the twenty-first century. Such things as communication or IT equipment do not have such a power. Architecture possesses an uncanny power and appeal.

**Ito** — You make a good point.

---

1. Kakunodate Denshokan (now, Kakunodate Kabazaiku Denshokan) (1978).
2. *Posuto modaan ni deguchi wa aruka* (Is Postmodernism a Dead End?), Dialogue with Kazuo Shinohara, *Shinkenchiku*, September 1983.
3. Naoshima Town Hall (1983).
4. Tsukuba Center Building (1983).
5. Shinonome Canal Court CODAN2 Block (2003).
6. *Shinkenchiku*, July 2004.

# Collected Works
# 2002-2014

# 6 意匠と構造の融合
## Integration of Design and Structure

伊東豊雄との対話　Conversation with Toyo Ito

### ブルージュ・パヴィリオン
Brugge Pavilion ［2002］

### サーペンタイン・ギャラリー・パヴィリオン 2002
Serpentine Gallery Pavilion 2002 ［2002］

### まつもと市民芸術館
Matsumoto Performing Arts Centre ［2004］

### TOD'S 表参道ビル
TOD'S Omotesando Building ［2004］

### 福岡アイランドシティ中央公園中核施設 ぐりんぐりん
Island City Central Park "GRIN GRIN" ［2005］

### 瞑想の森 市営斎場
Meiso no Mori Municipal Funeral Hall ［2006］

ブルージュ・パヴィリオン
サーペンタイン・ギャラリー・パヴィリオン 2002

——「せんだいメディアテーク」以降、海外のプロジェクトが入ってくるようになります。「ブルージュ・パヴィリオン」は市からの依頼ですが、クライアントとの出会い方や仕事の受け方は変わりましたか。

確かに90年代後半から、「せんだい」とは関係なく、海外のプロジェクトが少しずつ増えてきましたね。
「ブルージュ」は、突然、向こうの建築家のグループから、「2002年のEUカルチュラル・キャピタルにブルージュが決まった。そのイベントに関するインフォメーションセンターをまちの中心につくりたいので、それの設計を依頼したい」という話がきました。ただし、敷地はローマ時代のカテドラルの跡地だから、下にある遺跡を傷つけないような、軽いものでやってほしいという条件でした。そのころ、いくつかのアルミのプロジェクトを担当していた平田晃久君や中山英之君からのリアクションがあって、アルミでやろうという話になりました。

—— アルミのプロジェクトをいろいろやっていたというのは、アルミという素材への興味からですか。

アルミという素材への興味というより、アルミをストラクチャーにすることが一番の興味の対象でした。「せんだい」以降、"新しい構造"に目覚めたということもあります。これは新しい構造を発見するというより、「せんだい」で構造の強さにインパクトを受けていたことから、構造の強さが「建築」を元気にするようなことをやりたいと。構造によって力強い建築をつくるということと、アルミでつくることによって、カーテンウォールではなく、外皮にストラクチャーが出てくるという面白さ。それがひとつになって、いろいろなプロジェクトがそこから生まれます。

——「ブルージュ」でも初めから、構造で面白いことをやろうという意識があったわけですね。

ありましたね。最初の案は、パネルが展示などにも使えるような、内/外を隔てたプロジェクトでしたが、最終的にはブリッジのような外部空間になりました。そのストラクチャーを向こうの人たちが気に入ってくれて、できるだけピュアな形でやりたいから外だけでいい、インフォメーションセンターという機能がなくてもいいということになりました。それで、まちの人たちは別に渡らなくてもいいのに橋を渡って楽しんでいる(笑)。

—— あの橋を渡った後に新しい風景が感じられるような空間が、あそこにあるのではないかということは想像できます。通り抜けるというのはシンプルな空間体験のひとつで、葛飾の公園で制作したパヴィリオンでも、子どもが喜んで通り抜けたり水辺で遊んだりしていますね。

こういうミニマムなストラクチャーというのは面白いですね。

——「サーペンタイン・ギャラリー・パヴィリオン 2002」に関しても、先ほどおっしゃった構造の力強さ、プラス幾何学ということもありますが、幾何学云々というよりも、人がその空間を体験することによって、新しい身体の延長というか、身体を感じる枠が少し広がるような空間があるのではないかと想像しています。

いまになってみると、「サーペンタイン」の評価は非常に高いのですが、僕は「ブルージュ」のほうが好きですね。「ブルージュ」は構造と空間とがひとつになって、よく出来ていると思います。つまり、「構造」を感じさせない空間だけれど、一番構造的なんですよ。

——「ブルージュ」は、アルミという素材のもっている特徴が構造に生かされていると思います。「サーペンタイン」は、スチールの力技でつくっているのが視覚的にも表れているというところが違うと思います。あれは構造家のセシル・バルモンドさんからの提案があったのですか。

そうですね。平面で考えていることが現実に建ち上がりストラクチャーになってくると、別のものに変わっていく。
一方、「ブルージュ」はそういう転換はなくて、構造自体をテーマにしており、構造がもつかもたないかのギリギリを見極めた、極限的な状態をつくりました。そこから生まれるはかない感じが、ヨーロッパの人たちへのアピールになったのだと思います。
そうでないと、1年後に、カルチュラル・キャピタルの期間が終わり、取り壊すといったときに、あそこまで市民が擁護してくれなかったと思いますね。もともと1年で取り壊す予定で始まったプロジェクトでしたから。

Brugge Pavilion
Serpentine Gallery Pavilion 2002

– The office has been doing a great deal of overseas work since Sendai Mediatheque. Brugge Pavilion was a municipal commission. Has the way in which you find clients or receive jobs changed?

Overseas projects have gradually increased since the late 1990s, but this is not related to Sendai Mediatheque.
In the case of Brugge, a group of architects there contacted me out of the blue and told me the city had been designated the European Capital of Culture 2002. They wanted me to design an information center in the center of the city concerning that event. I was asked to create something lightweight that would not damage the ruins of a cathedral below-ground. Akihisa Hirata and Hideyuki Nakayama were in charge of a number of aluminum projects in the office at the time, and we decided to build this structure too out of aluminum.

– Was the office engaged in a number of aluminum projects because you were interested in aluminum as a material?

I was interested, not so much in aluminum as a material, but in making structures out of aluminum. Since Sendai, I'd become intrigued by "new structures." It doesn't mean that I wanted to discover new structures. The impact that a powerful structure had on Sendai convinced me that architecture could be revitalized by such power. I became interested in creating powerful buildings through structure and in expressing an aluminum structure on the outside instead of a curtain wall. All these different threads came together and led to diverse projects.

– So from the start you intended to do something interesting with structure at Brugge?

I did. In the first scheme, panels that could also be used for exhibitions separated inside from outside, but ultimately, the project became a bridge-like outdoor space. The people in Bruges liked that structure. They wanted the form to be as pure as possible and told me it could simply be an outdoor space and need not function as an information center. When it was built, the people of the city enjoyed crossing the bridge even when they had no particular need to cross it [laughs].

– I can imagine the space altering the way people saw the landscape. Passing through something is a simple spatial experience. Children enjoy passing through the pavilion created for the park in Katsushika and playing by the water.

Minimal structures of this sort are interesting.

– Serpentine Gallery Pavilion 2002 has a powerful structure as well as a geometry. However, it isn't so much geometry *per se*. Instead, the space there is such that, experiencing it extends the body in a new way. It increases the capacity of the body to feel.

People praise Serpentine now, but I myself preferred Brugge. Structure and space were integrated at Brugge. I think it was well made. That is, the structure did not draw attention to itself though Brugge was the more structurally driven of the two pavilions.

– Brugge made use of the characteristics of aluminum as a material. Serpentine on the other hand is a steel tour-de-force. I understand the idea for it was proposed by the structural designer Mr. Cecil Balmond.

Yes. An idea that is conceived in plan changes into something different as it is actually built and becomes a structure.

At Brugge, on the other hand, there was no such transformation. Structure itself was the theme. We created an extreme condition, ascertaining the very limit of stability of the structure. I think its sense of ephemerality appealed to people in Europe.

If that hadn't been the case, I don't think so many members of the public would have supported keeping it a year later when Bruges term as Capital of Culture ended and the structure was about to be dismantled. After all, the project was initially scheduled to last only a year.

「葛飾にいじゅくみらい公園」パーゴラ
Pavilion for Katsushika niijukumirai Parks Pergola

045

それから4～5年経って、市長がそろそろもう取り壊してもいいんじゃないかと言った時も、市民が存続のために立ち上がって、当時の文化大臣のところまで嘆願がいって、それで文化財に指定されましたからね。文化財としてメンテナンス費用を出すことが決まったので、メンテナンスのために新しい橋を設計して、予算を見積もるところまでいきましたが、大臣が代わって、予算が出ないままとうとう10年経って解体されてしまいました。

― 市民がキャンドルを灯して、保存運動をしていましたね。

あれは本当に僕も感激しました。保存しようという意志をまちの人たちがキャンドルをあそこに置くことで表明したわけですね。それが地元の新聞に載って、それで結局10年もちこたえましたが、特にポリカーボネートでつくった浮き桟橋みたいなブリッジは、傷みが激しくてボロボロになっていました。あれは取り替えないと保存するのは難しかったと思います。

― 最初からブルージュのような歴史的なまちの中に建てることに、市民からの抵抗はなかったのですか。

僕も最初にプレゼンする時は、アルミの、工業的な建築ともいえるようなものをもっていったら嫌がられるかと思っていました。ところが、特に依頼してきた建築家たちが感激してくれて、「こういう古いまちに住んでいると退屈する。だから新しいものを求めているんですよ」と言われました。建築家たちがそう言っても、まちの人たちは嫌がるだろうなと思っていたら、多くの人が感激してくれましたね。

だから、つくっている時も、通りがかったおばあさんが熱心に見ている。ヨーロッパの人は一般の市民も、新しく何かが出来ていくことに対して関心をもってくれているのだなと思いました。

― 壊されるとさびしくなりますね。

僕は自分の設計したものがなくなっていくということにはそんなに抵抗がないですね。もう使われなくなって、しかもメンテナンスが十分でないなら、僕は壊してしまったほうがさっぱりする（笑）。建築も人間と同じで寿命があって、そんな老醜をさらしていくことはないと思っています。

― 1年間の仮設の構造物が10年もったというのは、うれしいですね。

そうですね。ヨーロッパの人は、建築に対しても、まちに対しても、日本人と時間に対する概念が違いますから。
「サーペンタイン」は、いまでも建っていますよ。最初、ロンドンのセシルさんたちが元のパワーステーションを修復したテーマパークに置かれ、それからまた転売されて、いまは地中海に面した南仏のホテルの庭先にあります。でも購入する人がいるので、ヨーロッパはすごいと思いますね。

## まつもと市民芸術館

― 「せんだい」では構造と素材とファサードが切り離されているように思うのですが、「まつもと市民芸術館」の穴の開いているファサードは、外皮の扱いと構造素材の扱いが一体となって、力強さが出てきているように思います。

「まつもと」のコンペティション案はガラスのファサードとフラットな大屋根のある提案でしたが、実施設計の段階でGRCパネルにガラスをはめ込んだファサードになりました。ただ、外壁は構造体になっていないので、カーテンウォールの一種ですが、「まつもと」では、構造の問題より、非常に狭い敷地にどう収めるかが最大の課題でしたね。

― 「まつもと」は、この章で取り上げたプロジェクトの中ではちょっと異色だと思うのですが、コンペティション案はガラスのファサードで、基本的に水平なスラブの連続という印象が強い。それから「サーペンタイン」を手がける中間にあった「オスロ・ウェストバーネン再開発計画コンペティション応募案」でも、構造と軽快なものに水平ラインを強調するテイストがあって、このコンペティションも、水平性の中に「せんだい」の力強さがあります。その中で「まつもと」は、閉じる方向に進み始めていて、それがその後の「TOD'S 表参道ビル」や「MIKIMOTO Ginza 2」（p. 050）につながっているような気がします。

いつもコンペティションではいろいろなことをやって、問題の核心がどこにあるかを探っていくわけですが、「まつもと」の場合、一番大きいのは、フライタワーを真ん中に置いたこと、そして反転させたことに尽きると思います。

オペラが上演できるようにするには、大きなT字型のステージで4面舞台が必要になります。あ

「ブルージュ・パヴィリオン」、解体への抗議運動として市民がローソクの灯をともす
Brugge Pavilion: Local residents burned candles as part of a protest against dismantling the pavilion.

When, after four or five years had passed, the mayor suggested it might at last be time to dismantle it, many people protested and petitioned the then Minister of Culture. That was how it came to be designated a cultural asset. The decision was made to pay for maintenance of the cultural asset; a new bridge for the purposes of maintenance was designed, and a budget estimate was prepared. However, a new minister took office, and ten years passed without funds being actually budgeted. The structure was eventually dismantled.

– There was a public preservation movement, with people lighting candles, wasn't there?

I was quite moved by that. The people of the city expressed their desire to preserve the pavilion by placing candles there. The event was covered by a local newspaper, and thus the pavilion managed to last ten years. However, the floating bridge-like structure made of polycarbonate in particular suffered a lot of wear and tear and was in bad shape. Preservation would have been difficult without its replacement.

– Wasn't there public opposition at the start to build in a city as historic as Brugge?

When I had to make my first presentation, I myself thought that people would hate an aluminum, industrial-looking structure, but the architects who'd commissioned me were especially excited. I was told that living in such an old city was boring and that was why they were seeking something new. I thought that, even if architects felt that way, the people of the city would hate it, but many people were excited about it.

When it was being constructed, passersby, even elderly ladies, would look on with keen interest. It seems to me members of the general public in Europe take great interest in things under construction.

– It is sad that it was dismantled.

I'm not so opposed to seeing things I have designed disappearing. I would feel a lot better if a thing that is no longer being used, particularly a thing that is not being adequately maintained, were dismantled [laughs]. A building is like a human being. It has a lifespan, and there is no point in taking inordinate measures to preserve a building.

– It is wonderful that a temporary structure expected to last a year survived for ten years.

Yes. People in Europe conceive of time in the context of buildings and cities differently from the Japanese.

Serpentine is still standing. First, it was relocated to a theme park that a group in London including Mr. Cecil created from a former power station. Then, it was resold and is now in the garden of a hotel in the south of France facing the Mediterranean. I think it is amazing that there are people in Europe who would purchase things like that.

### Matsumoto Performing Arts Centre

– At Sendai, the structure, the material and the facade are treated separately, but in the perforated facade of the Matsumoto Performing Arts Centre, the treatment of the exterior skin and the treatment of the structural material are integrated, resulting in a more powerful statement.

The competition proposal for Matsumoto featured a glass facade and a large, flat roof. However, in the final design stage, the facade became GRC panels into which glass was fitted, and that was how it was built. The

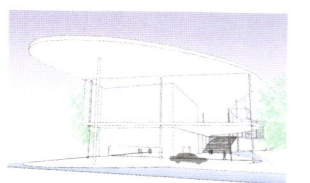

「まつもと市民芸術館コンペティション案」
Competition proposal for Matsumoto Performing Arts Centre

「オスロ・ウェストバーネン再開発計画コンペティション応募案」
Architect Competition Vestbanen, Oslo, Norway

の敷地でステージをT字状に置くとその後ろへ回り込めないから、片側に寄せて田の字型のステージにするのはどうだろうという話になった時に、東建男君が、ミュンヘンのオペラ劇場やコベントガーデンにその先例があると言い出したわけです。中山君のお父さんが二期会の理事でしたから、中山君のお父さんを通じて専門家に確認したら、「田の字型でも十分オペラはできますよ」という話でした。

さらに、反転することによって、搬入口が真ん中のホワイエの下になり、後ろに回り込まなくてよくなる。もし、反転しなければ、オペラの舞台のために10t級の大きなトラックが出入りできるように、後ろの大きな木を伐らなければならないし、隣の民家の真ん前にいかにも楽屋裏然とした場所をつくってしまう。反転すればそれも解決するので、この反転した案が評価されれば勝てるだろうし、評価されなければ最初に落ちるだろうという思いで案を提出しました。

コンペティションの後、もう一度敷地に行ってみると、周りが民家で囲まれていて、お互い内からも外からも見られるという問題点を抱えていました。また、市長が「松本は木造の城と石積みのまちだ。まつもとのホールでそれをどうシンボライズするか」と言っていたという話を聞いていました。このような点を考慮して、外壁を石積みのようなイメージのものにしようということから出来たのが、いまの象嵌のパターンです。

— そう言われたら、石積みにも見えてきますね（笑）。

市長は最初、そのモックアップを見てしばらく絶句していました（笑）。でも、すぐに思い直して、われわれがそれを一番いいと思うのだったらそれがいいのだろうと言ってくれました。出来上がるころには大変喜んでくれましたね。われわれも結果的にはガラスのファサードになるより、はるかに良かったと思います。

— 初期のスケッチでは、床は劇場なのでアップダウンしている所があって地形的ですが、屋根がフラットでしたね。敷地の印象から、フラットな屋根を強くイメージしていたのですか。

屋上庭園が最初から条件付けられていました。地上がもともと公園でしたので、それを上にあげてくださいということでした。そのことをどこかで意識したのだと思いますね。

— 観客も大階段を上りながらホワイエを通って客席に行くと、自然と日常の世界から舞台の世界に入る準備ができていく空間になっているように感じました。そのプロセスも観劇という行為の一部だと思いますが、あの大階段は最初からイメージされていたのですか。

反転した結果、エントランスの先に幅の広い緩い階段がきたということですね。あの勾配の緩い階段は印象的だと思いますが、スロープが欲しいと言われて可動のスロープも脇に付けられました。

もともと、演劇を観るとかコンサートを聴くというのは、劇場の中だけで完結するのではなく、道路からさまざまなシークエンスを経てホールに入っていく。そこで演目を観たり聴いたりして、終わったら夢見心地でホールから出て、いつの間にか現実に帰っていくという、その道行きが大事ですね。

江戸時代の勧進能の舞台を復元した絵巻物がありますが、それによれば仮設の劇場をつくり、朝早く、櫓太鼓の音が響き渡ると、みんなが集まってきて、屋台でおまんじゅうを食べながらのんびりと待っているという様子が描かれています。仮設の劇場には3つの入り口があって、武士のための桟敷席に行く入り口、一般大衆が枡席に行く入り口、演者が入って行く楽屋口が並列に置かれていて、触れ太鼓が鳴るとそれぞれの入り口から入って行く。

そして、お能の演目がいくつもあって、枡席の人たちは弁当を食べたりヤジを飛ばしたりしながら、武士は桟敷席で芸者を侍らせてお酒を飲みながら、一日ずっとお能を楽しんで、最後はぞろぞろと出て行く。お能を見るというのは一日がかりのエンターテインメントだったんですね。

— そういうゆったりとした時間の流れが、「まつもと」にもあるような気がします。そういう時間が演じる者と観る者の間に流れていて、それがう

exterior wall is not structural, so it is a kind of curtain wall. However, the biggest issue in Matsumoto was not a problem of structure but the question of how the building was to be accommodated on an extremely small site.

— Matsumoto seems a bit different from other projects discussed in this chapter. The competition proposal had a glass facade and basically seemed like a series of horizontal slabs. Then there was the Architect Competition Vestbanen, Oslo, Norway(2002), which the office developed while doing Serpentine. In that, horizontality was emphasized in the structure, and lightweight elements were used. The horizontality of this competition proposal had some power of Sendai. Matsumoto became more closed and is linked in that sense to subsequent works such as TOD'S Omotesando Building and MIKIMOTO Ginza 2 (p. 050).

Many different things are always attempted in a competition because we are trying to find the heart of the problem. In the case of Matsumoto, the biggest thing was the decision to locate the flytower in the middle and flip the positions of the stage and the audience.

To put on opera, one needs four stages, arranged in a T-shape in plan. With that site, it would have been impossible to get around the stages had they been arranged in such a way. That was when it was suggested that the stages be pushed to one side and arranged in a quadripartite square in plan. Takeo Higashi said there were precedents for that in opera houses in Munich and Covent Garden. Nakayama's father is a director of the Nikikai [an organization of vocalists], and so we consulted an expert through him. We discovered that such an arrangement is a viable one for opera.

Furthermore, reversing the positions of the stage and the audience resulted in the delivery entrance being located under the foyer in the middle. It was no longer necessary to go around to the back. If the stage and audience hadn't been flipped, then the large trees in the back of the site would have had to be cut down to accommodate the coming and going of large, ten-ton trucks and private houses next door would have been exposed to the centre's messy inner workings. Reversing them solved that. I thought we would win if the virtue of this reversed scheme was recognized. If not, then our scheme would be the first to be eliminated from consideration. That was my belief when we presented our scheme.

After the competition, I visited the site once more. The site is surrounded by private houses, and we were faced with the problem of being quite visible from without and of being able to see into those houses from within. In addition, the mayor said that Matsumoto was a city famous for its wooden castle and stonework. He wanted to know how that was going to be expressed in the hall. Taking that into consideration, we tried to make the exterior wall suggest stonework. That is how we arrived at the inlay pattern--the pattern of glass embedded in the panels--on the outside.

— Now that you mention it, it does seem a bit like stonework [laughs].

When the mayor first saw the mock up, he was at a loss for words [laughs]. But he quickly recovered and said that if we thought that was the best solution, it was all right. He was quite pleased by the time the building was completed. We too felt in the end that it was far better than having a glass facade.

— In early sketches, the floor went up and down because it was an opera house-it was topographical in character-but the roof was flat. Did your impressions of the site lead you to imagine the roof as flat?

A roof terrace was part of the program from the start. There was originally a park there at ground level, and we were asked to raise it to a higher level. I think that was in the back of my mind.

— When the audience pass through the foyer while ascending a grand stairway and proceed to the auditorium, the space seems to prepare people for a natural transition from the daily world to the ground stage. I think that process is part of going to the theater. Did you have an image of that grand stairway from the start?

The reversal of the stage and audience meant

「中野本町の家」 White U

047

まくいっているのかなと思います。

それは、「中野本町の家」（p. 047）をつくったころからいつも意識していたような気がしますね。これは建築をどう考えるかという、かなり本質的な建築の思想に関わってくることで、僕は体験の総和、経験の総和、空間化したものが「建築」だと思っています。それは日本庭園のような、いろんな要素を組み合わせて出来た体験ですから、庭を歩く人によって少しずつ体験が変わってくるように、ひとりずつ違った建築空間をつくり上げていく。そういう空間に興味があります。

これは「八代市立博物館・未来の森ミュージアム」でもそうですね。ひとつのボリュームの中に納まっていても、スロープや階段を上がったり下りたりしながら展示室を巡るシークエンスが出来ています。

— 伊東さんが時どきおっしゃる「ポルトガルの街角ではなんとなく人が集まっていて、そこに音楽が流れている。建築だけじゃなくて、人びとの行為そのものがまちにつながっていく」というのは、住宅も「まつもと」もそこらへんの意識がつながっているということですね。

そうですね。のちの「ゲント市文化フォーラム・コンペティション応募案」（p. 339）は明らかにそういう外部性を意識しながらやっていたし、「台中国立歌劇院」にもつながっていますね。

要するに体験するプロセスを「建築」と考えるかどうか。ル・コルビュジエの建築はそうですね。サヴォワ邸もスロープを上がっていく所から屋上庭園に至るまで、さまざまなシークエンスの変化があります。それがすごく楽しくて、そういう建築が好きですね。チャンディーガルの裁判所の3つの色のついた壁も、スロープを行ったり来たりするたびに景色が変わっていく。

— 「中目黒Tビル」でも、アトリウムがあって内側のテラスで会議をしたり、おしゃべりをしたりしていましたが、オフィスだから机の上で仕事をしているだけじゃなくて、いろいろな動きがある。それを一日の流れと関係付けるということですが、舞台でも「フィガロの結婚」（p. 090）の時はそのような動きがありましたね。

楽屋、ステージがあり、オーケストラピットがあり、客席があるという、その関係を結んでしまう、そのすべてが演劇空間なんだということですね。役者や小澤征爾さんが舞台奥から登場して、ステージやオーケストラピットに行き、役者も客席まで入ってくるとか。これは「まつもと」の芸術監督の串田和美さん流の演出と関わっていると思います。

昨年（2013年）7月に「まつもと」で公演された、串田さん作・演出の「空中キャバレー2013」は、観客が搬出入り口から入って行くと祭りの縁日のようになっていて、役者がそこで売り子になっていたり、大道芸をやっていたり、みんな30分ぐらいそこで楽しんでから舞台のほうに移動する。すると、役者が今度は演者として出てくる。串田さんも演出をしながら、役者として登場もするし、観客としてその周りを動き回って人びとと言葉を交わしたりしている。

— 串田さんの考え方は、建築といろんなところ

「八代市立博物館・未来の森ミュージアム」
Yatsushiro Municipal Museum

でつながっているということですね。

そうですね。串田さんは観客と演者との間の、見る・見られるという関係をなくしてしまいたいという思いが一貫していますね。

内／外の問題もそうですし、内においても舞台と客席とか、そういう壁を取り払いたいという思いがいつもあります。

僕もステージの上で一段高い所でレクチャーしている時と、同じテーブルで学生たちと話す時では、こちらの気持ちや雰囲気も違うし、話し方も変わりますからね。

### TOD'S表参道ビル

— 「TOD'S表参道ビル」は、ヨーロッパのクライアントからの依頼で東京に建築をデザインするとどうなるかという話になりますが、最初はどういう経緯から始まったのですか。

元朝日新聞のファッション担当の知り合いを通じて、「TOD'S」のCEOであるディエゴ・デッラ・ヴァッレさんから依頼がきました。ディエゴさん

---

that a wide, gently rising stairway would be situated at the far end of the entrance. I think the gently rising stairway makes an impression, but they wanted a ramp. That is why we installed a movable ramp to one side.

Going to a dramatic performance or a concert is not an experience limited simply to the theater itself. Diverse sequences are experienced starting on the street and leading to the hall. In the hall the program is seen or heard, and at the end of the program, the members of the audience leave the hall still basking in the afterglow of the performance. Eventually they find they have returned to reality. That entire journey is important.

There is a picture scroll that shows what a stage for *dengaku* and *sarugaku* performances, the antecedents for Noh, were like in the Edo period. A temporary theater was erected, and early in the morning, the beating of a drum would prompt everyone to gather. They would eat steamed buns at stalls and wait leisurely. There were three entrances to the temporary theater, all in a row, one leading to box seats for samurai, another leading to compartmentalized seating areas (*masu-seki*) for the general public, and one leading to the dressing room for the performers. People would start entering once the beating of a drum announcing the performance began.

There were a number of programs, and the people in the *masu-seki* would eat box lunches or heckle the performers, the samurai in their box seats would be entertained by *geisha* and drink *sake*. In this way, the audience would spend the entire day enjoying performances. At the end, they would all file out. Watching performances was a day-long form of entertainment.

– That leisurely flow of time seems to me to characterize Matsumoto as well. Time flows in that way for both the performers and the audience, and that seems to work quite well.

I think I have been conscious of that ever since I designed White U (p. 047). This is related to a fairly essential architectural idea, that is, how architecture ought to be conceived. I believe architecture is the spatialization of the total sum of experience. Experience is the result of a combination of diverse elements, as in a Japanese garden. Just as experience changes slightly for every person walking in a garden, every person's experience of an architectural space ought to be slightly different. I am interested in such spaces.

That is also true of Yatsushiro Municipal Museum. Although everything is contained within a single volume, there is a sequence for going through the exhibition rooms and negotiating ramps and stairs.

– You sometimes mention that in Portugal, people will gather on a street-corner for no particular reason, and there is always music playing there. The city is made up of not only buildings but people's actions itself. Awareness of that is evident in your houses and in Matsumoto.

Yes. Our later scheme for the Forum for Music, Dance and Visual Culture, Ghent (p. 339) was clearly developed with that sort of exteriority in mind. That is also connected to National Taichung Theater.

In short, if the process of experience was considered architecture. It is with Le Corbusier's works. In the Villa Savoye, diverse sequential changes take place from the moment one ascends the ramp to the moment one arrives at the roof garden. That is quite pleasurable. I like such buildings. The wall painted in three colors in the High Court in Chandigarh changes constantly in appearance as one goes back and forth on the ramp.

– T Building in Nakameguro also has an atrium, with people meeting or chatting on the inside terrace. Though that is an office building, people are moving in diverse ways; it isn't just desk work. The point is to connect all these movements to the passage of time during a day. There was that sort of movement on stage for the "Marriage of Figaro," (p. 090) wasn't there?

Creating a relationship between the dressing

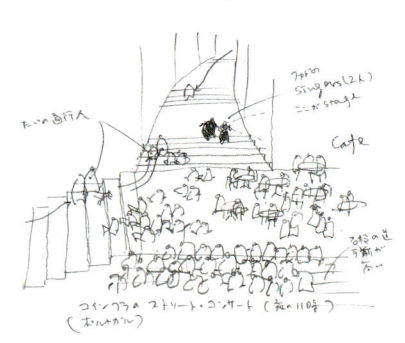

オルガンのストリートコンサート、伊東によるスケッチ
Ito's sketch of a street concert in Portugal.

の奥さんがインテリアのデザイナーで、奥さんにすすめられたらしいですね。

　その時に、なんとしてもコンクリート造で、カーテンウォールではなくて構造体がファサードに露わになっているものをやりたいと思いました。それは「サーペンタイン」の流れで、力強さが欲しいということですね。「TOD'S」は間口が狭いから、ガラス張りのファサードでは街並みに埋没してしまう。

― 同じ商業建築では「MIKIMOTO」がありますが、あれは鉄で出来ている。「TOD'S」は初めから、力強さという意味でコンクリートが一番いいということですか。

　そうです。ほかの表参道の建築に比べて小さな建築だから、強いシンボル性をもったものでないと対抗できないと思ったわけです。

　まず、最初にディエゴさんにプレゼンする時は、コンクリートに穴がぽつぽつ開いている案と、いまの原型になるような樹のパターンの案と、ふたつの小さな模型を持って行きました。そうすると、彼はしばらく黙っていたので、こちらから「この樹のパターンのほうが絶対面白いと思う」と話したら、意図を理解してくれたようで、それでやろうとその日のうちに決断してくれて、スタートしました。

　設計期間も工期も限られていたし、技術的にも難しい問題を抱えていましたが、新谷眞人さんの構造がすごく繊細で良かったし、竹中工務店のきわめて優秀なチームが施工してくれました。また、クライアントは資金もある。さまざまな意味で「TOD'S」に非常に恵まれていました。

― 「TOD'S」も「ブルージュ」も構造は新谷先生ですが、「TOD'S」は、構造体が表に出てくるというので、いかに構造の力強さを出せるか、それを最初に話しながら進めていかれたのですか。

　そうです。「TOD'S」の場合も樹のパターンの斜めのラインがクロスしながら交差するのは、基本的にはブレースのように横力に対して強いから成り立つと言われました。あとは、外側のストラクチャーに対してスラブをどう関わらせるかが重要なポイントでした。それを新谷さんがうまく解決してくれて、内側で斜めの柱に引っかかっているような、表まで強く出てこないストラクチャーにしてくれました。それが非常に良かったですね。

― それがファサードからスラブ自体が浮いているように見える要因かもしれないですね。スラブ板が出ていたら、普通の感じになってしまいますね。

　そうです。一気に「建築」になってしまいますね。樹木のシルエットが一気に消えてしまう。これは重要なことですね。

― スラブが出ると一気に建築化してしまうというのは、伊東さんは「不均質な抽象性」とおっしゃっています[1]が、樹のパターン自体がシンボルなのだけれど、それはまったくの抽象という意味ではなくて、建築から少し離れたところの抽象性のようなものがコンクリートのパターンとして前面に出てきていることがスラブを出さないということと関係していて、それが建築をつくるというよりも、新しい抽象性をつくるという方向にいっているということですね。

そうですね。

― 上のパーティールームに行くと、特にそう感じますね。内にいるのに、外にいるような感じがあります。このパターンがずっと続いていくような感じがあって、伊東さんのおっしゃるシークエンスの体験の総和というのがすごく感じられました。

　このファサードの面白さはいくつかあって、これで囲い込んでしまったことで、内に入っても、どちらが内か外かわからないようなところがありますね。これは「サーペンタイン」も同じで、「サーペンタイン」をやった時に、内にいるような気がしないのが面白いと思いました。

― ファサード面が表参道の通りに対して狭いということもあって、立体的に樹のパターンで巻いたというのが面白いですね。ファサードとしても一周回っていることで、続いているという関係がよくわかります。

　おそらく日本のクライアントだったら、「見えない所まで同じファサードでやる必要はないのではないか。そのほうが安くなるでしょう」と、必ず拒否されてしまうと思いますが、「TOD'S」ではそれを許してくれたわけですね。隣のビルが壊された時に、やはり全面同じファサードでつくっておいて良かったなと、あらためて思いました。

　特にパーティーをやる6階のスペースに入った時に、樹の上から風景を眺めているような、そういう内／外の関係がすごく面白いですね。

― そういう内／外の反転でいうと、反転の極致

---

rooms, the stage, the orchestra pit and the seats--all these constitute the theatrical space. An actor or Mr. Seiji Ozawa emerges from the back of the stage and goes to the stage or the orchestra pit, or an actor enters the seating area. That is related to the style of direction of Mr. Kazuyoshi Kushida, the artistic director of Matsumoto.

In "Kuchu Cabaret 2013" (Cabaret in the air), written and directed by Mr. Kushida, which was performed at Matsumoto in last July (in 2013), when the audience enters from the delivery entrance, they find things arranged like a festival fair, the actors are playing vendors or street performers, and after enjoying all this for about 30 minutes, they move to the stage. Then, the actors emerge as the cast this time. Mr. Kushida too emerges as a cast member while also directing the whole performance, and exchanges words with people who are moving around as part of the audience.

– Mr. Kushida's idea is that a performance is tied to various parts of the building.

Yes. Mr. Kushida consistently wants to eliminate the relationship of seeing and being seen between the audience and the cast. That's also true of the problem of inside and outside. Inside too, there is always a desire to remove the wall between the stage and the audience.

I find that my feelings or the atmosphere, the way I speak, changes, depending on whether I am lecturing from a high stage or sitting at the same table with students.

### TOD'S Omotesando Building

– With TOD'S Omotesando Building the question I would like to discuss is, what happens when one designs a building in Tokyo for a European client. But first, how did this project come about?

I was asked to do this by Mr. Diego Della Valle, the CEO of TOD'S, through an acquaintance who formerly covered fashion for Asahi Shimbun. Apparently, Mr. Diego's wife, an interior designer, recommended me.

I definitely wanted to make it a concrete structure, with the structure revealed on the facade instead of hidden behind a curtain wall. This stemmed from the same idea for Serpentine, the desire for a powerful expression. The frontage of TOD'S is narrow, so a glass facade would have simply blended into the streetscape.

– MIKIMOTO is also a commercial building but made of steel. With TOD'S, did you think from the start that concrete was the best way to create a powerful expression?

Yes. It is a small building compared with other buildings on Omotesando. I believed the only way it could stand up to other buildings was to create something with a powerful symbolic quality.

When we were making a presentation to Mr. Diego for the first time, we took two small models, one with holes punched into the concrete and another with a tree pattern that was the prototype for the eventually constructed building. He was silent for a while and then we said, this tree pattern is absolutely more interesting. He seemed to have understood our intention and decided on the scheme that day. That was how the project began.

We had little time for design and construction, and difficult technical problems had to be solved. However, Mr. Masato Araya designed an excellent structure--one that was quite delicate--and an extremely able team at Takenaka Corporation was in charge of construction. Moreover, the client had ample funds. We were quite blessed in many different ways on the TOD'S project.

– Mr. Araya was the structural designer for both TOD'S and Brugge. At TOD'S, the structure is revealed on the outside. Was the question of how to express the power of the structure discussed from the start of the project?

Yes. I was told that TOD'S would work because the intersecting diagonals act in much the same way as diagonal braces and resist lateral forces. The other important point was how the slabs relate to the structure on the outside. Mr. Araya solved that problem nicely. He designed the structure so that the slabs are caught on diagonal columns inside and do not reveal themselves that much on the outside. That was quite good.

– That may account for the way the slabs themselves seem to float and be detached from the facade. If the slabs were fully revealed on the outside, the result would feel ordinary.

Yes. It would instantly become a "building." The tree silhouettes would instantly disappear. That was an important point.

– When you say that showing the slabs on the outside would have instantly turned it into a building...You often talk about "a non-uniform abstract quality."[1] The tree patterns themselves are symbols, but not in the sense of being entirely abstract. There is a somewhat non-architectural abstract quality introduced in the form of concrete patterns, and this is related to the decision that was made to keep the slabs from being revealed on the outside. This is intended to produce, not so much a building, as a new abstract quality. Is that correct?

が「福岡アイランドシティ中央公園中核施設ぐりんぐりん」ですね。

ああいう反転とは全然違う反転で、藤森さんが1巻目で「下諏訪町立諏訪湖博物館・赤彦記念館」のことを"裏返った「中野本町」"という言い方をしていますが、それ以上に、僕は「TOD'S」とか「サーペンタイン」の裏返りというのを内部空間で実感しましたね。

　この建築は、竹中工務店の優秀なチームが自分たちの技術や能力に対するプライドをむき出しにして、われわれにチャレンジしてくるような意気込みでやっていましたから、現場はいつも緊張感が張り詰めていた。すごかったですよ。

— 出来上がったコンクリートの表情は、想像以上にきれいに出たという印象でしたか。

コンクリートがきれいに打てているかどうかというより、そういう気持ちがモノに表れるから、建築にハリが出てくるというか、その精神が感じられる空間になりますね。設計者ももちろんそうですが、明るい気持ちで建築を考えている時は、明るい建築になるし、気が滅入りながらつくっている時は、暗い建築になる。

　あと、「TOD'S」はファサードのガラスを象嵌のように見せるのが最大のポイントでした。そこでわれわれと竹中との間で、あるいはガラスを請け負った旭硝子との間で、目地を何ミリにするか、シールを何ミリにするかというやり取りは、ものすごい緊張感がありましたね。

— 新しく現場に職人さんが入ると、職長が自主的に10ページのマニュアル本をつくって教育していました。末端の作業員まで教育して、さらにモックアップでガラスとコンクリートの納まりを確認する。精魂を傾けてつくっていたという印象が強くあります。

— 象嵌が難しいのは、実は揺れる時に割れの心配があるということですね。「まつもと」はGRCのパネルで持ってきてはめ込んでいますので、パネル全体が揺れるわけですが、コンクリート打ち放しでも建物の構造に直接はめ込んでいる建物は、「MIKIMOTO」、「多摩美術大学図書館（八王子キャンパス）」もそうですが、そういう新しい試みが始まったのは「TOD'S」が最初になると思います。それに対しては、どのようにやっていったのですか。

まず、免震構造にすることですね。それで地震力を半減させる。それによって目地やシールの幅も半減すると思ったのです。ただ、そういう計算はできても、実際につくるのは相当恐ろしいことなので、構造屋さんとガラス屋さんと施工者の間でのやり取りで、施工者は当然安全側にいくから15mmとか20mmぐらいシールの幅をとってくださいと言う。われわれは5mmと言って、その間の8mmで決まったという経緯があります。地震時のコンクリートの可塑性とか、ひずみ感を見て決めていきましたね。

— 「TOD'S」は周りも全部免震が入っていますね。「多摩美」も入れているし、「MIKIMOTO」もそうですね。

ただ、「MIKIMOTO」は、2階から上は外壁のスチールパネルの奥にガラスが引っ込んでいるから、だいぶ難易度は下がりましたね。1階だけ裏からガラスの上に、もう1枚重ねて、表のガラスが外壁と面一になるようにしています。

— 「TOD'S」の時は、ガラスとコンクリートを面一に納めることへのこだわりが相当厳しかったですね。

そう。抽象的にものを見せるということが重要ですからね。樹というシンボル性をコンクリートで表現した時に、それが内側にガラスがいってしまうと生々しくなるというか、それをひとつの面のように見せることによって、美しくもあり抽象的でもあるというものが生まれてくるのではないかと思います。

— 「TOD'S」のころやっていた一連のプロジェクトは、屋根をどう扱うか、スラブをどう扱うか、ということと構造がファサードの表現として関係しているということがありましたが、これは伊東さんがおっしゃった、スラブが見えると一気に建築化してしまうという言葉に集約されているような気がします。最近は伊東さんの中でも、攻めるところが変わってきているということはありますか。

そうですね。力強さを求めているので、もう一度、抽象という概念をどう考えるかという問題を整理しないといけないと思っています。特に「台中国立歌劇院」が出来てくると圧倒される。もう面一に納まっていようがいまいが関係ないようなところがありますから。ああいう建築に比べると、

「MIKIMOTO Ginza 2」 MIKIMOTO Ginza 2

---

This facade is interesting in a number of ways. Because we enclosed the building with that facade, one is not quite certain on the inside if one is inside or outside. That was also true of Serpentine. When we did Serpentine, I thought it was interesting how one did not feel like one was inside.

— It is interesting that you wrapped the building three-dimensionally with a tree pattern, in part because of the narrow frontage of the site on Omotesando. The elevation goes all around the building, and one understands that it continues on.

If the client had been Japanese, he would probably said there was no need to continue the same elevation in places that are not visible. He would have pointed out that it would be cheaper to discontinue it. Our idea would have inevitably been rejected, but TOD'S OK'd the idea. When the building next-door was demolished, I was glad we had used the same elevation all around the building.

Especially the effect in the sixth-floor party space--it feels as if one is looking at the landscape from the tops of trees. The relationship between inside and outside is quite interesting.

— The ultimate example of a reversal of inside and outside must be Island City Central Park "GRIN."

That is an entirely different kind of reversal. In Volume 1, Mr.Fujimori called Shimosuwa Municipal Museum "a reversed White U." I believe the reversal at TOD'S or Serpentine is felt more in the inside space.

The excellent team from Takenaka Corporation took great pride in its skills and abilities on this project and seemed determined to challenge us to do our best. It was always quite intense on the site. It was amazing.

— Was the appearance of the concrete as cast more beautiful than you'd expected?

It wasn't so much a question of the beauty of the concrete as cast. The beauty was an expression of the determination with which people created the object. The intensity comes through in the building. One can feel that spirit in the space. This is of course true of architects as well, but when the people constructing a building are cheerful, the building becomes cheerful, when they are depressed, the building becomes gloomy.

One more thing, making the glass on TOD'S facade seem like inlay was a major objective. We had intense discussions with Takenaka and the glass contractor, Asahi Glass, concerning such issues as how many millimeters wide the joints should be, or how many millimeters wide the seals should be.

— When workmen who were new to the site arrived, the head workman prepared a ten-page manual on his own and educated them. He educated even the workers doing the lowest level of work. He would confirm the way glass and concrete met, using a mock up. As you said, they put their heart and soul into the project.

— The difficult thing about inserting glass is the possibility of cracks when there is vibration. At Matsumoto, the glass is installed in a GRC panel, so the entire panel vibrates. Installing glass directly into the exposed concrete structure of a building is something that has also been done in MIKIMOTO and Tama Art University Library (Hachioji Campus), but this experiment was, I believe, first atttempted at TOD'S. How did you go about this?

First, we used a base-isolated structure, that halves the seismic force. We thought this would halve the width necessary for joints and seals. However, even though calculations may indicate that is possible, actually making them that width was rather scary. The structural designer, the glass contractor and the builder had discussions, and the builder naturally wanted to be on the safe side and to make the seals 15 to 20 mm wide. We wanted five

Yes.

— That is felt particularly in the upper-floor party room. Though one is inside, one feels as if one were outside. It feels as if the pattern could extend forever. I could sense what you meant by the total sum of experiences undergone in a sequence.

「TOD'S」は繊細ですね。小さい工芸品のような建物です。

## 福岡アイランドシティ中央公園中核施設
## ぐりんぐりん

——「TOD'S」に比べると、「ぐりんぐりん」は力強いですね。これは3次元曲線にチャレンジし始めたものですが、「TOD'S」と「ぐりんぐりん」が始まった時期がほぼ同じというのが面白いと思います。これも職人技が試されるものでしたね。

あのねじる足元の所は非常に小さい曲率になってくるので、その部分をどうつくるかという問題がありましたね。そこは家具屋さんがつくった型枠です。

——型枠は力強いと思うのですが、「ぐりんぐりん」の模型を見ると、ちょっと衝撃的ですね。この時の内／外の考え方というのは、先ほど「TOD'S」とはちょっと違うと言われましたが、どう違うのですか。

「ぐりんぐりん」は、ダイレクトに内／外を反転していこうと考えましたからね。

——「リラクゼーション・パーク・イン・トレヴィエハ」も、言語としてはスパイラルというか、巻きながら開放していくような系統のものだと思いますが、「ぐりんぐりん」はもう少し大地と一体となって巻かれているような印象があって、開かれた部分がかなり地面、ランドスケープと一体となっている。「トレヴィエハ」は台座の上に載っていて、巻貝のような構造体がスパイラル状に伸びている。それとは全然違う開かれ方が「ぐりんぐりん」にはあるのではないかなと思います。だから、「トレヴィエハ」は幾何学的で、実際に幾何学が設定されていますが、「ぐりんぐりん」は本当に自由ですね。

「トレヴィエハ」も「ぐりんぐりん」もそうですが、スパイラルというのは開放系ですね。系が閉じていないから。それを建築にするというのは非常に難しいことだと思います。植物はなぜスパイラルを描くかというと、成長するために一番いい形なんですね。どんどん伸びていける。でもその分、不安定になります。だからスパイラルは、構造としては非常に難しいですね。

——この後、7章で紹介する「2009高雄ワールドゲームズメインスタジアム」も「トーレス・ポルタ・フィラ」もそうですし、スパイラルで何作品かつながっていくわけですが、「ぐりんぐりん」はそれの始まりの作品ですね。「せんだい」から、スパイラルのパターンは、縦にいったり横にいったりというのがいくつかのプロジェクトで出てきますが、一方で、「サーペンタイン」にあるような内／外を反転するという流れもあります。この時期、伊東事務所ではそういう2つの流れがありますが、スパイラルに対する興味と、内／外を反転することが「ぐりんぐりん」につながったのでしょうか。

そうですね。スパイラル状に開いたものをつくってみたいという気持ちが強くあったのだろうと思います。自然界の幾何学に近づけたいということですね。

——伊東さんがおっしゃった「成長」という意味での、開放系としてのスパイラル[2]に当時は興味があって、それが直結して内／外ということに関係する場合としない場合があると思いますが、建築に落とし込んだ時には、スパイラルにすることによって、開く・閉じるということがうまく表現出来たのが「ぐりんぐりん」だったのかなという気がします。

この時期が一番、新しいアルゴリズムとか、幾何学をベースに有機的なアルゴリズムを採用しながら建築をつくってみたいという気持ちが強かったのです。だから、開放系で建築をつくることをやろうとしていたんだと思います。ただ、本当にスパイラルで描くと難しい。構造的にはものすごく弱いのです。

## 床／水平問題

——伊東さんは「ぐりんぐりん」では、もう少し水平な、床のようなエレメントを入れたほうが良かったのではないかとおっしゃっていますが、もう少し建築的な部分があったほうが、逆に自由な有機的な建築が浮かび上がるということですか。

それは「せんだい」がそうですし、「TOD'S」も裏のほうで水平のスラブがスッと見えていることが効いていますね。それが曲面だけになってしまうと途端に、建築らしさが消えて単なる有機的なオブジェになってしまう……。建築は、水平な「床」があって初めて「建築」なんですよ。だから、抽象的な、自然界にないものをそこに持ち込む意味が生じる。でも全体の幾何学は有機的に出来

mm, and the decision was made to go with eight mm. We made the decision taking into consideration the plasticity and deformation of concrete during an earthquake.

– TOD'S is completely base-isolated. Same for Tamabi and MIKIMOTO.

Only, in MIKIMOTO, the glass is recessed on the exterior-wall steel panels from the second floor up, so the degree of difficulty was considerably reduced. It is only on the first floor that the glass is flush with the exterior wall. A second pane of glass is layered behind that front glass.

– The office was determined to make the glass flush with the concrete at TOD'S.

Yes. It was important to create an abstract quality. A symbolic tree form is expressed in concrete, but if the glass had been recessed, the tree form would have been too explicit. I think that because the glass is flush with the concrete, the result is beautiful yet abstract.

– The other projects the office was doing around the same time dealt with issues such as the treatment of the roof, the treatment of slabs, and the involvement of the structure in the expression of the facade. All these issues can be summed up by what you said earlier, about how showing the slabs on the outside instantly turns the work into a building. Do you feel that the things you focus on have been changing recently?

Yes. Because I am searching for powerful statements, I feel it is necessary to reconsider the concept of abstraction once more. National Taichung Theater, in particular, as it nears completion, is overwhelming. Whether things are flush or not is beside the point. Compared to such buildings, TOD'S is delicate. It is like small craftwork.

### Island City Central Park "GRIN GRIN"

– "GRIN GRIN" is powerful compared with TOD'S. This is where you began to take up the challenge of a three-dimensionally curved surface, but it is interesting that TOD'S and "GRIN GRIN" started around the same time. This too tested the skill of workmen.

Those twisted lower portions of the structure presented a problem of construction because they have extremely small radii of curvature. The forms for those portions were made by a furniture maker.

– The forms were powerful, but seeing the model for "GRIN GRIN" was a bit of a shock. You said earlier that your approach to the question of inside and outside here was slightly different from your approach to TOD'S. How was it different?

At "GRIN GRIN", the idea was to reverse inside and outside in a straightforward way.

– Relaxation Park in Torrevieja can also be described as a spiral--it coils and opens up--but "GRIN GRIN" seems more integrated with the earth as it coils. Torrevieja is set on a plinth; the conch-like structure grows in a spiral. "GRIN GRIN" is completely different. Torrevieja is geometrical, and the geometry is actually fixed, but "GRIN GRIN" is truly free.

Spirals are open systems, and that is true of both Torrevieja and "GRIN GRIN." The systems are not closed. It is quite difficult to make architecture out of them. Plants are in form of spirals because those are the best forms for growth. Spirals allow steady growth. But to that extent, they become unstable. Spirals are therefore structurally extremely difficult.

– There are several subsequent works that are connected by their spiral forms such as The Main Stadium for the World Games 2009 in Kaohsiung and TORRES PORTA FIRA which appear in Chapter 7. They all start with "GRIN GRIN," don't they? Since Sendai, the spiral pattern has appeared, sometimes vertically and sometimes horizontally, in a number of projects, but a reversal of inside and outside, of the kind seen in Serpentine, has also been a tendency. There are these two trends in works by the office during this period. Did these two trends--the interest in spirals and the reversal of inside and outside--come together in "GRIN GRIN"?

Yes. There was an interest in creating things that are open in spiral form, a desire to approach the geometry of the natural world.

– It seems that there was an interest at the time in spirals as open systems, in the sense of what you call "growth,"[2] and that there are projects in which that is tied to the question of inside and outside and projects in which that is not. I feel that GRIN GRIN was a project in which, from an architectural perspective, using a spiral form made possible the eloquent expression of open versus closed.

It was during this period that the desire was greatest to design buildings using new algorithms or organic algorithms based on geometry. That is why we tried to design buildings that were open systems. Only, true spirals are difficult. They are quite weak structurally.

051

東京オペラシティでの個展「伊東豊雄 建築｜新しいリアル」における波打つ床
The undulating floor in Tokyo Ito: The New "Real" in Architecture solo exhibition held at Tokyo Opera City.

ている。そういうコントラストが美しい建築をつくると思っていますね。

── それは「台中国立歌劇院」のシステムでも、広がっていくものを境界線でスパッと切るという問題とも直結しますね。

そうですね。

── 伊東さんの書いた文章[3]で、プリミティブハットの絵をみて、床に注目されているというのが面白いと思いましたが、床というのが、「原初の建築」の要素として一番強いと考えられているわけですか。

建築の発生というのは「床」だと思います。類人猿からヒトが出てきた時に最初につくったのは、屋根もあるかもしれないですが、床だと思う。自然から切り離されることによって「建築」が発生しているし、アジアのような地域でも、地上に住んでいた人間が「床」に気づいて、地面から浮上したということが、建築にとっては、「屋根」より大きいと思いますね。

── ミース・ファン・デル・ローエも床にはかなりこだわりがあったと思いますが、ベルリンのミースの建物で開催された展覧会[4]で「エマージング・グリッド」という、かなり衝撃的な、ミースに対する挑戦とまで言えるような床の扱いをされたのも、むしろこちらのほうが自然ではないかという提案だと思います。これも「床」に対する伊東さんの意識が、均質な空間に入った時の対比として顕著に出ているのかなと思います。

あの時は、ミースの建築をいかに触らないで展示ができるかということを考えていくと、床に触るしかない。壁を立ててしまうと展示が成り立たないと思いましたからね。

── 人間はたぶん、特に内部にいる時は、壁は視覚的な印象が非常に強いのですが、床は、足による身体的な感覚を感じやすいのでしょうね。だから、東京オペラシティの展覧会[5]の床であったり、「瞑想の森 市営斎場」の屋根を歩いたりした時に、自然に感じるというか、面白い空間になっていたということですね。

「瞑想の森」の屋根はみんなが上りたがりますからね。

── あれはむしろ屋根をつくるときに、床を持ち上げたというような感覚なのかもしれないですね。「台中国立歌劇院」も水平な床が入っていたりする

から、それが逆に「建築」にしている部分もあるし、すごく自由に感じる部分でもあると思いました。そういう点で、「ぐりんぐりん」はもう少し建築的にしておくべきだったと思いますね（笑）。

### 瞑想の森 市営斎場

──「瞑想の森」と「ぐりんぐりん」は建っている場所も環境も全然違います。「ぐりんぐりん」は埋め立て地の広い平面の上に建っているし、「瞑想の森」は山間の、むしろランドスケープと一体となったような環境に建っている。立地条件が全然違う所に、同じようなシステムをもってきていますが、その中での曲面に対して何か思いがあったのでしょうか。構造的には似て非なるものですが。

「ぐりんぐりん」は、型枠と配筋をした状態の時は非常にきれいだと思っていたのに、型枠が外れたら、エッジの所がスムーズじゃなくて、あまりエレガントな印象がなかったので、まずいと思いました。「瞑想の森」はかなりグリッドのモジュールを小さくしているので、その結果、曲面はスムーズになっていますね。

これも現場で型枠を見た時は、きれいだなあと思いましたね。いま行っても、柱回りの所は、よく合板でこんなきれいなコンクリートが出来たものだと感心します。

── これは初めから「屋根」という意識があったのですか。

そうですね。上から下りてきた屋根と、地面から上がってきた部分があって、それが干渉し合いな

---

#### The Problem of the Floor or the Horizontal

– You said it might have been better at "GRIN GRIN" if more horizontal, floor-like elements had been introduced. Did you mean by that that having more architectural elements would have conversely made the free, organic character of the building stand out?

That was true of Sendai, and at TOD'S too the fact that the horizontal slabs are visible behind the facade is effective. When there are only curved surfaces, it no longer seems like a building; it becomes simply an organic object...

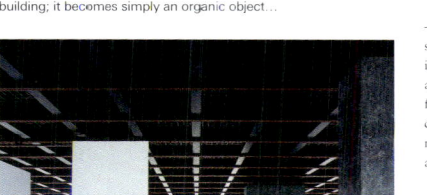

「東京─ベルリン／ベルリン─東京」展における波打つ床
The undulating floor in Tokyo-Berlin / Berlin-Tokyo Exhibition.

A building is a building only when there is a horizontal floor. The introduction of an abstract thing that is not found in nature is therefore meaningful. Nevertheless, the overall geometry is organically made. I believe that sort of contrast results in a beautiful building.

– That is also tied to the problem of clearly terminating with a boundary something that extends indefinitely, as with the system in National Taichung Theater, is it not?

Yes.

– I was interested to read something you wrote, that in looking at a drawing of a primitive hut[3], you were focused on the floor. Do you consider the floor to be the most important element in archetypal architecture?

I believe the floor is the generator of architecture. When humans evolved from the apes, the first thing they created was, along with the roof perhaps, was the floor. Architecture came about through separation from nature. Even in a region such as Asia, the fact that humans living on the ground discovered the floor and rose above the ground played a bigger role for architecture's development than the roof.

– Mies van der Rohe was also preoccupied with floors, but the fairly shocking treatment of the floor, which might even be considered a gesture made in defiance of Mies, in "emerging grid," your exhibition in Mies' building in Berlin, might be more natural. There too, your awareness of the floor is made markedly manifest by contrast inside that uniform space.

When I thought about how an exhibition might be organized without coming into contact with Mies' building, I concluded that the only solution was to come into contact with the floor. I did not think an exhibition would work if walls were erected.

– Walls probably make a strong visual impression on people, especially inside buildings, whereas floors are more easily sensed physically, through the feet. That's why, when one walked on, say the floor of the exhibition at Tokyo Opera City,[5] or the roof of "Meiso no Mori" Municipal Funeral Hall, one sensed quite naturally that…one felt that it was an interesting space.

Everyone wants to get up on the roof of "Meiso no Mori".

– There, it felt as if the floor had been raised to create the roof. At National Taichung Theater as well, the introduction of the horizontal floor is partly responsible for making it a "building." It is also the part of the building that feels quite free.

In that sense, "GRIN GRIN" ought to have been made slightly more architectural in character [laughs].

#### Meiso no Mori Municipal Funeral Hall

– "Meiso no Mori" and "GRIN GRIN" are completely different in place and environment. "GRIN GRIN" stands on a large level site on reclaimed land, and "Meiso no Mori" is in the mountains and integrated with the landscape. Similar systems are introduced under entirely different conditions of location. What were your thoughts on curved surfaces in that context? Structurally, of course, they are not authentic curved surfaces.

I thought "GRIN GRIN" was quite beautiful when the forms and reinforcement bars were in place, but once the forms were removed, the curved surfaces near the edges were rough and inelegant--I thought they looked awkward.

052

がら、その間に空間が出来ている。そのコンセプトだが外形にも明快に現れていますね。

― 最初から屋根のこの線というのは想定されていたのですか。

これはかなり初期に出てきたと思います。山間だからというのはもちろんありました。

― 愛されるという意味では、ここも葬儀場という使われ方以外に、ホールを使って演奏会が開かれたとうかがいました。そういう想定していなかった使われ方に対して、伊東さんはどう思われますか。新しい発見でしたか。

僕も「せんだい」では、「どこで本を読んでもいいし、どこでビデオを観てもいいんだよ」と言っていましたから、機能という概念からは常に自由でありたいと思っているし、「人間なんて場所さえあればなんだってできるんだよ」、というのが基本的な考え方です。だから、「葬儀場でコンサートをやりたい」と言ってくれたら、それは新しい発見でもなんでもなくて、われわれの建築をそういう言い方で表現してくれたんだなという感じですね。

でも屋根に上ると、屋根の上のほうがいい空間ですね。空間性を感じます。

― ひとりで上る経験と、何人かで上る経験は違うだろうなというイメージがあります。伊東さんから聞いた、戸田ツトムさんが「コンピューターと向きあっていると、足元が水に浸かっているように感じる」と言ったという話を思い出して、何人かでこの屋根に上って歩いた時には、屋根を伝ってみんなの感覚がつながっているような感覚になるのかなという気がします。

屋根のある建築は、床と同じように「建築」的になりますね。それは「建築」にしようとしているのだから当然かもしれないけれど……。そういう意味では、これは安定した建築ですね。誰が見ても、穏やかで、ああいいね！ という、そういう建築。

― 屋根があると安心感があるのでしょうね。教会もそうですが、天井が高くてヴォールト屋根があると、自然とその中心に人が集まってくるような状況が生まれる。屋根でいえば、結局ひとつの空間をつくっていく。「みんなの森 ぎふメディアコスモス」も、あのグローブがひとつの場所を定義していくようなところがあります ね。「ぐりんぐりん」もそうですし、「瞑想の森」も「ぎふ」につながっていくひとつの流れになっているように思います。

最近はそういう建築が多いですね。

確かに。屋根がいいか悪いかの問題ではなくて、どういう屋根を架けるか、だと思いますね。それで力強くもなり、穏やかになったり、きつくなったり、いろいろなことがある。勾配によっても違う。屋根が必要かどうかという議論は、あまり意味はないかもしれないですね。屋根があれば安心できるようなケースであれば、屋根を架けても全然悪いと思わないし、震災後、屋根はどうとか、陸前高田の「みんなの家」でさんざんそういう議論をしましたが、いまはもっと別のところにテーマというか関心があるように思っていますね。建築のもっている力とか、身体性とかが重要ではないでしょうか。

「台中国立歌劇院」が出来ていく現場を見ていると圧倒されますからね。われわれの理性を超えたというか、アルゴリズムと言いながらデザインしたのですが、いまでは別次元の空間に変わってしまっている（笑）。

― 伊東さんの中では、そういう理性を超えていく力強さ、人がその空間に入ってわくわくするという、そちらに興味があるから、最初の切っ掛けはアルゴリズムだとしても、それを超える強さを求めているということですね。

そうですね。「台中国立歌劇院」とインドのル・コルビュジエを見た影響は大きいですね。こんなひどいコンクリートでもこんな建築が出来るんだ、と思った。すごいことだと思います。

---

1.「不均質な抽象性」『新建築』2005年1月号
2.「アルゴリズム的思考と建築の「新しいリアル」」『10＋1』No.48、INAX出版、2007年
3.「シルバーハット：軽快な現代の小屋をめざして」『建築雑誌』Vol.101, No.1249、1986年
4.「東京―ベルリン／ベルリン―東京」展（2006年）
5. 個展「伊東豊雄　建築｜新しいリアル」（2006年）

---

We made the grid module quite small at "Meiso no Mori", so the curved surfaces there are smooth.
 I thought it was beautiful when I saw the forms on the site in that project as well. Even now, when I visit the building, I marvel at the beautiful way the concrete was cast around the columns, considering plywood was used for the forms.

– Did you imagine this as a "roof" from the beginning?

Yes. I imagined a roof descending from above and an element rising from the ground acting on one another and resulting in a space in between the two. That concept is clearly expressed in the exterior form.

– Did you have this sort of roof in mind from the start?

We arrived at it at a fairly early stage of the project. Of course, the fact that the site was in the mountains was a factor.

– Speaking of buildings that people love, I've heard that this is used not only as a funeral hall but as the venue for concerts. What do you think about the building being used in unexpected ways? Did you discover something new from this?

I basically feel people should be allowed to do anything they please with a place. At Sendai, I said that people ought to be able to read books or look at videos anywhere. From the perspective of function, I believe fundamentally that "people should always be free to use spaces in their own ways." Therefore, to find people wanting to use a funeral hall for concerts is not a new discovery for me. That is simply another expression of how we conceive our buildings.
 Nevertheless, when one gets on the roof--the rooftop is the better space. It seems to have a better spatial character.

– I imagine going up there alone is different from going up with others. I remember your telling us something that Mr. Tsutomu Toda once said, about how, when he goes online, it feels as if he were in water up to his ankles. Maybe when one goes up on the roof with other people and walks around, it feels as if all the people were somehow connected through the roof.

As with a floor, a building with a roof becomes "building-like." It may be only natural, since one is trying to make it into a building...In that sense, this is a stable building. It is tranquil, it looks good--it is that sort of building, whoever looks at it.

– I suppose one feels secure when there is a roof. It is the same with a church. When there is a high-ceilinged, vaulted roof, people naturally gather toward the center. In the end, a roof creates a single space. At Minna no Mori Gifu Media Cosmos, that globe defines a single place. That is also the case with "GRIN GRIN". "Meiso no Mori" seems also to be part of a trend that leads to Gifu.
 There seem to be many such buildings recently.

To be sure. The question is not whether a roof is good or bad, it is what sort of roof to construct. It can be powerful, tranquil, stern--it can be many different things. The pitch of the roof can also be a factor. A discussion on whether or not a roof is necessary may not have much meaning. If, in that particular case, the presence of a roof is reassuring, I don't think having a roof is a bad thing at all. After the Great East Japan Earthquake, there were many discussions regarding the roof in connection with the "Home-for-All" in Rikuzentakata, but I believe the focus of interest has since shifted elsewhere. The power, the physicality of architecture is important.
 Seeing National Taichong Theater going up on the site is overwhelming. It transcends reason--we talked about algorithms while we were designing it--but it is now changing into a space in a different dimension [laughs].

– Is it because you are interested in power that transcends reason, in spaces that get people all bubbling with anticipation, that you seek power, one that transcends even the initial algorithm?

Yes. National Taichung Theater and Le Corbusier's works in India have exerted a powerful influence on me. I was amazed that buildings like those could be built, even with concrete of such poor quality.

---

1. Non-uniform Abstraction: *Shinkenchiku*, Jan., 2005
2. Algorithmic Thinking and "The New Real" in Architecture: *10+1*, No.48 (INAX Publishing) 2007
3. Silver Hut: Seeking for a light modern hut: *KENCHIKU ZASSHI*, Vol.101, No.1249, 1986
4. Tokyo-Berlin/Berlin-Tokyo Exhibition (2006)
5. Solo exhibition Toyo Ito: The New *"Real"* in Architecture (2006)

# Brugge Pavilion
ブルージュ・パヴィリオン

2002　ベルギー　ブルージュ　Bruges, Belgium

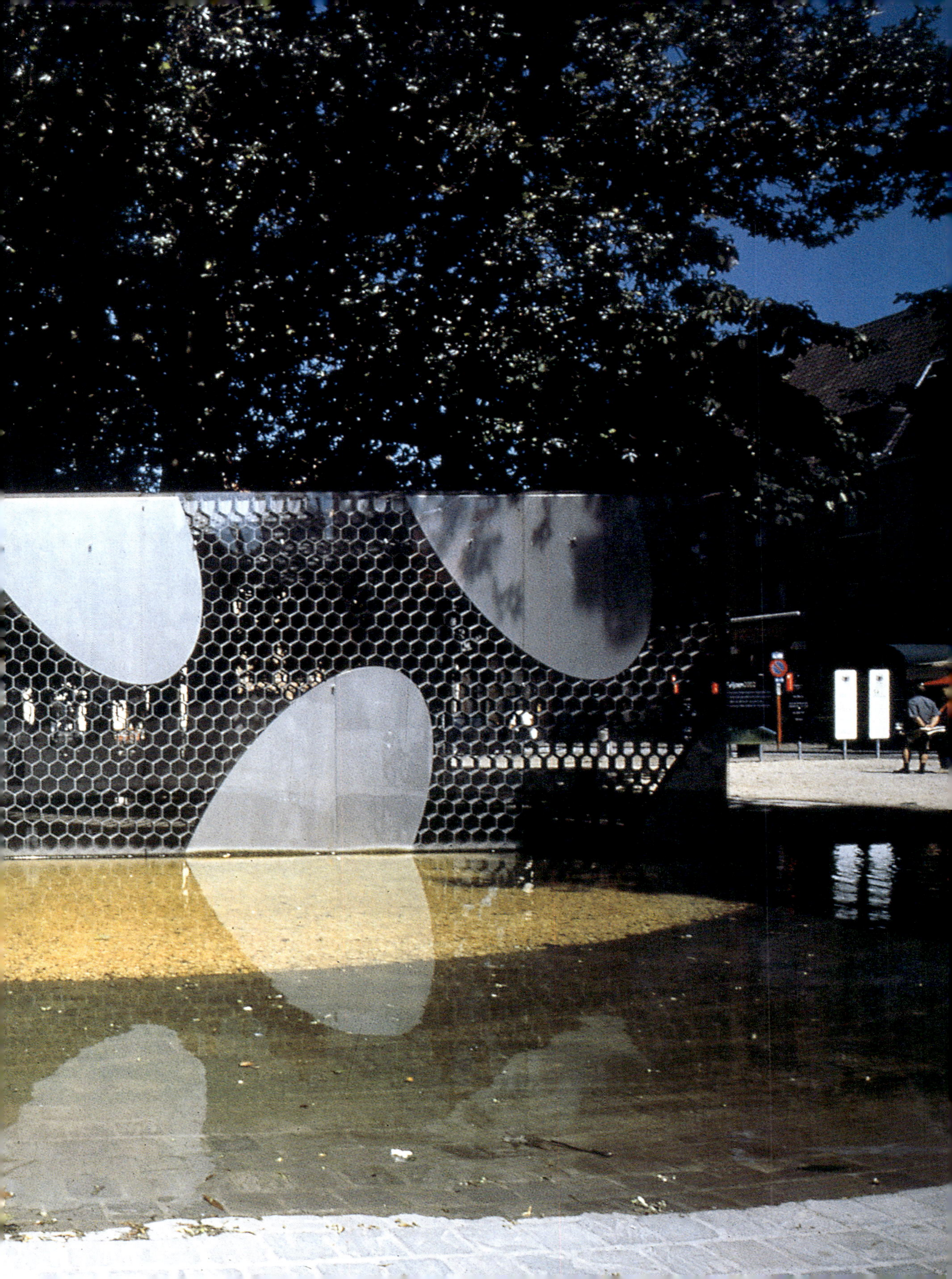

ブルージュ歴史地区ブルク広場中心のカテドラル跡地に建てられた
The structure was built on the former site of a cathedral in the center of Burg Square in Bruges historic district.

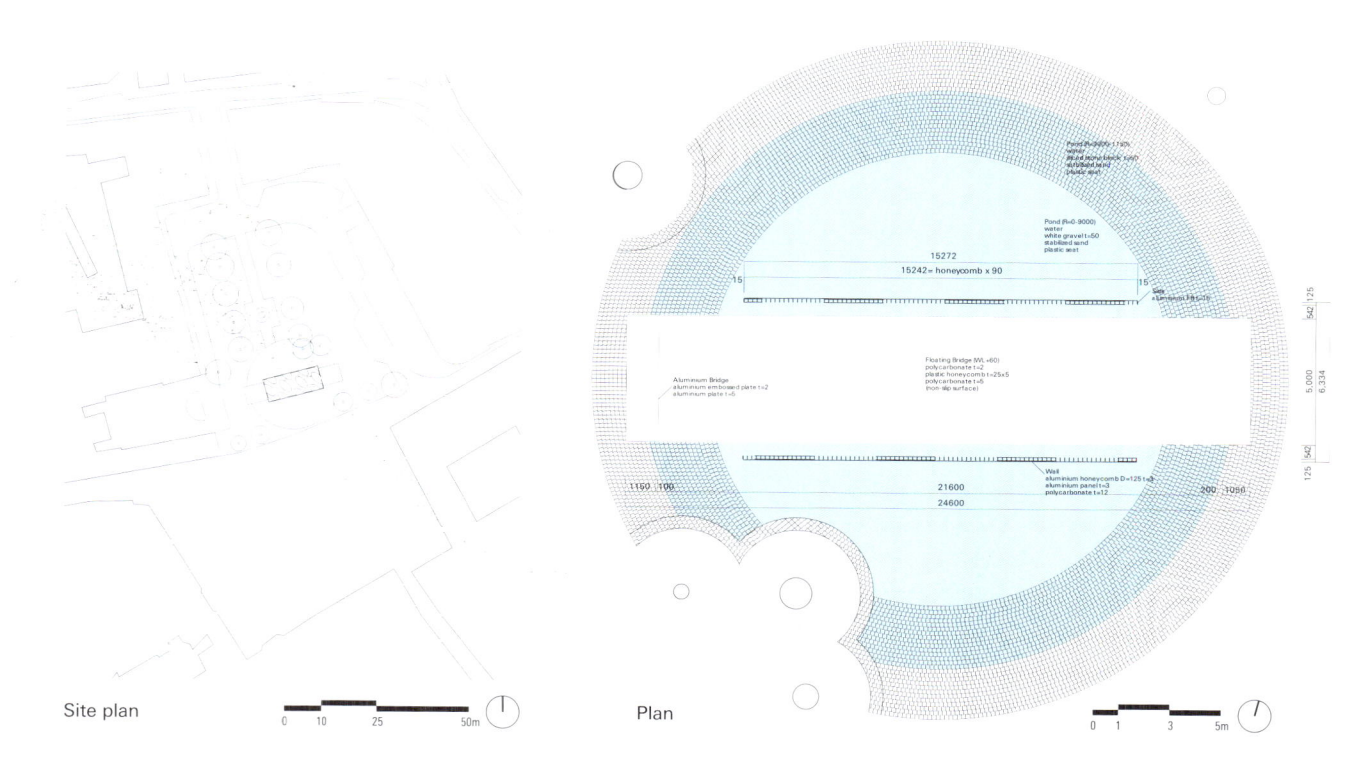

Site plan

Plan

パヴィリオンを通過する観光客
Visitors passing through the pavilion.

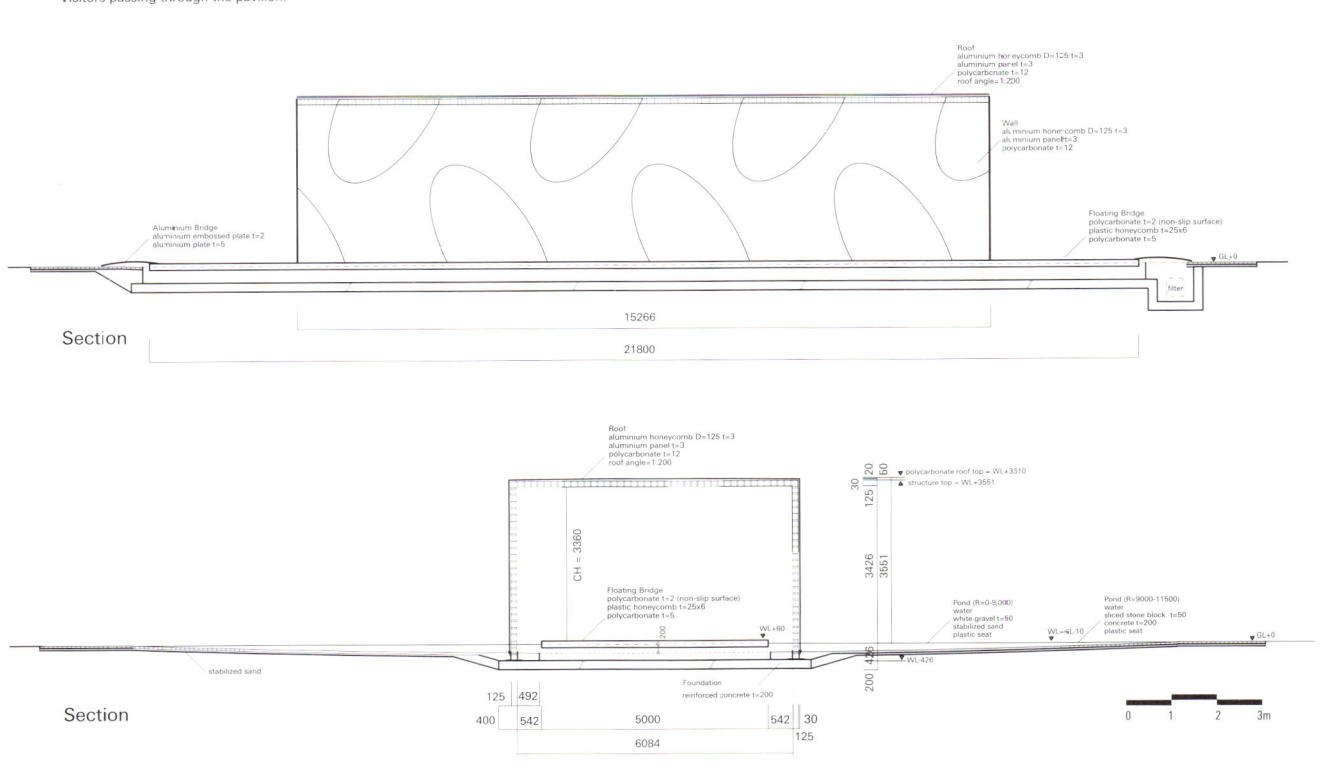

Section

Section

057

ブルージュ歴史地区ブルク広場のファサード
The facade of Burg Square in Bruges historic district.

Elevation

ベルギーの伝統工芸品のレースをモチーフにしたアルミハニカム構造
The aluminum honeycomb structure was inspired by lace, one of Belgium's traditional crafts.

2002年EUの文化首都に選ばれたことを記念して、ブルージュ発祥の地ブルク広場に建てられた。当初1年の予定であったが、市民の要望もあり2013年まで存続していた。

To commemorate the fact that the city was selected as the European Capital of Culture 2002, the work was erected in Burg Square, the birthplace of Bruges. It was initially scheduled to remain for one year, but ultimately, based n part to public demand, it stayed until 2013.

ハニカムを構造上ぎりぎりの地点で成立させるため曲げモーメントの大きなコーナー、脚部、スラブ中央部にアルミパネルを貼る
Aluminums surface panels are installed at critical areas such as large corners, legs, centre of the slab to bear extreme loads.

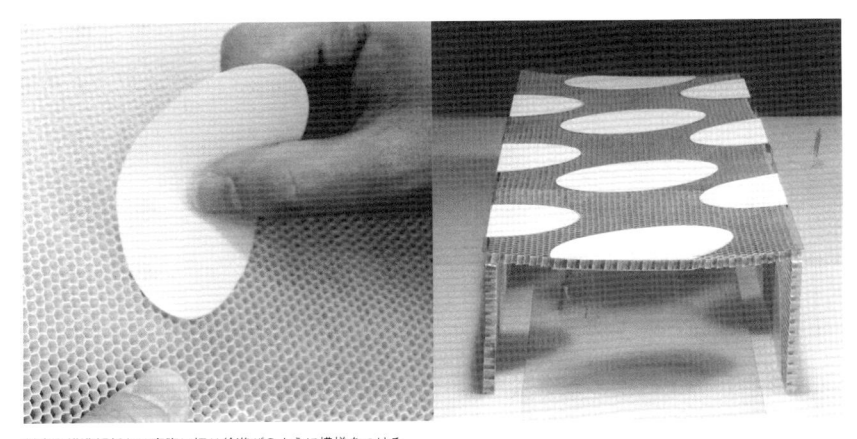

緻密な構造解析とは裏腹に切り絵遊びのように模様をつける
In contrast with this elaborate structural analysis, a pattern was applied to the reverse side – a process that was similar to playing with cutout pictures.

059

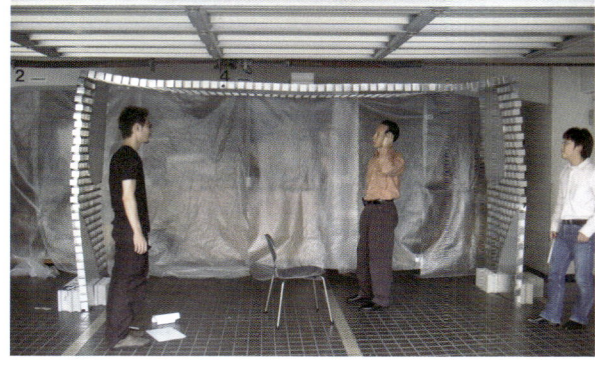

所内でのモックアップ検討。コーナー、スラブ中央部を固めると見違えるように強くなる
Inspection of the mock up at the office: When the corners and central slab were fixed, the structure becomes much stronger.

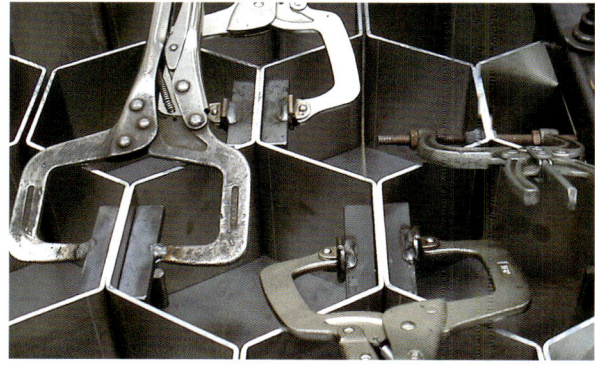

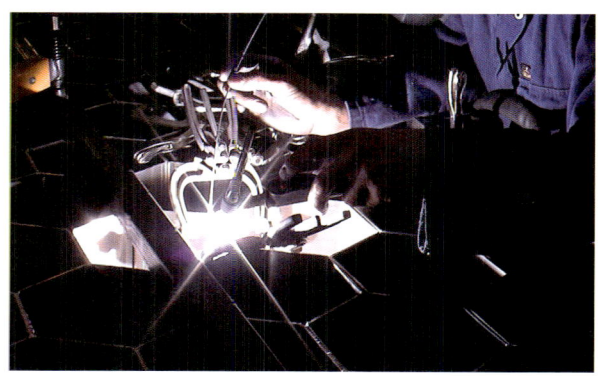

工場でのパネル製作現場、組立風景
Views of the panels being produced at the factory and assembled on site.

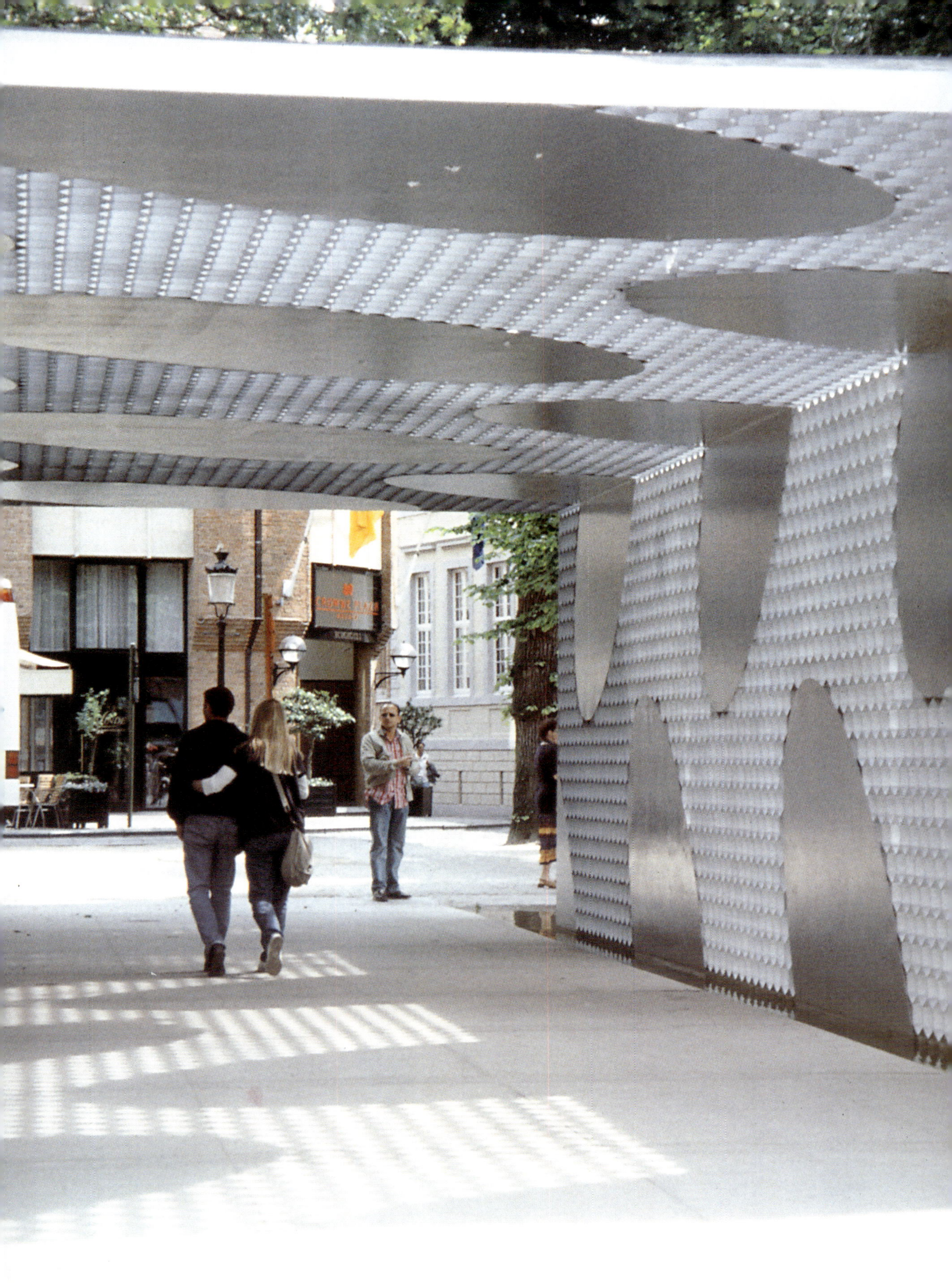

## Serpentine Gallery Pavilion 2002
サーペンタイン・ギャラリー・パヴィリオン 2002

2002 イギリス ロンドン London, UK

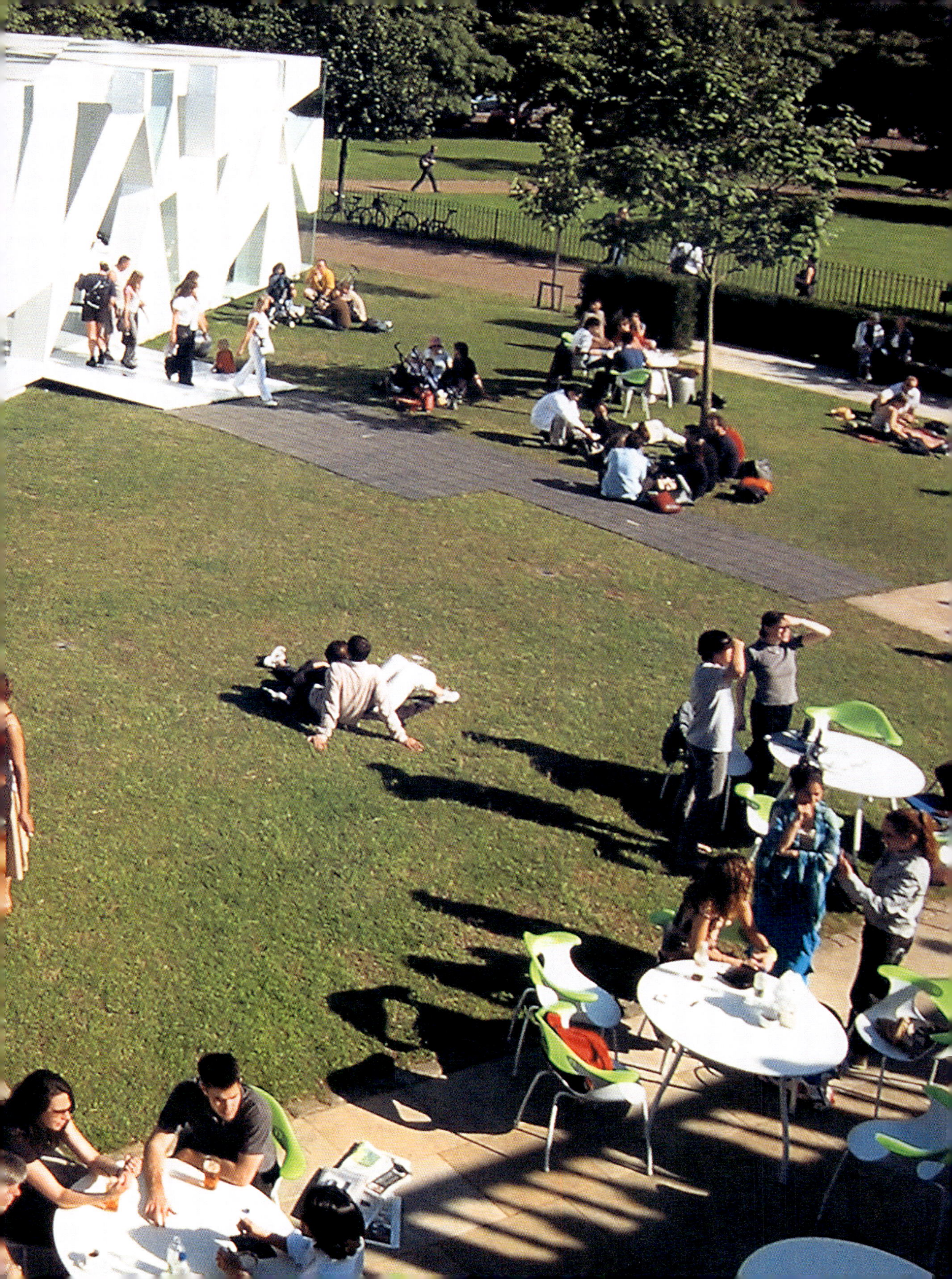

064

065

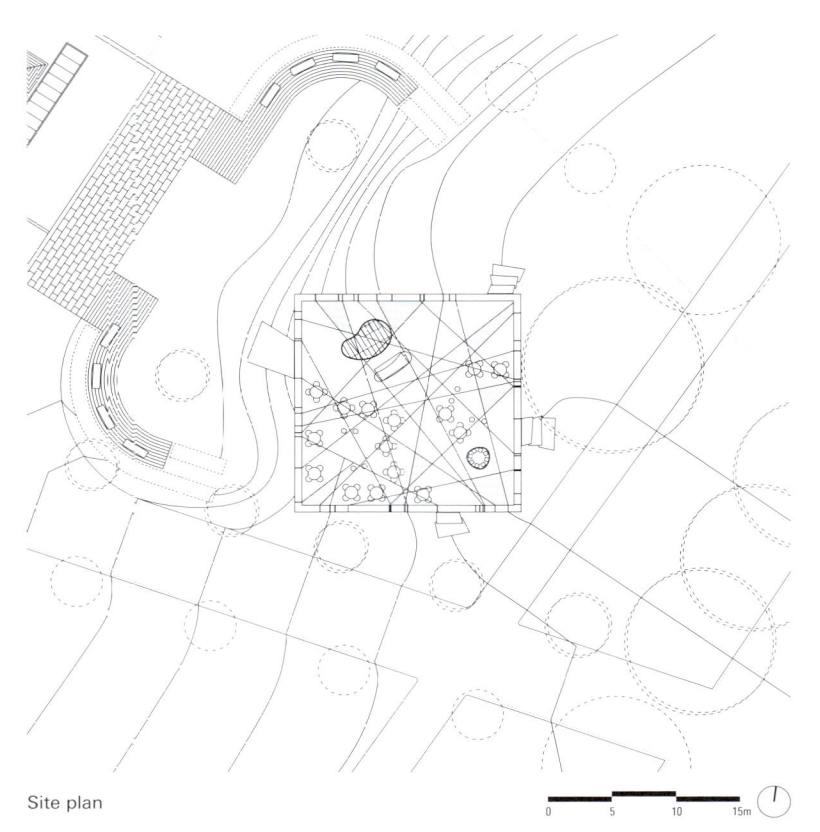

ロンドンのサーペンタイン・ギャラリー前庭に夏の3カ月間だけつくられたパヴィリオン。会期後、移築され、現在は南フランスのホテル庭先にある。

The pavilion was designed to stand for only three months during the summer in the front garden of London's Serpentine Gallery. Following the exhibition period, it was disassembled and now stands moved to the garden of a hotel in the south of France.

Site plan

外と内が連続するオープンエアのパヴィリオン
The exterior and interior of this open-air pavilion are continucus.

Expansion plan

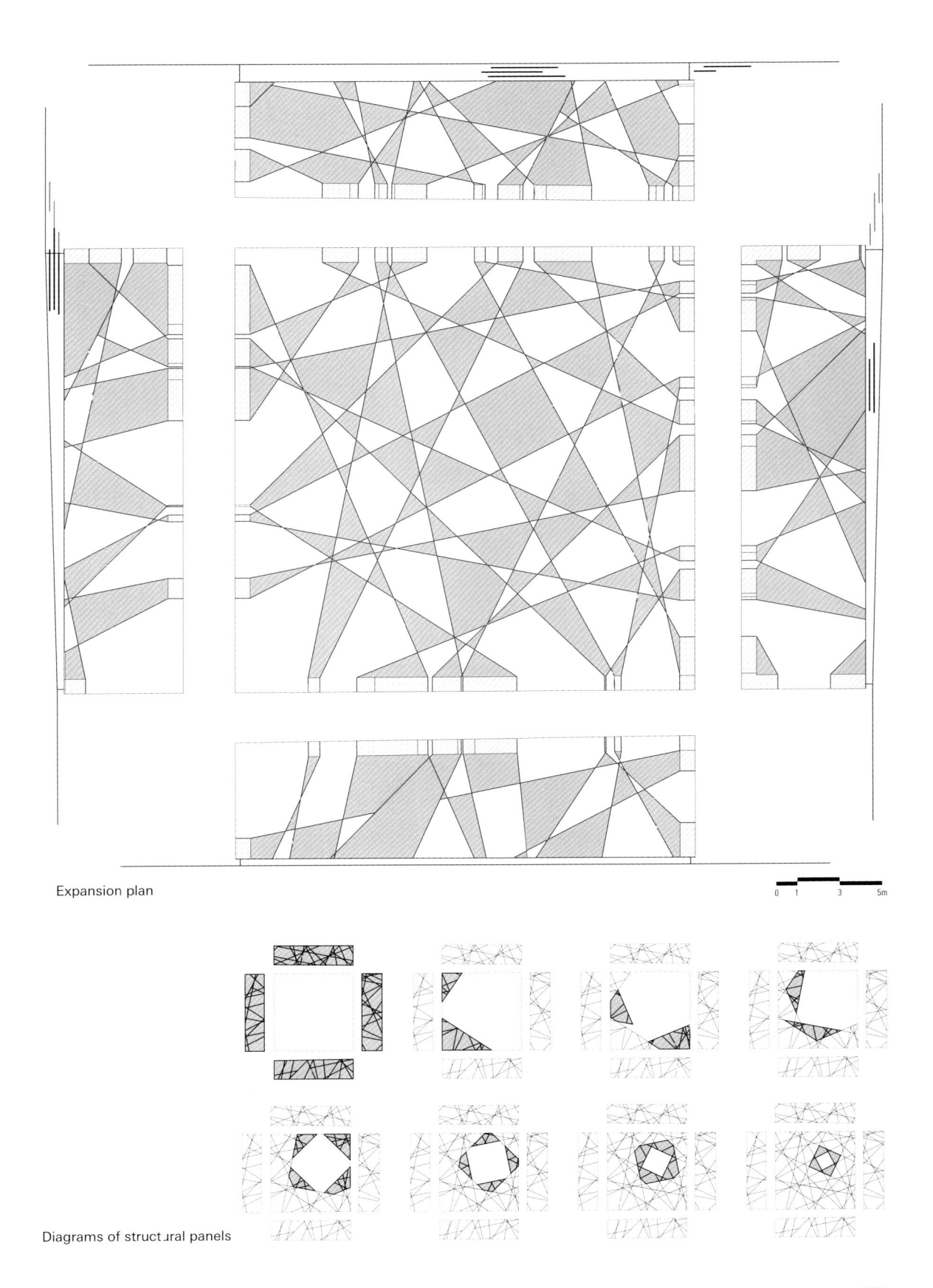

Diagrams of structural panels

067

- Exterior surface / pair glasses
- Exterior surface / aluminium plates
- Structure / grillage of flat steel bars
- Interior surface / aluminium plates
- Interior space
- Interior surface / aluminium plates
- Structure / grillage of flat steel bars
- Exterior surface / aluminium plates
- Exterior surface / glasses
- Floor / plywood, lawn
- Basement / steel grillage, wooden joists

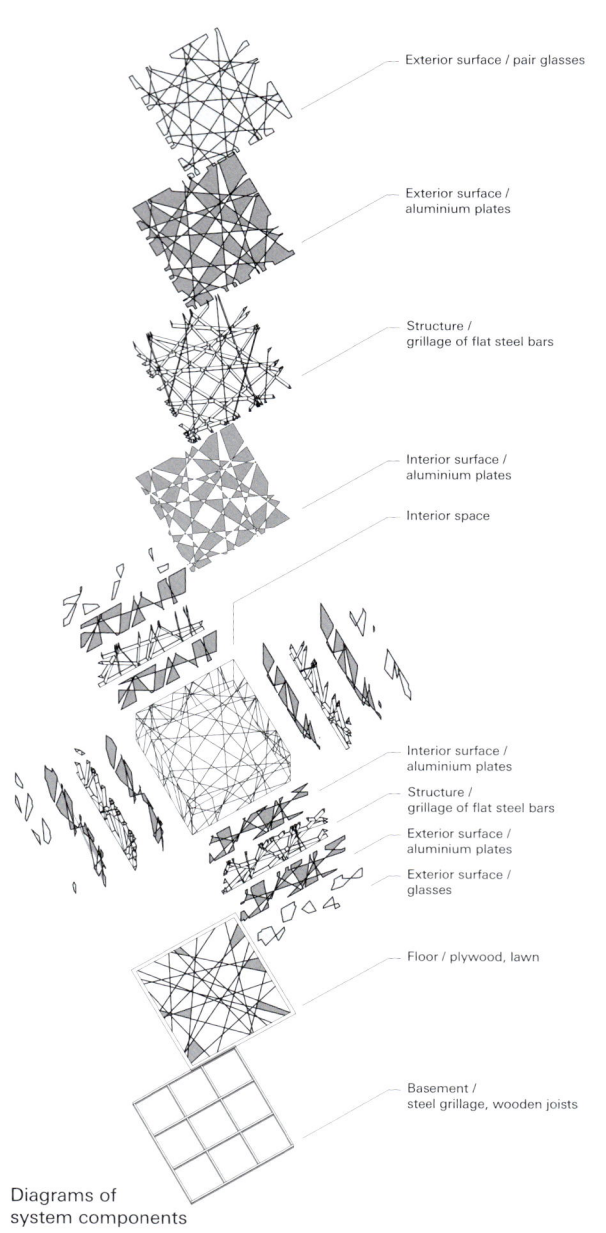

Diagrams of system components

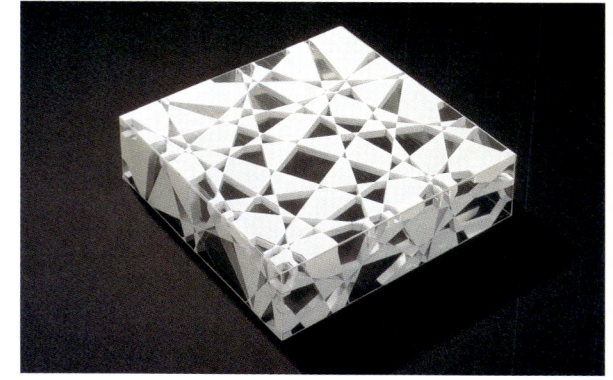

550mm幅のスチールプレートの組み合わせでつくられる構造体
The structure was made by combining steel plates, each with a width of 550mm.

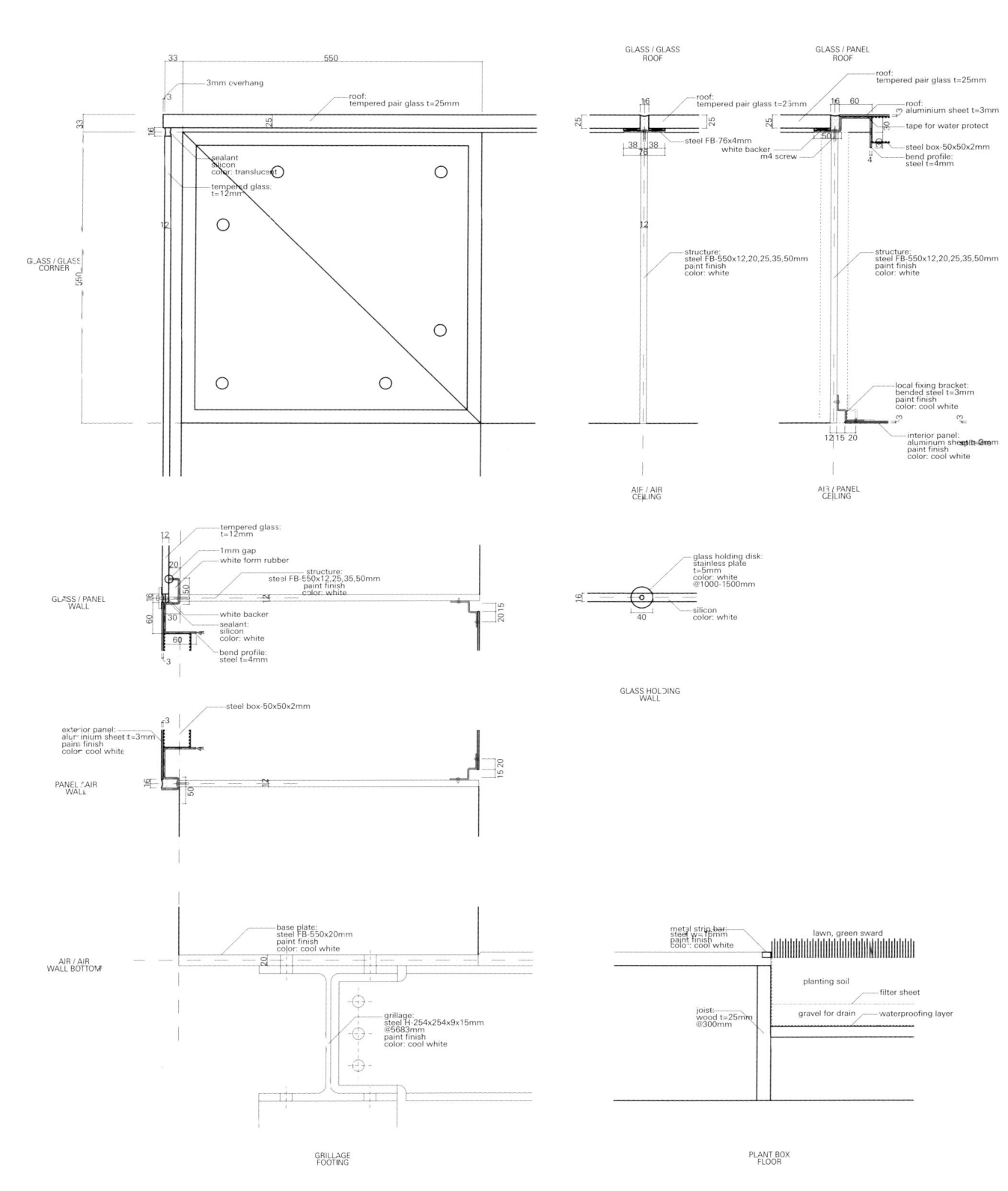

Detail

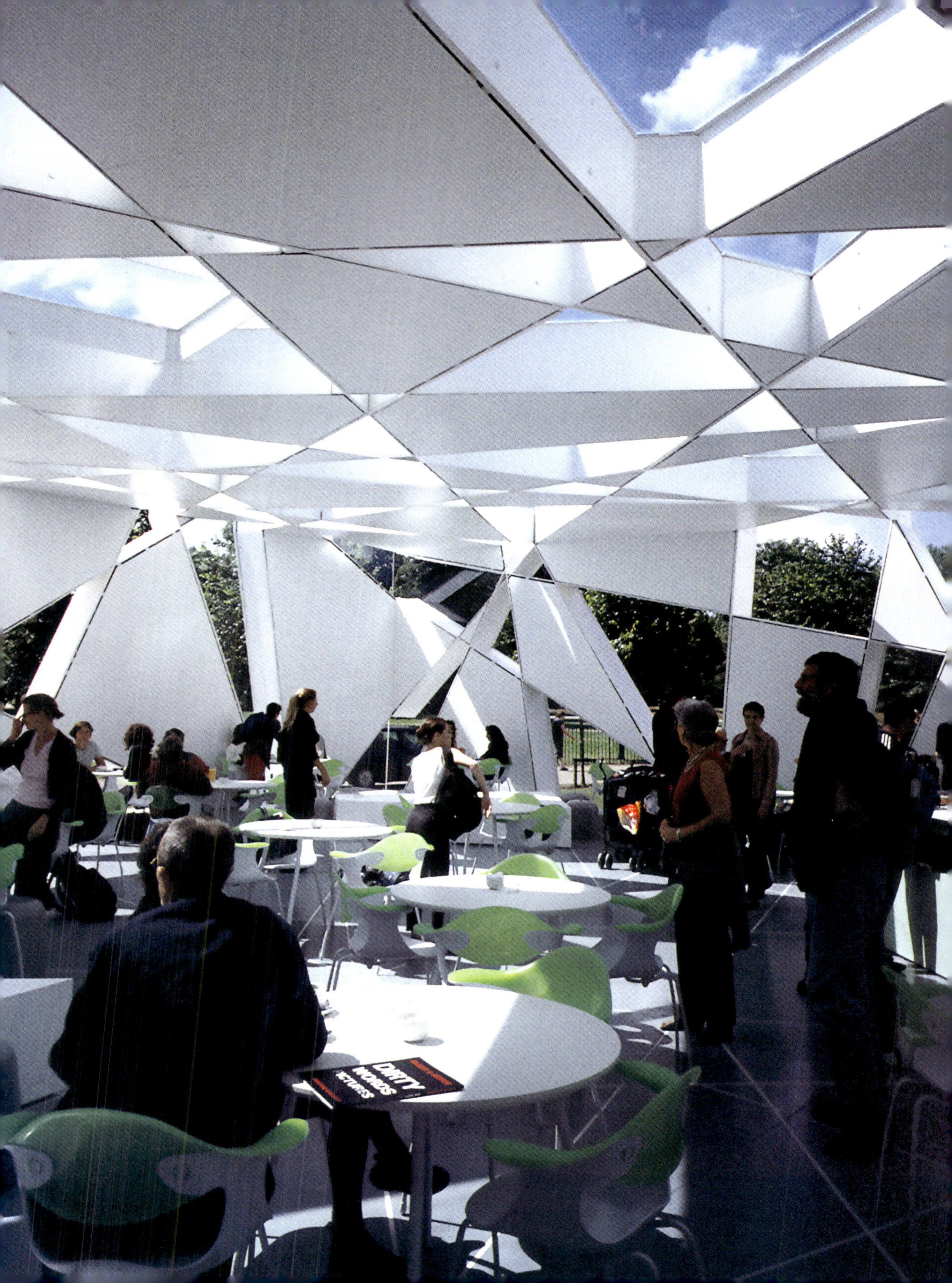
DIRTY
WORDS

木漏れ日のように差し込む光の下で思い思いに楽しむ人びと
Visitors relax just as they please in the sunshine as the light seems to stream through the trees.

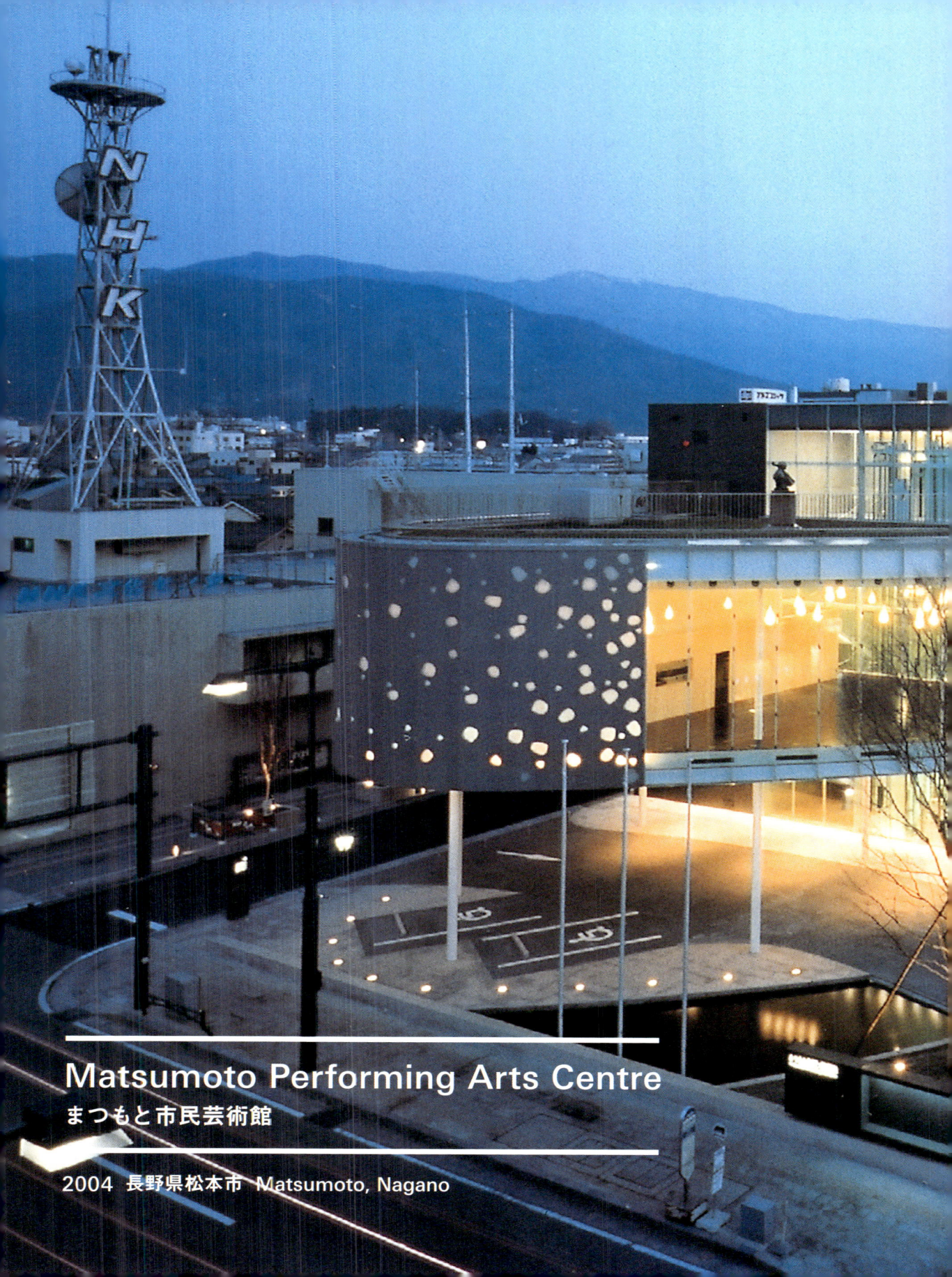

# Matsumoto Performing Arts Centre
まつもと市民芸術館

2004 長野県松本市 Matsumoto, Nagano

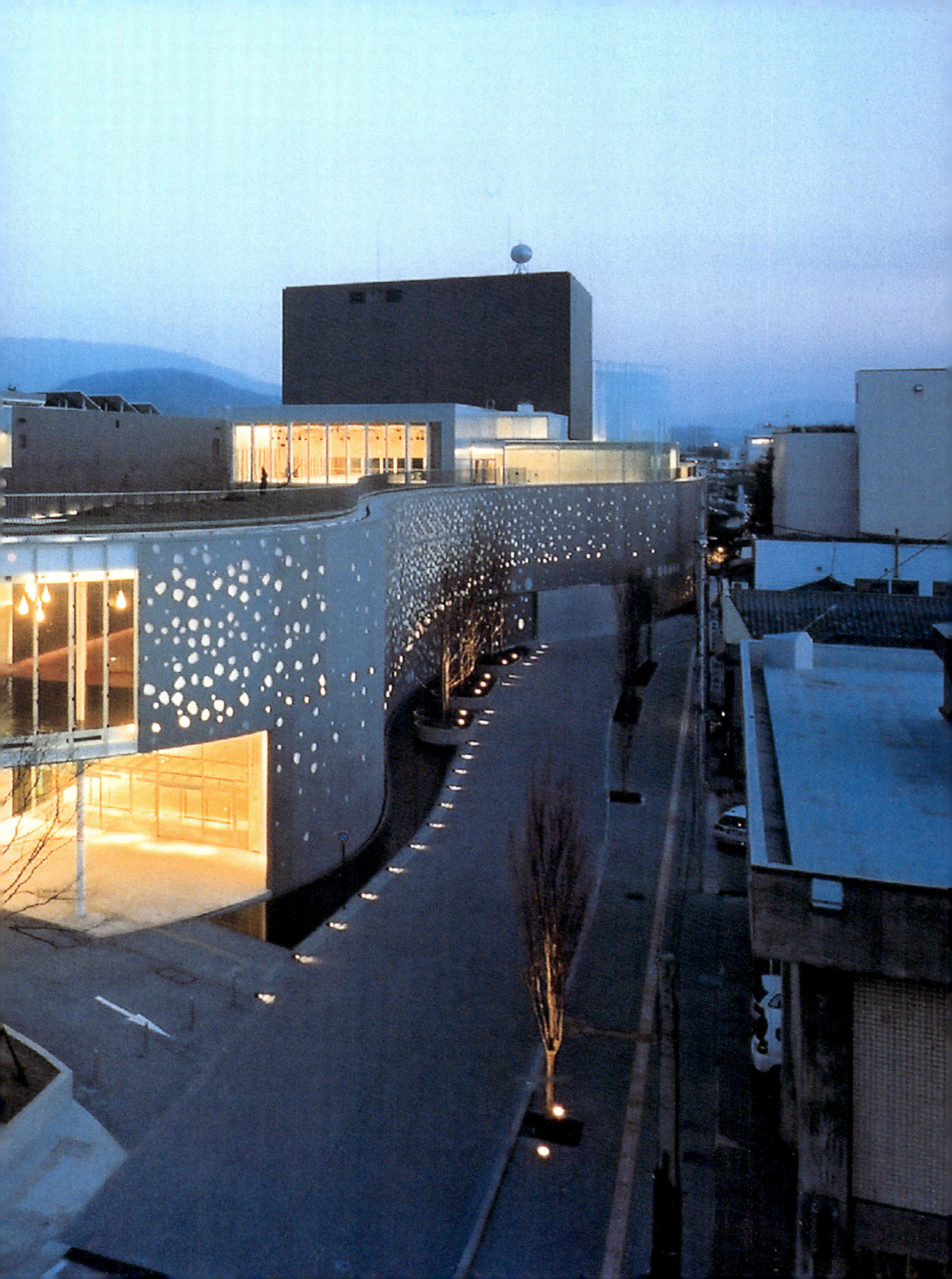

ルーフガーデン。奥にオープンスタジオが見える
Roof garden: The open studio is visible in the rear.

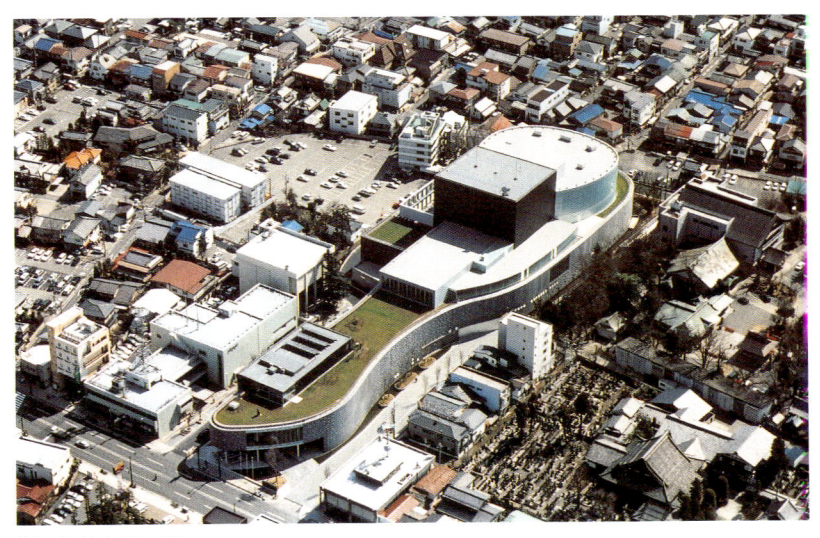

1959年に建てられた市民会館の老朽化に伴い、2004年に建て替えられた。1200〜1800席まで規模の調整できるオペラ上演可能な大ホールと240席の小ホール、折りたたみできる400席の客席を大ホール舞台場につくる実験劇場で構成される。

As the civic hall, built in 1959, had become decrepit, it was replaced with this building in 2004. The new facility has a large hall, which can be used for opera performances, and contains seating that can be adjusted to accommodate from 1,200 to 1,800 people, and a small 240-seat hall. There is also an experimental theatre on the stage of the large hall with 400 folding seats.

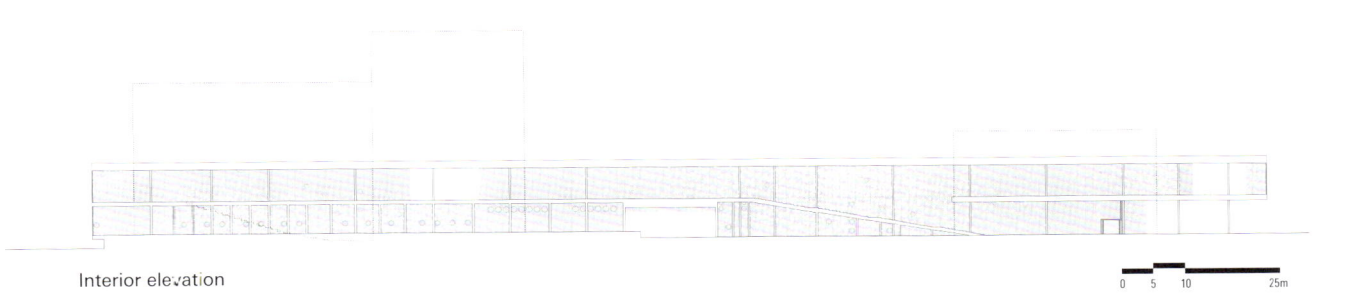

住宅に囲まれた細長い敷地
The long thin site surrounded by houses.

Interior elevation

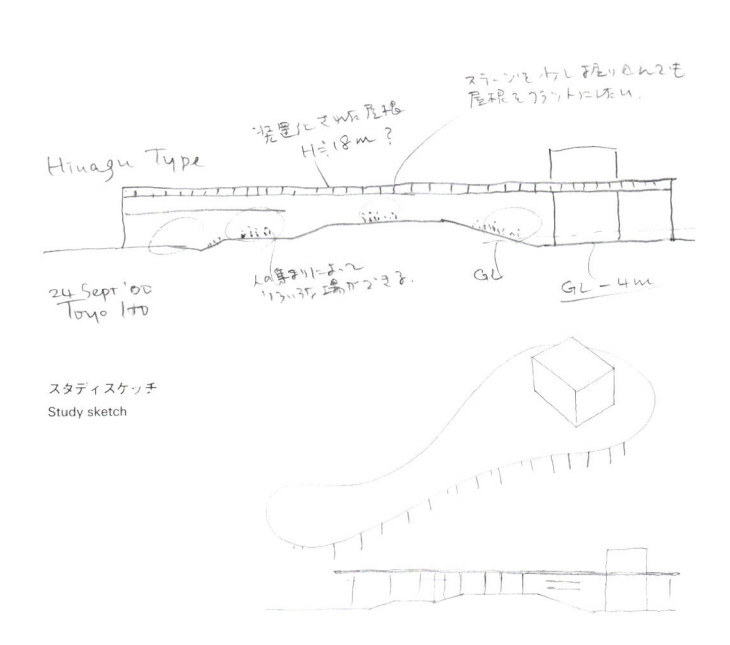

スタディスケッチ
Study sketch

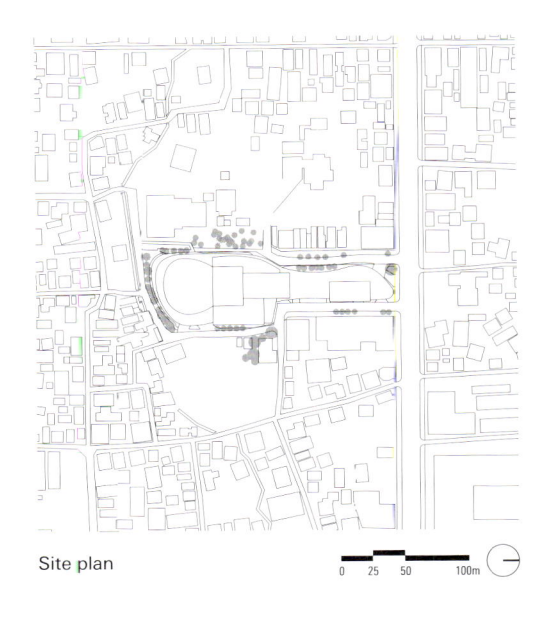

Site plan

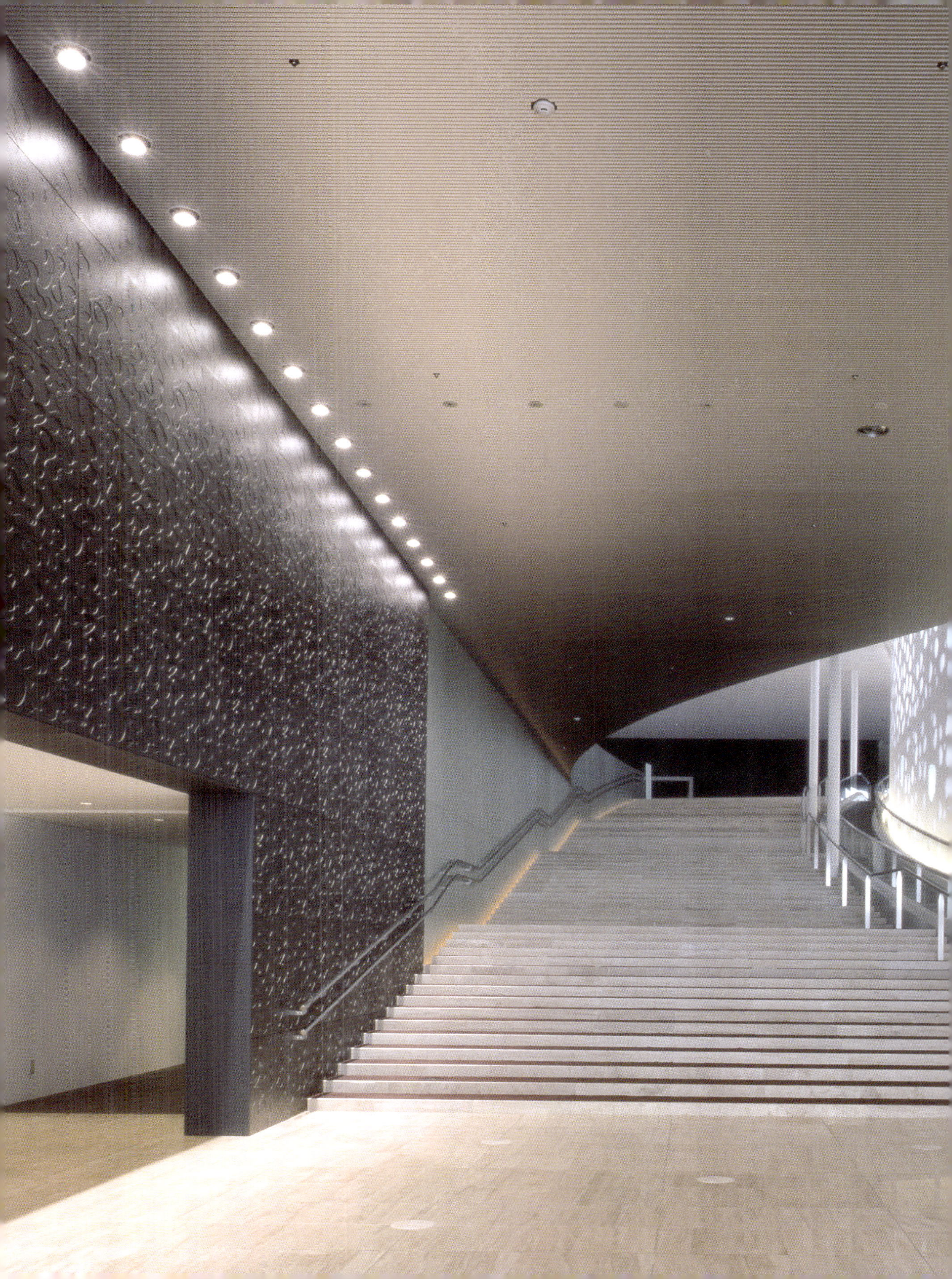

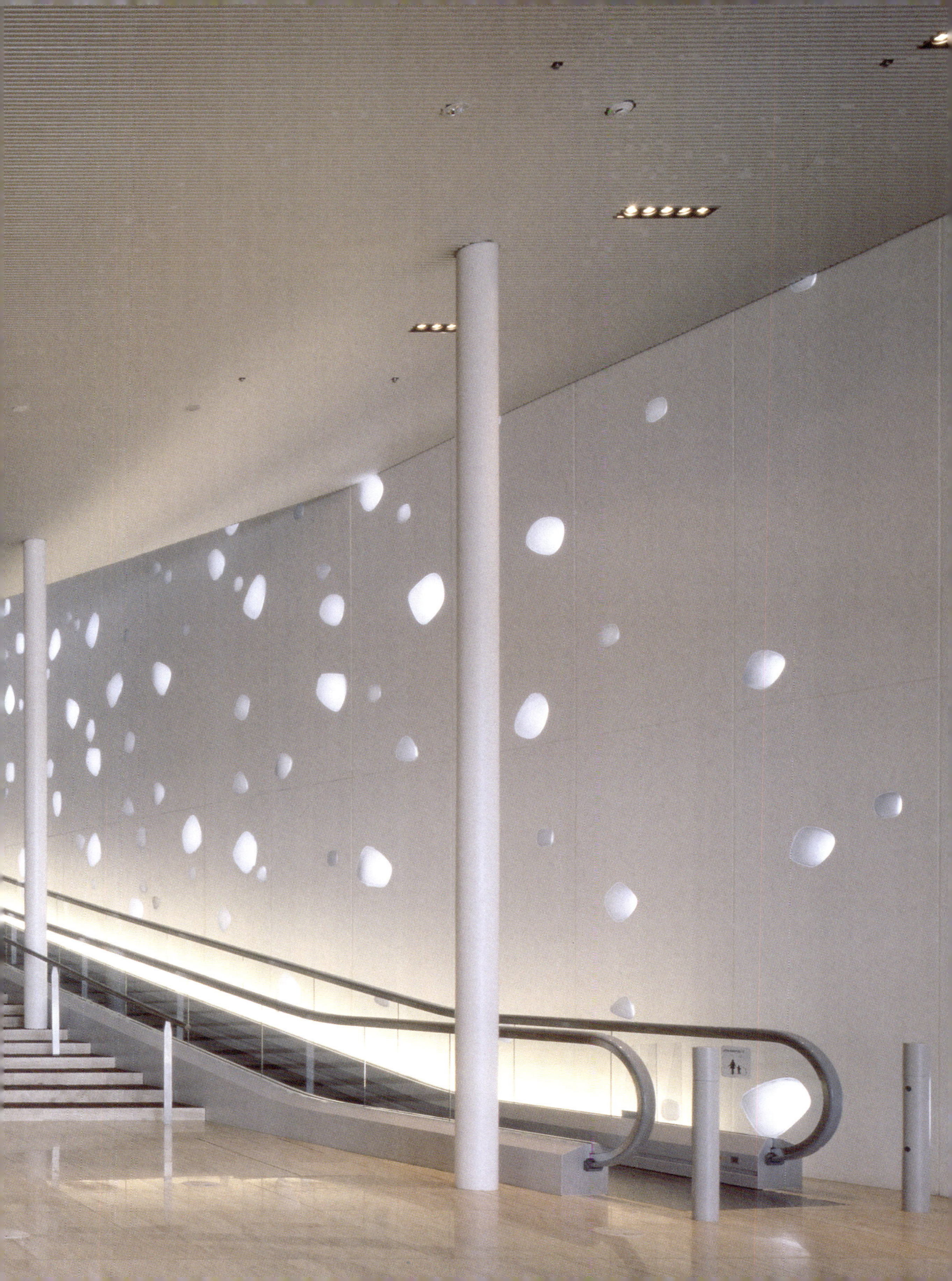

シアターパークから大階段、エントランスを見る
The large staircase and entrance as seen from the theatre park.

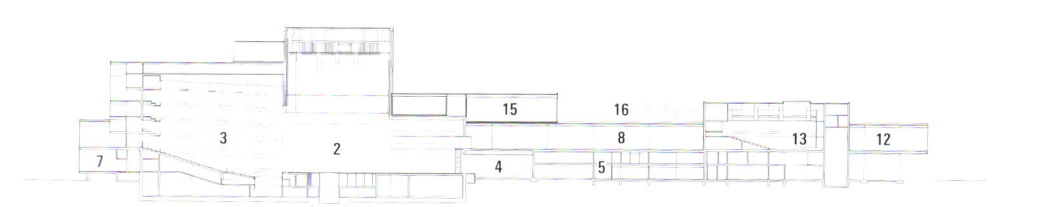

Section

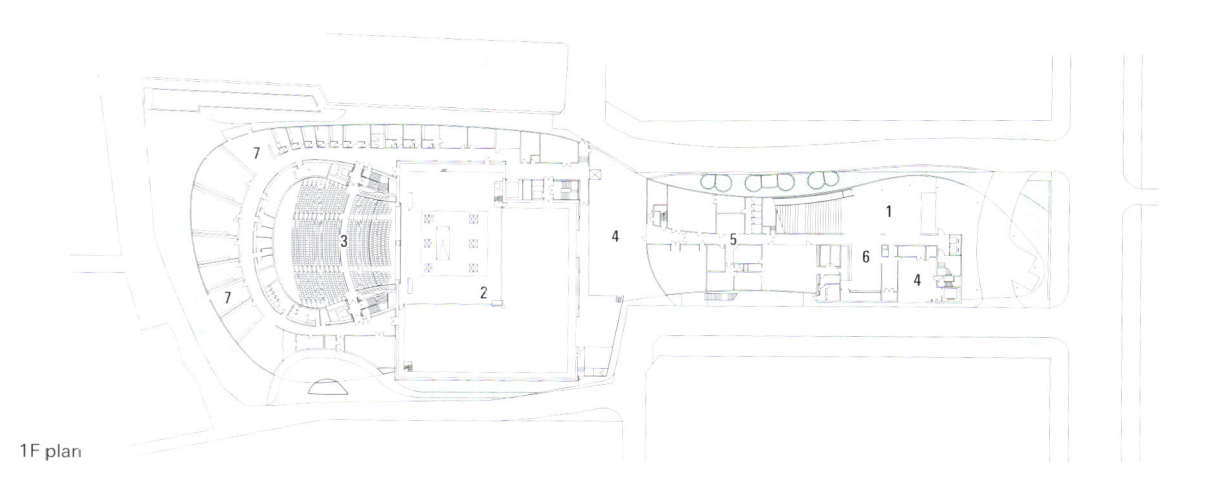

1F plan

開演前のシアターパーク
The theatre park prior to a performance.

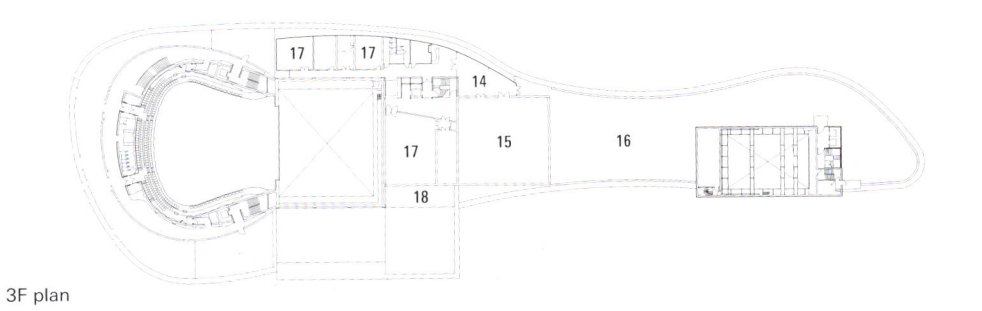

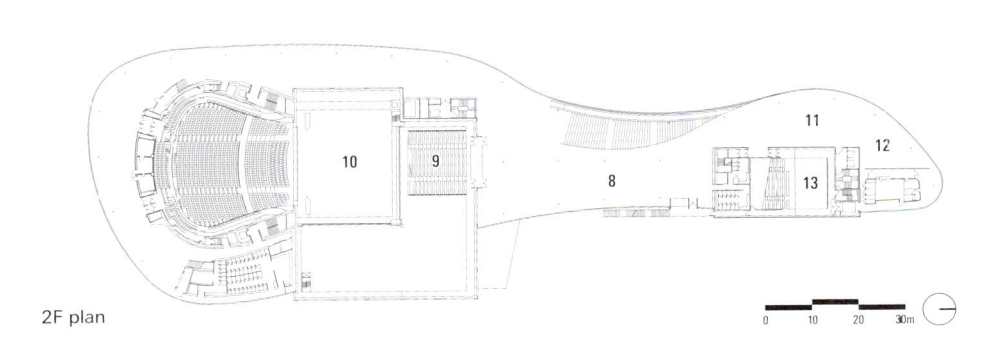

3F plan

2F plan

| 1 | entrance hall |
| --- | --- |
| 2 | stage |
| 3 | seat |
| 4 | back yard |
| 5 | office |
| 6 | information |
| 7 | backstage |
| 8 | theatre park |
| 9 | experimental theater |
| 10 | large hall |
| 11 | foyer |
| 12 | restaurant |
| 13 | small hall |
| 14 | lobby |
| 15 | open studio |
| 16 | roof garden |
| 17 | studio |
| 18 | terrace |

079

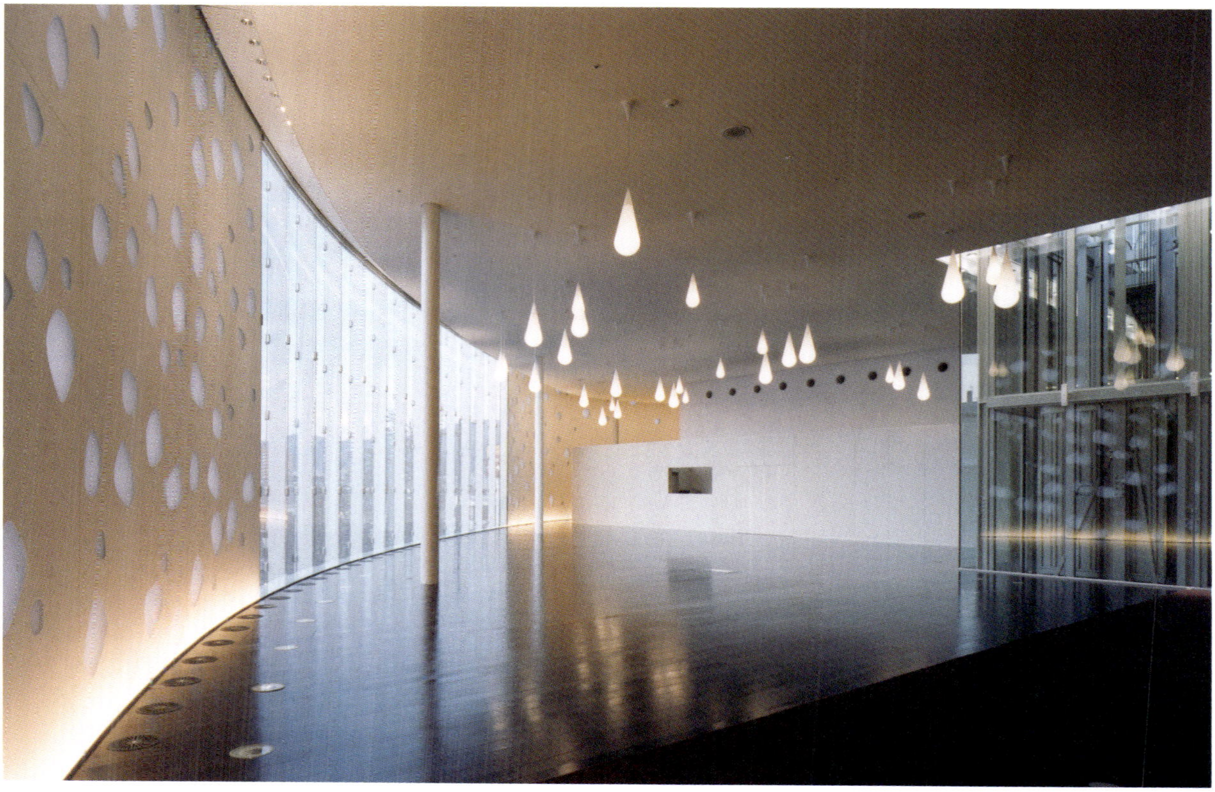

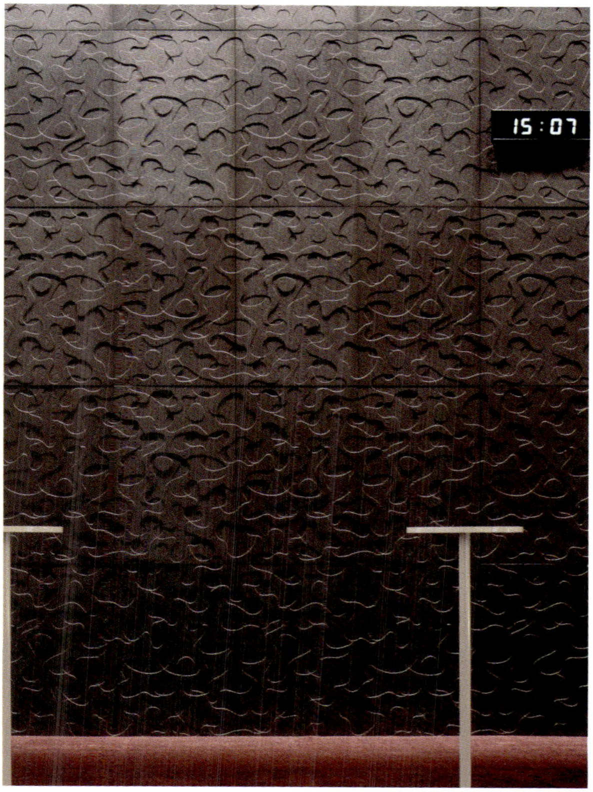
15:07

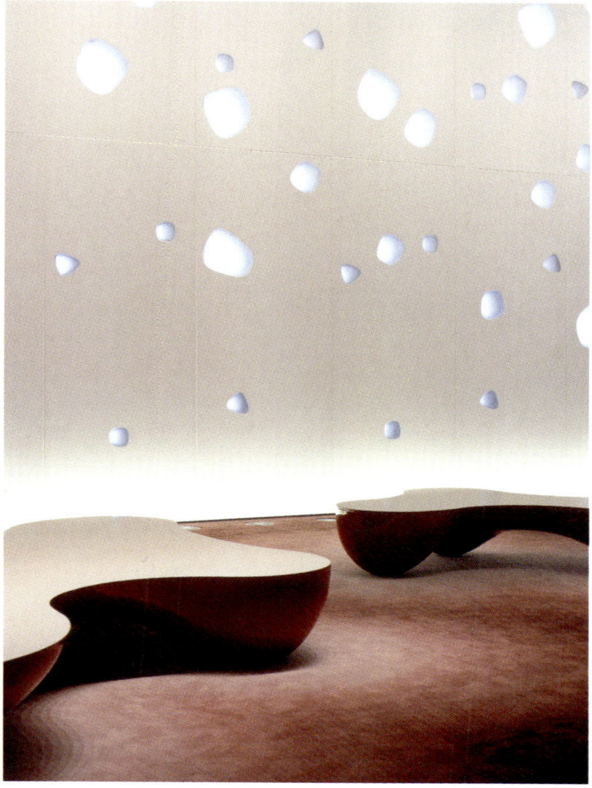

（左頁：上）レストラン
（左頁：左下）舞台外壁アルミキャストパネル
（左頁：右下）シアターパークベンチ
（右頁：上）楽屋ロビー
（右頁：下）楽屋廊下

(Left page: above) Restaurant.
(Left page: lower left) Cast-aluminum panels line the exterior walls of the stage.
(Left page: lower right) Benches in the theatre park.
(Right page: above) The backstage lobby.
(Right page: below) The backstage corridor.

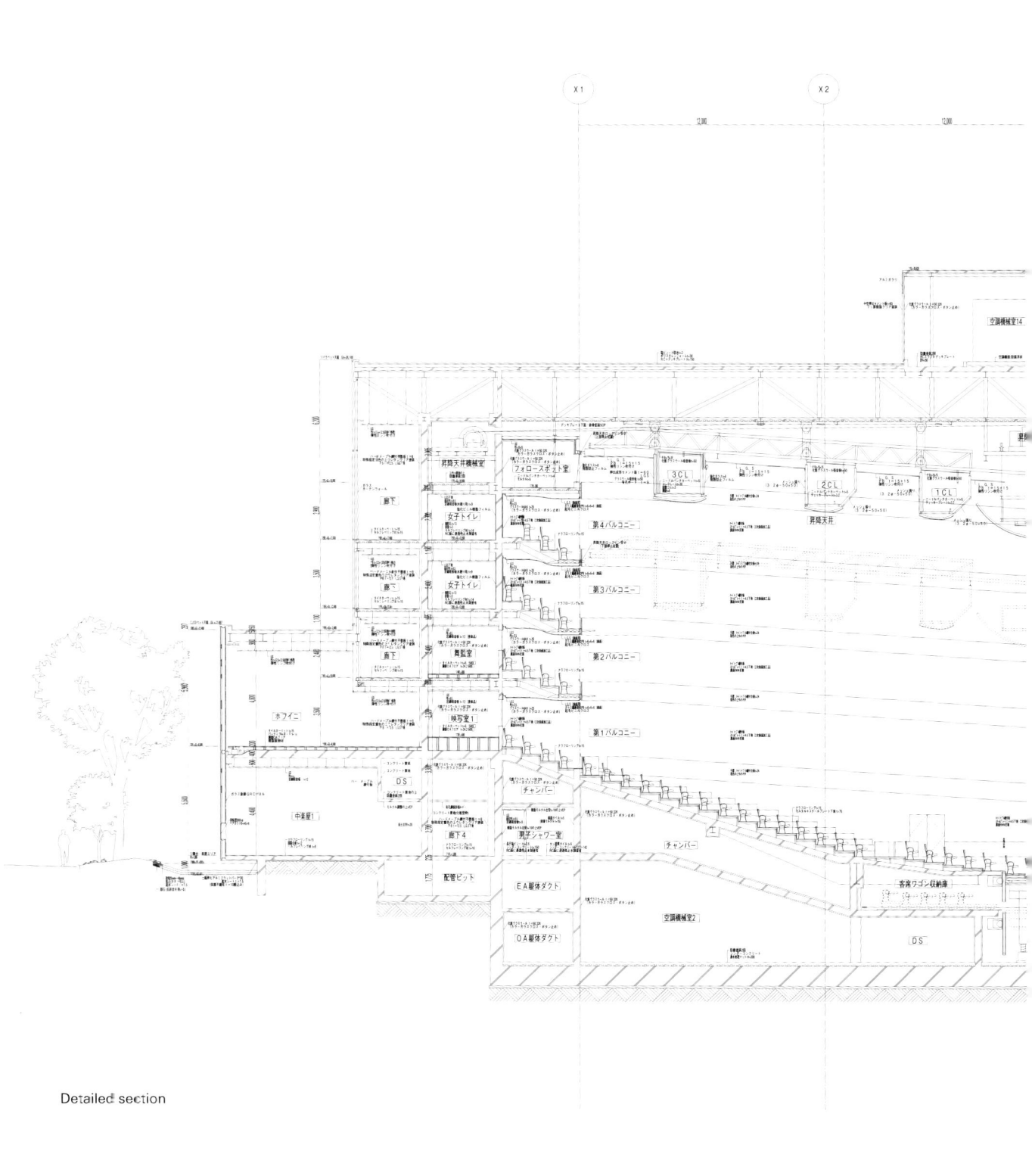

Detailed section

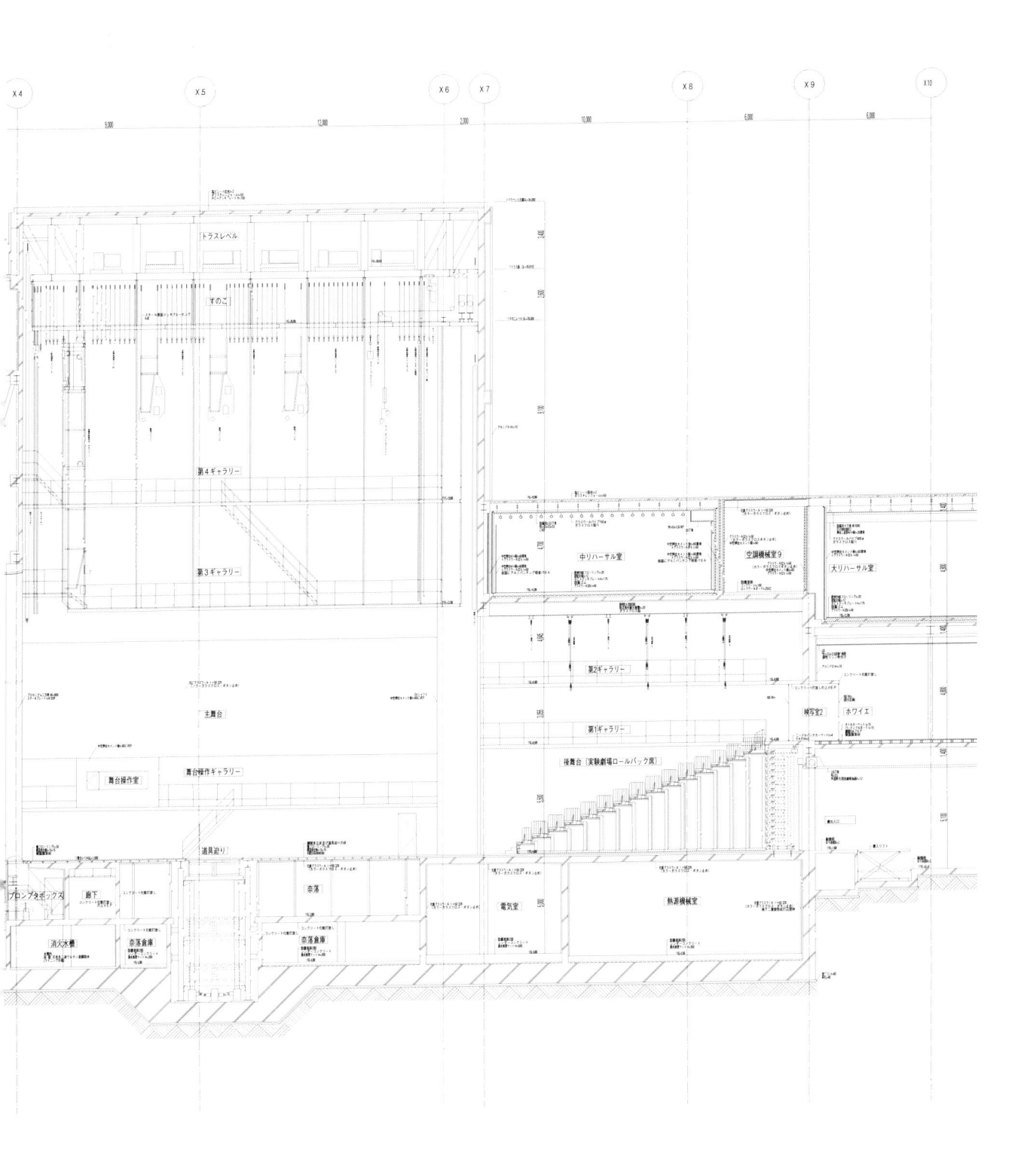

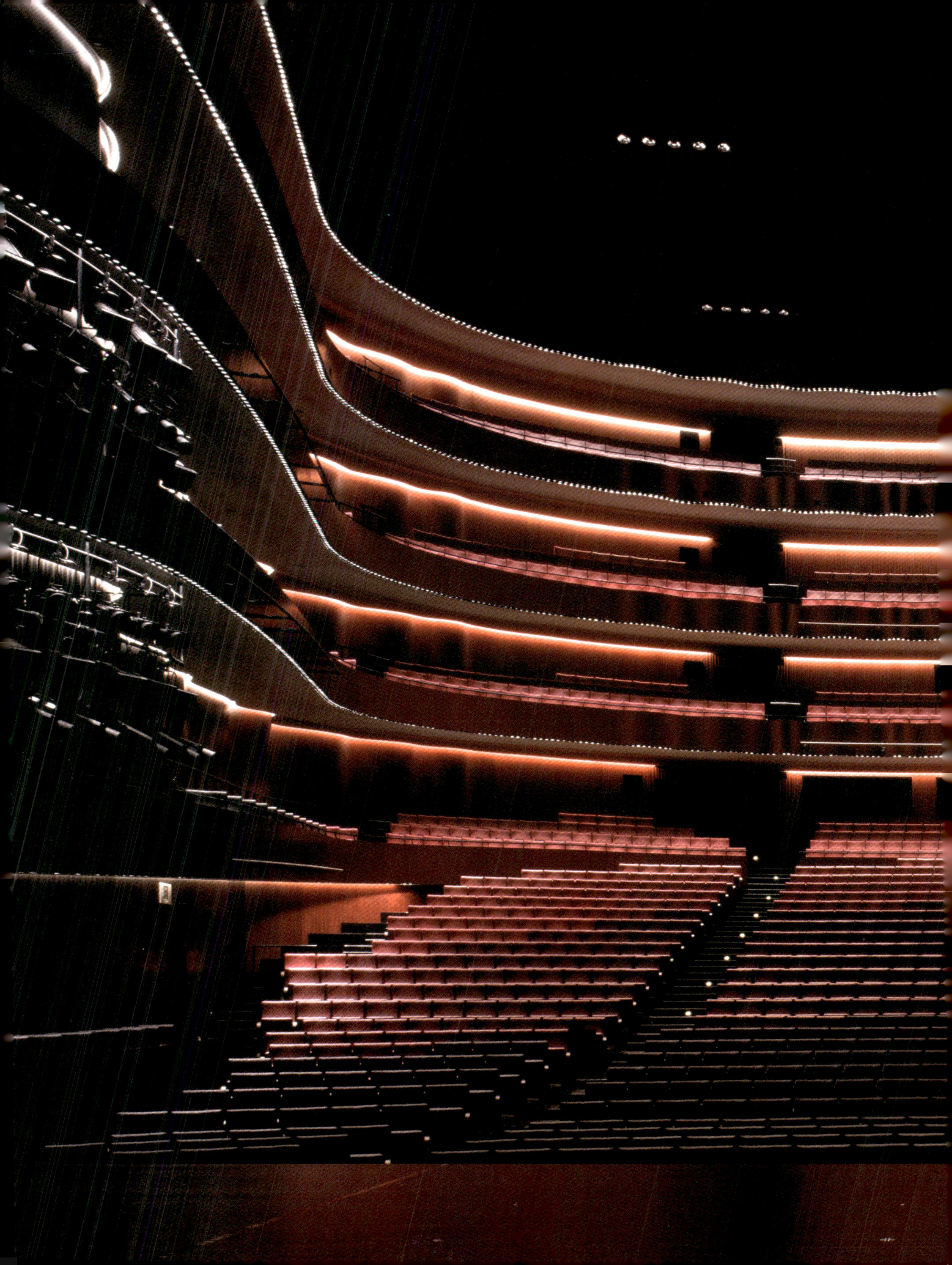

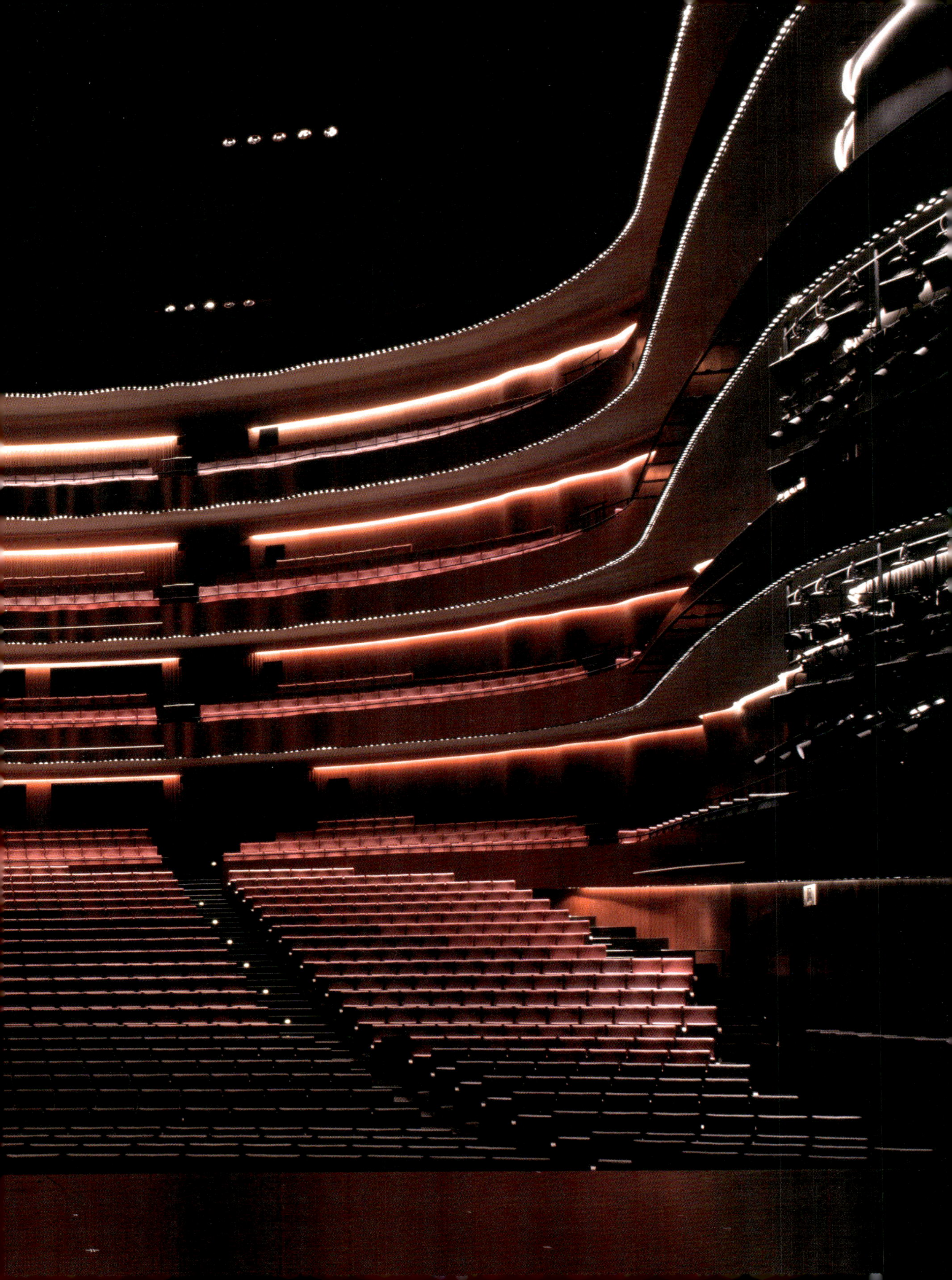

（左頁：上）大ホール客席　（左頁：下）実験劇場 折りたたみ可能な客席　（右頁）ステージを挟んで向かい合う実験劇場と大ホール
(Left page: above) Seats in the large hall. (Left page: below) The experimental theatre, equipped with folding seats.
(Right page) The experimental theatre and large hall face each other on opposite sides of the stage.

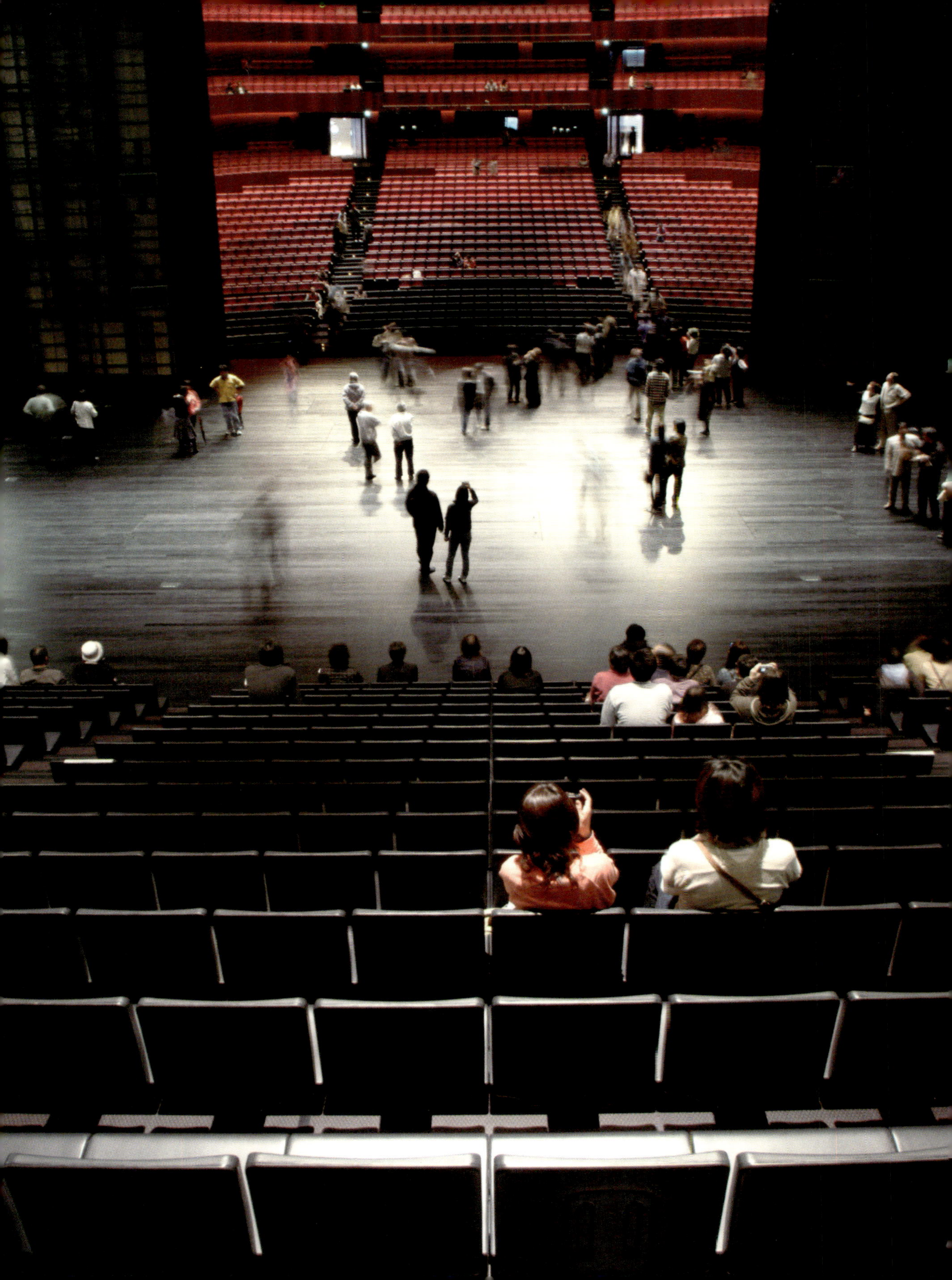

7パターンの手づくりのガラスを象嵌したGRCのサンドウィッチパネル
The sandwich panels made of grass fiber-reinforced cement with seven patterns of inlaid handmade glass.

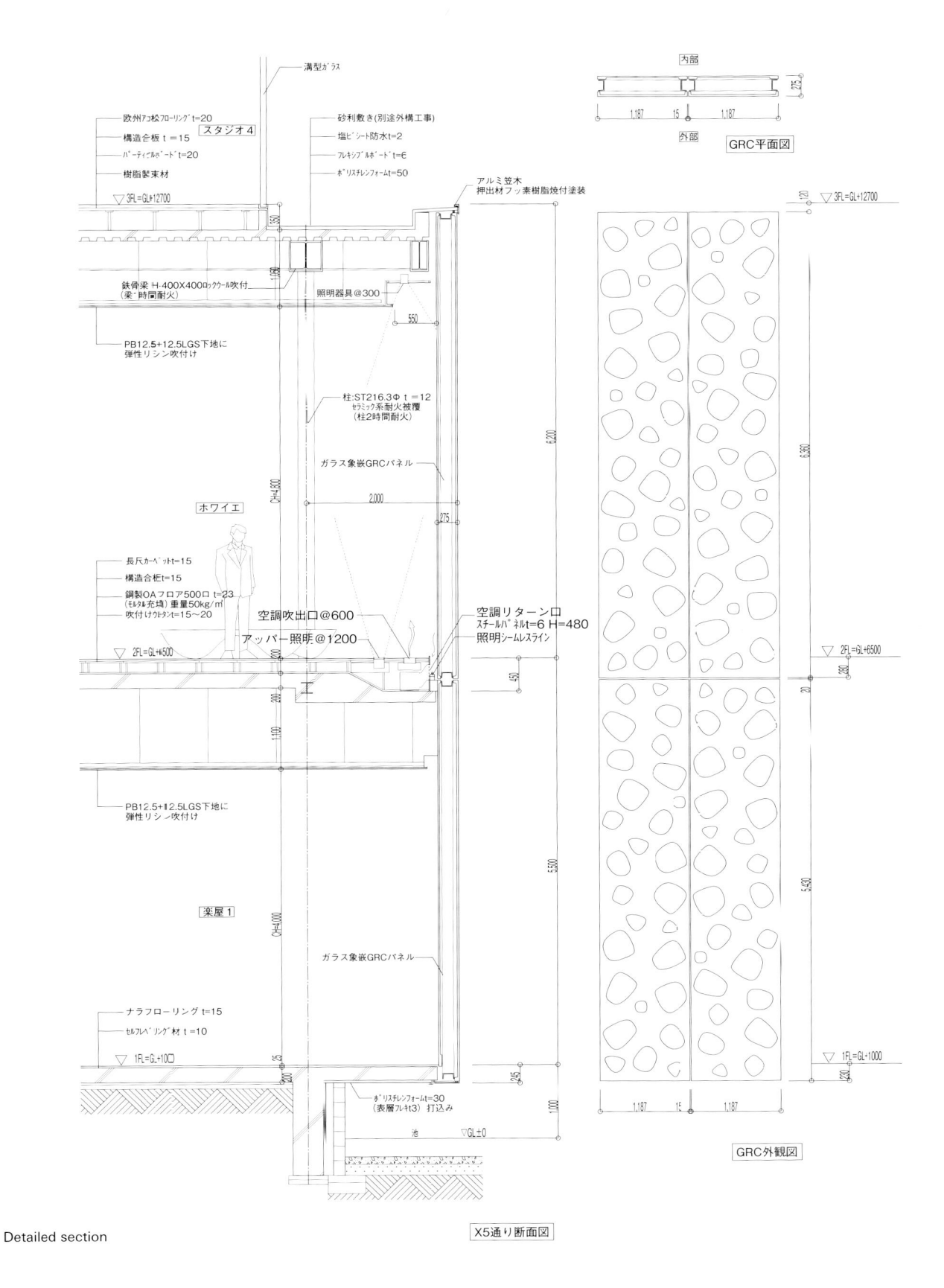

## Detailed section

**GRC平面図**

**X5通り断面図**

**GRC外観図**

- 欧州アコモ松フローリング t=20
- 構造合板 t=15
- パーティクルボード t=20
- 樹脂製束材

スタジオ4

▽3FL=GL+12700

- 溝型ガラス
- 砂利敷き(別途外構工事)
- 塩ビシート防水 t=2
- フレキシブルボード t=6
- ポリスチレンフォーム t=50

アルミ笠木
押出材フッ素樹脂焼付塗装

- 鉄骨梁 H-400×400ロックウール吹付
 (梁・1時間耐火)
- 照明器具@300
- PB12.5+12.5LGS下地に
 弾性リシン吹付け

柱:ST216.3Φ t=12
セラミック系耐火被覆
(柱2時間耐火)

ガラス象嵌GRCパネル

ホワイエ

- 長尺カーペット t=15
- 構造合板 t=15
- 鋼製OAフロア500□ t=23
 (モルタル充填)重量50kg/㎡
- 吹付けウレタン t=15～20

空調吹出口@600
アッパー照明@1200

空調リターン口
スチールパネル t=6 H=480
照明シームレスライン

▽2FL=GL+6500

- PB12.5+12.5LGS下地に
 弾性リシン吹付け

楽屋1

ガラス象嵌GRCパネル

- ナラフローリング t=15
- セルフレベリング材 t=10

▽1FL=GL+1000

ポリスチレンフォーム t=30
(表層フレキ t3)打込み

池 ▽GL±0

ステージの背後からステージ、オーケストラピット、客席までを結ぶ橋がかりとして合板を曲げてデザインされた舞台
Made of curved plywood, the stage is designed like a bridge reaching from the rear of the stage to the stage itself, and on into the orchestra pit, and the seats.

2005年に串田和美演出、小澤征爾指揮によって上演された子ども向け「フィガロの結婚（抄訳版）」の舞台。

A version of The Marriage of Figaro (abridged translation), made for children, was performed in 2005. It was directed by Mr. Kazuyoshi Kushida and conducted by Mr. Seiji Ozawa.

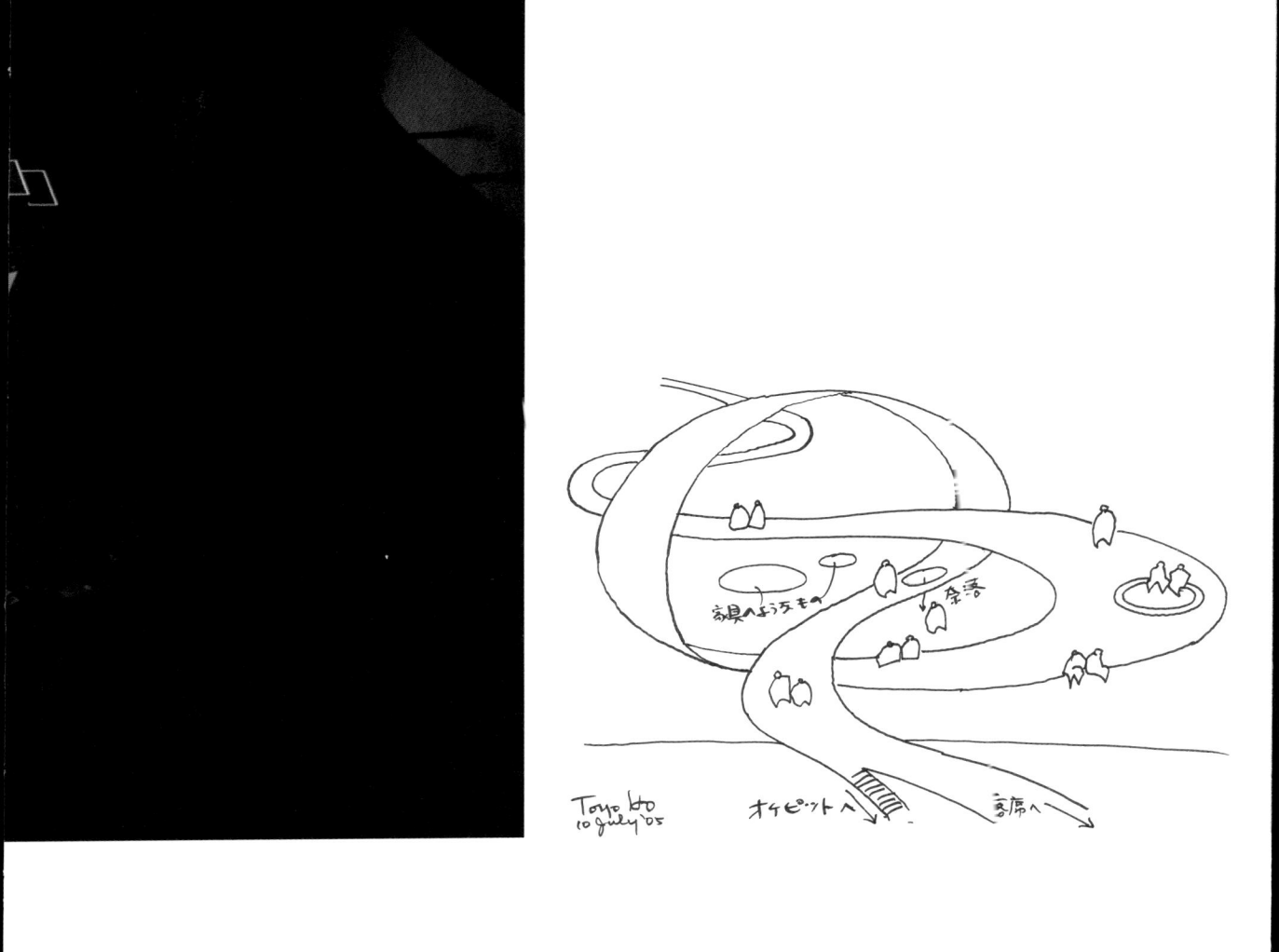

Toyo Ito
10 July '05

## TOD'S Omotesando Building
TOD'S 表参道ビル

2004　東京都渋谷区　Shibuya, Tokyo

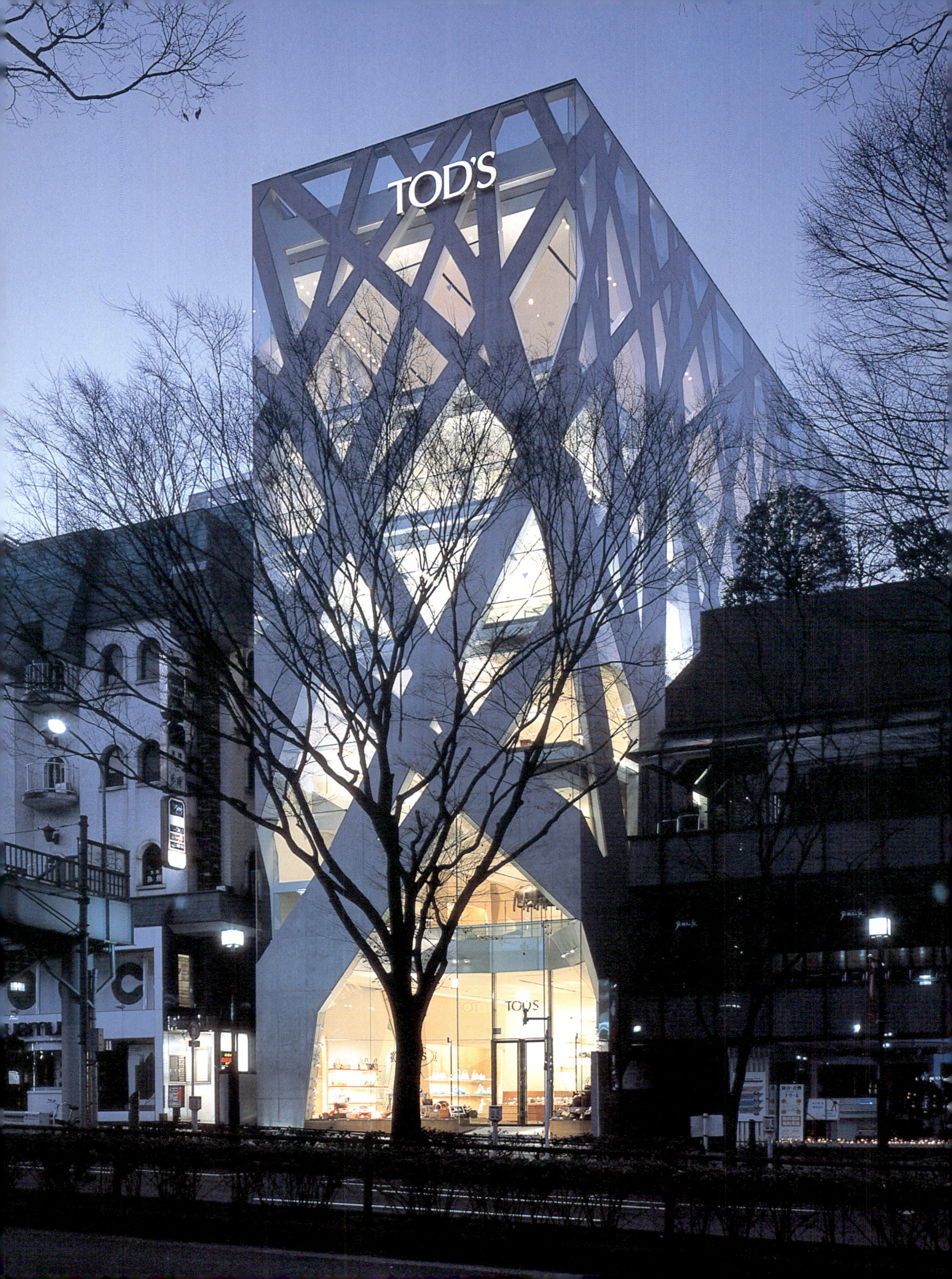
TOD'S
TOD'S

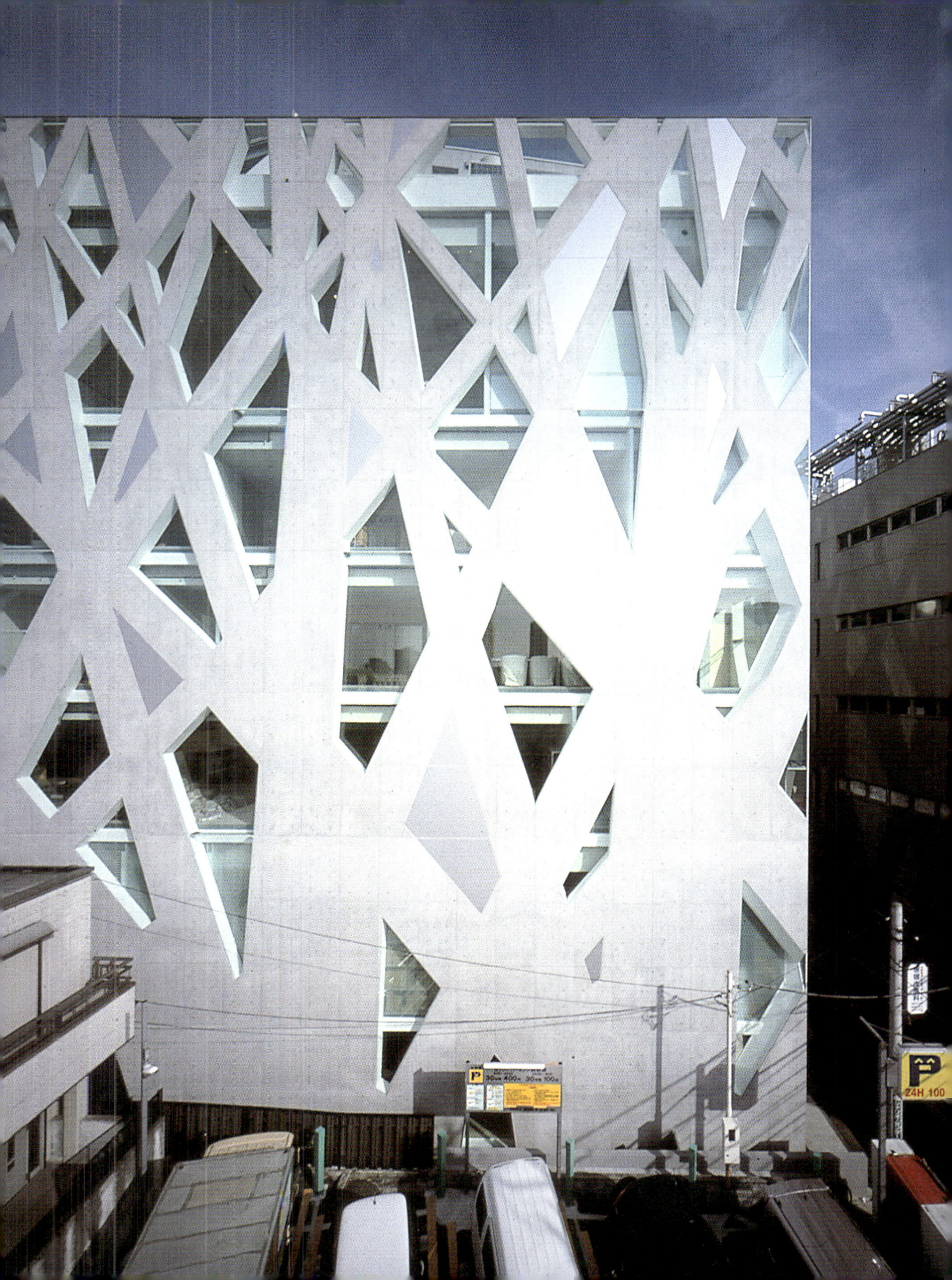
P
24H 100

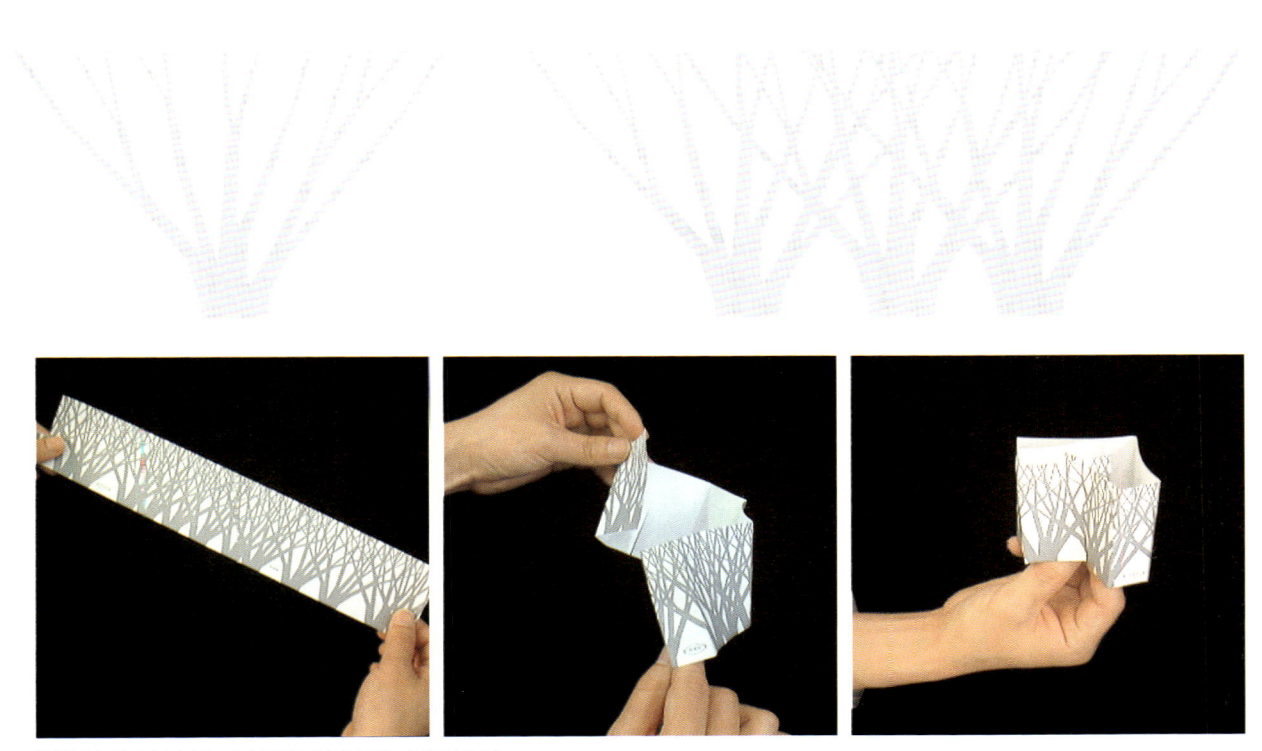

抽象化されたケヤキのシルエットを9本重ね合わせたパターンのストラクチャー
The pattern of the structure was created by juxtaposing the silhouette of nine abstract zelkova trees.

初期のファサードデザインのスタディ
Facade design study in the early phase.

095

ファサードの配筋
Reinforcements for the facade.

300mmの垂直躯体が500mmの
ヴォイド床スラブを支えている。接
合部を250mmまで絞り、床をファ
サードの表面より引込めることに
よってファサードのパターンが外側
からクリアに表現されている。

A 300mm vertical framework supports
the 500mm void floor slab. By reducing
the joints to 250mm, and retracting the
floor from the surface of the facade, its
pattern looks clear from the outside.

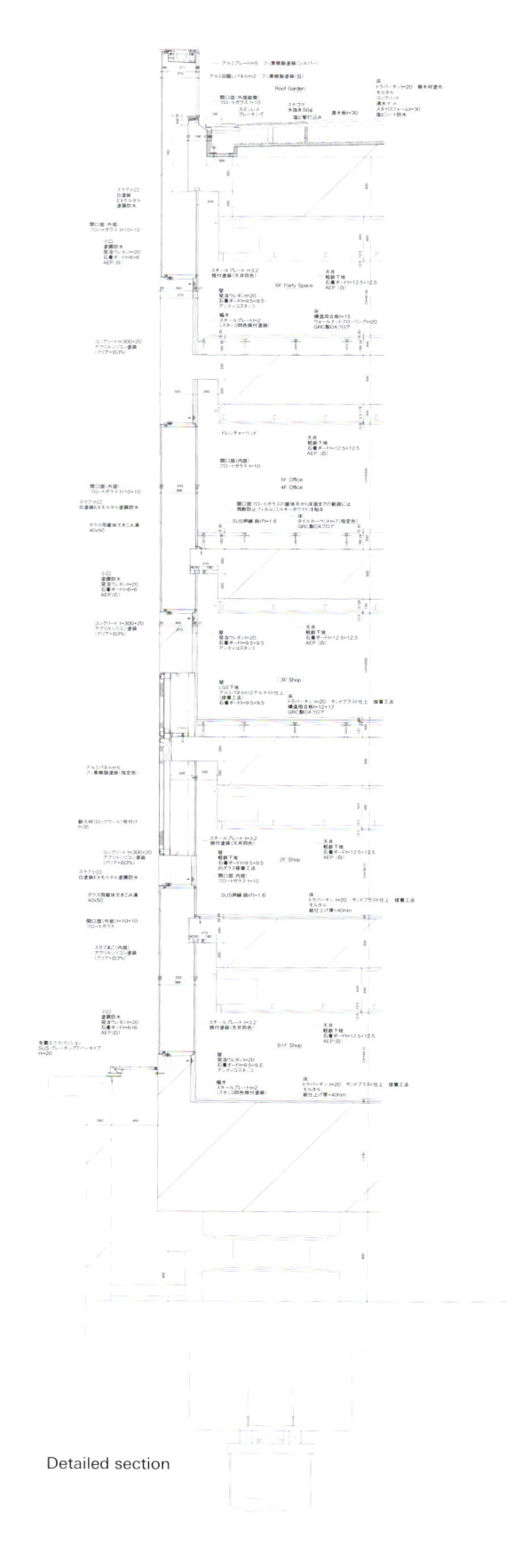

Detailed section

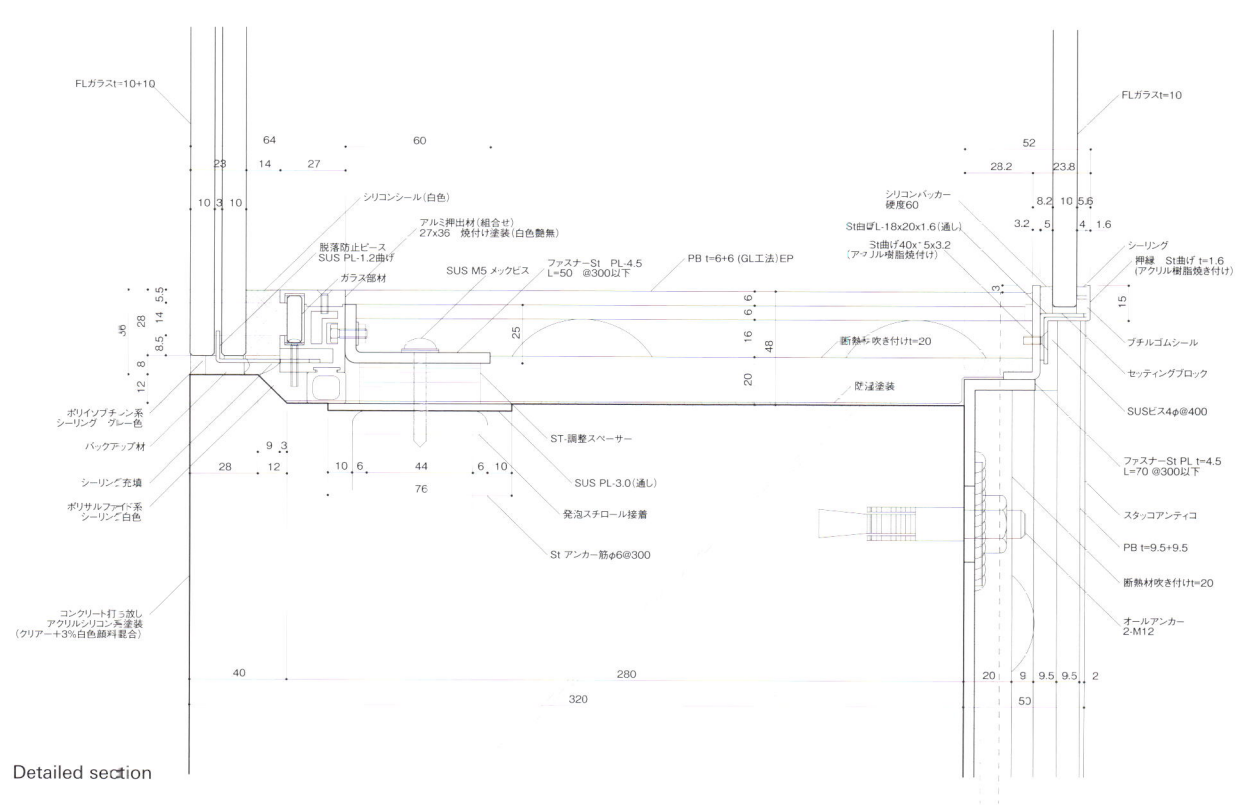

Detailed section

ショップ内階段
The staircase inside the shop.

4F plan

5F plan

6F plan

7F plan

B1F plan

1F plan

2F plan

3F plan

| 1 shop | 5 office | 9 meeting room |
| --- | --- | --- |
| 2 machine room | 6 locker room | 10 showroom |
| 3 stock room | 7 storage | 11 party room |
| 4 office entrance | 8 lunch room | 12 lounge |

Section

1 shop
2 show window
3 office
4 party space
5 roof garde
6 pent house

099

（上）ルーフテラス　（中）ラウンジ　（下）ショップ
(Above) Roof terrace.　(Middle) Lounge.　(Below) Shop.

木々の中からまちを望むような6階の内部空間
The sixth-floor interior makes it seem as if looking at the city through a group of trees.

東京、表参道に建てられたイタリアのブランドTOD'Sの専用ビルである。枝分かれする木の図式は、下層から上層にいくにつれて開口面積を増し、内部のプログラムに対応している。

This building was designed for TOD'S, an Italian fashion brand, in Omotesando, Tokyo. The size of the openings, patterned with branced trees, increases with each floor in relation to the interior program.

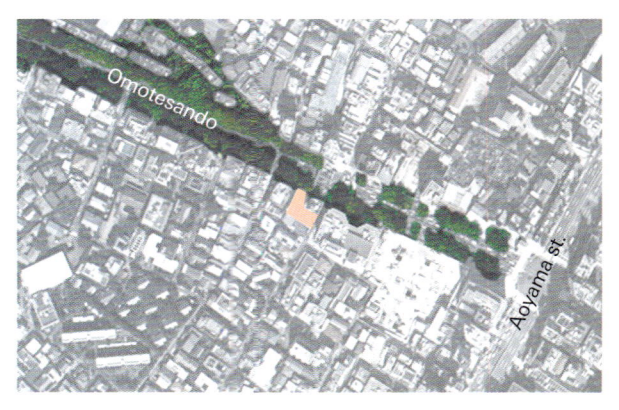

Site plan

**Island City Central Park "GRIN GRIN"**
福岡アイランドシティ中央公園中核施設ぐりんぐりん

2005　福岡県福岡市　Fukuoka, Fukuoka

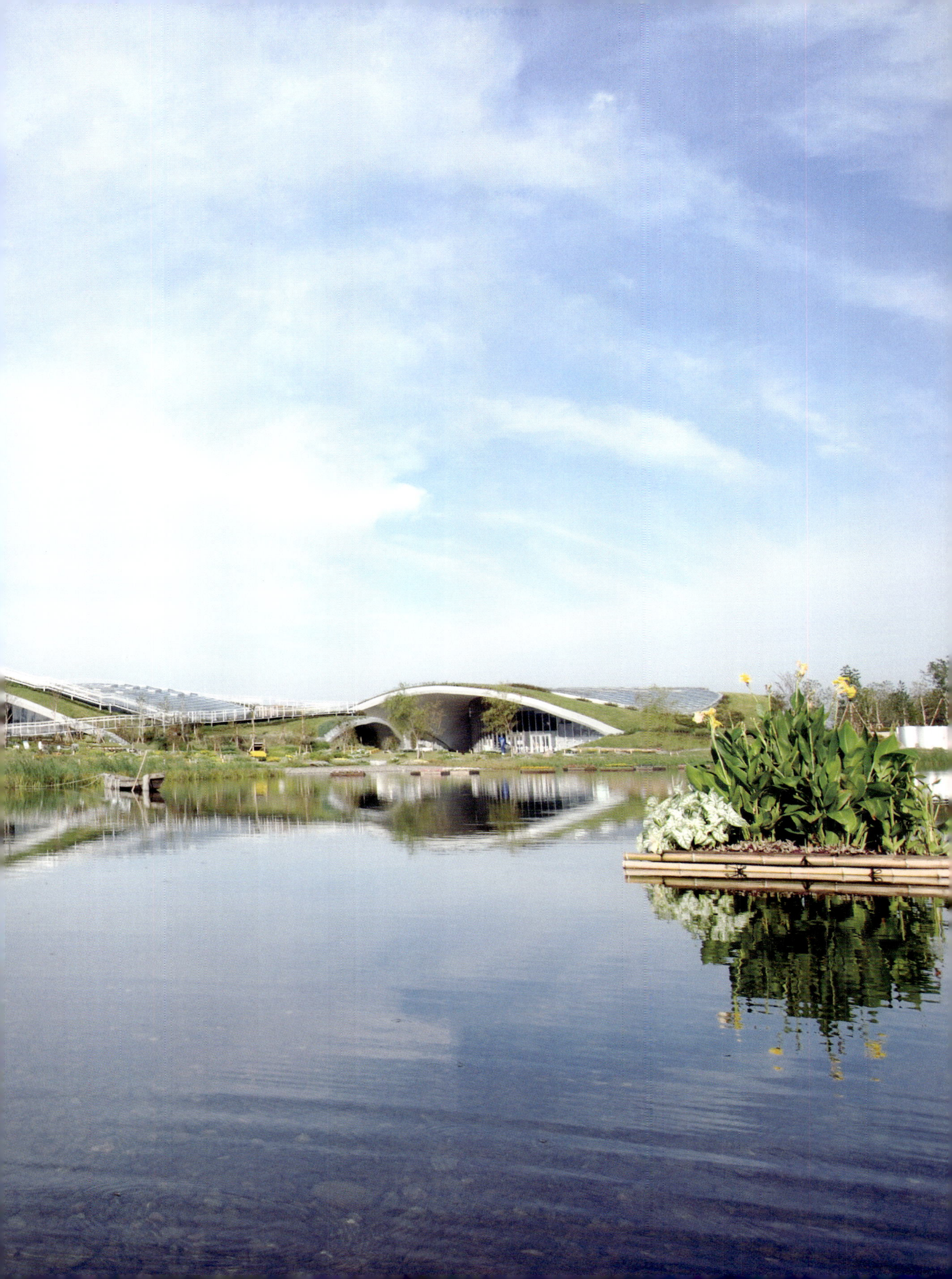

平坦な人工島に地形と連続した丘を作り出す
Producing continuous hills from the terrain on a flat artificial island.

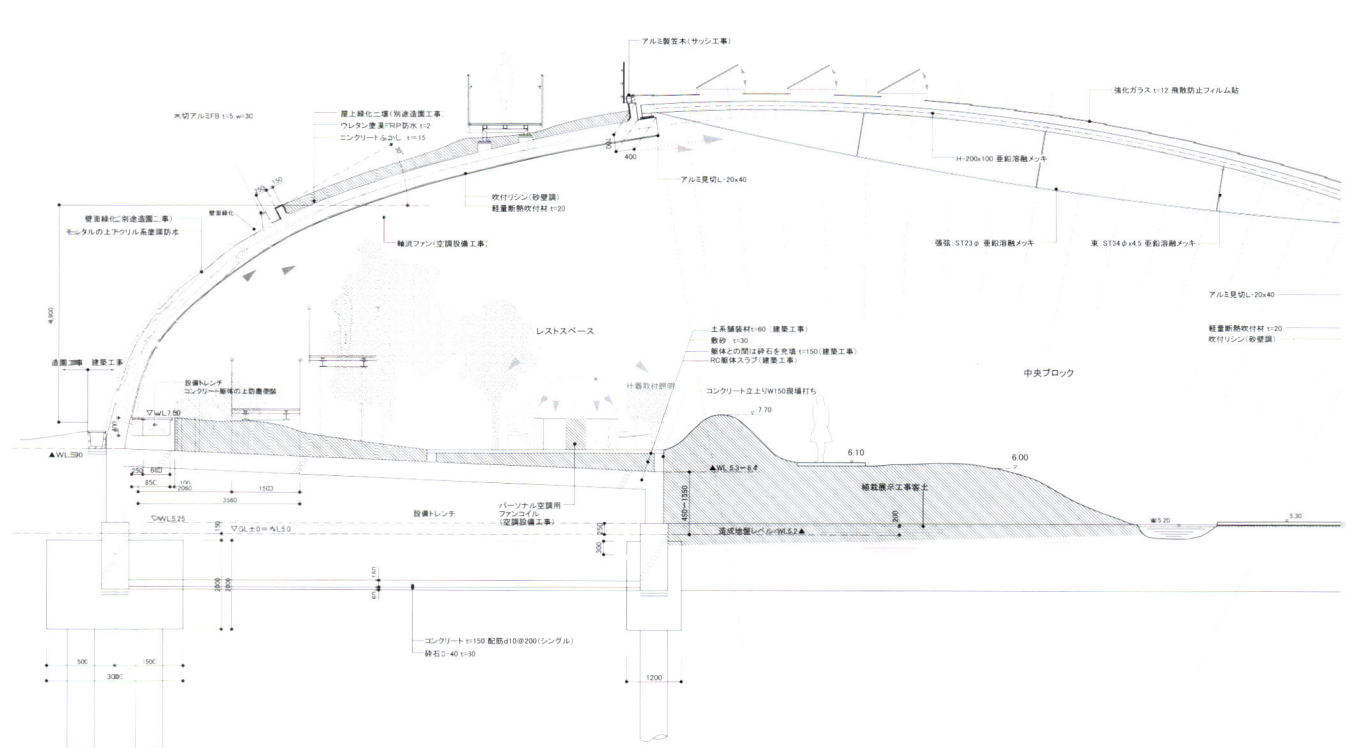

Detailed section

博多湾に浮かぶ400haの人工島の中央部に設けられた約1.53haの中央公園の中核施設。

Core facility of the Central Park of about 1.53ha, which is provided in the center of the artificial island of 400ha floating in Hakata Bay.

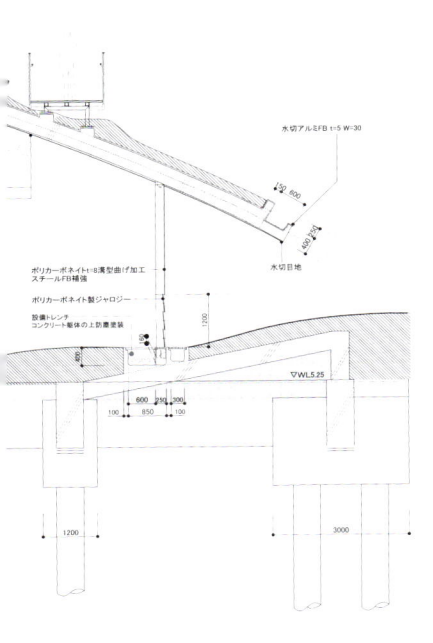

105

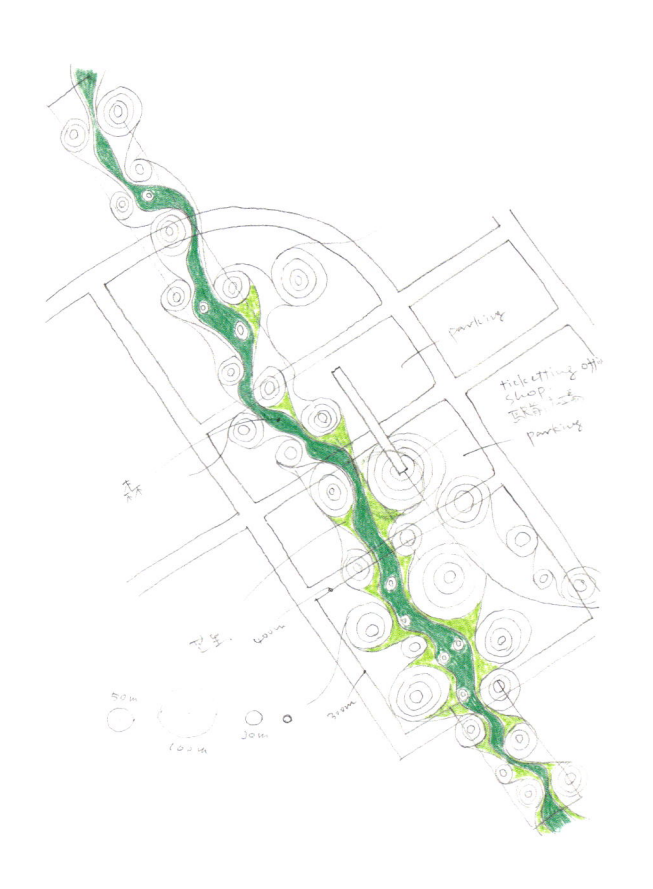

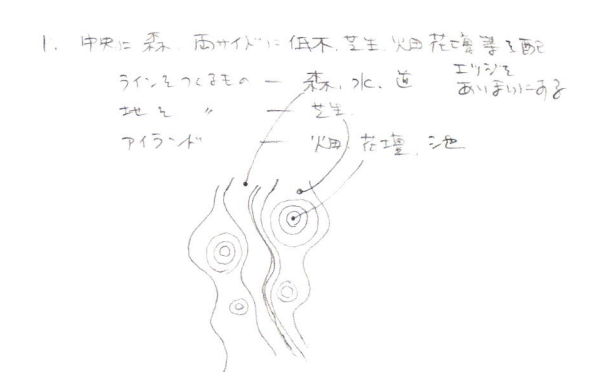

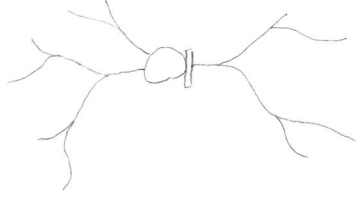

初期スケッチ
Early sketch.

スタディ当初より建築とランドスケープの連続した空間を目指した。

Beginning with the early studies, the aim was to create a space in which the building would be integrated into the landscape.

最終スケッチ
Final sketch.

107

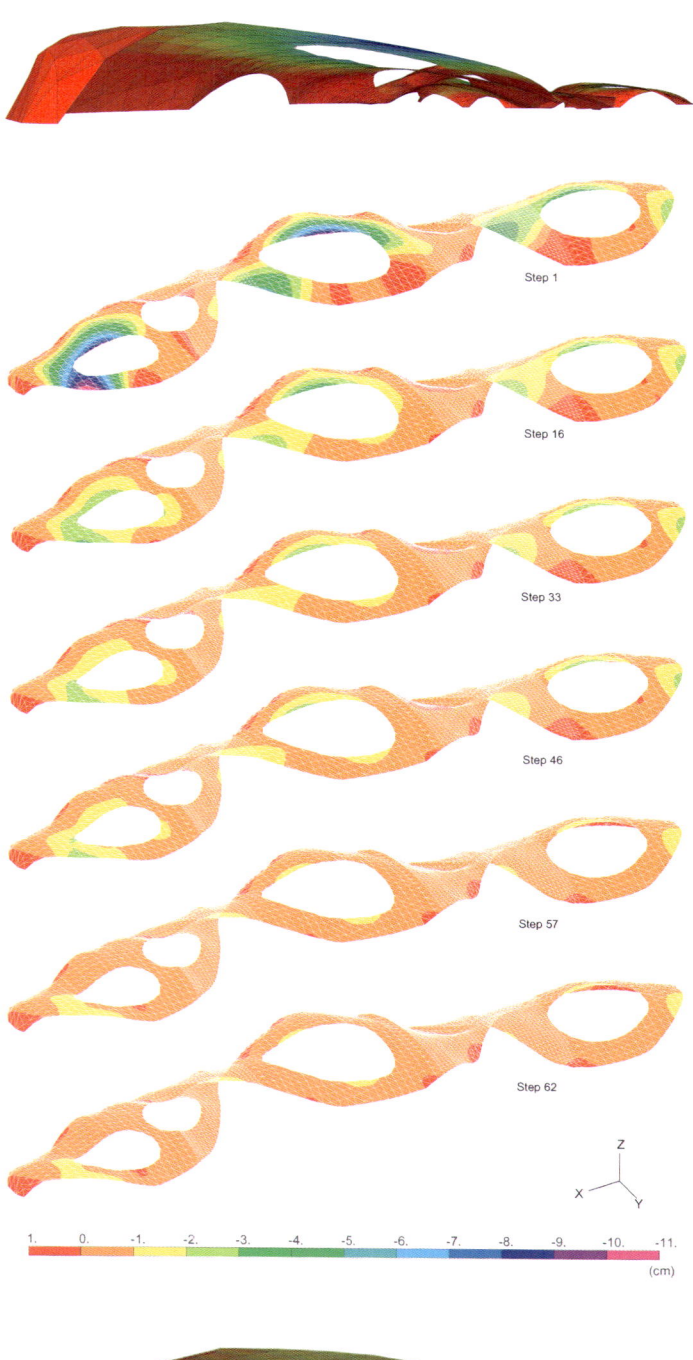

Step 1
Step 16
Step 33
Step 46
Step 57
Step 62

最適化のプロセス
Optimization process.

コンピューターでの形態解析によって最適化を繰り返すことで複雑な形態が可能となった。

It is now possible to make complex forms using repeated optimization and computer-based morphological analysis.

108

日本の伝統的な施工技術とコンピューターテクノロジーの融合。

The building is a hybrid of traditional Japanese construction techniques and computer technology.

109

Site plan

0  25  50  100m

航空写真
Aerial photograph.

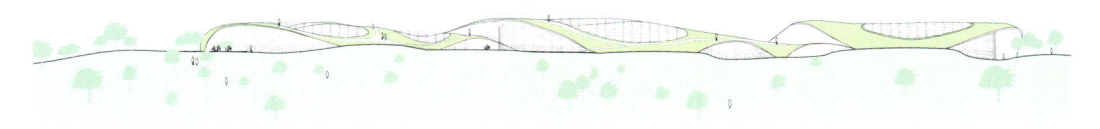

Elevation

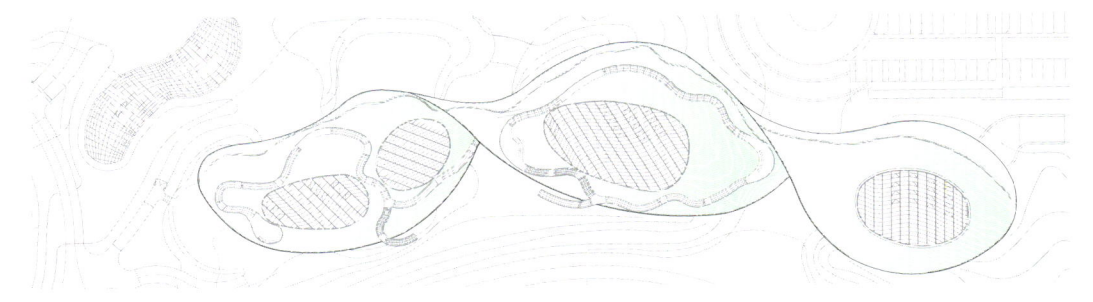

WL+17.0m level plan

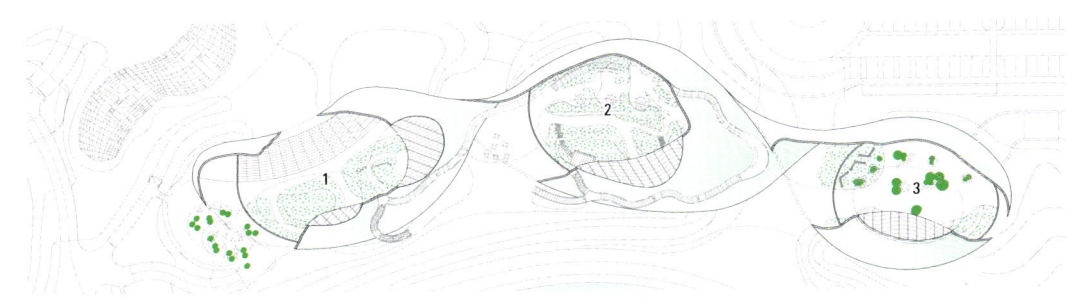

WL+11.7m level plan

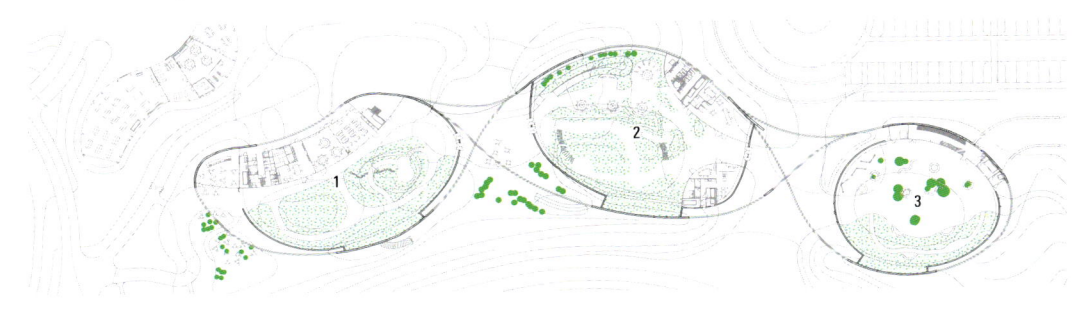

WL+5.0m level plan

1 south block
2 central block
3 north block

WL+4.5m level creation of the ground

0  10  25  50m

111

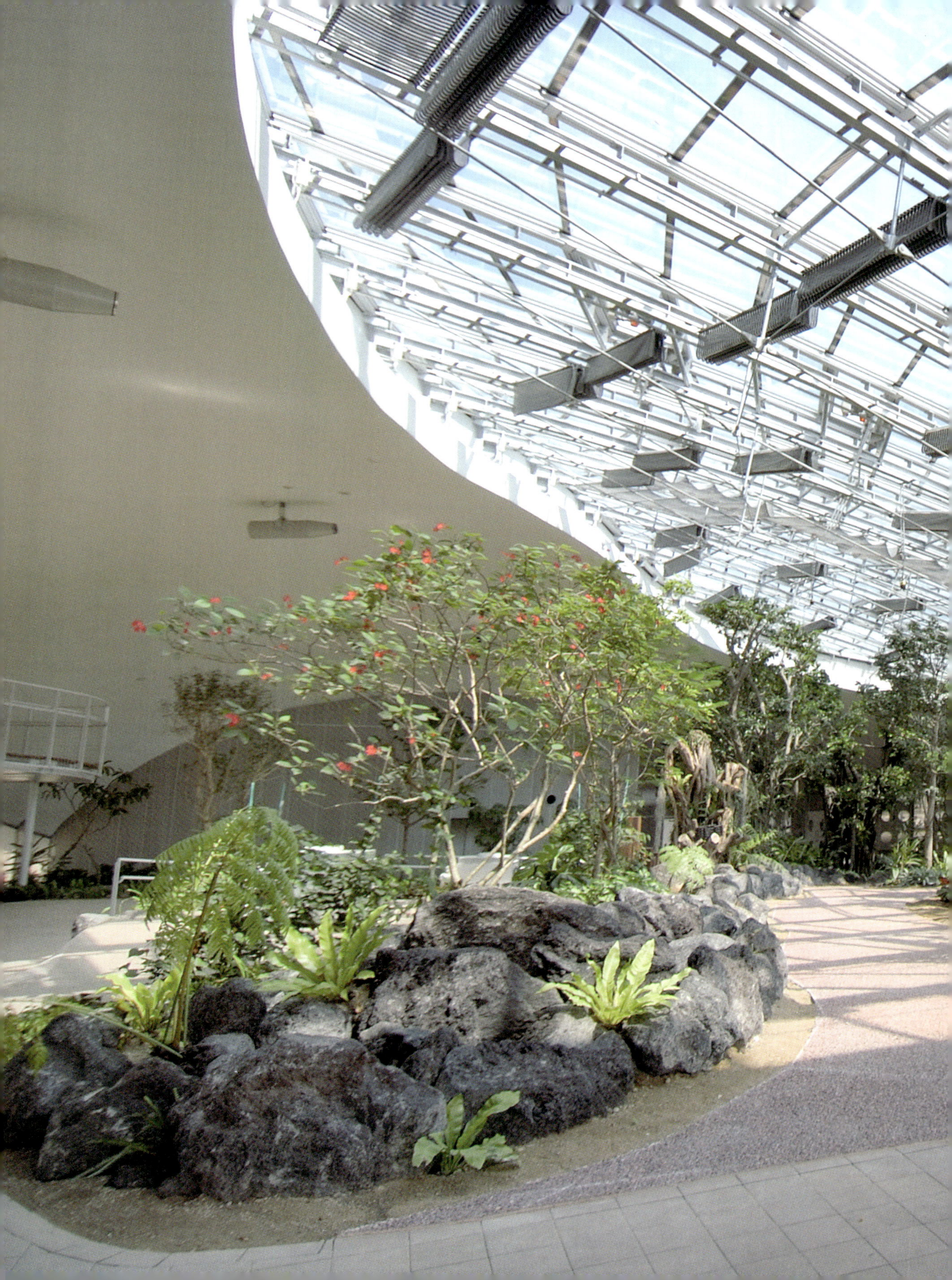

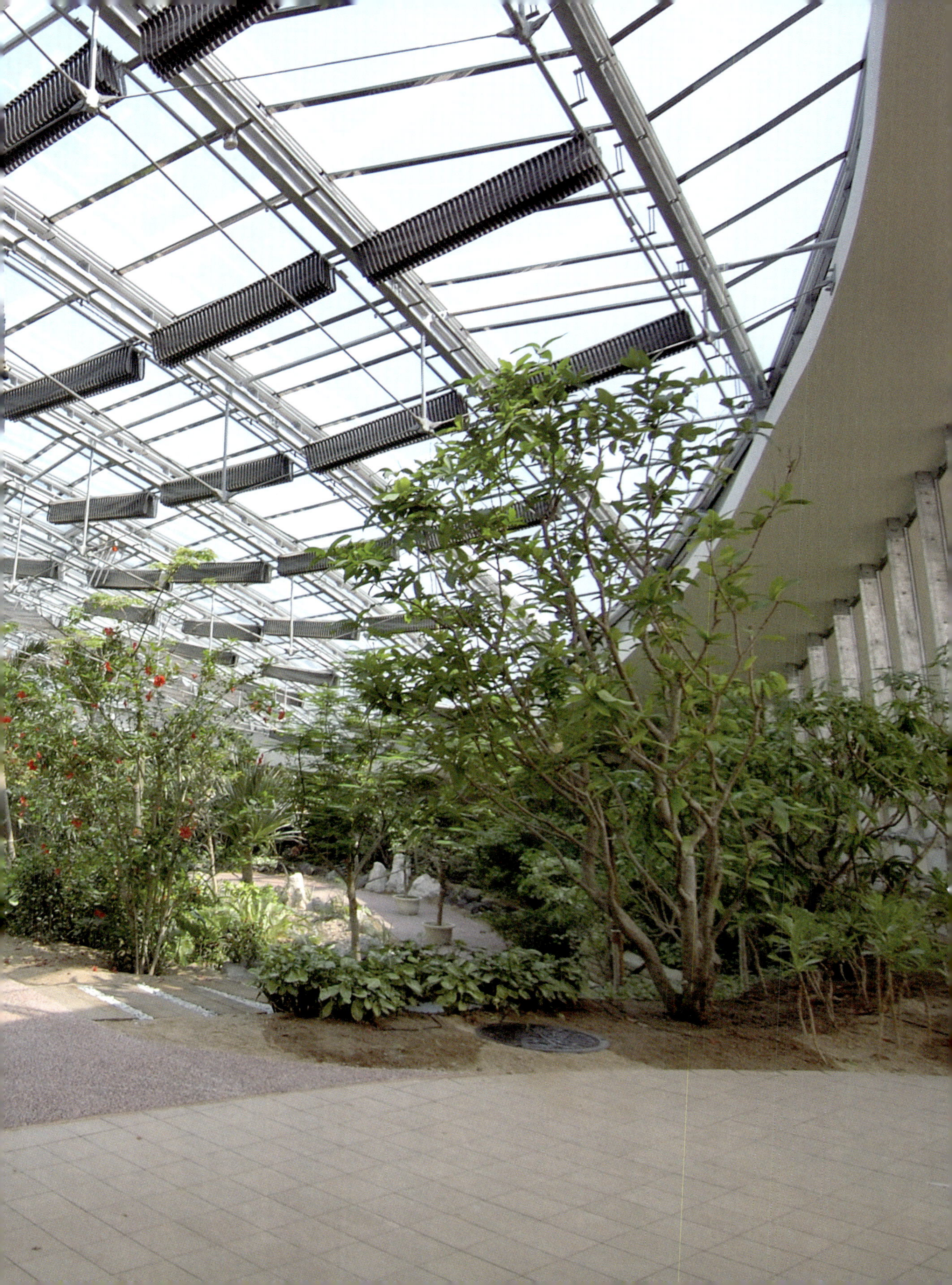

(下) スペインで製作されたPCのベンチ「Naguisa」
(右頁) 平坦な埋め立て地内の小さな丘のような建築。内部と外部が逆転するようスパイラルを描く構造体
(Below) Naguisa, precast concrete bench, was produced in Spain.
(Right page) The building recalls precast hills protruding from the flat landfill area. The spiral structure makes it seem as the interior and exterior are reversed.

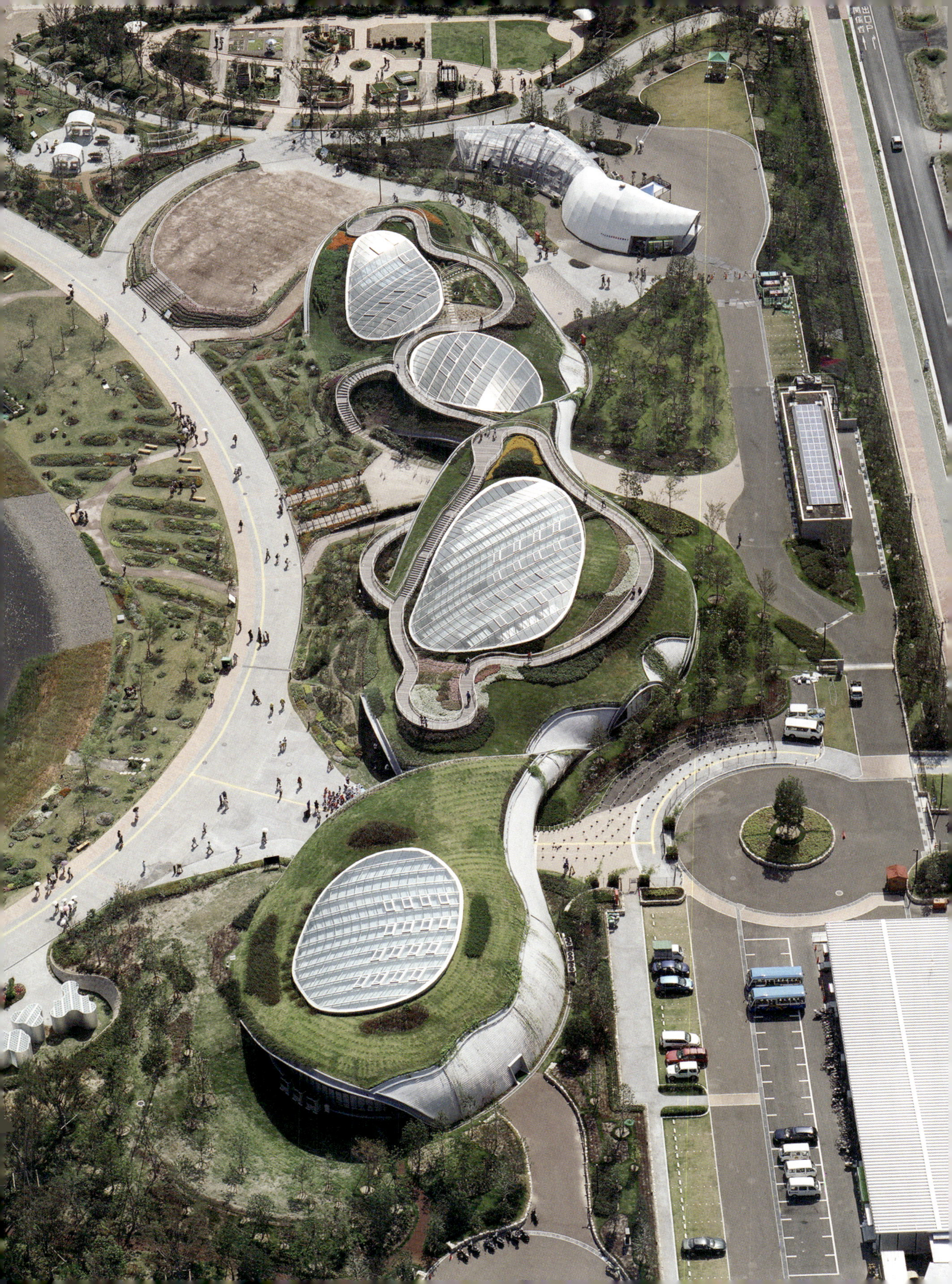

## Meiso no Mori Municipal Funeral Hall
瞑想の森 市営斎場

2006　岐阜県各務原市　Kakamigahara, Gifu

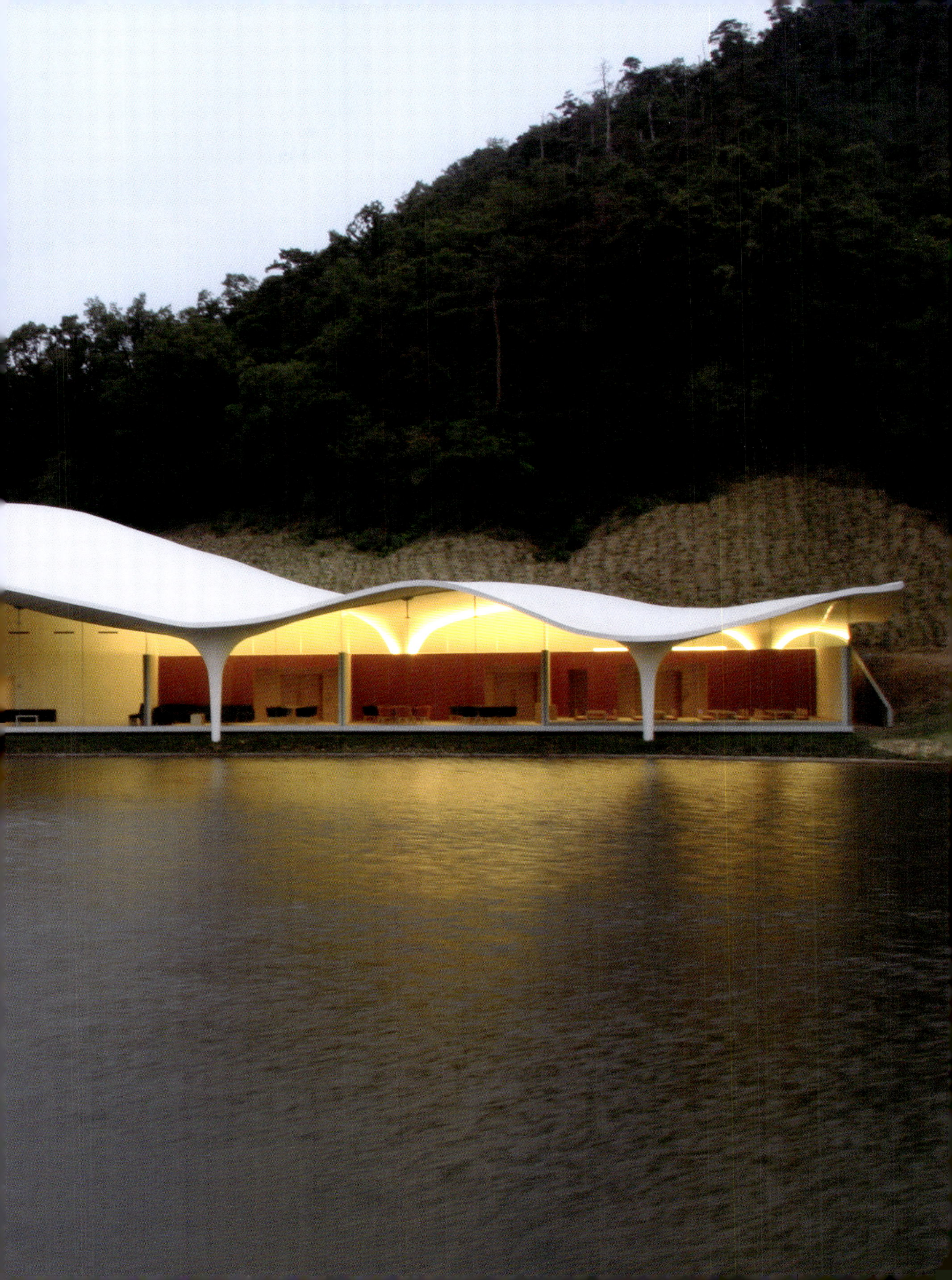

曲面天井が下方からのライトによって淡く面発光したかのように浮かび上がる
The roof appears to be floating above pale, soft light that is reflected on the curved ceiling below.

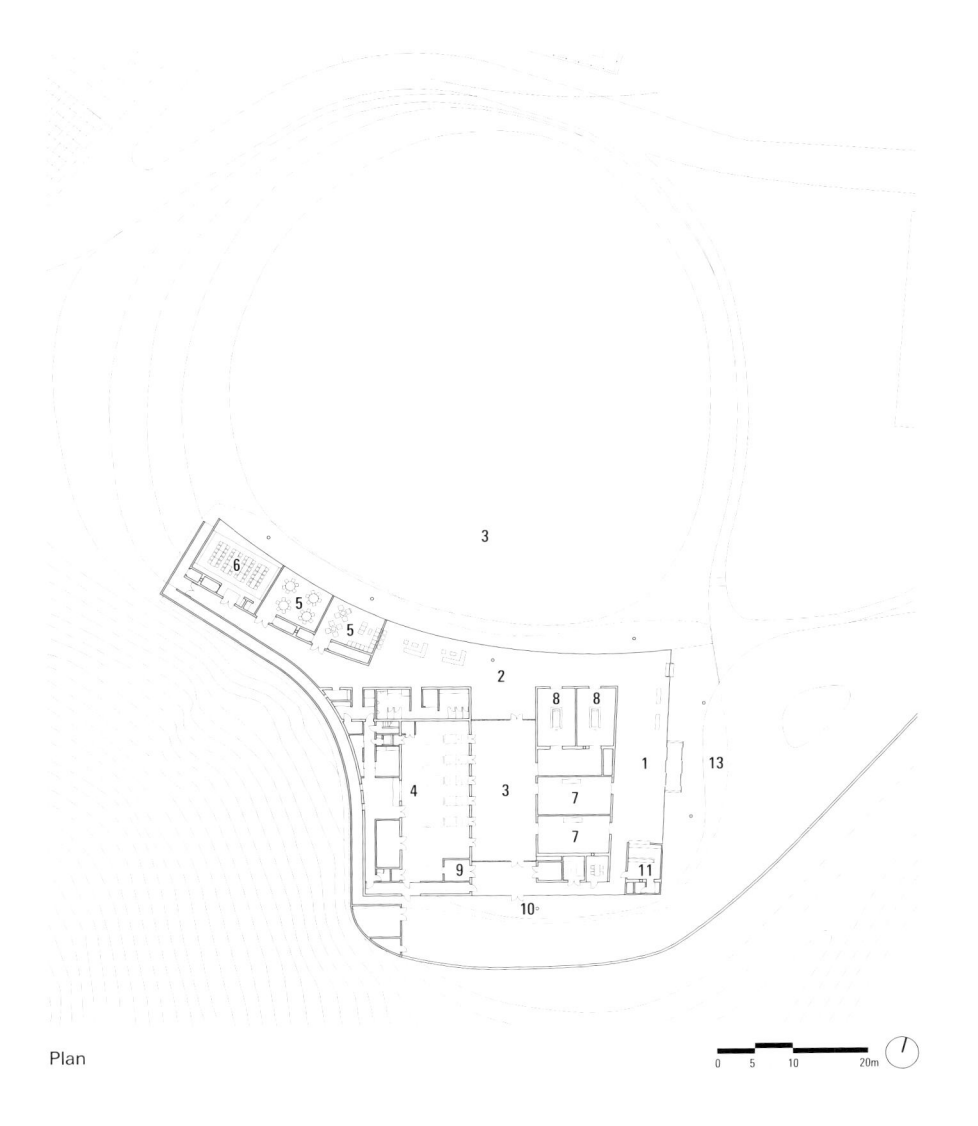

| | |
|---|---|
| 1 | entrance hall |
| 2 | waiting lobby |
| 3 | pre-cremation hall |
| 4 | crematorium |
| 5 | waiting room (western style) |
| 6 | waiting room (japanese style) |
| 7 | farewell room |
| 8 | bone collection room |
| 9 | anima pre-cremation hall |
| 10 | sub-entrance |
| 11 | office |
| 12 | driveway |
| 13 | pond |

Plan

敷地を含む公園墓地計画の一環として計画された火葬場。南側の里山、北側の溜め池の間に浮かぶ雲のようなやわらかな屋根が特徴的。

The crematorium was designed as part of a plan for a park cemetery that included the lot. The building is characterized by its light cloud-like roof, which seems to float between the wild forest on the south side and the reservoir on the north side.

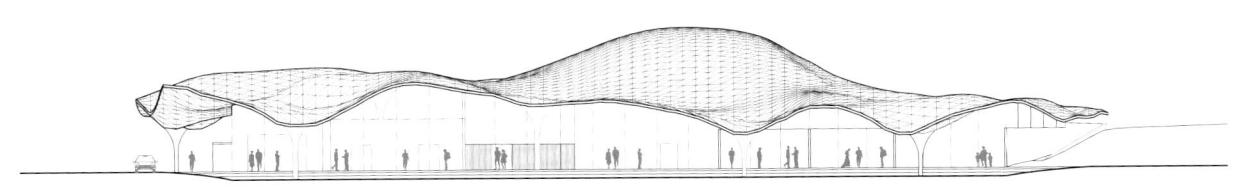

North elevation

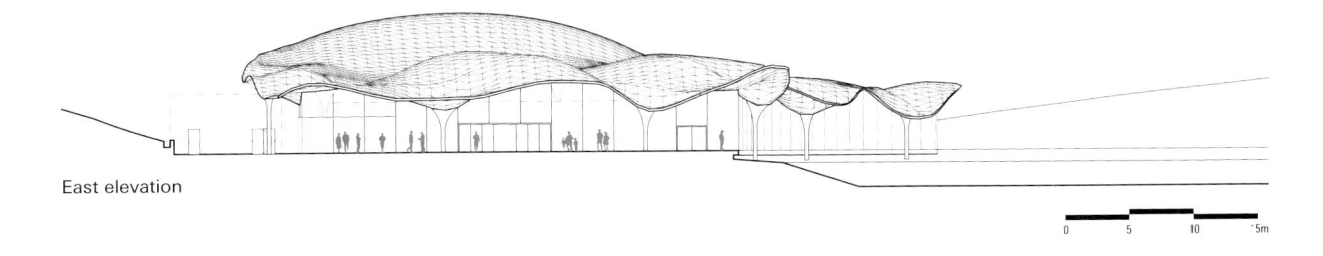

East elevation

炉前ホール。写真右側、火葬炉の扉が壁と同化している
The hall in front of the furnace. On the right hand side of the photo, the door of the furnace appears as a part of the wall.

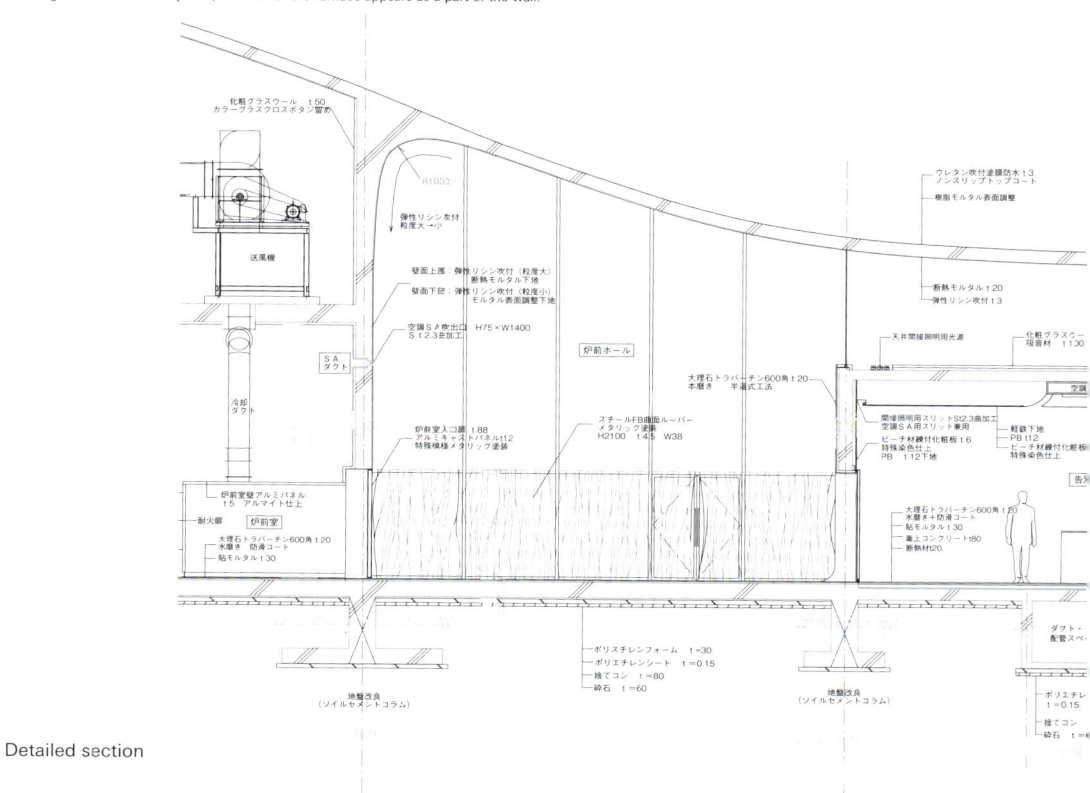

Detailed section

北側溜め池の静かな水面に面する待合室
Waiting room, facing the quiet waters of reservoir on the north side.

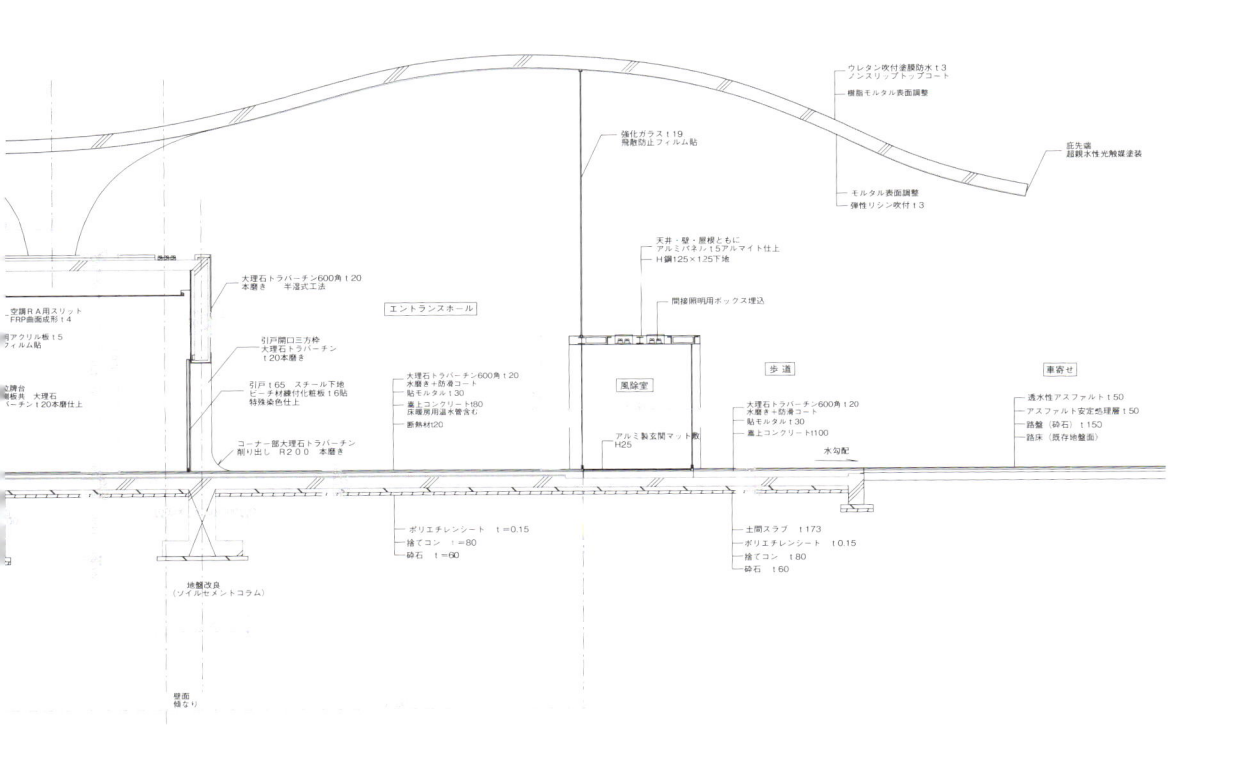

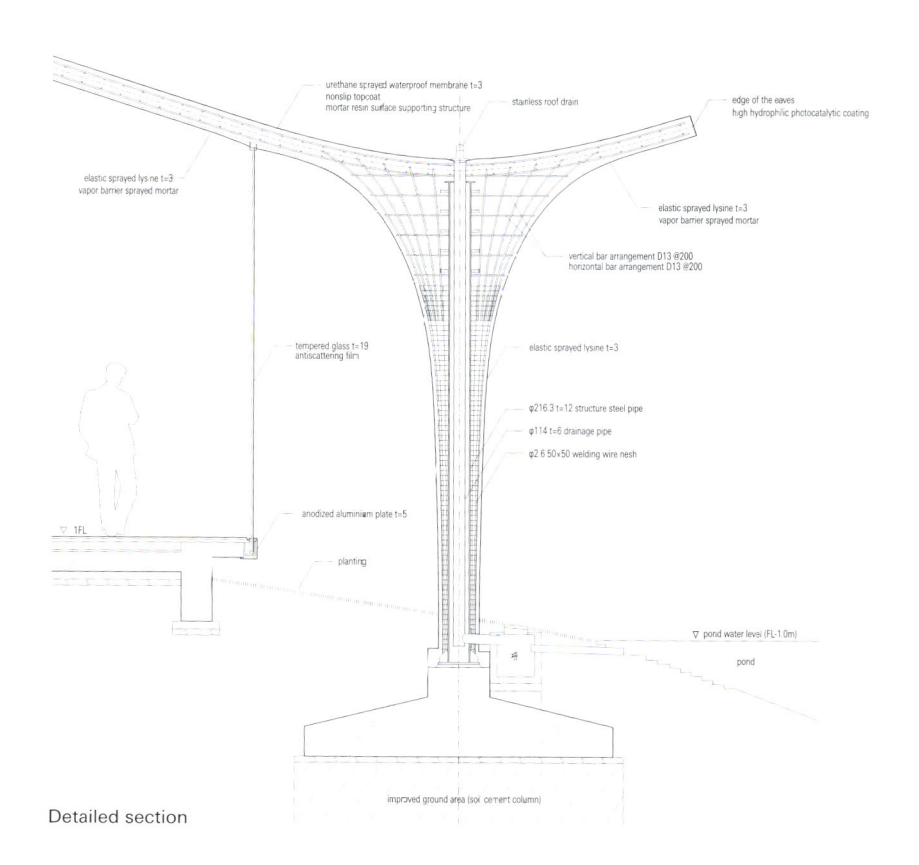

## Detailed section

- urethane sprayed waterproof membrane t=3
- nonslip topcoat
- mortar resin surface supporting structure
- stainless roof drain
- edge of the eaves
- high hydrophilic photocatalytic coating
- elastic sprayed lysine t=3
- vapor barrier sprayed mortar
- elastic sprayed lysine t=3
- vapor barrier sprayed mortar
- vertical bar arrangement D13 @200
- horizontal bar arrangement D13 @200
- tempered glass t=19 antiscattering film
- elastic sprayed lysine t=3
- φ216.3 t=12 structure steel pipe
- φ114 t=6 drainage pipe
- φ2.6 50×50 welding wire mesh
- anodized aluminium plate t=5
- ▽ 1FL
- planting
- ▽ pond water level (FL-1.0m)
- pond
- improved ground area (soil cement column)

大小さまざまな凹凸を繰り返すRC自由曲面シェル構造の屋根を、4つのコアと12本の構造用鋼管（雨水縦樋管を内蔵）円錐柱が支える。

The roof, a freely curved shell structure made of reinforced concrete contains various sizes of convex and concave surfaces. It is supported by four cores and 12 conical pillars (containing rainwater drainpipes) with structural steel hollow tubes.

現場での手作業で組み上げられた型枠
The molds were assembled by hand on site.

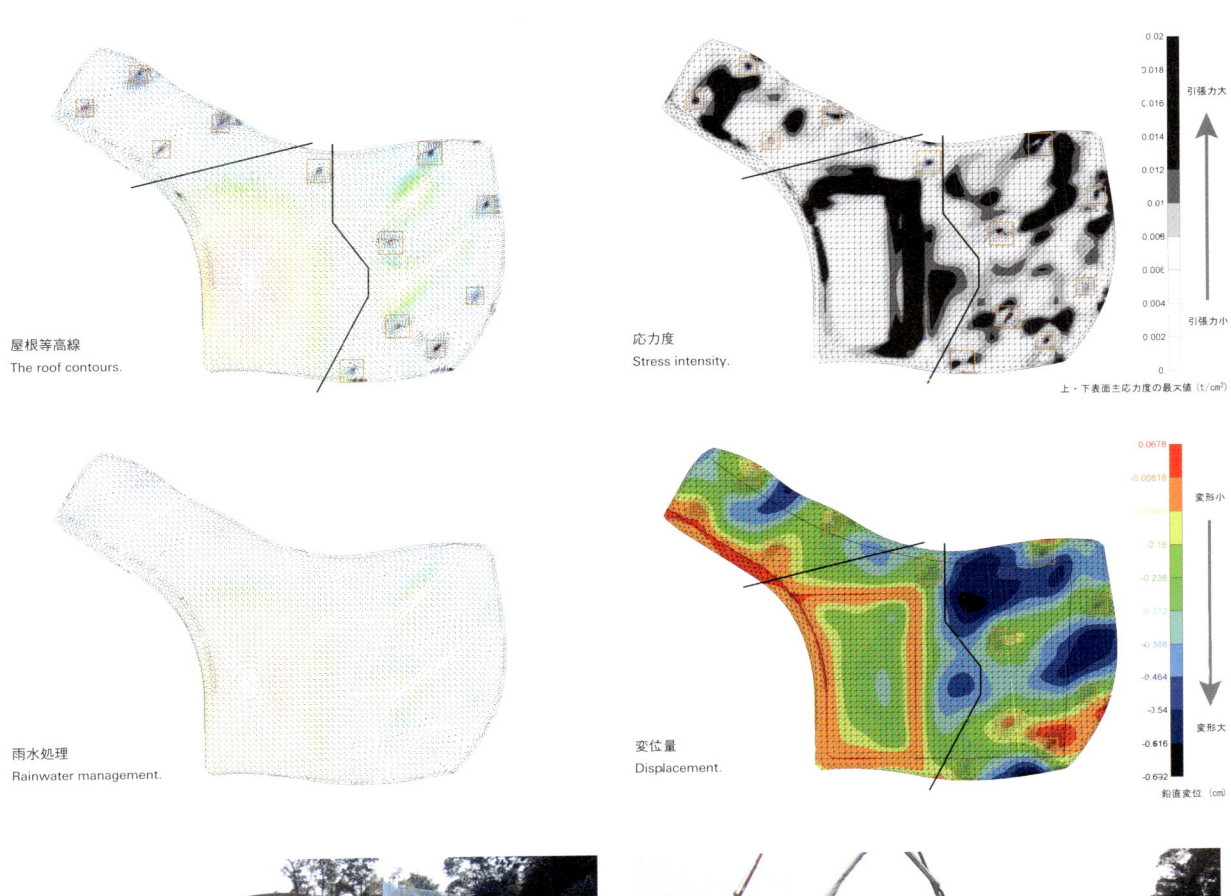

屋根等高線
The roof contours.

応力度
Stress intensity.

雨水処理
Rainwater management.

変位量
Displacement.

定点写真
A fixed-point photograph.

(上) 収骨室　(下) 時折ミニコンサートも催されるホール
(Above) The room for cremated remains.　(Below) Mini-concerts are occasionally held in the hall.

手前左側に収骨室、奥に待合室を見る
The room for cremated remains is visible in the left foreground; the waiting room is in the rear.

エントランスホール
Entrance hall.

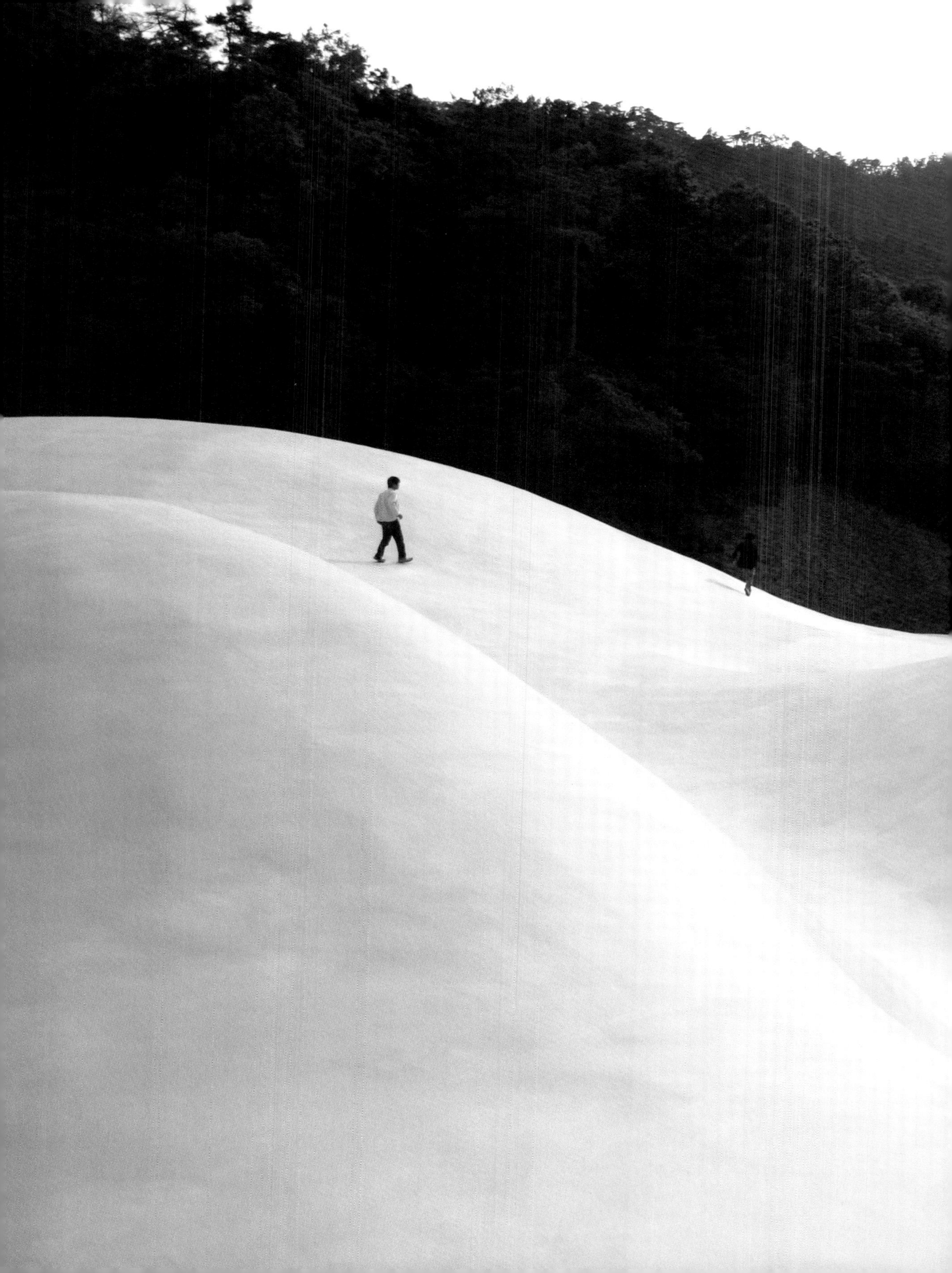

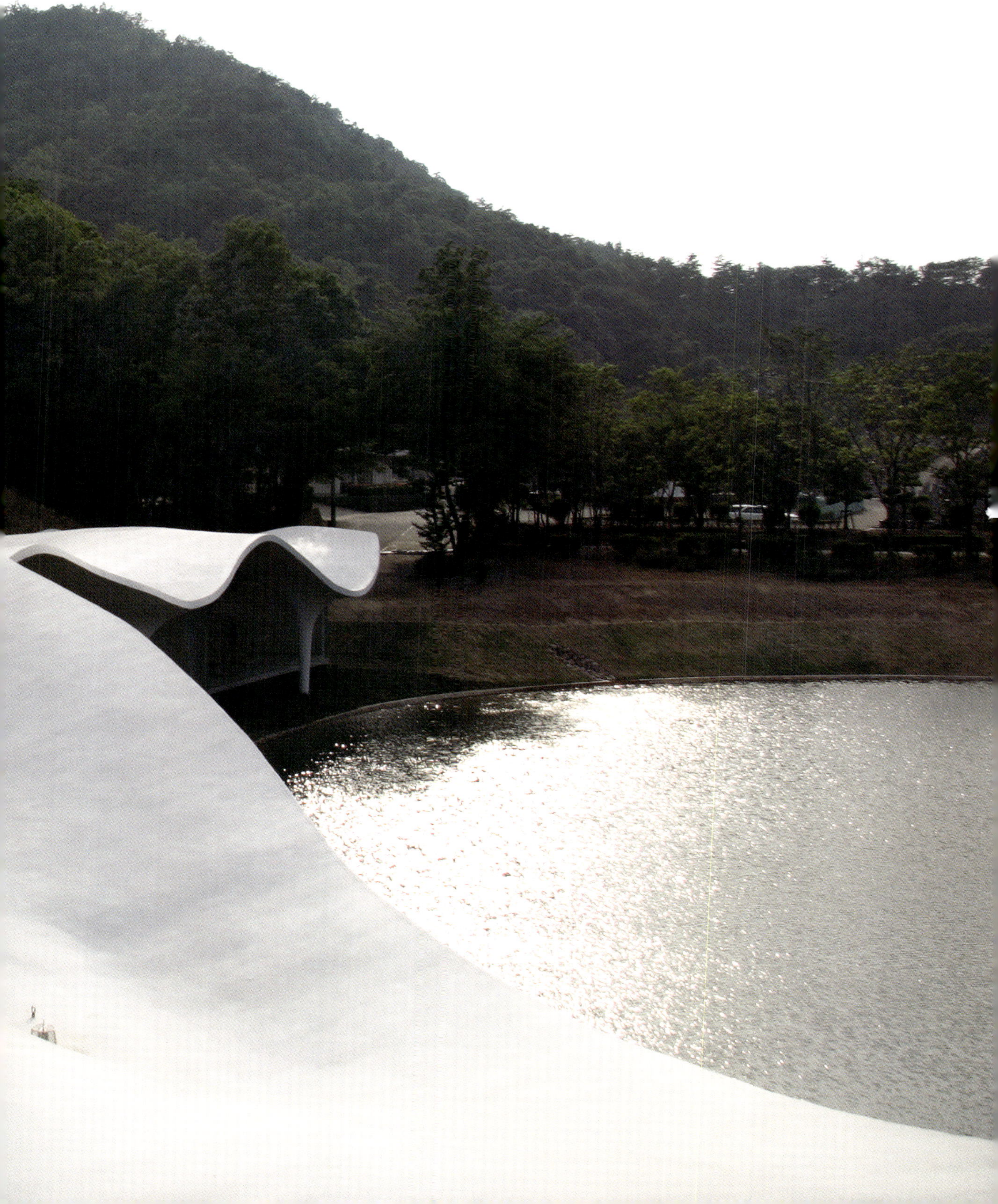

# 7 分節と連続
## Division and Continuity

伊東豊雄との対話　Conversation with Toyo Ito

多摩美術大学図書館（八王子キャンパス）
Tama Art University Library (Hachioji campus) ［2007］

座・高円寺
ZA-KOENJI Public Theatre ［2008］

2009高雄ワールドゲームズメインスタジアム
The Main Stadium for the World Games 2009 in Kaohsiung ［2009］

トーレス・ポルタ・フィラ／
バルセロナ見本市グランビア会場拡張計画
TORRES PORTA FIRA ［2010］／
Extension for the Fair of Barcelona Gran Vía Venue ［2003-］

今治市伊東豊雄建築ミュージアム
Toyo Ito Museum of Architecture, Imabari ［2011］

今治市岩田健母と子のミュージアム
Ken Iwata Mother and Child Museum, Imabari City ［2011］

**多摩美術大学図書館（八王子キャンパス）**

――「多摩美術大学図書館（八王子キャンパス）」は、伊東さんが多摩美術大学で教えられていることがきっかけで始まった仕事ですか。

そうですね。八王子キャンパスはそれまですべて、田淵諭先生を中心とする大学の八王子キャンパス設計室で設計されていました。図書館は新しいゲートと向かい合うような位置にあるので、シンボル的な意味もあるということで設計を依頼されました。

――ちょうどそのころ、多摩美のキャンパスが拡張されて計画が変わっていたと聞いています。それで図書館が新しいエントランスの近くになって、しかも坂の途中につくられるということになっていたわけですが、敷地についての第一印象はどうでしたか。

そうした条件をどう設計に取り込むかを考えた末に、初期は図書館の建築をすべて地下に埋める案を提案していました。ゲートと図書館の間に緑の「彫刻の庭園」が計画されていたので、地下空間を埋めて地上はすべて庭園にしてはと考えたのです。

ところが、ゲートのすぐ近くに大きなインフラが埋め込まれていて、物理的に不可能ということで、地上に出て来ざるを得なかったのですが、地上に出ても、地下＋1階というような案もありました。

――立体化しつつも、一部地下に埋め込まれた案ですね。ただ、アーチ状の構造体が少し出てきているような所もありました。

そうですね。地下にある時から、フラットスラブを支える柱は、「瞑想の森 市営斎場」の柱や「台湾大学社会科学部棟」の柱のような朝顔状に上で開く柱を意識していました。ところがあるとき朝顔状の柱頭が直交する2方向のみに変わって、それが連続した結果、アーチが生まれてきたのです。

――そうなると、その前段階で「福岡アイランドシティ中央公園中核施設ぐりんぐりん」や「瞑想の森」のような、自由曲面を使っていたものから一歩進めているという気がします。自由曲面を線状に置き換えたというか、アーチという幾何学に置き換えたというのは、「瞑想の森」と比べるとひとつ先のプロセスになったような、あるいは抽象化したというか……。

抽象化したとは言えるでしょうね。一説には、模型を作るのが大変だったので、省略形で作ったものがアーチになったというエピソードもあります。

――模型を作る時に、自由曲面という定義しづらいものを定義してつくらざるを得ないので、一種の幾何学に置き換えて作っていたということはありました。

図書館の場合、床は水平でないとまずい。「台中国立歌劇院」のような波打つ床にはできないから、水平であることが前提で、それに伴って、アーチが登場してきたと思います。

――当時、スタッフの中山英之君が、「ぐりんぐりん」や「瞑想の森」は、「建築」よりももっと溶けたような構造体、溶けた空間を表現しているもので、そこからもう一度秩序だったものというか、少し「建築」の側に戻すほうにスタディしようということを意識したと書かれていますね。[1]

アーチに置き換わったときに、アーチというローマ以来の建築要素を使うというのはどうなんだろうという疑問はありました。それと同時に、いまでも僕の中で持続している問題があります。「台中歌劇院」はある意味でもっと非建築的なものですね。「瞑想の森」に比べても三次元曲面を多用している。それはかなり僕の身体としてあって、逆に言うと、「多摩美」のような空間は僕の身体から遠いところにあると感じているので、抽象という問題もいろいろなレベルがありますね。

――「多摩美」をつくった直後に伊東さんは、アンリ・ラブルーストとかアントニン・レーモンドのような知的エレガンスというのか、コンクリートでも緊張感をもったつくり方や精度の高さについて書かれていますね。[2] 当時のラブルーストの図書館は構造的にも創意工夫されている。そういう理性的なものに対する憧れがあって、一方では「台中歌劇院」のように野性的なものもあって、そういう矛盾が伊東さんの中にはあるのでしょうか。

それは昔から常にあります。知的な部分、要するに頭で考える部分ですね。それに対して、もっと身体そのものから発せられてくるような無意識の部分というのがあって、誰の建築でも、相反するふたつの側面が常にオーバーラップしながら建築化されていると思います。そのどちらをより

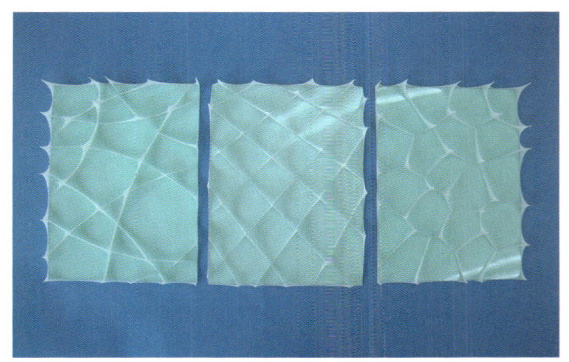

「多摩美術大学図書館（八王子キャンパス）」におけるアーチ自由曲線のスタディ
Study of freely curving arch for the Tama Art University Library (Hachioji campus).

強く出すかという問題がいつもあって、「台中歌劇院」は極めて身体的な空間ですが、「多摩美」は、意識で考えた部分が強い建築ということは言えるでしょうね。

— 建築史の授業でヨーロッパの伝統的なモチーフとしてアーチを習っていたので、現代建築にはまず使われないと思っていましたから、「多摩美」でアーチが登場した時には、かなりインパクトがありました。でも実際に「多摩美」を見ていると、そういう伝統的なアーチの建築とは相当違うと感じます。アーチの建物だと、まずアーチに囲まれた天井の高い空間が建物の中心にあって、そこがメインとなっているのに対して、「多摩美」は中心性をもたない、どこまでも広がっていけるような平面形になっていると思いました。

— 僕はアーチよりも、足元の細さ、ストイックさ、その精度が醸し出している緊張感のほうが強い気がしました。形式性を前面に出していても、それが建築的なものに感じられないというか、むしろ非建築的な要素——ストイックな要素、抽象化された模型により近いような状態の要素のほうが強いように感じますが、出来て訪れた時にも、そういう形式性の問題を気にされましたか。

それは現場を訪れた時に、アーチの列が湾曲しているし、スパンがそれぞれ違うし、壁も非常に薄いということで、いつも追求しているような迷宮的とか洞窟的な空間ではないけれども、しかし1階は軽い洞窟のような所もあって、これはこれで良かったんだと思うようになりました。現場に行って、アーチへの危惧はかなり消えたような気がします。

もうひとつ、1階は床がスロープになっていることの印象も大きいですね。水平だと、より建築的な印象が強かったと思います。

— 床に外の緑が映り込んでいるのも大きいですね。あと、家具がアーチの分節を横断していくことによって、人の動きも家具に沿って動いていくから、流動的な印象を強くしていますね。

そうですね。家具は藤江和子さんが提案してくれたものですが、すごく良かった。藤江さんも多摩美で客員で教えていたから、家具は藤江さんにやってほしいと考えていました。

— 家具の配置も、最初はアーチに沿って並べるなど、相当スタディとやりとりがありましたね。そこで一番重要だったのは、機能的でありながらも、空間の流動性をどう生み出すかということでした。

今回アーチにすることで壁的な要素もありますから、各ブロックが分節されるわけですね。その分節を書架が貫くことによって「分節」と「連続」という関係が生まれて、それはうまくいったと思います。この図書館の空間は、分節しつつ連続していく。これが単に柱とスラブだけだと、もっと連続性が強くなるから「せんだいメディアテーク」のようにひたすら連続的な空間になったのでしょうが、閲覧のためには少し遮られることが効いていると思います。

— 「せんだい」の場合は、チューブを中心にして、波紋のように広がる家具の配置の仕方をしていますね。

「せんだい」はチューブの存在がすごく強いから、その周辺に波紋が広がるように力が伝わっていくという印象が強い。しかし「多摩美」は遠心力はあまり働かないと思います。

— そうすると、「台湾大」も「点」としての柱があって、「多摩美」ではアーチがさらに「点」まで小さくなっていきながら、求心性もないというのか……。

used in contemporary architecture. But when I actually look at Tamabi, it seems quite different from traditional buildings in which arches are used. With a traditional building with arches, there is in the center of the building a high-ceilinged space surrounded by arches, and that is the main part of the building. Tamabi does not have a centralized character. It has an outspread planar form, which allows for infinite extension.

– The slenderness of the base, the stoicism and the tension produced by precision seemed to me stronger than the arches themselves. Though they obviously possess a formal character, they are not felt to be architectural. They are instead non-architectural elements--they seem stoic and abstract and are almost model-like in condition. Did the problem of formal character bother you when you visited the finished building?

When I visited the site, the rows of arches were curved, the spans were all different, and the walls were extremely thin, so it was obviously not the sort of maze-like cavernous space I am usually seeking. Nonetheless, there is a place on the first floor that is somewhat like a cavern, and I felt this is all right the way it is. The visit to the site dispelled for the most part misgivings I had had about the use of arches.

One other thing, the sloping first floor also makes quite an impression. If it had been level, the library would have seemed more building-like.

– The fact that the greenery on the outside is glimpsed beyond the floor has an impact as well. Also, articles of furniture cut across the articulations of the arches, making people move along those articles, reinforcing a sense of flow.

Yes. The furniture, proposed by Kazuko Fujie, is quite good. She was a visiting faculty member at the university, so I wanted her to design the furniture.

– Many studies were made and discussions held about the arrangement of furniture. For example, initially the furniture was arranged along the arches. Though the furniture is functional, the most important question was how to generate the flow of space.

The use of arches on this occasion meant introducing wall-like elements that articulated the library into blocks. The penetration of those articulations by shelves produced both "articulation" and "continuity"--I think it went well. The space of this library is continuous yet articulated. If this had been simply a structure of columns and slabs, continuity would have been stronger, and would have been a completely continuous space like Sendai Mediatheque. I think the fact that space is slightly screened off is better for reading.

– At Sendai, the articles of furniture were arranged like ripples emanating from the tubes.

The tubes are powerful objects at Sendai, and one does get the impression that force is emanating from them in ripples. However, there is not a centrifugal force at play at Tamabi.

「多摩美術大学図書館（八王子キャンパス）」の家具スタディ中のスタディモデル
Model for furniture study for the Tama Art University Library (Hachioji campus).

130

そうですね。求心性は弱まりますね。柱のレイアウトで「台湾大」はつくられていますから。3つの中心があって、そこから放射状に広がっていくから。それぞれ空間の流動感が違って見えるところが面白いですね。

── そうなると、「みんなの森 ぎふメディアコスモス」は楽しみですね。グローブを中心に考えると、「せんだい」のように、その周りに広がっていくイメージもあるでしょうし……。

それもありますが、屋根の曲面の影響が大きいでしょうね。東建男君が昨日現場を訪れて、合板で屋根の型(木造屋根架構の下地)が部分的に出来てきて、本体の屋根の形が想像できるようになってきたと言っていましたが、圧倒的に大きな空間だから、出来たらどんな空間になるのだろうね。

── ガラスのファサードの話では、よく最近、ガラスと面一に納めることが問題になっていますが、面一というのは、「TOD'S表参道ビル」、「まつもと市民芸術館」からですね。「せんだい」ではファサードはそのままカーテンウォールでつくっていますが、「多摩美」は構造とガラスが両方ともファサードに同じ次元で出てくるというのは、「せんだい」よりは開かれているというか、そういう意識があったのでしょうか。

いまになると、サッシの入っていない、でもアーチがある半屋外空間をつくれば良かったなとは思います。面一で仕上げることによって、建築としての完結性は強くなったと思うのですが、もう少しガラスを内側に入れておけば、外との連続性の印象は強くできただろうと思います。

このファサードが曲面ガラスになっているというのは、説明しても、初めて見る人は、見ても分からないような感じですね。

── 基準でやっているRも浅曲げですから、誤差の範囲内だと書いてありますね。

そう。1.8mの幅で最大5mmの曲げだったかな(笑)。

── そういうRに曲げることのほうがむしろ難しい。

だから、そこまでやったことがどうだったんだろう、という疑問は残りますね。日本の建築家はみんなそうやってセンシティブにものをつくっていっている。施工技術が伴うからますますそういう傾向が強くなっている。そうすると、こんな曲面ガラスは日本でしかできないから、その結果この建築は美しいけれども、それで果たしていいのかどうかという疑問もありますね。もっとラフにつくるやり方はないのか。こうやって洗練していく過程で、得るものと同時に、失うものもかなり大きいと思います。

── もっとラフなものでいいのではないかというのは、たとえばガラスをはめた瞬間にサッシが出てきたり、そこに建築的な納まりが必要になってきたりして、抽象的ではなくなっていくということがあって、出来た瞬間に「建築」になってしまうというような話をよく聞くことがありますが、そこに対する抵抗感がなくなったということでしょうか。

われわれのディテールは、「シルバーハット」が典型的ですが、いわゆる建築のプロフェッショナルな見地から言ったら落第ですね。建築にはこうやっておけば問題が起こらないというオーソドックスな、ディテールの長い歴史を積み上げてきたものがあります。けれども、われわれはそれよりももっと建築の全体を重視して、われわれが考えている建築の思想がそのまま伝わるような、それによってディテールも変化していくようなものをやりたいと思っているし、それはいまも変わらないと思います。

ただ、建築の思想そのものが変わってきているから、ディテールのあり方も変わってきていると思います。たとえば面一というのは、「まつもと」、「TOD'S」が一番典型的で、「TOD'S」は「まつもと」にならってやったから、象嵌するという意味合いが強くて、あれは面一じゃないと成り立たなかったと思うのですが、「多摩美」では面一にする理由はあまりなかったような気がします。

ファサードはほれぼれするくらいきれいですが、そのことでスポイルされる部分も結構あります。ひとつの面にしてしまうわけだから、抽象的な面になり過ぎてしまう。「抽象」は必要だと思いますが、いまわれわれの間では「抽象」の意味が変わってきている気がしているからね。もっと事務所全体で議論していかなくてはね。

### 2009高雄ワールドゲームズメインスタジアム

──「2009高雄ワールドゲームズメインスタジアム」は、台湾で最初のプロジェクトですが、これはコンペティションに応募したものですね。

― Does that mean that there are columns that are "points" at National Taiwan University too, and that the arches at Tamabi shrink to "points" and have no centripetal force…

Yes. There is diminished centripetality. National Taiwan University is based on the layout of the columns. There are three centers, and the plan radiates from those centers. The way each space seems to flow is different, and that is interesting.

― It will be interesting then to see what Minna no Mori Gifu Media Cosmos becomes. There is an image of force emanating, as there was at Sendai, but this time by the globe at the center…

There is that as well, but I think the effect of the curved roof will be powerful. Takeo Higashi, who visited the site yesterday, said that the plywood form of the roof (the substructure for the wood-frame roof) was partially built, and the form of the main roof could now be imagined. It is a space of overwhelming size, so I wonder what sort of space it will be when completed.

― With respect to the glass facade, making the glass flush with the structure is a problem that the office has often dealt with recently, ever since TOD's Omotesando Building and Matsumoto Performing Arts Centre. At Sendai, a curtain wall forms the facade, but at Tamabi, the structure and the glass occupy the same plane on the facade. Does this mean that Tamabi is more open than Sendai? Was that something you consciously strove to achieve?

Looking back, I think it might have been good to create a semi-outdoor space with arches and no window frames. Making the glass flush with the structure reinforces the impression of completeness as a building, but recessing the glass slightly might have made the inside seem more continuous with the outside.

People who see it for the first time cannot seem to see the curvature of the glass on the facade, even when it is explained to them.

― The best of the curve is quite shallow and supposedly within the allowed margin of error.

Yes. I think the maximum curvature is five mm over a width of 1.8 m [laughs].

― Using such a large radius of curvature is in fact more difficult.

We are therefore left wondering if all that effort was worth it. Japanese architects all go to the trouble of designing things sensitively in this way. Building technology is able to keep up with them, and that simply reinforces this tendency. This curved glass could have been produced only in Japan. As a result, this building is beautiful, but one is left wondering if this is a good thing or not. Is there not a rougher, cruder way of creating things? There are things gained by this process of refinement, but I believe there are also fairly important things that are lost.

「シルバーハット」 Silver Hut

― When you wonder if a work that has been more crudely put together might be all right, do you mean—there is often talk, for example, that having exposed window-frames for the glass makes building-like detailing necessary, and makes the work less abstract, so that the moment it is completed, it becomes a "building"--that you are no longer opposed to that happening?

そうです。これは設計施工一貫のコンペティションでしたが、竹中工務店と台湾の互助営造が組んで、竹中工務店の当時の副社長であった村松映一さんから誘われて、それに台湾の劉培森建築師事務所が加わった。この4者でJVを組んで応募することになりました。

設計は2006年で、竣工したのが2009年。4年で作ったことになりますが、互助営造の施工が素晴らしかったので、短い期間でスムーズに出来ましたね。

— この建築も繊細な部材を使った、精度が必要な建築のような気がしますが、日本の精度との違いを感じられたことはありますか。

そんなに繊細な建築だとは思っていない。それというのも構造設計が佐々木睦朗さんではなかったので、どうしても安全側に傾いてしまいました。われわれとしては、もっとスパイラル自体で構造をつくりたかったのだけれども、屋根の主構造は通常のトラスによる大きなキャンティレバーでつくり、それらを結ぶ横方向の力をスパイラル状のパイプでもたせている。つまりサブ的なものとしてのスパイラルですが、全体はダイナミックなスパイラル状の構造体が成立しているように見えるのかもね。

— スタジアムを開くことによって、いろいろなイベントで内と外が連続的に使われたりするようなことがあると聞いています。

この間、塾生たちと何年かぶりに行ったら、サッカーの試合をやっていましたが、まちの女の子が広場からぶらっと入って、散歩のついでに見ているという感じでした。そういう風景が日常的に見られるのはいいですね。閉じたスタジアムだと、競技を見ようと思って入らない限り、中には入れないから。

— 公園のほうからアイレベルで見えたり、競技をやっていないときはスタンドまで自由に出入りできるというのは、なかなかできない体験ですね。伊東さんが子どものころ、野球場の周りをぐるぐる回っても、音だけしか聞こえてこないのが嫌だったという体験を話しておられましたが、やはり開くということについては……。

だいたい大きな球場は、外側は観客席の裏側で美しくないんですよ（笑）。それとも壁を立ててしまうかどちらかでしょう。壁を立ててしまうとまたすごく閉鎖的になりますからね。

— 薄い帆地のようなサドルを並べることで、空間をその間につくっていますが、あのサドルもコンペ時はより壁的だったものが、実際はもっと単位が小さくなって、よりスレンダーになって、連続しているようなリズムがある感じになりましたね。

これは良かったですね。風が抜けるなど環境的な点は、うまく出来たと思います。

— このスパイラルのアイデアは、台湾の人にとっては流動性があるように感じてもらえて、これを「龍」にたとえていますが、こういうダイナミズムを入れることが、求められていたものと合致したということですか。

「龍」とは、できるだけコンペのときは言わないようにしていましたね。それは外国人が日本にきて「鶴だ」なんて言うと、「わかってもいないくせに……」と言われるじゃないですか（笑）。だから、絶対言わないようみんなに言っていました。

— 完成すると自然と「龍」と呼ばれるような状況になりましたね。

向こうの人が呼ぶならそれでいいですが、われわれが言うと的を外しているように思われる（笑）。

— このオープンというのがいいですね。日本の国立競技場もオープンで、スタンド越しに新宿のまちが見えている感じが良くて、全部閉じてしまうのは良くないなと思いました。風を避けるために一段掘り込まれているのも、アプローチしていった時に急に掘り込まれた場所が現れるのも、体験としていいなと思います。

フィールドをちょっと掘り込んで、そこは風の影響を受けないようにして、客席は風が通り抜けていくという、そういう設備計画的な構成はうまくいきましたね。

## 座・高円寺

— 「座・高円寺」は、「高雄」とは逆に閉じているということになります。これもコンペティションだったのですが、地下をここまで掘った案は他になかったということですか。

そうですね。われわれの案は、地上のボリューム

Our details--those of Silver Hut are typical--are no good from the point of view of professional architects. Orthodox details designed to prevent problems from occurring have been developed over a long period of time in architecture. However, our office places greater importance on architecture as a whole, and we want details to change in order to better communicate our architectural ideas. I believe that approach will not change.

However, architectural ideas themselves are changing, so the nature of details too is changing. For example, flush detailing is best represented by Matsumoto and TOD's, and TOD's was modeled on Matsumoto. Creating the effect of inlay was important, and it wouldn't have worked without flush detailing. However, I don't feel there was much reason for making the glass flush with the structure at Tamabi.

The facade is fascinatingly beautiful, but many things are to a certain degree spoiled by that. Because it is all flush, it has become too abstract a plane. "Abstraction" is necessary, but I think the meaning of "abstraction" amongst us is changing. There has to be more discussion by the office as a whole.

**The Main Stadium for the World Games 2009 in Kaohsiung**

– The Main Stadium for the World Games 2009 in Kaohsiung was our first project in Taiwan. Was this the result of a competition the office entered?

Yes. This was a design-construction competition Takenaka Corporation teamed up with Fu Tsu Construction Co., Ltd; Mr.Eiichi Muramatsu who was then vice-president of Takenaka, invited us to participate, and Ricky Liu & Associates Archtects + Planners Architects of Taiwan also joined the team. The four organizations formed a joint venture to enter the competition.

Design took place in 2006, and construction in 2009. We had only four years, but Fu Tsu Construction did excellent work and the project was completed without a hitch in a short period of time.

– This building too seems to be composed of delicate members and to have required precision. Did you sense any difference in level of precision between Taiwan and Japan?

I don't think this is such a delicate building. The structural design was not by Mutsuro Sasaki and inevitably erred on the side of caution. We wanted to make the spiral itself the structure, but the main structure of the roof is really a set of ordinary trusses that are cantilevered out, and the lateral forces linking them are borne by pipes arranged in a spiral. That is, the whole building may seem like a dynamic spiral structure, despite only the subordinate structure is in form of a spiral, the whole building appears as a dynamic spiral structure.

「2009高雄ワールドゲームズメインスタジアム」における通風のため細かく分割されたサドル
The intricately divided saddle used for ventilation in the Main Stadium for the World Games 2009 in Kaohsiung.

– I have heard that opening up the stadium has made it possible to use both inside and outside as one continuous space for holding diverse events.

I recently visited it for the first time in quite a

をできるだけ小さくして、地下を大きくしようというものです。これは周りへの配慮もあったのと、四角い箱であっても、芝居小屋というイメージをはっきりと出したいということですね。地上で積層されたものになると、芝居のための小屋というよりは、どうしてもビルの中の劇場という感じになってしまうので、3分の2ぐらいは地下になっています。それがうまくいったと思います。

— それは建築的なことがうまく働いているということですか。

実施に入ってから審査員でもあった佐藤信さんと直接話が始まって、天井高がもっと欲しいというリクエストでいまのような屋根に変わっていったし、ホールのデザインはもちろんのこと家具に至るまで、佐藤さんのチームと厳密な検討をしながらすべてが決まっていきました。その後そのまま佐藤さんが芸術監督になって、そのチームで運営もしていくことになりましたね。

それに、杉並区役所の方たちもこちらの話をよく聞いてくれました。そういうことが重なって、オープン後もいい運営がされています。

— 杉並区から職員が派遣されて、運営されているわけではないですね。

これはここのためのNPOを立ち上げて、そこに区が毎年予算をつけて運営しています。

「高円寺」がなぜうまくいっているかは、小規模ではありますが、まったく同じ規模の、演劇のためだけの劇場をふたつくったことですね。音楽や、演劇、レクチャー、何でもできる多目的ホールをつくると、結局中途半端になってしまう。演劇だけのホールを作っても、プロの人の使う劇場とアマチュア、市民が使う劇場では、設備や照明のあり方がかなり違います。

「高円寺」では、地上の劇場はさまざまなステージ設定ができます。その代わり、そのつど舞台設備や舞台照明を考えなくてはいけない。それに対して、伊東事務所の40周年記念イベントで使った地下の劇場はエンドステージ型だから、いつも照明が同じ方向を向いています。それだけでわれわれでも操作できるぐらいやさしいというか難易度が低い劇場になります。よって運用上の混乱がなくすんでいる。

プロでもアマチュアでも使えますということになると、中途半端になっていってしまうので、そこをはっきりさせたことが、「高円寺」がうまくいっている大きな要因ですね。

— この間ラジオで、「演者の人の間で評判がいい」という話を今度ここで演劇をする人がしていました。いまの話のように、2種類の劇場があることで、使い勝手が良く、さまざまな企画に対応できるということで、演者も喜ぶ劇場になっていますね。

それはうれしいですね。

ホールBで行われた、伊東事務所40周年記念イベント
40th anniversary party for to Toyo's office held at Hall B.

— 高円寺自体も、劇場を使う人がもともと多いまちですね。杉並はNPOもしっかりしていますし。

他にも、地下の練習室を使って毎日のようにスクールをやっているのも素晴らしいですね。あれに影響されて、われわれも塾をつくったということもあります。そこで脚本家も養成すれば、舞台設備、舞台照明のプロを養成するスクールもやっています。

— 2階のカフェでアルバイトしている人もそのスクールの人で、イベントをやっているのも演劇関係の人ですね。

週末に子どもに本の読み聞かせをしたりして、将来のお客さんを養成しているというのもあるし、全体が有機的に組織づくりされていますね。

— 「高円寺」が出来て、まちが変わったような感

---

while, together with my students of ITO JUKU, and a soccer match was being held there. Young women from town wandered into the stadium from the square; it was almost like they were out for a stroll and happened to pass by. It is nice to see scenes like that as part of everyday life. If the stadium were closed, people wouldn't be able to enter unless they were there specifically to see a match.

– Being able to see into the stadium at eye level from the park or to go up into the stands on one's own when there is no match going on is a rare experience. You have talked about how, as a child, you walked round and round outside a baseball stadium and hated that you could only hear the sounds of the game. Opening up the stadium was therefore…

The outside of a large baseball stadium is just the backs of spectator seats; it is not beautiful [laughs]. That, or they put up a wall. It becomes quite closed if a wall is put up.

– Thin, sail-like saddles are lined up, and they allow space to pass through them. At the time of the competition, those saddles were more wall-like, but they became smaller-size units and more slender. There is a rhythm, as if those saddles were continuous.

That was good. I think their environmental aspects, such as the way they let air through, are well done.

– People in Taiwan feel this spiral idea suggests fluidity and liken the stadium to a dragon. Does it mean the introduction of this dynamism was in accord with what was demanded?

We tried as much as possible to refrain from any talk of dragons during the competition. It is just like foreigners coming to Japan and talking about cranes--they are apt to be told they know nothing about the subject [laughs]. I told everyone not to mention dragons at all.

– Once it was completed, people began calling it a dragon quite naturally.

It is all right for them to call it that. If we had called it in first place, it would have seemed beside the point [laughs].

– The fact that it is open is nice. The National Stadium in Japan is open, and the way one can see the cityscape of Shinjuku beyond the stands is pleasant. It suggested to me that completely enclosing a stadium is not a good idea. The way the ground is lowered to avoid the wind blowing through…and the ground suddenly drops as one approaches, is also nice as an experience.

The field is lowered so that it will not be affected by winds, but air is allowed to pass through the stands. I thought the facilities were well organized.

### ZA-KOENJI Public Theatre

– ZA-KOENJI Public Theatre is the opposite of Kaohsiung; it is closed off. This too was the result of a competition. Did no other participant propose digging as far below-ground?

No. Our scheme made the above-ground volume as small as possible and enlarged the below-ground portion. This was in part out of consideration for the neighborhood, and also because, though the above-ground volume is in reality a square box, we wanted it to clearly suggest a theatre tent. If the above-ground portion had been several stories high, it would have seemed not so much like a theatre tent but like a theater inside a large building. That is why two-thirds of the building is buried. I think that worked out well.

– Do you mean by that that it works well architecturally?

In the final design stage, we began to talk directly with Mr.Makoto Sato, who had been on the jury. A request for a higher ceiling led to the present shape of roof. Everything was decided in close consultation with Mr.Sato's team--not only the design of the halls but even the furniture. He subsequently became the artistic director, and his team took charge of the management of the halls.

The people at the Suginami Ward office were also quite understanding about our ideas. All these things combined and have resulted in the theatre being well managed since the opening.

– Ward officials are not sent to manage the theatre, are they?

An NPO was established for that purpose, and Suginami Ward provides it with an annual budget for management.

The reason Koenji is working so well is that there are two theatres of the same size, albeit small, solely for dramatic performances. A multipurpose hall where anything--concert, drama or lecture--can be accommodated is, in the end, never fully satisfactory. Even with theaters for dramatic performances, a theater used by professionals and a theatre used by the public are quite different in mechanical equipment and lighting.

At Koenji, diverse stage settings are possible in the above-ground theater, but for that very reason, one has to think about stage mechanics and stage lighting each time. By contrast, the

133

じがします。コンペ前の古い建物の時は、暗くて、あまりいい雰囲気の場ではなかったのですが、いまは閉じることで、逆に人が集まってくる場所になったというのも面白いですね。

「まつもと」の芸術監督、串田和美さん流の演出を参考に、バックヤードを舞台の演出に使うこともできるような提案があり、舞台まで搬入車が入ってくることもできるような提案もあり、平面計画に関してもかなり大胆に出来ていますね。

「まつもと」での演出方法の経験もありますが、入り口の横にしか搬入口をとることができない(笑)。そこから地下に置くとか、上に置くとか、エレベーターで運ぶしかなかったのです。

ー「高円寺」はコンペティションの段階のボックスのときから、鋼板構造で計画されていますね。こういう有機的なかたちになったときも、このころの「TOD'S」、「多摩美」と同じように、鉄板とコンクリートの組み合わせでつくるという流れの中で、こういう構造形式を選んだのでしょうか。

これはコンクリートが表に出ていたら、ずいぶん印象が変わったと思いますね。本来幕でつくるテント小屋のイメージをどうやって保てるかということを考えると、コンクリートでつくったらそれが消えてしまう。鉄板1枚でやれば一番それに近いけれども、遮音性能という点から、内側にコンクリートを打つことになりました。

ー ボックスの時の薄いもので囲うというのが、覆いとしてそうなったということですか。

そうです。コンペティションの時はやや装飾的なパターンの開口もありましたが、あれはやらなくて良かったですね(笑)。

ー 外から見ると、鉄の塊ですが、中に入った時にパッと世界が一変するというか、中のインテリアの印象が外からは想像がつかないというのは、入った時のお客さんのわくわく感が高まるし、色の選択もつややかで、劇場として面白いと思います。

階段回りは、外のテント小屋というイメージとは違って、ぬめっとした感じがあって、官能的な空間になっていますね。建築関係者は階段回りに一番反応しますが、僕は逆に、この建築はもっと質素な、それこそテント小屋で芝居をやっているようなものだと思っていたので、この階段回りがすごく気になっていました。

ー これはどういう判断でされたのですか。かなり伊東さんの感性がそのまま出てきたというか……。

そんなに意識して官能的なものをつくろうと思ってはいないのですが、逆に出てしまう……。そういう意味でも、「多摩美」とはだいぶ違います。

### トーレス・ポルタ・フィラ／バルセロナ見本市会場拡張計画

ー スペイン、バルセロナの「トーレス・ポルタ・フィラ」は、本当に長いことやっていましたね。2002年にコンペティションがあって、2010年に完成しました。コンペティションの時から、この地区のランドマークとなるようなツインタワーが計画されて、それが実現されていますが、最初はどういうイメージをもたれたのですか。

これは空港からまちへ入って来るときに見えるサイトで、この2本がまちへのエントランスゲート的な意味合い、あるいはこの博覧会場に来るときのゲート的な意味合いをもっているということで、当初からシンボル的なものにしたいと思っていました。

ー これは建築というより、都市計画のレベルの大きなプロジェクトで、設計と拡張をずっと繰り返しながらプロジェクト自体も続いていったと聞いています。

コンペティションの時は、僕を含めて4人の建築家がいました。主催者は、それぞれの建築家にひとつずつプロジェクトを任せるという趣旨だったらしいですが、コンペティションが終わった後に、すべてを僕らのところに依頼してくれることになりました。

ー もともとは見本市が開かれるような、既存の展示場の拡張計画でしたね。

そうですね。バルセロナは19世紀末からアートと建築によって発展したまちだし、気候も良くて、明るいまちだから、見本市とか国際会議が多く開かれています。そういうイベントがまちの収入源になっていて、バルセロナはスペインの中でも経済的に豊かだったので、展示場を増やそうということになったようです。

---

basement theater, which we ourselves used to hold the event marking the 40th anniversary of the office, is an end-stage type of theatre and the lighting therefore always faces the same direction. It is an easy theatre to use, one that even we can operate. As a result, there are no mix-ups regarding its use.

A theatre that both amateurs and professionals can use ends up being not fully satisfactory. Making a clear distinction between the two types of use accounts in large measure for the success of Koenji.

– The other day I heard someone who is about to put on a play there say on the radio that this place has a good reputation among performers. He pointed out, as you just did, that there are two types of theatres. This makes things convenient and can accommodate diverse undertakings--hence its good reputation among performers.

I am happy to hear that.

– The Koenji district itself has always had many people using theatres. Suginami Ward also has reliable NPOs.

It is also wonderful how the basement practice rooms are used practically every day for a school. That inspired us to develop our own school. The basement school trains scriptwriters, and professionals in stage equipment and stage lighting.

– The people working part-time in the second-floor café go to that school, and the people working at events are also theatre-related people.

Everything seems organically organized. On weekends, there are book readings for children which in effect develop the audiences of the future.

– The creation of Koenji seems to have changed the community. The old building before the competition was dark and did not have a very good atmosphere. It is interesting how the new building, even though it is closed off, has become a place where people gather.

Taking a hint from the style of production of Kazuyoshi Kushida, the artistic director of Matsumoto, a proposal has been made to use the backyard as a stage as well. A way to get delivery vehicles to the stage has been proposed. Fairly bold plans are being devised concerning the layout.

We do have experience with the method of production at Matsumoto but there is only room for a delivery entrance to one side of the entrance [laughs] From there, items have to be taken by elevator to the basement or an upper floor.

– A steel-plate structure was planned for Koenji from the time of the competition, when the scheme was still a box shape. When this became an organic form...was the selection of the structural form part of a trend at the time, as in TOD's and Tamabi, to combine steel plate and concrete?

The building would have made a very different impression had concrete been used on the outside. The question then was how to suggest a theater tent, and using concrete would have made that impossible. Using a single layer of steel plate would have produced the nearest thing to a tent, but it was decided to cast concrete on the inside to improve sound insulation.

– The idea of the box had been to enclose the theatre with something thin. That was then replaced with the idea of covering the theatre with a thin material, is that correct?

Yes. At the time of the competition, there had also been somewhat ornamental openings. It is a good thing we did not include them [laughs].

From the outside, it is a mass of steel, but inside, it is an entirely different world. The unexpected character of the interior produces in the audience a feeling of eager anticipation, and the bright colors are also interesting for a theater.

The area around the stairway is different from the tent-like image on the outside--it is more sensuous. People from the architectural world respond most to the area around the stairway, but since I had imagined this building being simpler, like a theatre tent, I was quite uneasy about the stairway area.

– How did you arrive at your decision? It seems to express your sensibility fairly directly...

I wasn't consciously trying to create something sensual; it simply came out that way...In that sense, this is quite different from Tamabi.

### TORRES PORTA FIRA / Extention for the Fair of Barcelona Gran Via Venue

– The office was engaged in TORRES PORTA FIRA in Barcelona for a really long time. The competition took place in 2002, and the project was completed in 2010. From the time of the competition, the plan was to build a twin tower that would be a landmark for the area, and that objective was realized. What sort of image did you have in mind at first?

The site is on the way from the airport into the city. The two towers were to signify an entrance gate to the city or a gate to the exhibition grounds, so from the start I wanted

——スペインのクライアントの方は明るいし、スペインで仕事をするのは楽しいと伊東さんはよくおっしゃっていましたね。

　そうですね。スペインは新しい建築への期待がすごくあるし、特にバルセロナはそうですが、建築家のステータスも高いから、建築家は日本よりはるかに尊敬されています。
　ただ難しいのは、どうデザインをするかということですね。コマーシャルな面もあるし、ライブラリーや美術館をつくるのとは違うので、わかりやすいシンボル性をもちこむかは、難しい問題ですね。

　——その点ではシンガポールの「VivoCity」はかなり商業施設として成功していて、かつそこに大きなシンボル性があってということですね。

　でも「VivoCity」の場合も、構造的に他でやってきたような新しいことをやっているかといえば、やはり視覚的な部分だけで勝負していますね。

　——先ほどの「多摩美」で最後にきわめていった精度の問題とは全然次元が違いますね。シンボル性が海外での商業建築では求められているということですね。

　そうですね。

　——積層されているものと、平面的に広がりがあるものと、ここには両方ありますが、その場合のシンボルのつくり方に違いはありますか。たとえば積層されているものは、内部の連続性じゃなくて、ファサードやシルエットなど、もっと大きいところの操作で考えなければいけなくなってしまうと思うのですが。

　垂直なものは、構造的に、多少ねじったり曲がったりは可能だけれども、それくらいが限界だから、それ以上に何か革新的なことというのは極めて難しいですね。

　——タワーが2棟あって、それぞれキャラクターがありますね。オフィスタワーのEVコア部分はコンペティションの時は外に出ていなかったのですが、それをある時切り取ったような表現に変えたのは、現場で変えられたのですか。

　そうです。プラン上、EVコアが真ん中だと平面的に良いプランにならないので、それを寄せてきて、その時にそれをスパッと切った断面がエレベーションに表現されています。

　——このデザインについて、クライアントとどういうやりとりを行ったのですか。

　IFA（メッセコンベンションの協会）とは、最初からわれわれが自由にデザインして、デザインを含めて土地を売却するということになっていましたから、問題は起こらなかったのですが、ホテルの内装もわれわれがやったので、ホテルのテナントからの注文によって何度もやり直しています。ホテルのインテリアも難しい。われわれの苦手な部分ですね。

### 今治市伊東豊雄建築ミュージアム

　——「今治市伊東豊雄建築ミュージアム」はかなり中断期間も長かったとうかがっていますが、最初はどういうところから話が始まったのでしょうか。

　ギャラリー長谷川の長谷川浩司さんと馬場璋造さんが所敦夫さんを紹介して下さって、「ところミュージアム 大三島」に隣接したアネックスの設計を依頼されました。
　その時点では、場所も決まっていない状態だったのですが、最初は「ゲント市文化フォーラム」コンペティションのプロジェクトの一部みたいなモデルから始まりました。

「VivoCity」 VivoCity

---

to make them symbol c.

– This is an enormous project, one that is on the level more of city planning than of architecture. I have heard that the project underwent repeated design and expansion.

At the time of the competition, there were four architects including myself. It seems to have been the intention of the organizer to give one project to each architect, but after the competition, I was asked to design everything.

– It was originally a plan to expand an existing exhibition hall so that events such as trade fairs could be held, was it not?

Yes. Barcelona has developed since the end of the nineteenth century thanks to its art and architecture. Trade fairs and international conferences are often held there because the climate is good and the city is pleasant. Such events are a source of revenue for the city, and Barcelona was economically well-off, compared with the rest of Spain. That was why it was decided to increase exhibition facilities.

– You have often said that Spanish clients are of cheerful disposition and that working in Spain is enjoyable.

Yes. Much is expected of new architecture in Spain, especially Barcelona. Architects enjoy a high status and are much more respected than in Japan.
The difficulty, however, was deciding how to approach design. There was a commercial aspect to the project, so it was different from designing a library or an art museum. It was difficult deciding whether or not to introduce a symbolic character that is easily comprehensible.

– In that regard, VivoCity in Singapore is fairly successful as a commercial facility and quite symbolic in character as well.

But VivoCity, unlike other projects of ours, was not an attempt at something new structurally. We put our effort into the visual aspect of the project.

– This was on an entirely different plane from the problem of precision which we discussed earlier. You are saying that symbolic character is something demanded of commercial buildings overseas.

Yes.

– There are both stacked elements and horizontally extended elements. Does the way a symbol is created out of one type differ from the way a symbol is created out of the other? For example, with something that is stacked vertically, I would think one needs to consider, not internal continuity, but the manipulation of larger things such as the facade or the silhouette.

Slightly twisting or bending vertical elements is structurally possible, but that is about it. Being any more innovative than that is quite difficult.

– There are two towers, and they are different in character. At the time of the competition, the elevator core for the office tower was not exposed on the outside. The decision was made at some point to make it seem cut out. Was this change made at the site?

Yes. The plan was not working with the elevator core in the middle, so we pushed it to one side and decided to show its cut-away section in elevation.

– What sort of dialogue did you have with the client concerning this design?

There were no problems with IFA (the association of trade fair conventions). From the start we were free to design, and the land, including the design, was going to be sold. However, we were also in charge of the interior design of the hotel, and we had to redo it several times at the request of the hotel tenant. Hotel interiors are difficult. They are not our strong suit.

### Toyo Ito Museum of Architecture, Imabari

– I understand work on Toyo Ito Museum of Architecture, Imabari, was suspended for a long time. How did the project begin?

Mr. Hiroshi Hasegawa of Gallery Hasegawa and Mr. Shozo Baba introduced me to Mr. Atsuo Tokoro, who commissioned me to design an annex adjacent to Tokoro Museum Omishima.
At the time, the site had not yet been determined. We began with a model that was similar to a part of our scheme for the Ghent City Cultural Forum competition.

– It was referred to in the office as "mini-Ghent." This was directly after the Ghent competition.

A gently sloping area on somewhat lower ground than Tokoro Museum was selected, and we were designing for it. We wondered if it might be approached from the sea, but the question of the town's amalgamation with Imabari City occurred, and work on the project was suspended for a while.
During the stoppage, I had discussions with

—ミニゲントと言われていました。当時は「ゲント」のコンペの直後です。

「ところミュージアム」のやや下方にある多少ゆるやかな勾配の土地を選んで、そこにつくろうとしていたのです。できれば海からアプローチできないかと考えていたのですが、今治市との合併問題が起こり、しばらく中断しました。

その中断している間に所さんと、くまもとアートポリスの話や、大西麻貴さんたちと九州の公園で休憩所（フォリー）を学生とのワークショップでつくった話などをして、いずれ若い人を育てるような仕事をしたいという話をしたところ、所さんが「それならこのミュージアムでやったらいいじゃないか」と言われました。

初めのうちは、このミュージアムを貸してもらえるのだと思っていたのですが、いつの間にか「伊東ミュージアム」にしようという話になっていました。

— 建築のための教育の場だから、建築ミュージアムにしようということですね。

そうですね。所さんに「日本ではまだないから建築ミュージアムにしたらどうですか」と言われて、その後もいろいろ尽力していただきました。市の担当者であった白石さんは僕の建築にも理解が深く、当時の副市長だった藤原さんを説得して、僕らのほとんど知らないうちに建築ミュージアムの計画がオーソライズされていったのです。

— 大三島はものすごく景色のきれいなところですが、初めて行った時はどういう印象でしたか。

所さんが一度訪れたらほれこんでしまったという島で、最初に所さんと長谷川さんに案内されたときは、船で行きましたから、海からの印象が強くて、ものすごく美しい島だと思いました。今年の夏ミュージアムの展示替えの後は、宮浦港から小さな船で「伊東ミュージアム」と「今治市岩田健母と子のミュージアム」に行くようにしようと計画しています。

— 伊東さんの中で、子どもたちや若い世代の建築家を育てたいという思いは、「伊東ミュージアム」をやる前からあったのでしょうか。

くまもとアートポリスでコミッショナーになった経験が大きいと思います。何とかして若い人たちにチャンスを与えたいと考えると同時に、現在の大学の建築教育に疑問を感じていましたから、それを何とかしたいという思いがありました。

—「伊東ミュージアム」をやっている時に、伊東事務所でいままでつくってきたものをここで閲覧できるようなミュージアムにしようという話もあって、NPOを設立してアーカイブの管理をしたり、人を育てながら一緒に自分たちも刺激をされるような、そういう活動の場所にしようという話もありました。

そうでしたね。ただ、面積が小さいため、なかなかすべての条件を満たすのは難しいということで、建築の提案も二転三転しました。最初はアクロポリスのような案もあったし、石を積んで、そこにパーゴラがあるだけというような案もあったし……。

— そのころの展示はどういうものを考えていたのですか。

いまほどの展示までは考えていなくて、屋外でやろうというようなことすら考えていました。

— そうすると、「シルバーハット」の中庭みたいなイメージですか。

休憩所のような場所ですね。でも、上の道路からこの建築がどう見えるかを常に意識していましたね。というのは、ミュージアムの向こう側に日が沈むから、必ずシルエットになる。そのシルエットがどう見えるかはすごく気になっていました。

僕の場合、内部からふくらませるようにイメージを考えることが多いのですが、このミュージアムに関しては、外側からいつも考えていました。

— 最初のスタディを見ると、最初は地形に寄り添って建物を建てて、同じ言語の中でどう建築をつくっていくかというようなスタディをしていました。それがある時から幾何学が出てきて、最後にタワーみたいなものが持ち上がってきました。

その当時やっていたプロジェクトのイメージがいろいろオーバーラップしていますね。「ゲント」あり、「高円寺」あり、「オスロ市ダイクマン中央図書館」のコンペティション案あり、「瞑想の森」あり……。

— アーカイブの話もありましたし、壁面に展示

---

Mr.Tokoro about Kumamoto Artpolis and the design of a folly in a park in Kyushu with Ms.Maki Onishi as part of a student workshop. I told him that one day I wanted to be involved in training young people, and he replied that, in that case, I ought to design a museum.

At first, I thought I would be able to lease the museum, but at some point it became the Toyo Ito Museum.

– Since the idea was to create a place for education in architecture, it was decided to create an architectural museum.

Yes. Mr.Tokoro said, since there was no architectural museum yet in Japan, why not make it one. He has been very helpful. Mr.Shiraishi, the city official in charge, understands my architecture quite well. He persuaded the then vice-mayor, Mr.Fujiwara, and the project for the architectural museum was authorized almost before I knew about it.

– Omishima is a very scenic place. What were your first impressions of it?

Mr.Tokoro said he fell in love with it the first time he visited the island. When I was first shown the island by Mr.Tokoro and Mr.Hasegawa, we went by boat, so the view from the sea made a powerful impression on me. I thought it was a quite beautiful island. There is a plan to make it possible to go to Ito Museum and Ken Iwata Mother and Child Museum, Imabari City, by a small boat from Miyaura Harbor after a new exhibition is installed in the former this summer.

– Did you have the desire to educate children and train young architects even before the Ito Museum?

I think my experience as commissioner of Kumamoto Artpolis played a big part in that. I wanted to give young people an opportunity and also had misgivings about present-day architectural education in universities. So I wanted to do something about that.

– When we were doing the Ito Museum, there was talk about trying to make it a museum where work done up to now by the office could be viewed. There were also talk about establishing an NPO, administering an archive, and creating a place where we would train young people and where we ourselves would be intellectually stimulated.

Yes. But there being only limited floor area available, doing all these things proved difficult. The proposal for the building changed again and again. There was an acropolis-like proposal at first, and there was also a proposal to lay stones and build just a pergola…

– What sort of exhibition was considered at the time?

An exhibition as extensive as the one now in place was not considered. We even considered making it an outdoor exhibition.

– Was it imagined as something like the courtyard of Silver Hut?

A place that was like a resting place. However, I was always conscious of how the building would look from the road above. That

「今治市伊東豊雄建築ミュージアム」のオープニング展示、ルーム2およびルーム4
Opening exhibition in Room 2 and Room 4 at the Toyo Ito Museum of Architecture, Imabari.

しようという話も出てきて、いろんなことが重なっていたころでしたから。ただ、伊東さんはやはり見え方をずっと気にされていたような気がします。水平にもってくるとか。結局、ユニット的な考え方が「オスロ」で初めて出てきて、そのユニット内で展示していくというような、最終的には閉じたものになっていきましたね。

その場合でも、内部より外部のシルエットが……。

──「オスロ」で用いた幾何学が出てきても、初めのほうはただ地形に沿わせて配置しているのですが、それが最後にこのタワーが出てきたというのが印象的ですね。

地形が斜めになっているので、それに沿って足を下ろすような模型を作って持っていったら、伊東さんがそれをひっくり返して、「このほうがいいじゃないか。テラスができるし、タワーもできる」とおっしゃった。タワーとして見えてくると、親しみやすいような、愛嬌のある形も出てきたように思います。

あの形が見えた時に、シルエットとしてこれはきれいだなと思ったので、それで良しということになりました。

──あそこのテラスはすごく気持ちがいいですね。

そうですね。一般の人はあまり上れないですが。

実施設計では、「TOD'S」もそうですが、シングルラインで考えている時と違って、壁に厚みが出てきたときの幾何学は非常に難しいということを

嫌というほど思い知らされましたね。一つひとつがそれぞれ完結していて、重なるところをダブルにしていくといいのですが、そこを合わせて1枚にしようとすると、途端に幾何学が崩れる。

──そうですね。壁厚が二重になるのを避けるために、どちら側かを片寄せにしていくと誤差が生じてくる。最終的には内壁の壁厚が4種類ぐらいになりました。こんなに小さいのに種類が多かったですね。

「2種類の角度で単純な幾何学だから、施工しやすいですよ」と入札の時は言っていたのですが、実際はすごく大変でした。芯に対する距離とか角度で変わってくるから、正確な六角形じゃなくなって、長い辺が出てきたり、三角形の頂点で合わない、必ずずれてくるというので、現場では最後の最後まで苦労していました。

ひとつモジュールを決めてしまうと、高さから何から全部決まってしまうというのも、不自由なものだという感じがしましたね。

──一辺の長さが3m、これを斜めに使っているので高さにすると約2mになってしまう。しかも斜めに倒れているから、開口を取るとぎりぎりになってしまう。ただ出来た空間は、想像もしない

「オスロ市ダイクマン中央図書館・コンペティション応募案」
The New Deichman Main Library Competition.

広がり、想像もしない狭まりを内包していて、同じ平面系でもまったく異なる空間を壁の角度だけでつくったというのが面白いですね。

そうですね。

──ここにユニットを使っただけで、展示スペースの壁が倒れていたり迫ってきたりする。それによって展示が面白く見える可能性があるとか、そういうスタディもされたのですか。

そこも難しかったですね。せっかく壁が傾いているのに、そこからまた水平に台を出して模型を置いたらつまらない。それを何とかしてやめようというので、いろいろスタディをやりました。

──もしキュレーターがこの建築にいたら、かなりキュレーター泣かせの空間ですね。

---

is because the sun sets beyond the museum, so the building would inevitably be seen in silhouette. The view of that silhouette was something that was very much on my mind.

I usually imagine a building from within, but I always considered the museum from without.

– In the first studies, the building was adapted to the topography, and the same vocabulary was used to investigate how the building might be designed. Then, at some point, geometry appeared, and a tower-like object rose up.

Images from concurrent projects overlapped in various ways. There were Ghent, Koenji, the scheme for the Deichmanske Library competition, Oslo, and "Meiso no Mori"..

– There was talk of an archive; and also talk of exhibiting things on walls. Many different things overlapped. However, you were always concerned with the way it would look, for example, whether it should be horizontal or not. In the end, the idea of units was first conceived for Oslo, and it was decided to exhibit within those units. Finally, the scheme became enclosed.

But even then, my primary concern was not the inside but the silhouette of the exterior...

– Though the geometry that had been used in Oslo was adopted, it was arranged at first so as to conform to the topography. The final emergence of this tower was striking.

When we built a model of a scheme that conformed to the sloping topography and showed it to you, you turned it upside down and said, "Isn't this better? This way, we can build a terrace as well as a tower. When it was seen as a tower, it became more" friendly and appealing.

When I saw that shape, I thought it looked beautiful in silhouette and decided on the scheme.

– That terrace is quite pleasant.

Yes, though it isn't open much to the general public.

In the final design--and this was also true of TOD'S--we were made painfully aware of the difficulties presented by geometry when the thickness of a wall has to be considered. It was quite different from using a single line to represent a wall. It wouldn't have mattered if each one was self-contained and we could have had two where they overlap, but the moment we tried to make it a single layer, the geometry broke down.

– Yes. If we pushed the wall to either side in order to avoid having a wall that was twice as thick, an error resulted. In the end, there were about four types of thickness of interior walls. There were many different types for a building this small.

When bids were being solicited, we said that this would be easy to construct because there were only two types of angles and the geometry was simple. In reality, however, it was quite difficult. Because the distance to, and the angle with respect to, the center line of the wall changes, the wall may not be truly hexagonal--one side may become longer than the others--or the wall may not meet at the top of a triangle. There were always displacements, and work on the site was difficult to the very end.

Deciding on a single module that determines everything including the height can be quite restricting.

– One side is three meters long, but this is arranged at a diagonal, meaning it is approximately two meters in height. Moreover, because this is at a diagonal, it is barely enough to accommodate doors and other openings. However, the resulting space had unexpected expanses and unexpected constrictions. It was interesting to see how entirely different spaces could be created from similar layouts simply by changing the angles of walls.

Yes.

– The walls of the display spaces tilt backward or come forward through the use of units. Were studies undertaken to investigate the possibility of making displays more interesting?

That was also difficult. It would have been absurd to extend stands horizontally from walls and put models on them when we had gone to the trouble of tilting those walls. We undertook various studies to avoid doing that.

– If this building had had a curator, the space would have been a source of great aggravation.

Yes. It is a good thing it was our museum. If it hadn't been, it would have been impossible [laughs].

– For the opening exhibition, we decided not to use horizontal stands. Instead, models were attached directly to the walls, so that they could be viewed from different angles.

Because we wanted to suggest a completely closed world in which floor, walls and ceiling were continuous, we went through the trouble of laying a blue carpet and painting the walls and ceiling the same color.

– It produces a floating quality. Because everything is blue, one no longer has a sense of distance.

そう。うちのミュージアムだからまだいいけど、そうじゃなかったら、とんでもないことになりましたね（笑）。

——オープニング展示の時は、水平の台を止めて、壁に直接模型を付けることで、いろんな角度から模型を見ることができるような展示になっていましたね。

床、壁、天井がひと続きの、完全に閉じた宇宙だということを表現したいがために、わざわざブルーのカーペットを敷いて、同色で壁・天井も塗りました。

——浮遊感があるというか、全面ブルーにすると、全部ブルーで囲われてくるので、距離感がわからなくなってきますね。

確かに。だから寝っころがると面白いですね。

——最近は伊東塾の活動として展示もメインになってきていますね。

今年は3年経ったので、全部展示替えをしようということで、神奈川大学の曽我部研究室と昭和女子大学の杉浦研究室に手伝ってもらっています。また、塾生のOBも一緒になって、この島のこれからについてをテーマにした展覧会をやろうとしています。

実際にいまわれわれの拠点として、参道の中に1軒空き家を借りました。それをどう再生していくかとか、参道の将来をどう考えていったらいいかを考えています。また、集落が島のいろいろな場所に散在している理由を考えていますが、これは島自体がひとつの島というよりは、向かい合っている島と強く関係をもっているからではないかと。それによって集落の性格が全然違っているので、そこに曽我部研は興味をもっていますね。

——いつもミュージアムから見える島、憩いの家から見える島というのがあって、そこすごく近いんですね。同じ島の反対側より、見える島のほうが近く感じる。

そうですね。だからイノシシだって泳いでくるんだよ（笑）。

今年の展示替えではそこまではやっていませんが、僕は大三島をもっと面白い場所にしていきたいと思っていて、ミュージアムも今回の展示で終わるのではなくて、長い時間をかけて島のあるべき姿を考えていきたいと思います。

——ひとつのまいた種が島の中で広がっていって、最初に所さんが「ところミュージアム」を建てたことから、いろんな人が関係し合って……。

直島とはまったく違って、コマーシャルでないやり方でやっていきたいですね。

**今治市岩田健母と子のミュージアム**

——「岩田ミュージアム」も、いまの大三島の話の発展形のひとつだと思います。最初に考えていた敷地は大三島ではなかったですよね。「他にも敷地の候補はありますよ」と言って、岩田健さんを大三島に案内したことから始まったプロジェクトですね。

初めは豊島の予定でしたね。西沢立衛さんがミュージアムをつくった豊島を見に行きました。そうしたら、豊島でさまざまな開発が行われるという話を聞いて、一緒でないほうがいいと思いましたね。岩田さんの彫刻も具象で、豊島で展示されてるような現代アートとは一線を画したほうがいい。それで岩田さんを大三島に案内したら、岩田さんも即この島が気に入られました。それで、ここも敷地を探すことから始まって、「憩の家」、即ち海辺の元小学校の校庭だった場所がいいのではないかという提案をして、市がそれを許可してくれたので、ここに決まりました。

——「憩の家」は、廃校を借りて民宿にしたところですね。ここは海と山に囲まれた、ちょうど開けた場所ですね。千住真理子さんがここでバイオリンを弾いた時は、さざ波とかいろんな音と混ざり合って、すごく不思議な音環境になっていて感動しました。

まん幕のイメージがあって、伊東さんは初期のころ、「建築はないほうがいいんじゃないか。こんな所に作らないほうがこの彫刻にとっては幸せだ」とずっとおっしゃっていましたね。

大理石の彫刻が2、3体ありますが、それ以外は全部ブロンズだから、屋外に出しても大丈夫だということでした。大理石のものは、パーティションで雨がかからないようにしておけば大丈夫でしょうと。

——まん幕さえあれば建築になり得る、人が集ま

る仕掛けだけをつくって、あとは自由に使ってもらうというのは伊東さんの中で、ずっとあったのですか。

そうですね。要するに場所をつくるということですね。自然の中にはいろいろな場所があるので、その場所をちょっと際立たせれば人は集まってくる。そういうちょっとした仕掛けみたいなものですね。
　本当はこのようなリングが校庭に3つぐらいあると面白いと思っているのです。この建築は完全にひとつだけで閉じてしまっています。これがもし、子どもの遊び場でもなんでもいいけれど、ふたつあると、その間の空間が急に活き生きしてくるから、それをワークショップでやれるといいなと思いますね。

— いいですね。常設でなく仮設でもいいですから。

パーゴラみたいなものだけでもいいし。ここにひとつまるい畑をつくってもいいよ。パーゴラの中でバーベキューをやってもいい。

— 次のワークショップはそれをやりましょう（笑）。

— キャンプファイアをすると円陣になるし、みんなで大きな円を描くとか。そうすると、もっと「憩いの家」と一体となって使われるような、校庭を中心にしてそういう場所になりそうですね。
　大三島に行くと、いろんなことが実現できるような、そういういい関係が生まれています。

先週、中高生が「岩田ミュージアム」でバイオリンの演奏会をやっていたという話がフェイスブックでアップされていました。

いいですね。そういう試みが少しずつ動き始めるのは！

— 地元の人の意識が変わってきていますね。自分たちがやるというふうに。「憩いの家」のご主人も、最初は内気だったのですが、私たちが何度も行っているうちに、あれをやりたいこれをやりたいとすごく積極的です。

いいですね。

— やってみてうまくいったら、どんどんやれるんだという自信がついて、加速度的にいくのかもしれない。そういう刺激がいいですね。

その通りです。

1.『多摩美術大学図書館（八王子キャンパス）編』『PLOT』05《TOYO ITO 伊東豊雄：建築のプロセス》、A.D.A. EDITA Tokyo、2014年
2. 鈴木 明・港 千尋共編、多摩美術大学図書館ブックプロジェクト編『つくる図書館をつくる—伊東豊雄と多摩美術大学の実験—』、鹿島出版会、2007年

school ground in the centre.
　Good relationships that make it possible to realize many different things are established when we go to Omishima.
　There were comments made by junior and senior high school students on Facebook last week about a violin concert held at Iwata Museum.

It's good that experiments like that are gradually being tried!

– Local people are starting to take the initiative. The owner of Ikoi-no-ie was reserved at first, but as we continued to visit the island, he has become more active and expressed a desire to do this and that.

That's good.

– If he is successful in his efforts, he may gain even greater confidence. Things may accelerate. That sort of stimulus is good.

Exactly.

1. Tama Art University Library (Hachioji campus) *PLOT 05 TOYO ITO* (A.D.A. EDITA Tokyo) 2014
2. *Creating a Creative Library* (Kajima Institute Publishing) 2007

**Tama Art University Library** (Hachioji campus)
多摩美術大学図書館（八王子キャンパス）

2007 東京都八王子市 Hachioji, Tokyo

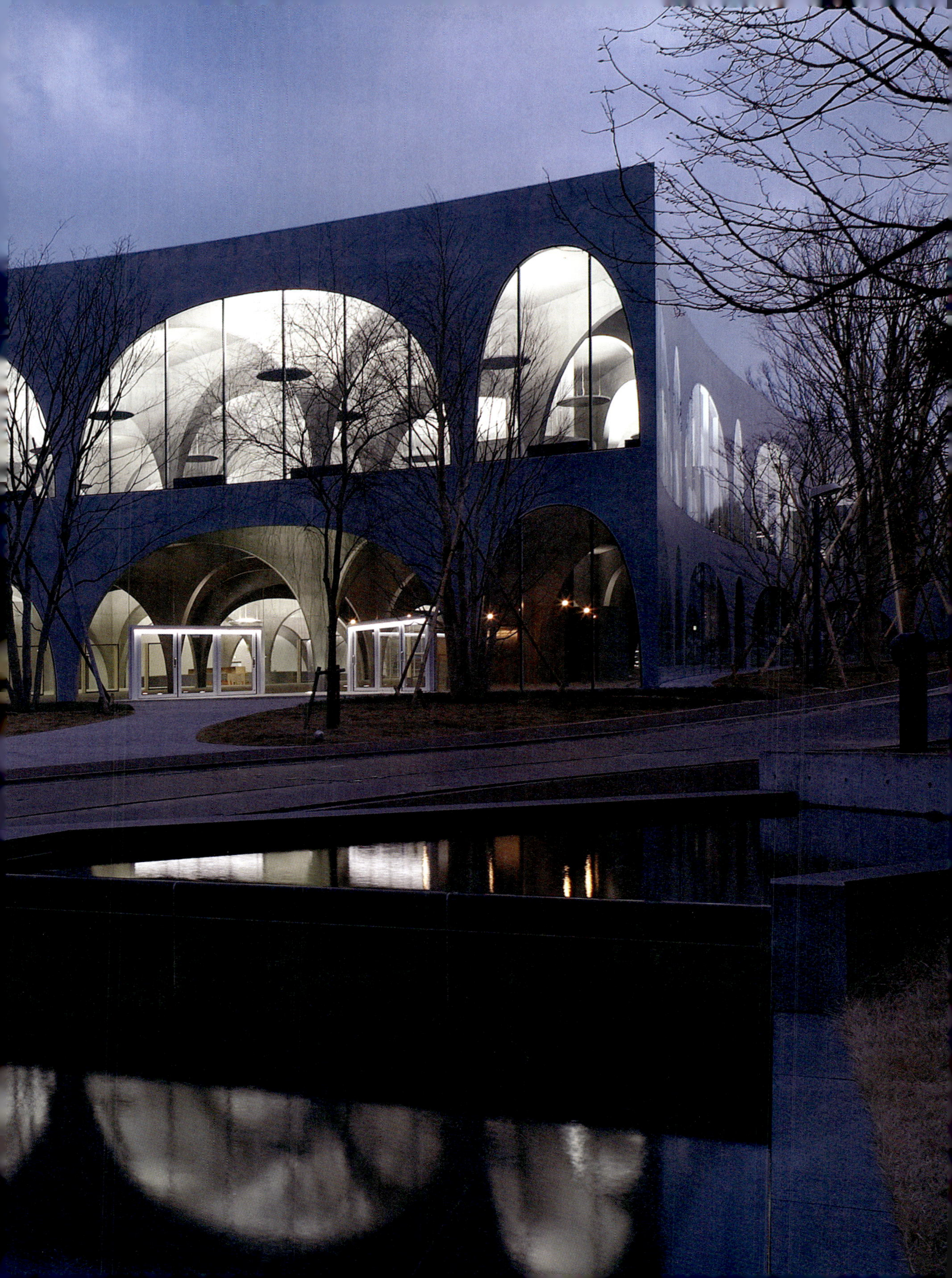

道路から東側ファサードを見る
The east facade as seen from the street.

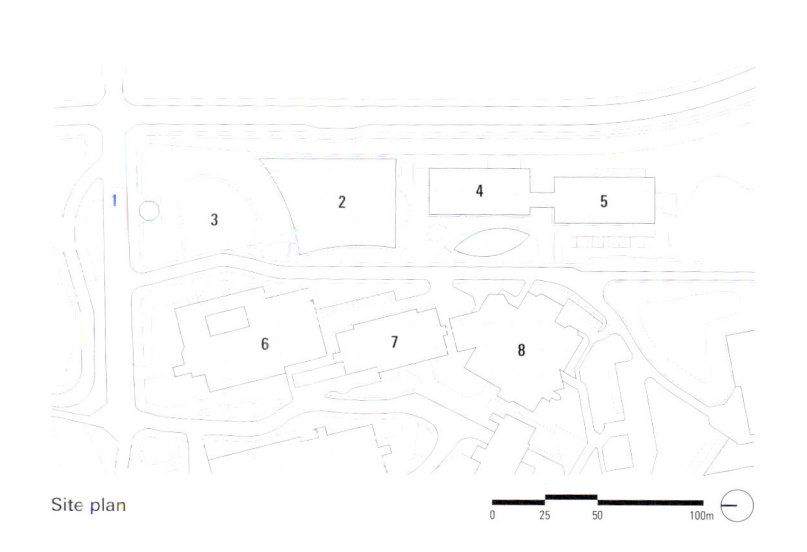

Site plan

1 main gate
2 library
3 sculpture forest
4 interaction design building
5 art science building
6 main building
7 media center
8 lecture hall

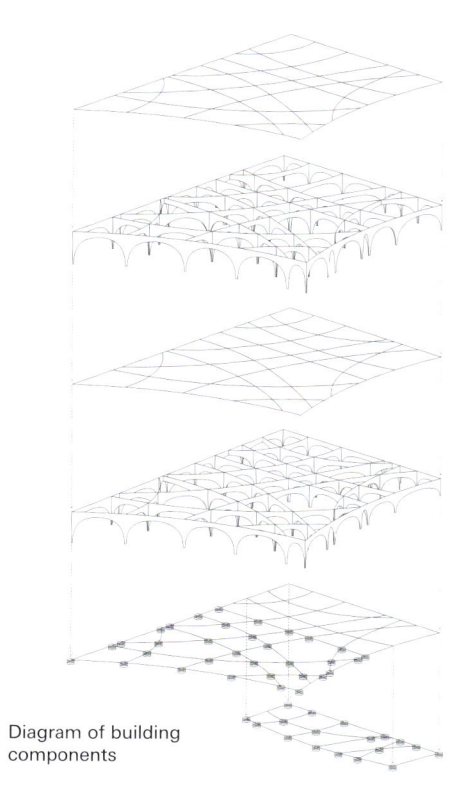

Diagram of building components

142

1F plan

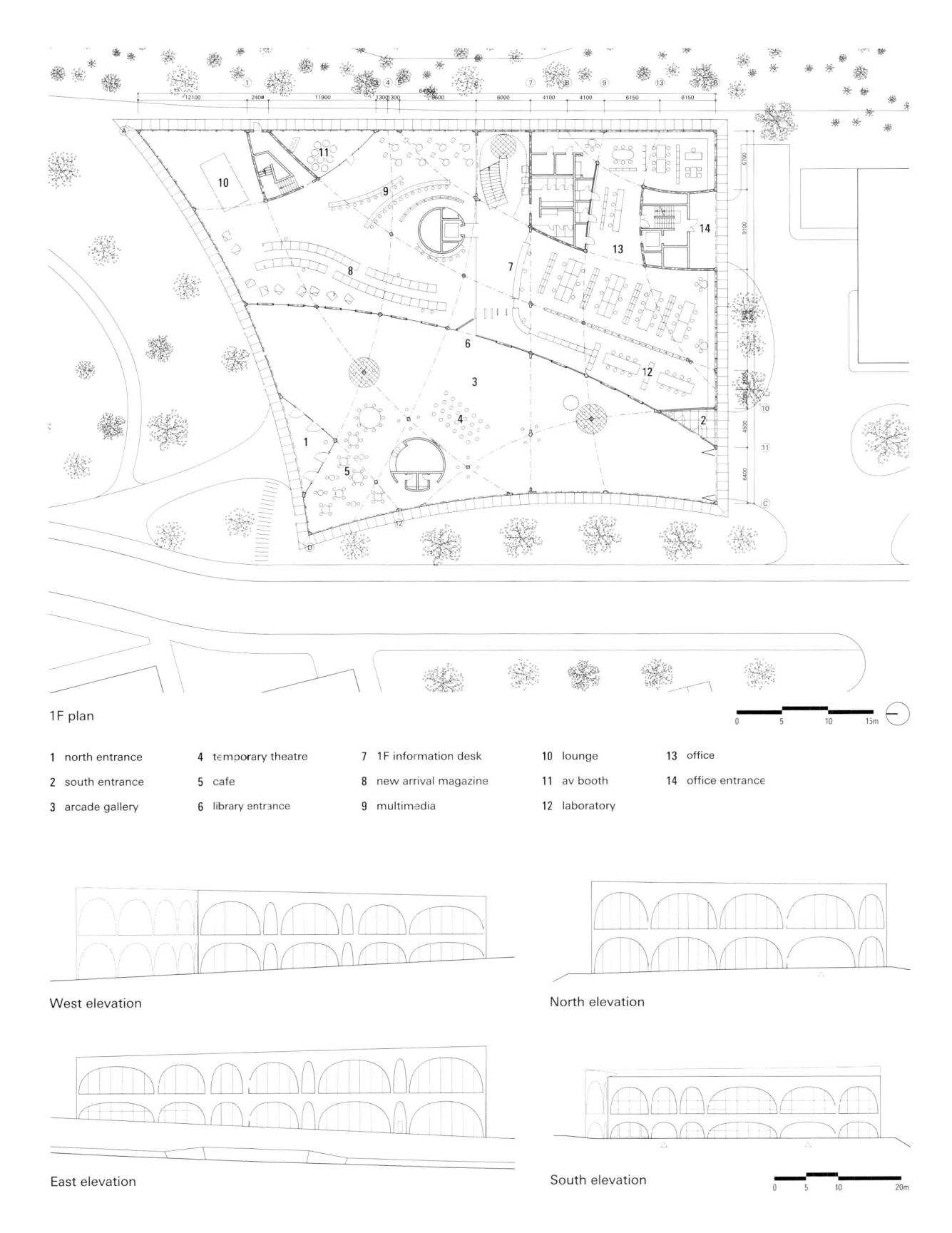

1 north entrance
2 south entrance
3 arcade gallery
4 temporary theatre
5 cafe
6 library entrance
7 1F information desk
8 new arrival magazine
9 multimedia
10 lounge
11 av booth
12 laboratory
13 office
14 office entrance

West elevation

North elevation

East elevation

South elevation

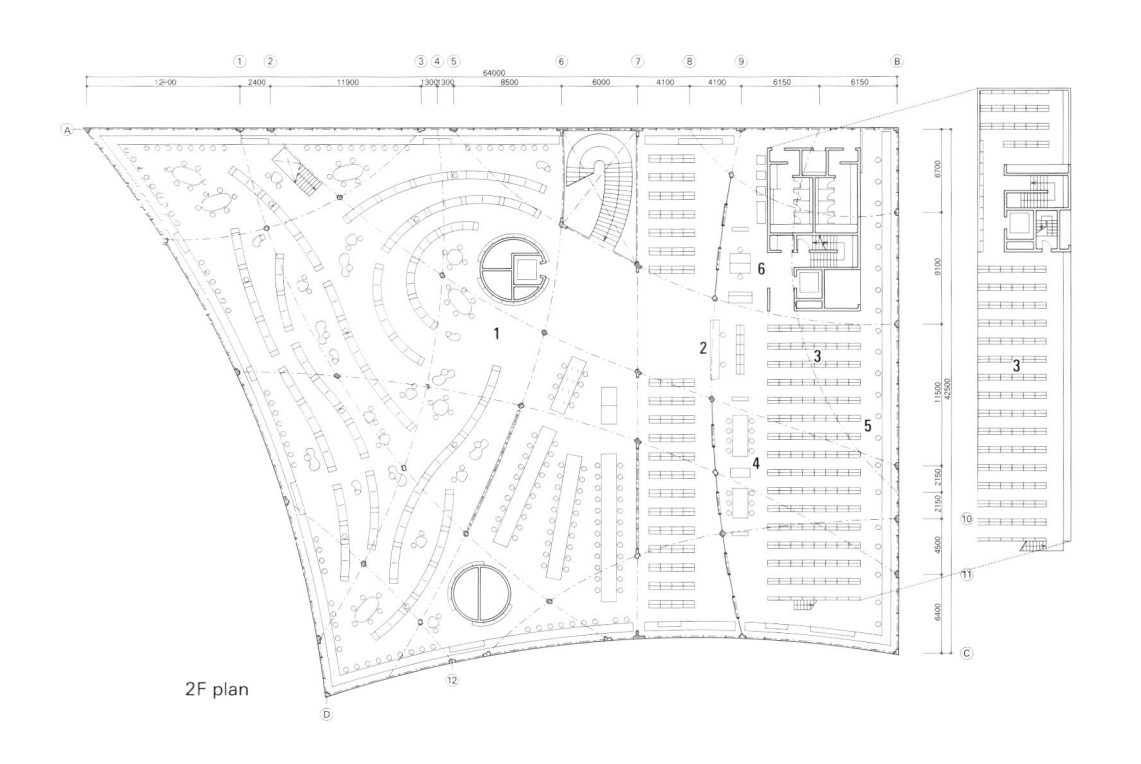

2F plan

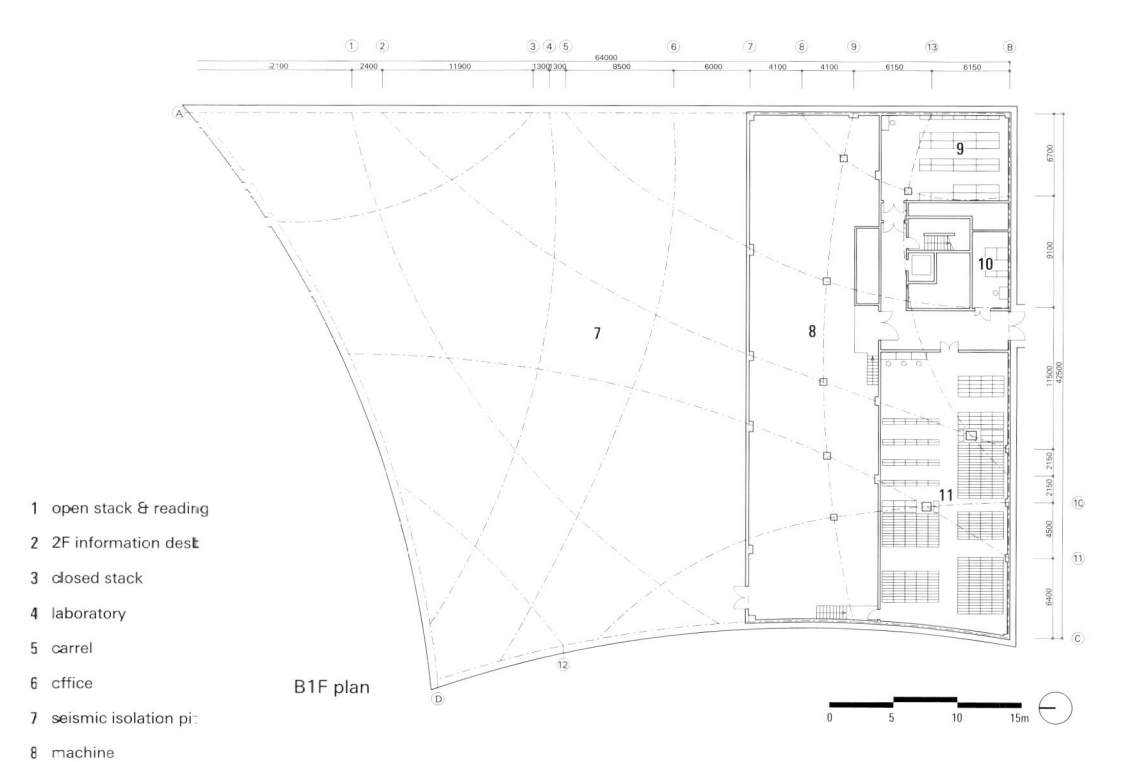

B1F plan

1 open stack & reading
2 2F information desk
3 closed stack
4 laboratory
5 carrel
6 office
7 seismic isolation pit
8 machine
9 valuable book stack
10 server
11 compact stack

144

（上）東側ファサードの一部　（下）敷地の勾配をそのまま取り入れた1階アーケードギャラリー
(Above) Part of the eastern facade.　(Below) The first-floor arcade gallery incorporates the original incline of the site.

中央部に鉄板でアーチをつくり、その両サイドにコンクリートを打って、厚さ20cmのスレンダーな架構を実現させた。地下に免震構造を採用している
The arches in the center were made with iron sheets and concrete, which was poured in both sides to create a thin, 20-centimeter framework. A seismic-isolation structure was installed underground.

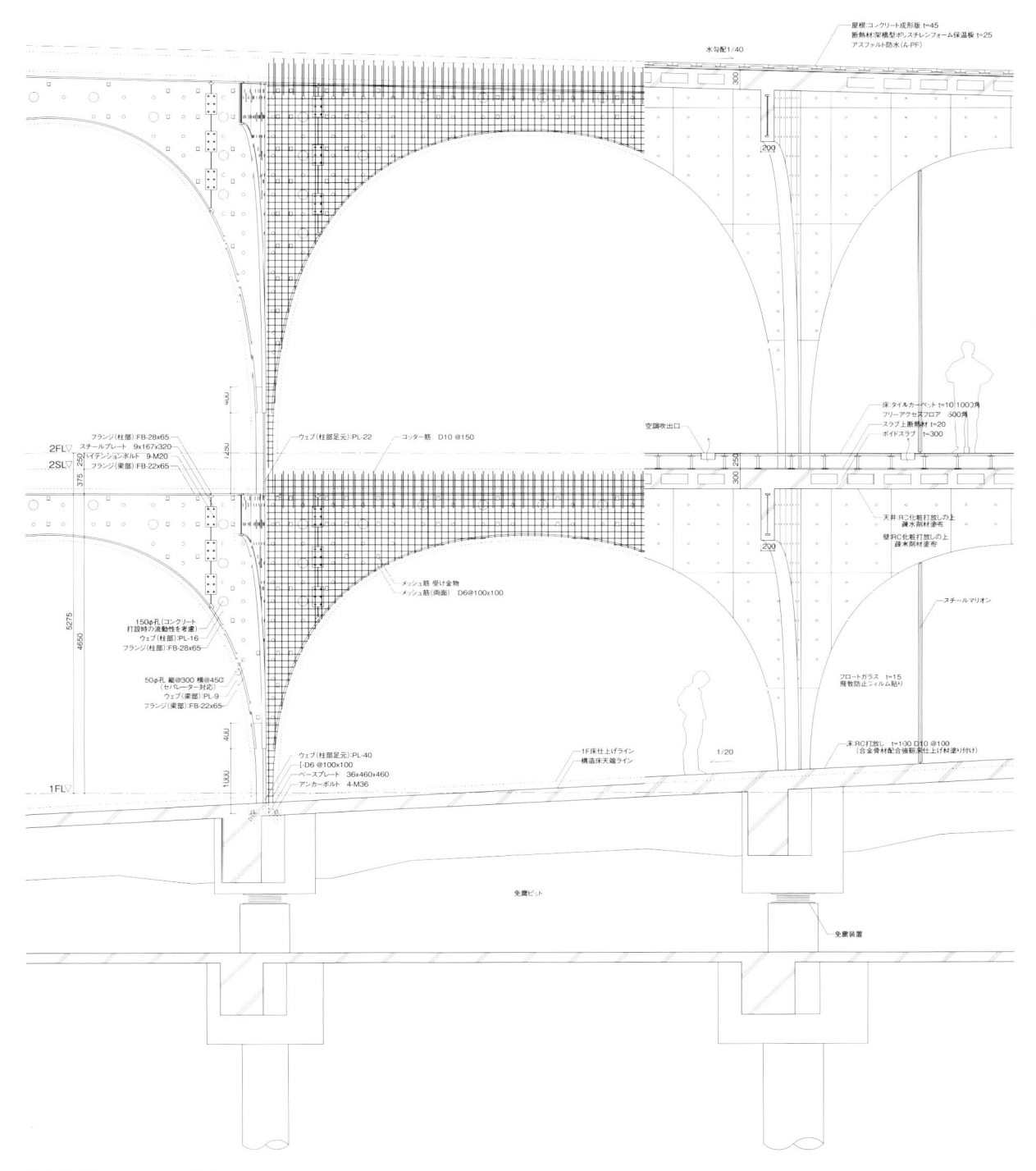

Detail of Construction Wall

東京郊外にある美術大学の図書館。スパンの異なるアーチラインが湾曲しながら交差して構造体を形成する。1階は南側が自由に通行可能なアーケードギャラリー、北側が雑誌、DVDカウンターのあるライブラリー。2階は大半が開架閲覧スペースで、一部にガラスパーティションで区切られた閉架閲覧スペースがある。

This library was designed for an art university in the suburbs of Tokyo. The structure is defined by arching lines of various spans that curve and intersect. There is an arcade gallery that can be traversed freely on the south side of the first floor and a library with magazines and a DVD counter on the north side. Most of the second floor is taken up with open shelving and a closed-shelf area that is divided by a glass partition.

1階から2階への湾曲する階段
The curved staircase that leads from the first to the second floor.

1階アーケードギャラリーのカフェ
The cafe in the first-floor arcade gallery.

1階アーケードギャラリー
The first-floor arcade gallery.

2階図書室、開架閲覧スペース。アーチによって分節されたブロックの間を湾曲する書架が貫く
The library and open-shelf area on the second floor. The curved shelves penetrate the blocks, which are segmented by the arches.

1階雑誌カウンター
First floor magazine counter.

1階AVブース
The audio-visual booth on the first floor.

2階窓際の閲覧カウンター
The reading counter next to the window on the second floor.

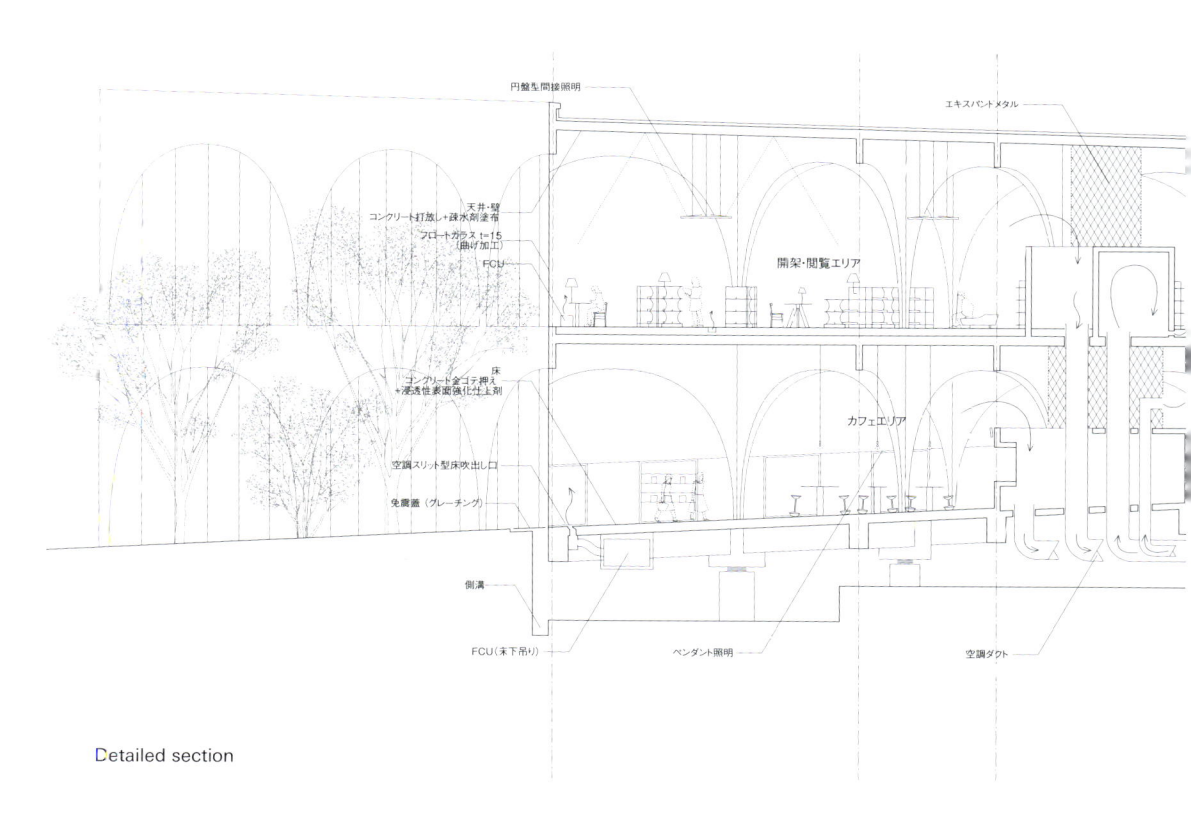

Detailed section

2階自習スペース
The study space on the second floor.

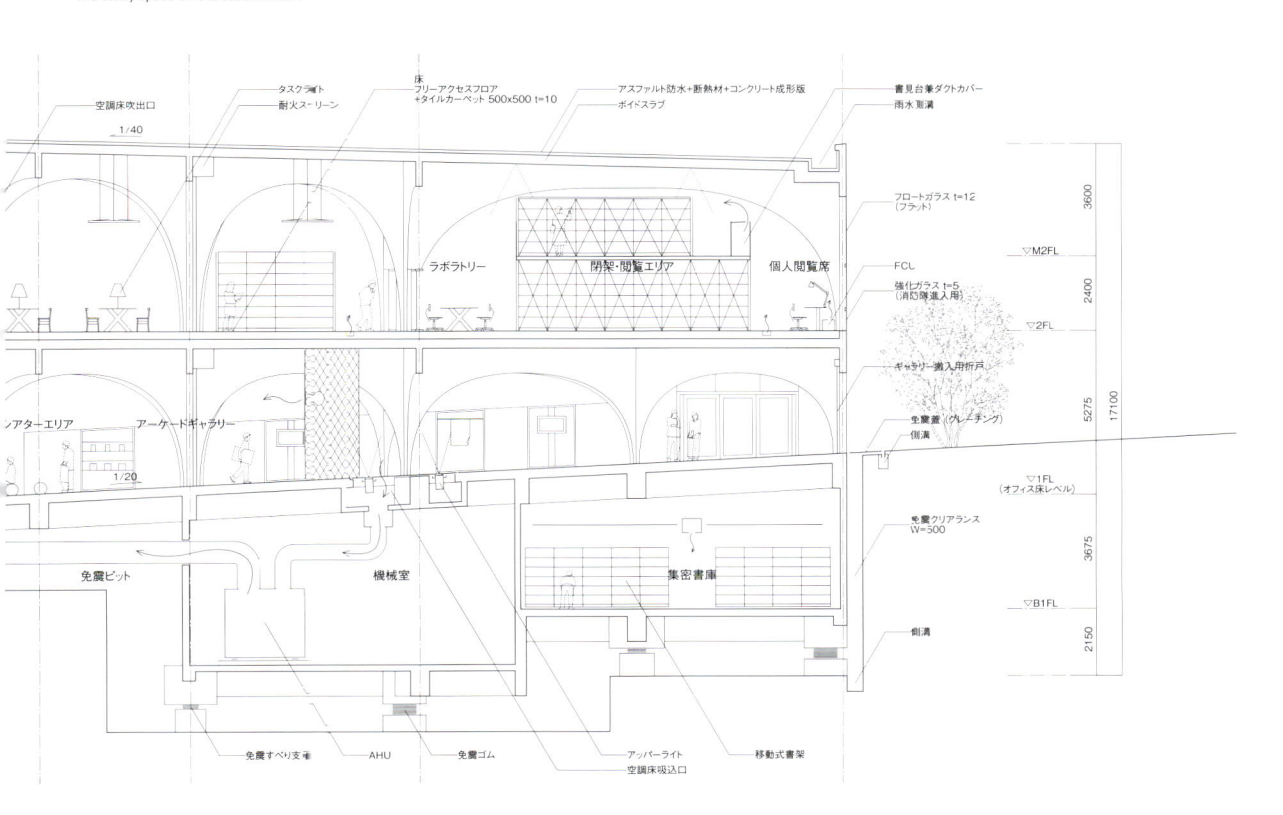

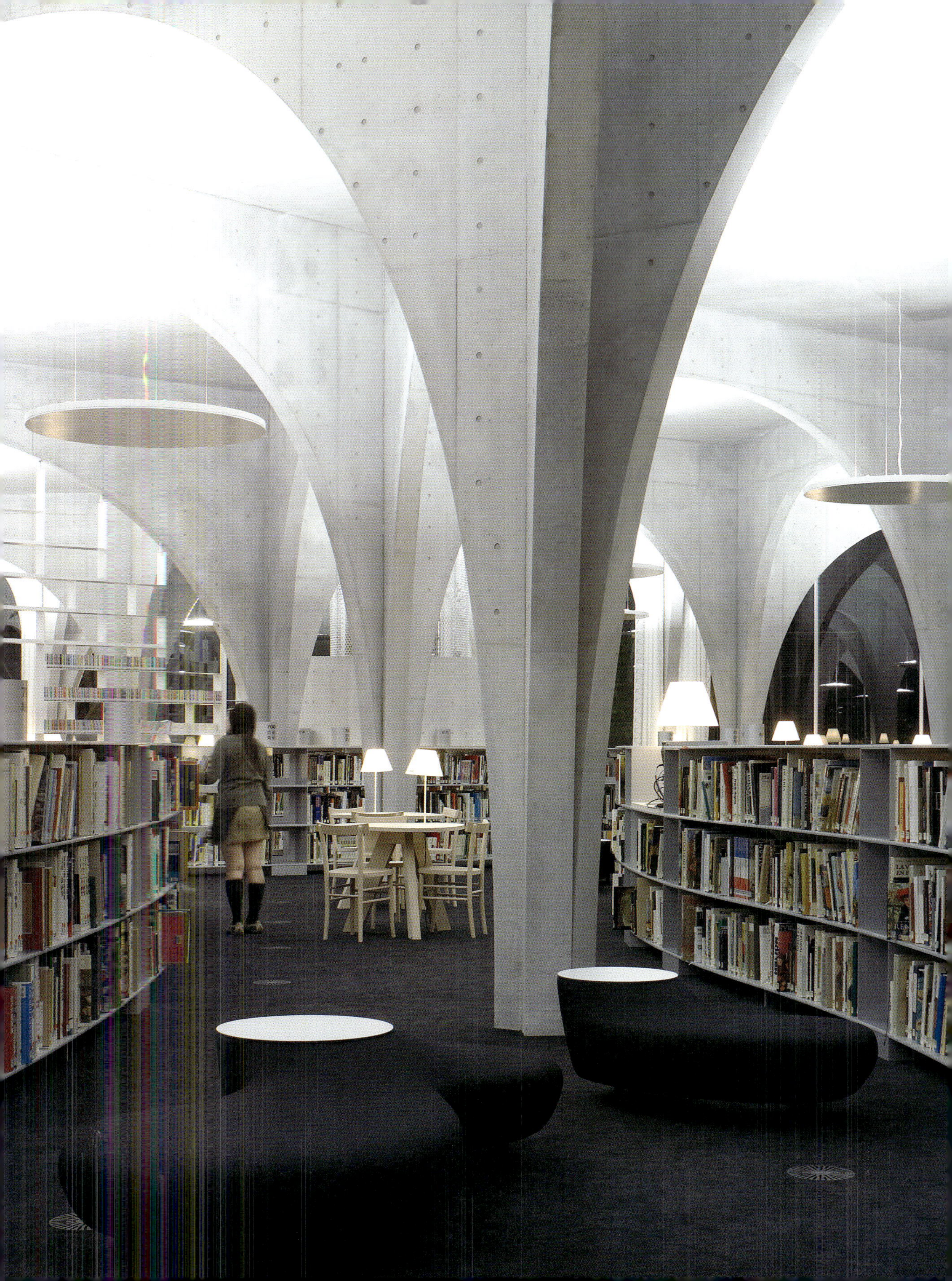

(左頁)2階開架閲覧スペース。アーチの柱脚は細く、浮遊感を生み出す　(上)1階映像閲覧カウンター。床は1/20のスロープ状　(下)外部より1階雑誌カウンターを見る
(Left page) The open-shelf space on the second floor. The column bases in the arches are thin, creating a floating sensation.
(Above) The video and reading counter on the first floor. The sloped floor has a gradient of 1:20.　(Below) The first-floor magazine counter as seen from the exterior.

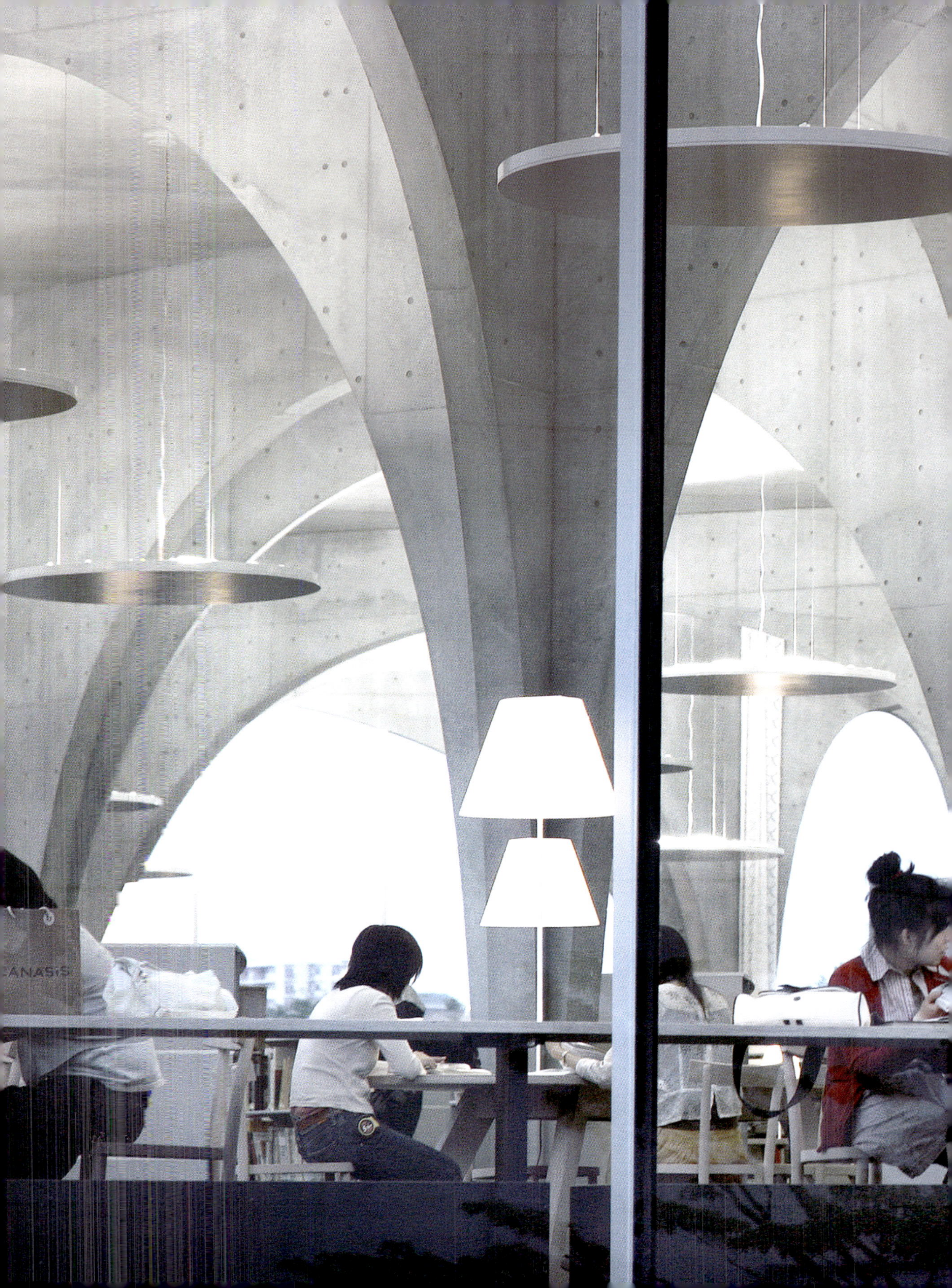

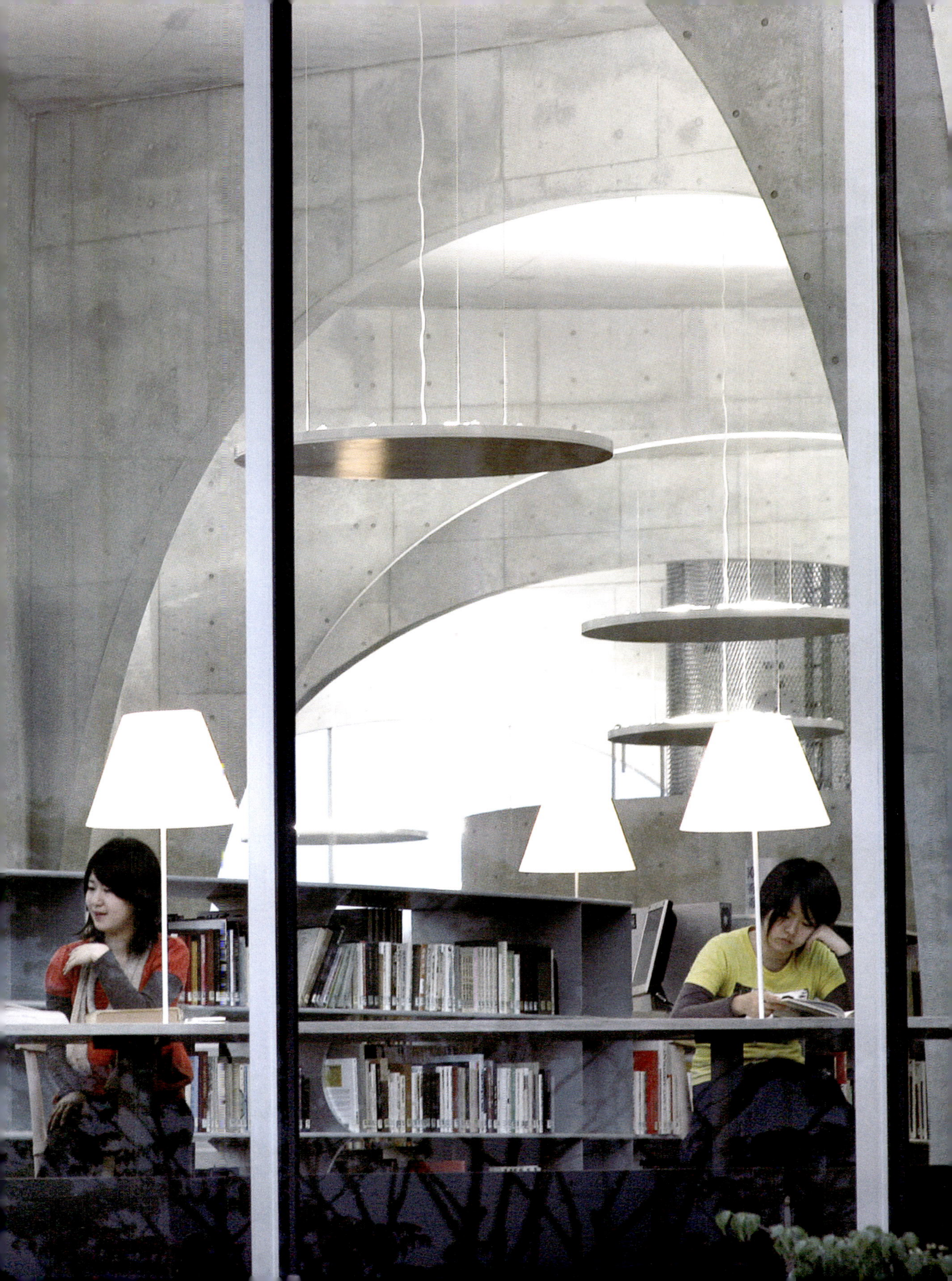

ZA-KOENJI Public Theatre
座・高円寺

2008 東京都杉並区 Suginami, Tokyo

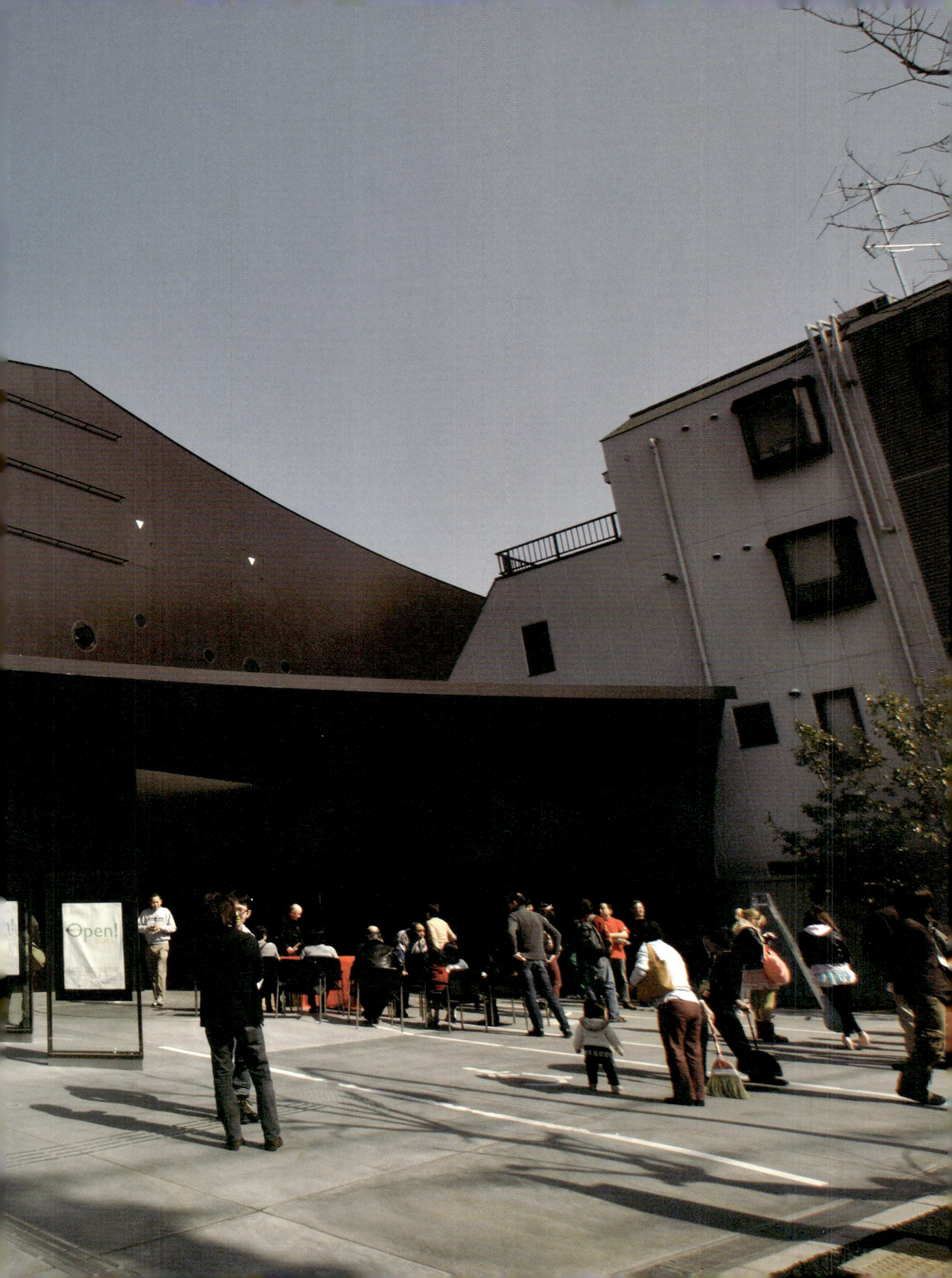
Open!

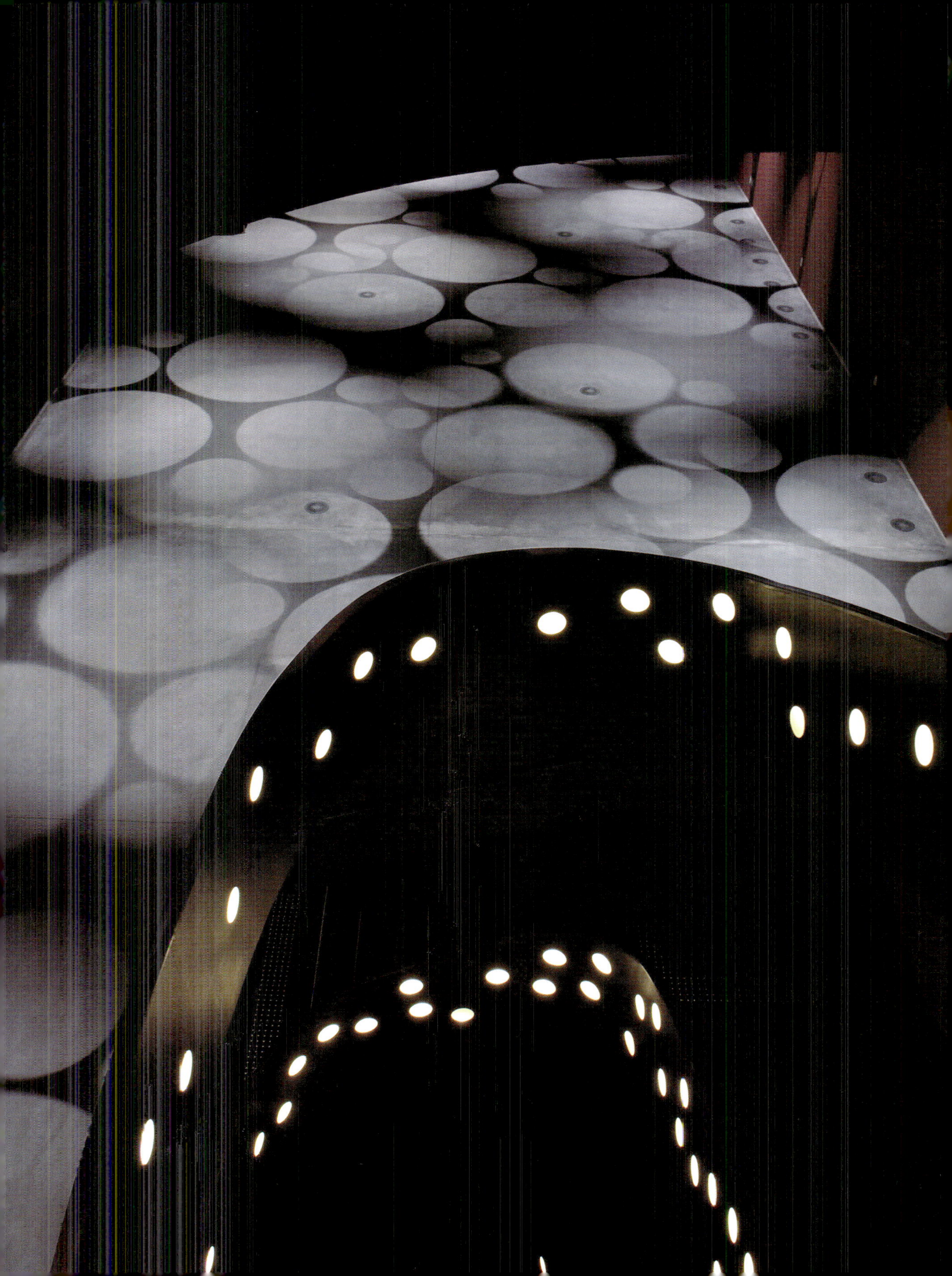

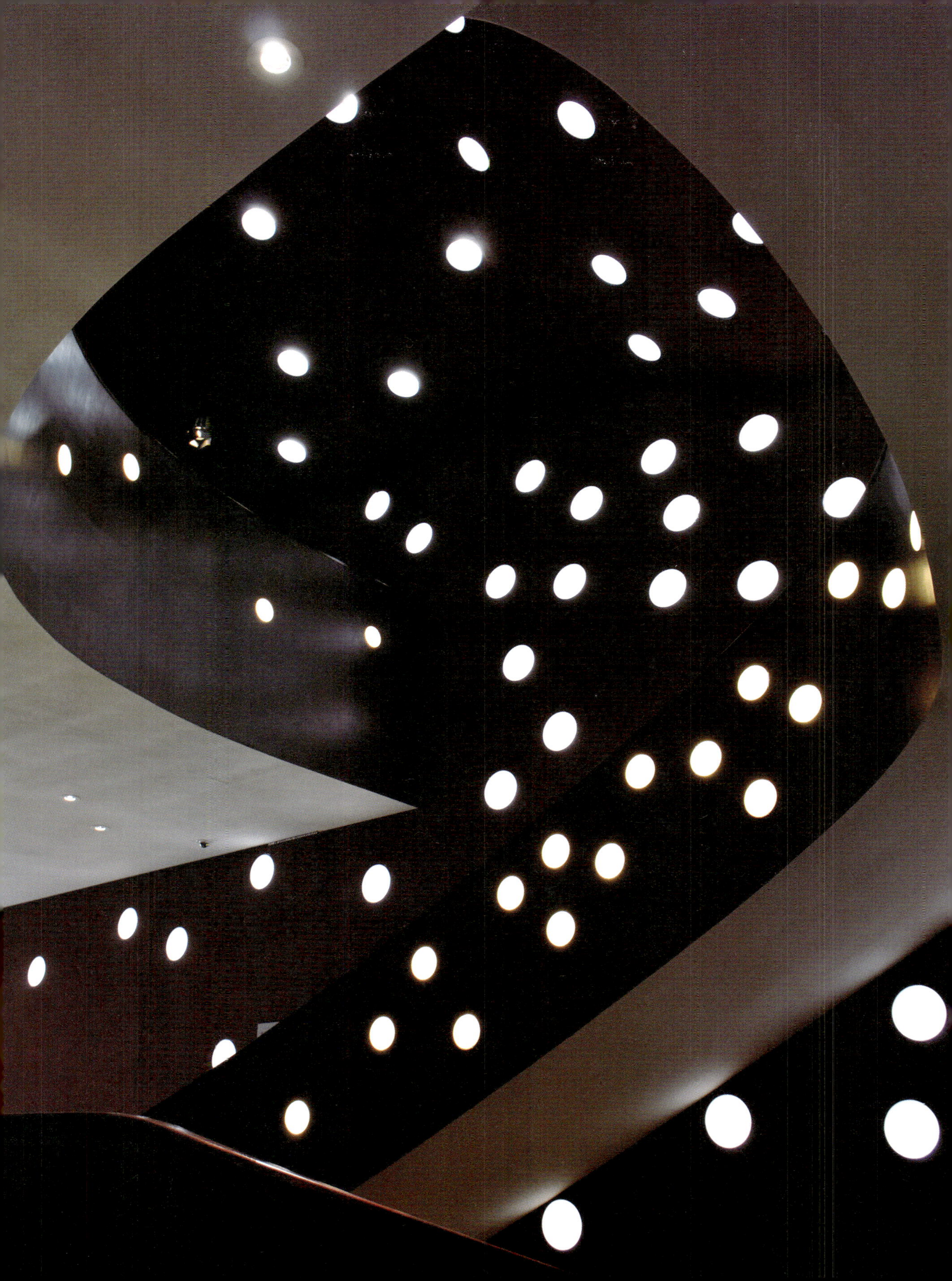

エントランス
Entrance.

| | | | |
|---|---|---|---|
| 1 plaza | 6 cafe | 11 technical store | 16 rehearsal room |
| 2 foyer | 7 reception | 12 ZA-KOENJI 2 | 17 wardrobe |
| 3 ZA-KOENJI 1 | 8 administration | 13 backstage lounge | 18 workshop |
| 4 loading bay | 9 first gallery | 14 dressing room | 19 av studio |
| 5 storage | 10 electric room | 15 AWAODORI HALL | 20 parking |

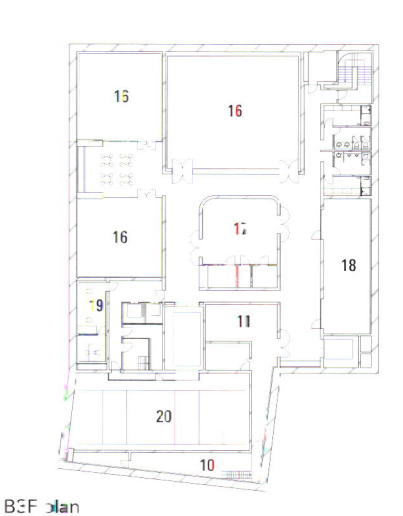

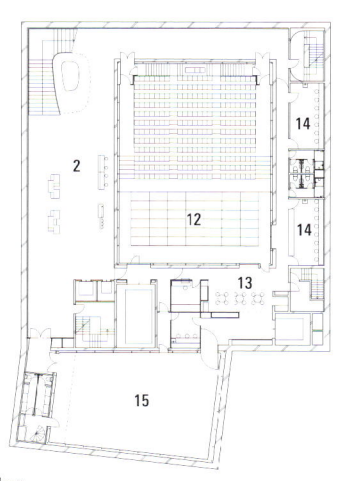

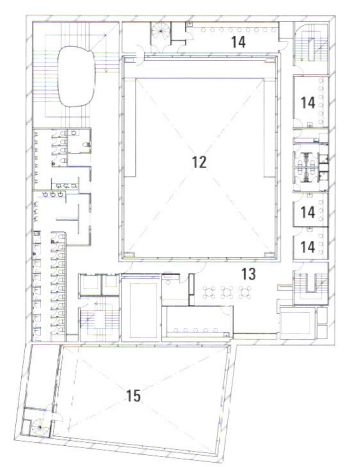

B3F plan    B2F plan    B1F plan

カフェ、レストラン
Cafe and restaurant.

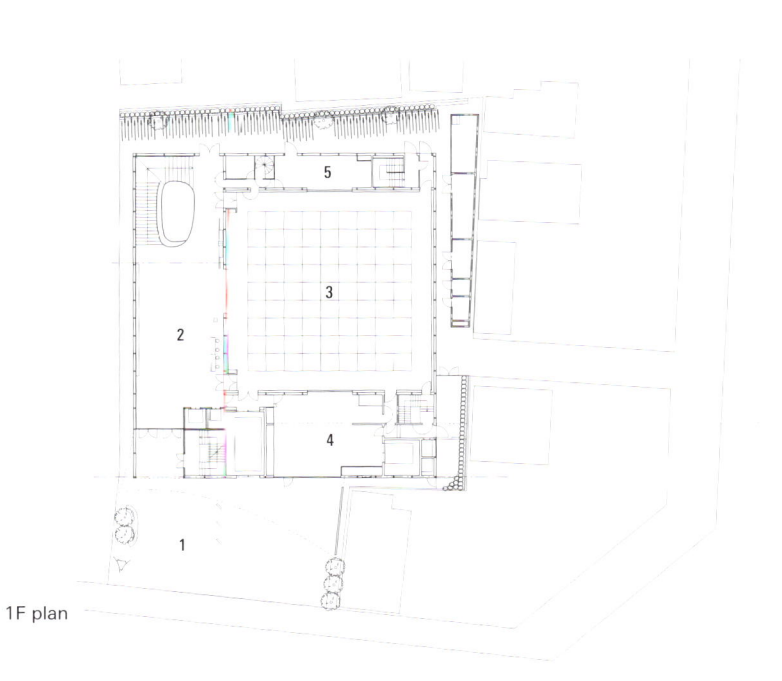

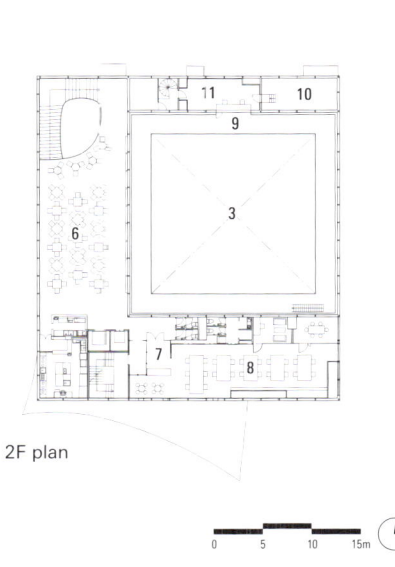

1F plan

2F plan

0  5  10  15m

〔上〕1階ホール「ZA-KOENJI 1」 〔下〕地下2階ホール「ZA-KOENJI 2」
(Above) Hall "ZA-KOENJI 1" on the first floor. (Below) Hall "ZA-KOENJI 2" on the second-floor basement.

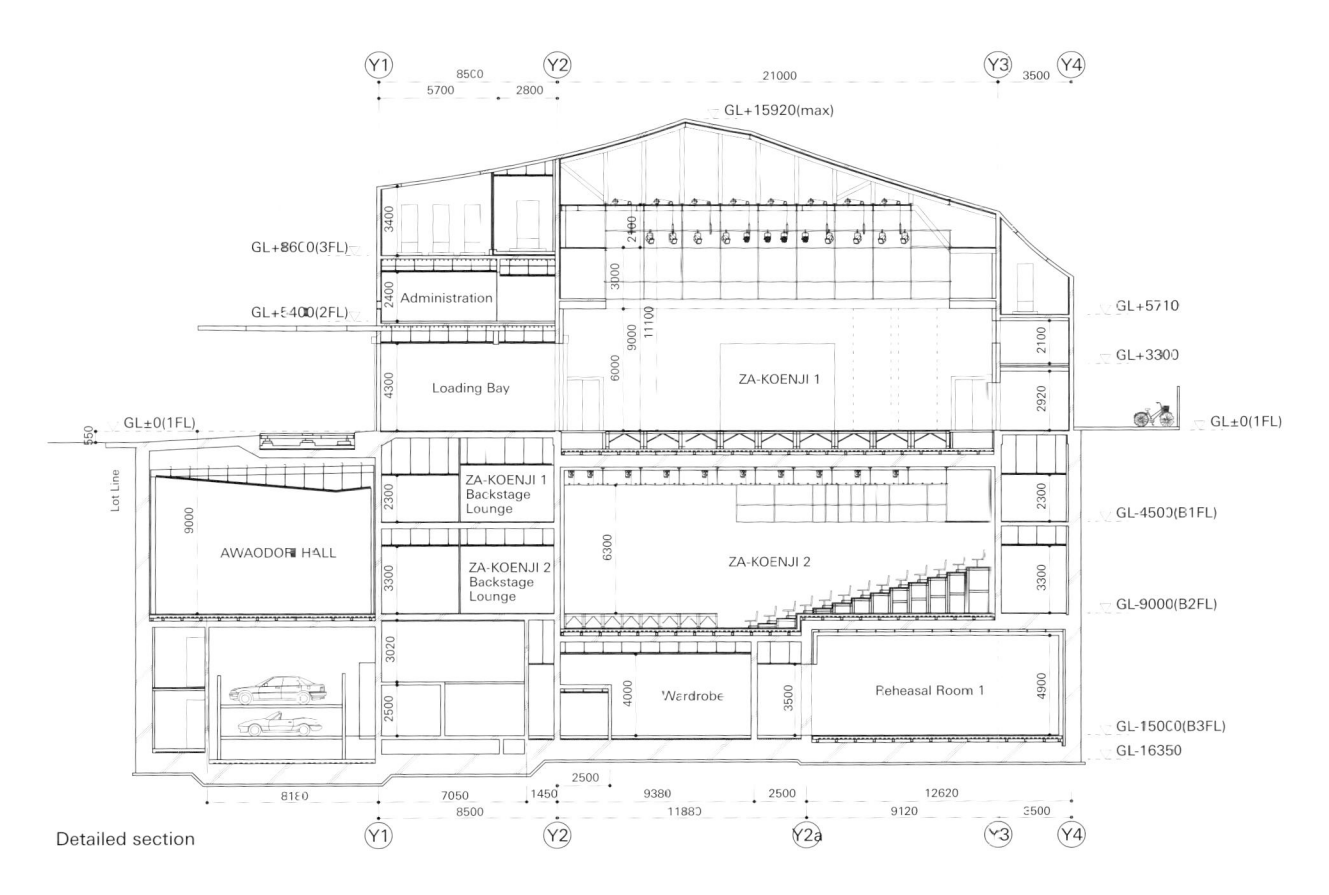

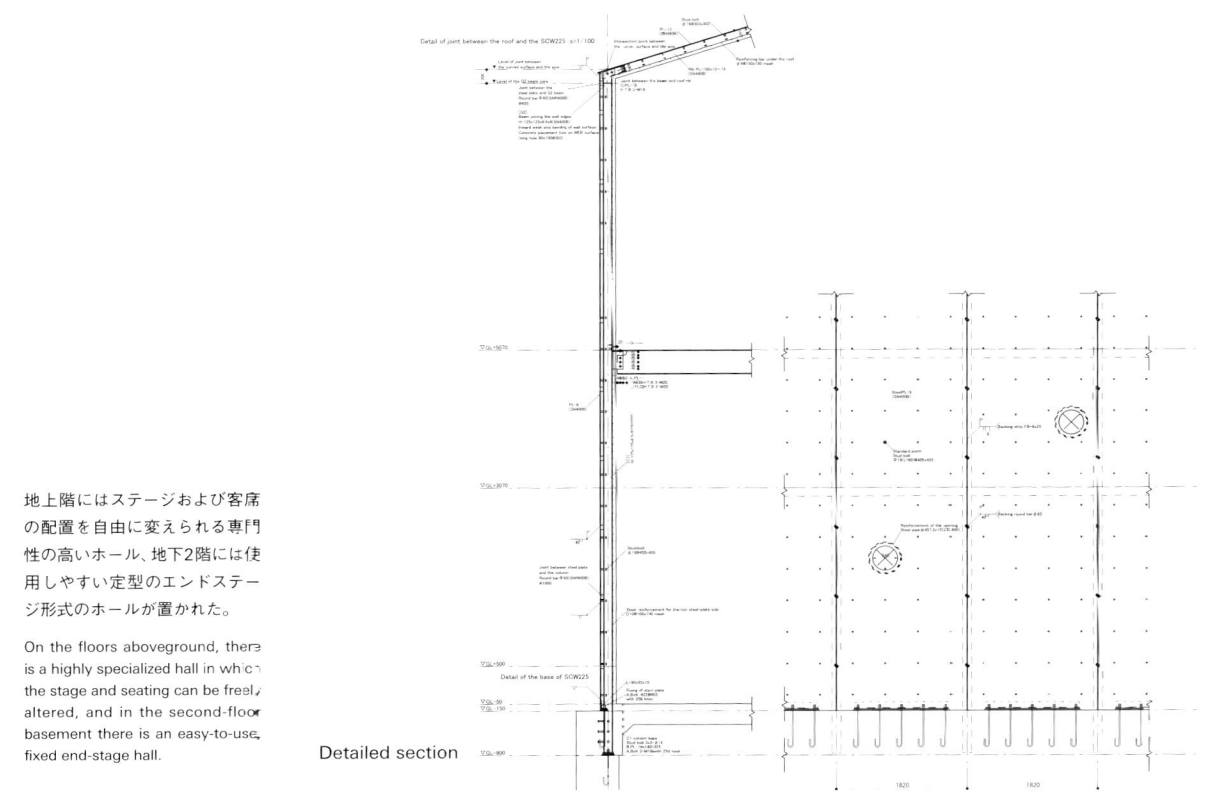

Detailed section

地上階にはステージおよび客席の配置を自由に変えられる専門性の高いホール、地下2階には使用しやすい定型のエンドステージ形式のホールが置かれた。

On the floors aboveground, there is a highly specialized hall in which the stage and seating can be freely altered, and in the second-floor basement there is an easy-to-use, fixed end-stage hall.

Detailed section

コンペティション時のフラットルーフ案
The flat-roof proposal submitted for the competition.

屋根のスタディ模型
The study models of the roof.

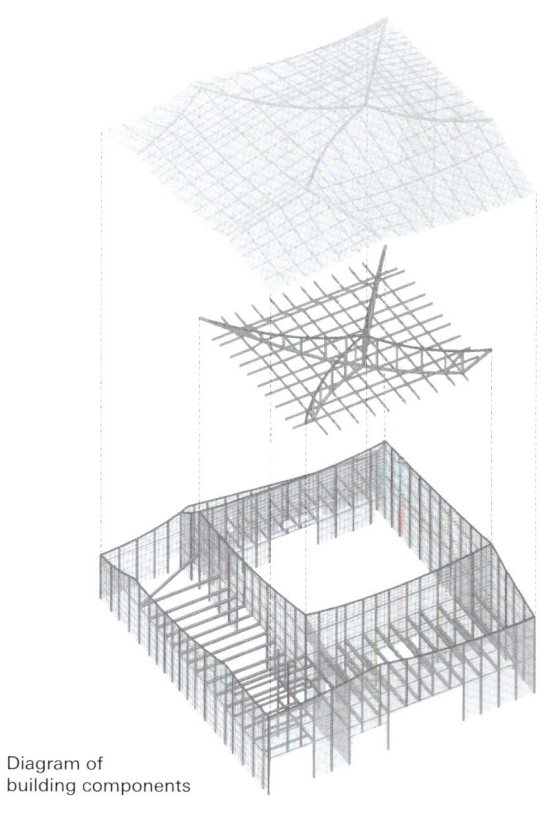

Diagram of
building components

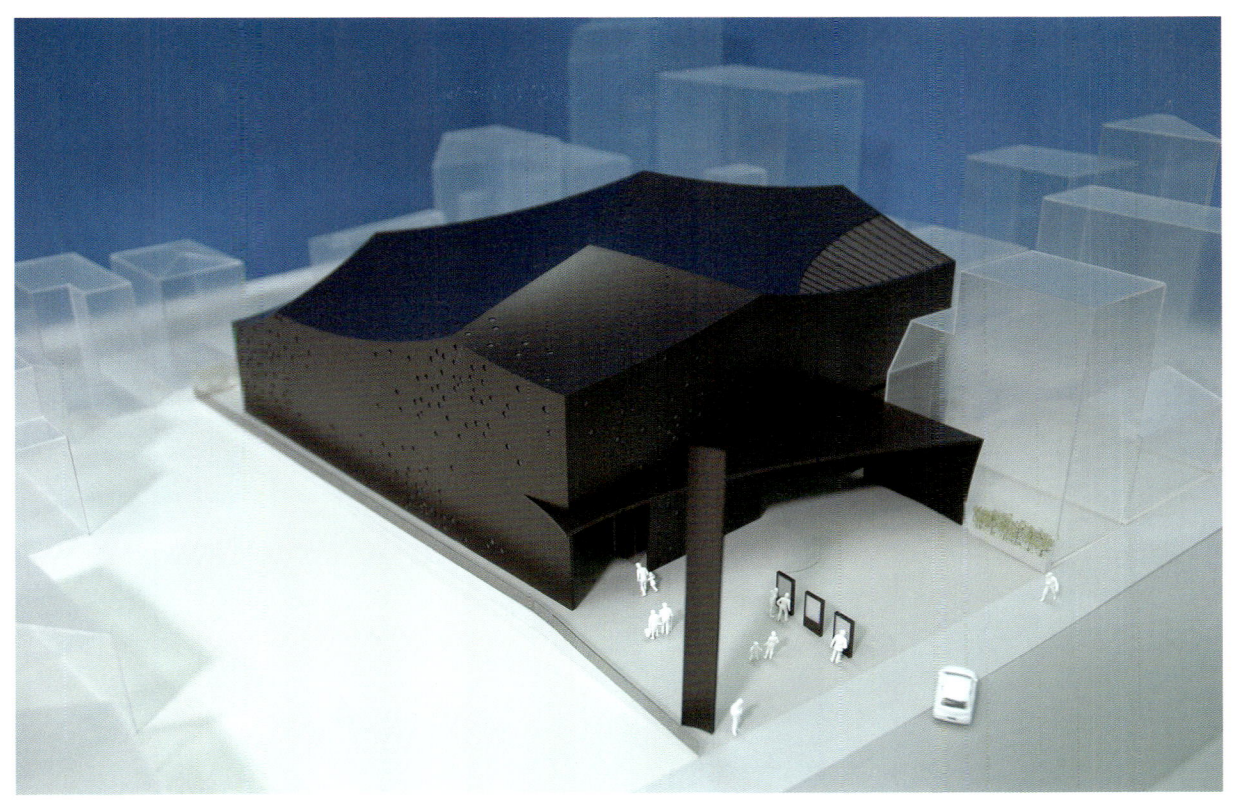

実施案
Working proposal.

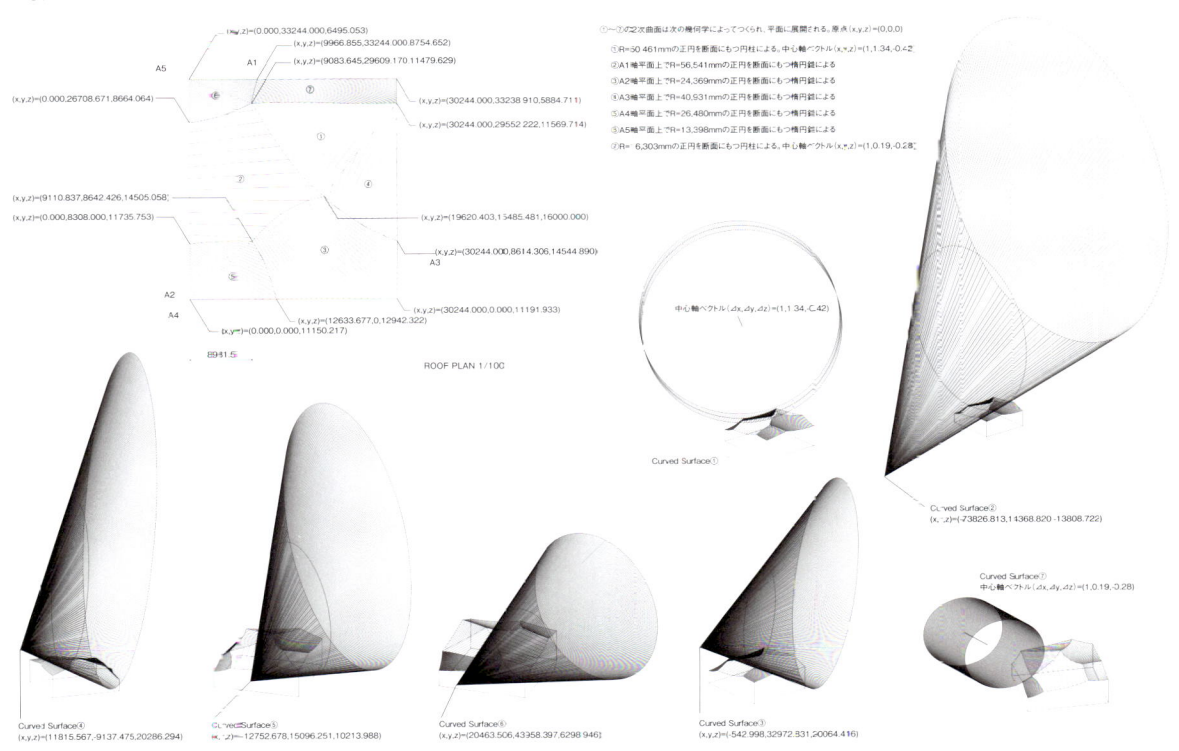

屋根のスタディ
Roof study.

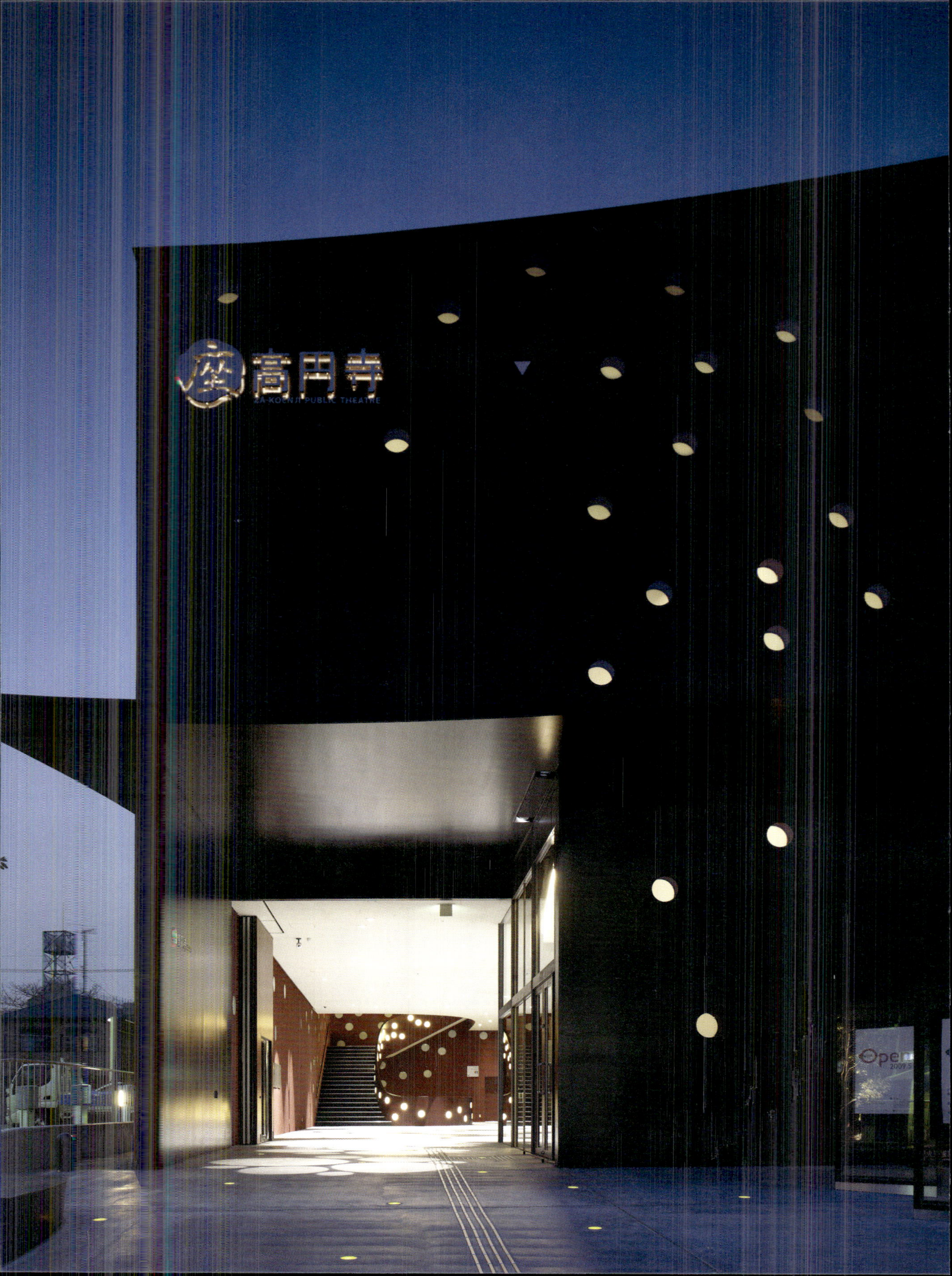

座高円寺
ZA-KOENJI PUBLIC THEATRE

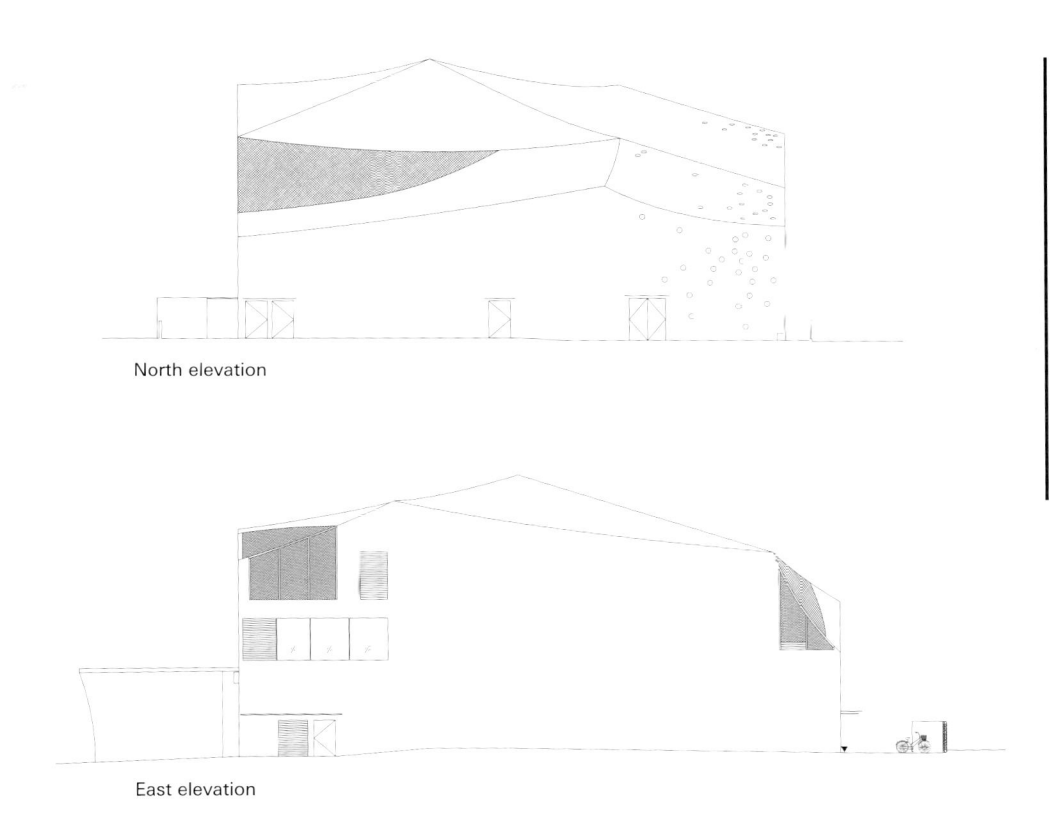

North elevation

East elevation

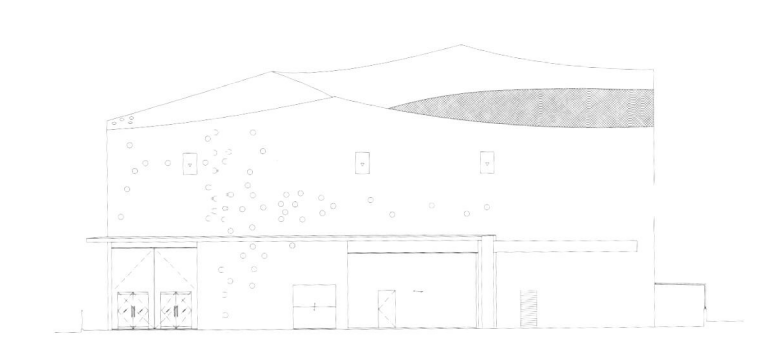

South elevation

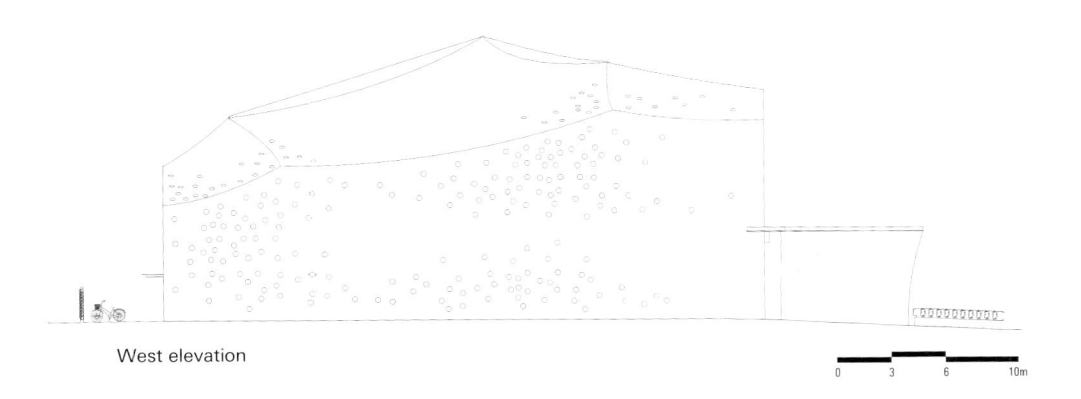

West elevation

0  3  6  10m

高円寺のパフォーミングアートの専用劇場、ふたつの250〜300席の劇場、平土間の阿波踊り練習ホール、3つのリハーサルスタジオ、カフェなどのコンプレックス。周辺環境に配慮して、全体の3分の2は地下に置かれている。

This specialty theatre for the performing arts, located in Koenji, is a complex consisting of two 250-300 seat theaters, a practice hall for Awa da cing Three rehearsal studios, and a cafe. In light of the surrounding environment, two-thirds of the building was placed underground.

東京都

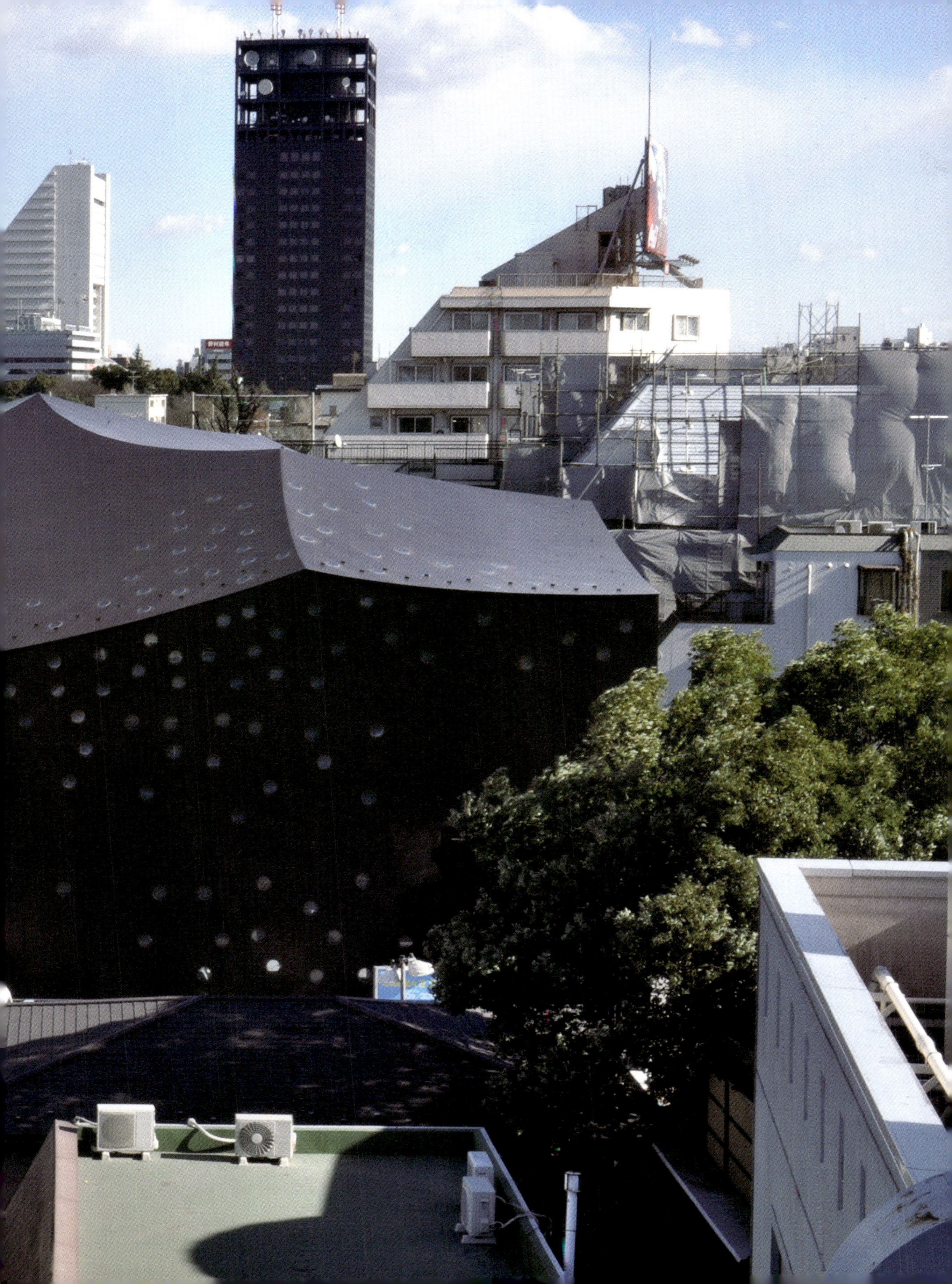

The Main Stadium for the World Games 2009 in Kaohsiung
2009高雄ワールドゲームズメインスタジアム

2009 台湾 高雄　Kaohsiung, Taiwan

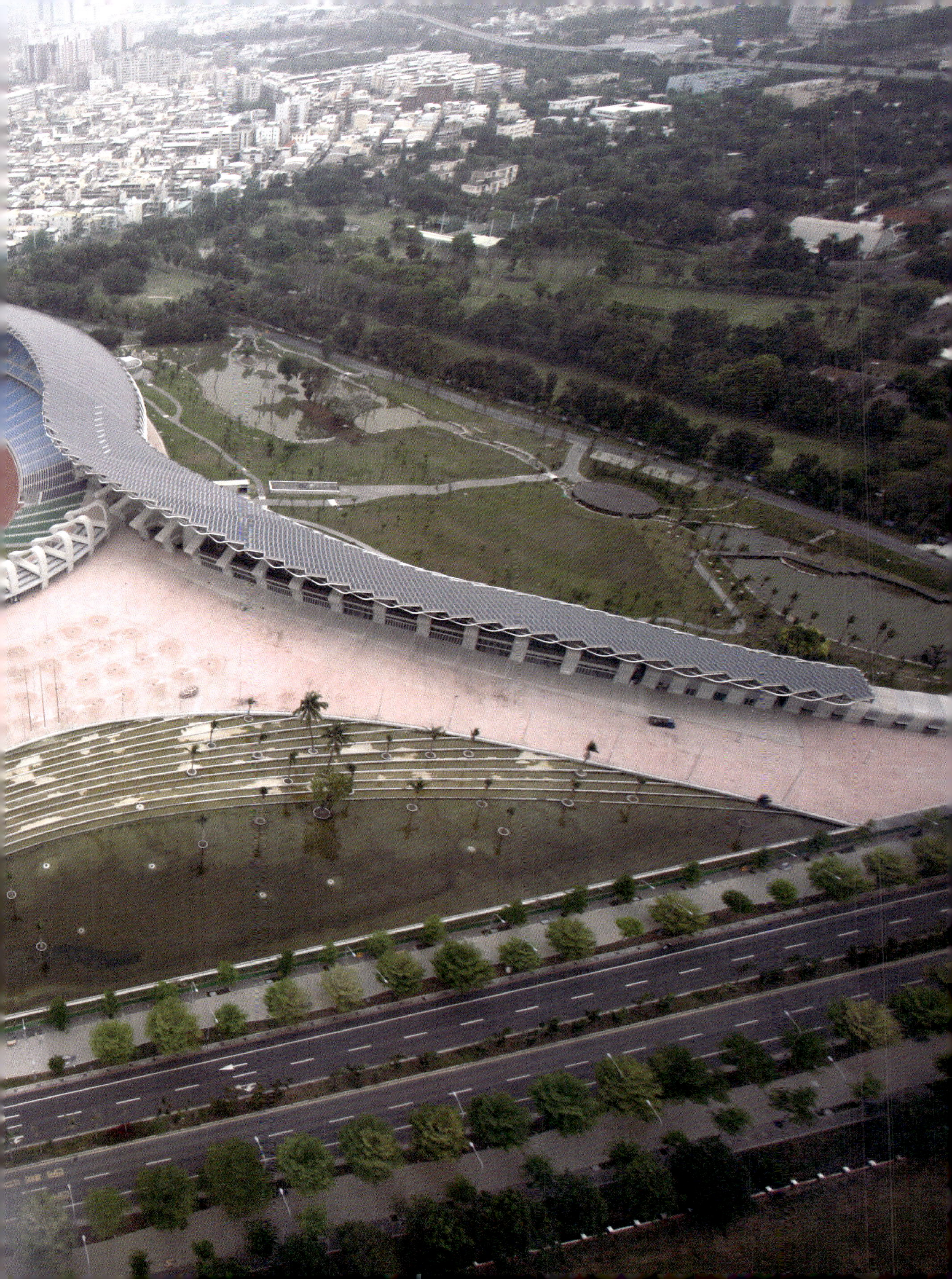

南側メインエントランスに向かって開かれたスタジアム
The open stadium as seen from the main entrance on the south side.

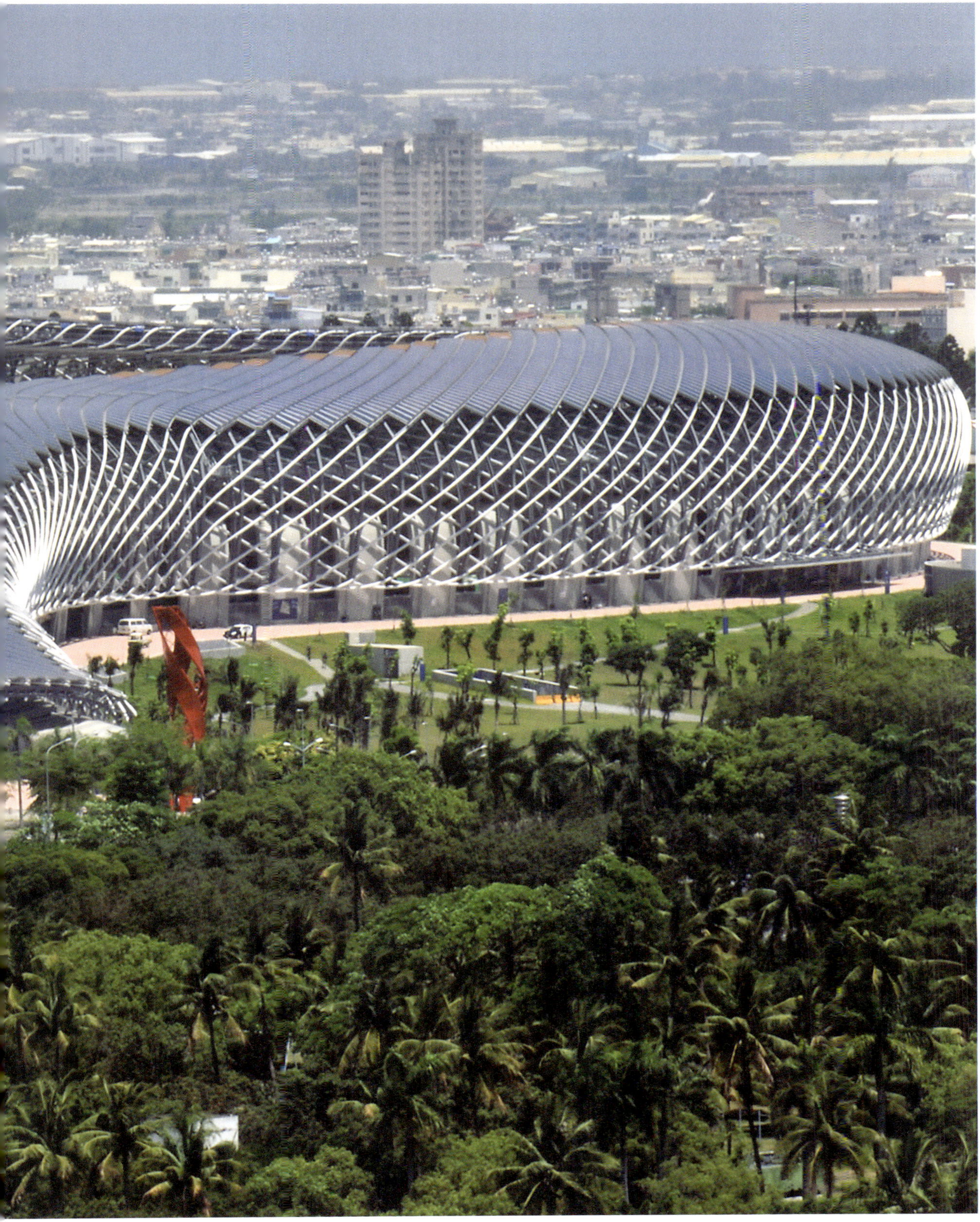

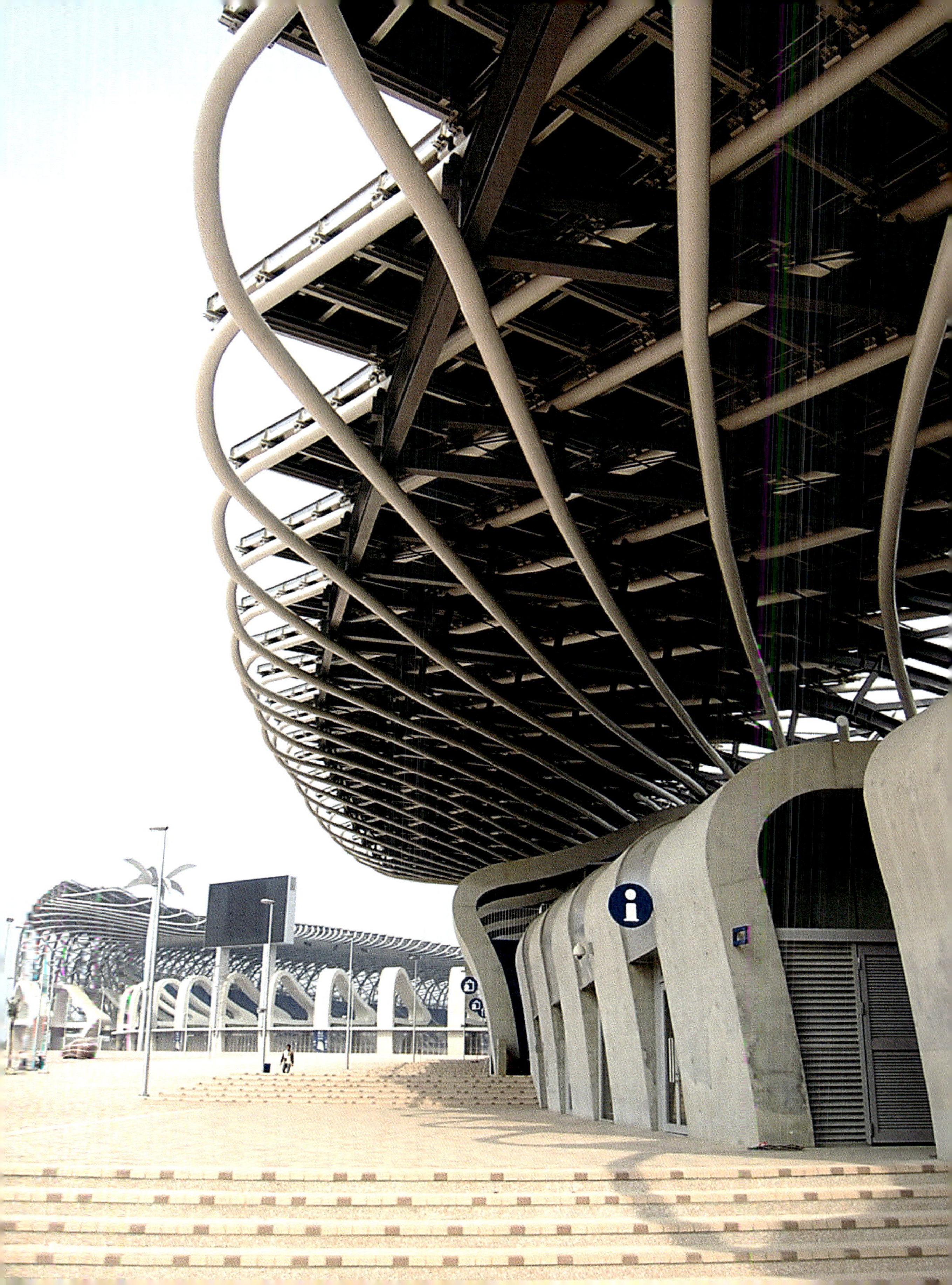

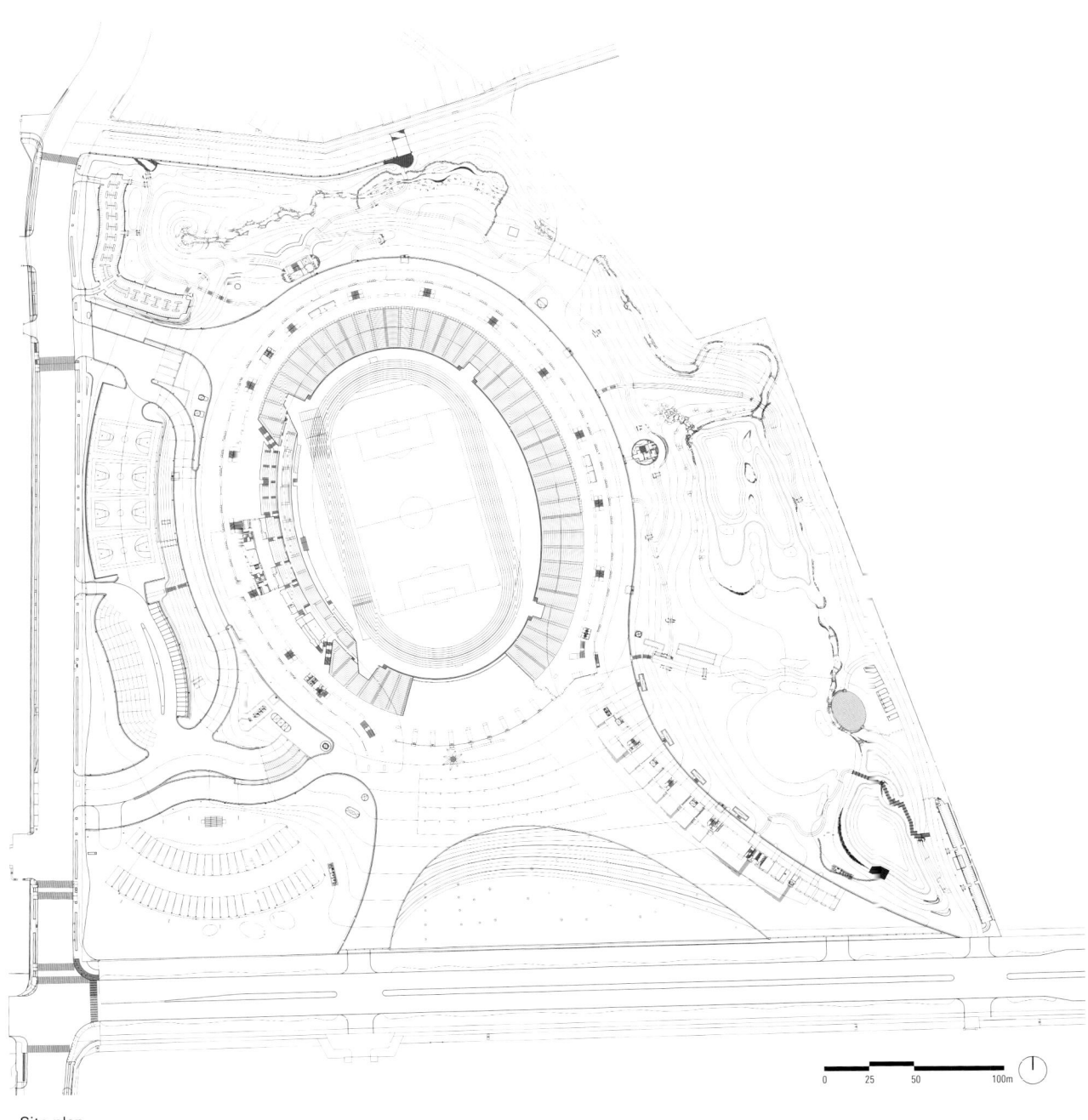

Site plan

台湾第2の都市である高雄市に2009年のワールドゲームズメイン会場として計画された4万人収容のスタジアム。メインゲート側を外部に開くことによって、日常的にエントランス前広場とフィールドを一体利用することが可能。

This stadium, with a capacity of 40,000 people, was designed as the main venue for 2009 World Games in Kaohsiung, Taiwan's second largest city. By opening the side of the main gate, the plaza in front of the entrance and the field can be used together everyday.

メインゲート側から見たスタジアム内部
The stadium interior as seen from the main gate.

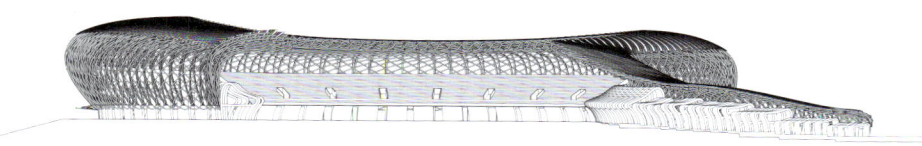

South elevation

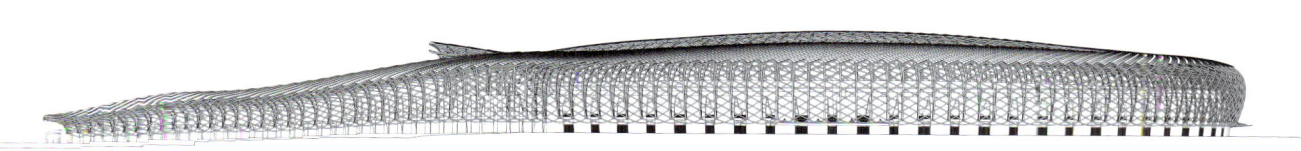

East elevation

東側のビオトープ越しにスタジアムを見る
View of the stadium beyond the biotope on the east side.

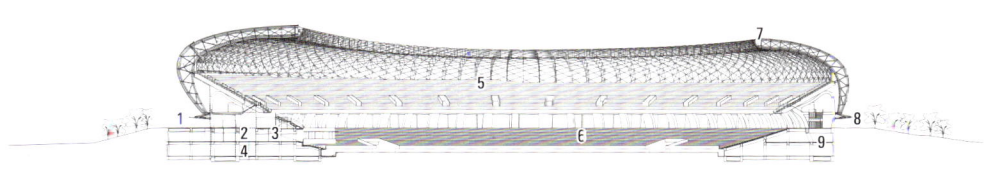

East-west Cross section

South-north Cross section

1 west entrance
2 VIP lobby
3 VIP room
4 athletes lobby
5 upper stand
6 lower stand
7 maintenance route
8 east entrance
9 car parking
10 LED display
11 lawn seats
12 north entrance

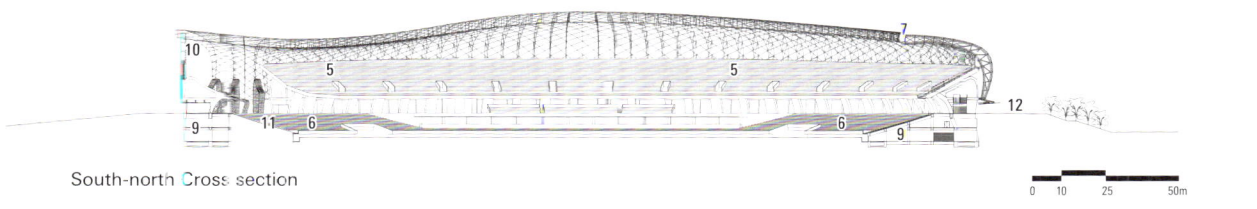

177

(上) モックアップ
(下) スタンドはサドルと呼ばれるPCユニットとスチールのトラスを組み合わせてつくられる
(Above) Mock up
(Below) The stands are made of a precast concrete unit called a "saddle" and a steel truss.

2F Concourse

FL +5

West Entrance (Main Stand Side)

1F Concourse

5500

1FL ±0

4700

B1FL -4700

9800

Car Parking Space (for VIPs and Staff)

Entra

5100

Car Parking Space (for Athletes and Staff)

Rest roo

B2FL -9800

1200

FL -11000

Rainwater St

Detailed section

6500　7400　8600

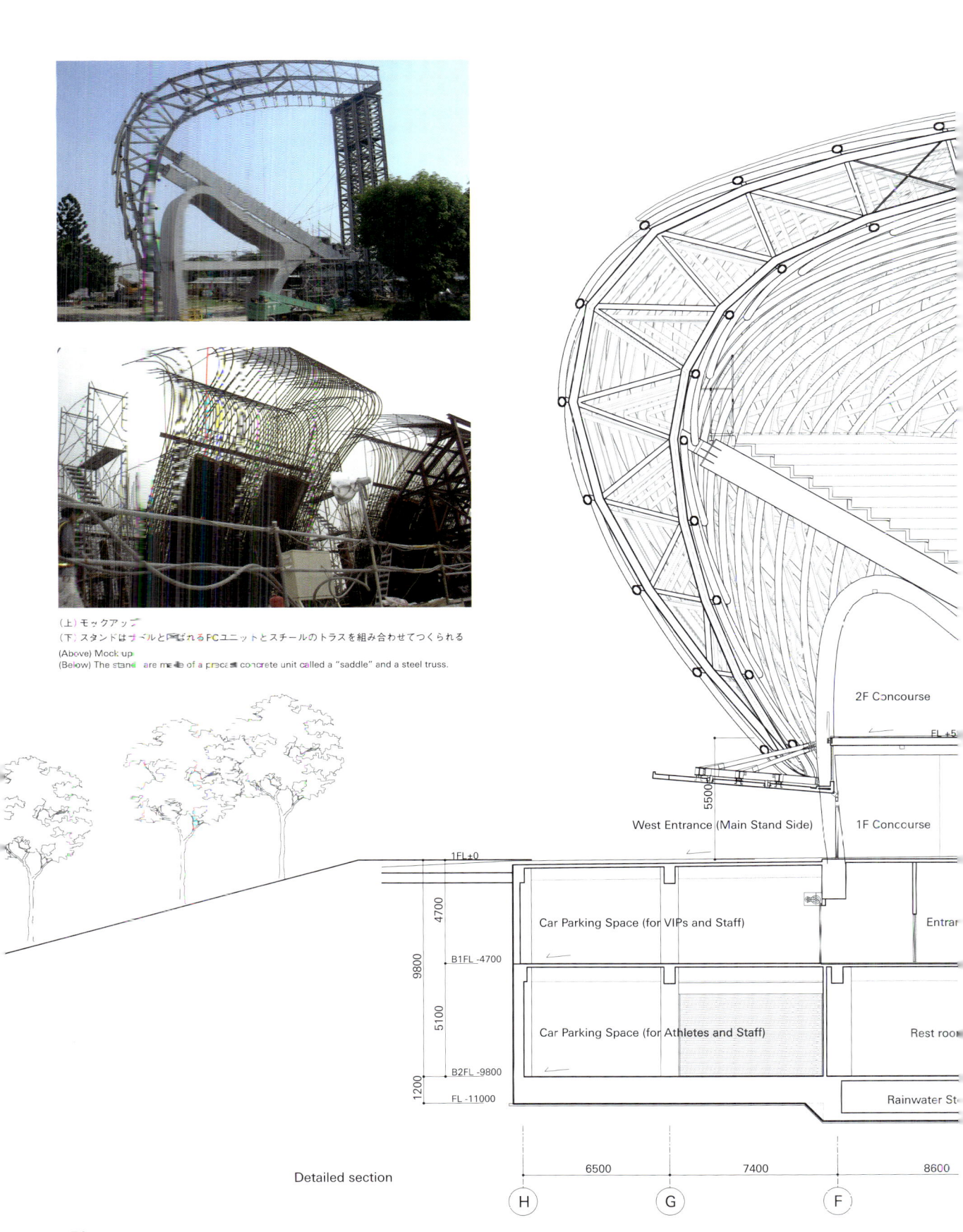

H　G　F

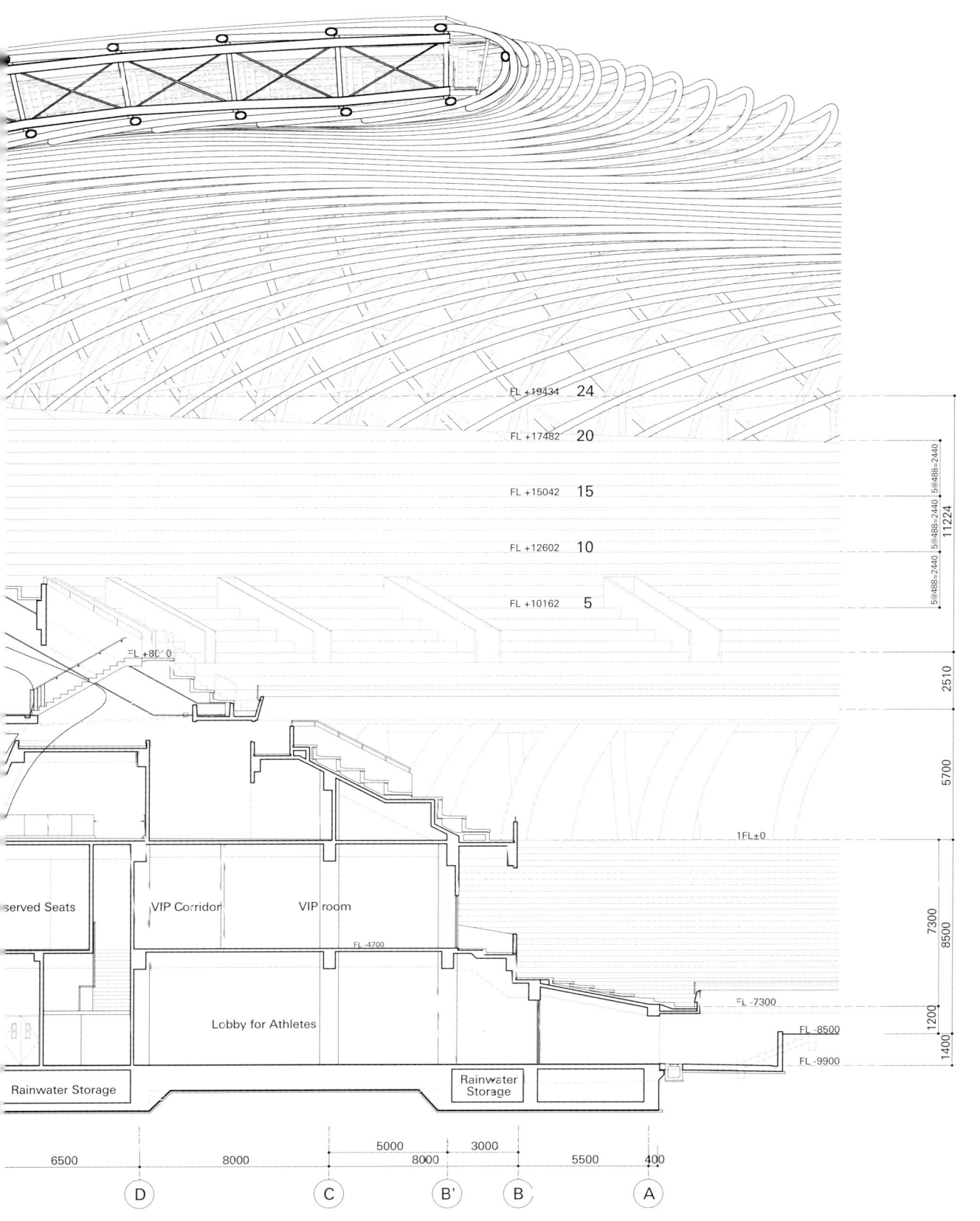

| | | |
|---|---|---|
| FL +19434 | 24 | |
| FL +17482 | 20 | |
| FL +15042 | 15 | |
| FL +12602 | 10 | |
| FL +10162 | 5 | |

FL +8010

1FL±0

FL -4700

Reserved Seats | VIP Corridor | VIP room

Lobby for Athletes

FL -7300
FL -8500
FL -9900

Rainwater Storage

Rainwater Storage

D — C — B' — B — A

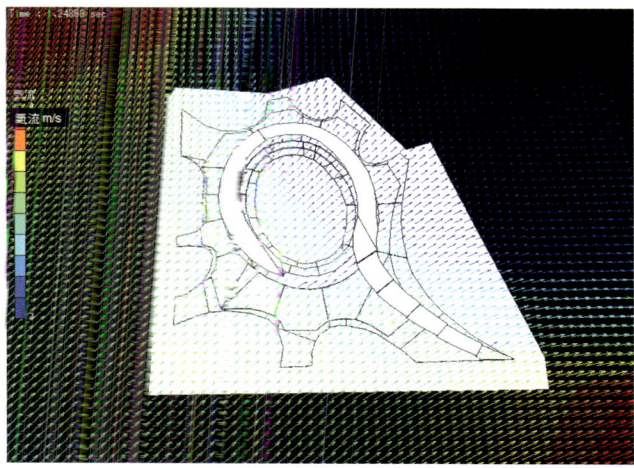

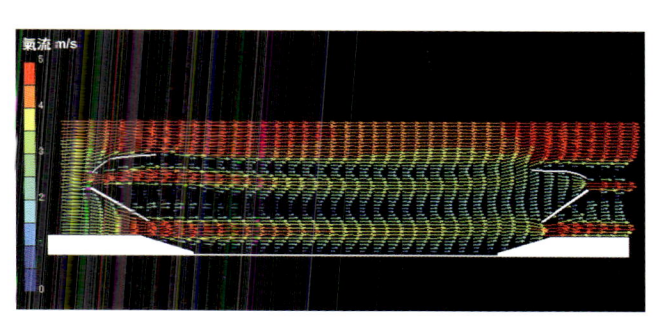

風のシミュレーション。フィールドを掘り下げることによって風を防ぎ、スタンドには心地良い風が流れるようデザインされた。

Wind simulation: Digging down into the field helped protect against the wind and create comfortable breeze in the stands.

約8,800枚のソーラーパネルがスタンドの遮光も兼ねる
The approximately 8,800 solar panels also create shade in the stands.

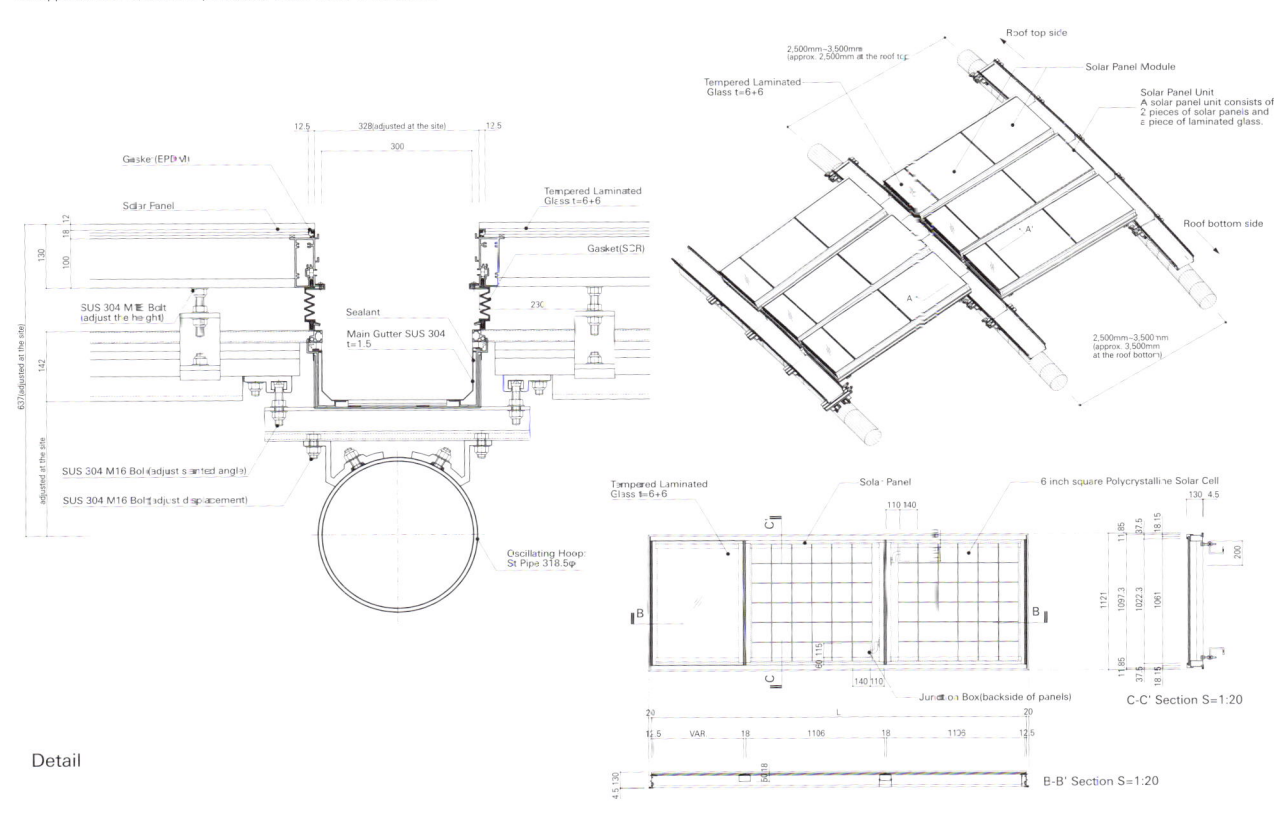

Detail

181

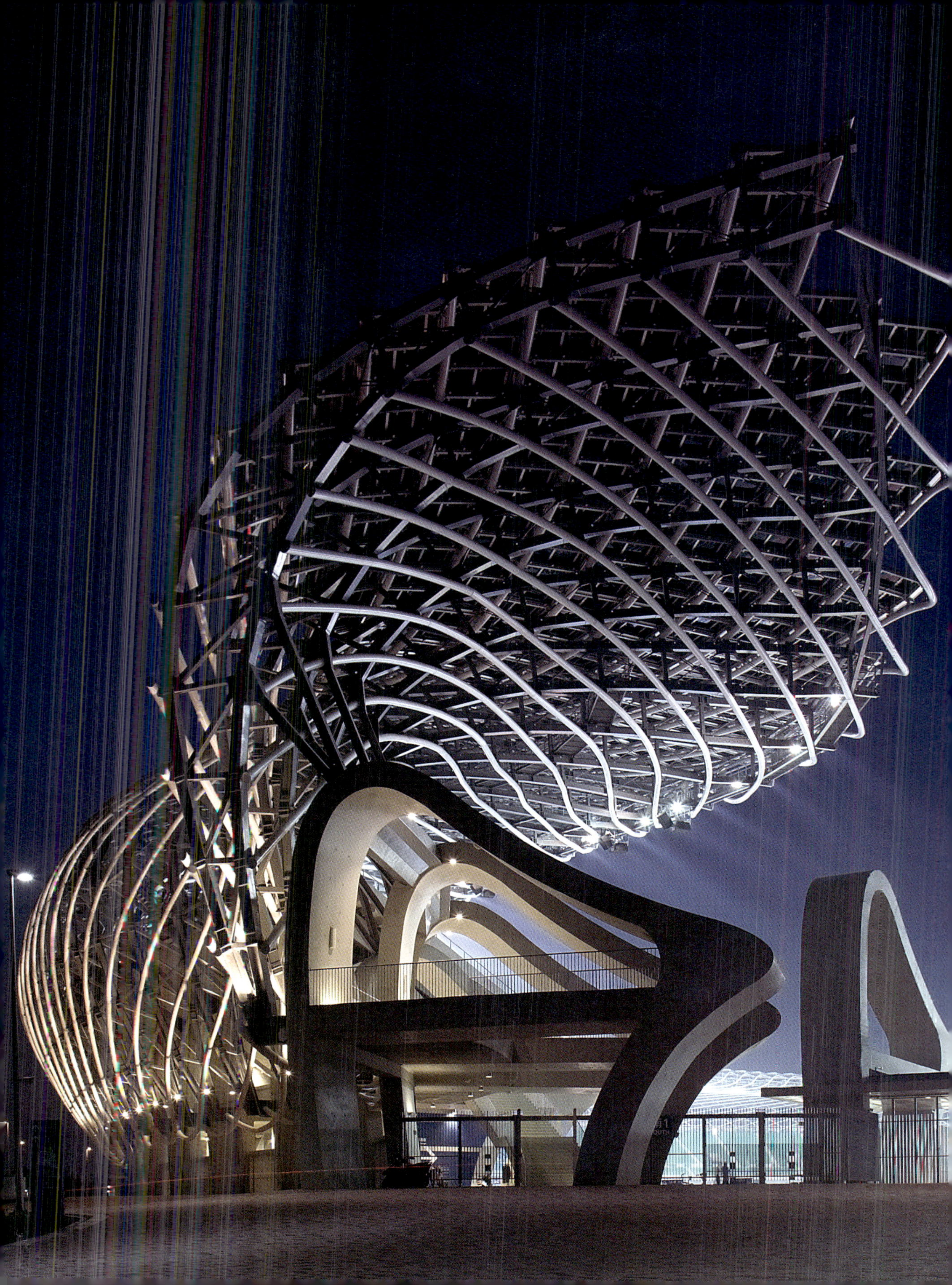

（上）夜景　（下）ワールドゲームズのオープニング
(Above) Night view.　(Below) Opening ceremony at the World Games.

183

TORRES PORTA FIRA /
Extension for the Fair of Barcelona Gran Via Venue
トーレス・ポルタ・フィラ／
バルセロナ見本市・グランビア会場拡張計画

2010／2003- スペイン、バルセロナ　Barcelona, Spain

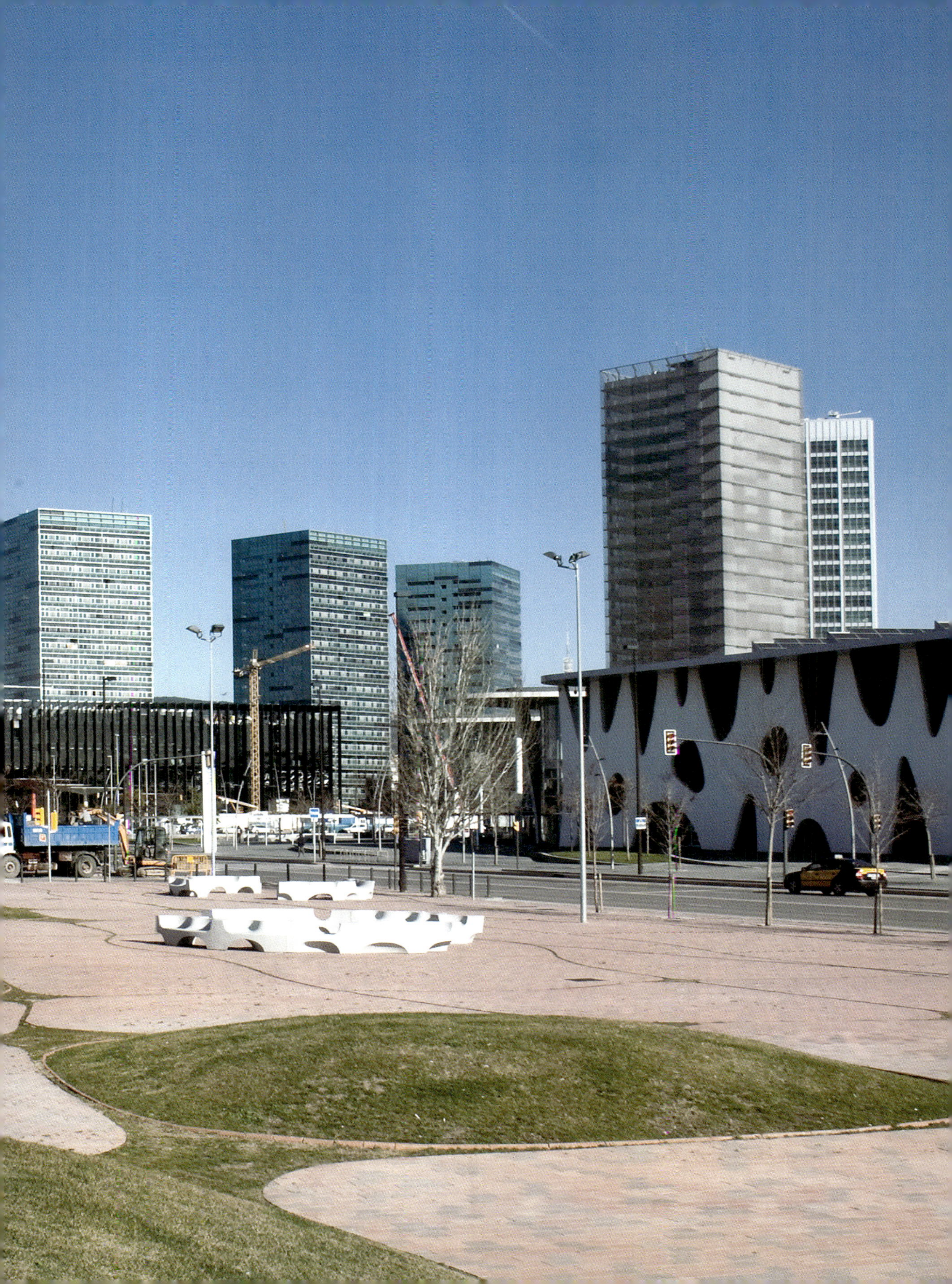

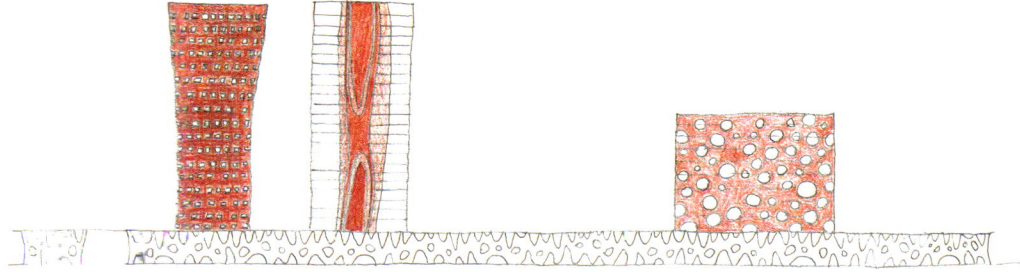

コンセプトスケッチ
Concept sketch.

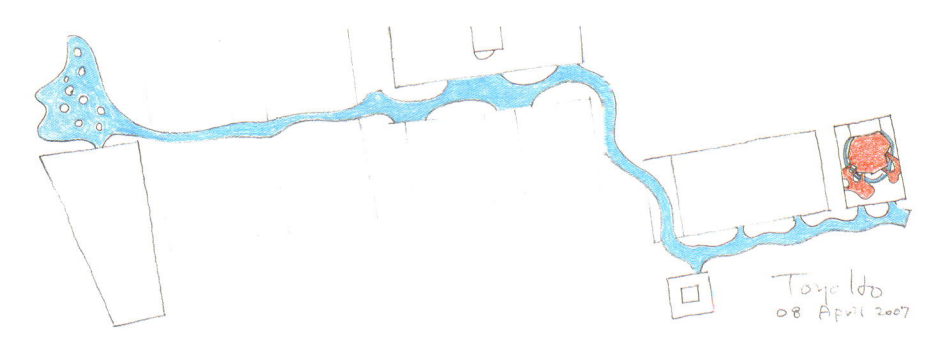

空港と市街の中間にあるバルセロナ見本市会場の拡張計画。既存展示場の間に4つの展示場、エントランスホール、それらを結ぶプロムナード、オフィス+ホテルのツインタワーが新たにデザインされた。

This was an expansion plan for a trade fair site, located between the city of Barcelona and the airport. Between the preexisting showroom venues, four exhibition halls, an entrance hall, and a promenade to link them were newly designed along with twin towers housing offices and a hotel.

オフィス(右)＋ホテル(左)のツインタワー
The tower on the right houses offices, and the left one a hotel.

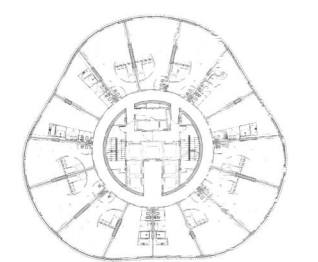

Hotel 23F plan

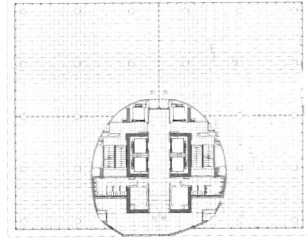

Office 14F-22F plan

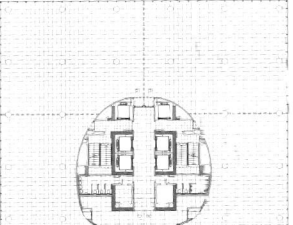

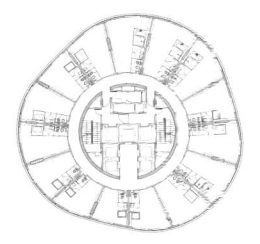

ホテルの平面形がオフィスのコア
部分とほぼ相似形になる。

The plan of the hotel has an almost similar shape of the core as the office.

Hotel 18F plan

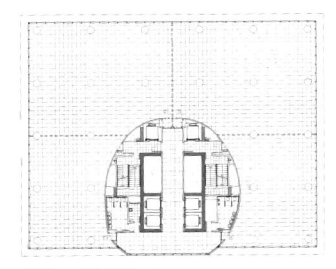

Office 1F-11F plan

1　entrance hall
2　reception desk
3　bar area
4　restaurant
5　lounge area
6　banquet hall
7　retail space

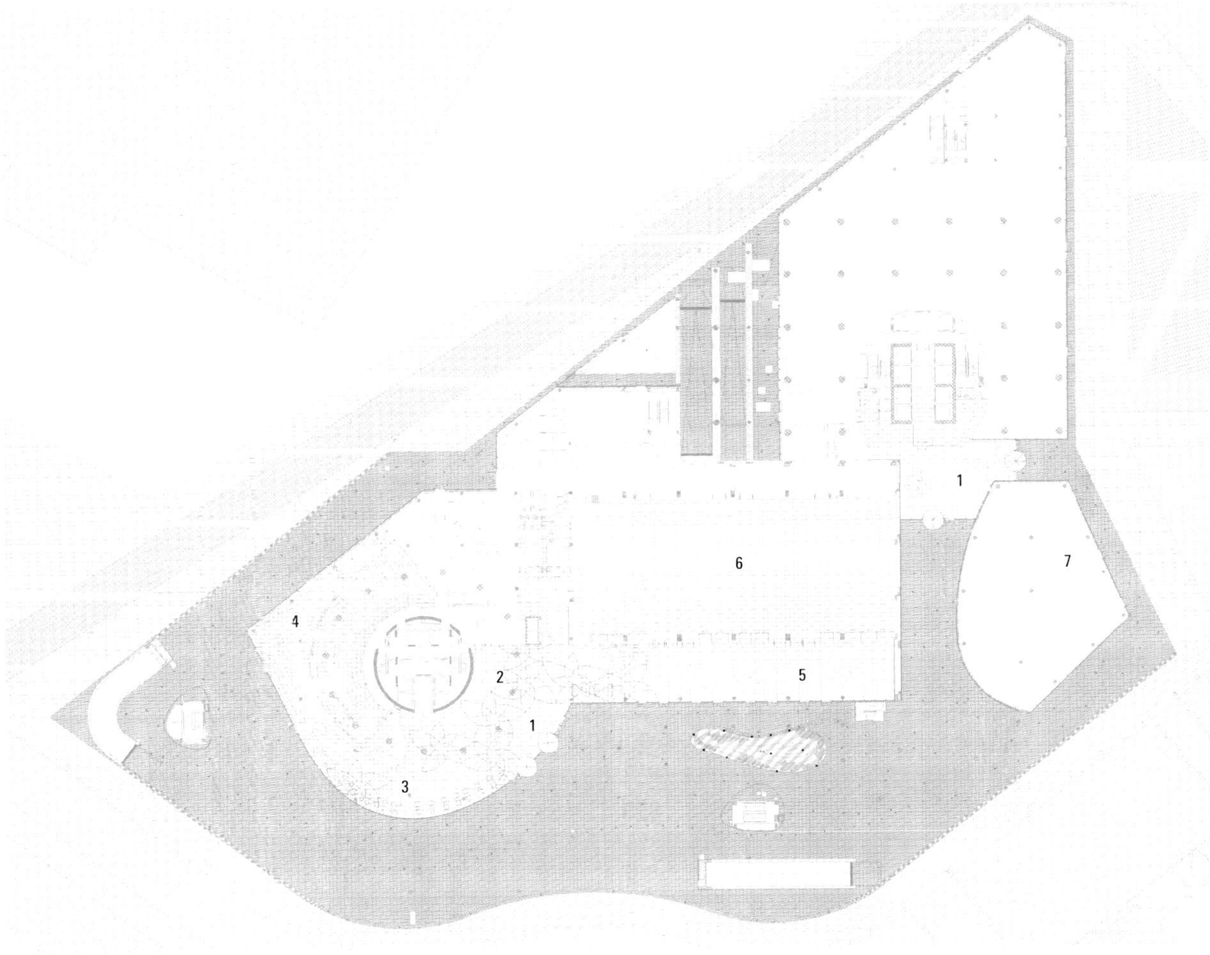

Site plan

0　5　10　20m

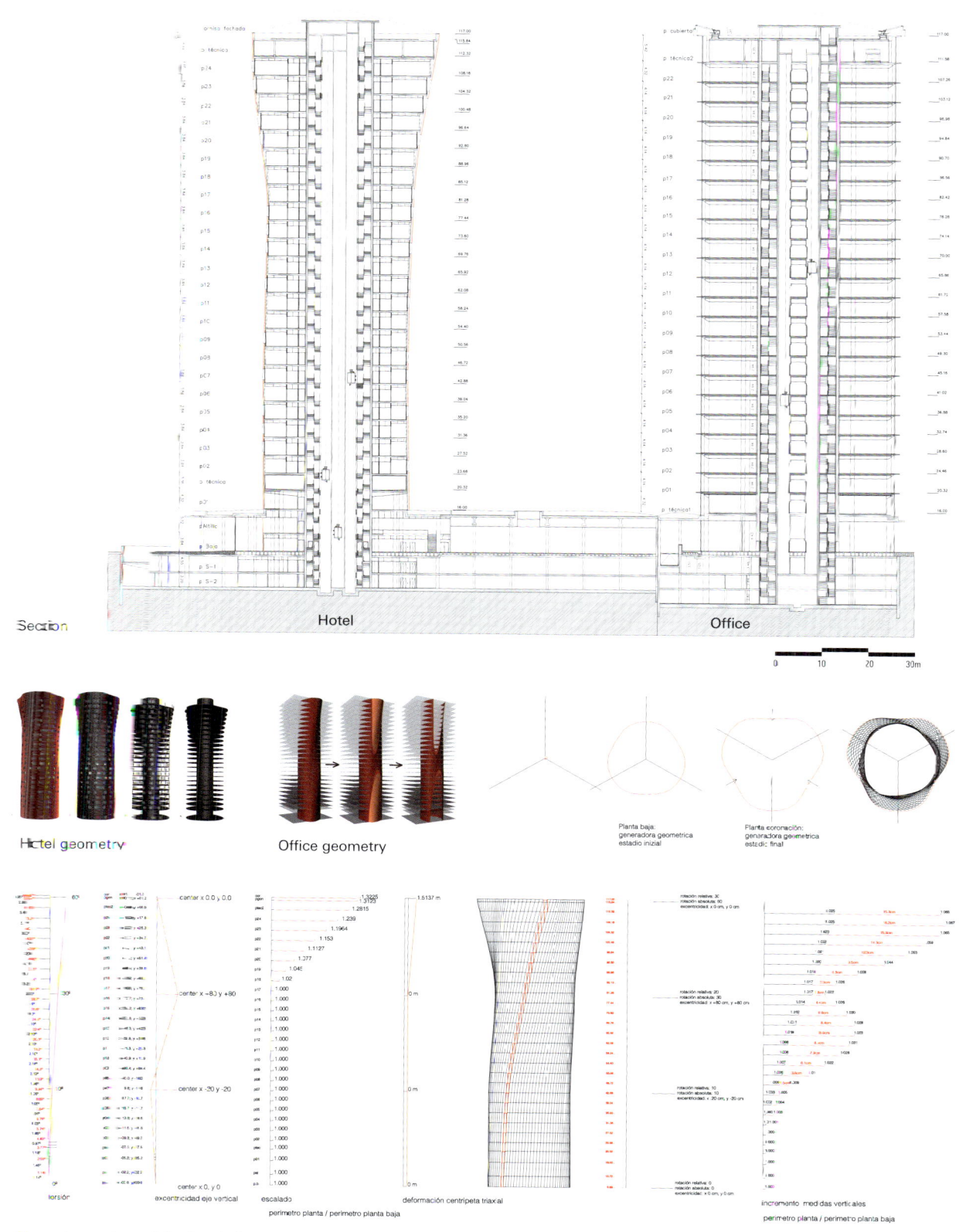

Section | Hotel | Office

0  10  20  30m

Hotel geometry

Office geometry

Planta baja:
generadora geometrica
estadio inicial

Planta coronación:
generadora geometrica
estadio final

Computer analysis of the facade line

（上）ホテル棟エントランスロビー
（左下）ホテル棟レストラン
（右下）ホテル棟バンケットホール
(Above) The entrance lobby in the hotel.
(Below left) The restaurant in the hotel.
(Below right) The banquet hall in the hotel.

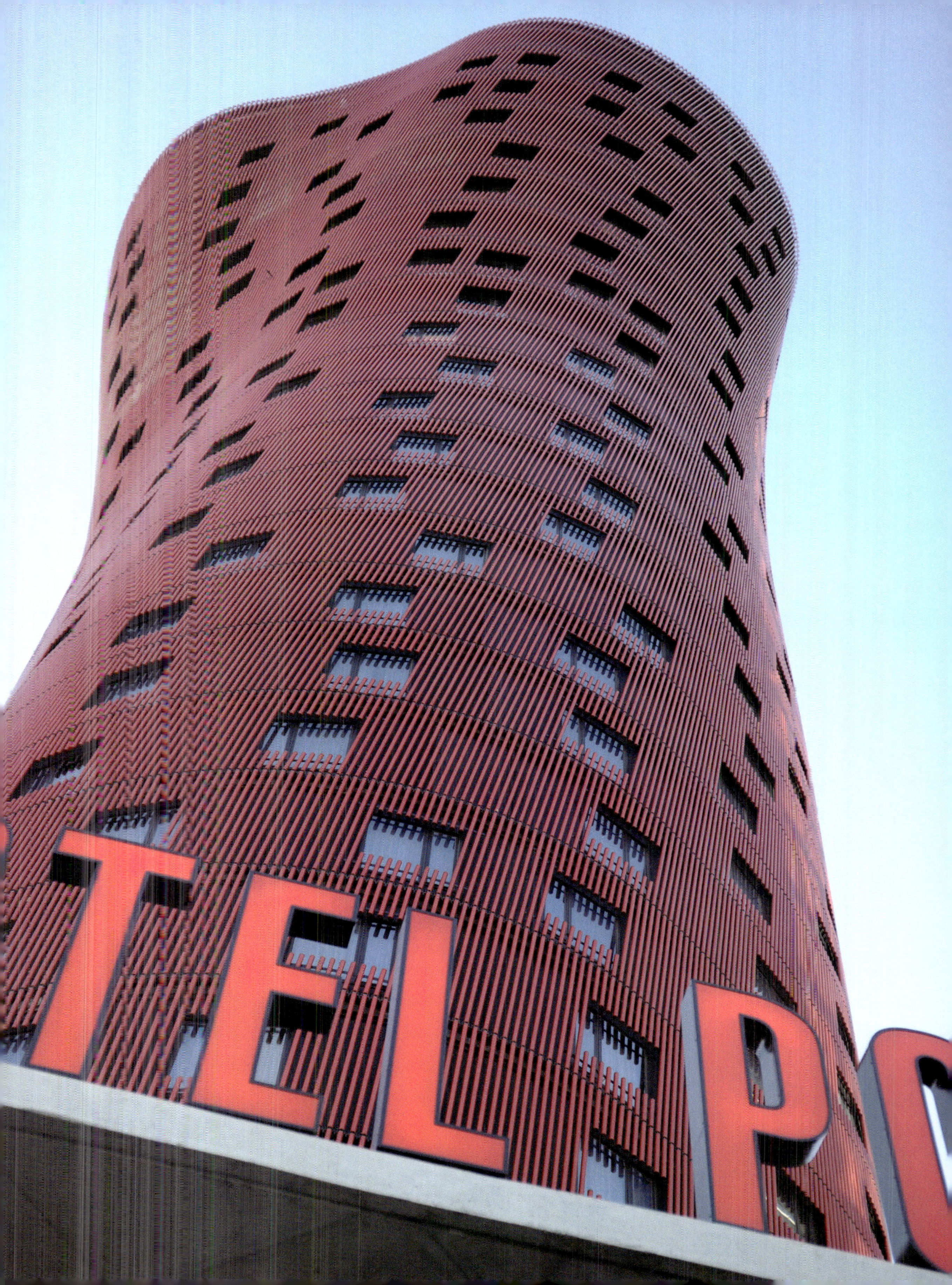
TEL PC

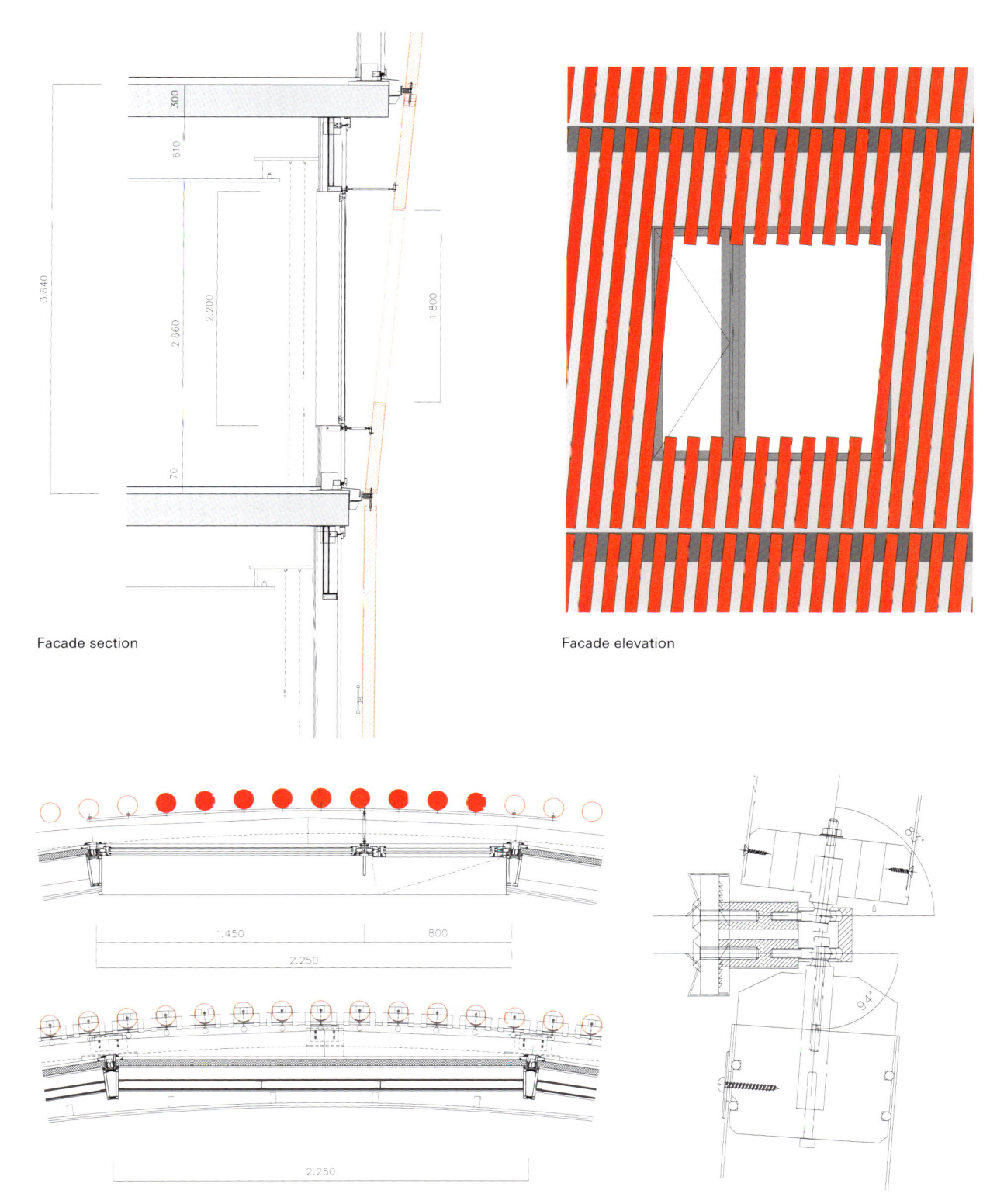

Facade section

Facade elevation

Facade details

(左頁) コンクリート壁の表面にスチールパイプをまわらせスパイラル状の形態を浮き上がらせる
(Left page) The spiral forms emerging by placing steel pipes around the concrete wall.

193

噴水の広場越しに見る
The entrance hall seen from across the fountain plaza.

Elevation

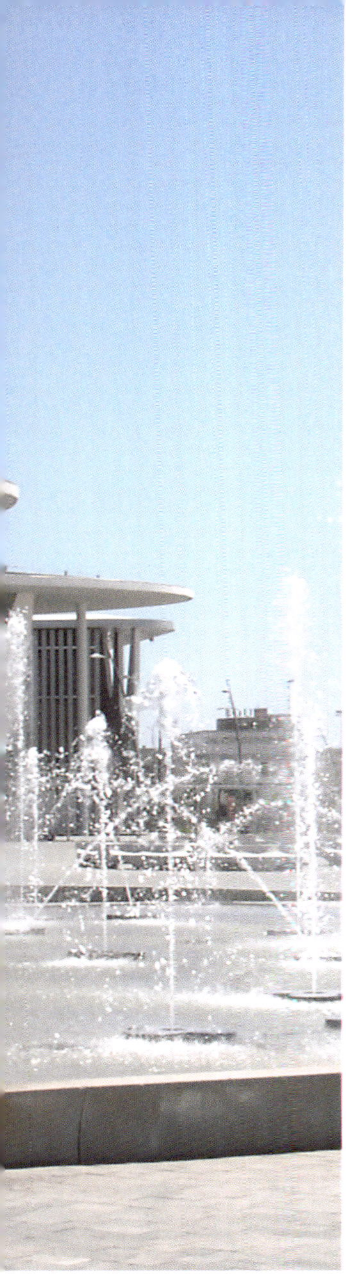

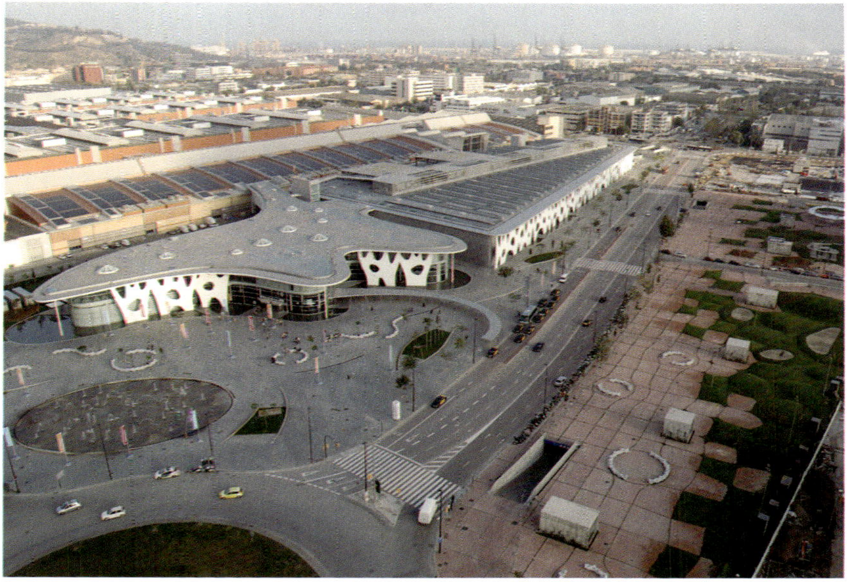

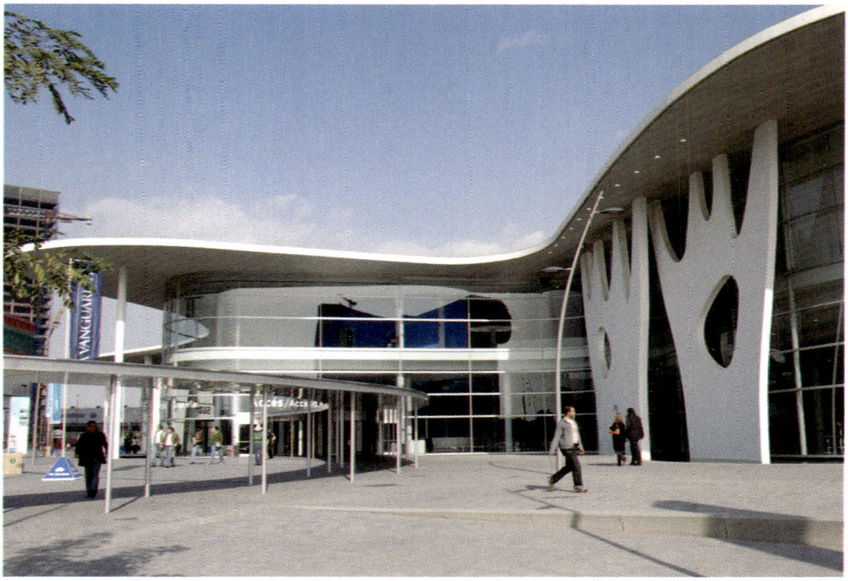

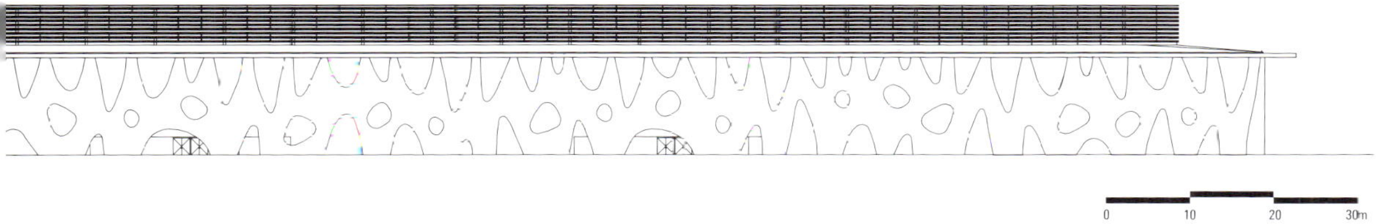
0
10
20
30m

セントラル・アクシス 展示場を貫通しながらつなぐ地上＋7mにつくられたプロムナード
The seven meter promenade penetrates and links the central axis and exhibition halls.

Plan+14.0m

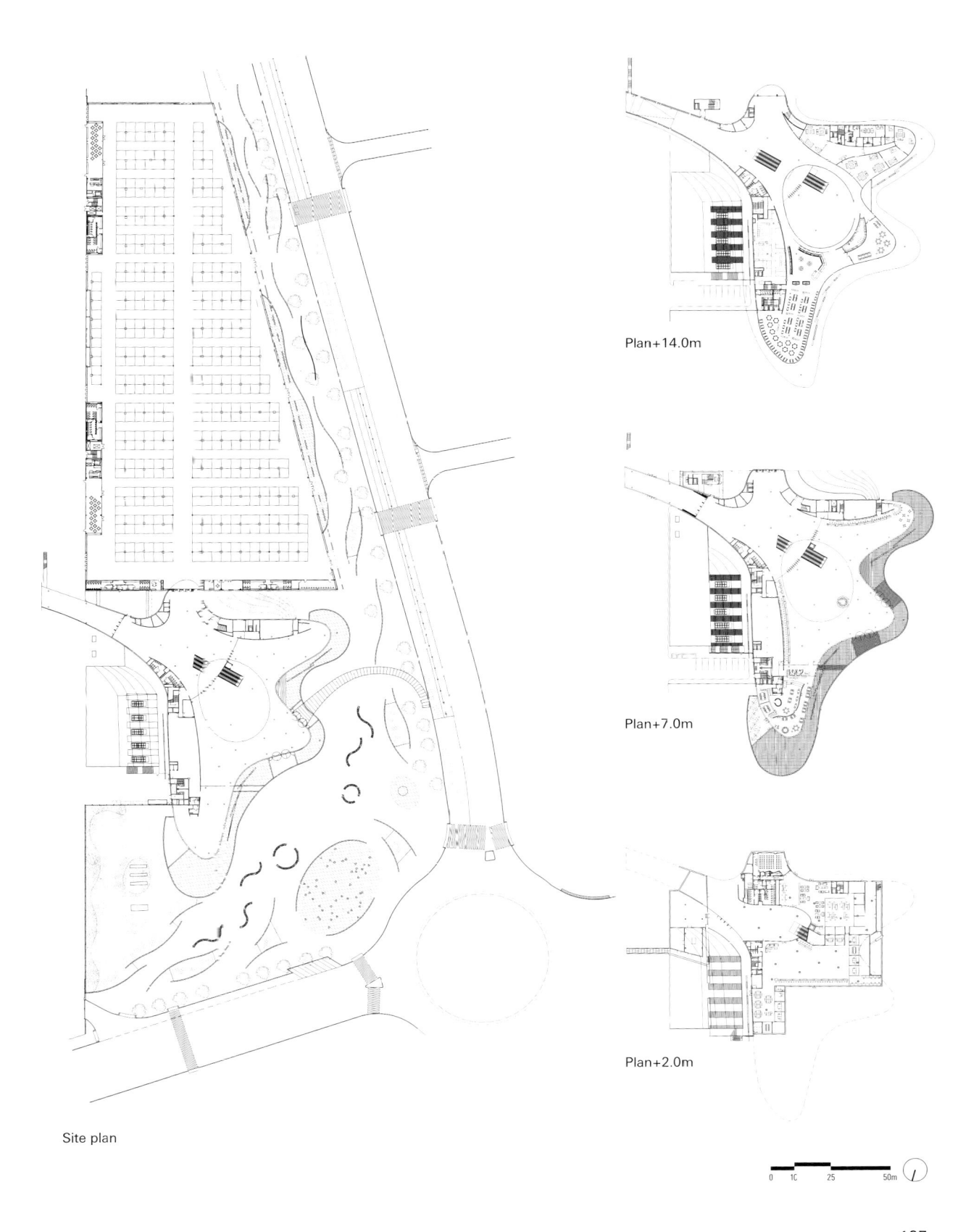

Plan+7.0m

Plan+2.0m

Site plan

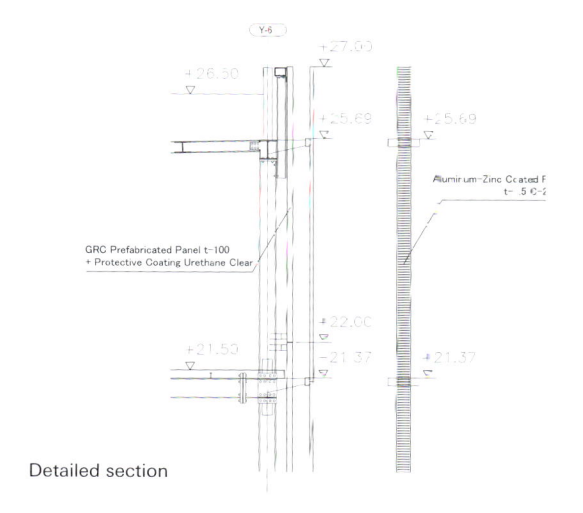

Detailed section

新築部分の延床面積25万m²に及ぶ拡張計画。複数の展示棟などを、広場やプロムナードによって有機的に結ぶ流動性の高い都市的空間を目指した。

This expansion plan created a total floor space of 250,000 square meters in the newly built section. The aim was to realize a highly fluid urban space in which several display wings were organically connected with a plaza and promenade.

セントラルアクシス
The central axis

施工中のファサード
The facade under construction.

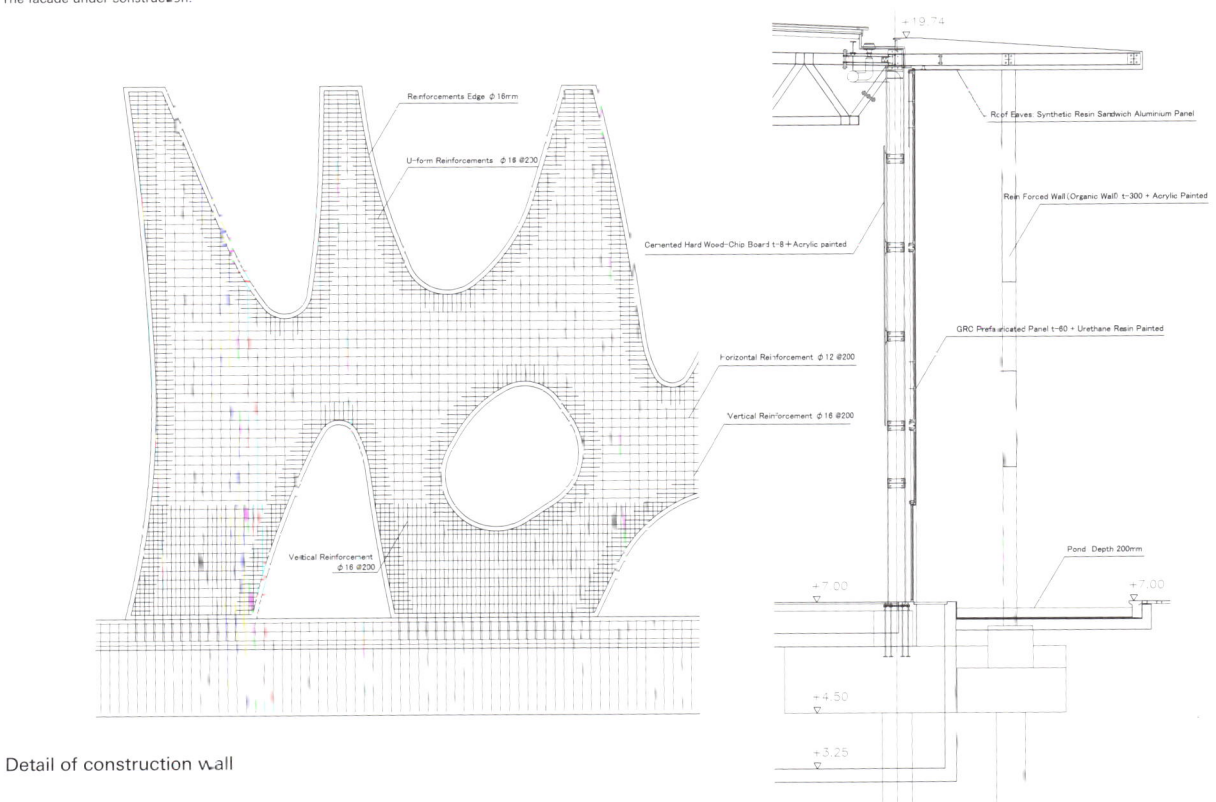

Detail of construction wall

Toyo Ito Museum of Architecture, Imabari
今治市伊東豊雄建築ミュージアム

2011 愛媛県今治市 Imabari, Ehime

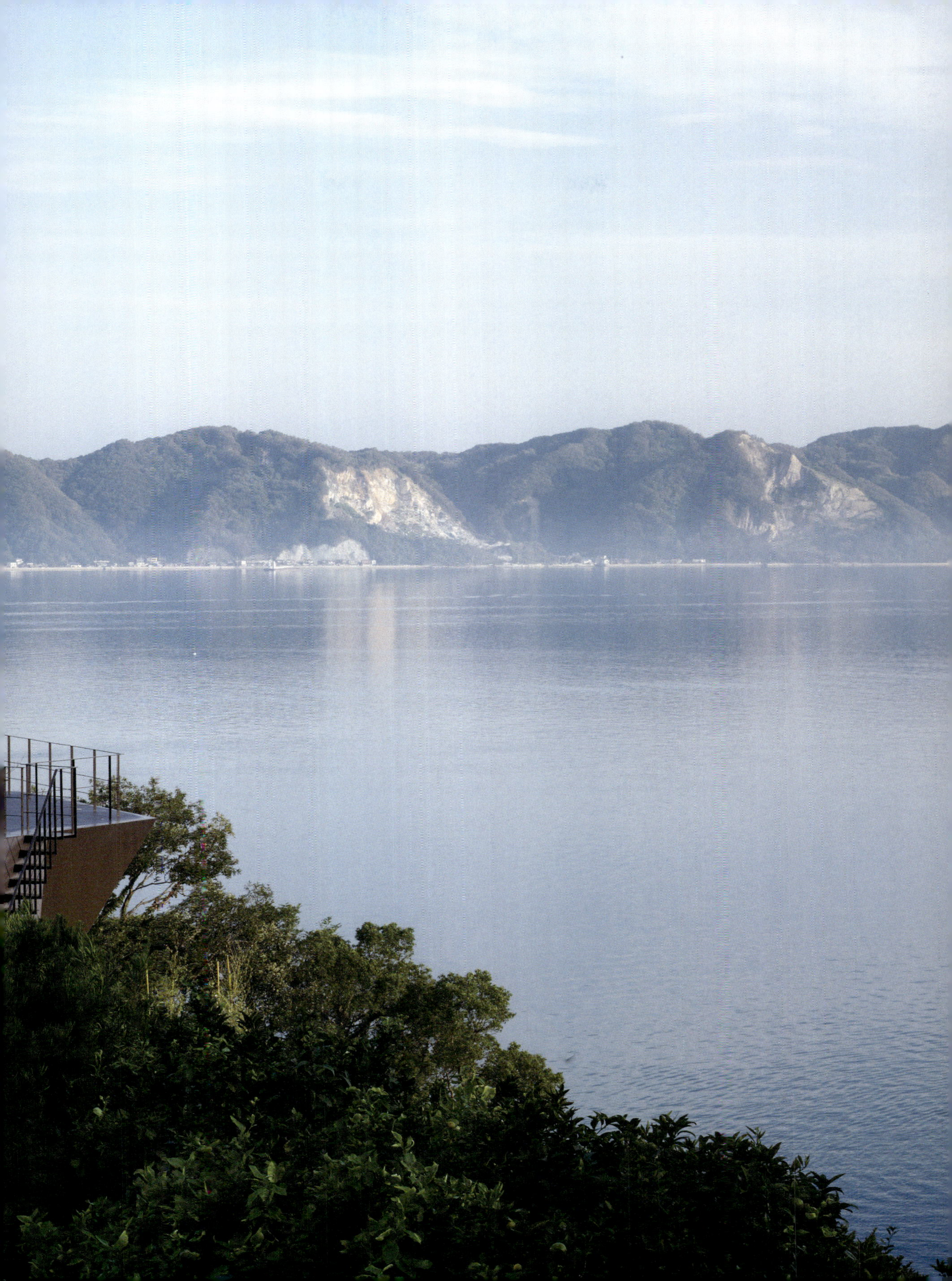

「シルバーハット」側から「スチールハット」を見る
View of the Steel Hut from the Silver Hut side

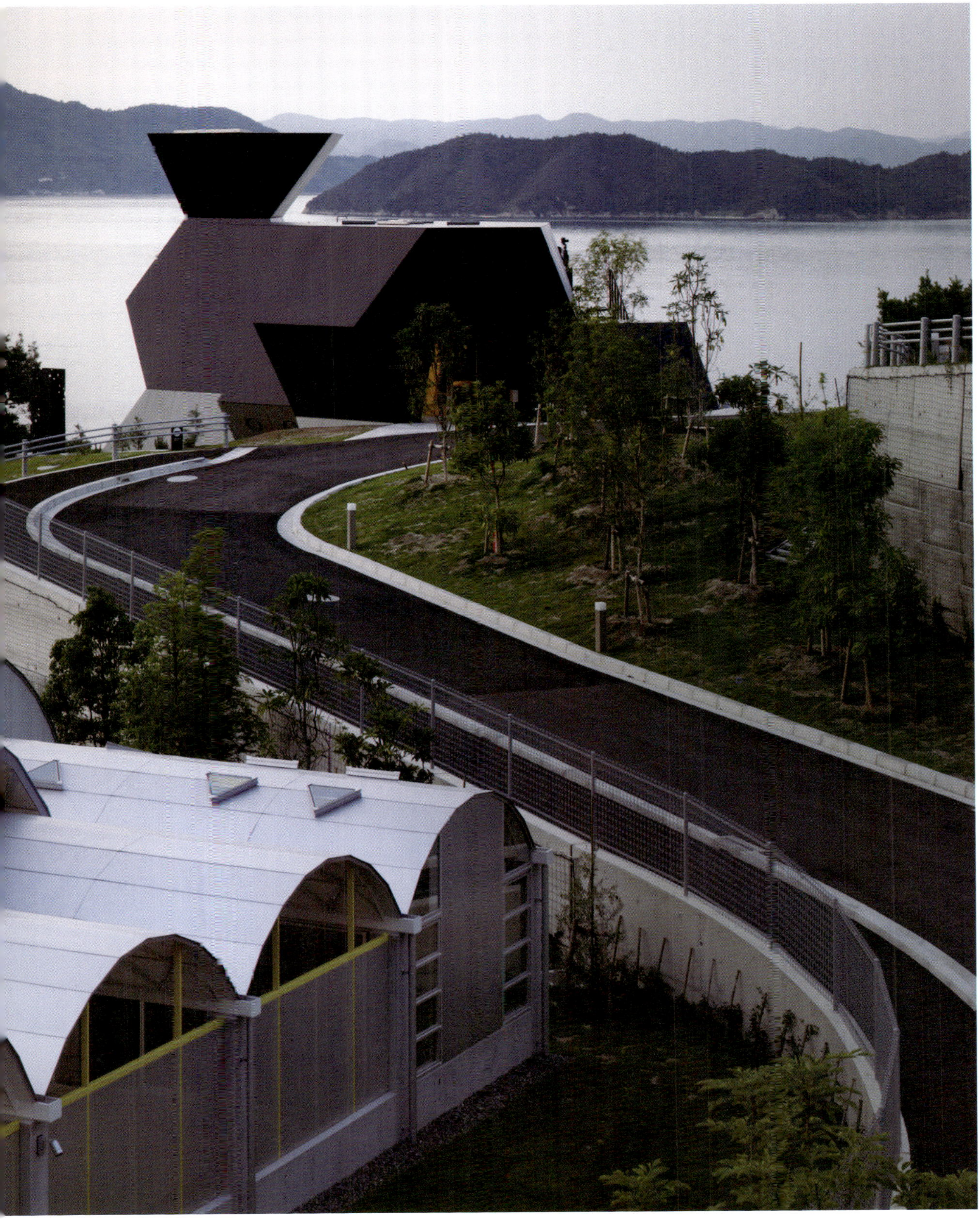

1 Steel Hut
2 Silver Hut
3 exhibition space
4 storage

Site plan

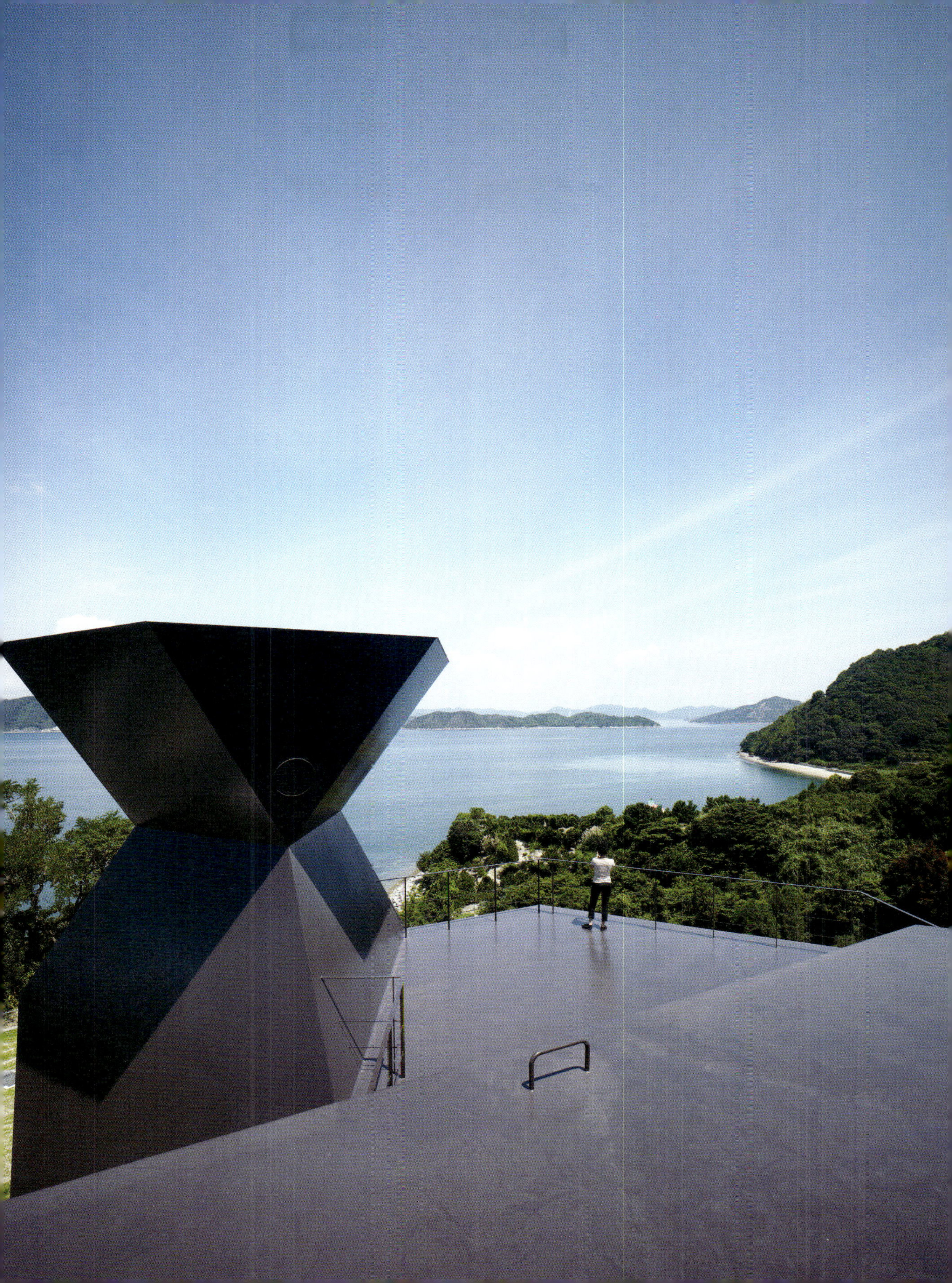

「スティールハット」と同じ幾何学で構成された「オスロ市ダイクマン中央図書館 コンペティション応募案」
Competition proposal for the New Deichman Main Library, Oslo, composed of the geometry as Steal Hut.

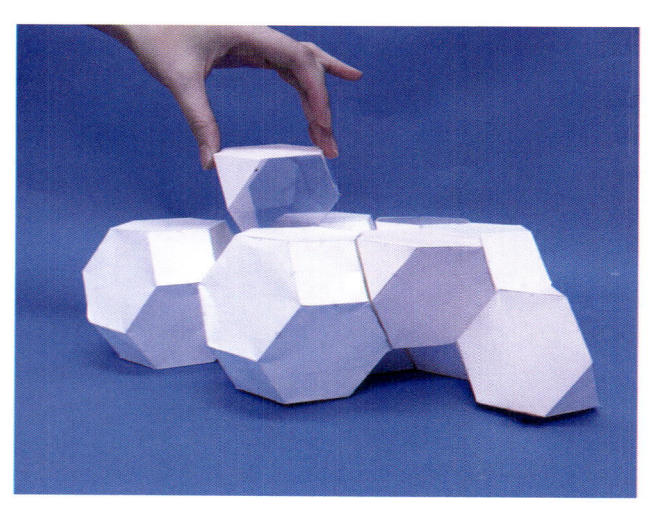

3種類の立体によって空間を密実に充填できる多面体のスタディ
The spaces are packed, using three types of solids.

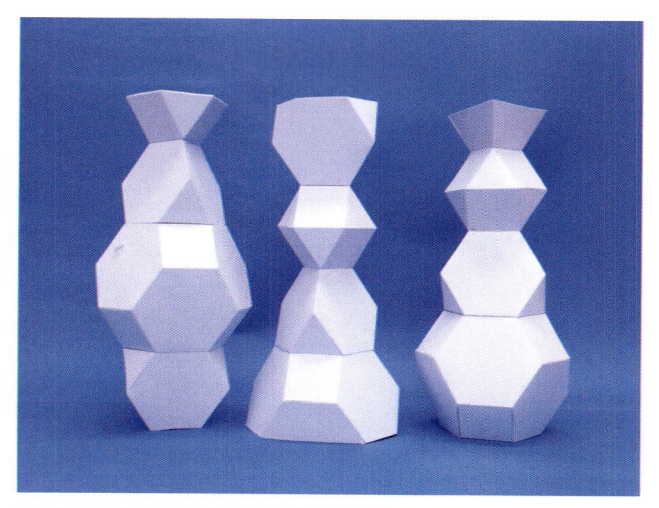

3種類の立体でできる多様な形態（ひとつの立体は上下を逆転）
Various forms were made with the three types of solids (one was turned upside-down).

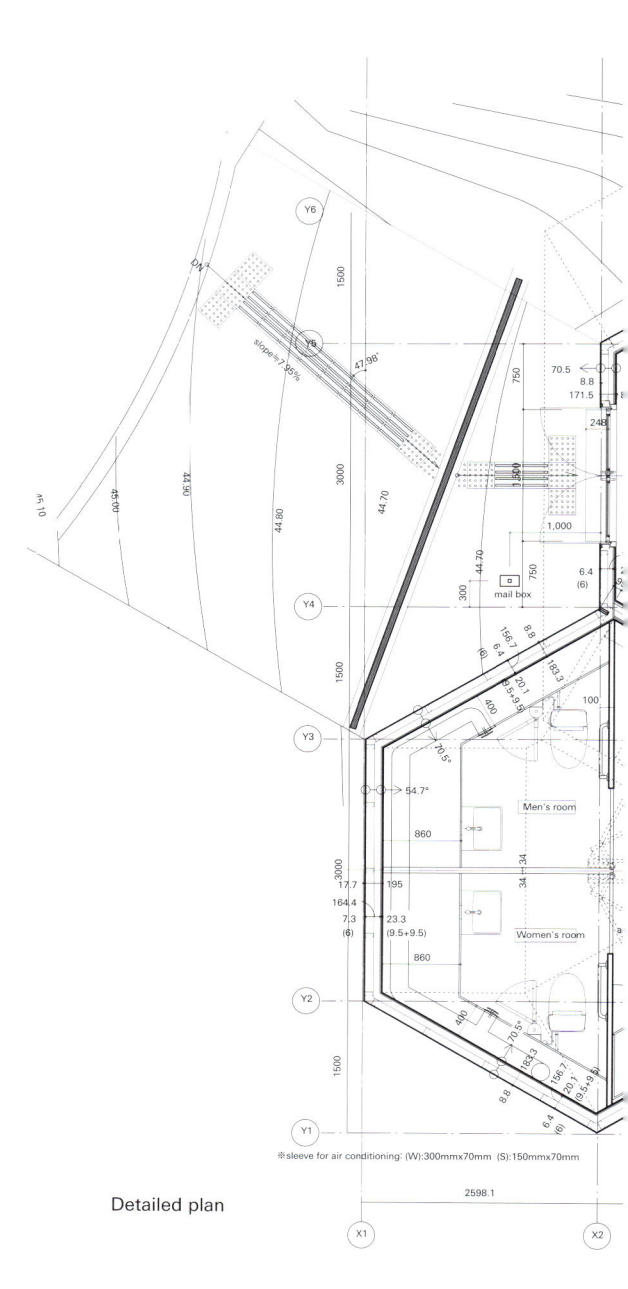

Detailed plan

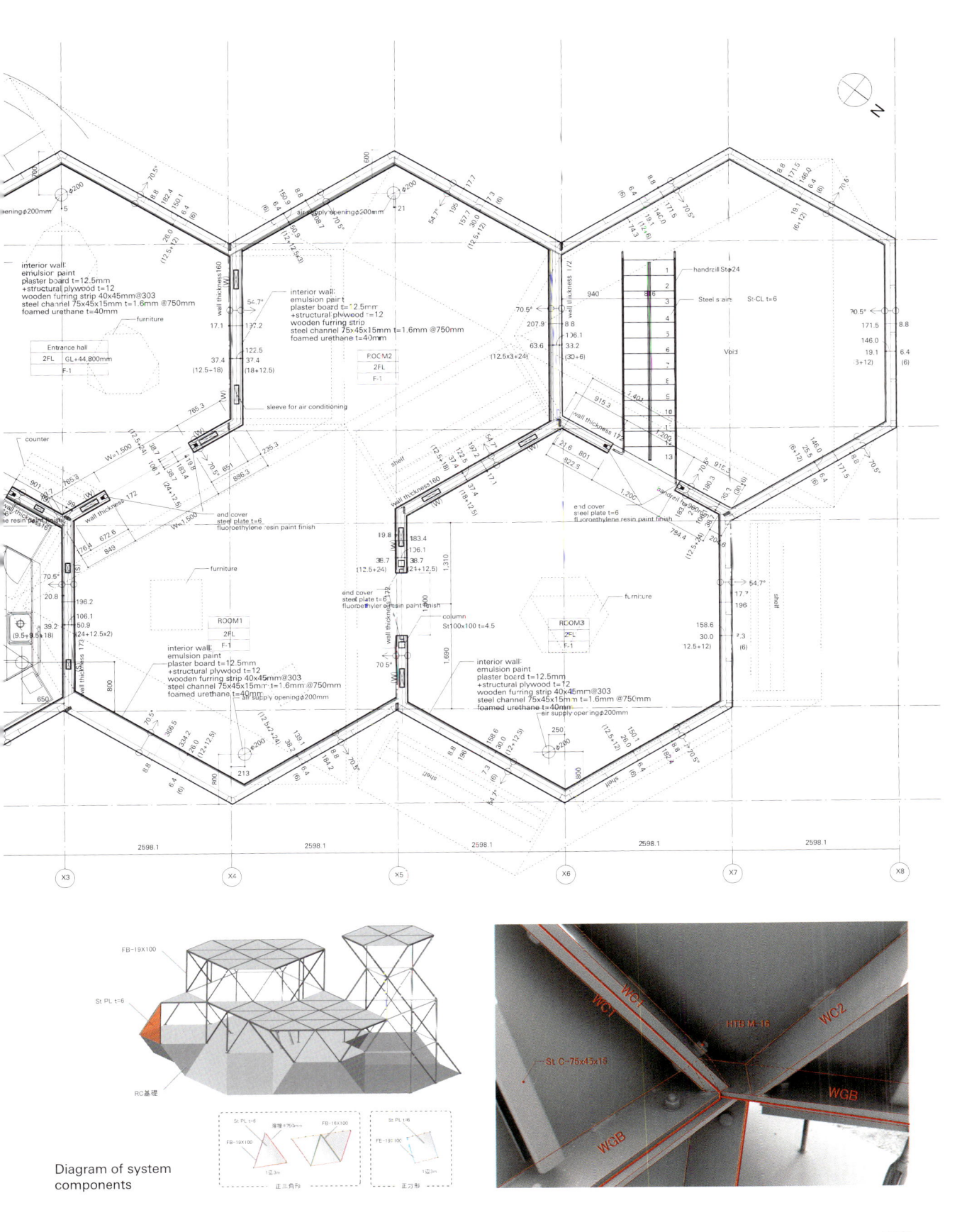

Diagram of system components

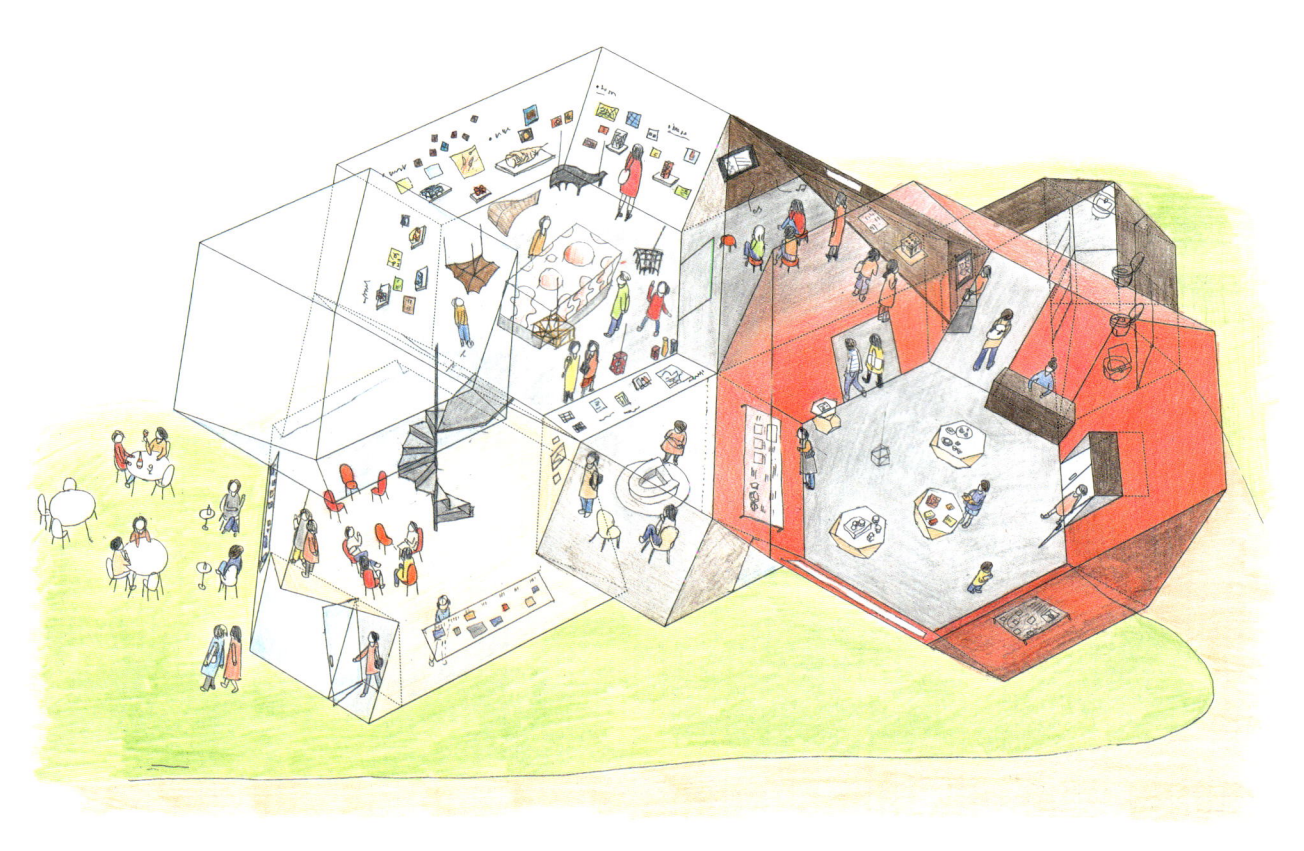

イメージスケッチ
Image sketch.

「日本一美しい島　大三島をつくろうプロジェクト2014」展 展示
Exhibition "Project Omishima 2014-Transforming into the most beatiful island in Japan."

瀬戸内海に浮かぶ大三島に建てられた伊東豊雄の建築ミュージアム。展示中心の「スティールハット」とワークショップ中心の「シルバーハット」の2棟より成る。

This museum, dedicated to Toyo Ito's architecture, was built on Omishima, an island inthe Seto Inland Sea. It consists of two wings: Steel Hut for exhibits and a Silver Hut for workshops.

サロン：部屋の窓からは瀬戸内海が見渡せる
Salon: The window of this room overlooks the Seto Island Sea.

「日本一美しい島 大三島をつくろうプロジェクト2014」展 エントランスホール
Entrance hall of the exhibition "Project Omishima 2014-Transforming into the most beatiful island in Japan."

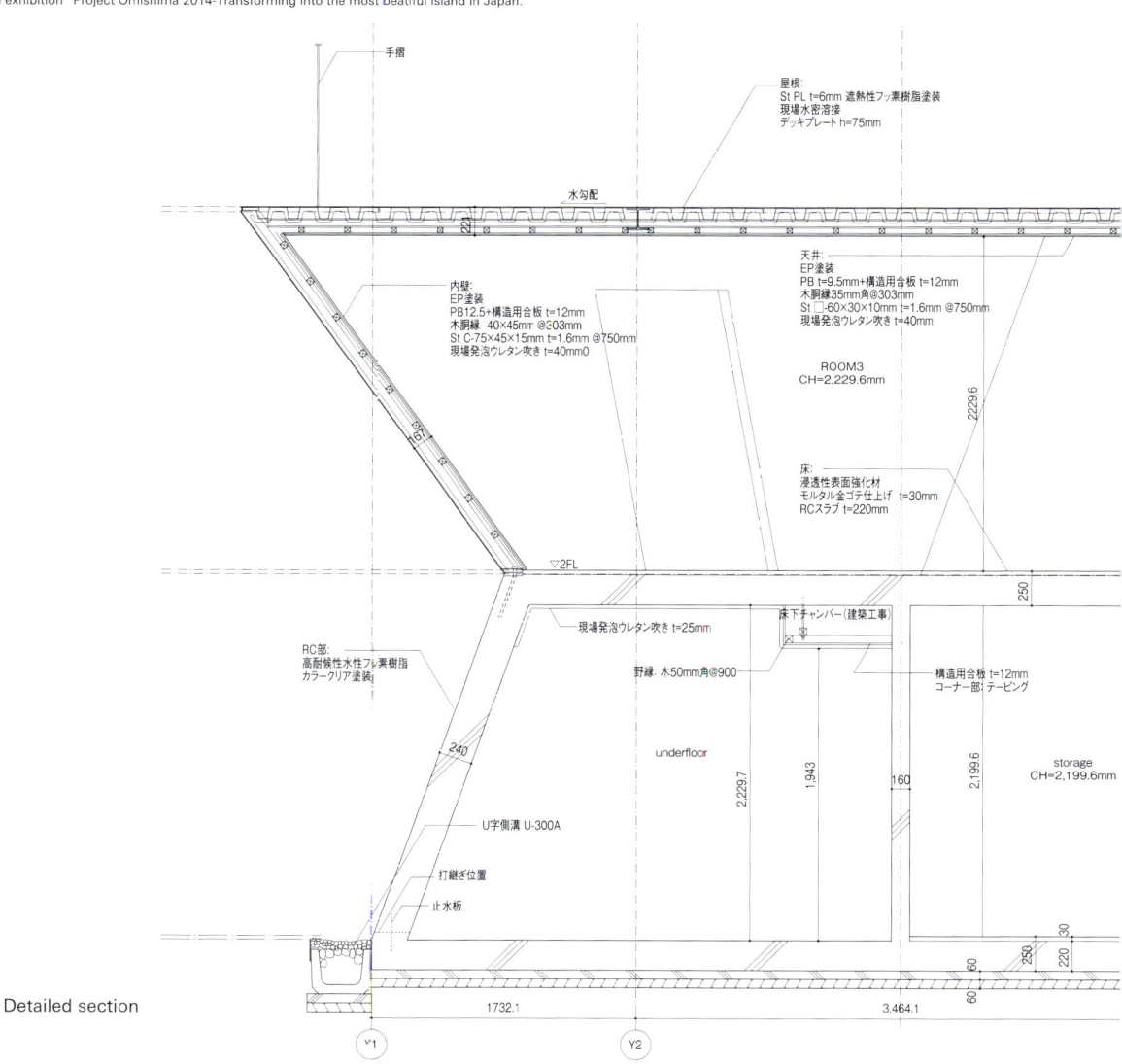

Detailed section

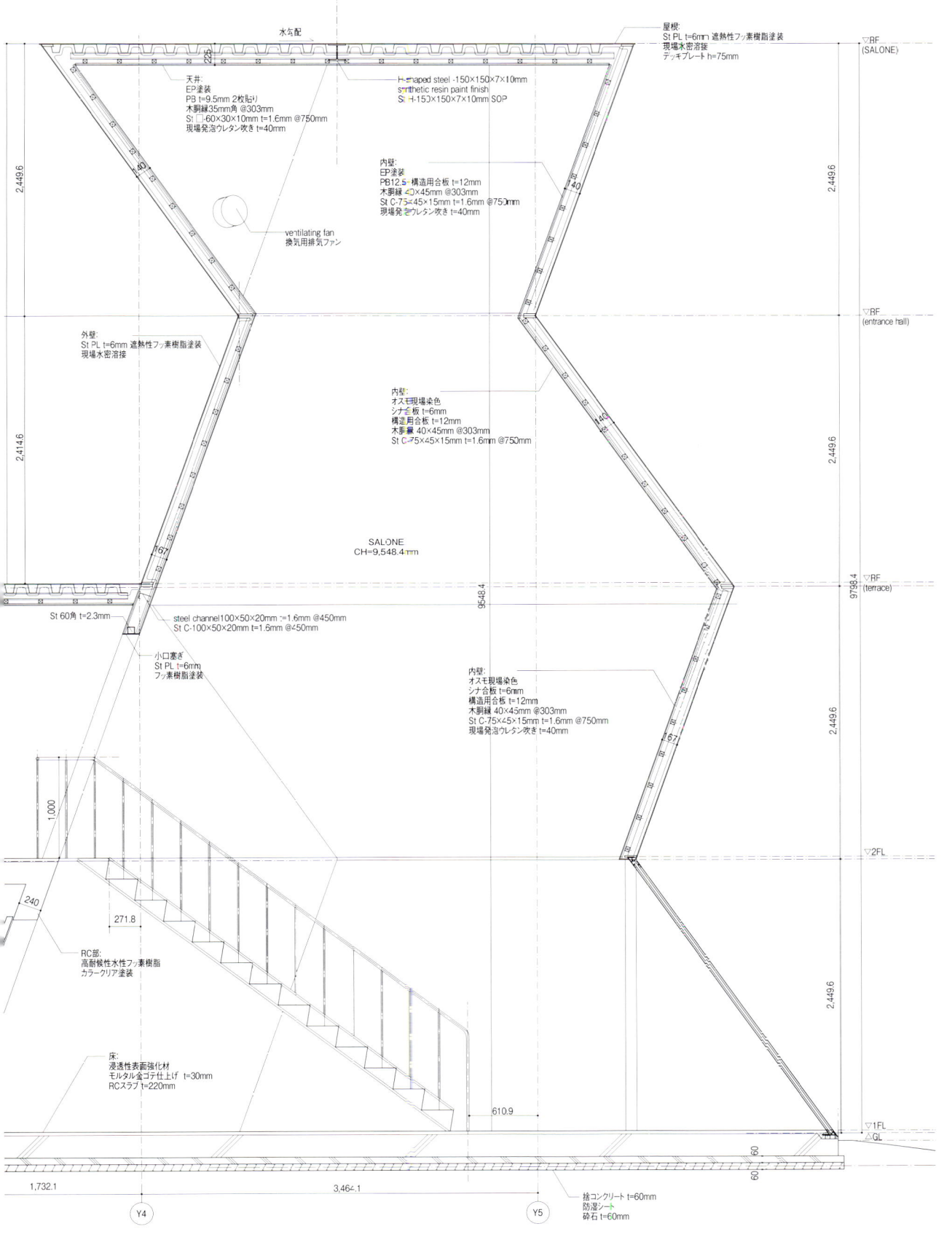

屋根:
St PL t=6mm 遮熱性フッ素樹脂塗装
現場水密溶接
デッキプレート h=75mm

水勾配

T-shaped steel -150×150×7×10mm
synthetic resin paint finish
St H-150×150×7×10mm SOP

天井:
EP塗装
PB t=9.5mm 2枚貼り
木胴縁35mm角 @303mm
St □-60×30×10mm t=1.6mm @750mm
現場発泡ウレタン吹き t=40mm

内壁:
EP塗装
PB12.5+構造用合板 t=12mm
木胴縁 40×45mm @303mm
St C-75×45×15mm t=1.6mm @750mm
現場発泡ウレタン吹き t=40mm

ventilating fan
換気用排気ファン

▽RF (SALONE)

2,449.6

2,449.6

140

▽RF (entrance hall)

外壁:
St PL t=6mm 遮熱性フッ素樹脂塗装
現場水密溶接

内壁:
オスモ現場染色
シナ合板 t=6mm
構造用合板 t=12mm
木胴縁 40×45mm @303mm
St C-75×45×15mm t=1.6mm @750mm

2,414.6

2,449.6

140

SALONE
CH=9,548.4mm

9,548.4

▽RF (terrace)

167

St 60角 t=2.3mm

steel channel 100×50×20mm t=1.6mm @450mm
St C-100×50×20mm t=1.6mm @450mm

小口塞ぎ
St PL t=6mm
フッ素樹脂塗装

内壁:
オスモ現場染色
シナ合板 t=6mm
構造用合板 t=12mm
木胴縁 40×45mm @303mm
St C-75×45×15mm t=1.6mm @750mm
現場発泡ウレタン吹き t=40mm

167

1,000

▽2FL

240

271.8

RC部:
高耐候性水性フッ素樹脂
カラークリア塗装

2,449.6

床:
浸透性表面強化材
モルタル金ゴテ仕上げ t=30mm
RCスラブ t=220mm

610.9

▽1FL
△GL

60
60

1,732.1    3,464.1

Y4    Y5

捨コンクリート t=60mm
防湿シート
砕石 t=60mm

211

## ⑥ 浦戸 (うらと)
「石積みに囲まれた豪壮な家々」

岡山と大山の間の谷筋に位置し、山を開いた畑と海を干拓した田からなる。昭和13年までくじ引きなどで一斉に田を交換するまわり田の慣習が残っていた。昭和30年代のみかん景気時代は豪壮な家の新築ラッシュが相次ぎ、結婚式の家はまさに石積みに囲まれている。大正13年には、農業の島・大三島で唯一の造船所が築かれた。

## ⑤ 宗方 (むながた)
「競い合う櫂伝馬精神」

関西に開かれ日当たりが良く住みやすい人口島の中でも数が多く、ことに旧暦6月11日、12日に勇壮を極める競い合いで神島をもらう櫂伝馬行事が盛んだった。最も心あふれる宗方の景色は最近消滅寸前とも呼ばれ、平成26年は15年ぶりに旧式石積みが復活した。大三島で最も愛媛松山寄りに近く、松山1時間足らずで今治と結ぶ。

ROOM 3

## ⑦ 口総 (くちすぼ)
「谷の水がつくる水田と棚田」

谷が多く水に恵まれ、みかん栽培以前は、平地に水田、山に棚田が作られ、神社の足元に静かな集落があたたかい暮らしを支え、海沿いにはかつて、宗方と同じ製塩業と酒造、昭和期の多い頃は小なるでは塩田が広がっていた。稲作条件で、譲り合いの精神が根づき、比較的今も方言との結びつきが深い。

## ⑧ 野々江 (ののえ)
「屋根並みをつくる瓦の土」

最西端島の山に挟まれ道に開けた集落。冬には冬に近づいて寒く、海を見れば伯方島が残しい。みかん栽培以前では約60年代以前は瓦の土を持つ焼瓦、地域の陶器を集散加工する小さな穴もあり、愛媛県産地として選ばれ、瓦の野々江瓦も屋根用瓦だった。時代が変わって瓦とした伝統の特徴。

## 大三島 の ⑬ の集落 と ⑬ の美しさ

大三島には13の集落があります。
古くから海上交通が発達し、周辺の島々との交流が盛んだったこと、
また、海や山の間の限られた土地に集落を築いてきた結果、
集落ごとに少しずつ異なる文化や生活習慣が形成されてきました。
この展示室では、大三島の「13の集落」と、長い歴史の中で紡がれてきた
自然や暮らしに関する「13の美しさ」を紹介します。

### 集落

① 盛（さかり）「人々の強い結束」

井口（いのくち）「の米どころ」

③ 甘崎（あまざき）「日本最古の水軍城跡」

菱摩芋

### 美しさ

① 大山祇神社「人びとの信仰の場所」

② 祭「受け継がれてきた人々の集い」

③ 楠「古くからのシンボル」

④ 地形「起伏に富んだ山、穏やかな海」

⑤ 集落「自然の豊かさと人びとの集い」

⑥ 舟

伊東の自邸として東京に建っていた「シルバーハット」を再生。構造体はほぼ同じだが、大半は屋根のある屋外空間となった
A reproduction of Silver Hut, which served as Ito's residence in Tokyo. The structure is nearly the same, but most of the new building is an outside space covered with a roof.

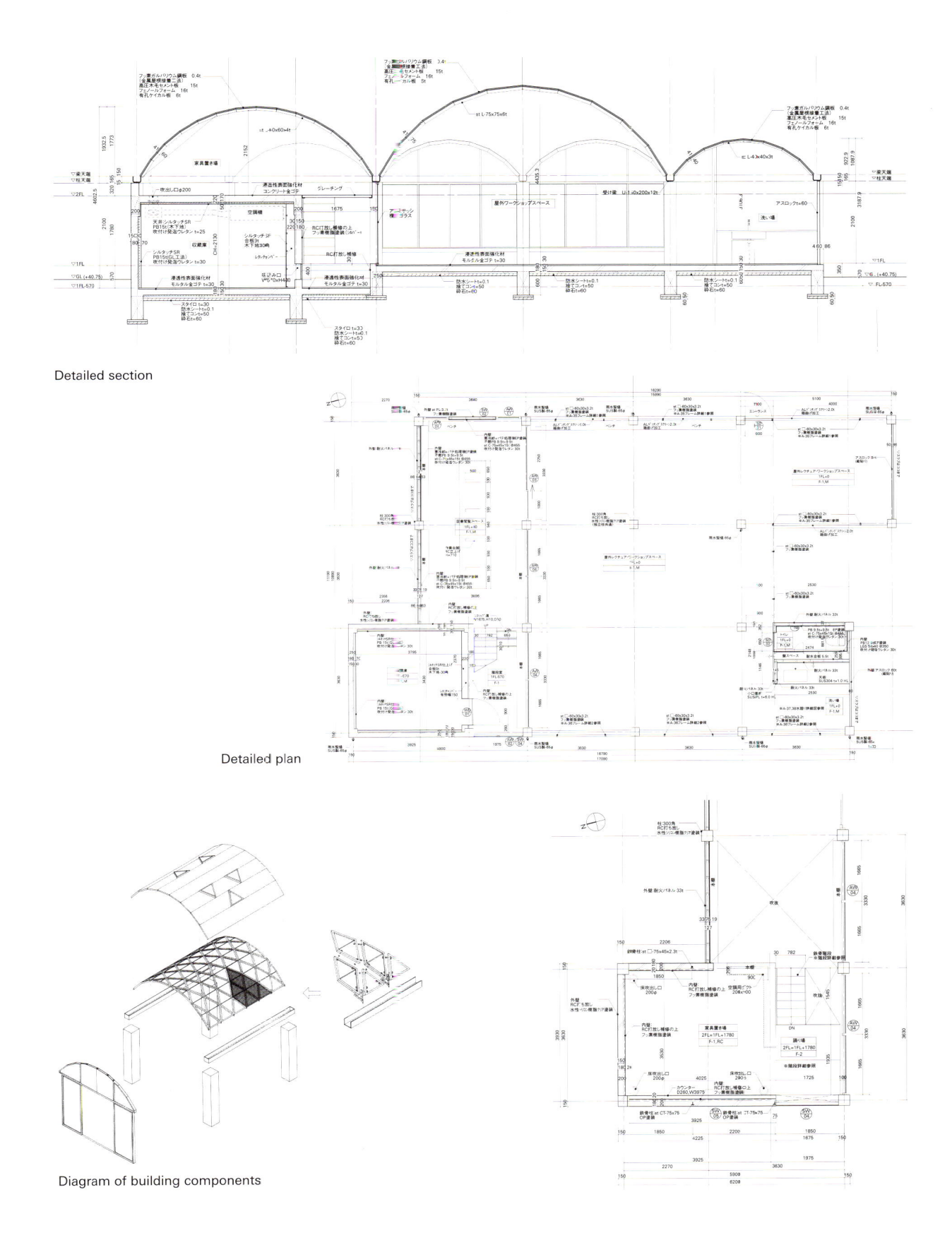

Detailed section

Detailed plan

Diagram of building components

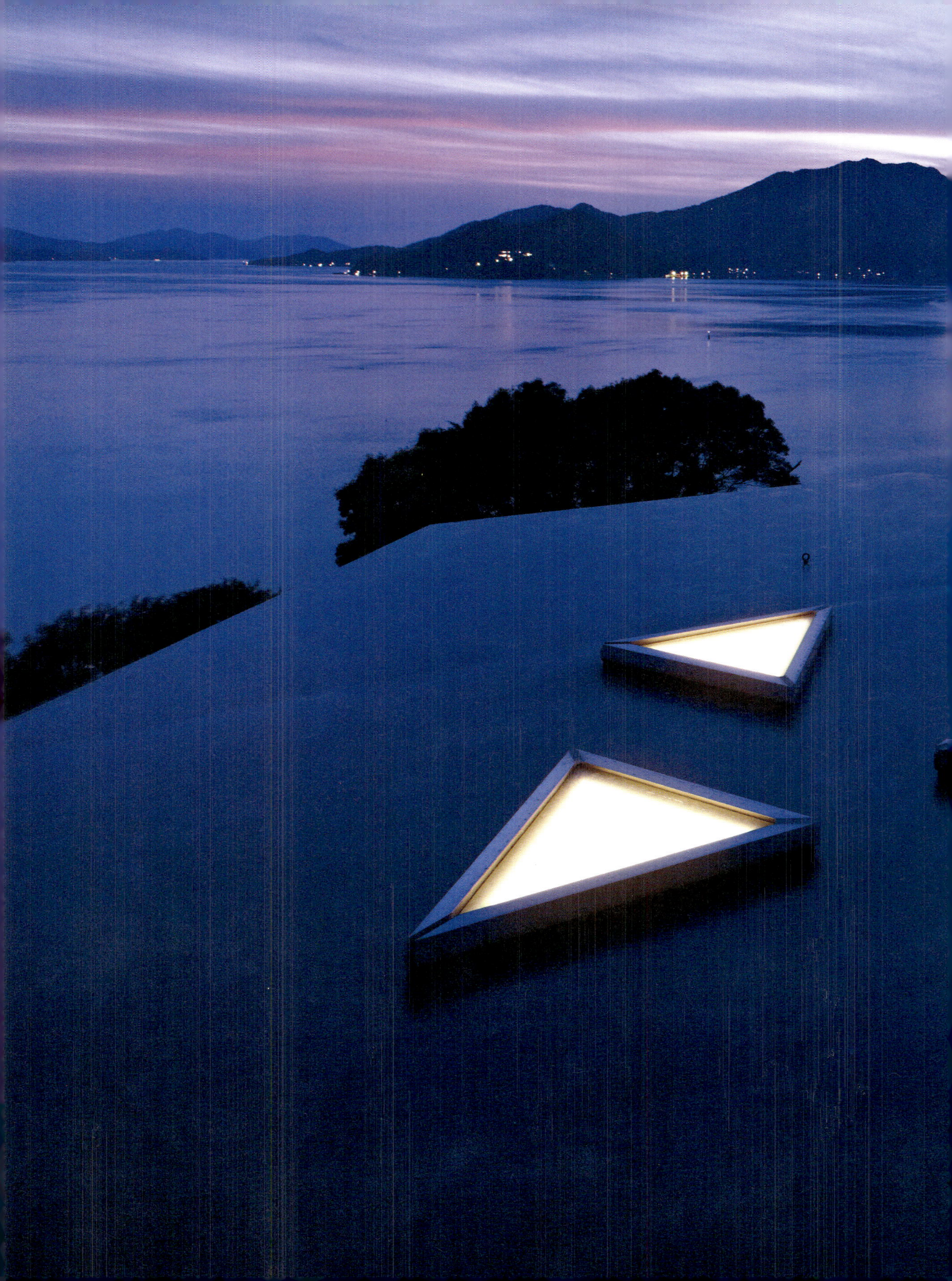

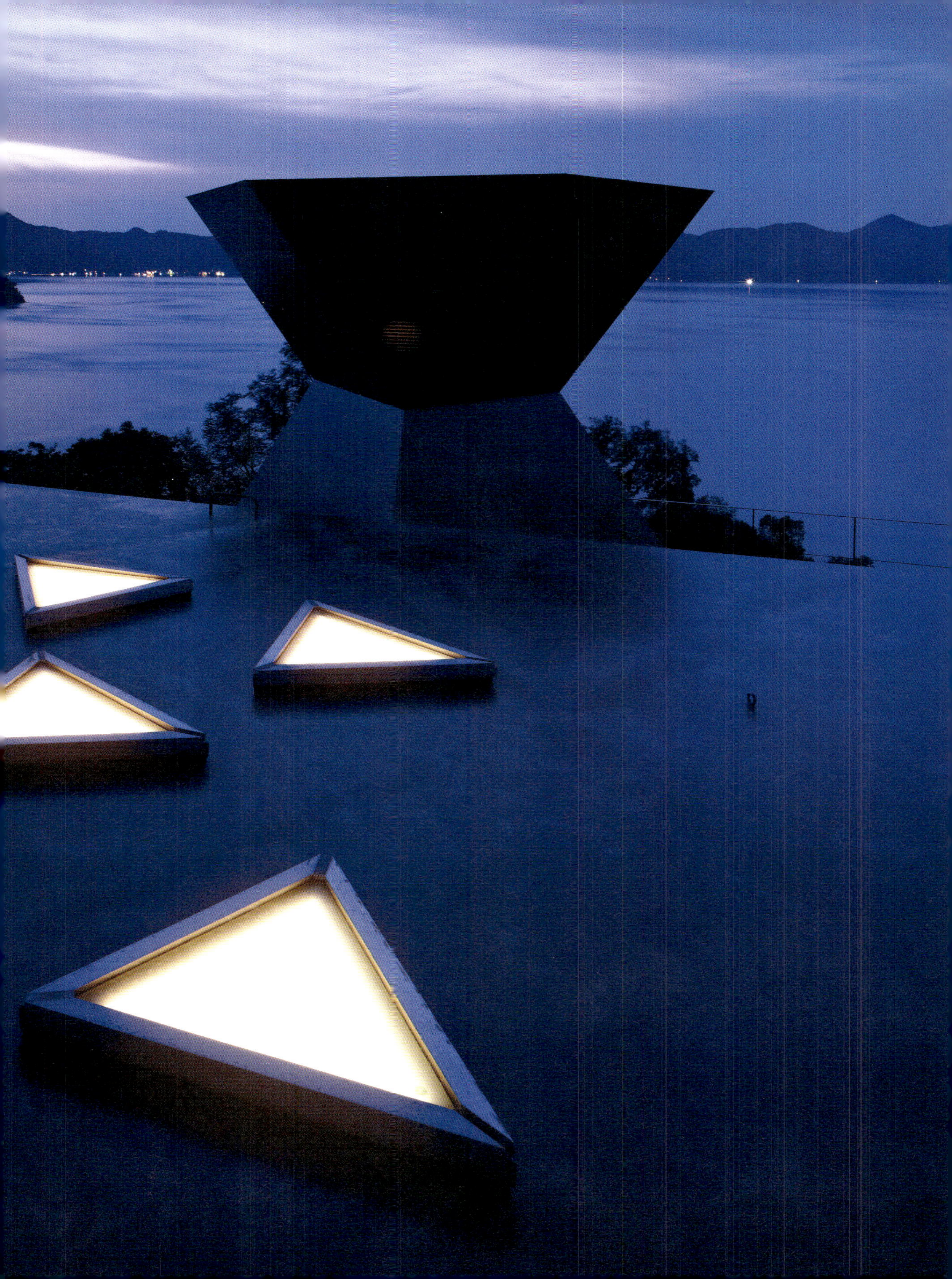

Ken Iwata Mother and Child
Museum, Imabari City
今治市岩田健母と子のミュージアム

2011　愛媛県今治市　Imabari, Ehime

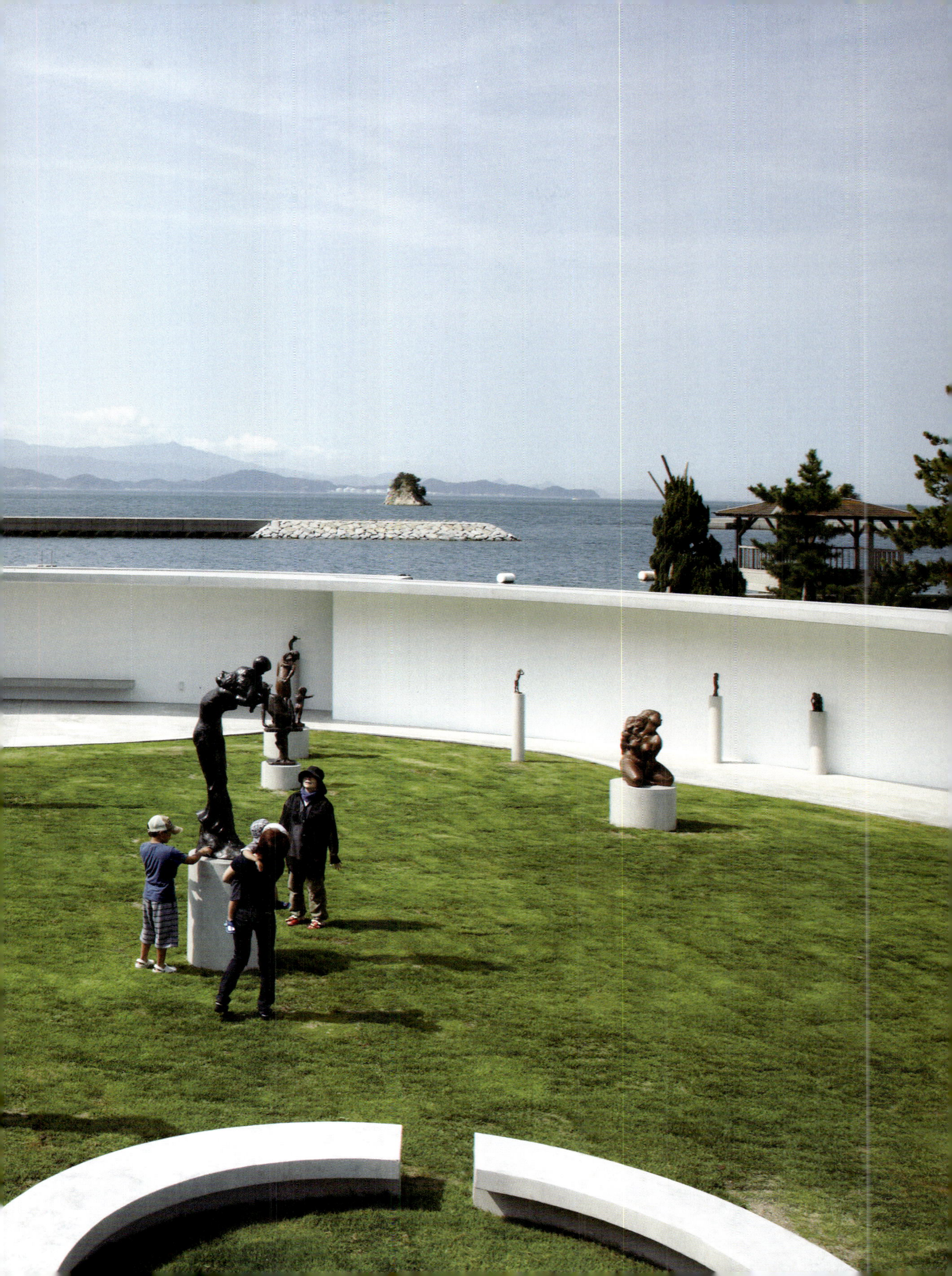

コンクリートを円弧状に巡らせた壁の中に44体の彫刻が置かれている
44 sculptures are contained within the arc-like concrete walls.

岩田健氏と
Ito with Mr. Ken Iwata.

オープニングでの千住真理子氏によるミニコンサート風景
A mini-concert was performed by Ms. Mariko Senju at the opening ceremony.

大三島の南西端にある旧宗方小学校（現在は宿泊施設）の校庭につくられた岩田健氏の彫刻ミュージアム（今治市立）

This museum, managed by the city of Imabari, is dedicated to Mr. Ken Iwata's sculpture. It stands on the grounds of what was once Munakata Elementary School (It is now an accommodation facility) on the southwest edge of Omishma

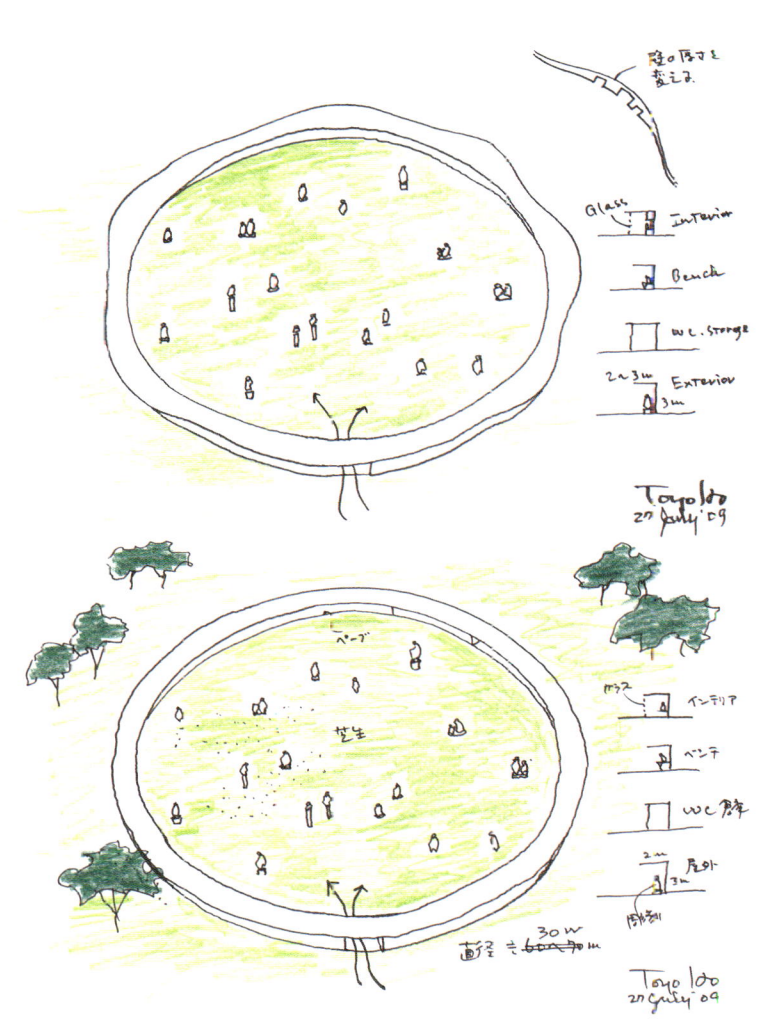

コンセプトスケッチ
Concept sketch.

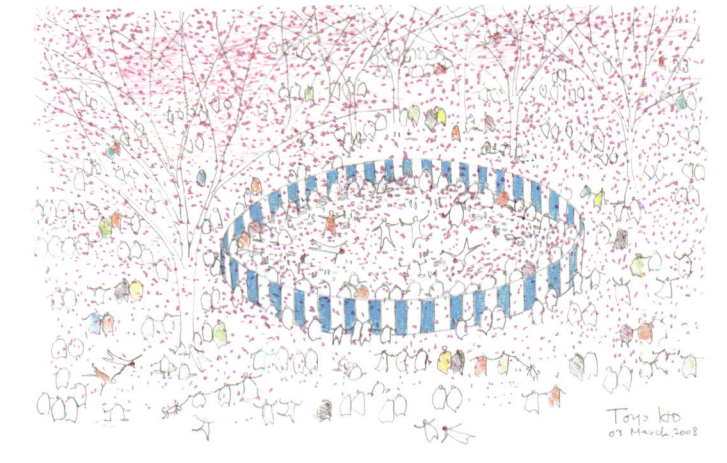

桜の下にまん幕を張るスケッチ
Sketch with hood curtain beneath the cherry trees.

221

エントランスへのアプローチ
The approach to the entrance.

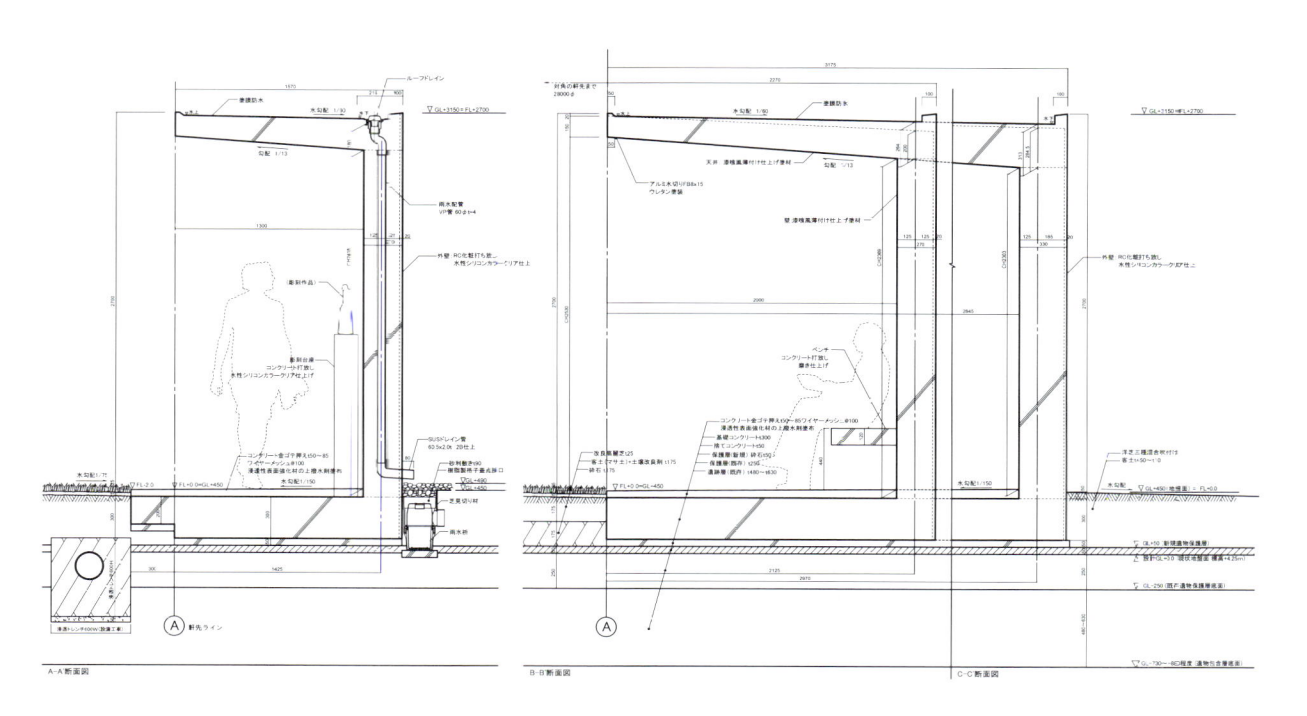

Detailed section

222

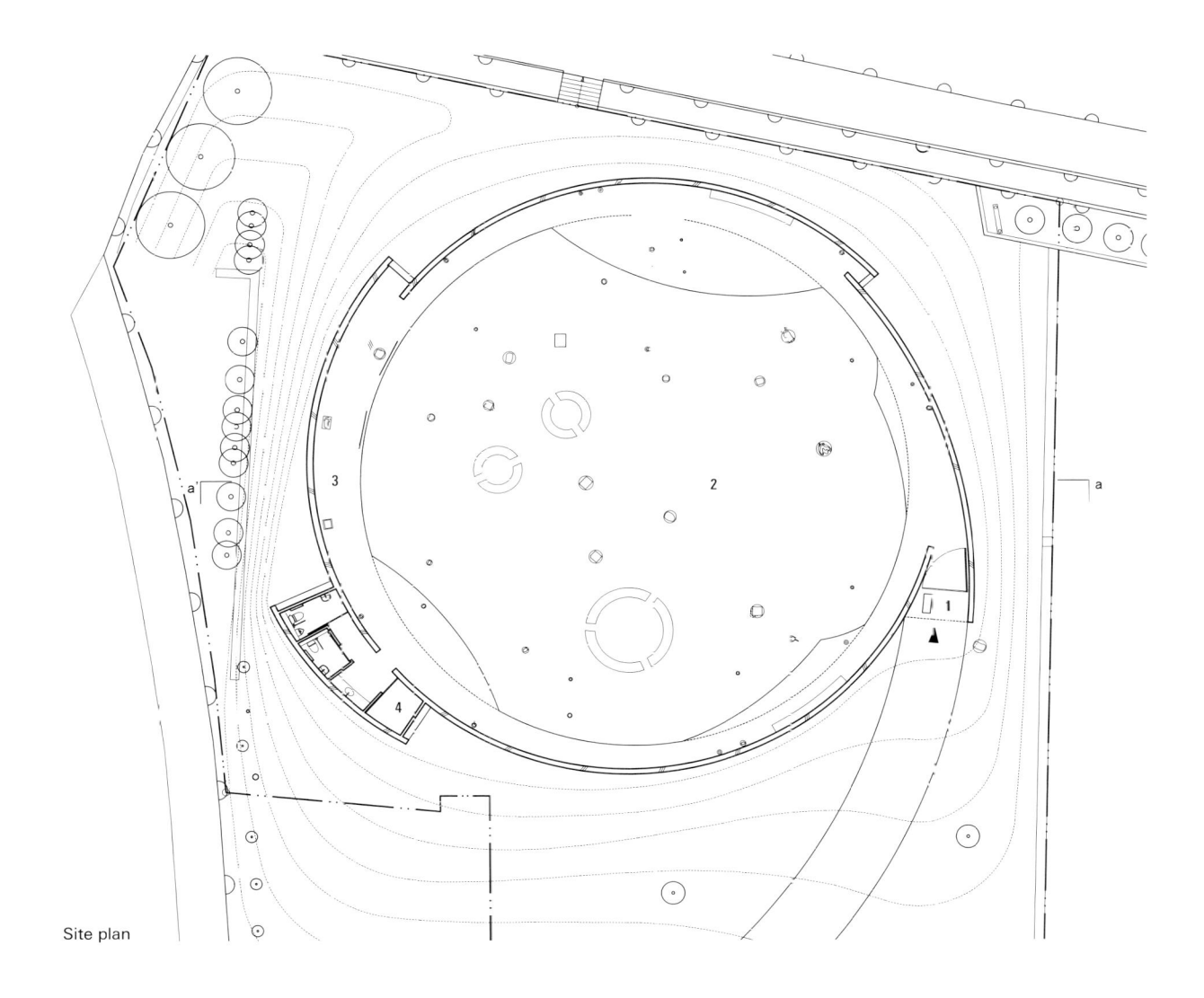

Site plan

1 entrance
2 courtyard
3 gallery
4 storage

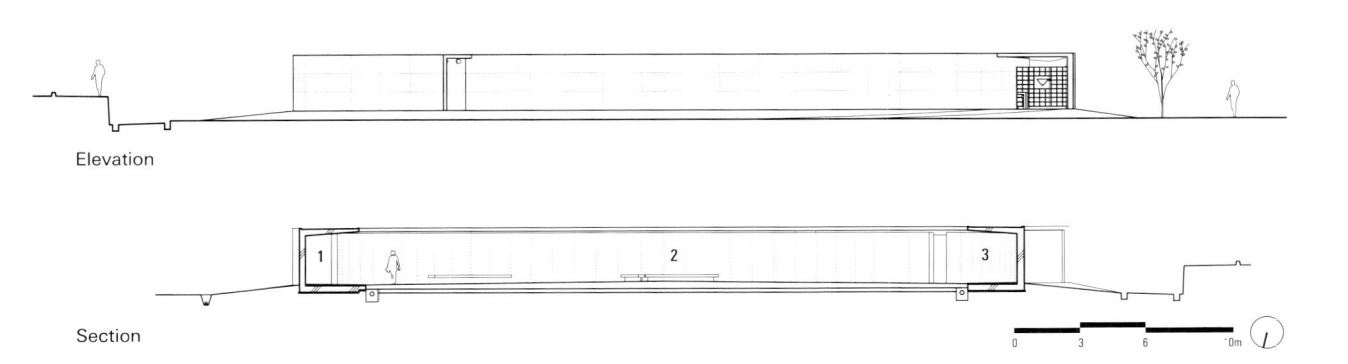

Elevation

Section

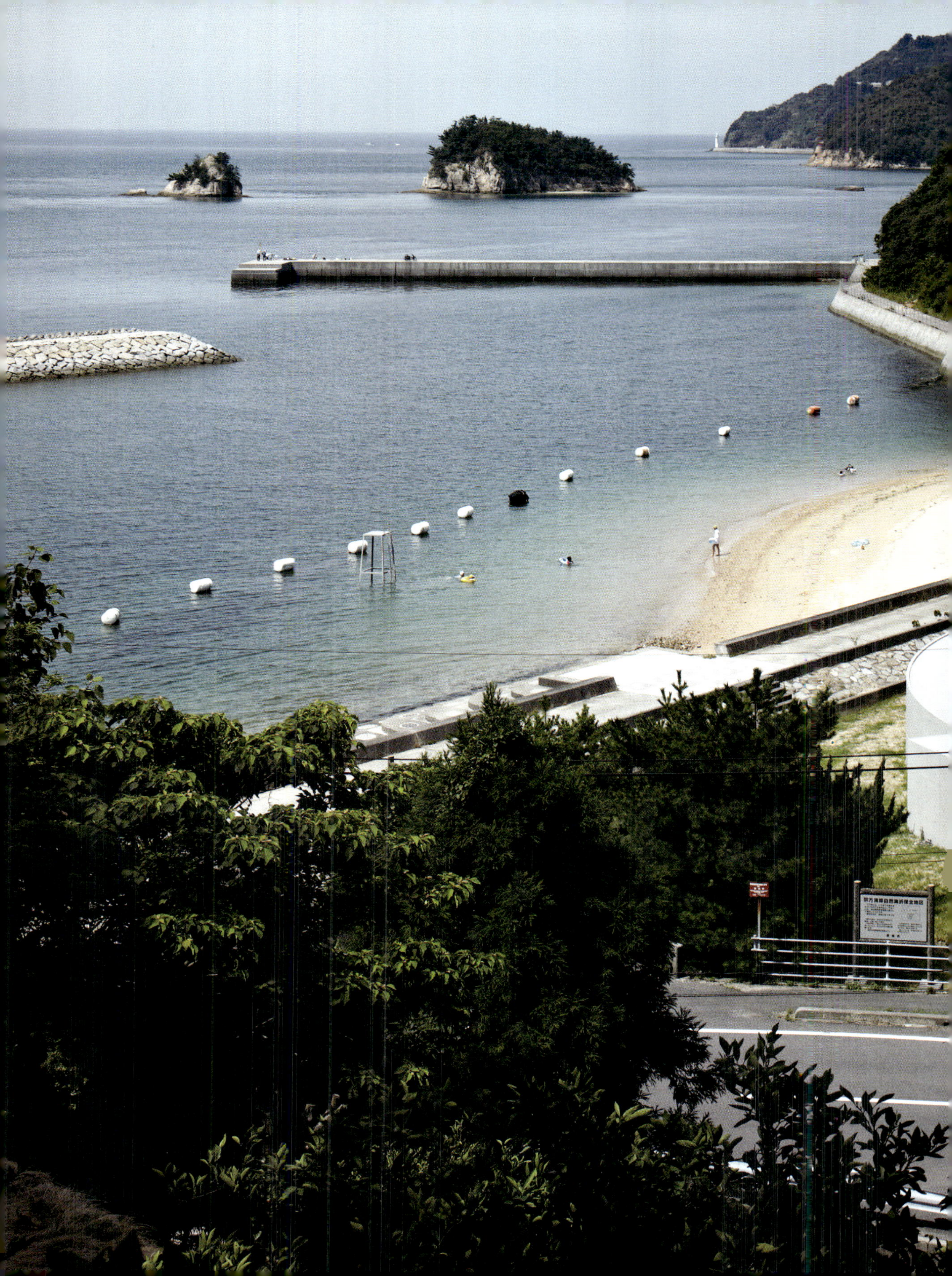

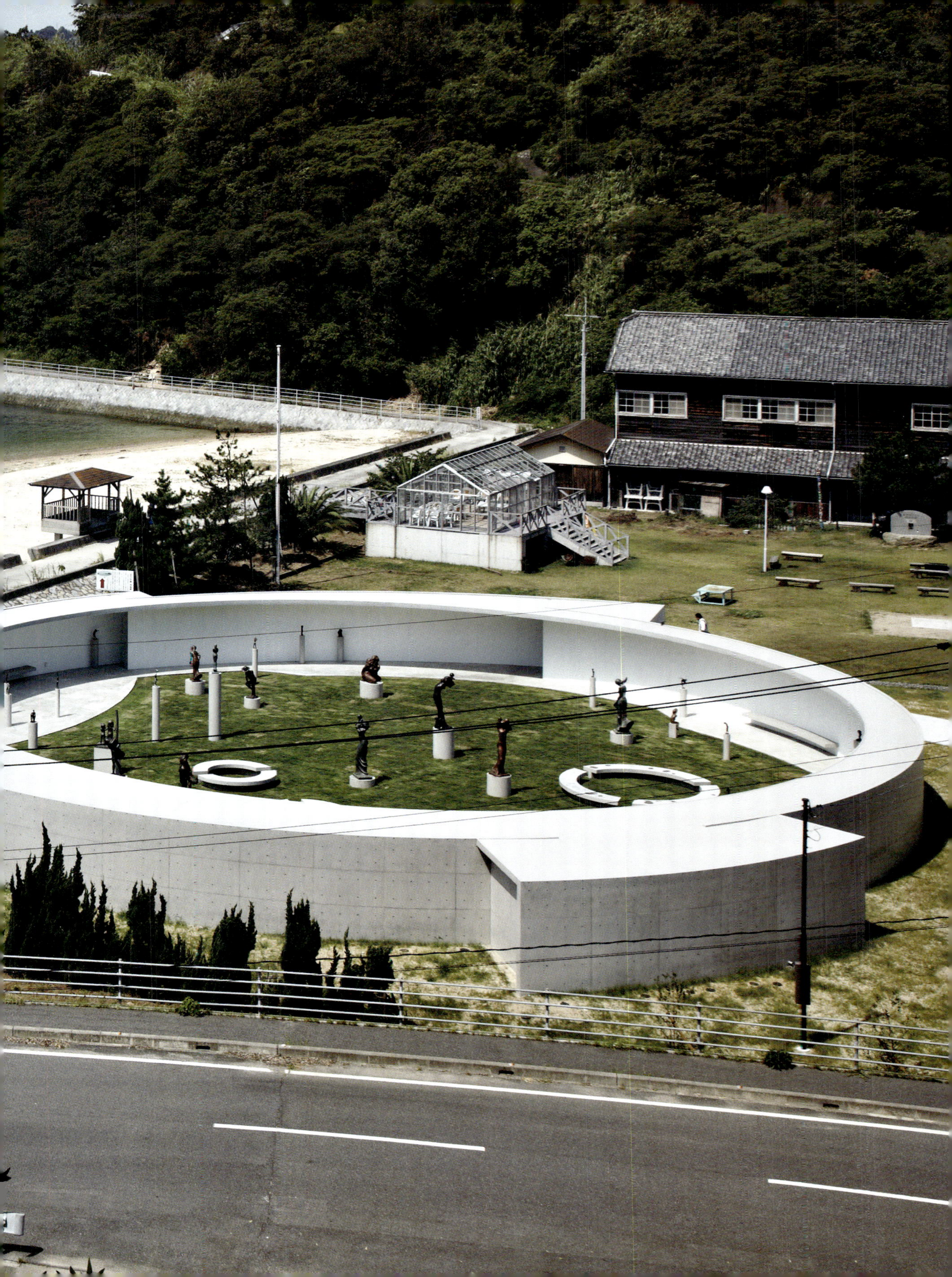

# 8 最新プロジェクト
## Latest Projects

伊東豊雄との対話　Conversation with Toyo Ito

### 台湾大学社会科学部棟
National Taiwan University, College of Social Sciences　[2013]

### 松山 台北文創ビル
Songshan Taipei New Horizon Building　[2013]

### みんなの森 ぎふメディアコスモス（建設中）
Minna no Mori Gifu Media Cosmos
(tentative title) (under construction)

### CapitaGreen（建設中）
CapitaGreen (under construction)

### （仮称）川口市火葬施設・赤山歴史自然公園（計画中）
Crematorium and Akayama Historic Nature Park in Kawaguchi
(tentative title) (under development)

### バロックミュージアム・プエブラ（計画中）
Barroco Museo Internacional (under development)

# CapitaGreen

ー「CapitaGreen」は、2007年から始まりました。「台中国立歌劇院」に次いで長いプロジェクトになります。

ー 先日、上棟式の写真を見て驚きました。シンガポールでも、各階のオフィスの前庭をこれだけ緑化しているというのはかなり珍しいですね。

ファサードの緑化率が50％以上ですからね。

ー「CapitaGreen」の設計のプロセスを見ていて面白いと思ったのは、当初の有機的なものから、さまざまな変遷を経ていまの形に落ちついたことです。都市の中に緑の立体的な森を立ち上げるという、強いメッセージ性を、具体的に緑ってどういうものだろう、緑の生々しさってどういうことだろうと考察した結果、表現的なものが整理された。具象と抽象のバランスの感覚に面白さがあると思います。その辺は伊東さんの中でどのように考えられていますか。

バランスについてはどう感じているの？

ー たとえば、全部緑というのもある、東西面だけを緑にして南北面はガラスにするというやり方も考えることができたと感じています。

ずっと「上昇」というイメージが強くあったと思います。容積率の関係で最初から、最上部の50m近くを森にするということが決まっていて、そこまで地上の緑をどうつなげていくかがテーマでした。半世紀前まではジャングルだったシンガポールが人工的な都市に変わった時に、もう一度その緑を取り戻すというコンセプトから始まって、地上の緑を屋上までどのように関係付けるかがずっと大きなテーマだったのです。その結果、こういうスパイラル状のイメージが残りました。

ー それは中にいる人というより、その周りを歩き回っている人や、そこで生活している人たちが感じるようなものでしょうか。

そうです。ですから、最終的に夜はどう見えるか、スパイラル状のパターンが感じられるかどうかというのは、まだわからないですが、一面は緑で一面はガラスというより、いまのデザインのほうがより流動的なものを感じることができると思いますね。
　オフィスの内側からも、緑の場所とガラス・スクリーンの場所がある程度混在していることが、環境として必要でした。

ー そういうオフィス環境が望ましいと？

日本のような場所だと、西日は避けたいという要望が強いですが、シンガポールの場合は太陽高度が高いから、東西南北の差がそれほどないことも影響していると思います。

ー それとオフィスを分割して貸す時に、各ゾーンに必ず緑とそうじゃない所とが両方出てくるように配慮して、全体のバランスは決めていきましたね。

そうです。

ー 緑の前面のガラスのルーバーは、密度が薄い状態になっており、それが風除けになっているということですね。

想像していた以上に隙間が多いという印象ですね。

ー その結果、ガラスと緑じゃなくて、そのふたつが混在し、ずっと続いていくという効果があります。

ここにルーバーがあったのが良かったなと思いますね。ルーバーがないと、完全にふたつのパターンになってしまう。ファサード全体がひとつの表層をつくっているということを前提にした上で、緑が現れてくるというところが、"おとなの建築"ではあると思います。

ー 日差しのパターンはわかりやすくて、プレゼンテーション時にみんな驚いたし、すごいものができるという期待感をもってもらえたと思います。一方で、いまお話にあったように、緑を入れ込もうとしているのに、むしろ対立が際立つというところが違和感になっていると思います。

この問題はなかなか悩ましいところですね。たとえばコンペティションなどでは、バルセロナの「トーレス・ポルタ・フィラ」は、表現としてある強さをもっているから通りやすい。一方で「CapitaGreen」のような建築はコンペティションだと勝てないと思います。そこの間でわれわれ

# CapitaGreen

— CapitaGreen started in 2007. It has taken the second longest time of any project the office has done; only National Taichung Theater is longer.

— I was amazed the other day when I saw photographs of the topping out. It is unusual even for Singapore to have such a green facade for the office floors.

Over 50 percent of the facade has been greened.

— Looking at the process of design for CapitaGreen, I find it interesting that after starting with an organic design, we made various changes and eventually arrived at the present form. Creating a vertical forest in the middle of the city sends a powerful message. But what exactly is "greenery"? What is the freshness of greenery? These questions were studied, and the form of expression was cut back. The balance maintained between representation and abstraction is interesting. What are your own thoughts on that?

How do you feel about the balance?

— For example, a scheme in which everything was greened, or in which just the east and west elevations were greened, and the north and south elevations were glazed, would have been possible.

I think I always had this strong image of something that was "ascending." For reasons of FAR, it was decided from the start to make nearly 50 meters at the top a forest, and the question was how to connect that to the greenery at ground level. The concept we started with was that Singapore, which had been a jungle only a half-century ago, had now become a man-made city, and that the time had come to restore the greenery. A major question was always how to relate the ground-level greenery to the roof-top. As a result, we arrived at this spiral-like image.

— Is that something that people who are walking around or living near the building, as opposed to working inside the building, perceive?

Yes. Hence the present design, which seems to flow more than a scheme in which one elevation is green and another elevation is glazed. It is still not clear how it will ultimately appear at night, or if the spiral pattern will be perceived or not.
　From the point of view of the office interior, an environment in which places that are green and places that have glass screens are mixed together was necessary.

— Such an office environment was desirable?

In a place such as Japan, there is a strong desire to avoid westerly sun, but in Singapore, the sun is so high in the sky that there is not much difference between east, west, north or south. That too has an effect.

— In addition, the overall balance was determined so that, when office space is divided and rented, each zone would always have both a green area and an area that is not green.

Yes.

— The glass louvers in front of greenery are not closely spaced; they serve as wind screens.

There are more gaps than I had imagined there would be.

— As a result, glass and greenery coexist, instead of there being one or the other.

I think it was good we installed the louvers. If they hadn't been installed, there would have been two distinct patterns. The facades together form a single surface. That is the basic premise. Then the greenery appears. That is what makes this an "adult" building.

— The pattern of sunlight is easy to understand. Everyone was amazed during the presentation and I think we managed to awaken expectations—they realized this could be something tremendous. On the other hand, as you said just now, what was incongruous was that, though we were trying to introduce greenery, there was marked opposition to the scheme.

This is a rather difficult problem. For example, a building that is quite expressive like TORRES PORTA FIRA, Barcelona, is more likely to be accepted in a competition. A building like CapitaGreen is not likely to win a competition. We are in something of a quandary, having to choose between two alternatives.

— CapitaGreen has gone through an interesting process in that sense. At first, it was easy to understand, symbolic, and directly expressed the concept. Having reached a shared understanding of the concept over time, however, we shifted from "expression" to actual "experience." As a result, the powerful form disappeared, and the scheme is one in which greenery and the city overlap slightly. I think such a transition would actually be good for many different projects.

That is true, but the emphasis of this building should be about the "cool void"—the way air is introduced through the red air intake at the

227

は戸惑っています。

— そういう意味で、この「CapitaGreen」は面白いプロセスを経て出来ているのではないかと思います。最初にわかりやすく、シンボリックで、コンセプトをそのままダイレクトに表現したものがあり、そこから時間をかけてコンセプトを共有した上で、「表現」から具体的な「体験」に移行した結果、強い形が消え、少し緑と都市がオーバーラップするようなものになった。そういう変遷が本当はいろんなプロジェクトにあるといいと思います。

それもそうですが、この建築で一番アピールするべき点は、上にある赤いエア・インテークから空気を取り入れて、それを各階に送り込んで空調するという「クールヴォイド」の存在。それが植物のような働きをしていることですよ。当初はもっと大きいクールヴォイドだったのが、細い静脈が通っているみたいになってしまいました。

しかしこのような提案は、コンペティションでいくらそういうことを言っても、審査員にはうけない。「新国立競技場国際デザイン・コンクール応募案」でも、われわれが提案したのは同じことだったと思います。このギャップの問題を超える強さをわれわれはつくり出していく必要があり、表現のみの強さでは意味がない。空気の循環の提案も、「みんなの森 ぎふメディアコスモス」ではある程度デザインといい形でバランスがとれたけれども、「CapitaGreen」でももっとできたのかもしれない。それを発見していくことが次につながるのではないかと思いますね。

ただ、超高層はやれることが少ない。

— ファサードとコア。いかに効率的にコア配置をするかが、重要視されていますから。

— ただ、緑化も、われわれが一方的に提案したわけではなくて、ある種の社会的な要望でもあったと理解しています。エア・インテークにしても、効果がわかれば、クライアントはもっとシンガポールでこれを導入したいと言っている。いま「CapitaGreen」はオフィス環境が外の環境と完全に切り離されているけれども、たぶんこれを見た人たちが「何でテラスに出られないのか」と言えば、それを切っ掛けにオフィス環境が変わっていくと思います。

そうですね。

— シンガポールのほうが日本よりも、そういう変化が起こりそうな感じはあるんですか。

新しいものを受け入れる意欲は、断然シンガポールや台湾のほうが強いから。こんな50％緑化をスカイツリーに配置するなんていうのは、日本ではあり得ない（笑）。

シンガポールでも、プランニングの時は、何十センチであっても貸せる面積を多くしろと言われましたが、緑をメンテナンスすることに関しては、なんの反対もなく受け入れてくれましたから。

— 経済大国であり、緑がマネーに置き換えられるような側面もあるから、合理的に割り切っていいと判断しているところもありますね。

それが売りになると、トップが直感的に思ったのでしょう。

— シンガポールはいま、緑化建築が流行しています。それとあわせて建築家の作家性を求めている。いろいろな付加価値になるものをシンガポールや台湾は求めていて、新しいものを提案できる土壌がある。

— シンガポールの人たちと話していて面白いのは、建築のことについて興味をもっている人が多いことだと思います。シンガポールでは、建築に触れる機会が多いのかもしれません。

中国でも海外の建築家を受け入れて開発が進んでいるし、台湾、シンガポール、韓国も、日本よりはるかに海外の建築家を呼んでいますね。日本では専門家以外の人が建築に興味を示さない原因はどこにあるんだろう。今度の新国立競技場の問題は、そういうことを議論を通じて高めていく、ひとつの突破口になるのではないかという期待もありました。

— 積層する建築では、空間の広がりではなく、ファサードのデザインと経済性が求められていると思います。伊東さんの中で積層のストラテジーみたいなものをどう考えていますか。

いや、特にないですね（笑）。ただ、今回のクールヴォイドがひとつのポイントで、そういう「働き」の問題をもう少し「表現」に変えていくことはできたような気がします。

— 最初に伊東さんが描かれたスケッチですが、

---

top and sent to each floor to be air conditioned. It functions like vegetation. The cool void was initially meant to be far larger but ended up being more like a thin vein running through the building.

However, jurors in a competition are never enthusiastic about such proposals, no matter how much we may talk about them. That was true of our proposal for the New National Stadium Japan International Design Competition (2012). We need to create something powerful that overcomes the problem of this gap; something that is powerful only as expression is meaningless. In Minna no Mori Gifu Media Cosmos, we were able to achieve to a certain extent a good balance between a proposal for the circulation of air and design. More might have been achieved with CapitaGreen. Discovering what that is may lead to further progress.

However, there is little that can be done with a high-rise building.

– Facade and core. Importance is placed on the efficient arrangement of the core.

– But greening is not something we unilaterally proposed; there is I believe social demand for it. The client has also said that if the air intake proves effective, they would like to introduce it more in Singapore. At present, the office environment of CapitaGreen is completely separated from the environment outside, but in all likelihood, if people who see this ask, "Why can't people go out onto the terraces?", that may provide an opportunity to change the office environment.

Yes.

– Do you think such a change is more likely to occur in Singapore than in Japan?

There is definitely greater eagerness to accept new things in Singapore or Taiwan. Greening 50 percent of something in Japan, say SkyTree, would be inconceivable [laughs].

There was demand in Singapore to increase the rentable floor area, even by just tens of centimeters, but they accepted everything concerning the maintenance of greenery without any opposition.

– Singapore is all about economic power, and in some respects greenery is a substitute for money. Therefore they are acting in a rational, matter-of-fact way and accepting it.

The corporate leadership probably intuited that it would be a sales point.

– Green architecture is now in fashion in Singapore. They are also seeking architects of an artistic character. Singapore and Taiwan are seeking different things that will add value and welcome new proposals.

– In talking with people in Singapore, it is interesting how many of them are interested in architecture. It may be that Singapore offers many opportunities for the public to come into contact with architecture.

Overseas architects are also involved in development in China. Taiwan, Singapore and Korea are inviting far more architects from overseas than Japan is. Why do people in Japan, excepting experts, show so little interest in architecture? I am hoping that the current problem over the New National Stadium will raise awareness of architecture through discussions

– In vertically stacked buildings, what is sought is not the extension of space but facade design and economy. What are your own thoughts on strategy with regard to vertically stacked buildings?

I have no particular strategy [laughs]. However, the cool void introduced in this project is an important point. I feel we were able to translate issues of "function" a bit more into "expression."

– In the first sketch you drew, the cool void seems transparent. Did you have an image of it from the start?

No, I was not thinking about the cool void. In the early schemes, I was thinking-- fairly expressionistically--about something resembling a wine glass.

「新国立競技場国際デザイン・コンクール応募案」
Proposal for the New National Studium Japan International Design Competition

クールヴォイドが透けているように感じます。当初からイメージをもたれていたのでしょうか。

いや、クールヴォイドは考えていなかったな。初期案ではかなり表現的に、ワイングラスみたいなものを考えていたところがありますね。

— この時は、緑というよりは、身体というか、内臓みたいなものが都市の中にあると面白いというようなイメージですか。

そう。

— そこから緑に移ったのは、やはりレギュレーションの話があったからでしょうか。緑化すると床の面積が増やせたので、緑化を増やしていく方針がクライアントと共有できたのが、一番大きかったと思います。

緑化以外にも「CapitaGreen」のテラスのように、中間領域を楽しむことができる部分が建築に見られるようになってきた。「CapitaGreen」は、最初は表層的な緑だったものが、空間の使い方、仕様の中に「緑」が現れ始めたひとつ目のプロジェクトという感じでしょうか。

そう。

— 「CapitaGreen」を見ても、インテリアの中に緑をもってきたりするのはなかなか難しい。だから、左官や煉瓦ブロックなど、自然な素材感のマテリアルの選択につながり、室内に緑がなくても、周辺の緑が半屋外的な場を介してつながっていく。

「The Crest(シンガポールコンドミニアムプロジェクト)」(p. 231)は少しそういうスペースの萌芽が出てきているし、「CapitaGreen」の場合は、外をまず緑にして、それに反応してオラファー・エリアソンさんが木の根のようなアートをデザインしてくれました。それに続いて、左官の壁とか煉瓦が出てきたわけですね。それは面白いことだと思います。オフィスビルでああいう左官の壁なんてない。

— そうですね。たいてい石ですね。

最初のころの有機的なものといまを比べると、緑の奥行きのイメージがちょっと違います。最初はテクスチャーとしての緑という感じがしますが、いまはガラスのルーバーがあってその後ろに緑があってと、重なりの奥に緑があり、タワーの内側まで緑がつながっている。だからこそ下にオラファーさんが根っこを想像するようなものをつくることになった。

初期のスタディをしている時に、ファサードがいかにも張り付けたみたいになったら嫌だと思って、どうしたらいいかたくさんスタディしました。

— ルーバーというのは、すごい提案というか、うまくいきましたね。

表面だけのデザインに終わらなくて良かったなと思います(笑)。初期のスタディもスケッチのように抽象的なレベルで見ている分にはいいけれど。

— 生々しさをもち始めると、急にこういうものが気持ち悪くなりますね。

厚さも出てくるしね。

### (仮称)川口市火葬施設・赤山歴史自然公園

— 「(仮称)川口市火葬施設・赤山歴史自然公園」プロジェクトが始まったのは2011年です。この計画は、広大なランドスケープも含めて、葬祭場と「(仮称)歴史自然資料館」と「(仮称)地域物産館」をつくるというものです。

「瞑想の森 市営斎場」を見た時に、あれは下から生えてきているようなボリュームとして各部屋があって、一方で天から舞い降りた羽衣みたいなものが屋根になっていて、葬祭場的な生と死の境目などが、大地と空みたいなコントラストとして表されていて、すごくわかりやすい建物だなと思いました。

「川口」を見ると、屋根は同じようなつくり方をしていますが、「瞑想の森」では軽い羽衣みたいなものだった屋根に山が載っていたり、違うものに置き換わってきています。「瞑想の森」には羽衣とか布みたいなものというイメージがあるとすると、「川口」にはどういうイメージをもっていますか。

僕の中では「大池」のイメージですね。上から圧力が掛かっているような、重いものでいいと最初から思っていた。どちらかというと「地形」に近いかもしれない。その中で、炉の機械室だけは、どう処理すべきかわからないというくらい苦労した場所ですね。

— 実際にボリュームとして現れてきてしまう絶対的な大きさがあって、それをどう建築の中に組

---

– Were you thinking it would be interesting to have, not so much greenery, but something corporeal, like an internal organ, in the middle of the city?

Yes.

– Did the shift from that to greenery take place because there was talk of regulations?

I think the biggest factor was we were able to arrive at an understanding with the client about increasing the greening of the building because greening made it possible to increase the floor area.
Besides the greening, parts that made the enjoyment of intermediate domains such as the terraces in CapitaGreen began to appear. CapitaGreen was at first only superficially green, but it was the first project in which "greenery" began to appear in the way space is used and specified, was it not?

Yes.

– It was rather difficult to introduce greenery into interiors, even with CapitaGreen. That led to the selection of materials with natural textures such as plaster and brick-faced blocks, so that even though greenery might be absent inside rooms, there was a connection, via the semi-outdoor places, to the surrounding greenery.

There was a hint of such a space in The Crest (Singapore condominium project) (p. 231). In the case of CapitaGreen, the outside was first greened, and in response to that, Mr. Olafur Eliasson created an artwork resembling the roots of a tree. That was followed by the use of plaster walls and bricks. I think that is interesting. Plaster walls are unusual for office buildings.

– Yes. They are usually clad in stone.

If we compare our early organic scheme with what exists now, the depth of greenery is imagined slightly differently. At first, greenery was imagined as texture, but now there are the glass louvers, and the greenery is behind those louvers. So the greenery exists deep inside layers. The greenery extends into the tower. That is precisely why Mr. Olafur imagined something like roots down below.

At first, we made many studies because we wanted to avoid having the facade seem like it had been simply applied to the building.

– The louvers were a great proposal--they worked out well.

I'm glad it was not just a surface design [laughs]. Though the early studies are nice too if one looks at them as abstract sketches.

– Such things suddenly become unpleasant when they become too real.

They also take on thickness.

### Crematorium and Akayama Historic Nature Park in Kawaguchi (tentative title)

– Crematorium and Akayama Historic Nature Park in Kawaguchi (tentative title) project began in 2011. This project also includes extensive landscaping and involves the creation of a funeral hall, the Historical natural information centre (tentative title), and the Regional products centre (tentative title).

In "Meiso no Mori" Municipal Funeral Hall, the rooms are volumes that have seemingly come up from below, and the roof is like a robe of feathers that has descended from the heavens. The fact that a funeral hall exists on the boundary between life and death is expressed through contrast between the earth and the sky. I thought the building was extremely easy to understand.
The roof in Kawaguchi is built the same way, but while the roof in "Meiso no Mori" was seemingly light as a feather here it is topped by a mountain; it is something else. In "Meiso no Mori" the roof was imagined as feathers or cloth. What was the image in Kawaguchi?

I imagined it as the earth. From the start I thought it could be something heavy, something on which pressure was applied from above. If anything, it is close to "topography." We had a lot of trouble with the machine room for the crematory--we didn't know how it ought to be treated.

– You mean that it was so large, it inevitably made itself known as a volume, and the problem was how to incorporate that into the architecture?

Yes. The overall image is therefore different from "Meiso no Mori." The architectural image we had in mind then and the architectural image we have in mind now are, I think, different. Materials too have changed.

– Yes. Is there a correlation between building type and schema in your own mind? For example, do you feel that the style used in Belle Vue Residences, the condominium in Singapore, suits housing? Or that a space arranged around multiple centers suits a library?

I think that develops naturally out of the relationship to the program. With multi-unit housing there is a limit to what can be done because units are stacked vertically.
The Crest (Singapore condominium project) was imagined as something plant-like, growing upward, but there was also a strong image of something "ascending." That was also true of

み込んでいくのかということですね。

そう。だから「瞑想の森」と全体のイメージが違いますね。あのころ考えていた建築像と、いま考えているわれわれの建築像は違っていると思うし、素材も変わってきましたね。

― そうですね。ビルディングタイプと図式の関係性みたいなことは、伊東さんの中に何かありますか。たとえば、住宅はシンガポールでのコンドミニアム「ベルビュー・レジデンシズ」のスタイルがしっくりくるとか、図書館だと中心点がたくさんあって、まわりに展開するような空間がしっくりくるのではないかとか。

それはおのずからプログラムとの関係でできているものだと思いますね。集合住宅では積層していったら、できることはかなり限られるから。「The Crest(シンガポールコンドミニアムプロジェクト)」では、上に向かって伸びていくという、植物的なイメージがあると同時に、「上昇」というイメージが強い。庇にしてもそうですね。「川口」は連続する波のような屋根ですが、これは相当平面が大きいから、ひとつの大屋根にするのは無理があると思いましたね。

― 最新の案を見ると、屋根という感覚とはちょっと変わってきていますね。平面と大きく関わりますが、中心に炉があって、その周囲に控え室とかの空間がある。その上に屋根が架かっているので、屋根というよりは大きな庇のように感じますね。

イメージとしては、民家の屋根の下みたいな、わりと暗くて、地面から盛り上がっていったようなイメージがありますね。だから、「瞑想の森」みたいな、ふわっとしたものとは全然違う。

― じゃあ、屋根が地面から出てきたみたいな感じですか。

そうですね。

― 同じ形態ですが、イメージが変わるものですね。

かなりごつい感じだしね。

― そうですね。炉が山になっているので、最後は弔われた人が山へ帰っていくような感じもあります。

以前の抽象的な、わりとミニマムにつくっていた時は、構造に重点があるというか、構造的なパラメーターを最大化するためのスタディをしていますが、いまはそれだけじゃなく、環境的なアプローチなど、要素が増えているような気がします。

その時に面白いと思っているのは、要素が増えてくると、設計の段階、特に初期でいろいろな調整が必要になる。たとえば断熱を良くしようとすると、窓が小さくなり、風も通らず、光も入らないものになってしまうというように、相矛盾するものを調整するような作業が出てきてしまう。

その時に、どういう指標で、何がいいのだろうというふうに考えていくと、もとのアイデアはミニマムなものがあるけれども、そこにいろいろな要素を足していき、さまざまな調整をしていった結果が新しい建築に結び付いていく。そのような中で、新しい素材を使うということについてはどのように考えていますか。

「川口」は初期から、いろんな素材を使おうとか、自然に近い素材を使おうと意識していましたが、最初からミニマムだとは思っていませんでしたね。基本的な考え方は、内外の関係をもっと曖昧にしていこうというような、日本の近代以前の家に近づけようということです。最近のわれわれのプロジェクトはそのような思想に始まるのですが、それがさまざまな矛盾と遭遇してしまう。

超高層には超高層の矛盾があるし、「川口」で難しかったのは、東京都内といってもいいぐらいの都心に近い所にあって、さまざまな人が利用する公園の中に、静かで、人目に触れないような葬儀場をつくってほしいというリクエストがありました。そのギャップの中でわれわれはデザインしていかなければならなかった。

たとえば、待合室の回りにテラスをつくって池に面するのだから、テラスに出てもいいだろうと提案しても許されない。小学生が通学途中に道路からこの屋根が見えてもいけない。その半面、ここでも友引の日は「瞑想の森」みたいにコンサートをやりたいという希望もあるし、非常に難しいですね。

― 本当は人が死ぬ所はもっと身近であるはずですが、そこは変えるのはなかなか難しいと思いますね。

最近、東京の葬祭場では葬儀をする人が減ってきていて、家族だけで密葬しましたとか、お別れ

---

the eaves. Kawaguchi has a continuous, wave-like roof. It was relatively large in area, so I thought it was unreasonable to make it one large roof.

– The roof seems slightly different in the latest scheme. It is closely related to the plan. The crematory is in the center, and the waiting rooms and other spaces are arranged around it. The roof is placed over that, so that it feels more like large eaves, that is like a large overhang, than a roof.

I imagine it as something that rises from the ground, rather dark, like the area under the roof of a *minka*. It is therefore completely different from the roof that seems to float in "Meiso no Mori."

– Do you mean the roof seems to have emerged out of the ground?

Yes.

– Roofs with similar forms can have different images.

It is rather hard and tough looking.

– Yes. The crematory forms a mountain, so it is as if the deceased in the end returns to the mountains.
When we were doing abstract, relatively minimal schemes in the past, we emphasized structure, or studied ways to maximize structural parameters, but now we seem to be considering not only that but an increasing number of factors including an environmental approach.
What is interesting is that as factors increase, various adjustments in the design stage, especially early in the design process, become necessary. Work must be done to adjust mutually incompatible things. For example, if we try to improve heat insulation, windows become small and limit the introduction of fresh air and light.
When we consider what sort of guideline to adopt--that is, what is preferable--under those circumstances, there was a minimalist idea previously. But now, as we add various factors to that, various adjustments are made, resulting in a new sort of architecture. In that process, how do you view the use of new materials?

I was intent on using various materials--materials that are close to nature--from an early stage in the Kawaguchi project, but I did not think the scheme would be minimal from the start. The basic idea was to approximate the premodern Japanese house, that is, to establish an ambiguous relationship between inside and outside. We have started with such ideas in our recent project, but in doing so, we encounter various contradictions.
Super-tall buildings have contradictions that are inherent in super-tall buildings. What was difficult about Kawaguchi was that the client wanted us to create a quiet funeral hall that is out of sight in the middle of a park used by many different people in a place that can be said effectively a part of Metropolitan Tokyo. We had to work under those contradictory conditions.
For example, we provided a terrace around the waiting rooms that faced a pond. When we suggested that people be allowed to go out onto the terrace, the proposal was rejected. We were also told that this roof should not be visible to elementary school students walking to school. On the other hand, they wanted to hold concerts at the hall on days when funerals

「ベルビュー・レジデンシズ」(シンガポール)　Belle Vue Residences (Singapore)

の会だけを行う、そういう人たちが増えているのはわかりますね。

― いろいろな矛盾がありますね。使う人にとっては隠された場所じゃなくて、最後に死者とお別れをする場所だから神聖なものであってほしいけれども、ふだん生活している時には目にしたくないという、矛盾がある。

矛盾があるし、「瞑想の森」だと、人口が少ないから1日に何組といってもそんなにかち合わないけれども、川口は都心だから数が多いわけです。それを、どうすればお互いすれ違わないようにするかとか、動線のことを考えなければならない。

― 伊東さんが言われたように、いろんな施設があって、公園があって、それこそ老若男女が出入りするし、公園で遊ぶ人もいる。そうすると、周辺の植木農家の方がたの中には「この山に自分たちの木を植える」とか、「おれはここで葬儀を行うんだ」と言われている人たちも出てきて、人びととの関係が築けているなと思っています。だから、死というものがここでは身近になるような気がします。都市の中にある火葬場として、隔離された山奥にあるものとはまた違う場になっていくといいなと思います。

ここに建築が出来ると、一つひとつの空間は静かだと思います。「瞑想の森」に共通するような空間が出来るはずで、それを感じた時に、いろんなことが見直されるだろうし、周りから隠さなくてはいけないという考え方も変わってくるような気がしますね。

― 現状を変えていくような切っ掛けが示しているし、ここで葬られたいという人も出てきている。これからいろいろ変わっていく契機になるかもしれませんね。

そうですよ。「瞑想の森」も、外国人が「ここで葬られたい」と言っているんだから。

― そういうことができるといいですね。グンナール・アスプルンドの森の葬祭場は、どんな宗教でも葬儀ができますから。

ここもそうだよ。だから仏教的にはしないと言われています。

― あと、公園の中に「歴史自然資料館」と「地域物産館」がありますが、全然性格が違うものが公園の中に散在しているほうがいいということですか。

違うほうがいいと、積極的に考えたわけでもないけれど……(笑)。

― 大きく言うと、「歴史自然資料館」のほうは展示スペースが主で、かつ、広場につながっていることもあり、子どもたちを見ながら休憩できるようなスペースが欲しいということで、わりと閉じています。「地域物産館」は、植木屋さんたちが植木などの展示をする。オリエンテーションスペースでは地元の小学生が奥のビオトープで勉強できる。また、遠足や社会科見学でも使う。公園の中に人が気軽に入っていけるようなスペースで、結構オープンな空間ですね。

何で「地域物産館」はフラットになって、「歴史自然資料館」はこんな屋根の付いたものになったんだろうね(笑)。

―「地域物産館」は、最初は2階建てで、温室がつながったようなものを考え、「今治市伊東豊雄建築ミュージアム」のような模型を作っていました。敷地が小高くなっており、開けていて池を見下ろせるので、積層するよりはフラットで、横に広がりがあるようなものがいいんじゃないかなという話から、ハスの葉っぱのフラットなルーフが出てきました。

ここにもいろいろな素材が使われていたりします。わりとシンプルストラクチャーに見えますが、ハスの部分は、少し生成りか白かというところですね。

屋根の形状はそれぞれ違います。柱はいま4タイプです。30本ぐらいありますから、ある程度タイプをつくり効率的にしました。

「台湾大学社会科学部棟」の図書館でのサッシの在り方が気になっています。内外のつながりが完全に切れてしまった。「川口」は内外の関係がだいぶ緩くなっています。それでも、もっと何かできたかもしれませんね。

― ミニマムにしようと思って、ガラスをきれいに納めようとした結果、境界が強くなってしまうということを、よく考えないといけないですね。

そう。「瞑想の森」も同じような問題を抱えていますね。

---

were not scheduled, as at "Meiso no Mori." It was extremely difficult.

– Places associated with death should actually be more a part of the everyday environment, but it is difficult to change that.

Fewer funerals are being held in funeral halls in Tokyo these days. Increasing numbers of people choose to hold private funerals or to have leave-taking parties instead, and that is understandable.

– There are many different contradictions. A funeral hall is not a concealed place for those using it, but it ought to be sacred since it is the place where they take leave of the deceased. However, they don't want to see it in the course of their everyday lives.

Contradictions exist. In the case of "Meiso no Mori," the population is small, so there is little likelihood of different groups bumping into each other. Kawaguchi is in the center of the city, so the numbers are greater. Paths of circulation have to be designed so that different groups do not come into contact with each other.

– As you said, there are various facilities, there is the park, used by the young and the old, male and female, people who also play in the park. Among the farmers nearby who make their living growing garden plants, there are those who come and say, "We will plant our own trees on this mountain," or, "We will have our own funerals here." This is a community, with relationships firmly established. That's why I believe death will become accepted as a part of the everyday environment here. I think it would be good if this, as a crematorium in the middle of the city, becomes a different place from an isolated crematorium in the mountains.

When the building is completed, I believe each space will be quiet. Spaces that have things in common with those in "Meiso no Mori" will likely be created. When people sense that, I think many different things will be reconsidered. I think the idea that a place of this kind must be concealed will also change.

– There are clues there of how the present situation can be changed, and people have started to express a desire to be buried here. This might provide an opportunity for various changes.

Yes. Even if non-Japanese people say they want to be buried at "Meiso no Mori."

– It would be good if that were so. People can have funerals at Gunnar Asplund's Woodland Cemetery whatever their religion.

That's true here as well. That's why they say they will not make the place Buddhist in character.

– There are also the Historical natural information centre and Regional products centre within the park. Does this mean you believe facilities that are entirely different in character ought to be scattered inside the park?

I wasn't actively promoting the idea that they should be different…[laughs].

– The Historical natural information centre is mainly exhibition space. It is also close to the square. That is why they wanted a space where people could rest while keeping watch over their children. The museum is therefore relatively closed. The Regional products centre is a place where growers of garden plants exhibit their plants. Local elementary school students can study in the biotope at the far end of the orientation space. It is also used for school excursions and civic study tours. It is a fairly open space where people in the park can casually drop in.

「The Crest(シンガポールコンドミニアムプロジェクト)」
The Crest (Singapore condominium project)

Why did the Regional products centre become flat and the Historical natural information centre end up with a roof like that [laughs]?

– The Regional products centre was initially two-stories and was connected to a hothouse. We built models that resembled the Toyo Ito Museum of Architecture, Imabari. Then, it was thought that it ought to be flat and spread out more because the site was on slightly higher ground and afforded a view of the pond. That led to a flat, lotus-leaf roof.

Diverse materials are used here as well, though it may seem like a relatively simple structure.
The lotus part is slightly unbleached or white.
The roof forms are all different. There are now

— あのガラスの異様さが目につきますね。奇跡的な、「こんなものが出来るんだ！」というガラスですが、気になるといえば、気になりますね。

フレームがないと、"開く"感じがしないから、閉じられているんだなと。

スクリーン的になっているわけですね。それが「川口」では無垢のサッシュになっている。ちょっと違いますね。

— サッシュがあると、ちょっとだけしか開かないのですが、「あ、開くんだな」という気になります。

ドアがひとつあると、それは開けるシンボルでありサインになるから、閉じられた部屋でも、ドアがひとつあるだけで安心するのと同じように、サッシュは外に出られるシンボルみたいなところがある。

— そうですね。前窓も"開く"というのがわかるし、建具というのは場所をつなげるものだから、そういうデザインをどんどん開発したいですね（笑）。

「歴史自然資料館」はシェル構造だったり、いろんなスタディをやっていましたね。

— そうですね。最初は1枚のシェルでやっていました。その時は、公園と一体になるような施設というコンセプトが面白かったのですが、ここで映像を展示したいという話になって、どうしても黒い、暗い、閉じたほうがいいということが出てきた。そうなると、公園と一体になったシェルの下に小さい箱があるというデザインに無理が出てきましたね。それで伊東さんとも打ち合わせを重ねて、いくつか家が建って、それを柔かい屋根でつなぐというような形のデザインに話が進んでいったと思います。

— これはなぜ3つが違うんですか。

三匹の子豚（笑）。

— 伊東さんが出張でどこかに行かれた帰りの飛行機で「三匹の子豚」が出てきて、それが切っ掛けに（笑）。煉瓦と土と木です。ワラではないですけど。

木は、結局木造ではなくなったんですよね。

— 鉄骨造で、仕上げに木を張ります。

これはみんな鉄骨造になったんだっけ。

— そうです。煉瓦の家も鉄骨です。鉄骨を中に入れて、両側に煉瓦を積む。

土の家は左官です。

たたずまいとして、これはかわいいですね。

かわいい。ランドスケープの石川幹子さんはあまり好きじゃないみたいですね（笑）。「地域物産館」はすごく気に入っていたけどね。

— 石川さんは、ランドスケープとの連続感があるので、閉じているものはだめだと。

家と家の間の空間は、石川さんがデザインしているのですが、家と家が近いと日が当たらないから育たないとか、さまざまな話があって、いろいろと難しそうでしたね。

大きな模型を作り、この地域の植木を見てまわり、「これはここに植えましょう」とその場で決めていかれました。最終的に周辺の地域の植木をここで見ることが出来るようになります。

— 「瞑想の森」や「台湾大」は、サッシュの話とかいろいろな要素が入ってきて、抽象的なものと物質的なものとのいい組み合わせが目指されていると思いますが、この「歴史自然資料館」を見ると、ものすごく抽象的だなという気もします。これは家型が強くて、それに3つの違う素材が割り当てられていて、それを屋根でつなぐというものですが、いろんな素材を使っているけれども、逆に抽象的だなという気がします。

— それはそうかもしれないです。記号的な感じがするからですね。煉瓦の家とか、一言で言えるから。

先日藤森照信さんと対談した時に、藤森さんはいつも「日本の民家は嫌だ。だから自分は畳も使わないし、障子も使わないし、竹も使わない。要するにそれは日本を象徴することになってしまうので、そういうのは嫌なんだ」と。そう言われれば、彼の建築では意外にも障子はないんですよ。それからゴザは敷くけれども、畳は使っていない。和風だと言われるのが嫌だと。素材もいろいろなものを使うけれど、手づくりでできるものばかり使っている。

つまり、「○○でない、△△でもない」という方法でいつもつくっているということで、これは面白い考え方だと思いました。そうやっていくことが、表現を消すことでもある。だから、藤森さん

---

four types of columns. There are about 30 columns in all, so we decided to develop several different types for the sake of efficiency.

I am uneasy about the sash in the library for National Taiwan University, College of Social Sciences. There is no connection between inside and outside. There is more of a relationship between inside and outside in Kawaguchi, but still more should have been done.

– Using clean details for glass in order to create a minimalist effect can lead to a more definite boundary. That is something we need to think about more.

Yes. There was the same sort of problem in "Meiso no Mori."

– The strangeness of that glass is striking. It is close to miraculous that such glass can be made, but it does make one uneasy.

It wouldn't look like it "opens" unless there was a frame. It would look closed.

It has a screen-like effect. In Kawaguchi, solid metal sash is used, so that is different.

– Where there is sash, though it opens only slightly, one picks up on that and thinks, "Oh, it opens."

Just as the presence of a door serves as a symbol or sign that a place opens and is reassuring in an otherwise closed room, sash serves as a symbol that one can go out.

– Yes. One understands that the front window "opens," and because doors and windows connect places, we ought to develop such designs [laughs].

We did many different studies, for example, the idea of making the Historical natural information centre a shell structure.

– Yes. Initially, we used a single shell. At the time, the concept of integrating the facility with the park was interesting, but then we were told videos would be shown there. That meant the place ought to be black, dark and closed. Having a small box under a shell that was integrated with the park seemed irrational. We had repeated discussions with you, and that led to the idea of having several houses that were connected by a soft roof.

– Why are the three different?

The Three Little Pigs [laughs].

– "The Three Little Pigs" was mentioned on a plane when you were returning from some trip, and that was the clue [laughs]. They are brick, earth and wood. There is no straw.

The wood one is not actually wooden construction.

– It is steel-frame construction finished in wood.

Did we end up making everything steel-frame construction?

– Yes. The brick house too is steel-frame. The bricks are laid on both sides of the steel frame.
  The earthen house is plastered.
  It is *kawaii*.

It is *kawaii*. Ms. Mikiko Ishikawa, the landscape designer, does not seem to like it much [laughs], though she liked the Regional products centre a great deal.

– Ms. Ishikawa objected to closed structures. She insisted the structures ought to be continuous with the landscape.
  She designed the spaces between houses. If the houses are built too close together, the sun does not reach those spaces and nothing will grow. There were various arguments she used to try to pull the houses further apart.
  She made a large model, studied the garden plants grown in the area, and decided on the spot which to plant where. People will be able to see the garden plants that are grown in the area.

– Various elements including sash were introduced in "Meiso no Mori" and National Taiwan University. The aim seems to have been to achieve a good combination of the abstract and the material, but this Historical natural information centre seems quite abstract. The house forms are assertive, three different materials have been assigned, and these are connected by a roof. Although various materials are used, it seems, on the contrary, abstract.

– That may be. It's because they seem symbolic. The elements can be described quite easily, for example, the brick house.

When I talked with Mr. Terunobu Fujimori the other day, he said that he dislikes Japanese *minka*. That's why he never uses *tatami*, *shoji* or bamboo. That is, those things inevitably symbolize Japan, and he hates that. Come to think of it, *shoji* is never used in his buildings, which is unexpected. He also may use rush mats but never *tatami*. He says he does not like to have his work described as *wafu* (Japanese style). He uses various materials but only things that can be hand-made.

That is, his method of design is to avoid being labeled. I think that is an interesting approach. To consistently adopt this approach is to eliminate expression. Therefore, a work by Mr. Fujimori is not a work by anyone else;

のものは、誰のものでもないし、どこにあったものでもない。そういう意味で「抽象」になる。

前に、藤森さんのもっている抽象性について書いたことがありますが[1]、藤森さんがある種のポピュラリティをもっているのは、山口百恵さんの「いい日旅立ち」にたとえられます。つまり、誰も反対しない「ああ、いいなあ」という懐かしさがあるけれども、それを具体的に「これだ！」と限定しないところが面白い。われわれもそういうことを別のやり方でやれるといいと思いますね。"個を超える個"と言っている、その意味はまさしくそういうことかなと思うんですよ。

― 家型をつくってしまうと、誰にでも共有されるけれど、それがシンボルというかサインになってしまう。でも、それがシンボルにならずに、誰にでも共有されるようなイメージをつくるということですね。でも、それがムチャクチャ難しいです。

難しいけれども、いろんな素材もいまは使える状態になりつつあるし、形もわれわれはどこかにこだわっているわけではないから、そういう考え方を共通のイメージにしながら発想していくと面白いかもしれないと思います。

― その「いい日旅立ち」的なものに、「みんなの家」は近いような気がして……。

そう、「みんなの家」はそれに近いことを目指しているんだと思いますね。これは東北地方独特のものだとかいった、地域性ではない。"どこにもあって、どこにもない"もの。藤森さんが、このあいだのレクチャー[2]で「縄文のこころと建築」というタイトルで話していたように、何千年も遡っていくと世界共通になる。そこまでいってしまえば問題ない。

― そこまでいかなくても、僕らが何十年か都市で生きてきて、同じような生活をしている人たちが同じ所に住んでいる中で、どこかしらで何かを共有していると思っています。心地いいと思う場所というのは、みんなが同じような所を想像してみたりとか。それは動物的な感覚もあるし、社会的なものもあり、みんなが共有する。でもその何十年も"どこにもない"ものって、あるかもしれないですね。

それは相当あるなあ（笑）。

― 菊竹清訓さんの初期の建物は、懐かしいなと思う要素があるような感じがしています。東光園にしろ出雲大社庁の舎にしろ。

そうね。菊竹さんも初期のものは、自分が育った環境からきているような、身体的なところから発している。モダニズムの最先端みたいなことを言いながら、そういう身体性がほとばしっているところに、あの新鮮な建築が生まれたのだと思います。スカイハウスもそうですね。

藤森さんも、なぜ茶室を必ず付けるんですかと聞いたら、「茶室は衣服みたいなもので、要するに身体的にものを考えられるから面白いんだ」と言っていますね。だから、藤森さんは全部具体的なものから考えている。例えばここにこの杉の木の丸太を1本切ってきて、枝振りから、この空間がどうなっていくのか、という順序で考えている。最後に「抽象」に行き着くところが面白い。ほかにいないタイプですね。

それは小さいからできることでもあると思いますが、図書館を考えるといった場合には、もっと大きいところから考えざるを得ない。でも、われわれは藤森さんと全然違う立場に置かれているからこそ、逆に新しい大法を発見する可能性があると思います。もしそれを発見できれば"21世紀の建築"になり得るはずです。ただ、「個」の表現で終始しているとそれは難しい。「台中国立歌劇院」はものすごく変なことをやっているけれども、あれは個人を超えているようなところがありますからね。

― それで言うと、ル・コルビュジエのユニテ・ダビタシオンを見ていると、個の表現ではあるけれども一般性をもっているというか、誰にでも受け入れられるようなイメージをもっているような気がして、そこがル・コルビュジエのすごいところなのかなという気がしますね。

そうですね。

― 思考がずっと「抽象」だけでなく、即物的に考えたり具体的に考えたりという、行ったり来たりができるのでしょうね。

やはり精神が開いているからでしょうね。

― 新しいものを考える時には、自分の身体を基準にして考えなきゃいけないけれども、そこからさらに踏み出した先で、一般性を獲得できるんですね。

---

it has never existed before. In that sense, it is "abstract."

I once wrote about the abstract quality of Mr. Fujimori's works. The kind of popularity his works enjoy can be likened to *Iihi tabidachi* (A Good Day for Departing), the song by Ms. Momoe Yamaguchi. The song has a certain nostalgic quality that everyone can relate to, but interestingly, there is nothing specific one can point to as the source of that nostalgia. I think it would be good if we could do something like that, only in a different way. I think that is what is meant by "transpersonal."

– If one creates a house form, it is shared with everyone, but it becomes a symbol or sign. What you are saying is that one should create an image that can be shared with everyone without it becoming a symbol. That is awfully difficult.

It is difficult, but today we are able to use many different materials, and we are not preoccupied with any particular form. It may be interesting to design while adopting such an approach to create common images.

– I think "Home-for-All" has a *Iihi tabidachi*-like quality…

Yes. I think the aim of "Home-for-All" projects is to create something like that. It is to create, not a thing that has a regional character unique to Tohoku, but a thing that "exists everywhere" and "exists nowhere." Just as Mr. Fujimori stated in his lecture the other day entitled "The Jomon Spirit and Architecture," if we go back thousands of years, a common architecture existed throughout the world. There are no problems if we go back that far.

– Even if we don't go that far back, we have lived in cities for decades. People who lead the same sorts of lives and live in the same places inevitably possess some things in common somewhere. The image of what constitutes a comfortable place may be the same for them. This may be an animal-like sense, it may be something social--it is shared by everyone. But things that "haven't existed anywhere" for decades may exit.

There are plenty of such things [laughs].

– Early works by Mr. Kiyonori Kikutake, for example, Hotel Tokoen and the Administration Building for Izumo Shrine, had elements that somehow seemed familiar.

Yes. Early works by Mr. Kikutake seemed to emerge from some corporeal place, from the environment in which he grew up. Though he talked as if he were at the forefront of modernism, those imaginative works were products of that sort of corporeality. Sky House too.

When I asked Mr. Fujimori why he was always designing tea houses, he said that tea houses were like clothing. They are interesting because they require one to think about things from a corporeal perspective. That is why Mr. Fujimori always starts from specific things. For example, if I cut down this cedar, which has this shape, and take the log to that place there, what will happen to the space? That is the sequence of his thought process. What is interesting is that he ultimately arrives at a form of "abstraction." He is one of a kind.

That is possible with small projects, but when one is dealing with, say a library, one must start from some larger place. But it is precisely because we are in a position entirely different from that of Mr. Fujimori that a possibility exists for us to discover a new approach. If we can discover that, then that may well produce the architecture of the twenty-first century. But that is difficult if it is always about personal expression. We are doing something quite unusual in National Taichung Theater, but the possibility exists because it transcends the individual.

– In that context, the Unité d'habitation by Le Corbusier is a work of personal expression but also has a universal quality--that is, I feel it has an image that everyone can accept. I think that is what makes Le Corbusier amazing.

Yes.

– I suppose it was because he didn't just think abstractly, he also thought realistically or materially. He was able to go back and forth.

I imagine it was because he was open-minded.

– One must use one's own body as a criterion when one is thinking of something new, but it is when one goes one step further that one is able to achieve universal quality.

Yes.

### Barroco Museo Internacional

– Barroco Museo Internacional in Mexico is an enormous building measuring 120 m x 120 m. We started by establishing a grid. That grid gradually was distorted, and we considered how light would enter. That was when the scheme suddenly took on a corporeal scale. We began with an idea similar to that of our scheme for BAM / PFA University of California Berkeley Art Museum and Pacific Film Archive, but when we began to think about such things, it became different from Berkeley.

233

そうですね。

## バロックミュージアム・プエブラ

— メキシコの「バロックミュージアム・プエブラ」の場合は、一辺120×120mという巨大なもので、最初にグリッドの設定がありました。そのグリッドがだんだんゆがんでいって、どう光が入ってくるんだろうと考えた時に、急に身体的なスケールに落ちてきた気がします。もともと「カリフォルニア大学　バークレー美術館／パシフィック・フィルム・アーカイブ」的な思考からスタートしましたが、そういうことを考え始めた段階で「バークレー」とは違うものになっている感じがします。

かなり違ったものになっていますね。

— その変化するターニングポイントは、光の入り方とか身体性について考えた時だった気がします。

そういうことを考えさせるのがメキシコの土壌というか、おおらかさですね。「バークレー」の時はそういう余裕がなかったように思えます。敷地が狭いというのもありますが、それだけではなくて、管理されながら設計が進んでいく気がしていました。

— 「バークレー」と比べると、だいぶ緩いというか、いろんなものを受け入れてくれるような大きさがある人が多いですね。

「バークレー」の場合は、日本と同じような管理社会の中でデザインするから、洗練されたきれいなものになっていきますが、「プエブラ」はきれいさというより、ダイナミックさとか、力強さとか、とにかく自由につくっていいよみたいな感じで、伸び伸びしていますね。

— 施主もそういうことを求めていたという感じですか。

施主はおおらかというか……(笑)。最初に、われわれがいままでどういうことをやってきたかを説明する中のひとつに「バークレー」があって、それを見た州知事が、「これは実現しなかったんだな。じゃあこれを建てよう」と言われたので(笑)、それで決まりました。

— 「バークレー」の時は、「ホワイトキューブからの脱却」というのが強くあったように記憶しています。これは一つひとつが回転体というような発想になっていて、その回転体が外部的な緑の空間でつながっていき、結節点を介して流動していくような空間になっています。これにより、流動性をうまく獲得出来た気がしています。
エッジを曲げる前は、グリッドが強く見えていたのですが、エッジを曲げてみると、急に消えてなくなる。

あるところまでシステマティックにいっているのですが…。

— グリッドを回転させていくと、あるところまではグリッドがきれいに残っているけれども、回転させ続けると隙間が出てきます。その隙間が出た所に光を入れようということになって、光について、さまざまな話をしていた時に、天から射すような光という話が出てきて、そういうものをカメラの絞りのような感じで考えたらどうだろうという話になりました。その時にグリッドが崩れていきました。

光の差し込む場所は休憩する緩衝地帯。中庭が見えたりしますね。

— 半外部的なものですね。

実際にはインテリアです。この博物館はすごく大きくて、7つのテーマがある部屋を一つひとつ巡っていく時に、そのまま全部屋つなげてしまうと長すぎてしまうので、途中途中に気分をリフレッシュするための場所を挟み込む意味合いでこの場所が必ずあります。そこで、中庭が見えたり空の光が見えたりするようにしています。

中庭も最初は小さいものがいくつかありましたね。

— 昔のプレゼンテーション案で、4×5のマス目でやっていた時は、ふたつ中庭があるというプランでした。その後大きな変更をして、大きな中庭ひとつを囲むように展示室を設けました。

それが結果的に良かったですね。初期案よりは単純化されている。

— そうですね。初期案では、すごく迷いそうな建物になっていました。それがシンプルに中庭をひとつぐるっと回るという体験にされたことで、迷

It is now considerably different.

– I believe our starting to think about the way light enters and corporeality was the turning point in that process.

The soil of Mexico, its tolerance, is what leads one to think of such things. We didn't have such leeway in Berkeley. Part of that had to do with the small site, but that wasn't all. It felt as if we had to design under supervision.

– Compared with Berkeley, this seems looser. The people seem willing to accept many different ideas.

In the case of Berkeley, we were designing in a managed society similar to Japan and arrived at a refined, beautiful scheme. But Puebla is not so much beautiful as it is dynamic or powerful. It is free and easy, as if we were under no restriction concerning the design.

– Do you think the client was looking for something like that?

The client is tolerant...[laughs]. When we first explained what sorts of things we had done up to then, we included Berkeley. When he saw it, the state governor said, "You say this was never realized? Well, let's build this." That was how it was decided [laughs].

– I remember that at the time of Berkeley, we were determined to break away from the white cube. These are all conceived somewhat like solids of revolution, each one connected to an outdoor-like green space. The space seems to flow by way of nodes. This enabled us to achieve a flowing quality.
The grid was quite perceptible until we curved the edges. Once we curved them, the grid suddenly disappeared.

Even though the scheme is systematic up to a certain point.

– When we rotate the grid, the grid remains up to a certain point, but when we continue to rotate it, interstices appear. The idea was to introduce light through these interstices. During discussions we had concerning light the idea of light that seems to come from the sky was suggested. We thought, Why not think of it like the aperture of a camera? That was when the grid broke down.

The places where light enters are buffer zones where people can rest. There are views of courtyards.

– They are semi-outdoor places.

They are actually interiors. This museum is enormous. There are seven rooms, each with a different theme. If all the rooms were connected, it would be too long for a visitor. We introduced these places in order to provide in-between areas where visitors can refresh themselves. People can see the courtyard or the sky in those places.

At first there were a number of courtyards.

– In an old presentation scheme, when we were still working with a 4x5 grid, the plan had two courtyards. After a major change in plan, the galleries were arranged around one large courtyard.

That was an improvement. It is simpler than the early scheme.

– It would have been easy to get lost in the early scheme. Now that visitors simply circle a single courtyard, there is little chance they will get lost. Though the museum is complex as a spatial experience, the exhibitions themselves are arranged in a simple way.

– There are two stories, with offices on the second floor.

「カリフォルニア大学　バークレー美術館／パシフィック・フィルム・アーカイブ」
BAM / PFA University of California, Berkeley Art Museum and Pacific Film Archive

– There are, in addition to offices, a restaurant, a library, an educational space for children, storage and a restoration room.

– In Berkeley, walls could be manipulated to create voids connecting multiple levels. Will there be something similar to that in Mexico, with multiple levels and the apertures of the walls?

– Berkeley was three-storied. With only two stories, there is not a sense of levels being stacked

わない。空間体験としては複雑だけれども、展示を巡る体験としては単純になります。

― 2層になっていますが、2階部分はオフィスですか。

― オフィスもありますし、レストラン、図書館、子どものための教育用のスペースと、あとは収蔵庫と修復室です。

―「バークレー」の時は、壁の操作で層をつなぐようなヴォイドが出来るような効果がありましたが、メキシコの場合は、積層と壁の絞りの部分とで同じような効果がありますか？

―「バークレー」は3層ですが、2層になるとあまり積層感がないです。むしろ積層していることよりも、上から入る光が1階までどう届くかというところに意識を置いていて、「バークレー」が垂直軸だとすると、「プエブラ」はより平面的に、XY軸で広がっていくような気がします。

「バークレー」のすごく抽象的なものに比べて、「プエブラ」は30cm以上ある壁の力強いもので、全然別の体験になっているような気がします。

吹き付けのざらざらした素材でね。

― 形が強いので、そういうものでやる予定です。

最初は打ち放しにしようとこだわっていましたが、きれいにコンクリートが打てるかどうか分からない。

― そうすると、展示としては、壁はほとんど使わないということですか。

それはこれからのスタディですね。
ただ絵を見せるという美術館とは違っていて、音楽とか文学とか、プログラムが部屋ごとに分かれている。その間に中庭を覗いたり、外側の水に面したり、いろいろな体験ができます。

― 新しい博物館ということもあって、展示方法もいろいろなやり方を試みるみたいですね。映像を模型に投影し立体的に表現するなど博物館の静的なイメージではなくて、よりダイナミックな展示になるイメージをもっています。
いろんな箱の寄せ集めのようにも見えますし、流動的な、箱を中心とした広がりを感じられるようにも見えます。「バークレー」の時は、切られた部屋がガーターでつながれているように感じたのですが、今回はそれぞれの部屋に違いが出てきていて、そこら辺が面白いですね。

それはメキシコのおおらかさにも関係していると思いますが、「バークレー」の時といまのわれわれの間には考え方の変化があって、「川口」と「瞑想の森」の違いと同じような、洗練された建築からもっとおおらかなというか、ダイナミックなものに変わっていくような力強さにこだわると言えるのではないかな。

― CGを見た時に、これがもし薄い壁だとするとシャープすぎて、ここに入りたくなるような気もするのですが、これはめくれている場所なので、そこがざらっとした壁になっていると、外と

内がつながりそうだなという気もするし、それはたぶん建築をやっていない人にも感じられるという気がします。

日差しが強いからね。

― だからメキシコというと、黄色とか赤とか、独特の色。

いまそういうスタディもしているところです。色はどうなるか分からないですが、こういうめくれあがったところに色を付けてというのをやってみようとしています。
そうすると、バロックがメキシコに入ってウルトラバロックになったみたいな話で、これもアメリカではモダンだったものが、メキシコにきてウルトラモダンになる（笑）。何かそういう萌芽が見られますね。
展示されるものにしても一つひとつは、そんなにすごい技術でつくったものではなく、すごく子どもっぽいんですよ。でも、相当のエネルギーを費やしてつくったんだろうと思います。

プエブラのバロック教会はキリスト教ですが、アジアのヒンズー教の寺院にも似ていますね。プリミティブな装飾で充満している。どこかで、植物と人間と動物とが一体になっているような、そういうコスモロジーを感じさせますね。それが幸せな気分になるのかもね。

― いわゆるモダンとかけ離れているというか、そういう思考ですね。

そう。まだまだわれわれはモダンな世界に浸って

---

one on top of the next. We are more focused on how light entering from above reaches the first floor. If Berkeley was organized on a vertical axis, then Puebla spreads horizontally along the X and Y axes.

– Berkeley was quite abstract, but Puebla has powerful walls over 30 cm thick. The experience will be completely different.

The material that will be sprayed on the walls will give them a rough texture.

– We are planning to do that because the walls are powerful.

Initially, we were going to give the walls an exposed concrete finish, but we aren't sure the concrete will be cast beautifully.

– Does that mean virtually no use will be made of the walls for exhibits?

That is something to be studied.
This will not be an art museum displaying only paintings. Each room will have its own program, such as music or literature. Between these rooms, visitors will be able to enjoy a variety of experiences, such as looking into the courtyard and seeing the water outside.

– I understand diverse methods of display will be tried in this new museum. Instead of the still images used in many museums, more dynamic displays are being planned, for example, film projected onto a model to create a three-dimensional look.
It may also suggest a patchwork of diverse boxes. It also suggests a flowing, horizontal extension centered on boxes. In Berkeley, the boxes seemed to be tied together by bands, but this time differences between the boxes are evident. That is interesting.

That may have to do in part with the tolerance of people in Mexico. Our thinking has changed since we did Berkeley, just as it did between Kawaguchi and "Meiso no Mori." We began with a refined building and are now concerned with something that is less uptight, that is, something that is strong and dynamic.

– This is something that occurred to me when I saw the CG. The walls, if thin, might seem too sharp-edged, and visitors might be wary of entering openings created by turning up the corners of walls. But if the walls are given a rough texture, that may help to connect inside and outside. I think even people who are not architects will sense that.

The sun is strong.

– That is why the colors used in Mexico are so distinctive, yellow, red, and so on.

We are currently undertaking such studies. We don't know what we'll do about the colors yet but are thinking about adding colors to the places where the corners of walls are turned up.
If that happens, then, just as Baroque became ultra-Baroque in Mexico, what was Modern in the United States will become ultra-Modern in Mexico [laughs]. We can already see signs of that happening.
The things to be displayed did not require great skill or technology--they are quite child-like. Yet great energy was no doubt expended to create them.

The Baroque churches of Puebla are Christian but resemble Hindu temples in Asia in some ways. They are covered with primitive ornamentation. There is a hint of a cosmology in which plants, humans and animals are all one--perhaps that accounts for the happiness one feels there.

– It is very different from the modern way of thinking.

Yes. By comparison, we ourselves are immersed in the modern world [laughs].

– It all depends on the client or the project in which we are involved.

In addition, the precision we are used to in buildings in Japan cannot be achieved in an overseas project. We need to be resolute and manage without precision. We have to consider what sort of architecture is possible under those circumstances.

– The same is true about the construction. There is also the question of whether we should disclaim responsibility for quality--responsibility for the completed building--because the project is an overseas one and things cannot be helped. When I walk around the first floor of Residential Hall at Nanyang Drive for Nanyang Technological University--it seems an interesting building because the original idea was well conceived. The things that make it good might disappear if the building's subtle shortcomings were corrected. We find ourselves torn in that way.

Exactly.
We become dour and serious when we must make things slimmer or thinner. However, we are able to enjoy ourselves and to think more freely if the problem is to make things fatter or thicker. We can consider more options with respect to arrangement or material. At least it seems that way to me.

– One begins to adopt an engineer's approach when making things slender, thin or flat. That is,

235

いますね（笑）。

— クライアント次第というか、関わるプロジェクト次第ですね。

それと、海外のプロジェクトでは、日本の精度で建築が出来ない。精度なんてどうでもいいやというたくましさみたいなところで、どういう建築が可能かを考えていく必要があります。

— つくる側もそうですね。クオリティに対する責任というか、海外だからしょうがないと、出来た建築に対する責任を放棄していいのかという問題もありますね。「南洋理工大学学生寮計画」を見ると、最初に考えた大きなストーリーがよく出来ているからか、1階部分を歩くと風景が変わっていくのが楽しくて、面白い建築だと思うんですが、微妙な所を直していくと、良さが失われてしまうのではないか。そういう葛藤はありますね。

その通りです。

細く、薄くというのは、われわれも難しい顔になっていっちゃうけれど、太く、厚くというのだと、「それならもっとこうできるんじゃない？」とか、「こういう素材を使えるんじゃない？」とか、開放的になるというか、楽しく考えられそうな気がします。

— 細く、薄く、フラットにとやっていくと、思考がエンジニア的になっていくような気がします。つまり、そのためにはどうしたらいいかという、そのひとつのパラメーターを極めるために頑張る。それはそれで必要ですが、ほかのところで

もっと良くしようという思考は、実は設計者しかできない部分ですよね。

クリエイティブではなくなっているのかもしれない。細ければいい、薄ければいい、枠を見せないでと、とりあえずそういう発想になってしまうのは、後ろを向いているような気がしますね。

さっきの藤森さんとの対談で最後に出ましたが、ムチャクチャでも自分たちが楽しんでやって出来たものの良さと、同じムチャクチャでも、わざとらしいムチャクチャの見せ方では、受ける印象が違うという言葉が印象的でした。自分たちがまず楽しんでやったら、出来たものはたぶんほかの人にも楽しんでもらえるし、自分たちが苦しんだら、苦しんだ感じの建築が見えてくるということなのかなという気がします。

苦しさもいろいろあるからね。「台中国立歌劇院」は苦しいことの連続だけれど、そこから共通の喜びが生まれてくるわけだから。

— そうですね。「プエブラ」も壁は斜めで、これは開口を開けるのもいろいろと難しい所が出てきているから、そういう難しさは相変わらずあると思うのですが、どんどんプラスにしていくような設計の仕方になってくるといいなと思います。

### 台湾大学社会科学部棟

— 台湾では、2013年、「台湾大学社会科学部棟」と「松山 台北文創ビル」のふたつが竣工しました。他の施工物件としては「2009高雄ワールドゲームズメインスタジアム」や「台北世界貿易中心広場」のプロジェクトがあります。「台湾大」と「台北世

「台北世界貿易中心広場」
Tapiei World Trade Centre Square Landscape Design

界貿易中心広場」ではアルゴリズムを使って大屋根やランドスケープが考えられています。アルゴリズムを最初に取り入れた「サーペンタイン・ギャラリー・パヴィリオン 2002」ではアルゴリズムをファサードで扱うという表層的なものでしたが、より積極的に使われ始めていると感じます。「台湾大」では、どういう経緯でこのような平面系のアルゴリズムをスタディしていったのでしょうか。

いろんなスタディをやりましたね。

— そうですね。最終案にいく前にはかなりの量の案を出しました。最初のほうは「台北文創」に少し近いような案をやっていったという記憶があります。

時期的にはどちらが先だったのかな。

— タイミングは、「台湾大」が先にあって、その第1案をプレゼンした後に「台北文創」が始まりました。

最終的に出来上がっている「台湾大」の教育棟

「南洋理工大学学生寮計画」
Residential Hall at Nanyang Drive for Nanyang Technological University

one tries to maximize each parameter in order to achieve the given objective. That is necessary, but it is in fact only the architect who tries to find other ways to achieve further improvement.

Perhaps one is no longer thinking creatively. The problem is solved if the thing is made slender or thin, or if the frame is no longer visible--that is how one looks at the problem. One is looking backward.

Toward the end of your talk with Mr. Fujimori, I was struck by what you said about how, even if a thing is absurd or unreasonable, if the people who created it enjoyed themselves, then it makes a good impression, whereas a thing that is absurd in a contrived way will probably not be enjoyed by others. If the people who create struggle, the

resulting building will seem tedious.

There are different forms of struggle. National Taichung Theater was a long series of struggles, but that gave rise to a shared joy.

– Yes. Puebla also has tilted walls, and creating openings has been difficult. Therefore, we will face difficulties as usual. It will be nice if the way we design steadily transforms those difficulties into advantages.

### National Taiwan University, College of Social Sciences

– In 2013, two buildings were completed in Taiwan: National Taiwan University, College of Social Sciences, and Songshan Taipei New Horizon Building. In Taiwan there are also The Main Stadium for the World Games 2009 in Kaohsiung and the Taipei World Trade Centre Square Landscape Design project. We used algorithms to design the large roof and the landscape of National Taiwan University and Taipei World Trade Centre Square Landscape Design respectively. Our first use of an algorithm was for Serpentine Gallery Pavilion 2002, and there it was used only on the surface, for the facade. Now we are using it more aggressively. What were the circumstances that led to our studying algorithms of this sort for the plan

for National Taiwan University?

We undertook many different studies.

– Yes. We produced many schemes before arriving at the final scheme. I seem to remember that at first we were working on a scheme slightly similar to Taipei New Horizon Building.

Which came first?

– National Taiwan University came first. After we presented our first scheme, the Taipei New Horizon Building project began.

The education building for National Taiwan University as built is 168 m wide, and Taipei New Horizon Building is 172 m wide. The question we considered was what to do with a site of nearly the same length. In the case of Taipei New Horizon Building, the site was for an extremely long volume.

The initial, basic study for National Taiwan University concerned how we might produce a unified building from a fairly detailed program. Should we accommodate the program in a single volume, or should there be separate volumes? The library became the key program, and we considered how to design it. From the start we wanted to make it attractive because the library was a space shared by students and other people.

The first scheme was somewhat lacking in that respect, and in the second scheme, which was

の横幅は168mあって「台北文創」の場合は172mです。だからほぼ同じ長さの敷地に対してどうつくるか考えました。「台北文創」の場合は非常に長いボリュームの敷地でした。

「台湾大」のほうは、かなり細かいプログラムをどうやってひとつの建築にしていくかが、最初の基本スタディでした。ひとつのボリュームに納めていくのか、別々にするのか。図書館がキープログラムとなり、どうやってつくっていくかを考えていきました。最初から図書館は学生やいろんな人たちの共有できる空間であるから、魅力的につくりたいと思っていましたね。

第1案は若干それが欠けているところがあって、それを発展させた第2案は、大学側からうまく利用してほしいと言われていた芝生のエリアと、図書館と教室・大教室が入っている場所とを一体化させながらつくりました。図書館と大空間をもっている大教室や共用スペースの境界が曖昧になるように考えていきました。

その後、プログラムの変更などもあり、図書館自体をキャンパス全体の中で、もう少し特別化できないかということから検討し、校舎棟の前に閲覧室だけ出すような案になりました。

スタディの過程を見ていると、最初はファサードを検討し、それから図書館で行われる活動を中心に考えるようになっていったと思います。

ファサードだけでなく、第1案、第2案でも、全体の細かいプログラムが入っている教室棟関係では、台湾の気候の中でどう快適な環境をつくるかということを主題に置いています。

今回のプログラムを見ていくと、基本的に研究室が一番小さい空間として必要で、他に大小の教室、会議室とかエントランス、さらにオフィスがありました。プログラムを組み立てていくと、上にいくほど小さな空間になる。なおかつ研究室や教室は、相当な量が必要になるので均質な空間の繰り返しでやらざるを得ない。上の構造が下にまで影響し、なかなか自由な空間がとれなくなる。でも、図書館とか会議室は、できるだけフリーな大空間をとりたいのです。

それをどう処理するかを考える時点で、ひとつのボリュームの中に入れ込むのはなかなか難しいということが分かってきて、図書館が目立っていったという経緯もあります。

それと、大学の建物ですから、メンテナンス的にも自然のエネルギーを利用したほうが良いことと、極力均質なものの繰り返しでグリッドにしておいたほうが経済的にすぐれていることから、上部は均質な空間である程度処理をして、グリッドから開放するという解決に至ったわけです。試行錯誤の末に分かってきたわけですね。

一方で、中庭に図書館がはみ出してくることに対して、既存の中庭との関係から抵抗もありました。そこでできるだけ図書館を周りの樹木に溶け込むように考え、実施案のようなアルゴリズムでつくる建物に変わっていったというプロセスをたどっています。だから、ある意味では理性的に出来ていると思いますね。

— そうですね。多くのスタディを行った結果、最終的に出てきたものです。当初、前庭にあまり建物を出さないで下さいと言われていましたから、それに対して図書館を出していくのは、きっとスタディを積んでいなかったら、強い提案にはならなかったと思っています。最終的にそれで納得していただけているのは、それまでの過程があったからこその証であると思います。

教室棟も、最初に2棟とか3棟に分かれていた時期もありますね。

— そうですね。最初のころ、プログラムは6,000㎡ほどで、途中、研究棟を追加で依頼されました。追加されたプログラムは3つで、出資者を表す3つの塔のような、アイコン性のあるものを求められました。残念なことに、第2案を出した後、ひとつのプログラムがなくなってしまいました。

そのプログラムというのは学部棟？

— いや、高等研究施設を追加でつくる予定でしたが変更され、なくなりました。この高等研究施設の占める面積は大きく、ボリューム自体のバランスが悪くなってきたので、図書館の在り方を考え直しました。同時に、図書館を前庭に出して、校舎棟に関しては、ふたつの塔もしくはひとつのボリュームで、真ん中は門型として抜ける、中庭と連続しているような場所をつくることを考えました。最終的には、ひとつのボリュームにまとめる案で落ち着きました。

スケッチを見ると、その考え方がよく分かりますね。

— ええ。ひとつのボリュームと図書館の関係ですね。

大学側からは、シンボリックなものを求められていました。立地としては、校舎が周りに建って

developed from it, we integrated the lawn, which the university asked us to use advantageously, with the library and the place accommodating the classrooms and large classroom. We tried to make ambiguous the boundary between the library and the large classroom and the common space, which are both large spaces.

There were subsequent changes in the program, and we studied if it was possible to make the library itself slightly more special on the campus as a whole. A scheme in which just the reading room was pushed in front of the school building was developed.

If we look at the process of study, I think we studied the facade first, and then focused on activities that would take place in the library.

It was not just the facade. In both the first and second schemes, the main focus in the case of the education building, which was programmed in detail, was on how to create a pleasant environment in Taiwan's climate.

If we look at the present program, basically the research rooms are the smallest rooms required, and then there are classrooms of different sizes, a conference room, the entrance and an office. When the program is put together, the rooms become smaller toward the top. Furthermore, a considerable number of research rooms and classrooms are necessary, so we had no choice but to accommodate them in repeated, uniform spaces. The structure at the top had an effect down below, making it difficult to create unobstructed spaces. Nevertheless, it would be preferable to make the library and the conference room large, free spaces.

It became evident, in thinking about how to deal with that problem, that accommodating everything in one volume was fairly difficult, and that was how the library became a separate volume.

And because it is a university building, which makes it desirable to use natural energy for maintenance and to create a grid formed from the repetition of uniform rooms for reasons of economy, we made the upper spaces uniform and arrived at a solution freed from the grid. This is something we arrived at through trial and error.

On the other hand, there was resistance to the library protruding into the courtyard because of the relationship to the existing courtyard. Therefore we tried to make the library blend into the surrounding trees as much as possible, and we arrived at the final scheme: a building created by an algorithm. That was the process we went through. In a sense, therefore, it was rationally designed.

— Yes. It is something that we ultimately arrived at after undertaking many studies. At first, we were asked not to let the building protrude into the forecourt too much. If we hadn't undertaken many studies, the proposal to let the library protrude would not have been so persuasive. It was the process that convinced the client in the end.

There was also a time when the classroom building was divided into two or three structures.

— Yes. At first, the program called for about 6,000 m². Then halfway into the project, we were asked to add a research building. There were three programs added; we were asked to design three towers, iconic in character, to commemorate the donor. Unfortunately, after we presented the second scheme, one of the programs was eliminated.

Was that the program for the faculty building?

— No. An advanced research facility was going to be added but eliminated. That advanced research facility occupied a large floor area, upsetting the overall balance and led to a reexamination of the arrangement of the library. At the same time, we thought about pushing the library out into the forecourt, and with respect to the school building, making a place continuous with the courtyard by creating two towers or a single volume with a gate shape in the middle that allowed people to pass through. In the end, we settled on a one-volume scheme.

The sketch makes the idea easy to understand.

— Yes. The relationship between the one volume and the library.

The university asked for something symbolic. The location is one surrounded by school buildings, and the library protrudes into the courtyard. The school buildings are arranged as if to enclose the site.

I thought that position was optimal in the sense of completing the courtyard. As we undertook studies based on that positional relationship, it became obvious that a 170-meter long volume was quite large, seen from the street. It was important to divide it in some way to soften its impact and to improve the flow of air.

— Yes. There was talk that, in the future, they want to treat the north gate much like the main gate in the overall campus plan. In addition, asking an overseas architect to design something is a new experiment for National Taiwan University. They hope for something that is original and eye-catching.

National Taiwan University is the most prestigious university in Taiwan and prides itself

237

いて、中庭に図書館が出てきている。校舎が、学校の敷地を囲うような形で建っている。

あの位置に建つのが、中庭を完成するという意味で最適だと思いました。そこでの位置関係を踏まえて、スタディしていくうちに、170mというのが、道路側から見るとすごく大きなボリュームだから、それをどう分節して柔らげていくかは、風の抜けの問題とあわせて重要でしたね。

— そうですね。全体のキャンパス計画の中で、将来的には北門を正門に近い扱いにしたいという話もありました。他には、台湾大学が海外の建築家に仕事を依頼すること自体が新しい試みで、斬新で、目を引くものをつくることが期待されていました。

台湾大学は、台湾で最も権威のある、古い伝統を誇る大学です。今回のプロジェクトは、たとえるとすると、東大のキャンパス内に外国人の建築家に頼んで建てるようなものですね。台湾では戦後、海外の建築家に依頼するのは稀だったと思います。コンペティションで通ってもなかなか実現していないから。

—「高雄」が切っ掛けになって、台湾大学から依頼されたのですか。

いや、それは分からないけれども、ペン先生という情熱的なプロフェッサーがいまして、彼が直接事務所にやってきて依頼されました。

— 台湾大学のキャンパスに、帝国大学として日本人の設計によって建てられたメインの建物がある。そのつながりもあって、日本の建築家に依頼することになったのでしょうね。

話は戻りますが、もともとアルゴリズムありきで話を進めていたわけではないと思っています。校舎とはまったく別の、ランドスケープの中に独立して建つ建築をどういう構造体でつくっていくかを考えていて、校舎は経済性を考えながら合理的に構成していったのに対して、図書館は違った要素でつくりたいと考えた。そこで初めて、アルゴリズムを使うことになったと思っています。

建築化して、アルゴリズムによって発生してくるものをつくり上げることができたのは、校舎棟によるところが非常に大きいですね。トイレやオフィスなどの機能的に閉じた要素が閲覧室には必要ないので、ピュアにアルゴリズムというものが見えてくるというか、建築化できた。

— 最終的には、アルゴリズムを使ってハスに近い円形となりました。そこに行き着くまで、どのような考え方をされていましたか。

図書館の閲覧室は、そんなにスパンの大きな大空間である必要はないわけで、むしろ柱があった方が落ち着いて本が読めると考えました。それ以前にも、「多摩美術大学図書館（八王子キャンパス）」や「せんだいメディアテーク」のように、柱なりアーチで分節されつつ連続しているというような空間が、われわれの閲覧室に対するひとつの形式のようになっています。「台湾大」でも大きな円形を描いて、その円形の中をどう分節していくかをいろいろ考えました。「多摩美」のようにさまざまな曲線が交差するようなパターンがあって、その間に自然光が落ちてくるようなものを考えながら、このアルゴリズムに行き着いたということですね。

— プランについてですが、ランドスケープの中での在り方に関して、最終的に出来上がったものの中からいろいろと感じるところがあります。もう少し具体的なつながりをつくり、境界を曖昧にするような、連続性を高めるつくり方があり得たかもしれない。

今回、内部空間の環境を整えるためにLow-eガラスを使っていますが、光が強くて、昼間、外から見たら境界をつくってしまう。直線でバシッと入っているため、非常に存在感のあるものになっている。

もう少しテラスを張り出して、外に出られるようにすることは、周辺に池を巡らせておけば、できたのかもしれない。

— そうですね。内部をもう少し開放するようなことを考えた方が、より良くなったかもしれない。

環境を整えるために、「ぎふ」でも使われている床輻射冷房のシステムを取り入れていて、同時に空調システムを使用する場合は、空間を閉じる必要性が出てきます。実際に夏の暑い時、もしくは湿度の高い時に、開放して冷房をかけると結露の心配があります。屋外空間と空調のシステムを両立させるということが難しかったし、境界がはっきりと出てきてしまったということが、反省点としてはありますね。

それはこれからの本質的な問題で、どこかで何か形式にこだわるということと、自然のエネルギー

---

on a long tradition. This project is like a foreign architect being asked to build something on the campus of the University of Tokyo. I think few overseas architects have been commissioned in Taiwan since the war. Even those who win competitions haven't had their schemes realized.

– Did National Taiwan University ask you because of Kaohsiung?

I don't know about that. There is an enthusiastic faculty member named Professor Peng. He came directly to our office and asked me to do the design.

– The main building on the campus of National Taiwan University was designed by a Japanese when the institution was an imperial university. Perhaps their commissioning a Japanese architect has something to do with this connection.

Going back to something that was said earlier, I don't believe we began with an algorithm. We were considering what sort of structure to use for a building that was going to be quite distinct from existing school buildings and would stand by itself in the landscape. School buildings are rationally organized with an eye toward economy, but we wanted to consider other factors for the library. That was when we first thought about using an algorithm.

The reason we were able to translate into architecture, that is, to create something generated by an algorithm, has a lot to do with school buildings. A reading room does not require functionally closed elements such as toilets and offices. We could envision a pure algorithm and translate that into a building.

– In the end, an algorithm was used to produce a lotus leaf-like circle. What sort of approach led to that?

The reading room of the library did not need to be a large space with a large span. I thought that on the contrary, having columns would make it more tranquil and easier to read books. One form we have adopted in the past for a reading room is a space that is continuous yet subdivided by columns or arches, as in Tama Art University Library (Hachioji Campus) or Sendai Mediatheque. We started with a large circle for National Taiwan University and considered how to subdivide it. We thought about a pattern of various intersecting curves as in Tamabi, with daylight introduced in between them. That was how we eventually settled on the algorithm.

– This has to do with the plan, but there are several things I want to say about the way it is arranged in the landscape in the final scheme. There may have been a way of arranging it so that there was a bit more actual connection to the landscape—a way of making the boundary more ambiguous and enhancing continuity.

Low emission glass is used to create the environment for the interior space, but the light is strong. During the day, it creates a boundary when the building is seen from outside. Because light enters directly, the glass makes its presence known.

If we had encircled the place with a pond, we might have been able to project the terrace out a bit more and allowed people to go out.

– Yes. The scheme might have been improved if we had given more thought to opening up the inside a bit more.

Introducing the radiant floor cooling and heating system installed in Gifu and using an air conditioning system at the same time makes it necessary to close spaces. When it gets hot in summer, or when humidity is high, there is the worrisome possibility of condensation if windows are opened and the cooler is switched on.

「大社文化プレイス」 T hall, Taisha

Making an outdoor space compatible with an air conditioning system was difficult, and making the boundary so visible is something we need to reflect on.

That is a problem we need to consider: How to reconcile a concern for form with the desire to create a space that uses natural energy. I don't think the two are entirely incompatible, and resolving this is a very important problem.

#### Minna no Mori Gifu Media Cosmos

– Minna no Mori Gifu Media Cosmos began in fall of 2010 and after the first and second stage

を利用した空間をつくるという、そのふたつの間でわれわれがどう考えていくか。そのふたつがまったく両立しないわけではないと思いますが、そこをどう乗り越えていくかは、すごく重要な問題ですね。

## みんなの森 ぎふメディアコスモス

——「みんなの森 ぎふメディアコスモス」は、2010年の秋に始まって、1次、2次審査を経て、最終審査が2011年2月にあって、次の月に東日本大震災が起きています。それから足掛け3年半、今年(2014年)の冬に竣工予定です。

「ぎふ」のプロジェクトは、図書館として、「せんだい」、「多摩美」、「台湾大」、「ぎふ」、それ以外にも、本のスペースがある「大社文化プレイス」も入れて5つ目のプロジェクトです。大きな平面に対する考え方もその都度変化してきました。

初期スケッチでは、「大きな家」の中に「小さな家」があって、そこに人が集まるというものから、少し境界を曖昧にすることによって人が集まってくるという考えかたに移っていったというのは、どのような経緯があったのでしょうか。

2010年の正月に、「いままで構造がデザインのベースになって、そこから形というか構成が決まっていたけれども、もっと設備の問題、つまり空気の流れとか光といったテーマをデザインのベースに据えることはできないかを今年は考えてみよう」という話をしました。その後依頼を受けた「Tプロジェクト」で「大きな家と小さな家」というコンセプトに行き着いた。あいにくこのプロジェクトは、待ったがかけられてしまった。そんな時期にこの「ぎふ」のプロジェクトが始まりました。

だから当初は、大きな長く続いていく二場の切り妻の屋根の中に「小さな家」が存在するというスタディを、ずいぶんやりました。

——考え方としては、「大きな屋根」というのは、まず少し外界から切るという考えですか。

——「大きな家」は半屋外空間として扱っています。「Tプロジェクト」の時も、工場の中でどう働いていくかということを考えて提案していきました。「小さな家」という仕事をする場所があって、一歩出ると、打ち合わせをしたり、コミュニケーションができる開放的な場所があるような、新しいオフィスの提案を試みました。それがオフィスだけではなく、図書館でも同じようなことができないかということですね。

半屋外といっても、結局は屋内でないと成り立たないんですよ。風が吹きさらしの所に本を置いて大丈夫かとか、セキュリティの問題とか、環境的な問題もあって、どうしてもそれは屋内にせざるを得ない。ただ、「大きな家」が屋内であっても、さらにその中に「小さな家」として、より性能の良い空間をつくれば、そこが読書をする空間として最適、光も上から落ちてくるという空間にできるだろうと思ってやりました。

ところが、いざ模型を作ってみると、ものすごく閉鎖的で、そこには入りたくない(笑)。形態的には「せんだい」のチューブに代わるような存在として、面白い、不思議なインテリアが出てくるのですが、そこで本を読むだろうかというと、入りたくない閉塞感がある。それをどうしたらいいだろうと一生懸命考えた末に、「グローブ」という概念に到達したのです。

——初期案は違和感がありますね。ふたつの空間が切り離されていて、入った瞬間プライベートな空間になりすぎてしまう。

家の中にいるような雰囲気は出たんだけれども。

——オフィスの構成としては、可能性のあるものだったと思います。使われる場所としては、使う人も決まっていくような形の中で、機能性という意味でもある程度安定した場所が確立されている必要がありますから。

図書館というプログラムでは、本を読む際に、自然と場所を探し出せるよう、ひとつの空間の中で、分節が緩やかに行われていたほうがいい。グローブというものが出てきたことで、緩やかに分節された空間が形成できたということですね。

「台湾大」の図書館では、家具で分節されていて、領域みたいなものがつくられていくような所があります。建築としては、均質な空間の中に図書館というものがセットされている。「ぎふ」の場合だといえばふたつの場所をつくろうとしている、というところに差異があると思っています。

でも、均質な空間をどう変えるかということで、「せんだい」の場合はチューブという存在で、「多摩美」の場合は交差するアーチという存在で、「台湾大」の場合は柱の粗密によって、場所を変えようとしている。自然の中に近いような空間に…。

そういうことは毎回やっていますが、「ぎふ」の場合は、屋根をはずした模型を見ると集落のような場所があって、それはそれでチューブに代わる

---

screening, the final selection was made in February 2011. The Great East Japan Earthquake took place the following month. Three and a half years have passed since then, and the project is expected to be completed in winter of this year (2014).

Gifu is our fifth library project–others include Sendai, Tamabi and National Taiwan University, and there is also T hall, Taisha. Our approach to a large plan has changed with every project.

An early sketch showed people gathering in "small houses" arranged inside a "large house," but the idea has changed, and now it is to draw people by making the boundary slightly ambiguous. What were the circumstances for this change?

At New Year's in 2010, I said that we had based our designs up to then on structure but that that year we should consider the possibility of basing designs more on issues having to do with mechanical systems, that is, the flow of air or light. We received the commission for the T Project soon thereafter and developed the concept of a large house and small houses. Unfortunately, the project was put on hold. That was when this Gifu project began.

That is why at first we made many studies of "small houses" standing under a long, large gabled roof.

– Was the large roof intended to first cut off the place under it slightly from the outside world?

– The large house is treated as a semi-outdoor space. We considered how people would work in the factory for our proposal for T Project. We tried to develop a proposal for a new kind of office. There would be a place for work called "small houses," and outside them there would be an open place for meetings and communication. We thought this would work for not just offices but libraries.

Though we imagined it as a semi-outdoor space, the "large house" idea doesn't really work unless it is an indoor space. Books are put at risk if wind is allowed to blow through it; there is the problem of security; there are also environmental problems. The space has to be indoors. But even if the "large house" is indoors, we thought we could create inside it "small houses," higher-performance spaces that would be optimal for reading, with light falling from above.

However, when we actually built a model, the "small houses" were extremely closed–no one would want to enter them [laughs]. Formally, they were not unlike the tubes in Sendai. They would create an interesting, strange interior, but they are so sealed up that no one would want to enter them to read books. So after much thought, we arrived at the concept of "Globe."

– The early scheme was incongruous. The two kinds of space were cut off from each other. The moment one entered a globe, it became too private a space.

Though the atmosphere was like being inside a house.

– I think it had potential as a way of organizing an office. Only certain people would come to use the place, and so, it would become functionally stable.

In a program for a library, space should be divided indefinitely so that people themselves can search for places to read that suit them. The globes make it possible to form a loosely divided space.

In the library for National Taiwan University, the space is divided by furniture. Places that are like territories are created. Architecturally, the library is set within a uniform space. In the case of Gifu, there are two places. That is the difference.

However, there are different ways of changing a uniform space. In Sendai, there are the tubes. In Tamabi, there are intersecting arches. In National Taiwan University, an uneven distribution of columns is used to charge the place. A space that is close to being natural...

We do this kind of thing each time. In the case of Gifu, when one takes off the roof and looks down on the model, there is a village-like place. They take the place of tubes, though I am hoping for something that's slightly more

「みんなの森 ぎふメディアコスモス」大きな家と小さな家の初期イメージ
Minna no Mori Gifu Media Cosmos the concept of big and small house during the early phase.

「みんなの森 ぎふメディアコスモス」初期グローブ模型
Minna no Mori Gifu Media Cosmos the starting model.

「みんなの森 ぎふメディアコスモス」屋根架構をとりはずした2階グローブの模型写真
Minna no Mori Gifu Media Cosmos, the model of 2nd floor Globe without the roof.

ものとして、もう少し開放的な楽しさを期待していますが、反対に、グローブの中にいる時に、どういう居心地の良さがあるのか、悪さが残るか、それがまだ不安で仕方ないですね。想像できる？

── 難しいですね。

コンペの時からずっと、「小さな家」といったグローブの中は一体どんな空間なのかというのは、ここ何年もみんな分からないところがあって……。

「せんだい」の時も、あのチューブがどういう存在になって、その間のスケールがどうなのかは、実現してみるまで分からなかったですからね。

──「ぎふ」では、グローブが特別な場所になっています。大きな屋根の中に「小さな家」があって、多様な環境が出来上がっている。外側ではテラスみたいなものとして扱われたり、さまざまな違いが体験できる。グラデーションみたいな場所にもなっていて、空間として面白いものになると思っています。

「台湾大」の場合は地上レベルにあることによって、周辺と切り離されたものなのかと感じてしまうことがありますが、「ぎふ」は2階にライブラリーをもってくることによって、外に向かって開くことができるという逆転が起こっているわけですね。自然と切り離すことによって、もう一度逆に開放できる。そこが西のプロムナードに向かっては西日を避けたり、並木に向かって緑と接しながら本を読むというリニアなテラスが出来ました。また、南の広場に面しても広場を見下ろすテラスが出来たし、金華山の側もそうだし、一歩前進したということは言えますね。

そういう具体例はひとつずつ積み上げていかないと、簡単にできるようでいて、なかなかできないことです。いままでは概念的に図上のパターンで自然を感じさせるとか、「台中国立歌劇院」もそういうところがありますが、人間の身体にあるチューブのような空間だと言いながら、外と内が物理的には切れてしまう。それを一歩ずつ克服していかなくてはいけない段階にきているのですね。「台湾大」も、教室棟のほうはそれがうまくいっています。

台湾のような暑い所でも、ああいう風を通すというのは結構有効な手段であって、恵比寿の「伊東塾」でも、同じようなことをやっていますが、結構暑い（笑）。

── 風が上に抜けていかないです。

密集しているから、風が通らないのです。その辺がなかなか大変で、そう簡単ではない。でも気持ちのいい時はすごく気持ちいいですね。

「ぎふ」で進化しているのは、積極的に関わってくれている日比野克彦さんの存在が大きいですね。日比野さんが岐阜の若い人たちとずっと付き合って、コミュニティを育ててくれていたのです。特に市民活動交流センターという1階の西側のエリアがどんな活動をしていくかに関して、積極的に意見が交換されていて、そういう意味では、ソフトの面でも「せんだい」よりはるかにいい感じで進んでいると言えますね。

── 2013年、「暦の夜舟」という日比野さんが企画したイベントに参加したのですが、日比野さんが中心となって、岐阜出身の植木屋さんなどを呼んでワークショップを開いていました。設計する側だけで建物を考えるのではなくて、今後一緒に使う人たちがその場所をどう使っていくかを深めていくためのイベントで、とても面白いと思いましたね。

以前からもそのような市民活動は行われていたのでしょうか。

「暦の夜舟」みたいなイベントは行われていましたが、それぞれ舟をつくる場所もばらばらだし、そういう場がなかったのですね。既存の図書館はそういう場にはなっていないですね。

── そういうものを統合するような場所になっていくということですね。

そう。そういう若い人の中には、市民活動交流セ

open and pleasant. But is it comfortable inside the globes, or is it uncomfortable? I am still uneasy about that. Can you imagine what that will be like?

– It is difficult.

Ever since the competition, for several years now, all of us have wondered what sort of space is inside the globe we call a "small house"...

It was like that at Sendai too. We didn't know what those tubes were going to be like and what the scale of the space between tubes was going to be like until the building was actually constructed.

– The globes in Gifu are special places. There are "small houses" under the large roof, and diverse environments are provided. The outside is treated as a terrace. One can experience various differences. There are gradations too–I think it will be an interesting space.

In the case of National Taiwan University, the library is on the ground level and seems cut off from the surroundings. In Gifu, the library is on the second floor, so it can be opened to the outside. Detaching it from nature paradoxically makes it possible to open it. The western sun is avoided on the west promenade––a linear terrace where one can face trees and read books has been created. A terrace looking down on the south square has been created, and the same is true on the side facing Kinkazan. Progress has been achieved.

We need to take such specific measures, one at a time. Unless we do so, this will be more difficult to achieve than it seems. Up to now, we have suggested nature conceptually, through patterns on drawings. That is also true in some ways of National Taichung Theater. We talk about the space being like a tube inside the human body, but the inside is physically cut off from the outside. We are at a stage when we must surmount difficulties one by one. That is going smoothly on the classroom building for National Taiwan University.

Letting the wind flow through a space is a fairly effective measure for a place as hot as Taiwan. We are doing something similar in the ITO JUKU Ebisu Studio, but it is still fairly hot [laughs].

– The air doesn't flow out at the top.

It's crowded in there––that's why the air doesn't flow. That is where things get difficult––it isn't that simple. But when it is comfortable, it is quite comfortable.

The active involvement of Mr. Katsuhiko Hibino is one reason Gifu has been evolving. He has been associating for some time with young people in Gifu and is helping to develop a community. In particular views are being actively exchanged concerning what sorts of activities will take place in the so-called civic activity and exchange center on the west side on the first floor. In that sense, far greater progress is being made in its soft, programmatic aspects than was the case in Sendai.

– I participated in an event planned by Mr. Hibino in 2013 called *Koyomi no yobune*. He invited gardeners from Gifu and held a workshop. Instead of having just the architects think about the building, he wants to get future users of the building to think about how it ought to be used. I thought it was quite interesting.

Have civic activities of that sort taken place previous to that event?

Events like *Koyomi no yobune* had taken place, but the boats were constructed in different places. There was no fixed venue. The present library is not used as such a place.

– So this place will help consolidate such activities.

Yes. Some of the young people engaged in such activities have expressed a desire to join the staff of the civic activity and exchange center.

In that sense, this is perhaps the first instance of public participation in which the public and the organizers are working side by side. KOENJI is working out well, but in that case, things are being decided mainly through talks with the administering NPO.

ンターのスタッフになりたいという人も現れています。

そういう意味では、住民参加といっても住民と向かい合うかたちだけではなくて、同じ方向を向いてものが進んでいくという状態は、おそらく初めてじゃないかなと思いますね。「高円寺」もうまくいっていますが、「高円寺」の場合は、主として運営のNPOとの話し合いの中でいろいろなことが決まっていましたし。

— 取りまとめてくれる人と話すだけで終わらせないところに意味があると思います。

そうですね。本当に市民が参加してきてくれるという、そういう公共建築が初めて出来そうなところまできている。これは素晴らしいですね。

— 企画を積極的に考えてくれる人のおかげでソフト面が強化されていくわけですが、「ぎふ」の場合は、建物が出来上がる過程と、運営者の人たち、そこを使う人たちの意識が同時進行で進んでいる。伊東さんが言われたように、何もなくてもみんながそこに集まってくるというのが公共としての新しいことであって、本来の在り方なのかもしれない。「ぎふ」を通して、さまざまな人たちから「岐阜を盛り上げたい」という思いがとても伝わってきます。

もちろん自治体も積極的にそれを推進していくという意味では、岐阜市はかなり例外的だと思いますね。

— そうですね。岐阜に行った時も、公共の人が率先して市民に声をかけてくれますし、三者がとてもいい関係でいられている。

いまの市長が元商社マンなので、ものすごく話がしやすい。それと、日比野さんが市長に信頼されているから、良い関係が生まれています。

特にこの市民活動交流センターの部分は、当初もっと閉鎖的な空間でした。コンペティションのあと、役所から閉じられた部屋をたくさんつくるように言われていたから、そういう方向で進んでいたのですが、市長にプレゼンした時に、「せんだい」みたいに、もっと開いてほしいと言われた（笑）。それでだいぶオープンな空間になりましたね。「せんだい」のことをすごく気に入ってくれている。

— 特に「せんだい」の1階の部分を気に入っているようですね。各階いろいろキャラクターはあると思いますが、1階は本当に開かれていて、さまざまなイベントが企画され、人びとが集まる場所になっています。

7階もすごくいいスペースとして使われていて、市民の側からさまざまな企画が持ち込まれて、いろんな催しが行われていますね。

— あそこに行けば何かしらやっているとか、そこにいれば一日過ごせるような所は、公共にはなかなかないですね。

そういう意味では、図書館というのは、毎日でもふらっと行って本や雑誌を読んだり、DVDを見たりできる、ギャラリーや交流センターで何かやっているのを見たりもする。岐阜ぐらいのまちだったら、必ず誰か知っている人が仙台以上にいるわけだから、「ここで何やっているんだ？」みたいな話から「おまえもやれよ」みたいな話になっていくし、子どもも「あそこのおじちゃんがいた」といった関係が生まれていく。

— 地方は、図書館の利用率が非常に高いですし、活発に市民と交流しています。そういうところに対して、地方自治体が協力することによってすごく有効的に物事が進んでいきます。

そうですね。

— いまはネットショッピングで本は買えるし、情報も個人で入手しやすい。その影響からか、図書館の必要性を考えなければならないこともありましたね。

紙の本はだんだんなくなるとか、図書館になくてもいい、というような議論がされた時期もありましたが、まったく逆の方向になっている。不思議な状況ですね。コンサートだったらその時間に行って、終われば帰ってしまうけれども、図書館は好きな時間に行って、特に人と話をしなくてもいいという、そういう気楽さが若い人にもお年寄りにも行きやすくしているのでしょうね。だから、いまの現代的なコミュニケーションの在り方を図書館が体現しているんだと思います。本というメディアを媒介にして。

本当にグローブの下は一体どうなるんだろう。光環境は良さそうだけど、その内部感、包まれ感がどうなるのかがなかなか分からない。8月にはモックアップでグローブがひとつ出来ますから、それ

— The fact that it doesn't just end after talks with the person doing the coordinating is meaningful.

Yes. A public building in which the public will actually participate is about to be completed. That is a wonderful thing.

— The soft, programmatic aspects are being developed thanks to someone who is actively thinking about the project. In the case of Gifu, the awareness of the administrators and users is being raised as the building is being constructed. As you said, to see people gather even when there is as yet nothing there is something new for a public facility, but that may be the way things ought to be. The desire of many different people "to rouse Gifu" can be sensed in this project.

Gifu City is exceptional in that the local government is actively promoting this.

— Yes. When I went to Gifu, people in local government took the initiative and contacted people for me. The three sectors there are in a good relationship.

The current mayor used to work for a trading company, so he is quite easy to talk to. And Mr. Hibino enjoys the trust of the mayor, so a good relationship is forming.

This civic activity and exchange center was initially a more closed space. After the competition, we were asked by city hall to design lots of closed rooms, and so that was the direction we were taking. However, when we made a presentation to the mayor, he said he wanted something more open, like Sendai [laughs]. That led to us making the space more open. He likes Sendai a great deal.

— He seems to like the first floor of Sendai in particular. Each floor has its own character, but the first floor is truly open and diverse events are planned for it. It has become a place where people gather.

The seventh floor is also used in a very good way. The public suggests diverse projects, and various events are held there.

— There are few public facilities where something is always happening and where one can spend an entire day.

In that sense, a library is a place one can drop in every day to read books or magazines, look at DVDs, and see what is happening in the gallery or the exchange center. In a city like Gifu, there is more likelihood of encountering an acquaintance than in Sendai. "What are you doing here?" someone will ask, and then, "Why don't you try this as well?" Children will see a neighbor. Relationships develop.

— The rate of use of libraries in local areas is quite high. They are in active communication with the public. The cooperation of local governments with such places can be quite effective in making things happen.

Yes.

— Today, one can easily buy books and get information on one's own on the Internet. That has an effect on the need for libraries--that is an issue that must be considered.

There was a time when the argument was

「伊東建築塾 恵比寿スタジオ」 ITO JUKU Ebisu Studio

を見て、良かったと思えればいいんだけどね(笑)。

**松山 台北文創ビル**

この建物は、いくつかの円弧をベースにしながらプランをつくっており、敷地に対してもプログラムに対してもすごく理にかなっていると思います。

　長手方向は172mあって、相当な長さですが、僕はこれを絶対2棟に分けたくなかった。なぜかというと、敷地の前で台湾ドームがいまつくられていて、その横にはホテルが高層で出来る。それぞれ大きなボリュームです。その間に、わずか2層しかない古い煙草工場を改修した文化施設がありますから、それを囲い込むような都市的スケールな空間がここにないとだめだと思ったのです。後ろは高架道路が通っているし、分棟にして視線が抜けたらだめだと思いました。

　だから、これがひとつの壁になるということが重要で、そういう大きな視点からのボリューム感と、一方で、たばこ工場の低層に向かい合うヒューマンスケールと、両方をどう満足させられるかを考えた時に、円弧が登場しました。なおかつその円弧が広場に向かって階段状に下りてくる。ホテルのほうは、既存の池に向かっているし、オフィスのほうは広場に向かっているという、その関係もうまくいったかなと思います。

── 都市的なスケールで、「壁」が必要だと考えたのですね。

そうです。これもまた都市計画の委員会では、「こんなアンチヒューマンな建築をつくるべきではない」と言われた。

── 「台湾大」の初期案と同じですね。

もっと分節できないかと言われましたが、絶対に大きさが必要だと思った。

── 都市的に引いた視点ではボリュームとして存在感があります。けれども、近づいていくとボリュームがスケールダウンしているところは、この分節の方法が有効に働いていると思います。クライアントの反応自体はどうだったのでしょうか。

委員の中には反対の人もいましたが、一方でクライアントのトップは、最初にこれでプレゼンした時に即、気に入ってくれました。細かいところまでプレゼンでしっかり聞いて、的確な反応をしてくれます。

── 初期は階段状の段差がなかった。伊東さんが「これではおかしいね」と言って、下2層だけ張り出した。その後、「上層と下2層をつなげたい」と言って、最終案になりました。

それと同時に、上層も変化した。

── 全体的にもっともっと緩やかにスケールダウンさせるグラデーションをつくり、緑が徐々に上がっていくようになりました。

最初は箱状になった緑が上に上がっていくという感じでしたね。

緑をつくる場所に2層でヴォイドみたいなものが開いていました。いま「台湾大」にあるようなものです。

でも「台北文創」の場合、穴を開けるヴォイド的な考え方が、オフィスには向かない。開けられないということで、表面的なものは止めることになった。

でも、円弧で抜いていることによって、オフィスの使い方とか奥行きとかそういったものにも変化ができているから、違ったタイプのオフィス空間にはなっています。かなり面白いオフィスになっているかなと思います。

通常の四角いオフィス空間に比べたら、なかなかいい感じのオフィスになっていると思います。

── 外壁に面した部分が大きくて、細長い感じが出て、自然光でも結構明るい状態ですね。

湾曲しているのが効果的でしたね。これが直線だったら、あの長さが退屈だと思うけれども。

── 欄間も効果的で、全面ガラスという感じがまったくしない。安心感をもてますね。

そうね。庇の深さもね。

── ガラスのファサードが面にきているというのとは、全然違う。この、奥行きを格子でもたせるというのは、最初から出てきたのですか。

そうですね。

── 「台北文創」は日本ではなく台湾でつくったことでうまくいった部分もあると思っています。それは何かというと、日本では効率よく工場生産して、現場に持ってきて組み立てますが、台湾では部材を標準化できない建物でも、「つくろう!」

---

made that printed books would gradually disappear or that libraries were no longer necessary, but we are going in the opposite direction. The situation is strange. One goes to a concert when it is scheduled, and then one goes home. However, one can go to a library whenever one likes, and there is no particular need to talk to someone else. That carefree quality is what makes it easy for the young and the old to go. The library embodies the contemporary form of communication, with books serving as the medium.

What will happen to areas under the Globes? The lighting environment seems good, but it is difficult to know how it will feel like inside--the sense of enclosure. A mock up of a Globe will be built in August. I hope it creates a favorable impression [laughs].

**Songshan Taipei New Horizon Building**

This building has a plan based on a number of arcs. I think it is quite reasonable for the given site and program.

It is 172 meters long. That is rather long, but I was quite certain I did not want to divide the building into two. That is because Taiwan Dome is now being constructed in front of the site, and next to that a high-rise hotel is going to be built. These are both large volumes. Between them is a cultural facility converted from an old cigarette factory only two stories high. I thought the location demanded a space on an urban scale enclosing that facility. There is an expressway in the back. Dividing the building into two would divert the eye elsewhere--and that was no good.

Therefore, it was important that it be one wall. A large volume was demanded from a broader perspective, but human scale was demanded in response to the low-rise cigarette factory. The arcs appeared when we considered how to reconcile these two demands. In addition, those arcs step down toward the square. The hotel faces an existing pond, and the office faces the square. That relationship works well.

– You believed a "wall" that was built on an urban scale was necessary.

Yes. The city planning committee told us such an anti-human building ought not to be constructed.

– The same thing happened with the initial scheme for National Taiwan University.

I was asked if it was possible to divide it more, but I thought this large size was absolutely necessary.

– From an urban point of view, this volume has presence. However, as one approaches it, this volume is scaled down. The way this was divided is working effectively. What was the client's reaction?

Though there were people opposed to it on the committee, the top executive on the client side liked it immediately when we made our initial presentation. He listens to even small details at a presentation and responds aptly.

– The arcs didn't step down in stages at first. You said, "This is odd," and extended just the lower two levels out. You subsequently said you wanted to connect the upper level and the two lower levels, and that was how we arrived at the final scheme.

At the same time, the upper level changed as well.

– We scaled down the volume gradually, and so greenery gradually rises.

Initially, greenery that was boxed rose up.

A two-level void exists in the place greenery is created. It is similar to what exists in National Taiwan University.

But in the case of Taipei New Horizon Building, a void-like approach does not suit offices. It was decided to eliminate a superficial void because it could not be opened.

But the arc creates change in the way the office is used and the depth of the office. It is a different type of office space. I think it has become a fairly interesting office.

It is a rather pleasant office compared with an ordinary, square office space.

– A large area faces the perimeter. The space seems long and slender. There is also plenty of daylight.

The fact that it curves is effective. If it were a straight line, that length would make it boring.

– The transom is also effective. It does not feel at all like it is completely glazed.

Yes. The depth of the overhang as well.

– It would be completely different if the glass facade were flush. Was it the idea from the start to support this depth on a lattice?

Yes.

– There is an advantage to building Taipei New Horizon Building in Taiwan rather than Japan. In Japan, this would be produced efficiently in a factory and then assembled on the site. In Taiwan, there is a willingness to construct buildings with non-standardized parts.

Mr. Riken Yamamoto saw this building and

となるからです。

この建築を山本理顕さんが見て、「台湾でもこんなきれいな建築が出来るんだ！ 頑張らなくちゃ」と言ってくれました。「台湾大」もきれいに出来ている。もちろんきれいに越したことはないけれども、台湾では施工がどんなに悪くても大丈夫という建築にチャレンジできると思います。

— 確かに僕は「台北文創」を見た時、きれいだと思いましたね。ただ同時に、きれいすぎるとも感じました。

これはわりと骨太な建築だから、そんなに精度がなくても、それなりに成り立つ建築ではあると思いますね。「CapitaGreen」もすごくきれいに出来ている。

— 職人に向上心がある国だと思いますね。いいものをつくろうという意識が、職人たちにはすごくあります。

「台中国立歌劇院」はそうですね。
　「台北文創」のファサードもそうだし、全体の分節の仕方もそうですが、建築が全体として醸す華やかさはないけれども、以前の美学——面一に全部納めるとか、細く繊細に仕上げていくとか、そういうことから少しずつわれわれがこのような彫りの深さになじんできていると感じます。もっと本当に居心地のいい空間をつくるために、美意識を少しずつ変えて、それがストックされてきた時に、新しい建築がどう花開くのか、そういう時期にそろそろきているのかなと思います。

現在も99％は相変わらずモダニズムの美学で、できるだけ要素を少なくして、単純にいう、"Less is More"の美学でつくっている。それを超えるためには、新しい美学にまで広めていくという、それはわれわれがつくり上げていかないといけないと思っています。それぐらいの自負をもっていたいし、そういう議論が事務所の中でもっと起こらないといけないと思いますね。
　どういうものが"成熟した建築"であるのかというのが、われわれの中である程度できていると思いますが、もうひとつそれを乗り越えて、新しい刺激をどうつくり出していくか。

— ある形式じゃないけれども、自由に思想をもちながら、それを統合していくようなことが具体的にできていくといいですね。

先ほど藤森さんとの対談に関して話をしましたが、藤森さんが「自分は日本の民家は嫌だ。だから畳も障子も竹も自分は使わない」と。それで「日本の民家も江戸ぐらいに出来たものまでで、それ以降の民家は絶対に自分はコピーをしない」と。だから、「自分は何かをやるときに、○○風とか、どこかに△△があったとか、そういうことをすべて避けて、不思議なものに到達するということをいつも目指している。材料も、工業製品が工業的に使われるというのは嫌だ。手で曲げられるぐらいのことしかやらない」と。
　前に藤森さんのことを文章で書いたことがありますが、ひとつは抽象の仕方だと思うんですね。つまり、モダニズムの場合は、あるひとりの個人の創作とか発明によって、ひとつの特殊な形態を際立たせることで成り立っていると思いますが、藤森さんのはそうじゃなくて、全部を否定していったような。そうやって浮かび上がってきた建築というのは、どこかである古代の、世界に共通するようなものに行き着くはずだと。そこまで彼は言わないですが、それに近いような気がします。そうすると、地域性とか、日本とかスペインとか、そういうものがはずれたところでの建築になる。
　そこで僕が言ったのは、〈ある抽象〉。モダニズムというのは、ひとつの、誰もやっていない特殊な形態ということですが、「サーペンタイン」もそうですが、そういうものじゃないところで浮かび上がってきて抽象性を獲得する。それを考えていくのが面白いと思っています。
　そうすると、誰のものでもないけれども誰のものでもあるような"個を超える個"みたいな、そういうものになる。そういうところに行き着くとすごくいいなと思っていますね。こういう大きい建築は、モダニズムという社会の枠組みの中でしかつくれないから、藤森さんのように簡単にはいかないけれども、でもそういうことを考えながらつくっていくというのは、面白いなと思います。

1. 2010年茅野市美術館「藤森照信展　諏訪の記憶とフジモリ建築」展図録に収録された、「抽象化のワナに陥らない唯一の建築家」
2012年 The Museum Villa Stuck "Terunobu Fujimori, Architect Works 1986-2012" 展図録に収録された、「藤森照信の建築は何故宙に浮かぶのか」
2. 伊東塾会員講座「縄文のこころと建築」2014年7月12日の講座

**National Taiwan University, College of Social Sciences**
台湾大学社会科学部棟

2013 台湾 台北 Taipei, Taiwan

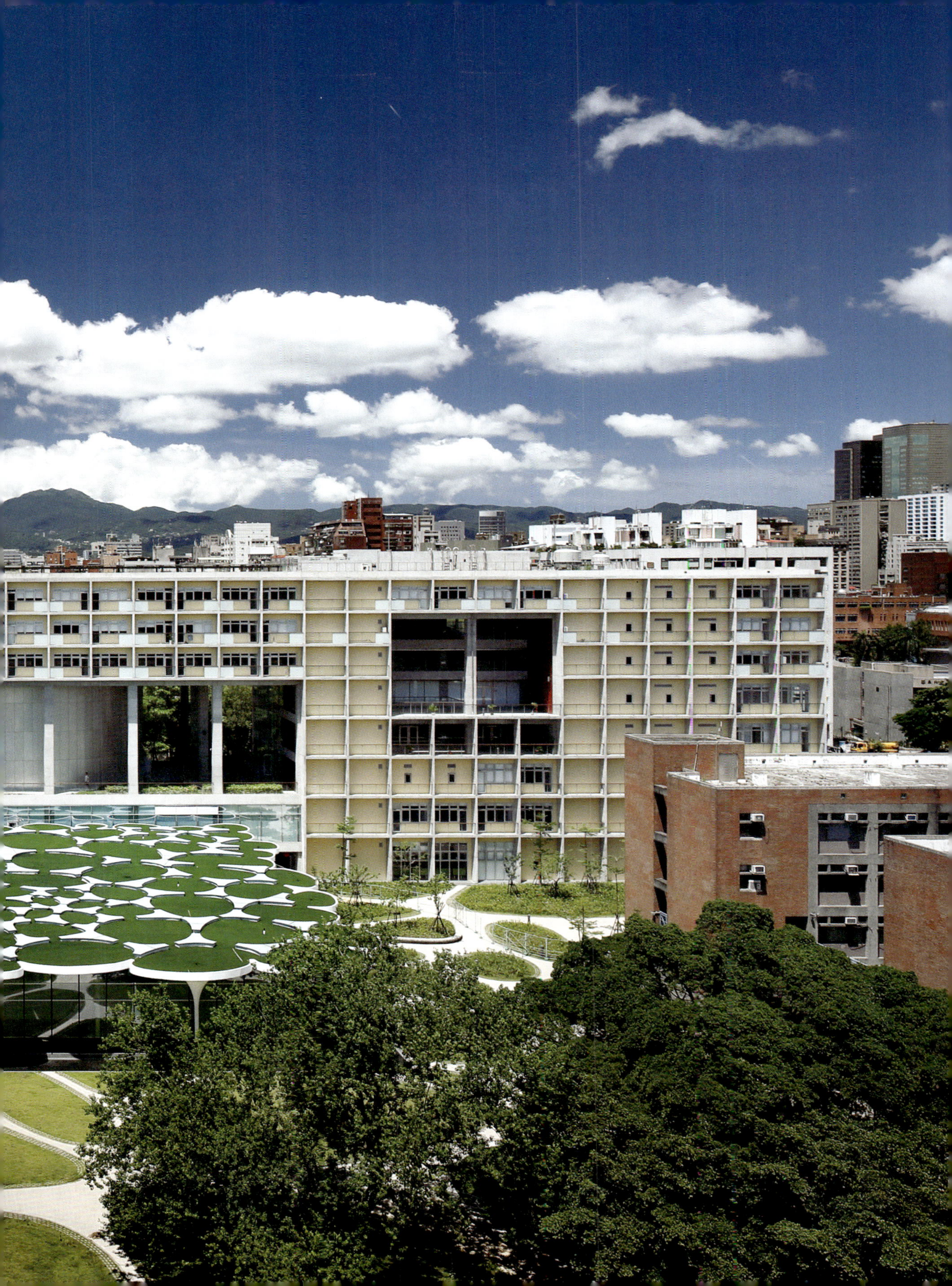

7F plan

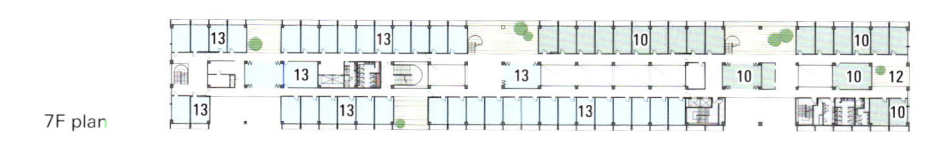

3F plan

1F plan

1 entrance
2 exhibition hall
3 porch
4 conversation room
5 classroom
6 library entrance
7 front desk
8 concierge
9 open-shelf reading room
10 conference room
11 staff room
12 balcony
13 laboratory

図書館棟越しに教室棟を望む
View of the classroom block beyond the library.

台湾大学社会科学部棟の建築は、2棟に分かれている。8層の教室、研究室、会議室を中心とした棟と低層の図書館棟である。外部道路に沿って168mに及ぶ教室棟を配置して中庭を完結させ、その中庭内に1層の図書館棟を配置することによって、環境への配慮を徹底した。

Two buildings were designed for the College of Social Sciences at National Taiwan University. The first, an eight-floor structure, primarily houses classrooms, research labs, and conference rooms, and the second, a low-rise building, contains a library. Special consideration was given to the surrounding environment by placing the 168-meter-long classroom block along an external road, creating a courtyard, and positioning the single-story library in the courtyard.

1 exterior corridor
2 library entrance
3 reading room
4 sky garden
5 VIP room
6 faculty room
7 recreation room
8 terrace

Section

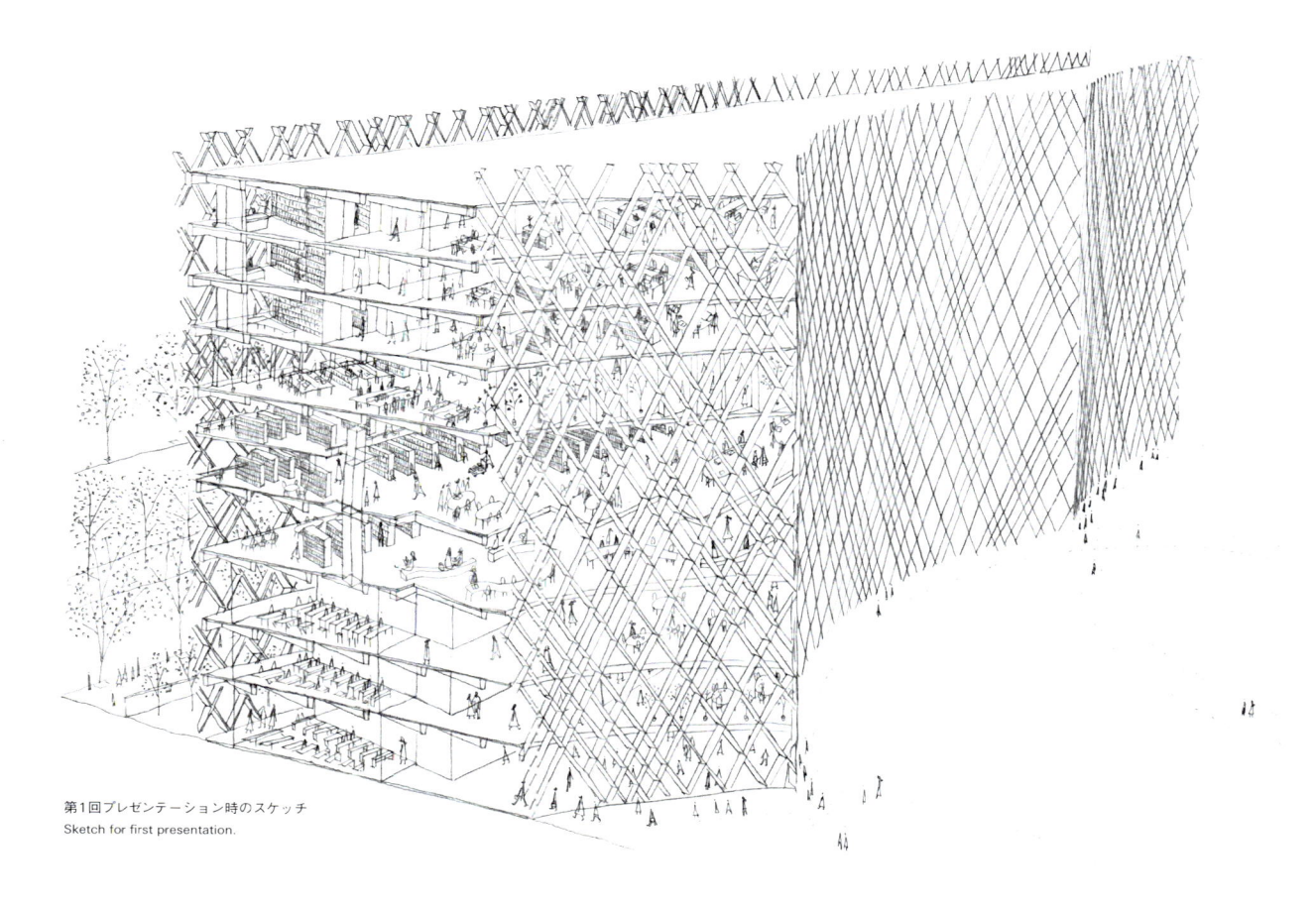

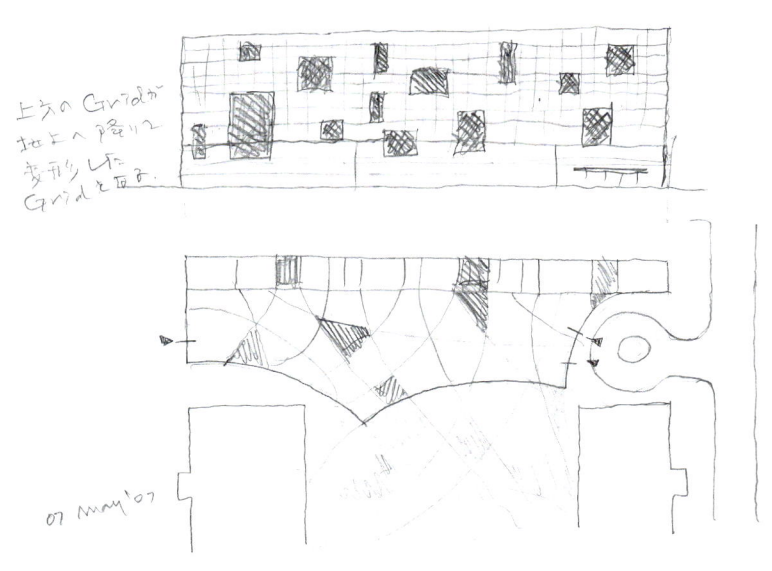

第1回プレゼンテーション時のスケッチ
Sketch for first presentation.

第2回プレゼンテーション案。高層棟と低層棟が生まれる。またエマージンググリッドを取り入れる

Proposal for second presentation. A high-rise and low-rise building appeared at this point, and an emerging grid had also been incorporated into the design.

中庭に図書館棟を出すスタディ
Study related to placing the library in the courtyard.

柱形状のスタディ
Study for column shape.

Site

最終案
Final plan.

249

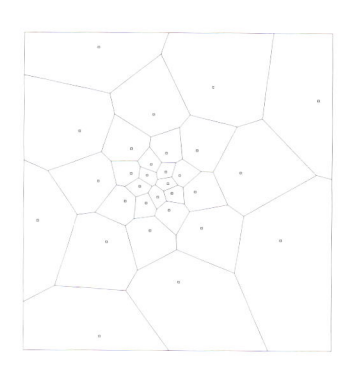

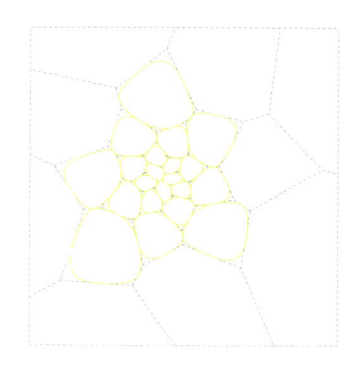

スパイラルを描きながら放射状に広がる幾何学を用いた柱と屋根の構造
The structure of the columns and roof makes use of geometrical principles, creating a spiral and extending into a radial form.

樹木のような構造体である柱の位置と屋根の形状は、3つの中心からハスの花のようなパターンを描く幾何学によって決定された。中心に近い部分は柱が密に立ち並び、中心から遠ざかるにつれて粗になっていく。こうした柱の粗密は場所の違いを生み、林の中にいるような自然の感覚をもたらしている。

Position of the columns and shape of the roof in the structure, resembling a grove of trees, were determined geometrically by creating a lotus-like pattern with three cores. Near the center, there is a dense forest of columns, which gradually become sparser as one moves away from the center. Making places with various densities of columns gives rise to a natural sensation, as if one is in the woods.

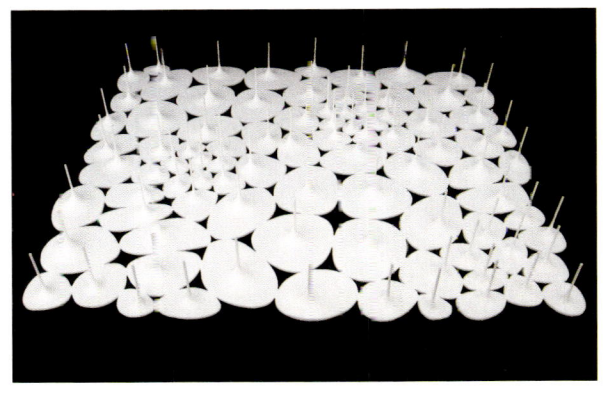

柱と屋根の模型写真
Photograph of column and roof model.

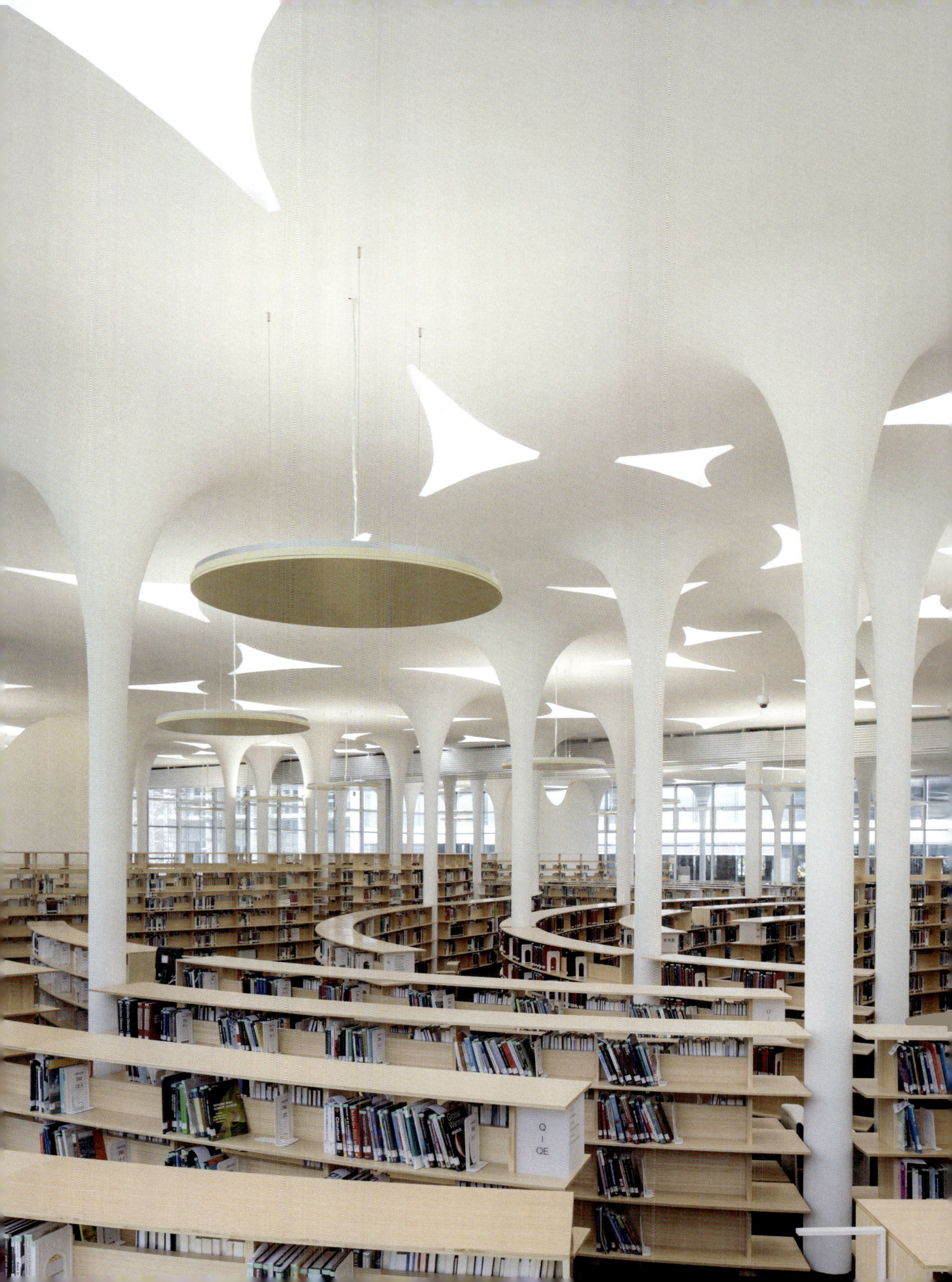
Q
QE

アルゴリズムに基づいて決定された柱の疎密が場所の違いを生み出す
The density of columns, determined by an algorithm, gives rise to differences in the space.

屋根とスカイライト
Roof and skylight.

スカイライトを見上げる
Looking up at the skylight.

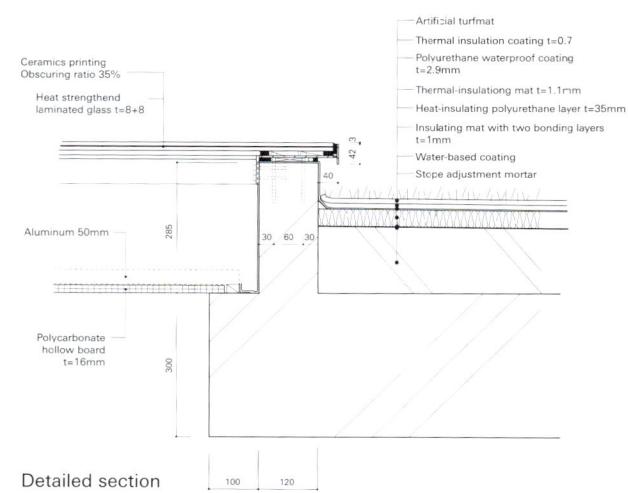

Detailed section

スカイライトの室内側は乳白のポリカーボネイト中空板を使用し、光を拡散させている。また閲覧室では台湾で初めての施工となる「床輻射＋床下冷房方式」を採用。快適性だけでなく省エネルギー性に配慮している。

Using white and translucent, polycarbonate hollow boards causes the inside of the skylight to diffuse light. The reading room is equipped with the first floor radiant cooling and heating system ever constructed in Taiwan. This was intended not only to provide greater comfortable but also to reduce energy consumption.

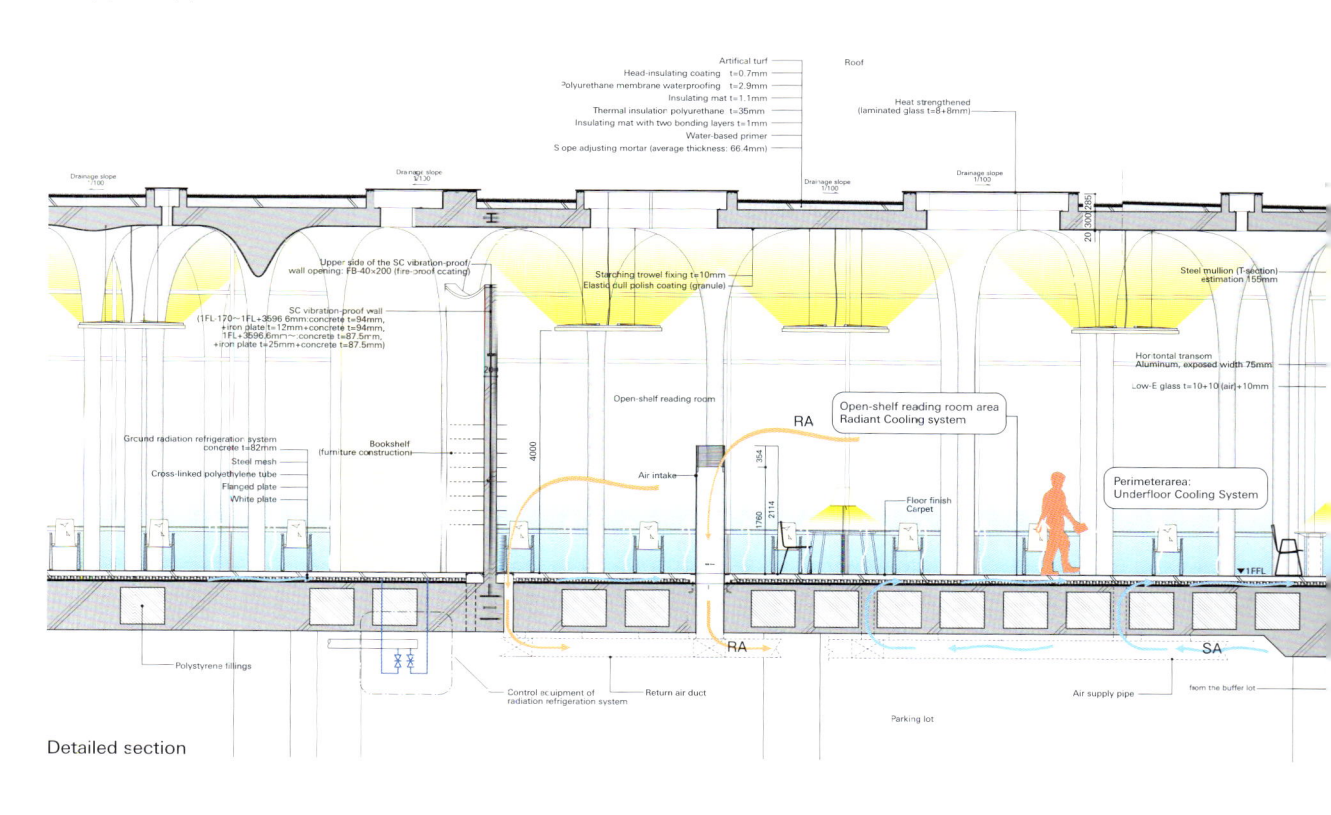

Detailed section

254

柱頭の配筋工事
Reinforcement work on the capitals.

FRP型枠とSC耐震壁の施工
Constructing the fiber-reinforced plastic molds and steel-reinforced, earthquake-resistant walls.

柱のモックアップが何回も行われた
A series of mock up of the columns were created.

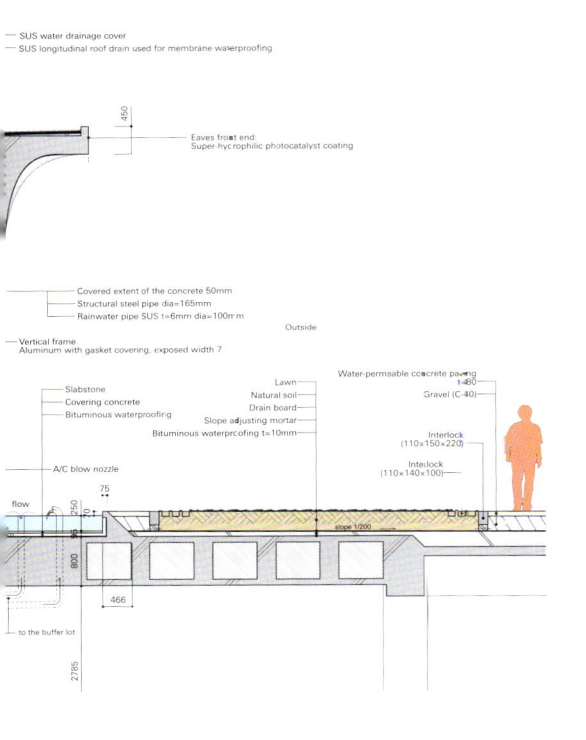

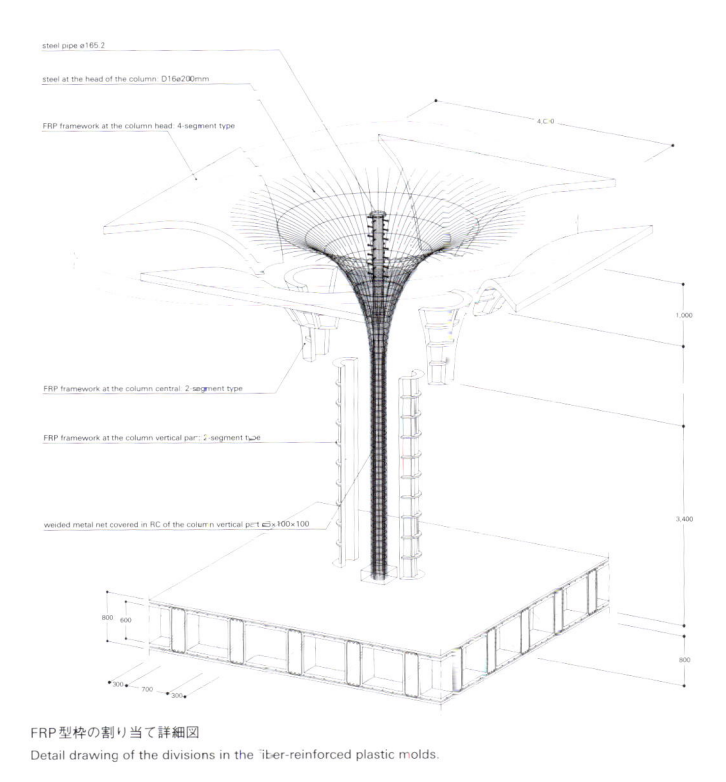

FRP型枠の割り当て詳細図
Detail drawing of the divisions in the fiber-reinforced plastic molds.

大通り側からの教室棟全景
Panoramic view of the classroom block from the main road.

Natural Ventilation  Natural light

Section

256

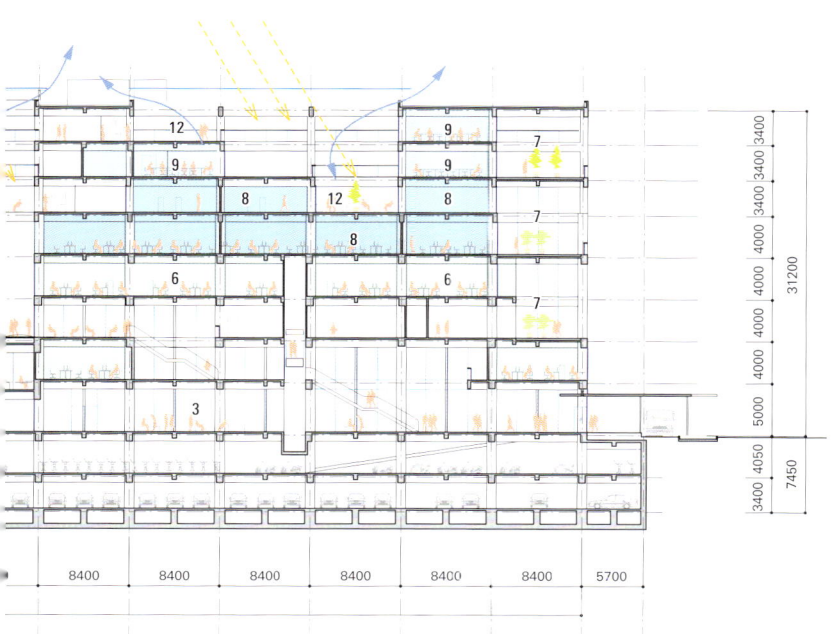

| | |
|---|---|
| 1 reading section | 8 research center |
| 2 library counter | 9 discussion room |
| 3 college history exhibition | 10 ready room |
| 4 classroom | 11 faculty recreation |
| 5 international conference hall | 12 lounge |
| 6 department office | 13 toilet |
| 7 common terrace | 14 closed stack |

257

教室棟ファサード
Facade of the classroom block.

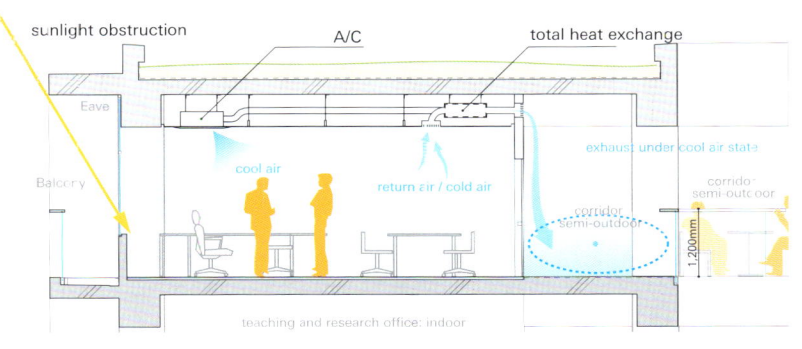

sunlight obstruction    A/C    total heat exchange
Eave
Balcony    cool air    return air / cold air    exhaust under cool air state
    corridor semi-outdoor
    corridor semi-outdoor    1,200mm
teaching and research office: indoor

パブリック空間の快適な環境実現のため、室内に供給された冷気を共用部に排気し、冷気の効率的な活用を行っている
To create a comfortable environment in the public space, the cool air produced by the indoor air-conditioning is discharged in the common area college in order to make the most effective use of the air.

各研究室、教室にはテラスを設け、彫りの深い外観とした。また、吹き抜けと廊下を組み合わせることによって、水平、垂直両方向の通風にも十分に考慮した。

By utilising both the double height open space and the external corridors, airflow is constantly ensured in both horizontal and vertical direction.

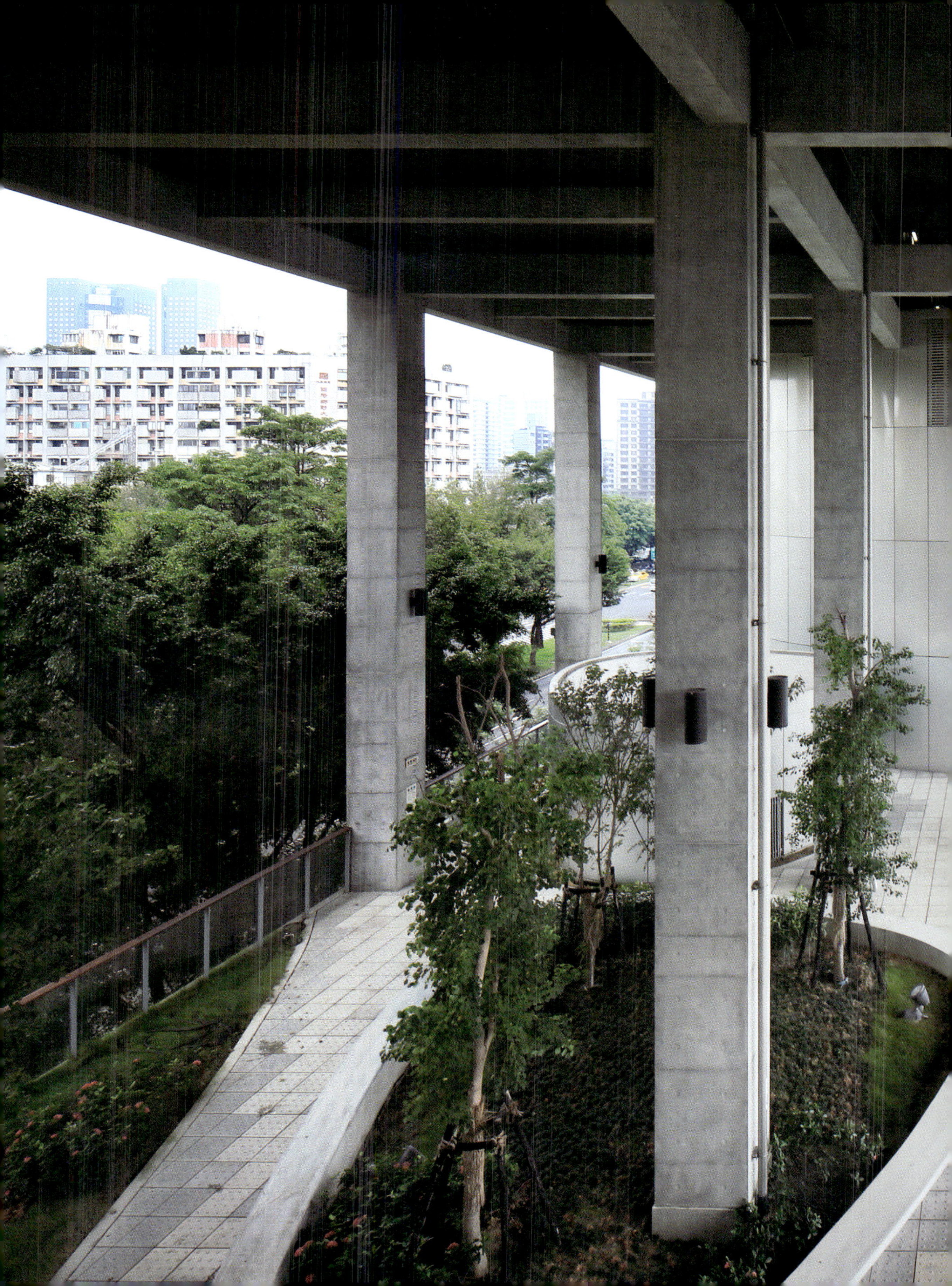

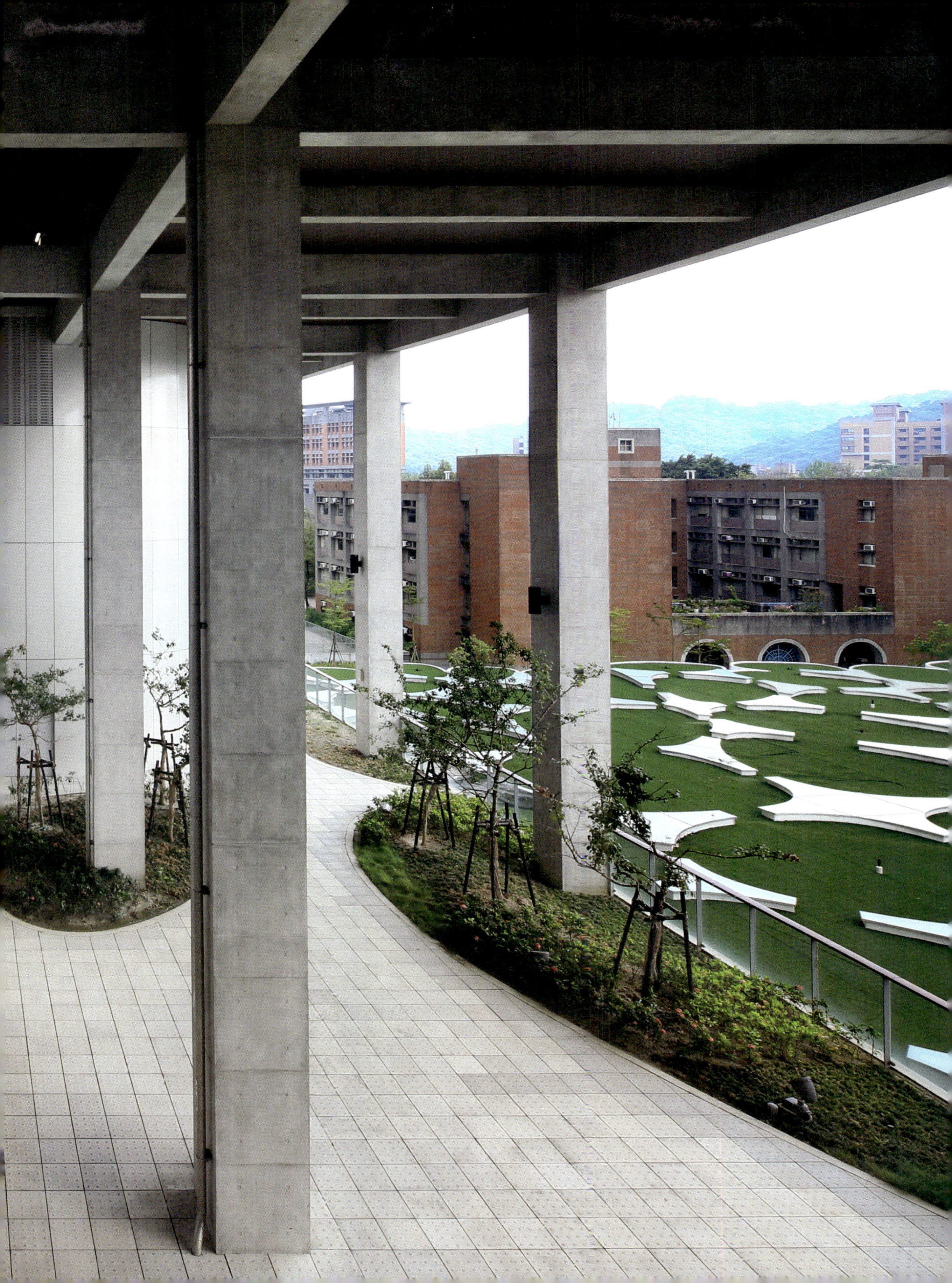

Songshan Taipei New Horizon Building
松山 台北文創ビル

2013　台湾 台北　Taipei, Taiwan

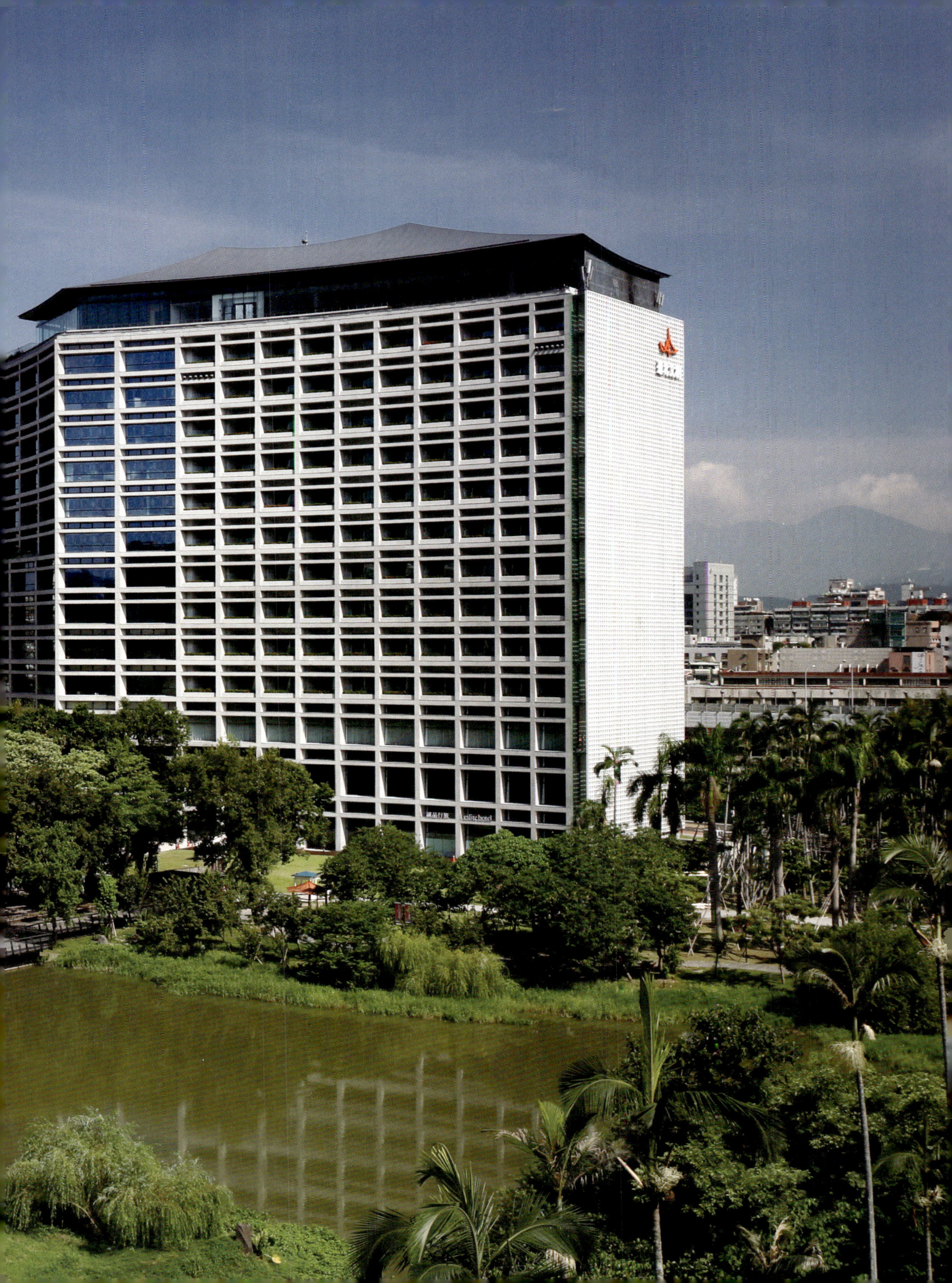

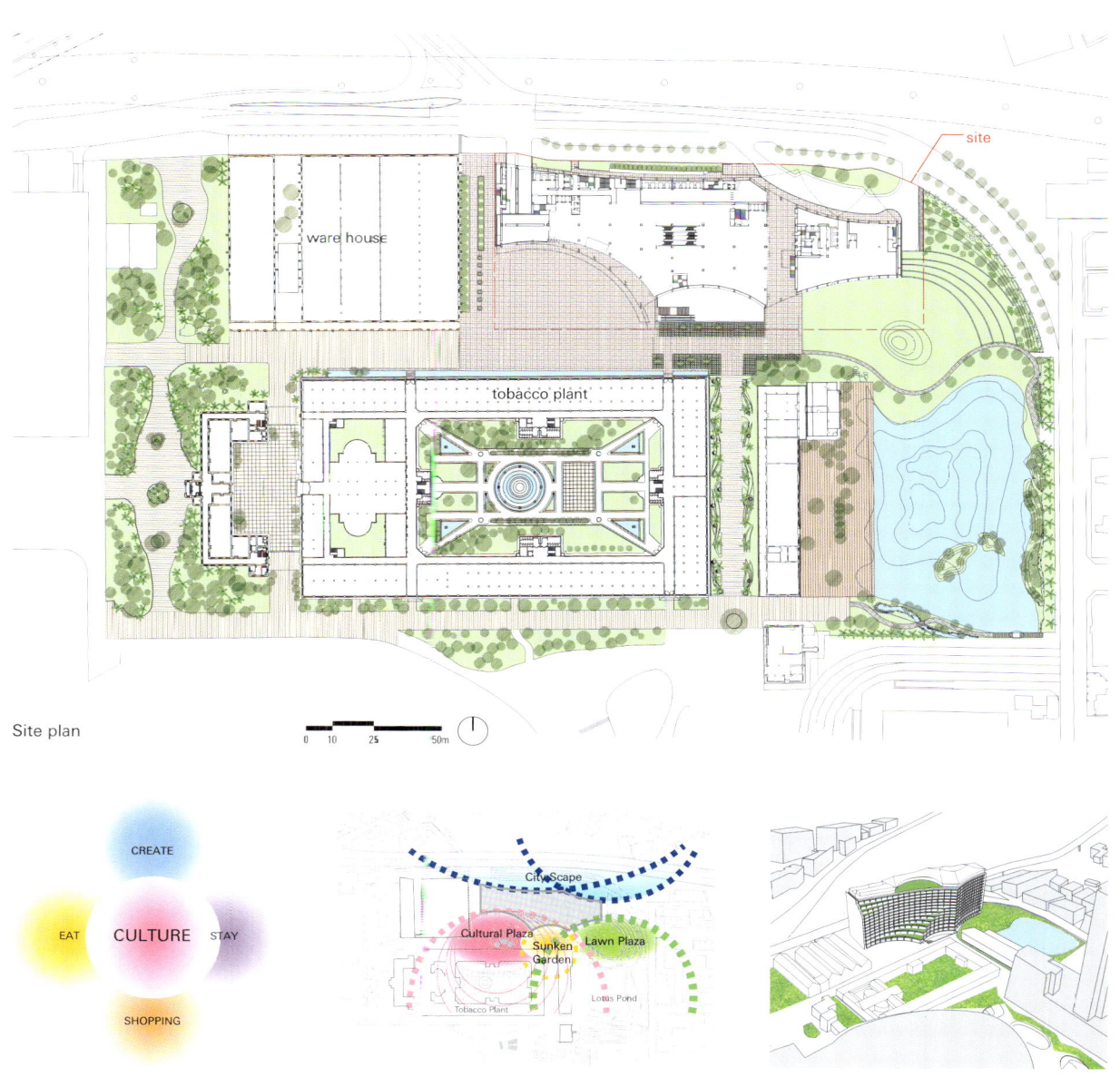

Site plan
0 10 25 50m

New Lifestyle

Human Scale

Green Network

松山文創区の俯瞰
Bird's-eye view of the Songshan Cultural Zone

1937年に整備された煙草工場
This tobacco factory was established in 1937.

椰子の木通りより望む
View from the palm-tree-lined street.

台北市の中心に位置する1930年代に建設された煙草工場の跡地における再開発計画。計画ではオフィス・商業施設・ホテル・文教施設から成る約10万㎡の複合施設を建設することで、古跡の保存や活用を行う別事業とともに文化活動の基盤をつくることが求められた。

This redevelopment plan was created for the former site of a tabacco factory, built in the 1930s, which is located in the center of Taipei. By creating an approximately 100,000-square-meter complex, made up of offices, commercial businesses, educational facilities, and a hotel, the plan satisfied the need to preserve the historic spot, generate new businesses, and lay the foundation for various cultural activities.

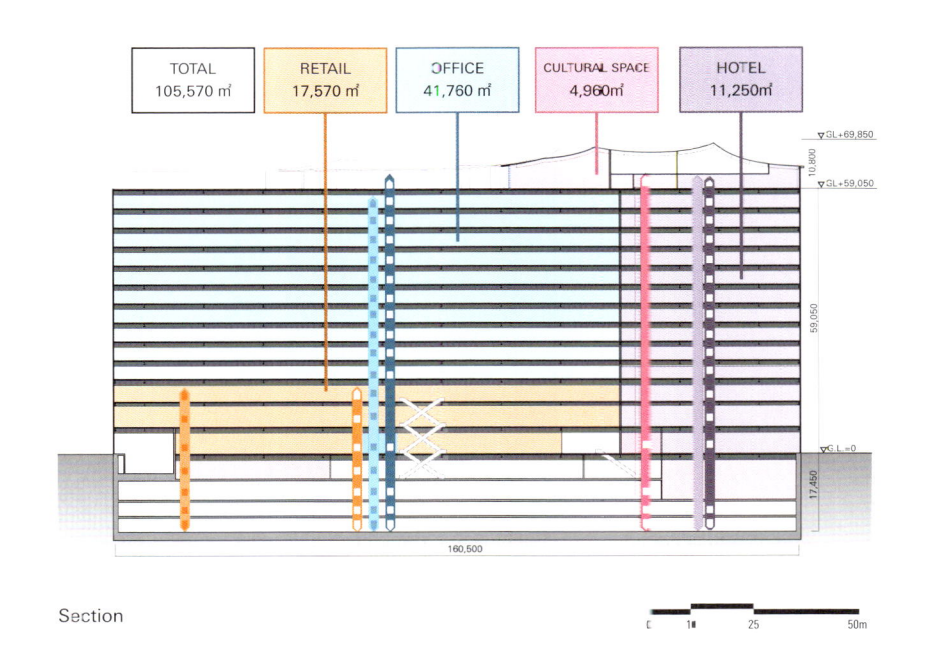

| TOTAL | RETAIL | OFFICE | CULTURAL SPACE | HOTEL |
|---|---|---|---|---|
| 105,570 ㎡ | 17,570 ㎡ | 41,760 ㎡ | 4,960 ㎡ | 11,250 ㎡ |

Section

265

(上) 保存される古跡とその間に見えるにぎやかな文化広場　(左下) 段上テラス
(Above) The lively cultural square between the historic buildings.　(Below left) A stepped terrace.

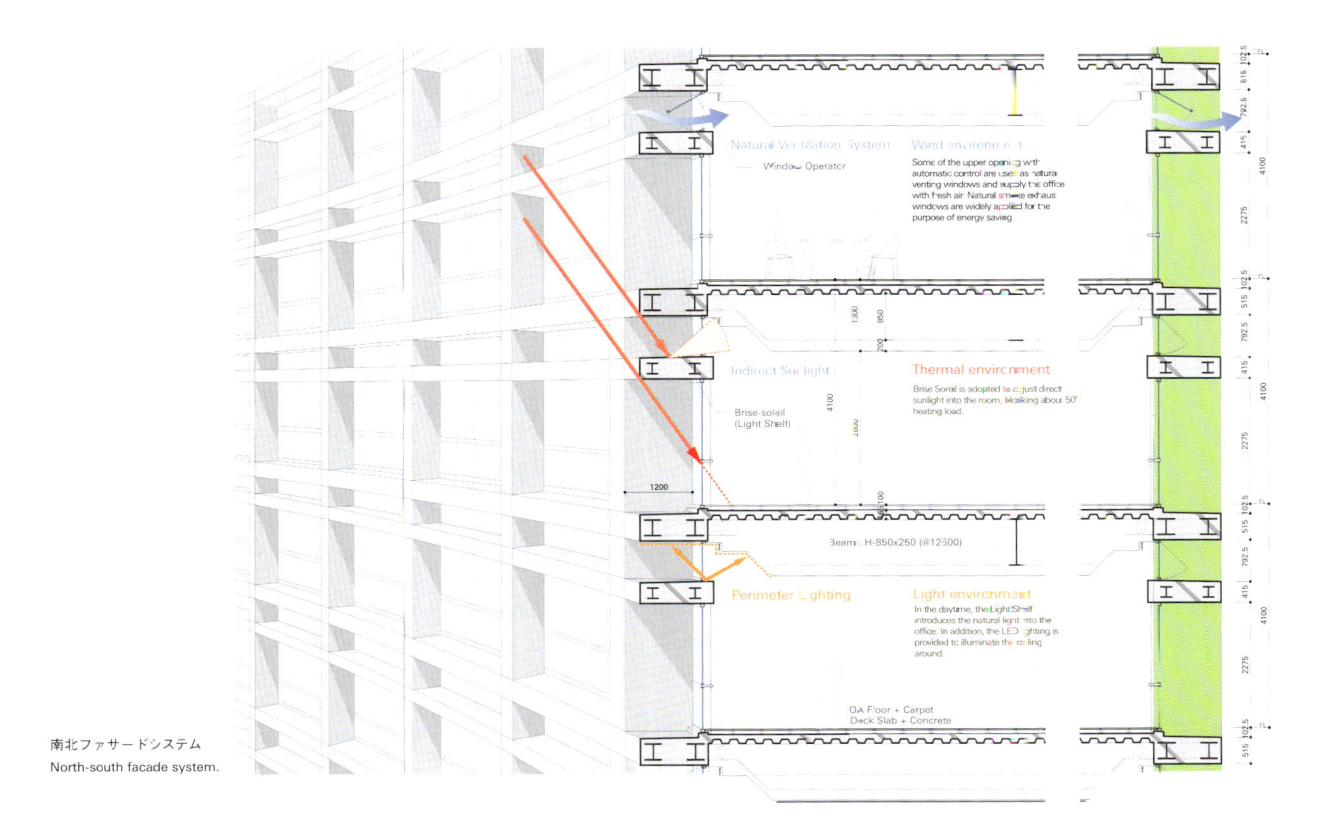

南北ファサードシステム
North-south facade system.

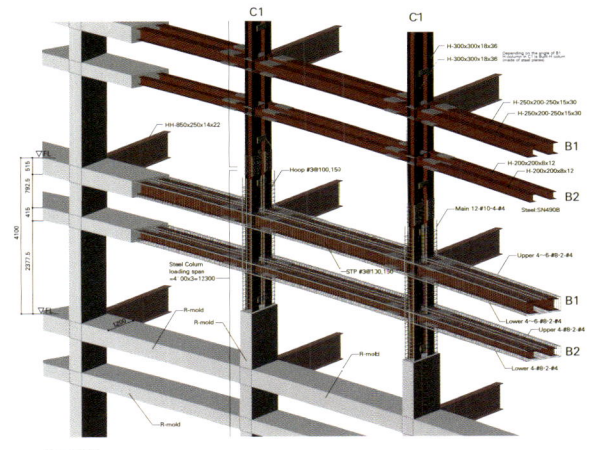

SRC格子構造
Steel-reinforced, concrete lattice structure.

南北のファサードはSRC格子構造であり、奥行1200mmの
ブリーズソレイユを形成している欄間部には自然排煙兼用
の通風窓を設けて、自然エネルギーの最大利用をはかる。

The north-south facade has a steel-reinforced, concrete lattice structure, and the transom, equipped with a brise-soleil shading system (measuring 1,200mm in depth), is furnished with windows that provide natural smoke exhaustion and ventilation to make the best use of natural energy.

(上)配筋工事　(下)型枠工事
(Above) Reinforcement work.　(Below) Mold work.

14F plan

9F plan

1F plan

culture square

greenland square

B2F plan

| | |
|---|---|
| 1 | retail |
| 2 | EV hall |
| 3 | sunken garden |
| 4 | promenade |
| 5 | hotel |
| 6 | kiss and ride |
| 7 | office |
| 8 | food court |
| 9 | cinema |
| 10 | concert hall |

(上)緩やかな円弧に囲まれたサンクンガーデン。立体的な緑の壁面が、地上の緑を地下へ連続させる
(左中)361席のコンサートホール。音響効果をつくりだす水平反射リブは本体建物の構成と調和をとる
(右中)3つのシネマのためのホワイエ空間
(左下)黒い吸音材と星屑のようなランダムな照明がちりばめられているシネマシアター内部

(Above) The sunken garden is enclosed by gentle arcs. The three-dimensional green wall create a link between the vegetation above and below ground.
(Middle left) The 361-seat concert hall: The horizontal reflective ribs improve the acoustics and create a harmony with the overall structure.
(Middle right) The foyer for the three cinemas.
(Below left) The interior of the cinema is lined with black sound absorption material and randomly positioned lights that resemble stardust.

(上)屋上庭園から台北中心部の夜景を望む　(下)イベントスペース使用時の様子
(Above) Night view of central Taipei as seen from the rooftop garden. (Below) View of the event space in use.

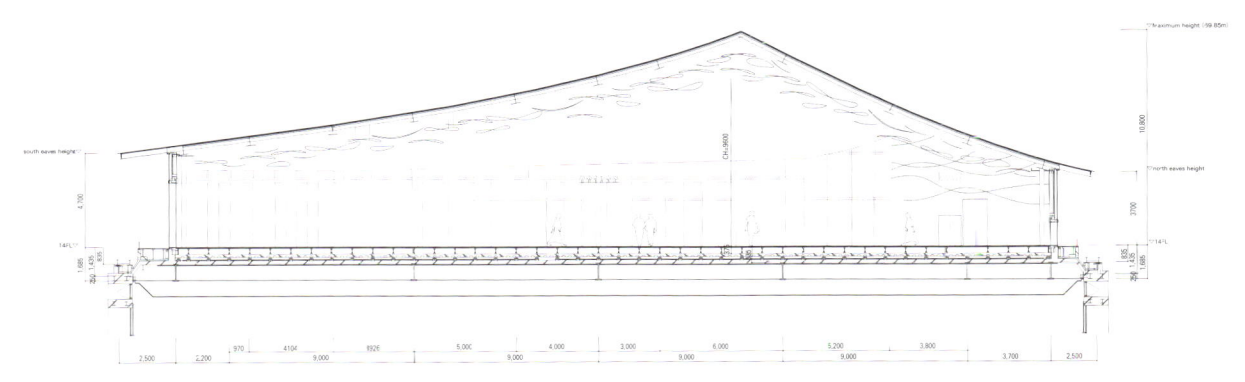

Detailed section of 14F

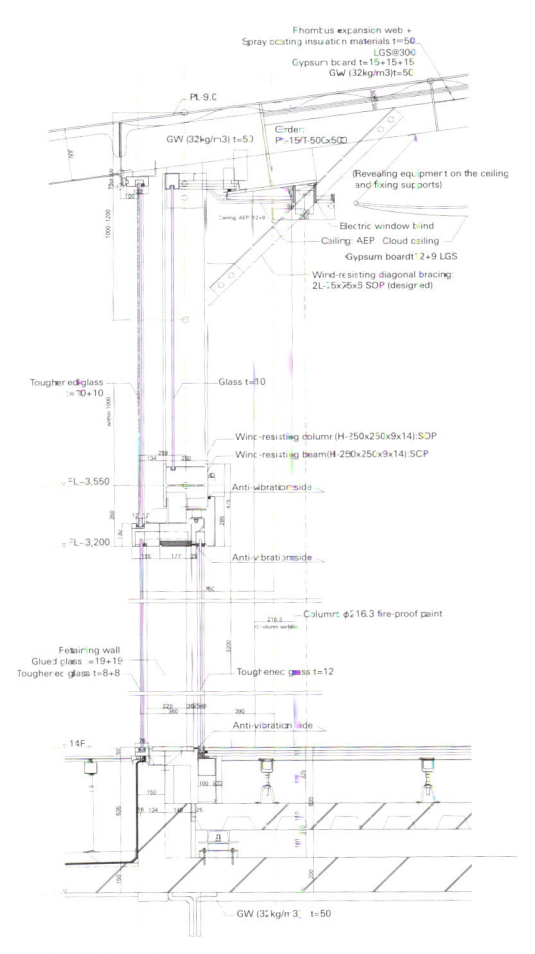

Detailed section

(上) 高雄の造船工場にて屋根鋼板と構造を一体的に製作する
(中) 運搬サイズに切断し、現場に搬入後、溶接して一体化する
(下) 躯体、塗装完成

(Above) The structure and steel sheets for the roof were integrally produced at a shipbuilding factory in Kaoshiung.
(Middle) After cutting the units into a portable size and transporting them to the construction site, they are welded together.
(Below) View of the structure after the framework and painting were completed.

271

(上)北側ファサードは、柱の奥行方向に彩色を施し、高架道路からの視覚効果を高めている
(Above) The columns in the cross-sectional direction on the north facade were painted to increase visibility from the freeway.

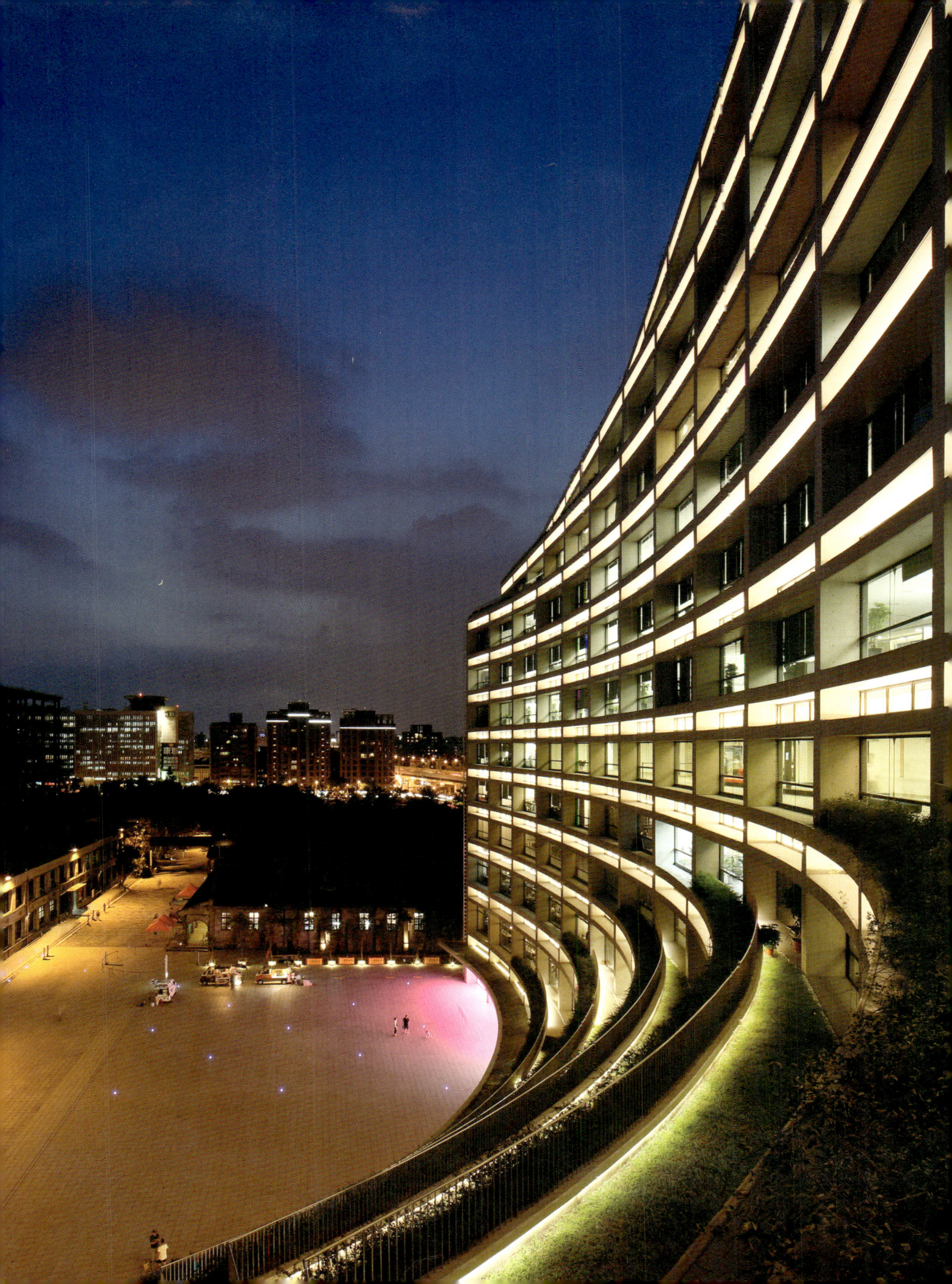

Minna no Mori Gifu Media Cosmos
(tentative title)

みんなの森 ぎふメディアコスモス

建設中 under construction  岐阜県岐阜市  Gifu, Gifu

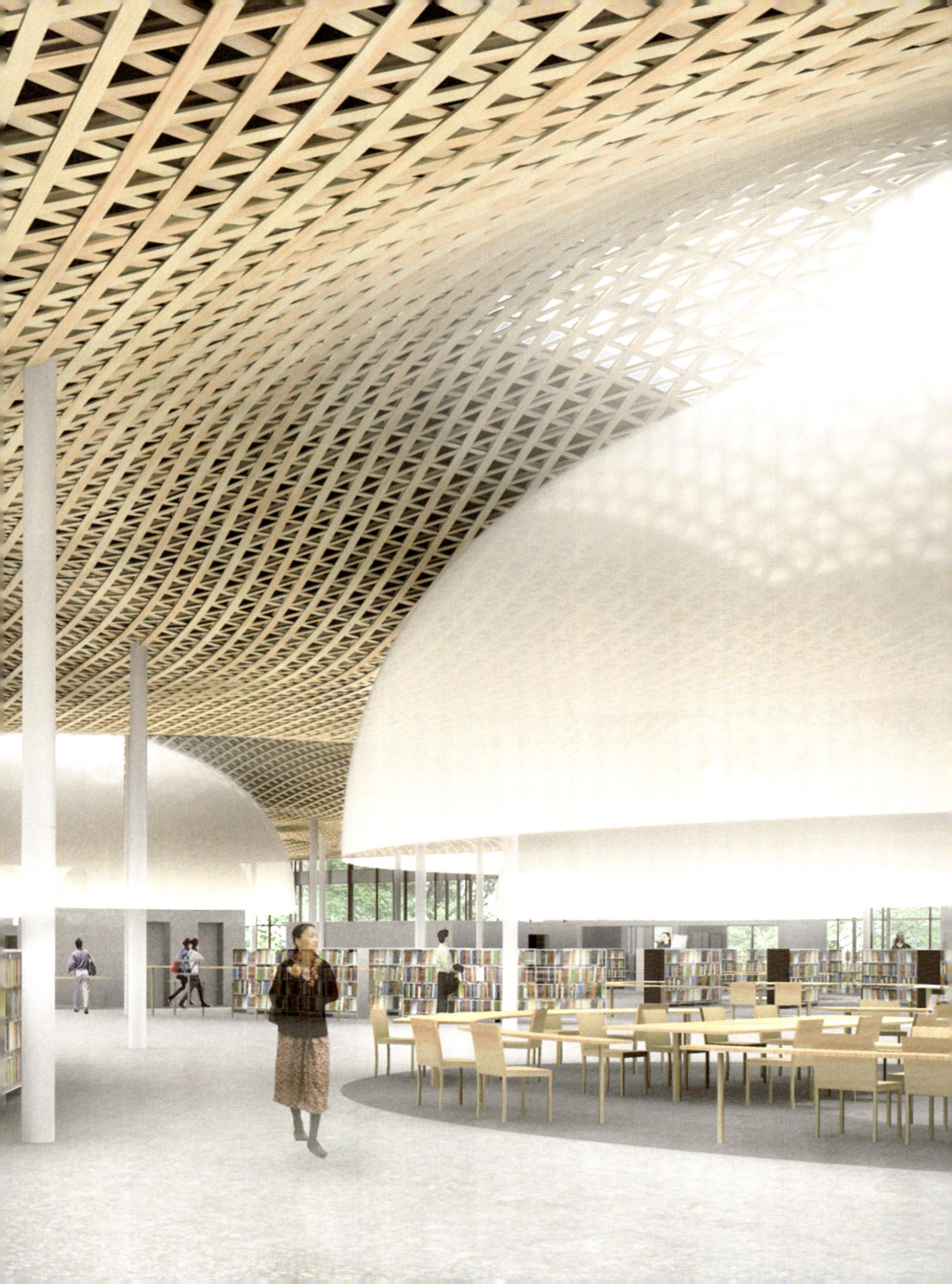

エントランスイメージ
Image of entrance.

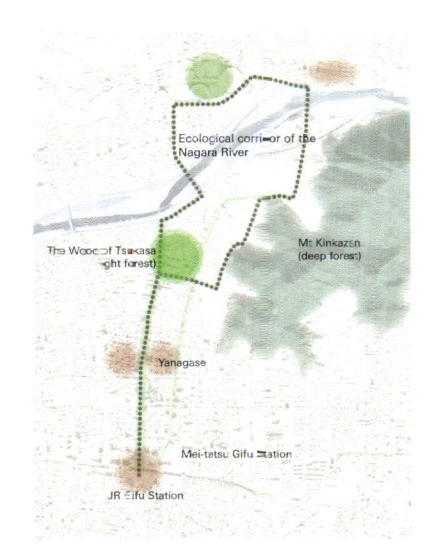

岐阜市航空写真
Aerial view of Gifu city.

鳥瞰イメージ
Bird's-eye image.

岐阜市中心部に計画中の図書館を中心とした文化複合施設。約80m×90mという大きな平面形が2層積み重なる構成をもち、1階には展示ギャラリーや市民活動交流センター、ガラスで見える公開書庫など、2階には開架閲覧スペースが広がる。

This complex cultural facility, mainly housing a library is in central Gifu. The building is made up of two stories, roughly 80 by 90 meter in dimension. On the first floor here is a gallery, a civic activity and exchange center, and a book archive visible through the glass. There is a vast area of open shelves on the second floor.

せせらぎの並木 テニテオ
Seseragi no Namiki TENITEO (Park lined with trees).

| # | Label | # | Label |
|---|---|---|---|
| 1 | entrance hall | 16 | browsing Globe |
| 2 | general information | 17 | exhibition Globe |
| 3 | exhibition entrance hall | 18 | reference Globe |
| 4 | exhibition hall | 19 | research Globe |
| 5 | multipurpose hall (open and closable) | 20 | reading Globe |
| 6 | space of exchange and conversation | 21 | concierge Globe |
| 7 | public square | 22 | fast reading Globe |
| 8 | work room | 23 | studying Globe |
| 9 | shop | 24 | children reading Globe |
| 10 | restaurant | 25 | parent-child reading Globe |
| 11 | office | 26 | browsing terrace |
| 12 | book vault (public stack room) | 27 | Kinka mountain terrace |
| 13 | multifunctional hall | 28 | consultation desk for children |
| 14 | yard | 29 | tea drinking area |
| 15 | main entrance | | |

2F plan

Legend:
- general
- philosophy
- history and geography
- society and science
- natural science
- technology and industry
- arts
- language
- literature
- teenager
- children's books
- fashion information
- luxury binding books
- finger reading, recording books
- visual and auditory data
- local information
- newspaper
- new publication
- reservation books area
- browsing area
- others

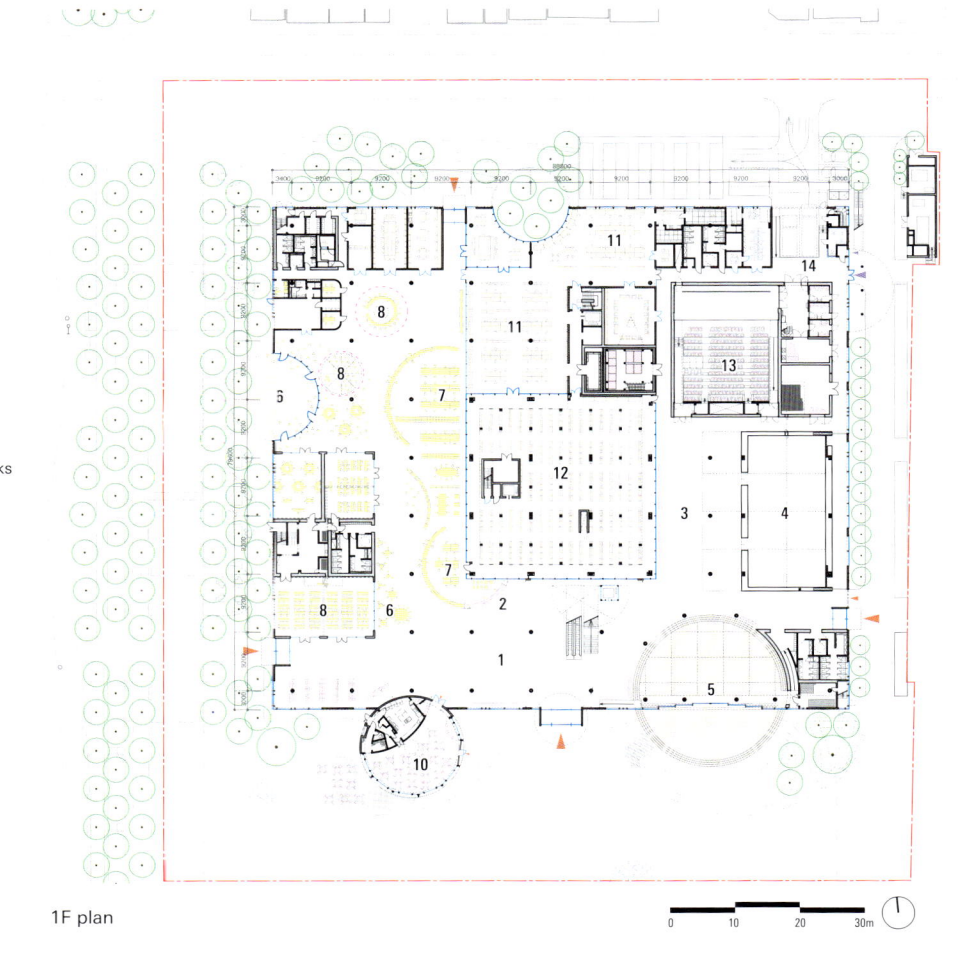

1F plan

278

模型写真
Photograph of model.

| | | | | | | | |
|---|---|---|---|---|---|---|---|
| 1 | cloister hall | 4 | interactive square | 6 | book archive | 9 | concierge |
| 2 | exhibition room | 5 | communication, conversation space | 7 | studio | 10 | study area |
| 3 | cloister | | | 8 | reading area | | |

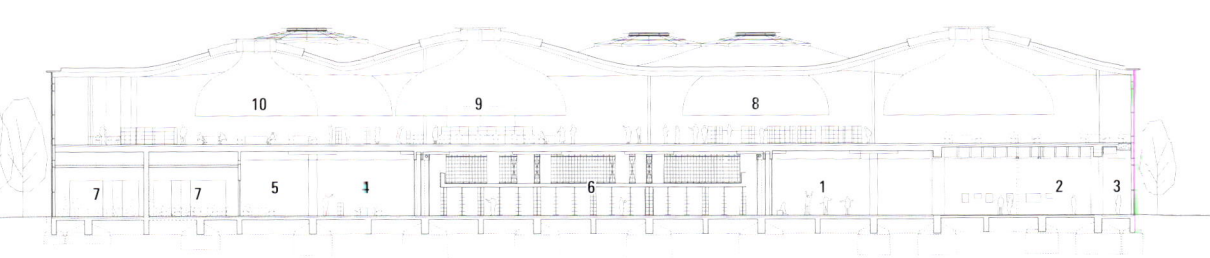

Section

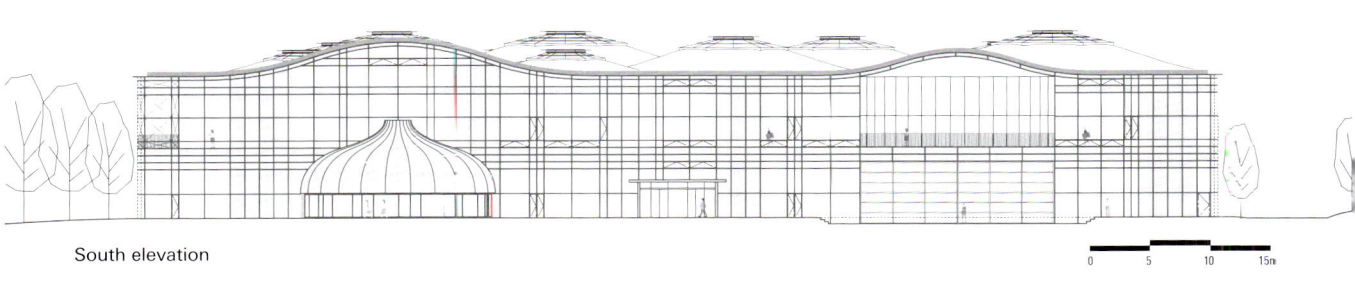

South elevation

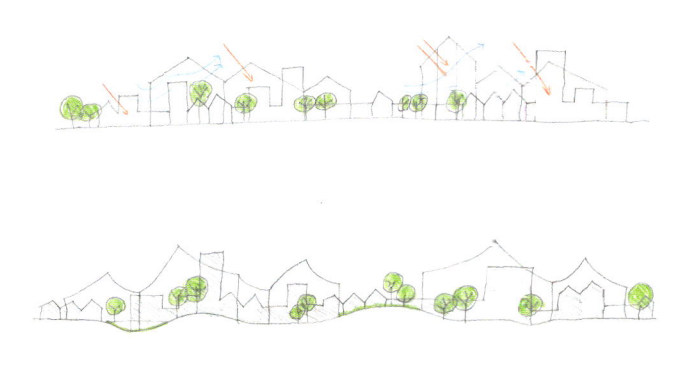

小さな家を内包する大きな家というコンセプトに基づく初期のスタディ
Study during the early phase with the concept of small houses with in a big house.

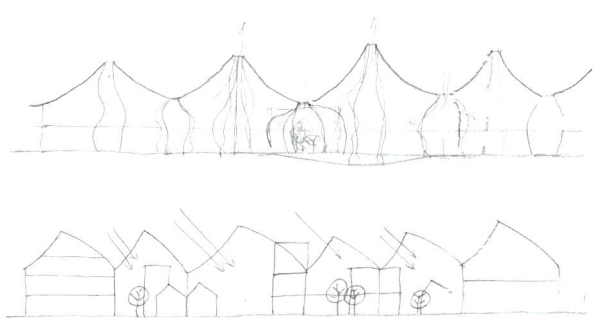

大きな家と小さな家の相互関係の変容。光と風を取り込む呼吸する大きな家
Transformation of the interrelationship between small and large houses. The big houses captures light and wind.

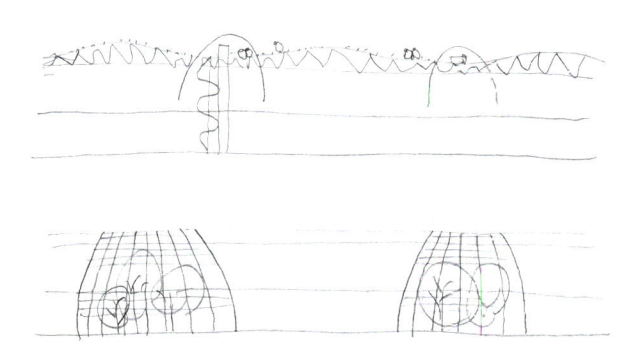

チューブが抽出され構造と環境面で大きな家を支える
Extracting tubes and supporting the large houses with environmental aspects and the structure.

チューブと小さな家の融合によるグローブの誕生。
環境装置であると同時に「家」としての場をつくる
Globes were made by combining tubes and a small house.
This creates a place that is both an environmental mechanism and a "house".

場と境界の設定
Determining the place and boundary lines.

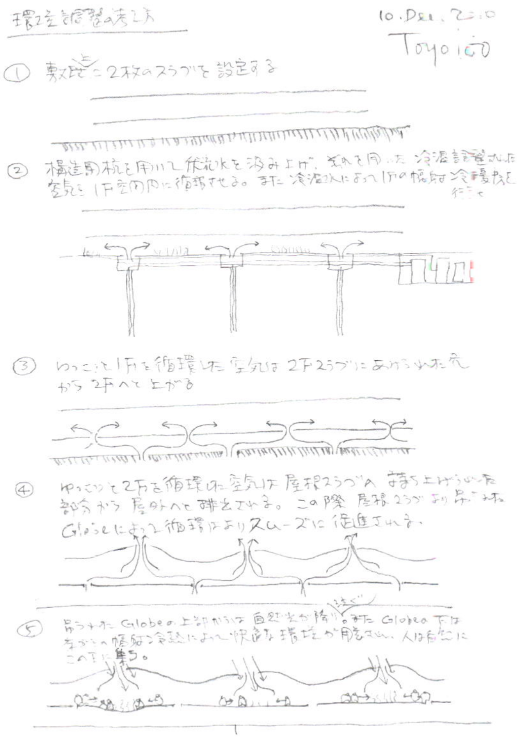

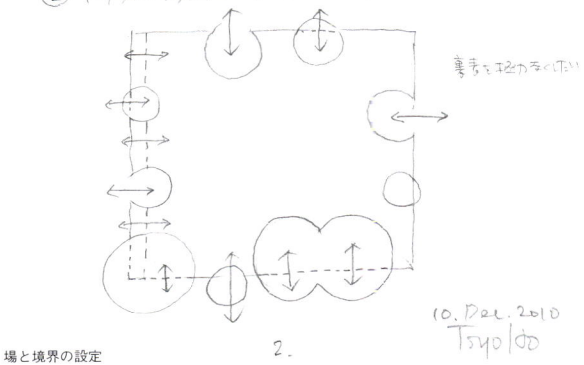

グローブの働き
Function of the Globe.

大屋根の下に集落のような本のまちが形成される
Under the large roof, a collection of books similar to a village is created.

冬

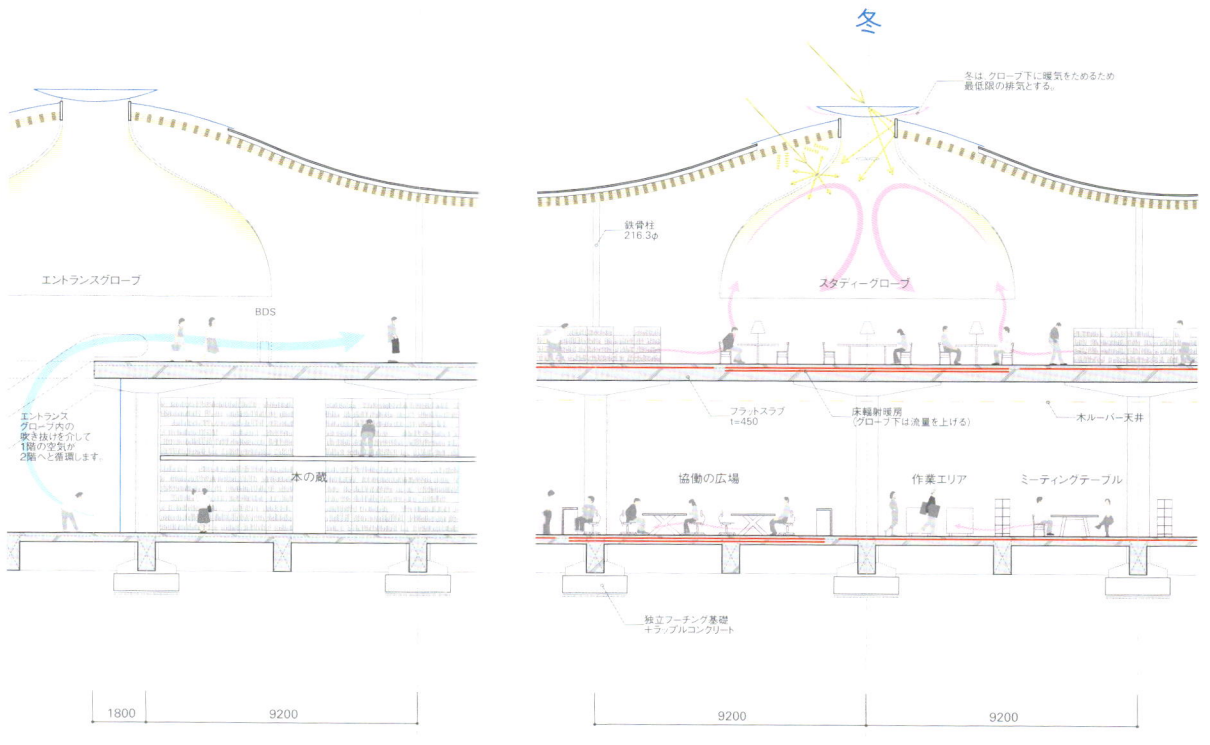

場と環境構成のメカニズム
Configuration of space and environmental mechanisms.

1階市民活動交流センターのイメージ
Image of the civic activity and exchange center on the first floor.

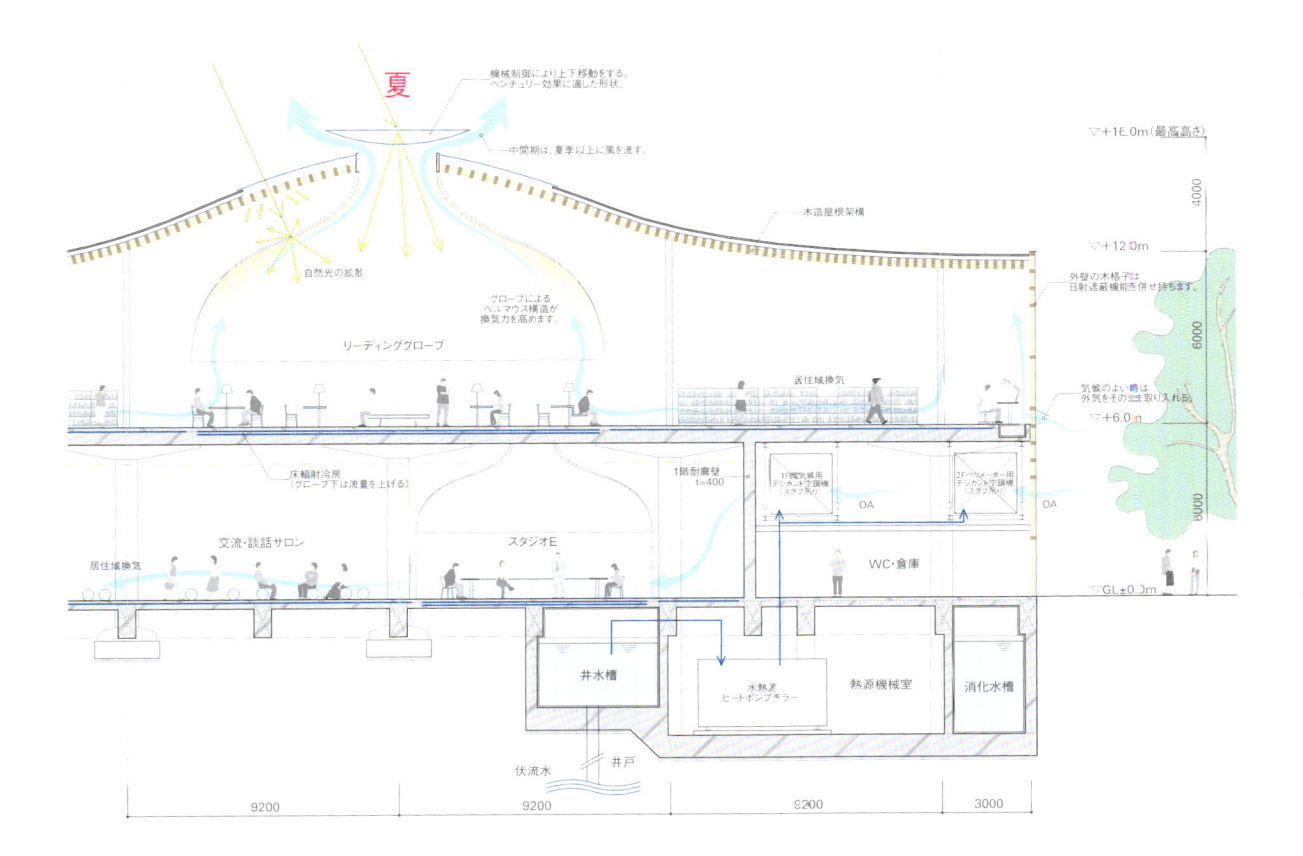

2階窓際の閲覧スペースイメージ
Image of the reading space next to the windows on the second floor.

豊富な地下水を利用した高効率な熱源システムを導入して床輻射の冷暖房等を行う。さらに床からの冷気、暖気を自然力によって室内循環させ、グローブ内に導く。このほか太陽光パネルの利用等によって消費エネルギーが従来同規模施設の2分の1になることを目指している。

A floor-radiating air conditioner is used a highly efficient heating system is made possible by means of the abundant underground water. Then cool and warm air from the floor are circulated around the room using natural forces and guided inside the Globe. By using other mechanisms such as solar panels, an attempt was also made to halve the amount of energy that would normally be consumed in a facility of this size.

283

グローブモックアップ
Mock-up of the Globe.

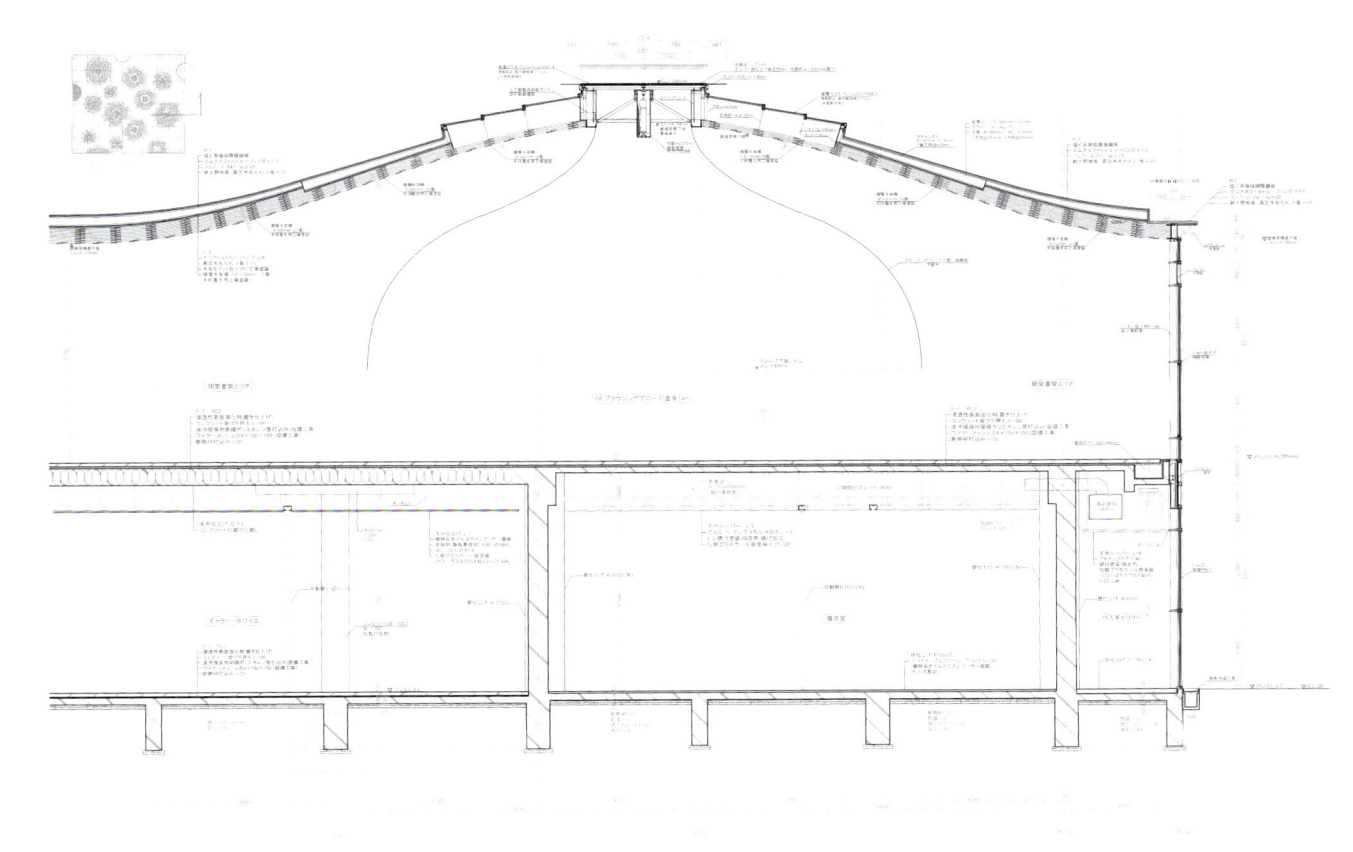

Detailed section

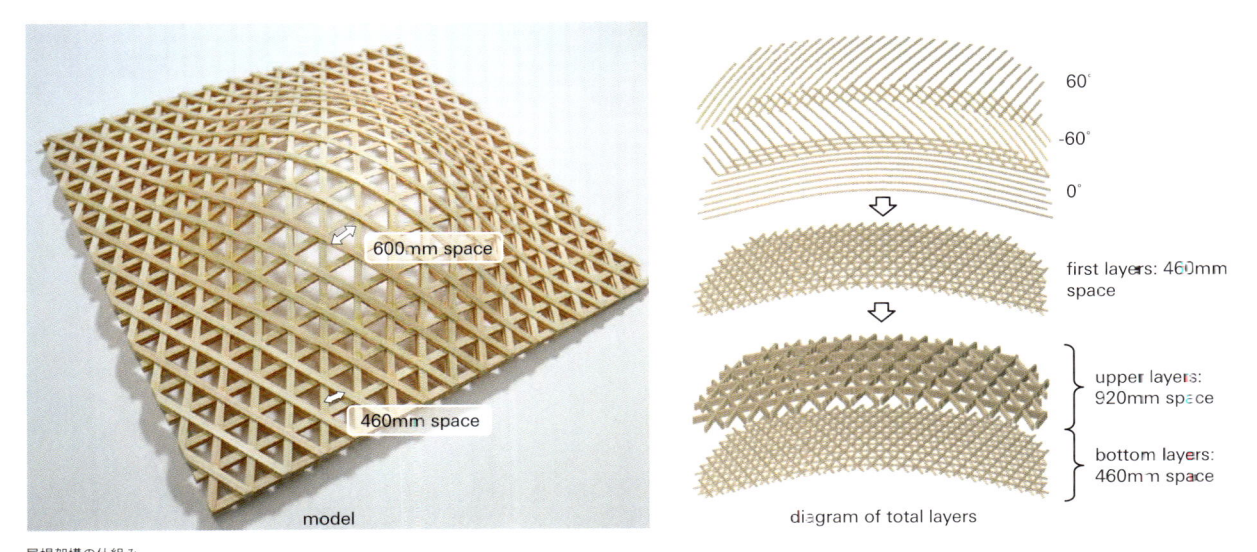

600mm space
460mm space
model

60°
-60°
0°

first layers: 460mm space

upper layers: 920mm space
bottom layers: 460mm space

diagram of total layers

屋根架構の仕組み
System of roof frame.

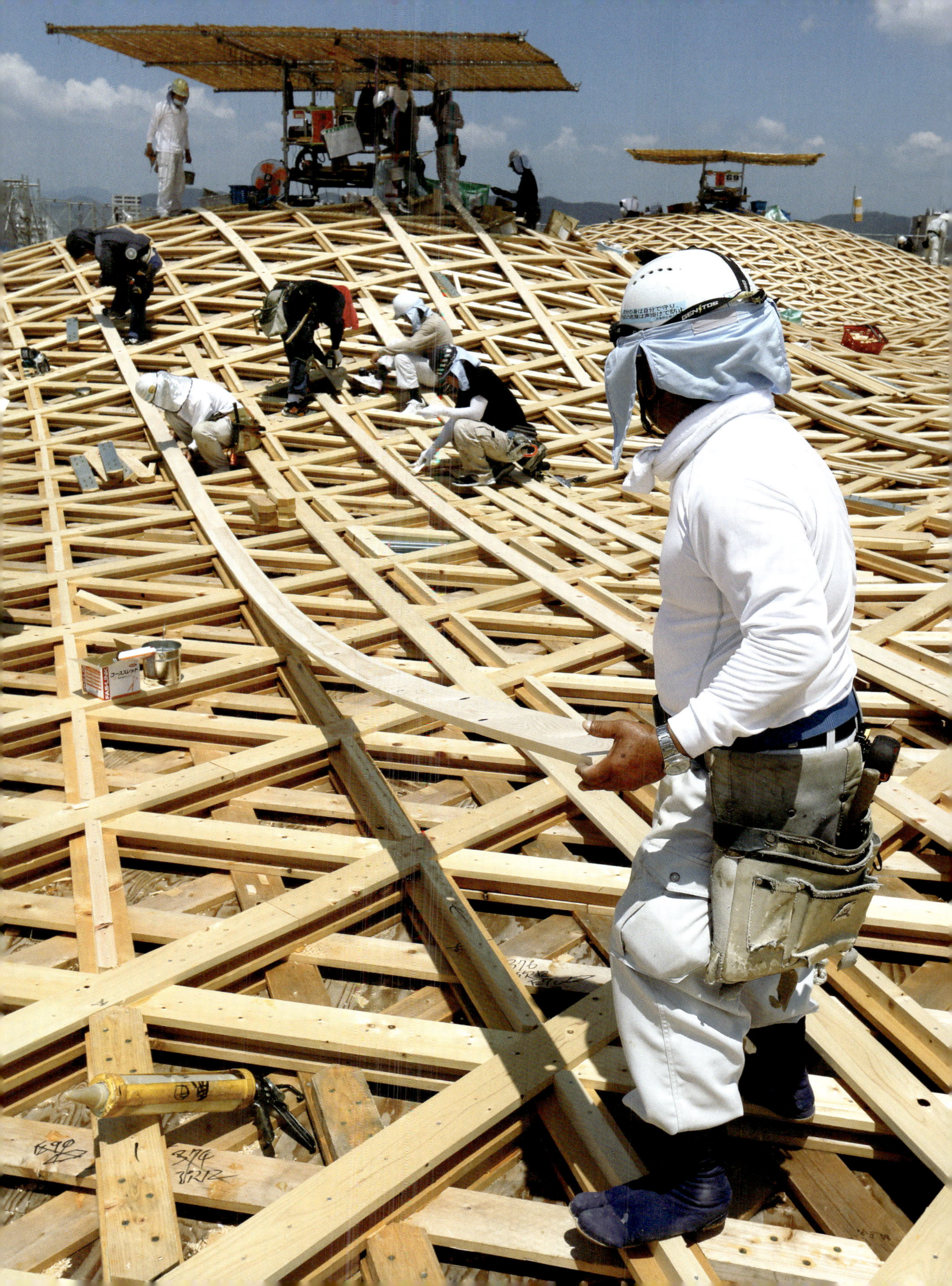

287

CapitaGreen
CapitaGreen

under construction　シンガポール マーケットストリート　Market Street, Singapore

シンガポールはかつて森があった。
私は新しい建築によって森を
再生したい。

私は生命体のように
呼吸する建築をつくりたい。

空に向かって上昇する植物の
ような建築、それがMSTである。

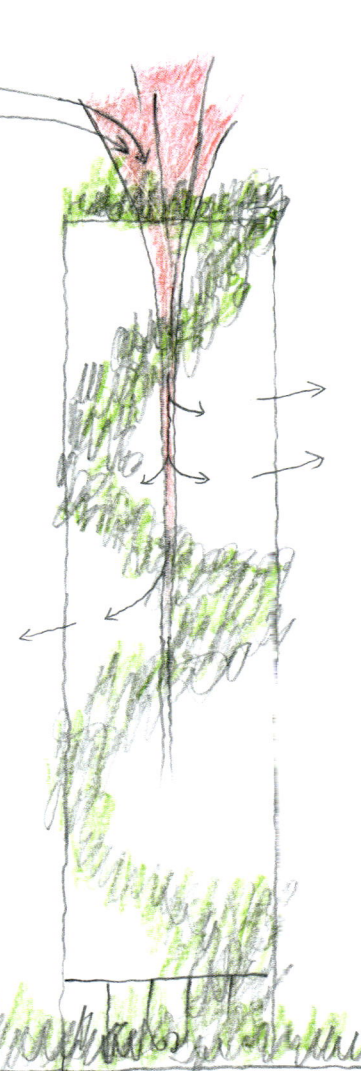

Toyo Ito

Site plan

シンガポールの金融ビジネスエリアの一角、高さ245m、40階建て、約8万㎡の高層オフィスビルの計画である。1本の樹木が大きく成長するイメージのもと、地上の緑が上昇し、頂部の森へと結ばれる。頂部のシンボル的役割を果たすエアインテークは地上より2〜3℃低い空気を下部に送り、各階の空調に使われる。まさしく樹木のような建築である。

This plan for an approximately 80,000-square-meter, high-rise office building with a height of 245 meters and 40 floors, was devised for a corner in Singapore's financial district. Based on the image of a single tree growing tall, greenery was elevated from the ground to create a forest at the top of the building. The air intake, symbolizing the top of the building, conveys air, which is two to three degrees cooler than ground level, to the lower part of the structure and can be used to cool every floor. The building looks very much like a tree.

Section

1 covered plaza
2 office lobby
3 office
4 cool void
5 roof garden
6 restaurant

1F plan

26F plan

40F plan

5F plan

14F plan

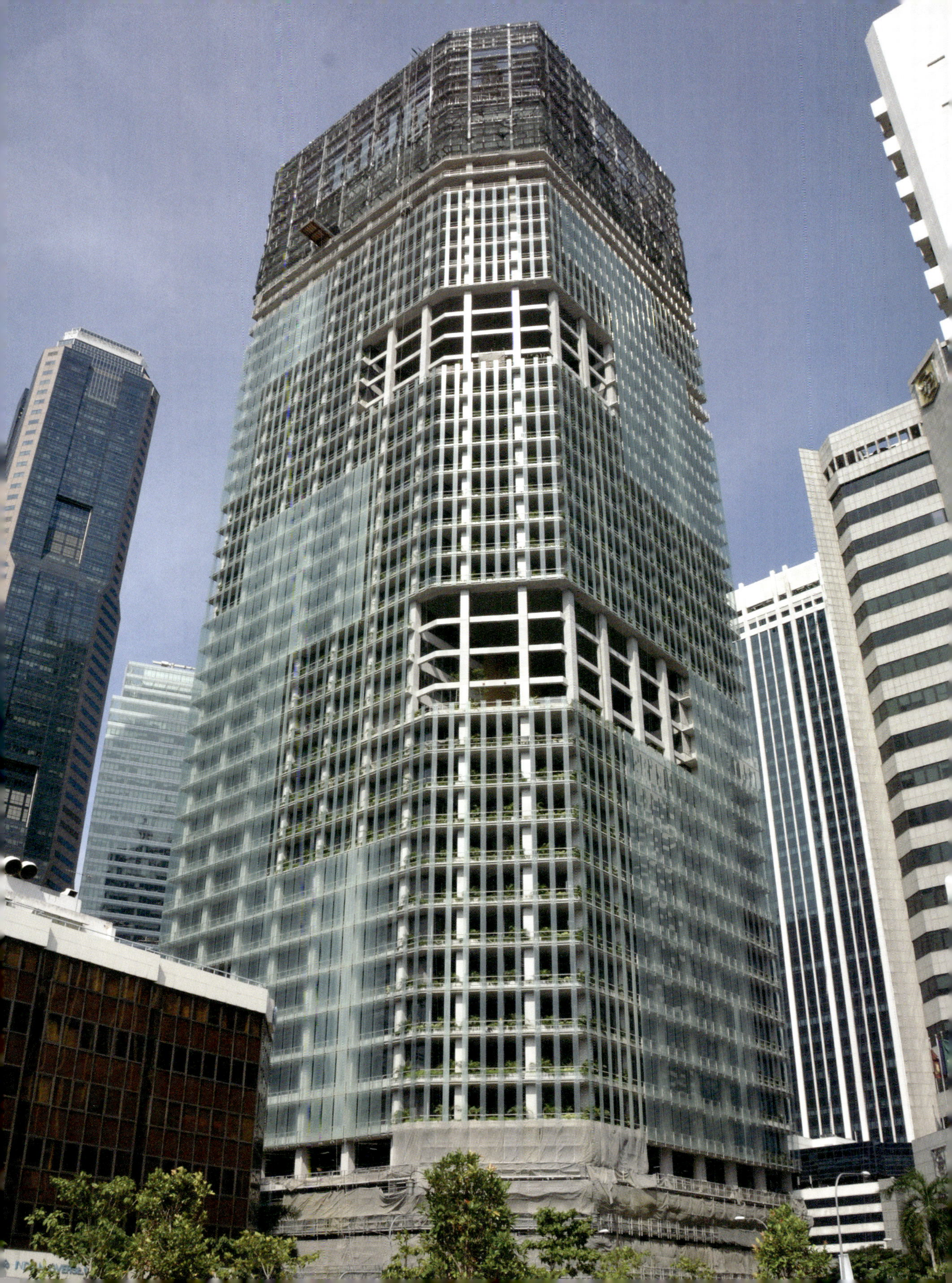

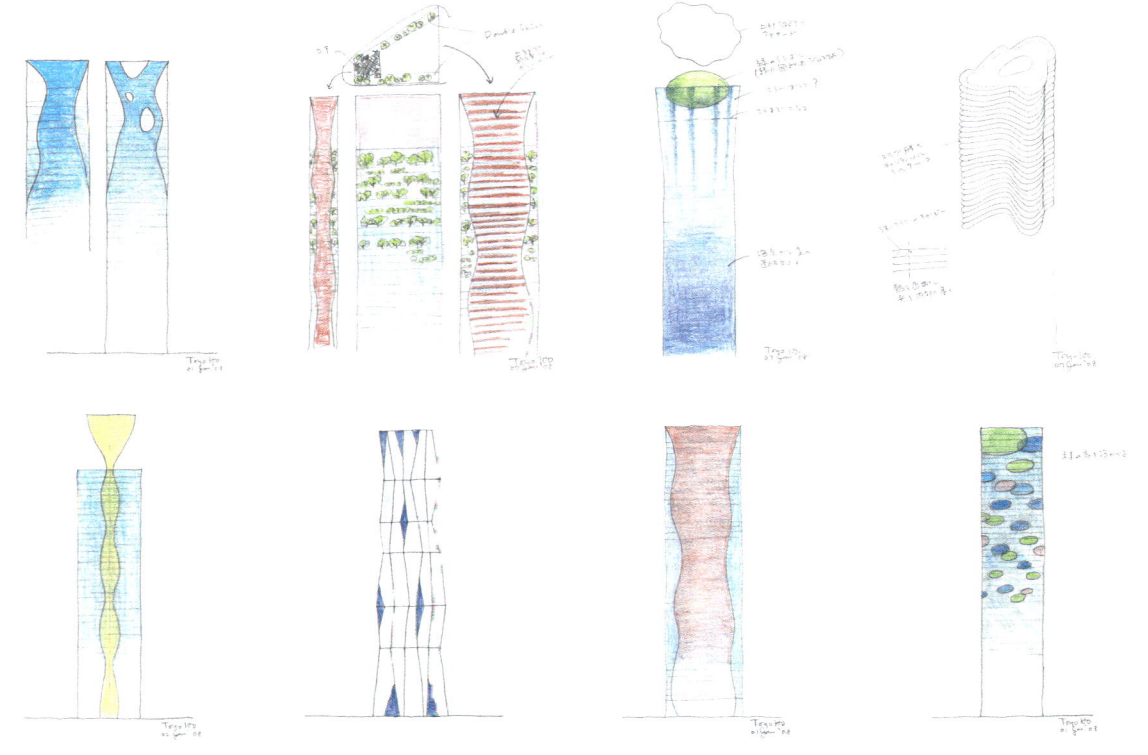

初期のスケッチ
Sketch of the early phase.

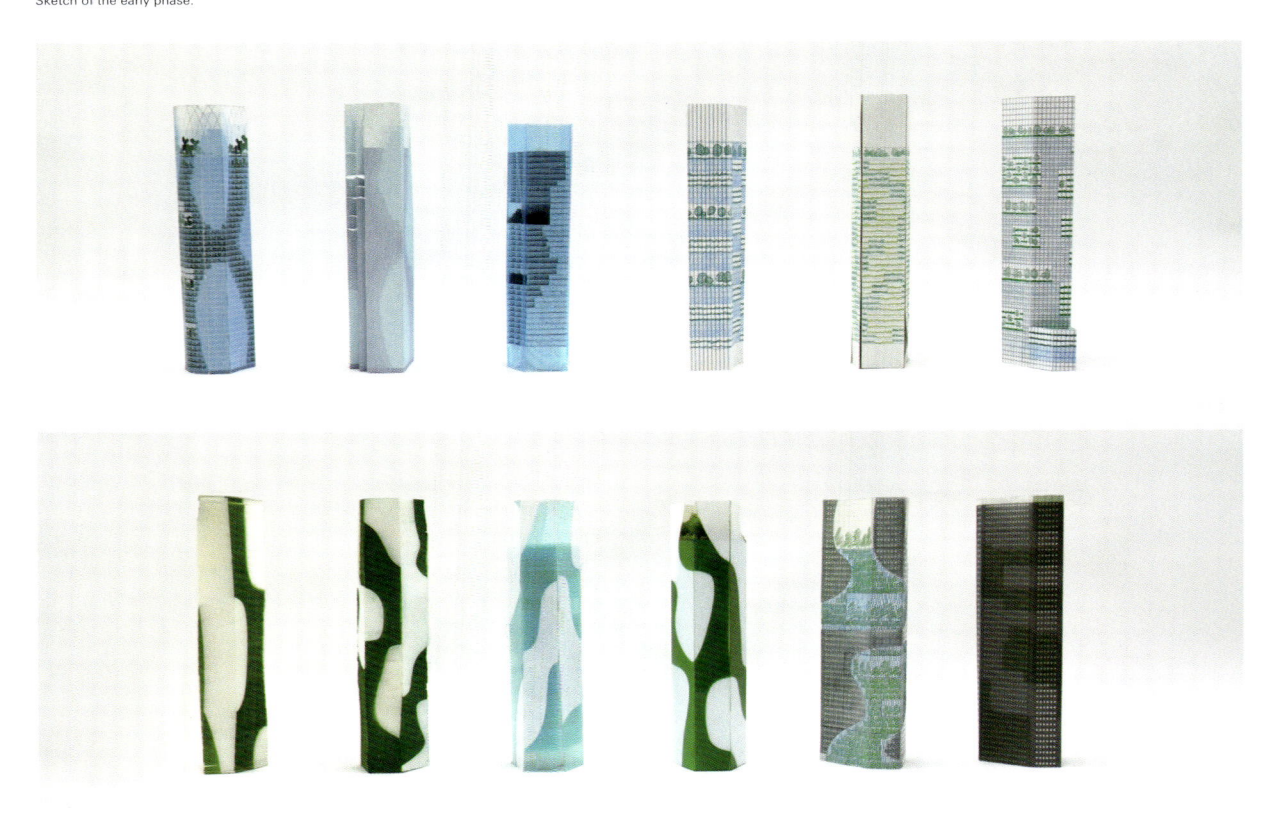

初期からのファサードモデル
Facade model of the early phase.

| West | South | East | North |

Total Wall Area : 58%
Total Green Area : 42%

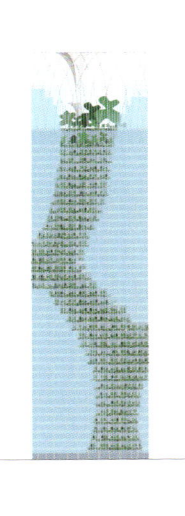

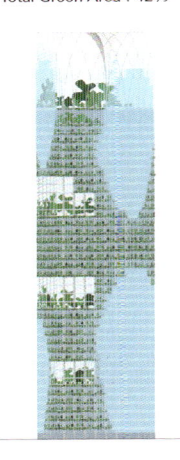

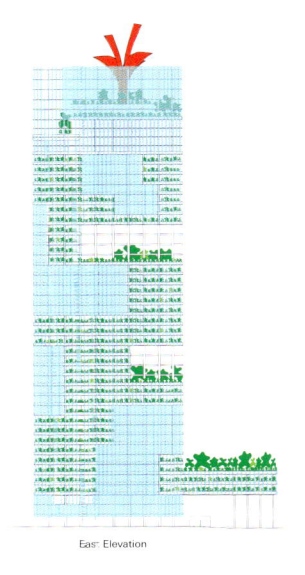

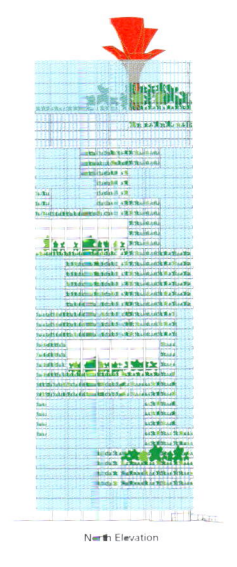

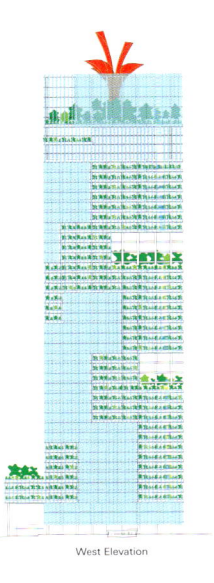

South Elevation | East Elevation | North Elevation | West Elevation

ファサードの変遷
The transformation of the facade.

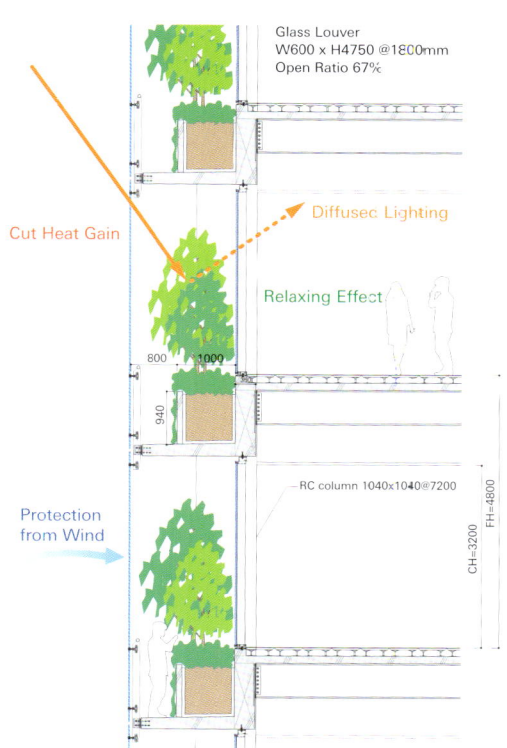

Section diagram of the green facade.

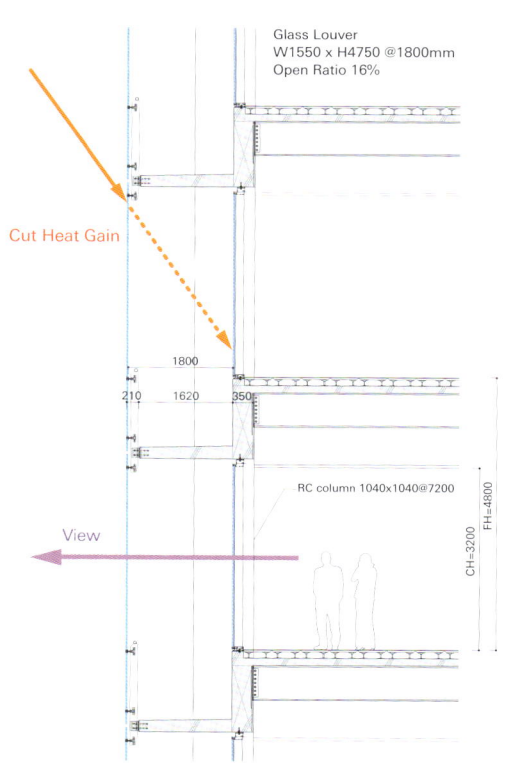

Section diagram of the urban facade.

294

立面はオフィス外周部に配された植物による視覚的な安らぎと日射の拡散効果が期待される「グリーンファサード」と、ガラスのダブルスキンによって日射をカットし、熱負荷を抑えた「アーバンファサード」の2種類のファサードが組み合わされて構成される。

The elevation is visually comforting because of the plants that are arranged around the perimeter of the offices, and the building consists of two different facades. The green facade is intended to diffuse sunlight, and the urban facade, with its double skin, reduces sunlight and the heat load.

（左中）グリーンファサード／アーバンファサード
（右中）グリーンファサードを内観から望む
（下）施行中のダブルスキン内側
(Middle left) Green facade / Urban facade.
(Middle right) View of the green facade from inside the building.
(Below) Inside of the double skin, under construction.

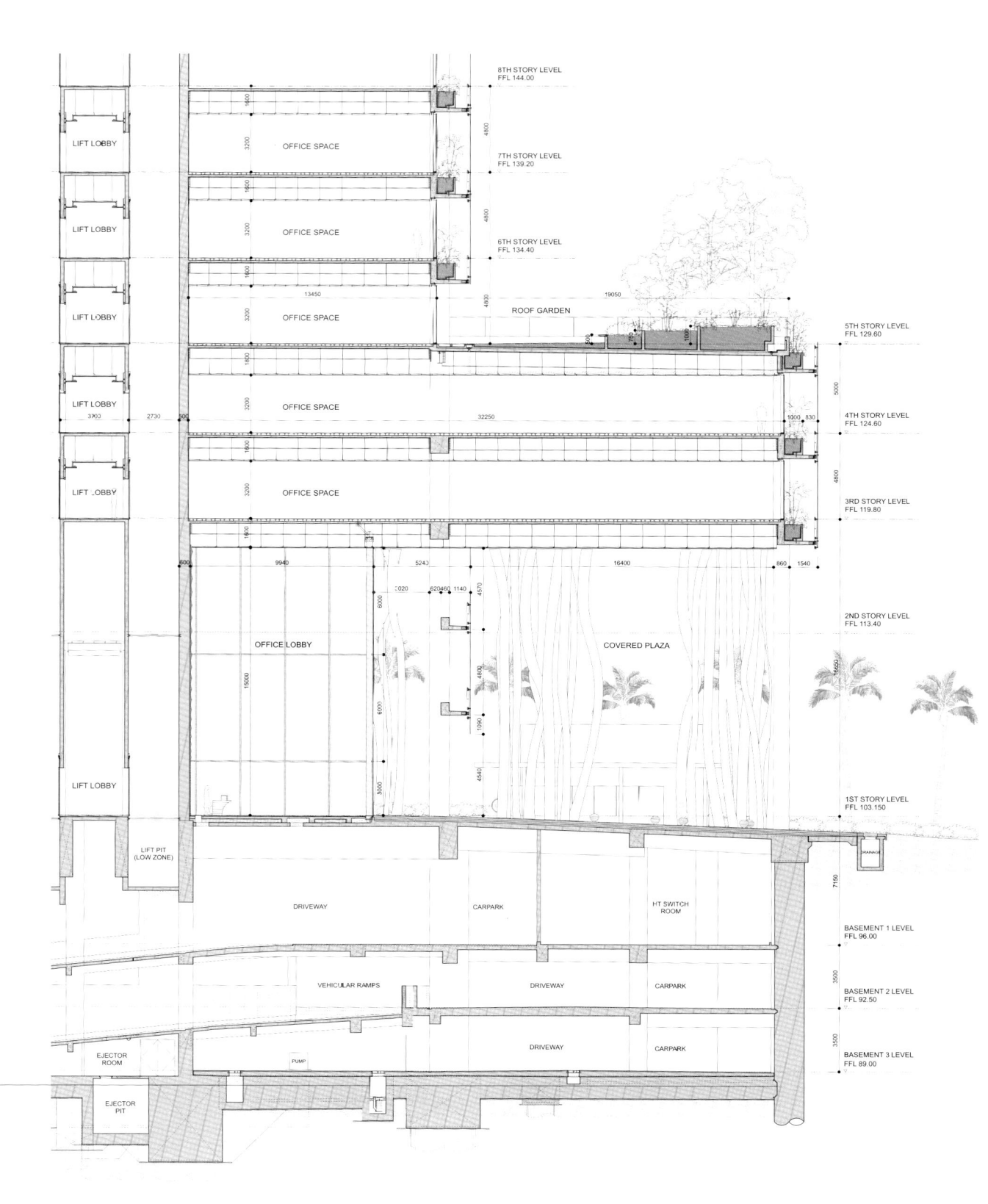

Detailed section

(上) エントランス現場写真
(左中) エントランス外観イメージ
(右中) エントランス内観イメージ
(左下) 久住有生氏による左官壁モックアップ制作の様子

(Above) Site photograph of entrance.
(Middle left) Image of entrance exterior.
(Middle right) Image of entrance interior.
(Below left) Mock up of earthen plaster walls, being created by Mr. Naoki Kusumi.

ウインドキャッチャー施工風景
Constructing the wind catcher.

最上階にあるウインドキャッチャーが上空の清涼な空気をつかまえ、「クールヴォイド」を介して各階のオフィスフロアに送り込まれる。

The wind catcher on the roof of the building captures refreshing air from the sky and conveys it to the offices on each floor in form of cool void.

スカイフォレストのイメージ
Image of the sky forest.

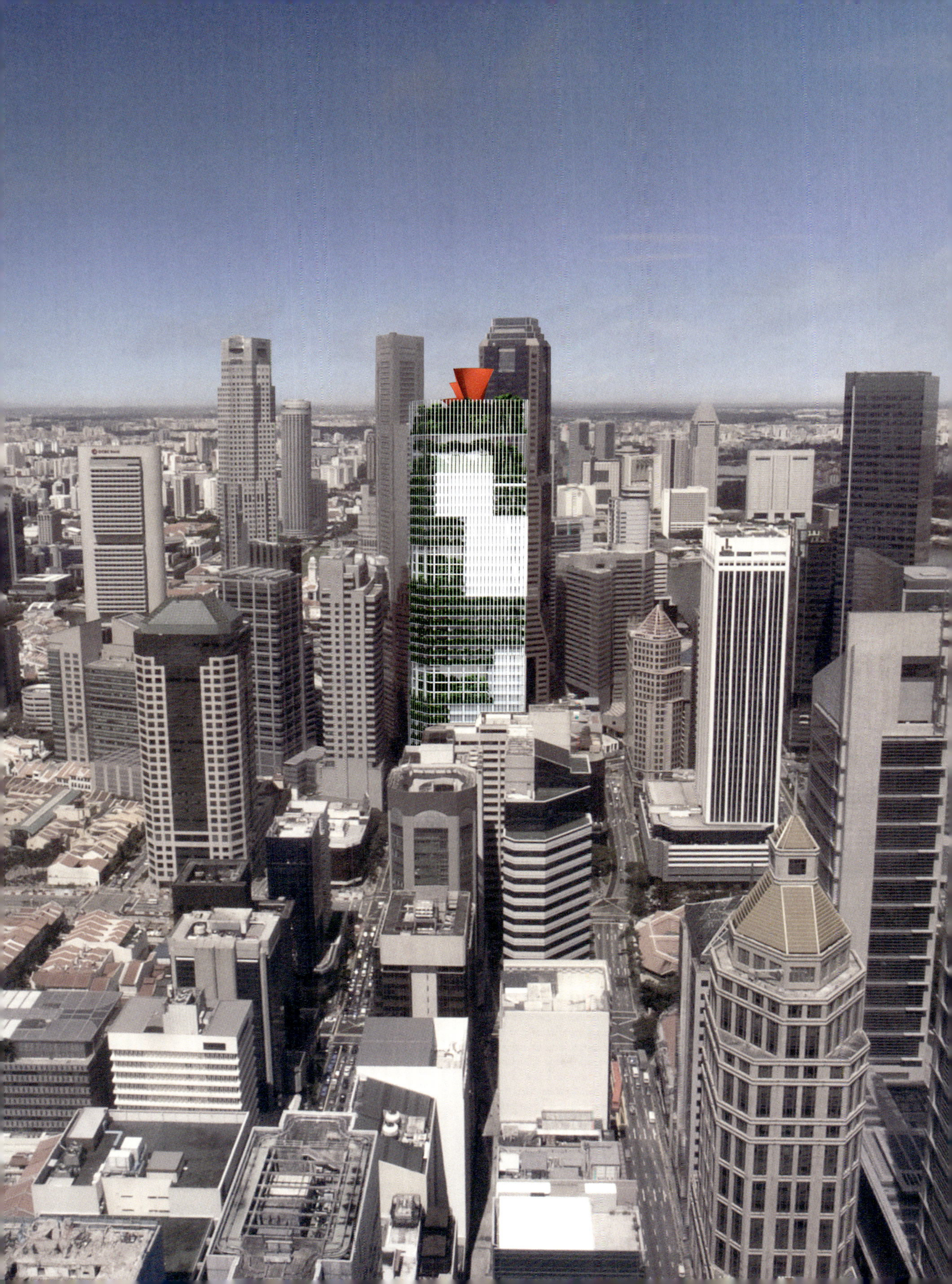

Crematorium and Akayama Historic Nature
Park in Kawaguchi (tentative title)
（仮称）川口市火葬施設・赤山歴史自然公園

計画中 under development　埼玉県川口市　Kawaguchi, Saitama

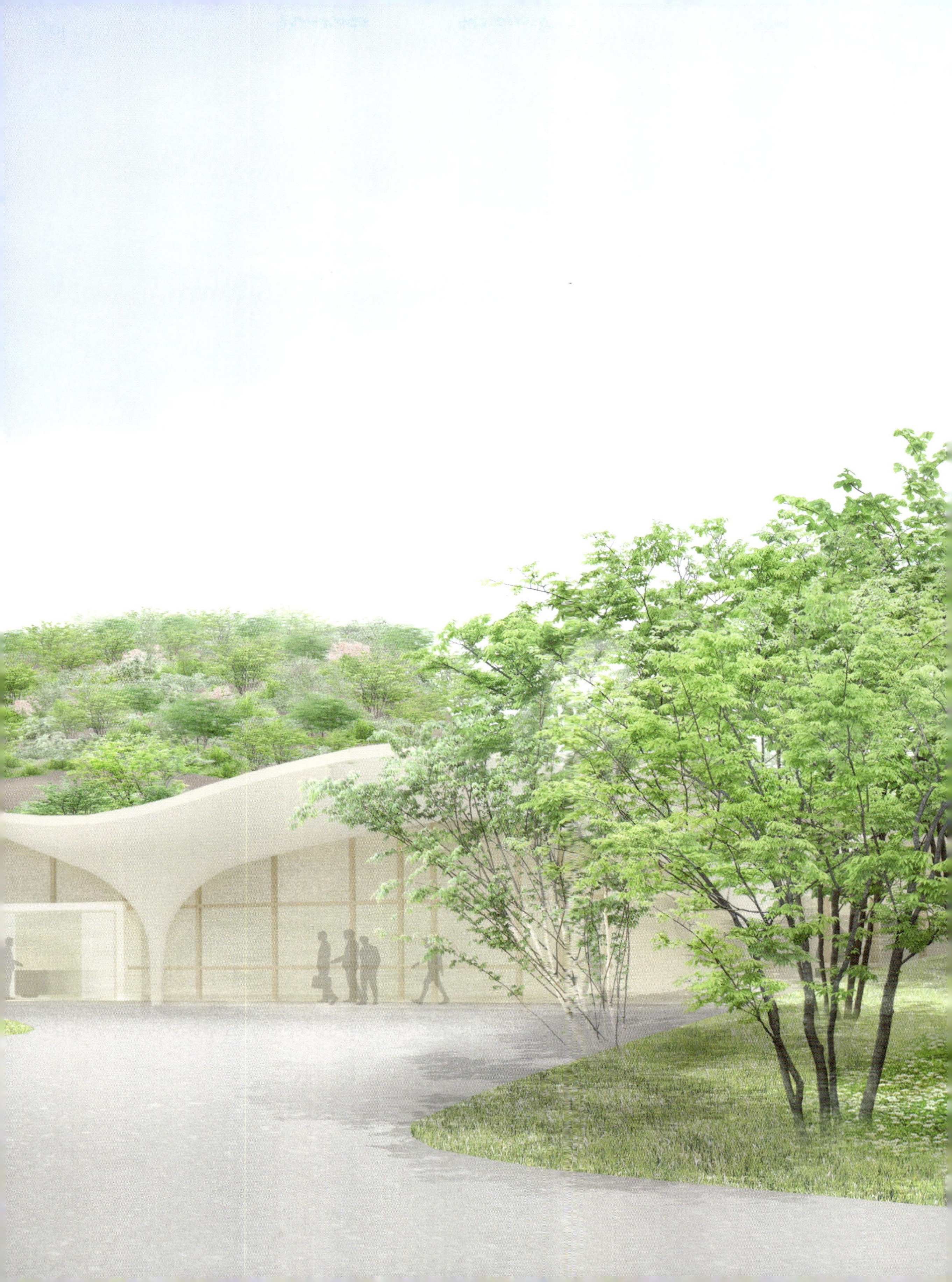

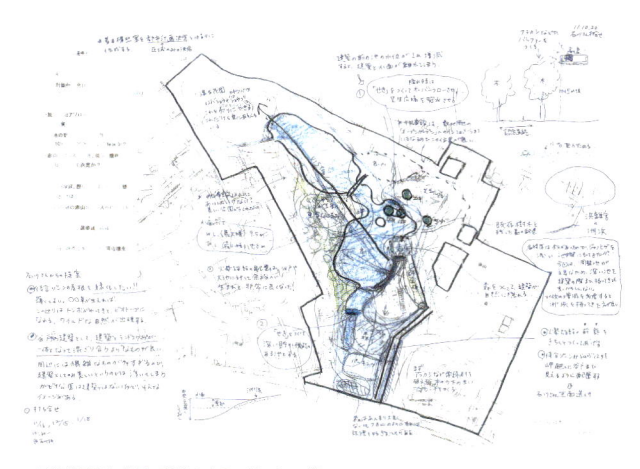

石川幹子氏と共同で製作したランドスケープ案
Landscape proposal Ito created with Ms. Mikiko Ishikawa.

視線の抜けの検討スタディ
Study related to eliminating the line of sight.

基本構想時の大屋根案
Proposal for large roof created as part of the basic concept.

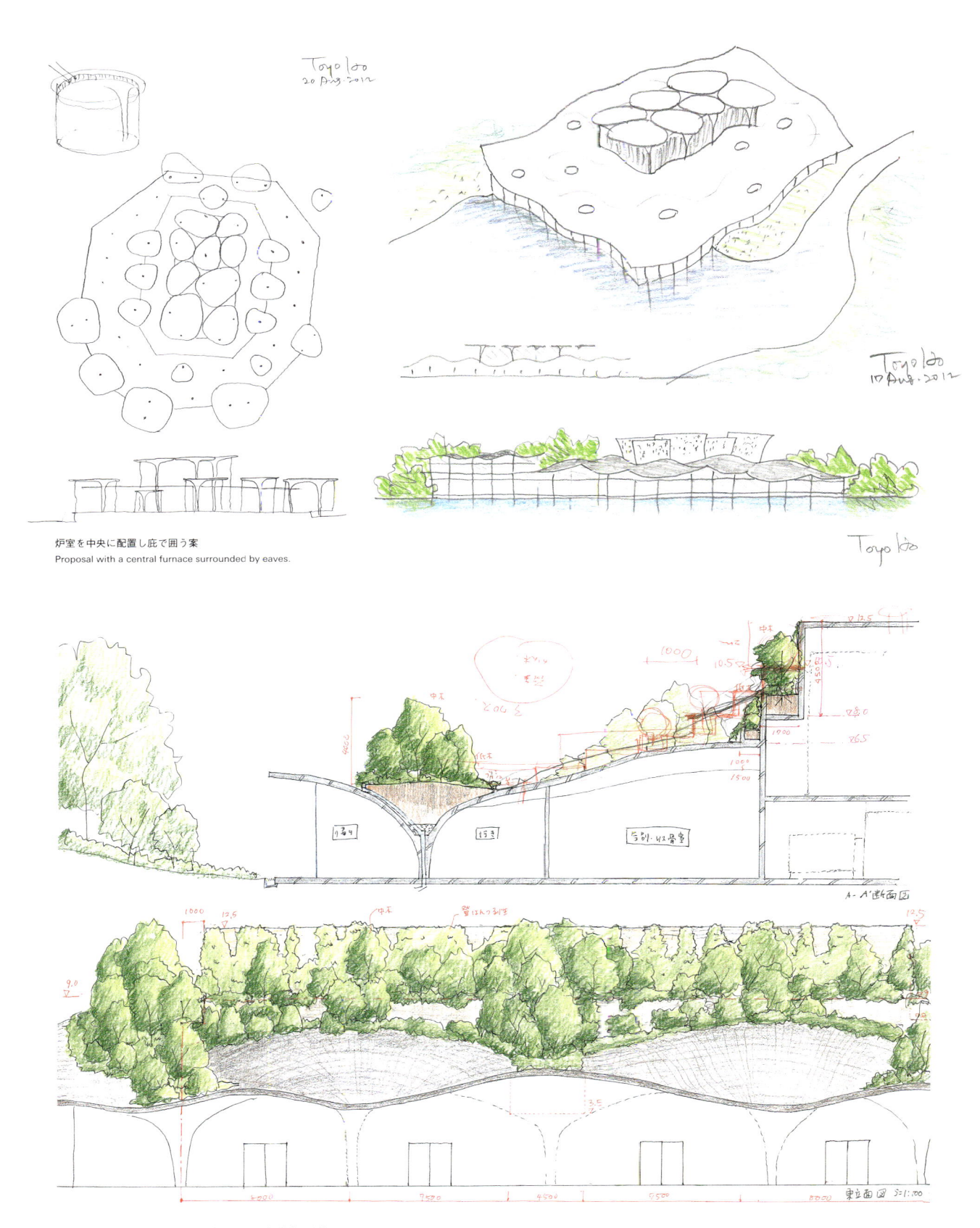

炉室を中央に配置し庇で囲う案
Proposal with a central furnace surrounded by eaves.

中心部を周囲に溶け込ませ、建物ボリュームを極力小さく抑えた
The volume of the building was minimized as much as possible to make the center blend in with the surroundings.

(仮称)川口市火葬施設・赤山歴史自然公園
Overall plan for Crematorium and Akayama Historic Nature Park in Kawaguchi (tentative title).

| | | | |
|---|---|---|---|
| 1 | crematorium | 7 | playground |
| 2 | entrance | 8 | biotope |
| 3 | service station | 9 | Regional products center (tentative title) |
| 4 | observation terrace | 10 | open nursery |
| 5 | Historical natural information center (tentative title) | 11 | tour bus station |
| 6 | management office | | |

埼玉県川口市に計画中の約11haの公園の中に建つ火葬施設。周辺のランドスケープになじみ極力目立たぬように設計された。低く抑えられた曲面スラブによる屋根と、炉の機械室周囲を緑化することによって風景に溶け込ませている。

This crematorium was designed as part of a plan for an approximately eleven-hectare park in Kawaguchi, Saitama Prefecture. The plan was intended to keep the building from standing out too much from the familiar setting. By using a curved slab with a reduced height for the roof and planting trees around the furnace's machine room, a further attempt was made to integrate the building into the landscape.

1 entrance
2 foyer
3 waiting hall
4 office
5 ash collection & farewell room
6 furnace
7 multi functional room
8 waiting room

1F plan

305

告別・集骨前ホールイメージ
Image of the hall in front of the room used to bid farewell to the deceased and collect their remains.

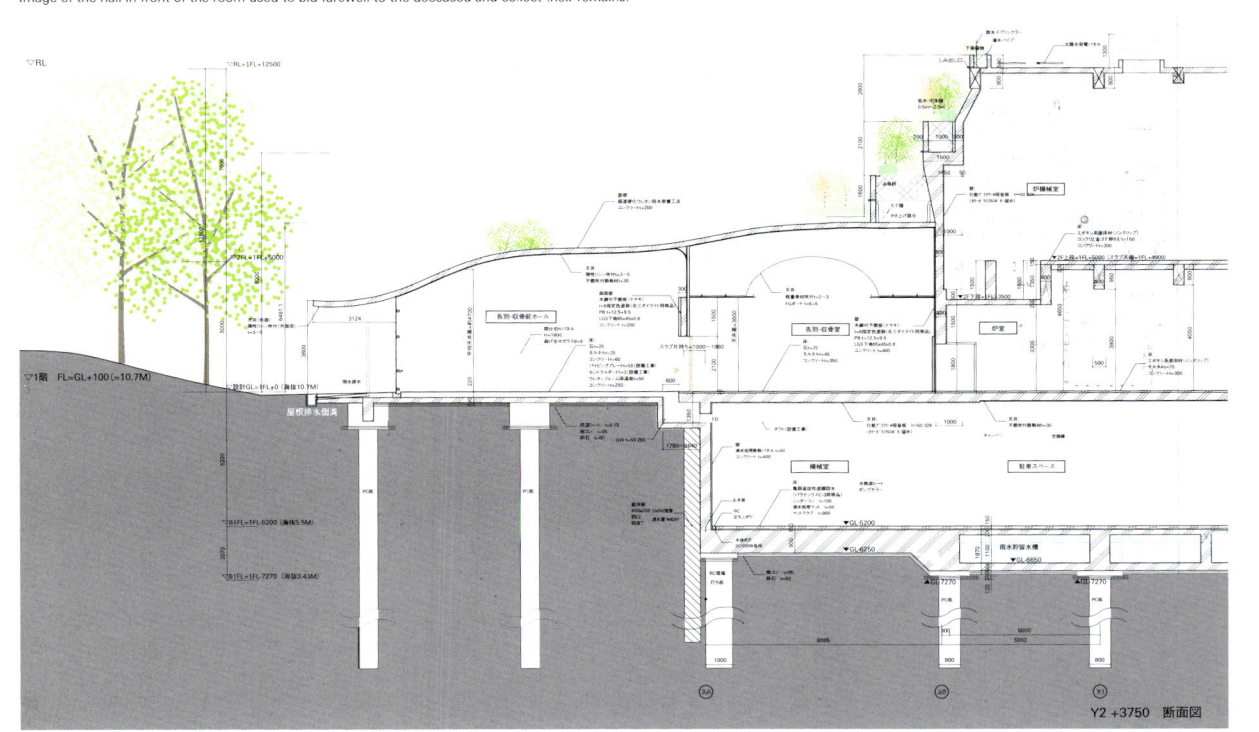

Detailed section

告別時照明の模型写真
Model of lighting effect in the room used for bidding farewell to the deceased.

集骨時照明の模型写真
Mode of lighting effect in the room used for collecting the remains of the deceased.

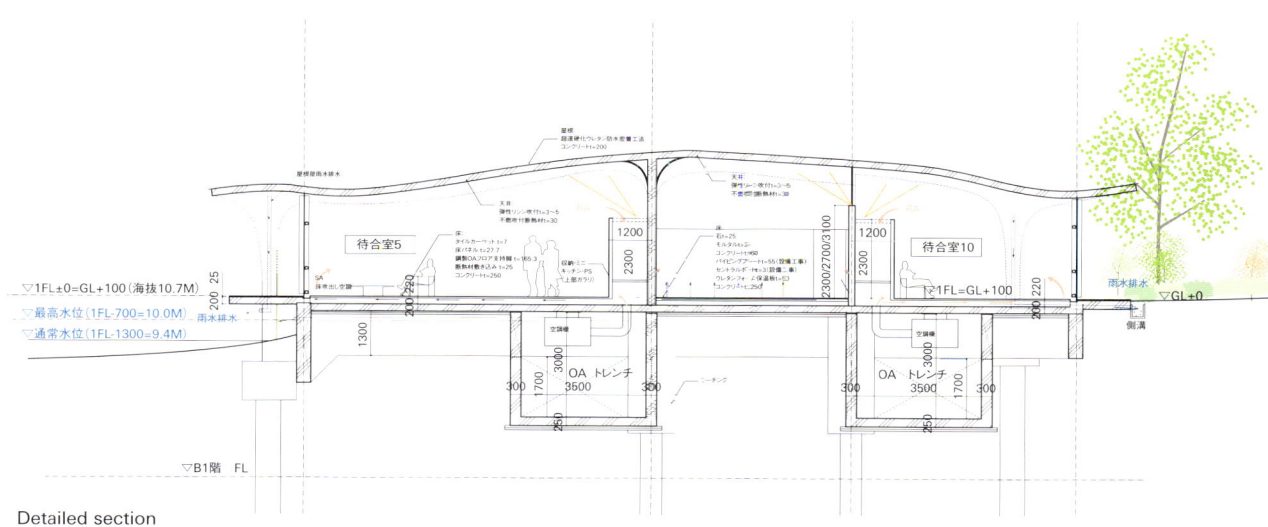

Detailed section

待合ホールイメージ
Image of waiting hall.

待合室イメージ
Image of waiting room.

| | |
|---|---|
| 1 | entrance |
| 2 | exhibition and sale corner |
| 3 | cafe terrace |
| 4 | cafe / exhibition |
| 5 | shop |
| 6 | front / office |
| 7 | kitchen |
| 8 | storage room |
| 9 | toilet |

The Regional products centre (tentative title) plan

公園内に建つ(仮称)地域物産館。カフェやショップ、週末に植木市を行うための展示直売コーナーが蓮の葉のような屋根の連続する空間に並ぶ。

The Regional products centre (tentative title) in the park: A cafe, shop, and display and sales corner, where a plant market can be held on weekends, are positioned in the space to form a link with the lotus-like roof.

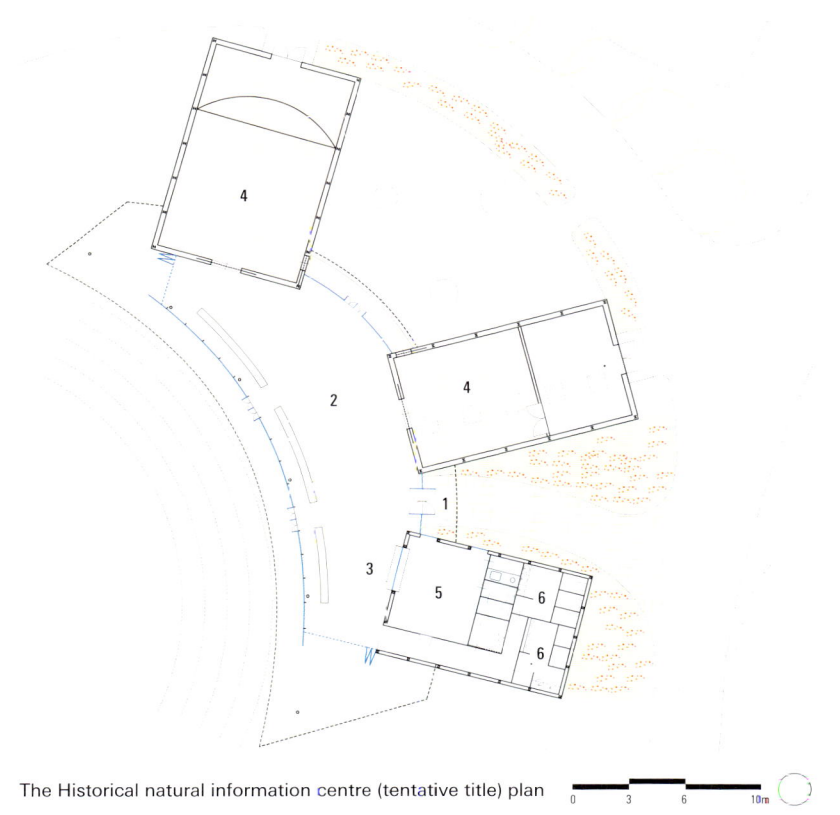

| | |
|---|---|
| 1 | main entrance |
| 2 | foyer |
| 3 | front |
| 4 | exhibition room |
| 5 | office |
| 6 | toilet |

The Historical natural information centre (tentative title) plan

公園内に建つ(仮称)歴史自然資料館。管理事務室、展示室、映像ギャラリーをそれぞれ「木の家」「土の家」「レンガの家」とし、それらをフラットルーフの下のホワイエでつないだ。

The Historical natural information centre (tentative title) in the park: A management office, exhibition room, and video gallery are housed in "wood house", "earth house" and "brick house" respectively, and connected by means of a foyer beneath their flat roofs.

## Barroco Museo Internacional
バロックミュージアム・プエブラ

計画中 under development　メキシコ プエブラ　Puebla, Mexico

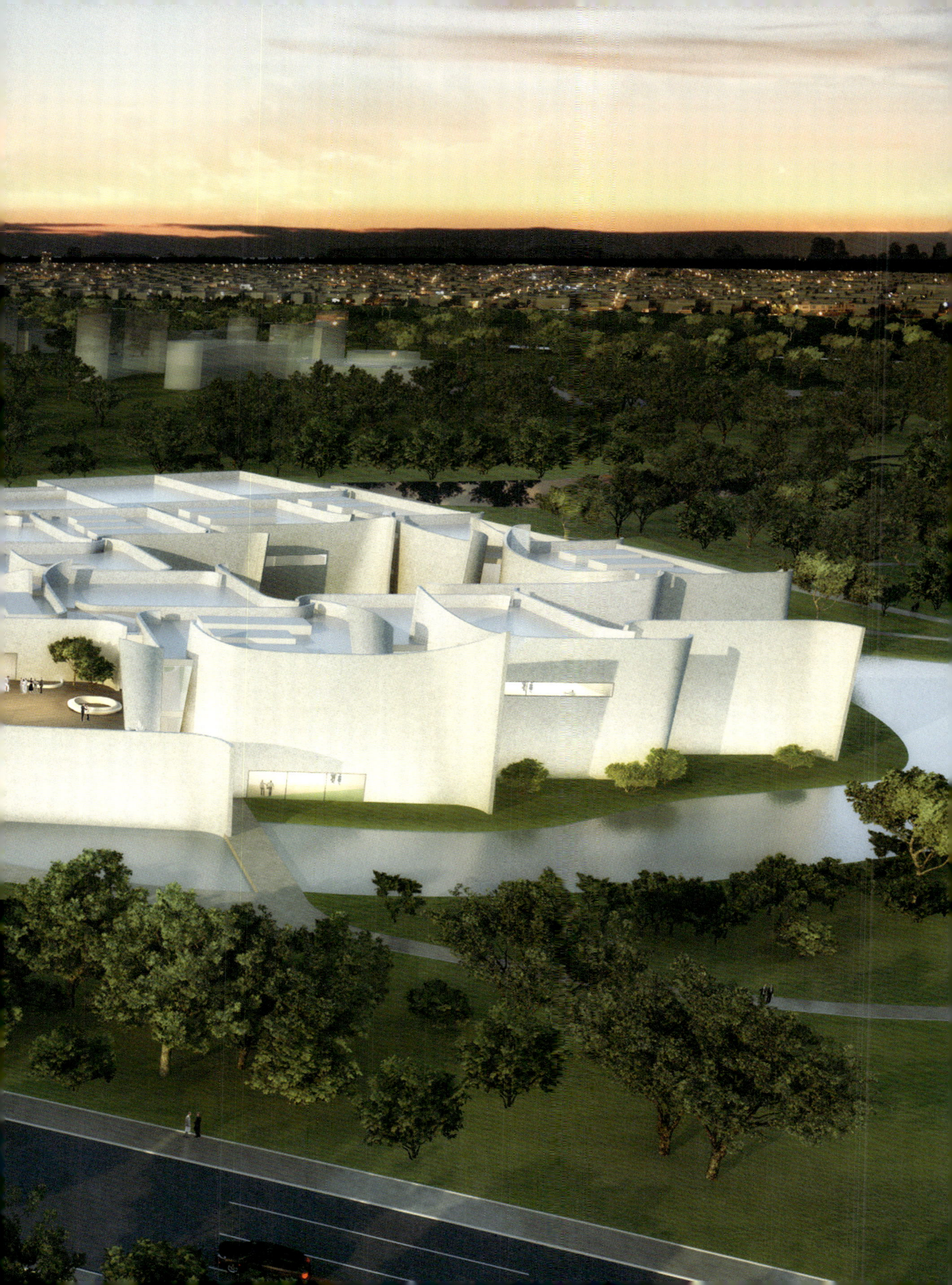

| | | |
|---|---|---|
| 1 | entrance hall | |
| 2 | foyer | |
| 3 | exhibition hall | |
| 4 | exhibition room | |
| 5 | temporary exhibition | |
| 6 | shop | |
| 7 | auditorium | |
| 8 | collection storage | |
| 9 | information | |
| 10 | international salon | |
| 11 | terrace | |
| 12 | restoration atelier | |
| 13 | education atelier | |
| 14 | museography atelier | |
| 15 | library | |
| 16 | office | |
| 17 | restaurant | |
| 18 | kitchen | |
| 19 | storage | |

Site plan

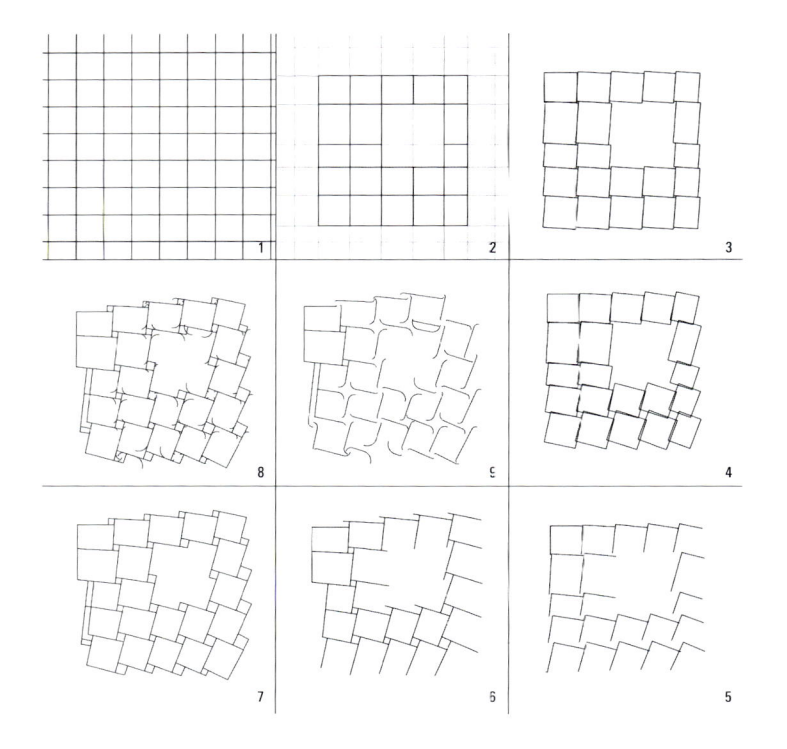

バロックミュージアム・プエブラはメキシコ4番目の都市プエブラ郊外に計画され、バロック芸術を紹介するミュージアムである。この計画において意図されているのはグリッドの幾何学が歪み、流動し始める空間である。グリッドに回転を与え、そこに生じる小さな緩衝空間を介して展示空間を結びつけることで、グリッド間や内外の関係に流れを生み出す。

The Barroco Museo Internacional is being planned in the suburbs of Mexico's fourth largest city, Puebla. The museum will concentrate on baroque art. The plan calls for a distorted geometric grid and a space that looks as if it is beginning to flow. By turning the grid, and linking it to the display area via a small buffer space that emerges there, it is possible to create a flow within the grid and between the interior and exterior.

2F アクソノメトリック
Axonometric drawing of 2F.

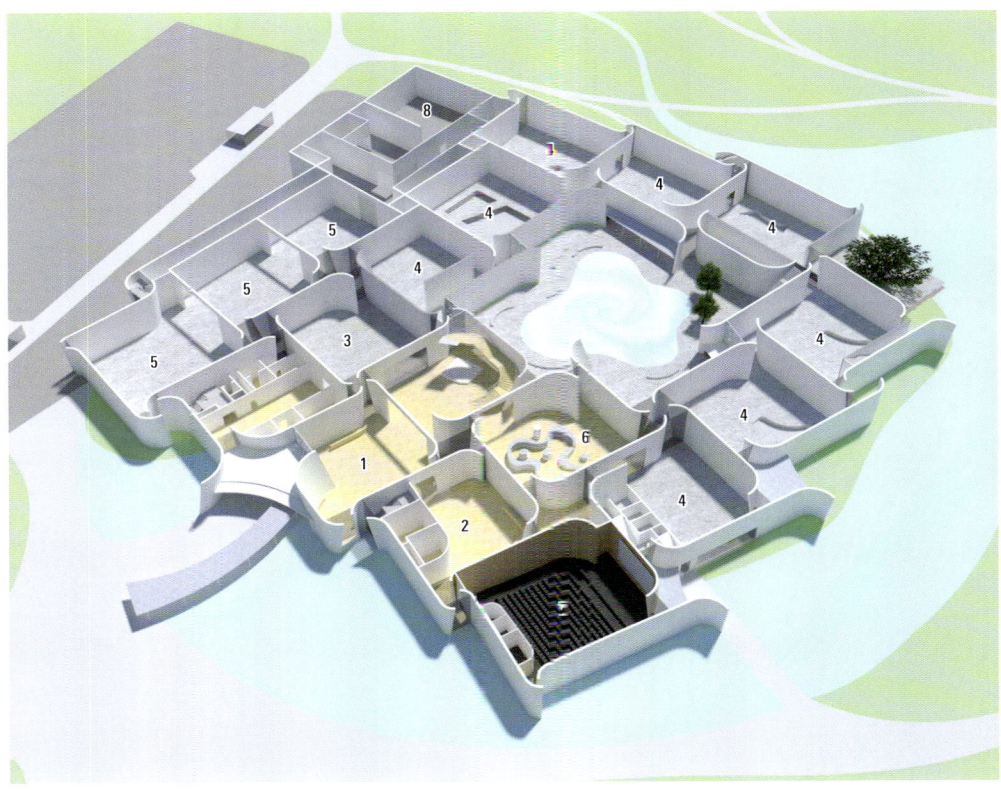

1F アクソノメトリック
Axonometric drawing of 1F.

313

整形グリッドによるプログラムの分析、それらをつなげるためのグリッドの操作、グリッド間に生まれる緩衝空間とスタディーは進んだ。緩衝空間の壁を曲げることで、カメラの絞りのように、差し込む光をコントロールする。

After analyzing the programs with a formal grid, the grid was manipulated to link the programs, and the buffer space that emerged between the grids was studied further. By making the walls in the buffer space curved, it was possible to control the amount of light in the same way that a camera lens controls light.

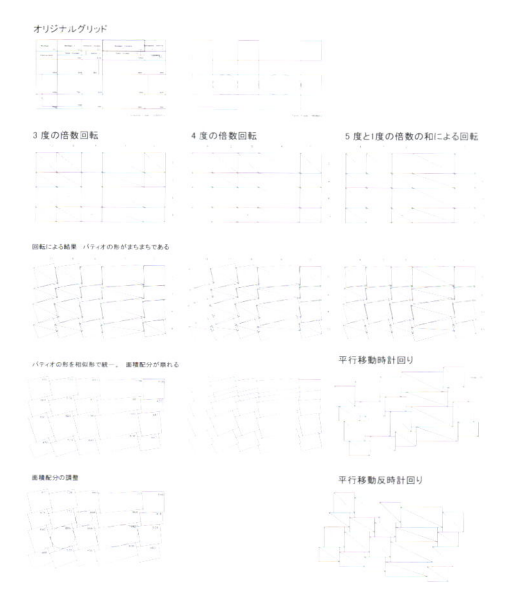

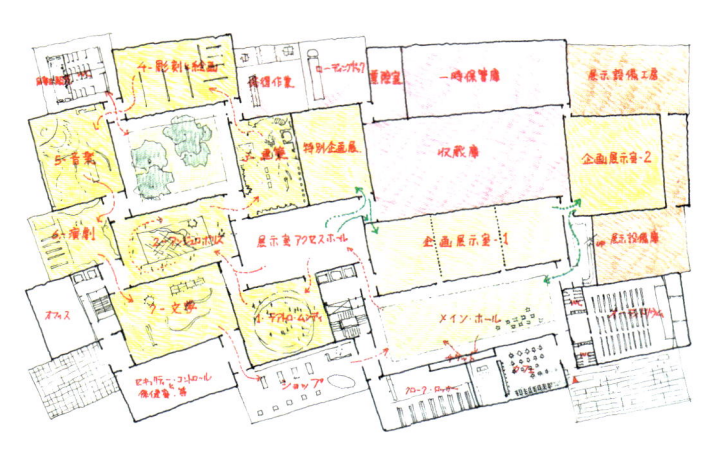

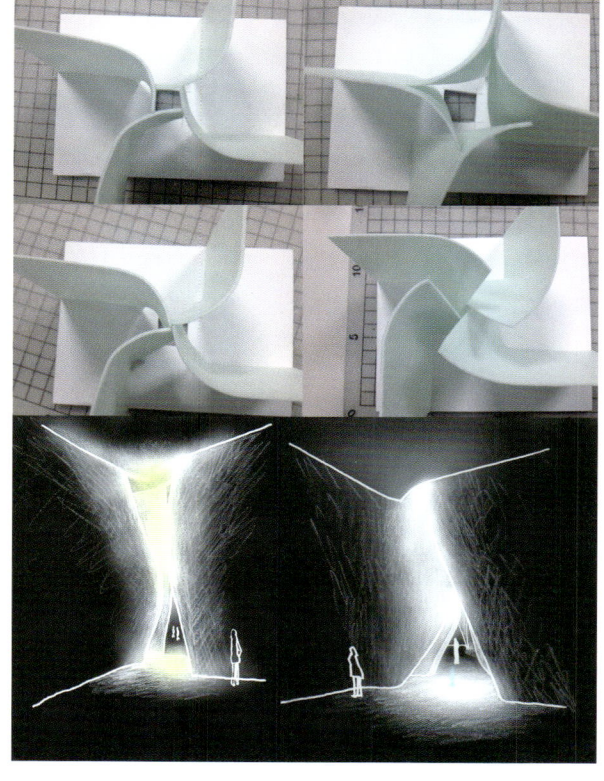

初期案では4×5のグリッドで構成され、迷路のようであったが、大きな中庭を配置し、それを回るような動線とすることで、シンプルかつ、より動きのあるプランに変更された。

The initial plan made use of a 4x5 grid that resembled a labyrinth, but by inserting a large courtyard and creating flow lines that went around it, the plan became simpler and incorporated more movement.

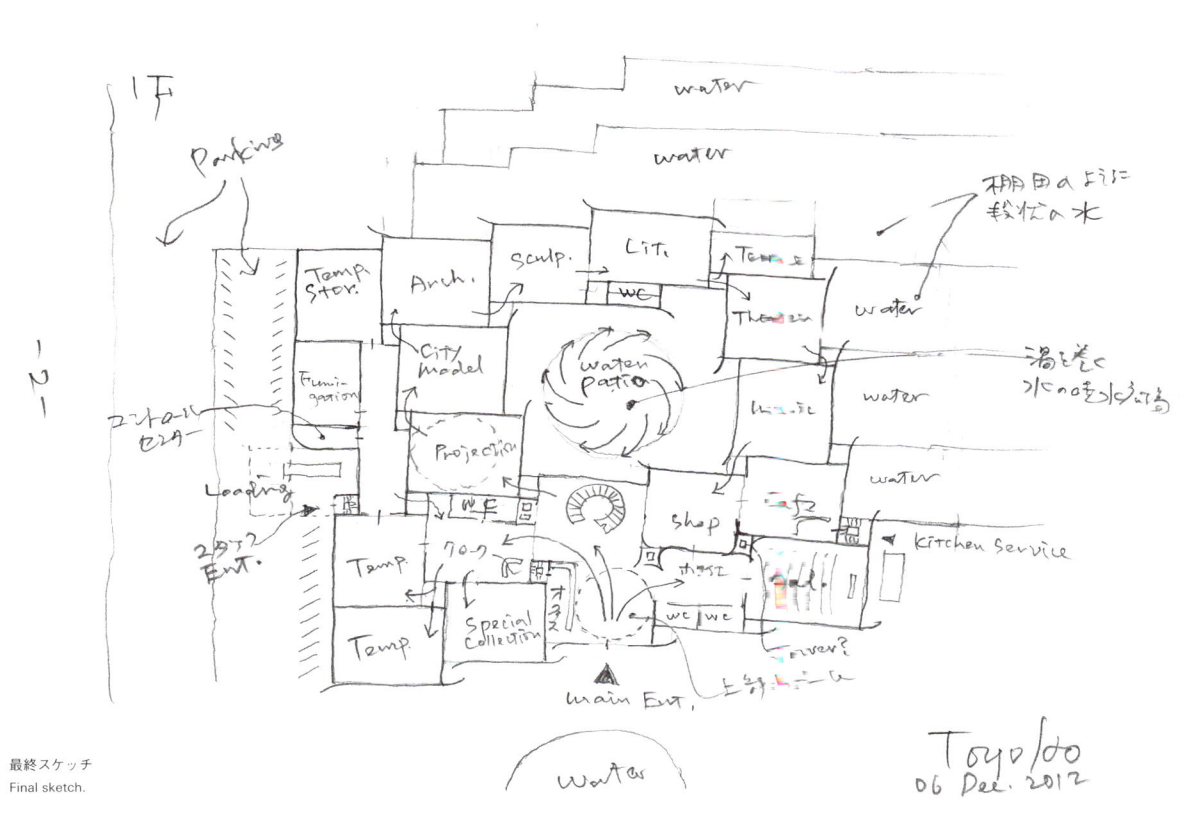

最終スケッチ
Final sketch.

315

プラン中央の中庭。大きく渦を巻く噴水を見る
The courtyard in the center of the plan. A fountain with large whirls is also visible.

メインエントランス
The main er trance.

エントランスロビー奥に大階段が見える
The large staircase is visible behind the entrance lobby.

(上) 緩衝空間のトップライトを見上げる
(中) ロビーの大階段
(下) 2階テラス
(Above) Looking up at the top light in the buffer space.
(Middle) The large staircase in the lobby.
(Below) The terrace on the second floor.

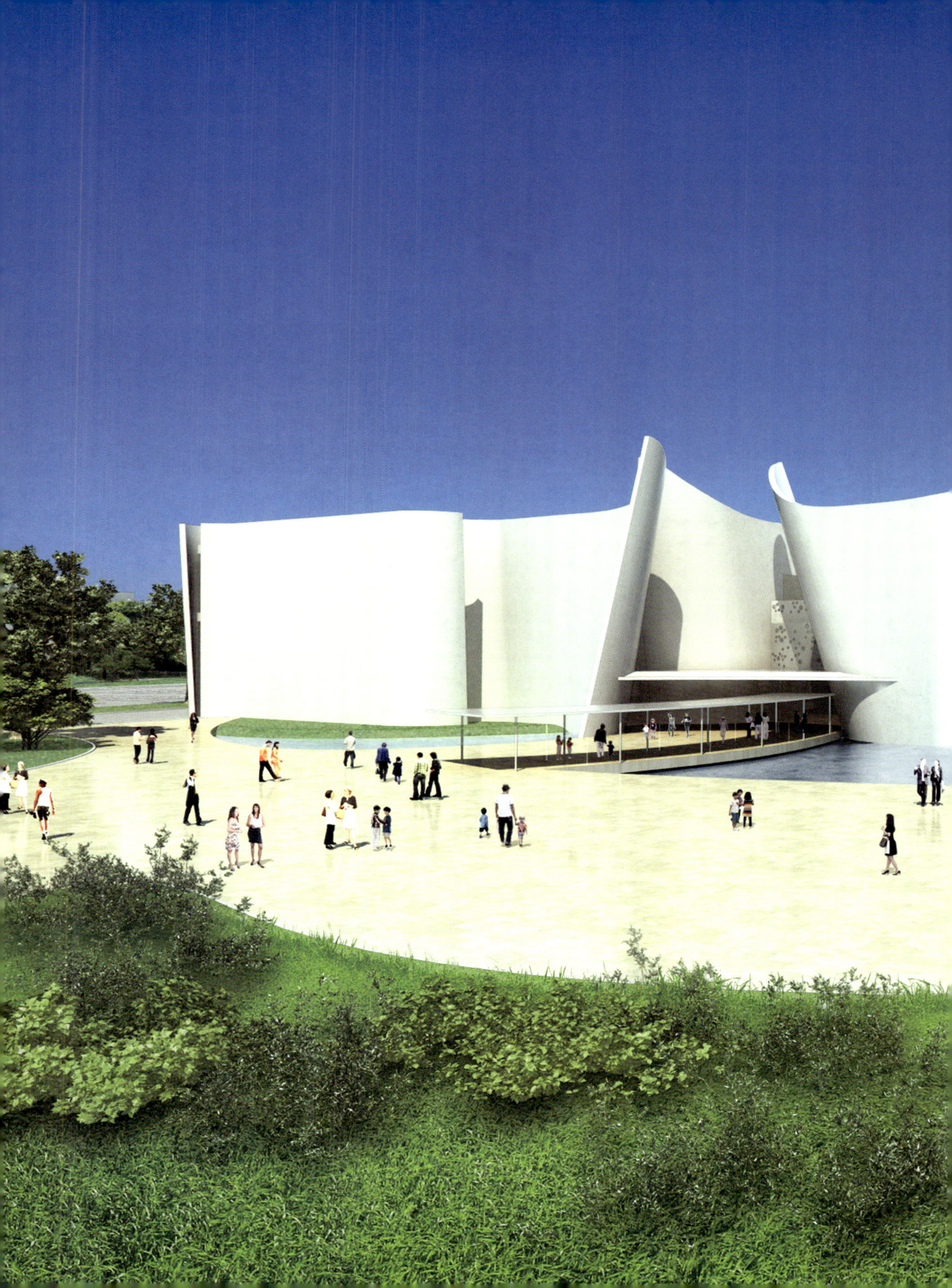

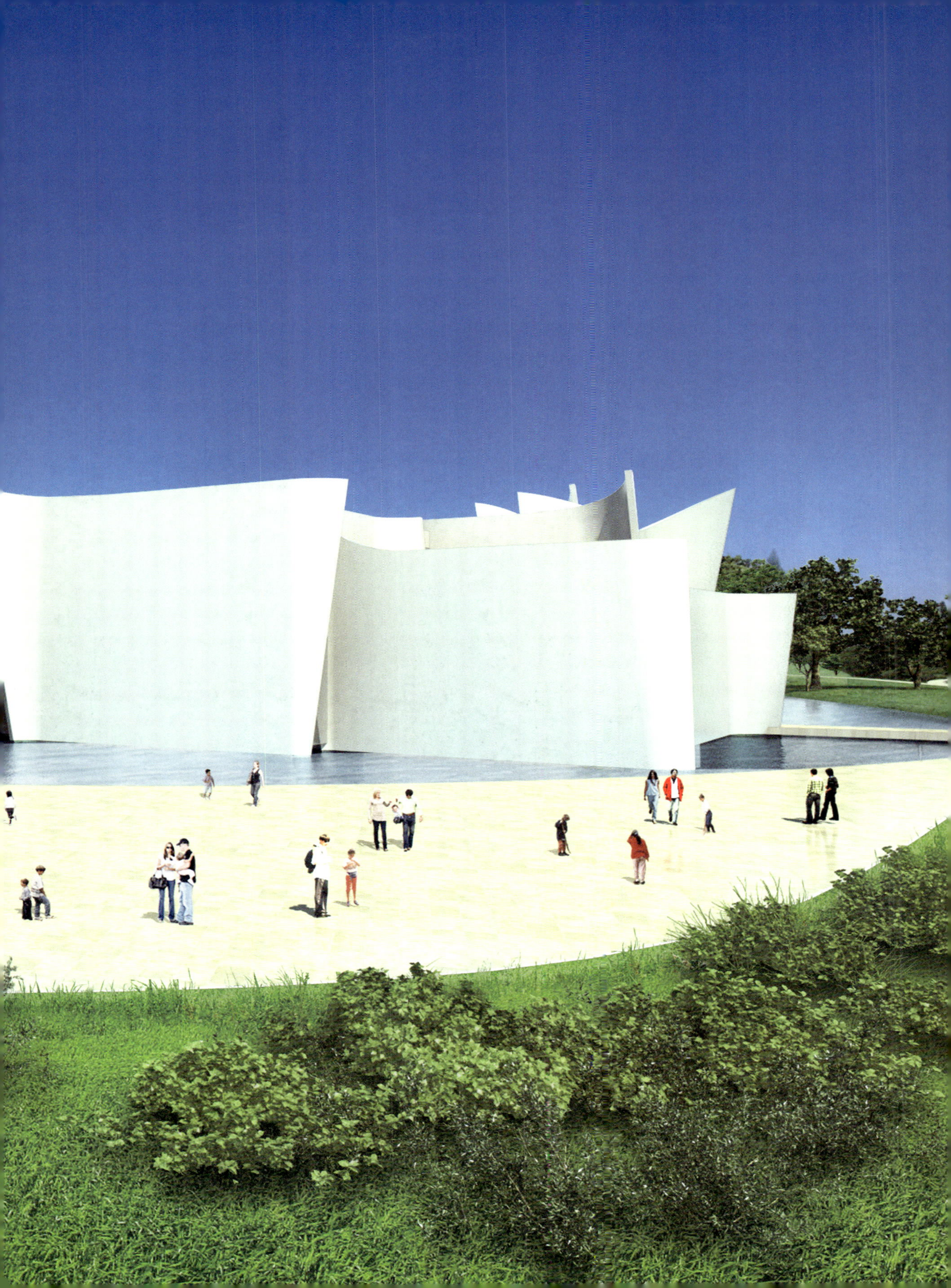

# 9 みんなの家
## Home-for-All

伊東豊雄との対話　Conversation with Toyo Ito

## みんなの家
### Home-for-All ［2011-］

——「みんなの家」は2011年3月の東日本大震災以降、進行中も含めて全部で15（2014年9月時点）プロジェクトあって、そのうち11プロジェクトが完成しています。最初に出来たのが仙台市宮城野区の「みんなの家」ですが、そこから2年3年経って、少しフェーズが違ってきていると思うので、「みんなの家」の流れに関してどのように考えていくかという話を中心に進めていこうと思います。

みんながどう思っているかを聞きたいですね。

——宮城野区の「みんなの家」が出来た時は被災直後で、支援のためにすぐつくらなければならないというような切迫した状況でした。けれども、それ以降出来てきた「みんなの家」は、復興支援というより、地域の人が集まる場所というような役割になってきています。例えば岩沼「みんなの家」も、みんなが「支援」という気持ちで集まっているわけではなくて、ゆとりを求めているというか、自分の生活をもっと豊かにしていきたいと考えていて、自分の生活に密着した場所として楽しんで使ってくれているように思います。いまの日本の社会の状況を考えると、「みんなの家」は公共的な建物をつくっていく上での原点のような場になり得ると思っています。

震災が起こったのが修士課程1年の時でしたから、私自身はあまり支援活動ができなかったのですが、伊東さんが宮城野区で「みんなの家」をつくったという情報が学生の間を駆け巡って、あの写真を見て驚いたと同時に、伊東さんが地元の人たちと一緒につくったという事実が、学生としては衝撃的でした。

いまから当時を振り返ってみると、「みんなの家」で問いかけたことは、自治体に対して、ちまたの公共建築はマニュアル通りにつくられていて、ほとんど住民のことを考えていないように思われるので、公共の意味をもう一度問いかけてみたいという点がひとつ。

もうひとつは、建築界に対しての問いかけで、建築家の表現偏重に対して、もっと社会的な存在としての建築を考え直す必要があるのではないかという点ですね。

映画監督の石山友美さんが、磯崎新さん、安藤忠雄さん、チャールズ・ジェンクスさんとピーター・アイゼンマンさん、レム・コールハースさん、僕の6人へのインタビューを編集して「Inside Architecture – A Challenge to Japanese Society」というDVDをつくっていますが、その中で僕がコメントしているのは、70年以降、磯崎さんと篠原一男さんが社会を批判するようなポーズで建築をつくり始めた。60年代までは、建築家はもう少し社会の内側にいて、明るい未来があることを信じて都市的な提案をしてきたけれど、70年の日本万国博覧会でおもちゃのような未来都市を見せられたことから、篠原さんと磯崎さんが社会を文化的に批判する方向から「建築」を主張し始めた。僕たちの世代は、そこに共感を覚えて自分の建築をスタートした。

僕らも、そうやって社会の外側からいつも建築

を批判しながら「建築」を考えて、抽象的であったりミニマムであったりするような、批評性の強い建築をつくり続けてきました。それは批評性という力をもっていたから評価されてきたわけですが、それがいまの40代の建築家にまで継承されている。

でも、批評性をテーマにしながら、実際には批評する相手が見えない。しかし、本当は批評する相手はむしろ以前よりもはるかに巨大な存在となっているはずだから、そうした存在へのアンチテーゼとして「みんなの家」もあったはずだし、今度の新国立競技場の問題もそうだし、原発の問題も防潮堤の問題もそうですね。全部その相手は同じ立ち姿を見せているけれども、肝心の若い世代の人たちは、それに対して批評的なポーズで建築をつくりながら、批評する相手には何も立ち向かっていないという、不思議なことが起こっている気がします。

── いまの若い世代は、批評というよりも自己表現というか、むしろ閉塞感が漂っていて、自分にしか向かっていない。伊東さんのもっと前の世代のような批評性というのとは全然違う、外に向かっているものではなくてもっと内向的なものなので、批評性さえないような気がしています。

── 批評というより、結局それが「表現」になってしまっていると思います。常に新しいものを表現していかないと自分は建築家として認めてもらえないという強迫観念みたいなものがあって、「みんなの家」でも、伊東さんの「みんなの家」とは違うものを自分たちはつくっていかないといけないという思いにさいなまれながら、デザイン

をされているように思います。

「みんなの家」は、先ほど話したように、一方で自治体とか、いまの社会を覆っている制度に対する批評という意味は大きくあったと思いますが 一方で、住民と一緒につくるとか、住民と話し合いながらつくるという点では、逆に批評性をやめて建築が出来ていくことへの期待と楽しさがありましたね。

そのふたつの間には大きなギャップがあって、被災地へ行きながら「みんなの家」をつくっても、一方で防潮堤をつくる自治体とか制度の壁があって、それに対してまったく対話のない住民、ある意味で無力感にさいなまれている住民がいて、その間に「みんなの家」がはまり込んでいるような感じになっています。

「みんなの家」に対して唯一反応してくれたのは熊本県ですね。熊本県では知事の主導で県内にふたつの「みんなの家」をつくって、いまも使われていますし、仮設住宅自体も木造でつくって、これから仮設がなくなったらそれをどうするかという議論がされている。また、今度アートポリスのアジア国際会議をやる時に、5つの大学で、阿蘇の病院の中に「みんなの家」をつくるというプロジェクトを県の主導でやろうとしています。

ところが、肝心の東北ではほとんど反応がないのは、復興計画という上からの使命を3つの県と各地方自治体が重く受け止めていて、なかなかそこまで踏み込めないのかもしれません。

── かさ上げの問題も、その結果何が起こるのかを自治体があまり考えていないような気がします。陸前高田はかさ上げの工事がかなりのスピー

ドで進んでいて、陸前高田の「みんなの家」をもしかしたら壊さないといけないというような状況です。「みんなの家」の存在自体が小さいこともあって、市役所のほうでは「みんなの家」に対する配慮や計画の修正はほとんど考えていないように思います。

── 「みんなの家」は、運用していく人というか、そこをどう使っていけるかということにかかっていると思います。本当にみんなが集まるような場所になるには、それを受け入れる自治体とか使う人たちが、意識を共有しないといけないと思いますね。

自治体が好意的に受け入れているのは、仙台市宮城野区、宮城県東松島市、岩手県釜石市。福島県の相馬市や南相馬市も好意的に受け入れてくれています。

── 岩沼の場合は、市はあまり関わっていないのですが、玉浦地区の人たちが主体的にNPOを最初に立ち上げてやっていたので、使う人たちがかなりエネルギッシュで、非常に活用されているし、また、大きな企業が付いているというのが大きいですね。

東松島の場合は、Tポイント・ジャパンが建設資金を協賛して建てたものですが、実際に運営しているのは住民たちです。ゴミの管理などを住民が自主的に始めたことから中心メンバーが固まっていって、そのメンバーが社団法人をつくって、運営費も自分たちでまかなったりしています。ただ、仮設住宅地なので、今後いつまでその場所が使えるかという話もあると思います。

最初のころは、伊東事務所が企業に「一緒にこ

---

– Since the Great East Japan Earthquake of March 2011, there have been 15 "Home-for-All" projects [as of September 2014], including several that are on going, and 11 are actually completed. The first to be completed was "Home-for-All" by Kumamoto Artpolis Tohoku Support Group in Miyagino-ku, Sendai. In the two, three years that have passed since then, the projects seem to have entered a slightly different phase. I would like to focus the talk on people's perception of the direction taken by "Home-for-All" projects.

I would like to hear what everyone is thinking.

– "Home-for-All" in Miyagino-ku was completed right after the disaster, and there was a sense of urgency, a sense that this had to be built immediately to provide support for reconstruction. However, "Home-for-All" projects that have been completed since then do not so much support reconstruction, but serve as places where people of the local community can gather. For example, people do not gather in "Home-for-All" in Iwanuma to provide support but to make their lives richer. They enjoy using it as a place that is closely connected to their everyday lives. When one considers what circumstances in Japanese society are like today, "Home-for-All" can be a place that is the starting point for the creation of public buildings.

The disaster occurred when I was in the first year of my master's program, so I was unable to engage very much in support activities. But the news that you had created "Home-for-All" in Miyagino-ku spread among students. We were amazed to see photographs of it and also shocked as students to learn that you had worked with local people to build it.

Looking back now, I was questioning the meaning of public buildings. Local governments seem to design public buildings according to a manual and with little consideration of the people who use them.

I was also questioning the architectural world--that is, the excessive importance architects attach to expression. I believe the social significance of architecture needs to be reconsidered.

Ms. Tomomi Ishiyama, the film director, has edited interviews with six people, Mr. Arata Isozaki, Mr. Tadao Ando, Mr. Charles Jencks, Mr. Peter Eisenman, Mr. Rem Koolhaas and myself and made a DVD entitled "Inside Architecture--A Challenge to Japanese Society." In it, I commented that in the 1970s, Mr. Isozaki and Mr. Kazuo Shinohara began to use the design of architecture as a way of criticizing society. Architects were more integrated into society in the 1960s; believing in a brighter future, they developed urban proposals. However, after seeing the toy-like vision of a future city presented at the Osaka Exposition of 1970, Mr. Shinohara and Mr. Isozaki began to approach architecture from the perspective of social and cultural criticism. Our architectural careers all started sympathetic to that approach in our generation.

We too approached architecture from a critical position outside society and designed abstract and minimal architecture that was strongly critical in character. Our works were praised because they possessed a critical character, and that approach is maintained today by architects who are in their 40s.

However, though they adopt critical character as a theme, it is not clear that they are actually criticizing anyone—even though those we ought to be subject to criticism have meanwhile become even more enormous and powerful in the world. "Home-for-All" ought to have been their antithesis. The current problem of the New National Stadium, the problem of nuclear power, and the problem of seawalls all have to do with them. They all take the same form, yet strangely, members of the younger generation, even though they adopt a critical stance in designing architecture, do not confront them.

– Members of the young generation today are concerned, not much criticism but with self-expression. It feels claustrophobic--they confront only themselves. It is nothing like the extroverted critical character of the older generation you mention; it is so introverted that it does not seem critical in character at all.

– I would not call it criticism; it has become a matter of expression. It is almost like an obsession, that one must always express something new or one will not be recognized as an architect. With "Home-for-All" as well, it seems other architects felt compelled to design something that was different from what you had done.

As I said earlier, "Home-for-All" was quite meaningful, on the one hand, as criticism of local government or of the present system of society. On the other hand, however, in working together with local residents, a critical posture was abandoned. There were simply the hopes raised by, and the enjoyment of, the process of creating a building.

There was a huge gap between the local government and the system of society on the one hand and the local residents on the other. When we went to a disaster-stricken area and tried to create "Home-for-All," we had a local government, which intended on building a seawall, and obstacles placed by the system on one side, and the local residents who were not engaged by the local government or the system in any dialogue and tormented by a feeling of powerlessness on the other, and "Home-for-All" was mired between these two sides.

321

伊東建築塾 塾生による大三島の「みんなの家」プロジェクト
"Home-for-All" Project on Omishima by ITO JUKU students.

ういうことをやりませんか」と声をかけていったところから始まって、そういう活動を見ていた他の企業もだんだん参加するところが増えてきた。企業と住民を新しく結び付けたという意義も「みんなの家」にはあると思うのですが、一方で公共とはうまくつながれないという問題を抱えています。あと、そういう企業の活動が今後増えていくと、「みんなの家」の色合いもまた違う意味をもってくるのかなという気がしますが、そのあたりに関してはどう考えていますか。

第1の問いに対しては、自治体にはあまり期待できないというのが3年間の結論ですね（笑）。むしろ企業に期待したい。企業が公共に働きかけるという意味では、岩沼はインフォコムという存在があって、うまくいっているし、Tポイント・ジャパ

ンは、いまのところそんなに運営には関わっていないけれども、2つ目3つ目をつくろうとして、しかも規模が大きくなっている。そういう活動に積極的に関わっていこうとしているところを見つけて企業を動かしていくほうが、はるかに動きが早くて、うまくいく可能性は高いと思います。

— 企業の人たちは自分たちでやりたいことをやっていて、しかも採算もどこかで考えているから、こんなふうにしたらもっと楽しいじゃないかとか、そういうアイデアがどんどん出てくる。

大三島でもわれわれは、「みんなの家」をつくりたいと思っています。大山祇神社のすぐ近くに伊東塾で空き家を1軒借りて、それをみんなでリノベーションして大三島での活動拠点にしていこうというものです。あの参道はヒューマンなスケールでつくられていて魅力的な場所であるにもかかわらず、さびれてしまっている。われわれが拠点をつくって、まちの人に集まってもらえる場所にしていきたいと思っています。

— 大三島ももとは小さなまち単位での公共事業だったわけですね。まちに寄付されたお金で事業

が始まって、いまだに市の人たちはそんなに積極的ではないですが、そこから広がりを見せているというのは、つくって終わりではなくて、その後もずっと続いていくことが重要だと思います。それもひとりの人の熱い思いと熱心な動きから始まっているので、やはり「人」が重要ですね。

第2の問題に対してはどうだろう。

— 伊東さんが「建築は社会的な存在である」とおっしゃっていますが、そう思うようになったのはいつごろからですか。

批評的に建築をつくるということの矛盾を僕らもずっと引きずってきましたね。ヨーロッパの建築家は批判をするし批評もするけれども、それは前提として、建築家は社会の内側で正当な位置を確保されているし、その上で批判をしている。しかし日本の場合は、社会の外側にいながら、「建築家が勝手に批評しているだけ」と無視されている。それはむなしいとずっと思っていました。

組織事務所が公共の大規模建築をほとんど設計していて、とりわけ今度の新国立競技場はその問題がものすごくあらわになっています。そういう現状をただ批判するだけでなく、どうやったらわれわれも同じ土俵に立つのか、ということを建築家は考えないとだめだと思います。それが「みんなの家」のひとつの狙いでもあったし、震災後の僕らの考え方ですね。

特に若い建築家たちは、これから日本の中でつくっていかなくてはいけないわけだから、そのことをもう少し真剣に考えていかないと、いまよりますますひどいことになると危惧しています。完

— The only one to respond to "Home-for-All" was Kumamoto Prefecture. Under the direction of the prefectural governor, two "Home-for-All" were built and are still being used, wooden temporary houses themselves were also constructed, and a discussion is on going regarding what to do when temporary houses cease to exist. In addition, a project in which five universities will construct "Home-for-All" inside a hospital in Aso when an Asian international conference on Kumamoto Artpolis is held is being considered by the prefecture.

However, there is practically no response in Tohoku, the region directly affected by the disaster. That may be because the three prefectures and local governments are already dealing with the reconstruction project, a mission imposed from the top, and have no spare time or energy for such activities.

— I don't feel that local governments have much considered the consequences of raising embankments. The raising of embankments is proceeding with considerable speed at Rikuzentakata. The situation is such that "Home-for-All" in Rikuzentakata may have to be torn down. In part because "Home-for-All" is small, I don't believe the city government has taken "Home-for-All" into account or considered revising plans for its sake.

— I think it all depends on the people operating "Home-for-All," or how "Home-for-All" is used. If it is truly to become a place where everyone gathers, the local government and the people using it need to be on the same wavelength.

The local governments that have been sympathetic toward "Home-for-All" are Miyagino-ku, Sendai, Higashi-Matsushima City, Miyagi Prefecture, and Kamaishi City, Iwate Prefecture. Soma City and Minami-Soma City in Fukushima Prefecture have been sympathetic too.

— In the case of Iwanuma, the city is not much involved, but the people of Tamaura district, on their own initiative, established the first NPO. "Home-for-All" is used quite actively, and the fact that a large corporation is involved is a major factor.

In the case of Higashi-Matsushima, "Home-for-All" was constructed with donation from T Point Japan, but residents are actually operating it. The residents took the initiative in managing garbage, and that was how the core members came together. Those members formed a corporation, and they are paying for operating costs themselves. However, there is the question of how long they will be able to continue to use that place, since it is a temporary housing area.

It began with our office going around to corporations and asking if they would work with us on something like this. Seeing such activities, other corporations have gradually come on board as well. That is another way in which "Home-for-All" has been meaningful—it has established new ties between corporations and residents. However, the fact that there are no good relationships with public institutions is a problem. If such corporate activities increase in the future, the character of "Home-for-All" may change. What are your thoughts on that?

In response to the first question, the conclusion reached after three years is that we should not expect much from local governments [laughs]. I would pin our hopes instead on corporations. In the sense of corporations pressuring public institutions Infocom is a major presence for Iwanuma, and that is going well. Tpoint Japan is not that involved in operations yet, but there are plans to create a second and a third "Home-for-All" that are even bigger in size. I think seeking out places where corporations want to become actively involved would be far quicker and is more likely to be successful.

— Corporations are doing what they want to do themselves, and, moreover, have thoughts of profits somewhere on their minds. They offer many ideas about how to make things more enjoyable. We are thinking of creating "Home-for-All" on Omishima as well. The idea is for ITO JUKU to borrow a vacant house near Oyamazumi Shrine and renovate it for use as a center of activity on Omishima. The approach leading to the shrine is a human-scaled and attractive place, yet deserted. We want to create a base and make it a place where local people will gather.

— Omishima was originally a public project on a small municipal scale. The project began with a donation made to the town, and town officials are still not that actively involved. However, I think, in light of the growing influence the original project has had, it is important, not just to create something and leave, but to continue its activities. It all began because of the enthusiasm of one person, which goes to show that people are important.

What about the second problem?

— You have said that architecture is a social object. When did you begin to think that way?

I have been wrestling with the contradiction of adopting a critical stance to the design of architecture for a long time. European architects criticize and offer critical commentary, yet they all have a proper position inside society. It is on the basis of the position they enjoy that they criticize. However, in the case of Japan,

全に組織事務所に公共の領域を固められて、海外に行って建築をやるか、住宅をやるしかないというような状況になりつつありますよ。

― 今回の新国立競技場の問題でも、ニュースで取り上げられたし、改修案に賛成する人がかなり増えてきているように思います。

そうした住民の声や動きを建築家が吸い上げて、行動を起こしていくことは必要なのかもしれないなと思います。「みんなの家」の活動全般を見ても、「みんなの家」をつくろうと言って、みんなに賛同してもらって、いろんな人たちが協力してくれて、住民と話し合って、どんどん出来てきた。公共も、そういう動きがかたちとして目に見えれば、何かしらのアクションを起こしてくれる。それがもう少し大きく公共の建物に対してもやっていけるようなかたちをつくっていければ、大きな組織と同じ土俵に立てるようになると思います。

新国立競技場の問題も、「市民たちも反対しています」と言っても、世の中の人びとはそんなことに全然関心もないし、反対もしないのかもしれません（笑）。

ところがパリで「コニャック・ジェイ病院」(p.385)をやった時に、最初に病院のオーナーが、僕らの提案に対してどうしてそれをやりたいのかを根掘り葉掘り聞いて、それを説得するのに半年かかりました。でも、いったん納得したら、どんなに周辺住民の反対を受けても、彼は「これ以上いいものはない」と断言して、前面に立って住民と対話をする。住民たちも集まってけんけんごうごう議論をしていますが、それが終わったらみんなで一緒にシャンパンを飲んで、和気あいあいと談笑している。そういう「対話」が日本にはまったくないですね。

― 自分たちの意見を言うことさえしてくれない。無関心ですね。

自治体も「うるさいのはマスコミだけで…」と言っている（笑）。

台湾でも韓国でも、学生はものすごく元気がありますね。われわれのまわりにいる塾の人とか事務所のスタッフは、大三島にみんな自主的に行ったり台湾に行ったりして、住民たちと一緒に原点からもう一回考え直そうとしてくれています。

― それを求めているようなところがあります。都会の事務所の中でずっと仕事をしていると、たまには泥の中に足を入れたり、自然の中で汗をかきたくなる。大三島の人は率直に話してくれるので、自分も率直になれる。そういうことを繰り返すと、自分にとっても精神的にバランスがとれてくるように感じます。

そういう事実が「みんなの家」を一緒にやった、若い建築家たちにも響いているのだろうか…。もちろん、大西麻貴さんのように気仙沼に通って一生懸命やっている人もいますよ。柳澤潤君がこの間メールをくれて、「自分は何か被災地でやりたいと思ってコンペティションに何度も応募したが、力及ばず実現しなかった」ことを言っていたので、今度の福島のTポイント・ジャパンの「みんなの家」は彼にやってもらおうと思っています。また、「みんなの家ネットワーク（NPO HOME-FOR-ALL）」をいまつくっていますから、KDAのマーク・ダイサムさんやアストリッド・クラインさんたちも一生懸命やってくれているし、アトリエ天工人の山下保博さんもそうですね。そうやって少しずつ地道にやるしかないからなあ。

ただ、震災の直後に「批評はしない」と僕は言ったし、どんな小さなことでもできることからやろうということ、個を超えられるかという問題、この3つが震災後の最初のシンポジウムで提案したことですから、批判しているよりは、そういう活動のほうが意味があるかもしれない。

― あとから自治体のほうもついてくるのかもしれないですね。「みんなの家」を広げていくことによって、逆に自治体のほうが刺激されてくる。

まあ、気仙沼でも、渡辺謙さんが「K-port」を自ら投資して実現した結果、市も遅まきながら動き出そうとしていますね。あんな所に人は絶対集まらないと市では思っていたのに、すごく集まるから。

― 建築家ってそういうことですよね。そういうモデルを提示する、それによって場所が変わる。

それは「せんだい」もそうだったし、いろんなレベルで、これからもそういう発見が必要ですね。

---

architects are viewed as outsiders who offer criticism without being asked—that is why they are being ignored. I have long thought that it is pointless.

Almost all large public buildings are designed by organizational architects. The problem has become quite public with the New National Stadium. It is not enough for us architects to criticize this state of affairs. We need to consider how we can compete on equal terms with organizational architects. That has been one of the objectives of "Home-for-All" and my thought since the disaster.

Young architects in particular who must work in the future in Japan—I am afraid the situation will become even worse unless you think more seriously about the problem. Organizational architects have a secured position of obtaining work in the public sector. Conditions are such that the only possibilities open to architects in the future may be to work abroad or to design houses.

– The present problem of the New National Stadium has been taken up in the news, and increasing numbers of people seem to favor revising the plan.

I believe architects need to channel the opinions and actions of people and start movements. When we look at "Home-for-All" activities as a whole, for example, a call was made to create "Home-for-All," support was gained from everyone, cooperation was provided by many different people, and after discussions with residents, one "Home-for-All" after another was created. Public institutions themselves will take action in some way if such movements take visible form. I believe we will be able to compete equally with large organizations if we develop an approach that will work with slightly larger public buildings.

With respect to the problem of the New National Stadium, even if we hear local people are also opposed to it, the general public has no interest in it and may not even oppose it [laughs].

But when we did Hospital Cognacq-Jay (p. 385) in Paris, the owner of the hospital initially was quite persistent and asked us detailed questions about why we wanted to design it that way. It took us half a year to persuade him. But once he was persuaded, he was adamant that there was no better way to design it, even in the face of opposition from local residents. He took the initiative and engaged in a dialogue with the residents. The residents gathered and there was a clamorous discussion. But once it was over, everyone drank champagne, and a friendly atmosphere prevailed. That sort of "dialogue" never happens in Japan.

– People don't even offer their own opinions. They are uninterested.

Local governments insist that it is only the mass media that is making a fuss...[laughs].

Students have great energy, not only here but in Taiwan and Korea. The students at ITO JUKU and the staff at our office, I go to Omishima or Taiwan on their own initiative and try to rethink things from square one together with local residents.

– We are looking for such opportunities. After working for a long time in an office in the city, we want to wiggle our toes in the mud and work up a sweat in a natural setting occasionally. People in Omishima speak in a straightforward manner, and that allows us to be straightforward too. Such experiences seem to restore our psychological balance.

I wonder if that has had an effect on young architects who worked with us on "Home-for-All"...Of course, there are people such as Ms. Maki Onishi who commutes to Kesennuma and works as hard as she can. Mr. Jun Yanagisawa sent me an e-mail the other day saying he'd entered a number of competitions because he wanted to do something in disaster-stricken areas, but that regrettably he hadn't won any. I am thinking of having him design T Point Japan's "Home-for-All" in Fukushima. Then, I am in the process of creating NPO HOME-FOR-ALL. Mr. Mark Dytham and Ms. Astrid Klein are hard at work on that, as is Mr. Yasuhiro Yamashita of Atelier Tekuto. We have to keep at it, that is all we can do.

Only, at the first symposium held immediately after the disaster, I proposed three things: to refrain from criticism; to do whatever we can, however small; and to see if we can transcend the individual. Therefore, such activities may be more meaningful than engaging in criticism.

– Local governments may eventually follow our lead. The fact that "Home-for-All" is becoming a broader movement may stimulate local governments.

Well, as a result of Mr. Ken Watanabe investing in and building K-port in Kesennuma, the city is belatedly starting to take action. The city didn't think people would ever gather in such a place, but it is drawing large numbers of people.

– That is what architects can do. They can suggest such a model, and that can change a place.

That was also true of Sendai Mediateque. Such discoveries will continue to be necessary on many different levels.

# Home-for-All
## みんなの家

### 「みんなの家」主旨

「みんなの家」は、東日本大震災を受けて自分たちにできることを模索しようと集まった5人の建築家グループ「帰心の会」によって提唱されたプロジェクトです。仮設住宅での厳しい暮らしを目の当たりにした時、悲しみや心の痛みを共有したいひとりの生活者として、同時に建築を生業とする者としてできることを考え、始まりました。当初は家を失った人びとが集い、暖を取り、飲み、食べ、語り合えるささやかな憩いの場をつくることを目指し、以下3つをコンセプトとしました。

- みんなが一緒に考え一緒につくる
- 人と人の心のつながりを回復する
- 生きるエネルギーを育む

最初の「みんなの家」は熊本県の協力のもと、宮城県仙台市の仮設住宅の中に、2011年10月に完成しました。竣工式で涙を流して喜ぶ住民の人たちを見ると、このプロジェクトの必要性を改めて実感しました。その後、伊東豊雄、妹島和世、山本理顕が中心となって若い世代の建築家たちに呼びかけ、2014年9月までに被災各地に11軒の「みんなの家」が完成し、現在も4軒の計画が進んでいます。それらは仮設住宅地内や被災した商店街、漁港の周辺に建てられ、その主たる用途も仮設住民たちの集まり、コミュニティの回復、子どもたちの遊び場、農業や漁業を再興しようとするNPO団体の拠点としてなど、多岐にわたるようになりました。震災から3年半が経過したいま、「みんなの家」は単に被災地支援という役割を超えて、これからの公共施設、さらにはこれからの社会の在り方に言及し得る可能性を秘めていると思っています。「みんなの家」がもつ意味を、私たちは次のように考えています。

1. 人びとの心を癒し、人と人を結ぶヒューマンな場として、公共施設の最もプリミティブな意味を問う。従ってそれは平時の公共施設のあるべき姿を示し得る
2. 利用者（住民）、設計者、施工者が一体となってつくることにより、近代主義的な個を超える可能性をもつ
3. 〈他者を想い、他者に尽くそうとする精神〉によって経済至上主義の社会から自立し、人間の尊厳を蘇らせ、人びとに未来への希望を育む可能性をもつ

「みんなの家」のさらなる発展を目指し、さまざまな試みが続いています。

NPO「HOME-FOR-ALL」設立に際して　2014年7月

### "Home-for-All" concept

"Home-for-All" is a project proposed by KISYN-no-kai, a group of five architects who got together to see what we could do in response to the Great East Japan Earthquake. We wondered what we, as individuals who wanted to share the sadness and pain with those living in temporary housing and as architects, could do. First, three principles were adopted with the aim of creating modest places to relax where people who had lost their homes could gather, take warmth, drink, eat and talk.

"Home-for-All" is to:
- **to be created and built by all.**
- **to recover connections between one another.**
- **to nurture the energy to live.**

With the cooperation of Kumamoto Prefecture, the first "Home-for-All" was completed in October 2011 in a temporary housing area in Sendai, Miyagi Prefecture. The need for this project was impressed on us once more when we saw the tears of joy of residents at the ceremony to celebrate its completion. Toyo Ito, Kazuyo Sejima and Riken Yamamoto subsequently rallied young architects. Eleven "Home-for-All" projects have been completed in disaster-stricken areas as of September 2014 and four more are in progress. They have been constructed in temporary housing areas and near shopping areas and fishing ports that were hit by the disaster. They have become quite varied in character and include gathering places for residents of temporary housing, places intended to restore communities, places for children to play, and centers for NPOs trying to revive farming and fishing industries. Today, three and a half years since the disaster, "Home-for-All" has gone beyond its initial object to provide support for disaster-stricken areas. We believe that it has the potential to suggest the way public facilities and society ought to be like in the future. "Home-for-All" is meaningful in the following ways.

1. As a place that gives people psychological comfort and helps establish human relationships, it suggests the most primitive form of public facility. It can therefore define what public facilities under ordinary circumstances ought to be like.
2. It has the potential to transcend the individual as defined by modernism because it is created by users, architects and builders working together.
3. Its guiding spirit-to care for and to serve others-has the potential to make us independent of a society that places priority on economic concerns, to restore human dignity and to nurture people's hope for the future.

Diverse efforts are continuing in order to further develop "Home-for-All."

"Home-for-All" concept for setting up NPO HOME-FOR-ALL, July, 2014

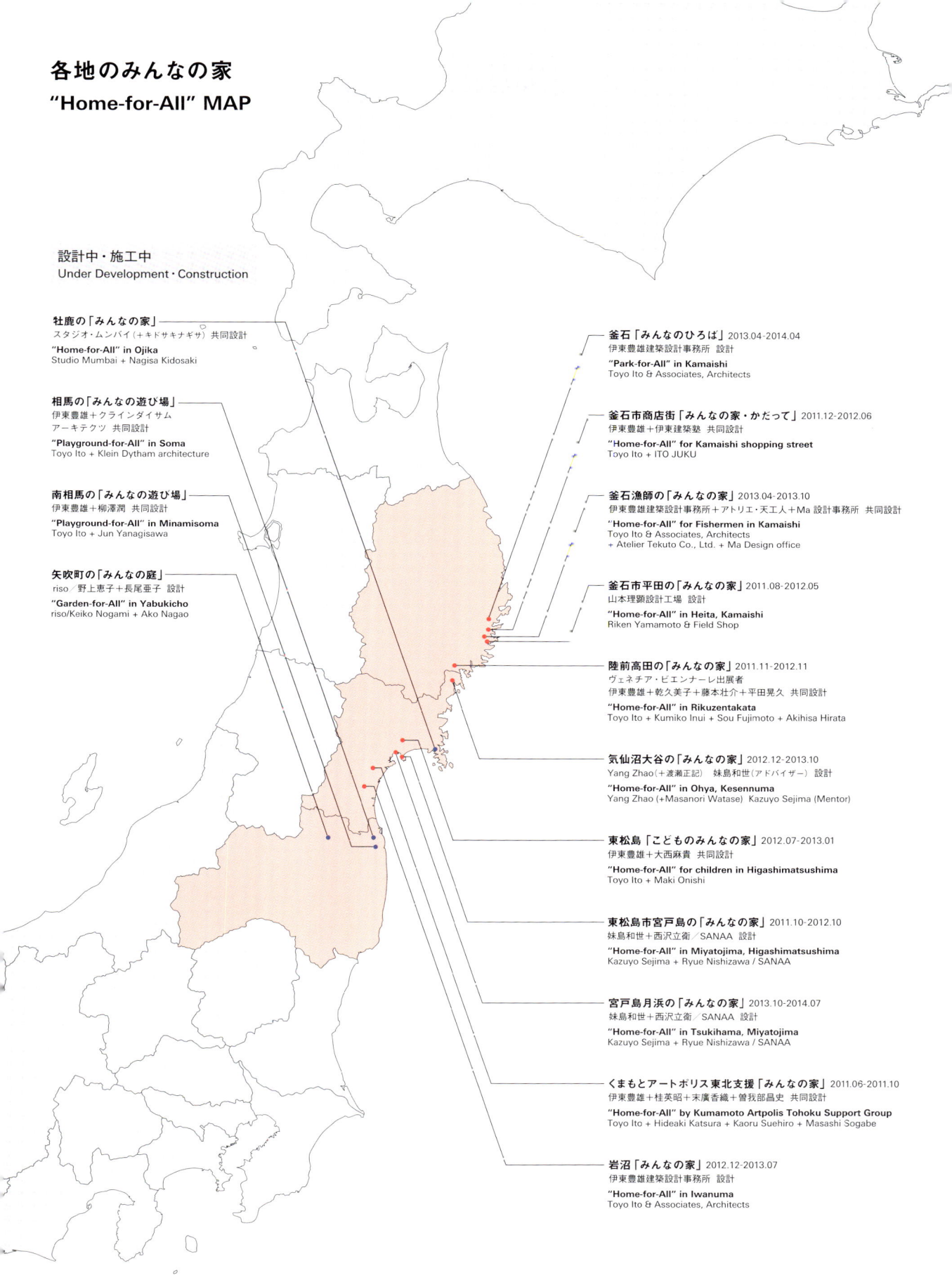

# 各地のみんなの家
## "Home-for-All" MAP

設計中・施工中
Under Development・Construction

牡鹿の「みんなの家」
スタジオ・ムンバイ（＋キドサキナギサ）共同設計
"Home-for-All" in Ojika
Studio Mumbai + Nagisa Kidosaki

相馬の「みんなの遊び場」
伊東豊雄＋クラインダイサム
アーキテクツ 共同設計
"Playground-for-All" in Soma
Toyo Ito + Klein Dytham architecture

南相馬の「みんなの遊び場」
伊東豊雄＋柳澤潤 共同設計
"Playground-for-All" in Minamisoma
Toyo Ito + Jun Yanagisawa

矢吹町の「みんなの庭」
riso／野上恵子＋長尾亜子 設計
"Garden-for-All" in Yabukicho
riso/Keiko Nogami + Ako Nagao

釜石「みんなのひろば」 2013.04-2014.04
伊東豊雄建築設計事務所 設計
"Park-for-All" in Kamaishi
Toyo Ito & Associates, Architects

釜石市商店街「みんなの家・かだって」 2011.12-2012.06
伊東豊雄＋伊東建築塾 共同設計
"Home-for-All" for Kamaishi shopping street
Toyo Ito + ITO JUKU

釜石漁師の「みんなの家」 2013.04-2013.10
伊東豊雄建築設計事務所＋アトリエ・天工人＋Ma 設計事務所 共同設計
"Home-for-All" for Fishermen in Kamaishi
Toyo Ito & Associates, Architects
+ Atelier Tekuto Co., Ltd. + Ma Design office

釜石市平田の「みんなの家」 2011.08-2012.05
山本理顕設計工場 設計
"Home-for-All" in Heita, Kamaishi
Riken Yamamoto & Field Shop

陸前高田の「みんなの家」 2011.11-2012.11
ヴェネチア・ビエンナーレ出展者
伊東豊雄＋乾久美子＋藤本壮介＋平田晃久 共同設計
"Home-for-All" in Rikuzentakata
Toyo Ito + Kumiko Inui + Sou Fujimoto + Akihisa Hirata

気仙沼大谷の「みんなの家」 2012.12-2013.10
Yang Zhao（＋渡瀬正記） 妹島和世（アドバイザー）設計
"Home-for-All" in Ohya, Kesennuma
Yang Zhao (+Masanori Watase) Kazuyo Sejima (Mentor)

東松島「こどものみんなの家」 2012.07-2013.01
伊東豊雄＋大西麻貴 共同設計
"Home-for-All" for children in Higashimatsushima
Toyo Ito + Maki Onishi

東松島市宮戸島の「みんなの家」 2011.10-2012.10
妹島和世＋西沢立衛／SANAA 設計
"Home-for-All" in Miyatojima, Higashimatsushima
Kazuyo Sejima + Ryue Nishizawa / SANAA

宮戸島月浜の「みんなの家」 2013.10-2014.07
妹島和世＋西沢立衛／SANAA 設計
"Home-for-All" in Tsukihama, Miyatojima
Kazuyo Sejima + Ryue Nishizawa / SANAA

くまもとアートポリス東北支援「みんなの家」 2011.06-2011.10
伊東豊雄＋桂英昭＋末廣香織＋曽我部昌史 共同設計
"Home-for-All" by Kumamoto Artpolis Tohoku Support Group
Toyo Ito + Hideaki Katsura + Kaoru Suehiro + Masashi Sogabe

岩沼「みんなの家」 2012.12-2013.07
伊東豊雄建築設計事務所 設計
"Home-for-All" in Iwanuma
Toyo Ito & Associates, Architects

## くまもとアートポリス東北支援「みんなの家」
### "Home-for-All" by Kumamoto Artpolis Tohoku Support Group

宮城野区の福田町南1丁目公園の仮設住宅地内に完成した12坪の「みんなの家」。2011年6月〜7月にかけて住民たちの希望を入れつつ設計が進められた。木材はすべて熊本県でプレカットされ、現場に運ばれた。

This "Home-for-All" is 40 square meters in floor area, completed in a temporary housing area in Minami 1-chome Park in Fukuda-machi, Miyagino Ward. Design took place in June through July 2011, with input from residents. Wood material was all pre-cut in Kumamoto Prefecture and delivered to the site.

## 釜石商店街「みんなの家・かだって」
### "Home-for-All" for Kamaishi shopping street

釜石のNPO＠リアスと、津波によって被害を受けた商店街の中に、復興の拠点をつくりたいという思いが一致し、実現した。瓦礫の中に立ち、復興へ向けて人びとが集まり、語り合う場となった。

This was built because we and @Rias, an NPO in Kamaishi, both wanted to create a base for reconstruction of the shopping area that had been damaged by the tsunami. Rising amid debris, it became a place where people gathered to discuss reconstruction.

## 陸前高田の「みんなの家」
### "Home-for-All" in Rikuzentakata

陸前高田市高田町大石の、まちが見下ろせる場所に5人のチーム（伊東豊雄、乾久美子、藤本壮介、平田晃久、畠山直哉）によって設計が進められた。たびたび現地に赴き、ヒアリングと議論を重ね、被災杉を用いて実現した。

A five-person team (Toyo Ito, Kumiko Inui, Sou Fujimoto, Akihisa Hirata and Naoya Hatakeyama) designed this for a place in Oishi, Takata-cho, Rikuzentakata City, looking down on the town. The site was visited many times, repeated hearings and discussions were held, and "Home-for-All" was built using cedar from the disaster-stricken area.

## 東松島「こどものみんなの家」
### "Home-for-All" for children in Higashimatsushima

東松島市最大の仮設住宅地であるグリーンタウンやもと応急仮設住宅地内に建てられた子どものための「みんなの家」。現地に足を運び住民の人びとや運営をする集会所の人びととと話し合いを重ねた。仮設住宅に暮らす子どもたちが、友だち同士で集まって話し合える、心と心の通じ合う場となった。

This "Home-for-All" for children is built in the emergency temporary housing area Green Town Yamoto, the biggest temporary housing area in Higashimatsushima City. The site was visited and repeated discussion were held with residents and people from the assembly hall who would operate it. This became a place where children living in temporary housing could come with friends and talk.

### 岩沼「みんなの家」
"Home-for-All" in Iwanuma

岩沼に、農業を再興しようとするNPO法人「がんばっと！玉浦」のために、さまざまな人の協力のもと、完成した。深い庇のある木造平屋で、三和土土間やかまど、土壁などを、設計者や利用者、出資者が、一緒になって力を合わせてつくった。農業支援活動を継続的に行う拠点として、次の世代に地域の農業を継承することができるような場として活用される。

This was completed in Iwanuma with the cooperation of various individuals for Gambatttto!! Tamaura, an NPO trying to revive the farming industry. A one-story wooden construction building with deep eaves, it has an earthen work space, a hearth and clay walls. The architects, users and the investors worked together to construct this. A base for sustainable activities in support of agriculture, this is being used so that the next generation can continue to farm in the area.

### 釜石漁師の「みんなの家」
"Home-for-All" for Fishermen in Kamaishi

2011年秋、前年のヴェネチア・ビエンナーレで金獅子賞を受賞したバーレーン館の漁師小屋が東京で展示された。海辺の再開発による海岸線の埋め立てのため解体の運命にあった小屋である。この漁師小屋を展示終了後譲り受け、釜石市の漁業復興の拠点にと釜石市に提言し、小屋の一部として実現した。

In fall of 2011, a fisherman's hut which had been part of a Bahrain Pavilion exhibition that had received the Golden Lion at the Venice Biennale the previous year was exhibited in Tokyo. The hut was destined to be dismantled because the coastal area of Bahrain was being reclaimed for redevelopment. After the exhibition, the hut was given to us. We added a new structure to it to form "Home-for-All" for fishermen. It is a base for the reconstruction of the fishing industry in Kamaishi.

### 釜石「みんなのひろば」
"Park-for-All" in Kamaishi

子どもたちのスポーツ活動を支援するために、既存のグラウンドの整備とともに子どもたちや地区住民が活用できるクラブハウスをあわせもつ施設。さらには復興まちづくり協議会の活動の拠点として、活用される。

The construction of a facility serving as a clubhouse that children and local residents can use was combined with the improvement of an existing athletic field in order to support children's sports activities. This is also used as a base for activities by the reconstruction and community development conference.

くまもとアートポリス東北支援「みんなの家」　"Home-for-All" by Kumamoto Artpolis Tohoku Support Group

1. 設計者・施工者・住民が一緒になったオープニングイベント 2. 竣工式での集合写真 3. 仮設住宅にはない、温かい光に住民が涙を流す 4. 仙台市の小学生が訪問し、住民から被災体験を聞いた 5. 住民との対話を重ねながら設計を進めた 6. 熊本県から仙台に向けた木材の出発式 7. みんなで囲めるテーブルは、学生ボランティアによってつくられた 8. 住民参加で行われた、座布団をつくるワークショップ 9. 棚が拡張され、全国からの贈り物で埋まっている 10. 住民によって植えられた、「みんなの家」の前の花壇

1. At the opening event, designers, contractors, residents were together. 2. Group photo at the completion ceremony. 3. Residents shed tears not in the temporary housing, but in the warm light. 4. Elementary school in Sendai City visited the site and heard the disaster experience from residents. 5. Presenting a more developed design while dialoging with residents. 6. Dispatching of wood toward Sendai from Kumamoto Prefecture. 7. Table, which can be surrounded by many people, was made by student volunteers. 8. Workshop to make cushion was held with the participation of residents. 9. Shelf is extended, it is filled with gifts from all over the country. 10. Flower beds in front of "Home-for-All" planted by residents.

# 釜石商店街「みんなの家・かだって」 "Home-for-All" for Kamaishi shopping street

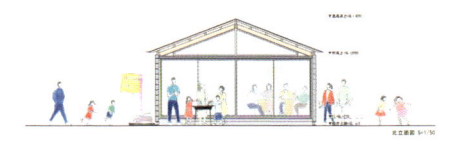

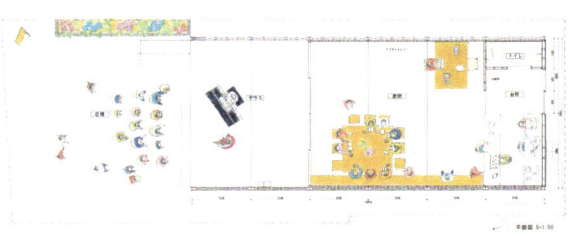

1. 住民ワークショップで製作された家具 2. 塾生のボランティア作業による塗装作業 3. オープニングセレモニーでの集合写真 4. 被災した商店街の中に、「みんなの家」の灯りがともる 5. 今後の復興を巡って話し合いが日常的に行われている風景 6. テラスを使ったイベント風景

1. Furniture is manufactured at residents workshop. 2. The paint job by volunteer students at ITO JUKU. 3. Group photo at the opening ceremony. 4. In the shopping district affected by the disaster, the lights of "Home-for-All" blink on. 5. Everyday scenery, residents having an ongoing discussion over the future of the reconstruction. 6. Events scenery, using a terrace.

331

# 陸前高田の「みんなの家」 "Home-for-All" in Rikuzentakata

東松島「こどものみんなの家」　"Home-for-All" for children in Higashimatsushima

1. 被災者の代表者である菅原みき子さんと、繰り返し行われた設計の打ち合わせ 2. 第13回ヴェネチア・ビエンナーレ国際建築展日本館で設計の過程を展示した 3. ストーブを囲む、内部の風景

1. Design meetings were repeatedly held with Ms. Mikiko Sugawara, who is the representative of the victims. 2. Study models that have been exhibited at the Japanese Pavilion of the 13th International Architecture Exhibition, Venice Biennale. 3. Interior space around the stove.

1.「テーブルの家」に集まり、映画を見る子どもたち 2. 住民との話し合いの様子 3. 3つの建物をつなぐ縁側を、子どもたちが自由に駆け回る 4. 子どもたちへのクリスマスプレゼントとして、気仙沼から運ばれた野外ステージ

1. Gathered in the house of the table, children are watching a movie. 2. Discussions with residents. 3. Children run around freely along the edge that connects the three buildings. 4. Outdoor stage as a Christmas gift to the children, which was carried from Kesennuma.

# 岩沼「みんなの家」 "Home-for-All" in Iwanuma

1.がんばッと!!玉浦、インフォコム（寄付者）、仲介する中田英寿氏らと行った最初の打ち合わせ 2.さまざまな方が一体となってつくり上げる土間やかまど 3.完成したかまどの前で記念撮影 4.さまざまな催し物が開かれる前庭 5.ハーブガーデンに面した縁側は地元住民の憩いの場となっている 6.毎週末に行われる直売イベント

1. The first meeting event with Mr. Hidetoshi Nakata who mediates Infocom and Ganbatto!!Tamaura and (donors). 2. Various people worked together to make *Doma* (dirt floor) and furnace. 3. Commemorative photo in front of the completed stove. 4. Many kinds of events are held in the front garden. 5. *Engawa* (veranda-like porch), facing the herb garden became a recreation area for resicents. 6. Products sales event takes place every weekend.

335

# 釜石漁師の「みんなの家」 "Home-for-All" for Fishermen in Kamaishi

# 釜石「みんなのひろば」 "Park-for-All" in Kamaishi

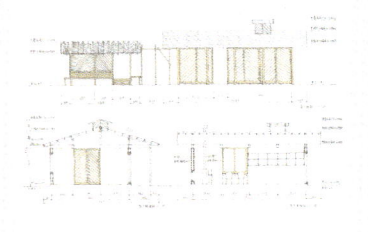

1.バーレーン漁師の小屋と、そこから結ばれた新棟の2棟から成る「みんなの家」 2.囲炉裏付きの大きなテーブルに人びとが集まる風景 3.利用者との話し合い 4.バーレーンから運ばれた小屋

1. The hut for fishermen of Bahrain and "Home-for-All" that consists of new two buildings and that is connected to the hut. 2. People gather around a large table with fireplace. 3. Meeting with the users. 4. The hut, sent from Bahrain.

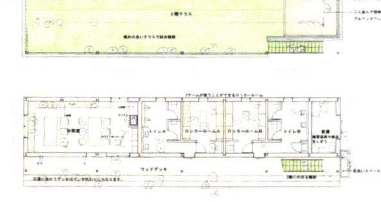

1. 地元の小学生と行った1回目のワークショップ 2. 竣工式での記念写真 3. 2階ブルペンでの始球式の様子 4. 休憩室の様子 5. ナイキジャパン主催の野球教室

1. First workshop with the local elementary school students. 2. Commemorative photo at the completion ceremony. 3. Opening pitch ceremony at the second floor bullpen. 4. Appearance of the resting room. 5. Baseball classroom sponsored by Nike Japan.

# 10 台中国立歌劇院
National Taichung Theater

伊東豊雄との対話　Conversation with Toyo Ito

## 台中国立歌劇院(建設中)
National Taichung Theater (under construction)

## ゲント市文化フォーラム・コンペティション応募案

― 「台中国立歌劇院」は、2005年にコンペティションがありました。それからになりますから長いプロジェクトです。台中で使われている幾何学が生まれたのは、2004年の「ゲント市文化フォーラム・コンペティション応募案」ですね。

そうですね。当時ベルギー・ゲントに住んでいたエディ・フランソワさんにすすめられて、応募しました。残念ながら今年（2014年）亡くなってしまいましたが、エディさんは建築ディレクター、アートディレクターみたいな方でした。彼はすごくピュアな人で、このコンペティションに落ちた時はボロボロ涙を流したし、このコンペティションがなくなってからも、このプロジェクトでやるべきだと市に再三働きかけていました。またこのコンペティションはミラノのデザイナーであるアンドレア・ブランジさんとの共同発表です。ブランジさんとエディさんは親しく、エディさんはブランジさんのアートワークをコレクションしたりしていました。この3者でディスカッションをしながら進めたプロジェクトです。

計画は川に沿って敷地があり、敷地は前面道路に接続していない。まちの真ん中なのに不思議な土地でした。クルマがやっと通れるような細い道を入っていくと敷地に至りますが、もう一方は石段で車は入れない。最初のイメージはストリートコンサートのような自由で気楽なホールをつくれないかということでした。そこでアプローチの細いストリートが建築の内にまで続いていて、それらの合わさった広場のような場所をメインのコンサートホールにしては、と考えたのです。

― 建築の中に入っても、まだ細い道が続いているような感覚があります。まちの構造とこの案の立体的な道というのは密接に関係しているわけですね。

そうです。だから、これはものすごく不思議な案ですが、コンテクストが確立されています。近隣の住宅と向かい合っている場所はどうしようとか、川に面している所は散歩できるようにしようとか、使われなくなった古いサーカス小屋も将来は組み合わせて使おうとか、周辺との関係をひとつずつ考えました。

― まちの延長としてホールをつくることで、建築を単体でつくっているというよりは、まちをつくるというか、まちの延長で「場」をつくるというような印象がありますね。その中にホールが埋め込まれている。

それは「空間」の感覚の違いからですね。空間という言葉をヨーロッパではポシェと言います。ポケットですね。つまり、もともと中身が詰まって

「ゲント市文化フォーラム・コンペティション応募案」コンペティションモデル
Model for competition proposal, Forum for Music, Dance and Visual Culture, Ghent.

「ゲント市文化フォーラム・コンペティション応募案」航空写真
Aerial photograph for competition plan, Forum for Music, Dance and Visual Culture, Ghent.

### Forum for Music, Dance and Visual Culture, Ghent

– National Taichung Theater was the subject of a competition held in 2005. The project is still ongoing, so it has been a long-term one. It was in the 2004 competition for the Forum for Music, Dance and Visual Culture, Ghent that the geometry used in Taichung first appeared.

Yes. We entered at the suggestion of Mr. Eddy François, was residing in Ghent, Belgium. Sadly, he passed away this year [2014]. He took on a role similar to an architectural and art director. He was quite pure at heart and cried when our scheme failed to win the competition. Even after the competition was over, he tried to convince the city to undertake this project. Our scheme was a collaboration with Mr. Andrea Branzi, a designer from Milan. Mr. Branzi and Mr. Eddy were close friends, and had a collection of artworks by Mr. Branzi. The three of us held discussions concerning this project.

The project site was along a river and did not face a street. It was a strange site though located in the middle of the city. The site was accessed from one direction by a road barely wide enough for a car, and from the other direction no cars could enter, as there were only stone steps. I first imagined the facility as a casual concert hall for events such as street concerts. I thought of the narrow access streets continuing into the building and meeting in a square-like space, which would have been the concert hall.

– It does feel like the narrow streets continue into the building. There is a close relationship between the organization of the city and the three-dimensional network of streets in this scheme.

Yes. This was quite a strange scheme, but there was a definite context for it. I considered the relationship of each part of the scheme with the surroundings: how to treat the places that face neighborhood houses, whether or not to make the place facing the river an area for strolls, whether or not to incorporate and use in the future an old circus structure.

– You were not so much designing a single building, a concert hall in a city. You were instead designing a place as an extension of the city, and embedding the hall in that place.

It stems from a difference in the perception of space. In Europe, space is referred to as *poché*, meaning "pocket." The space is a place that has been hollowed out from something solid. In Japan, however, space means the interval between two or three supporting posts. In short, it is *ma*. Therefore, the European concept of space is quite different from the Japanese concept of space.

The competition scheme for Ghent was a solid from which "streets" had been scooped out. Many old streets in Europe are narrow passageways that seem like they have been carved out of rock. So the space of the scheme was conceived in that image.

– Streets were carved out--in places they widened out into squares--and were lined with houses. These "streets" also led upwards.

Yes. It was an interesting project. However, I did not have a favorable impression of the jury. After the presentation, I did not feel the jurors understanding the scheme at all. When I showed them the model, I was asked if a place where I had made the floor transparent was made of glass. I was quite disappointed [laughs].

– I remember there were comments in the competition guidelines that stirred the imagination. The people who wrote the guidelines were different from the people who served on the jury?

No, there were such people on the jury. The

いるものをえぐったところを「空間」としています。しかし日本では、柱が1本、2本、3本とあった時に、その間を「空間」とします。要するに「間」ですね。だから、スペースといった時に、ヨーロッパの人が考えることと、われわれが考えることは随分違うんですよ。

「ゲント」のコンペ案は、ヨーロッパ的に詰まったものがいっぱいあって、その間に「道」があるというものですが、ヨーロッパの古いまちは、岩をくりぬいて道にしているような、ぎちぎちに詰まったような細い道が多いですから、そんな空間のイメージに近いですね。

— くりぬかれて広くなった所が広場になっていたり、それに面して建物が並んでいたりするつくり方ですね。その「道」がさらに上にもつながっていくことがある。

そうです。面白いプロジェクトでしたね。
でも、この審査会での印象は決して良いものでなく、プレゼンが終わったあとに、この案が全然理解されてないと感じましたね。模型を見せても、透明な床がある所を指して「ここにガラスがはまっているのか」と質問されて、ガッカリしました(笑)。

— コンペの要綱では、イメージを刺激するような言葉があったように記憶していますが、その要綱をつくった人たちと審査員の人たちは違ったのですか。

いや、審査員の中にそういう人もいました。フランスのオペラ座の芸術監督もいたように思います

「ゲント市文化フォーラム・コンペティション応募案」コンペティションモデル
Model for competition proposal, Forum for Music, Dance and Visual Culture, Ghent.

が、そういう人たちも全然理解が及ばなかったようですね。要するに均質な平土間の床があって、それがグリッド状に分割され、それぞれがアップダウンできるようにして、客席配置を変えられるようなものを考えていたのだと思います。ある意味で「座・高円寺」の1階のようなものですね。

— コンペに参加した時には、伊東事務所では「長岡リリックホール」や「まつもと市民芸術館」など、いくつかホールをやっていましたが、当初からそういうホールとはちょっと違ったチャレンジをしようという考えがあったのでしょうか。

そうですね。コンサートホールの形式を解体してしまおうと思っていました。イタリアのパッラーディオの「テアトロ・オリンピコ」は、放射状に通路が抜けていて、その先はまちにつながっているのですから、それに近い考え方ですね。

完結したホールで何かをやるというのは、近代以降の話であって、20世紀的なかたちです。そうではなく、もっと外とつながって、コンサートをやっていると遠くから音が聞こえてくるとか、1幕目はここでやって、2幕目はみんなが移動して別の所でやるとか、そういう外ともつながるようなコンサートが面白いと思っていたのです。

artistic director of the Opéra in France was among them, but even they did not understand the scheme at all. There was a uniform, level floor, divided into a grid, with each unit being adjustable vertically change the seating arrangement of the audience. In some sense it was like the first floor of ZA-KOENJI.

– At the time of the competition, the office was doing a number of halls such as Nagaoka Lyric Hall and Matsumoto Performing Arts Centre. Did you intent from the start to take on the challenge of something slightly different from such halls?

Yes. I was thinking of disassembling the form of the concert hall. The idea was close to Palladio's Teatro Olimpico in Italy, which has radiating passageways that suggest streets connecting to the city.

Putting on performances in self-contained halls is a modern idea, a twentieth-century form. I thought a hall that was more connected to the outside—perhaps sounds from a distance might be heard during a concert, or the first act might take place here, and for the second act, everyone might move to a different place—a concert that was connected to the outside in such a way would be interesting.

### National Taichung Theater

– At the time of the National Taichung Theater competition, you said you wanted to realize the theatre connected to the outside that had originally been conceived for Ghent. You saw it as a second opportunity to do that [laughs].

Initially, yes. I thought it would be wasteful not to use this geometry. I was waiting for a chance, and then the competition for a opera house in Taichung came along. I thought it was a golden opportunity, since Mr. Hiroshi Hara was a juror and Mr. Mohsen Mostafavi, the Dean at Harvard University, was the chairman of the jury [laughs].

– Why do you think the jury selected the scheme by the office over other entries?

I think one reason was that the curved surface we designed was conceived as a systematic structure. I say structurally conceived, though in fact, it subsequently caused us considerable problems.

– There was a fundamental reconsideration of the structure halfway through the process.

Yes. At first, Mr. Cecil Balmond's team was in charge of the structural design, but halfway through the process, Mr. Mitsuhiro Kanada was named structural designer and took over.

– Arup analyzed the wall thickness, which had been 800 mm during the basic design stage, and said it could be made 400 mm.

A team that was designing automobiles whose strong suit was thin membrane structures took over the analysis at Arup, and they immediately said walls could be 400 mm.

「ゲント市文化フォーラム・コンペティション応募案」コンセプトスケッチ
Sketch for the competition proposal for Forum for Music, Dance and Visual Culture, Ghent.

### 台中国立歌劇院

――「台中国立歌劇院」のコンペの時は、「ゲント」の外までつながっていくような劇場を実現させたいということで、リベンジマッチと伊東さんは言われていましたね(笑)。

最初はそうでした。とにかくこの幾何学をこのままお蔵入りさせるのはもったいないと思ってチャンスを狙っていたところ、台中でオペラハウスのコンペが始まりました。原広司さんが審査員でいましたし、ハーバード大学の学部長のモイセン・モスタファヴィさんが審査委員長でしたから、これは絶好のチャンスだと思いましたね(笑)。

――伊東事務所の案が他のコンペティターより評価された点は何でしょうか。

ひとつの理由は、われわれのつくり出した曲面がシステマティックな構造体として考えられている点だと思います。もっとも、構造的とは言いながら、のちにずいぶん苦労しましたけれども。

――途中で根本的に構造を考え直したことですね。

そうです。当初セシル・バルモンドさんのチームがずっとやっていましたが、途中から金田充弘さんが指名され引き継ぎました。

――壁厚が、基本設計時は800mmだったものを、アラップで解析し、「400mmにできる」という話がきましたね。

それはアラップの解析チームが、薄膜構造みたいなものを得意としていた車のデザインをやっているチームに代わり、代わった途端に「400mmでいける」という話になりました。

――膜というか曲面の考え方がそこで一気に変わったということですね。金田さんに「台中国立歌劇院」の構造に関して聞く機会があった際に、ブラジャーのワイヤーフックや車の高張力鋼板などをたとえに、曲線のつくり方で形を保つ方法が「台中国立歌劇院」の構造にも使われていると聞きました。

800mmだと本当の洞窟みたいになりましたね。

いやあ、それは大変なことになっていたと思います。

――「台中国立歌劇院」が出来つつあるのを見て、みんなはどう考えていますか？ 他のわれわれがこれまでやってきた建築とかなり違いますが、それをどう受け止めるべきか。

――現場を体験してきたのですが、写真にとらえきれない空間ですね。建物内を進んでいくたびにいろいろ違う体験があり、その連続で刺激的だと感じました。

迷宮的ですが、明かりがあるから記憶に視覚情報として残るところがあって、本能的に適切な方向へ進んでいける感じがあります。

工事中の現場は真っ暗で方向感覚がつかめません。その中で光が差し込んでいる場所が見えます。大体そこが広がりのある空間になります。いままで壁で切れていた所が連続して見えてくるというのは、本当に面白いと思います。

「福岡アイランドシティ中央公園中核施設ぐりんぐりん」が出来たころ、「ぐりんぐりん」と「台中国立歌劇院」、「ゲント」の比較論を事務所の中で行いました。「台中国立歌劇院」はグリッドで分けられ、縦つながりの空間と横つながりの空間が繰り返される。空間の繰り返しは、次の空間への予感みたいなものを生むが、予感通りの空間であったり逆に予感を裏切る空間であったりすることで建築的な体験を生むはずだと書いてありました。

伊東事務所がこの時代にアルゴリズムというルールを重視していたというのは、そういうものの中で建築的な体験を生み出そうということを実験的にやっていたのかなと思いました。

まあ、そうですね。その話と関係しているかと思いますが、「台中国立歌劇院」では最初にグリッド状のパターンを立体的につくってしまって、そこに2000席と800席の劇場を強引に突っ込んだわけですね。その時にその部分がぐわ〜っとゆがんで、幾何学に変形が生じる。

普通、劇場というのは、「まつもと」でもそうですが、最初に劇場というスペースがあって、舞台があって、客席があってという順序で考えていきますね。ところが、「台中国立歌劇院」は"まず幾何学ありき"で、そこに力づくで劇場を入れ込んでいるから、本当にこの劇場を入れるのは大変でした。金網で手を傷だらけにしながら模型を作っていたから、ほんとに血と涙の結晶ですよ(笑)。

――金網じゃないと模型が作れないからみんな金網でやりましたが、硬くて手が痛くなる。最初のころは慣れなくて、本当に苦労しました。

– There was an abrupt change in thinking about membranes or curved surfaces at that point. When I had an opportunity to ask Mr. Kanada about the structure of National Taichung Theater, he likened it to the wire-hook of a brassiere or the high tensile strength steel plate in automobiles and said a method of maintaining a form by means of the way curves were created was used in the structure of National Taichung Theater.

If it had been 800 mm, it would have really been like a cave.

It would have been awful.

What do all of you think, having seen National Taichung Theater in the process of construction? It is quite different from the buildings we have done up to now--what do you make of this difference?

– I have been working on the site, and the space cannot be fully understood through photographs. Every time I go inside, I experience something new, and the series of experiences has been stimulating.

It is mazelike, but because there is light, visual information is retained in one's memory. One instinctively advances in the proper direction.

During construction, it was completely dark, and I had no sense of direction. But places where light enters could be seen, and those are generally broader spaces. Seeing continuity in places that had been cut off by walls up to now is truly interesting.

Around the time Island City Central Park "GRIN GRIN" was completed, there was a discussion in the office comparing "GRIN GRIN," National Taichung Theater and Ghent. National Taichung Theater is divided by a grid, and vertically connected spaces and horizontally connected spaces are repeated. The repetition of space produces expectations about the next space to come. It has been written somewhere that meeting or not meeting such spatial expectations generates an architectural experience.

I thought that in emphasizing algorithms or rules at the time, the office was experimenting with the generation of architectural experience through such things.

Yes. This may be related to that, but in National Taichung Theater, we first created a three-dimensional grid pattern and forcibly introduced 2,000-seat and 800-seat theatres inside that pattern. When we did that, those parts were distorted, and deformations of the geometry were generated.

Ordinarily, when one is designing a theatre --and this was true of Matsumoto--one first considers the space called the theatre, with a stage, and then an audience. But in National Taichung Theater, the geometry came first, and we forcibly introduced theatres into that geometry. Introducing those theatres was quite difficult. We suffered many cuts and bruises building models out of metal mesh, so this was truly the product of blood, sweat and tears [laughs].

– We used metal mesh because it was the only way we could build models, but it hurt our hands trying to shape the metal material. At first, we still hadn't the knack and it was truly hard work.

When we were wondering how to introduce the theaters, we changed the shape by spreading and pushing together the metal mesh bit by bit.

In The New Deichman Main Library, Oslo (p. 137), competition scheme, we had decided on a system which did not have much flexibility, but this system could be stretched--it was a soft, flexible system to a certain extent, one that could be adapted to a program like an opera house.

A program for a library can be accommodated with relatively small spaces, so a series of small spaces like the proposal for The New Deichman Main Library Competition can work. However, a theatre has a clear form and the space is large, so it is difficult to dismantle the form. I marvel at how we were able to achieve such a space with the arbitrary approach--I think that was the key point with respect to this building. The thing that is coming into being--the hall is taking on the form of a hall--but we took a completely opposite approach. What is distinctive about this building is that its spaces --the hall, the areas around it, the offices above it, the restaurant--are all related to one another.

– The use of a reverse process--instead of designing a space so that it can be used in a certain way, one considers how a space that has been created might be used. Somewhat like a spelunker discovering a space, one can create an unexpected space, a space with the potential to transcend one's imagination.

– We call a floor introduced into a "Catenoid" (p. 359) a "Plug." (p. 370) A plug creates a place in a cave made solely of curved surfaces where people gather or engage in activities. That is what changed it into a space for people.

Deciding at what level to introduce a horizontal floor was difficult in itself. If it were lowered slightly, there would be many convexities and concavities, and if it were raised slightly, it becomes practically all horizontal. The floor area would have been different if the floor had been ten cm higher.

– At first, we introduced a level plane, thinking of it like a surface of water. I seem to remember that it was only after considerable time had passed that we discovered what it would look like.

When we were undertaking this study, we created an undulating floor for the exhibition in Tokyo Opera City.[1] In that study, an attempt was made to

劇場をどうやって入れるかという時には、金網をちょっとずつ広げたり狭めたりしながら、形を作っていきました。

「オスロ市ダイクマン中央図書館 コンペティション応募案」(p.137)では、あるシステムで固まってしまい融通がきかないという面がありましたが、このシステムは、引き延ばしたりという、ある程度柔らかい融通性のあるシステムであるというところで、オペラハウスみたいなプログラムに対しても適応できているのかと思いました。

図書館ですと、わりと小さい空間でも成り立つプログラムですから、「ダイクマン中央図書館」のように小さな空間の連続もあり得ると思いますが、劇場は形式がはっきりしているし、大きい空間なので形式を解体するのが難しいですね。そういう空間をよくこんな方法で強引にやったなと思って、そこがこの建築の最大のポイントだったと思います。出来上がりつつあるものは、ホールはホールとしてある形式を備えつつありますが、発想の仕方がまったく逆だったというわけです。ホールの中にいても、周りを歩いていても、上のオフィスにいても、レストランにいても、ある一連の関係性をもった空間になっているのは、この建築独自の特徴だと思います。

— 逆のプロセスを使ったということですが、こう使うためにこうつくるというのと同時に、出来てしまった空間をどうやって使おうかと後から考える。洞窟を探検してスペースを発見するようなところが予期せぬ空間を生み出しているというか、想像力を超えられるような可能性をもっているのかなと思います。

— カテノイド (p.359) に入れた床のことを「プラグ」(p.370)と呼んでいます。プラグにより曲面だけの洞窟に人が集まったり活動したりする場所が出来ていく。それによって人間のための空間に変わったような印象もありました。

水平の床をどういうレベルに入れるかというのは、それはそれで難しかったですね。ちょっと下げると凹凸だらけになるし、ちょっと上げるとほとんど水平になってしまう。10cm上がったら床面積が変わりますから。

— 最初は水面のような考え方で水平面を入れていくと、こういう見え方をするのかというのが、だいぶ後になってから見えてきたような記憶があります。

このスタディをしていたころ、東京オペラシティの展覧会で「うねる床」をつくっていたと思いますが、そのスタディの中で、水平でない床でもいけるのではないか、実際には使いづらいだろうなという、その辺のバランスを図っていたということもあるのでしょうか。

そうですね。劇場のフロアはいずれにしても段状につくる必要がありますが、オフィス、レストラン、ギャラリーといったような上層階は、フラットにしてしまうのか、うねる床はどこまでやっても大丈夫なのかを、かなりスタディしました。

—「ゲント」のころから一貫して、屋外空間がそのまま建築の中に入ってきたような、内部か外部かわからないような空間を目指されているかと思います。曲面の幾何学を構成している「カテノイド」に対して、水平、垂直なスラブや壁を構成している「プラグ」は、機能を成立させるためにホール境界や、ファサードに使われていますね。

そうですね。あれは構造的にもすごく効いています。本当は「ゲント」のように考えれば、2000席のホールと800席のホールは時に連続する空間にしてしまえば一番ラディカルでしたが、遮音の問題などで、そこまでは無理でした。

でも、こんな強引なことをよくやり遂げたと思うし、これを施工するのに、本当に何年間もゼネコンと毎日毎日言い争いながら、それでも担当スタッフが頑張ってくれている。

— これを実現するということが重要なことですね。コンペで終わったというのではなく、これが本当に出来るというのはすごいなと思っています。

そうですね。藤森照信さんが「これが日本にないのが悔しい」と言ってましたが、本当に日本でこういう建築にチャレンジできないのが残念です。

— 日本ですと、管理の問題や、運営でもいろいろな問題が出てきそうですが、台湾の劇場とか運営はおおらかなのでしょうか。

決しておおらかというわけではなくて、台中の役所も「こんなものは許さない」、「どうして遅れているんだ」と言い続けながら、でも最後通告はしない(笑)。それでも進んでいくところが、日本と台湾の違いだと思いますね。

achieve a balance between the idea that an uneven floor might work and the idea that such a floor would in all likelihood be difficult to use?

Yes. The floor of the theatre has to be made stepped in any case, but we undertook many studies to see if the upper floors such as offices, restaurant and gallery ought to be made level, and to what extent an undulating floor might be introduced.

– Ever since Ghent, the objective has consistently been to create a space that could be inside or outside–it is difficult to tell which–to suggest that outdoor space has been introduced directly into the building. "Plugs," which form horizontal slabs and vertical walls as opposed to the "Catenoid" forming the geometry of the curved surface, are used at the boundary of the hall or the facade in the service of function.

Yes. They are quite effective structurally. If we had considered it as we had for Ghent, then we might have made the 2,000-seat hall and the 800-seat hall spatially continuous, which would have been most radical, but that was impossible for reasons such as the problem of sound insulation.

Nonetheless, I marvel at how we were able to achieve such an uncompromising work. The staff persevered, even though they had to argue constantly with the general contractor for years.

– The fact that this idea is being realized is important. I think it is amazing that this did not just end with the competition but is actually being built.

Yes. Mr. Terunobu Fujimori said it is maddening that this is not in Japan, and I think it is truly regrettable that we cannot take up the challenge of a building of this kind in Japan.

– Various problems of supervision and administration are likely to arise in Japan. Are requirements with regard to theaters or the administrations of theatres less stringent in Taiwan?

They are by no means less stringent. Officials in Taichung are just as likely to say, "We cannot permit this sort of thing," or, "Why are you behind schedule," as officials in Japan. The difference is that they don't issue ultimatums [laughs]. The project proceeds despite such objections.

– A comment that you made at some discussion that you wanted to create a dreamlike space, like a space in Shangri-La, made a strong impression on me. It was right after the Great East Japan Earthquake, a time when people were wondering if it should be business as usual in architecture. Your words made me more hopeful with respect to architecture. They awakened a sense of hope with respect to the power of architecture.

National Taichung Theater has continued for nearly ten years since the competition. Has the place or meaning of the project changed for you in that time?

「台中国立歌劇院」メッシュによるモデルでのスタディ風景
Landscape study with mesh model for the National Taichung Theater.

― 以前、ある打ち合わせの中で、伊東さんが「ここでは夢の中にいるような、桃源郷のような空間をつくりたいんだ」とおっしゃった言葉が非常に印象に残っています。ちょうど東日本大震災直後の時で、建築はいまのままでいいのかと悩んでいたところでしたが、建築に対して希望を感じたというか、建築の力に対する期待感がわいてきました。

「台中国立歌劇院」はコンペティションから10年近く続いていますが、その間にプロジェクトの位置づけや意味合いが、伊東さんの中で変わってきているところはありますか。

例えば「みんなの家」は、管理というコントロールの網の目からはずれたところでつくっているという意味で、あるユートピア的な状態ですね。一方、「台中国立歌劇院」の場合は、管理の壁をぶち壊す、蹴飛ばしてでもつくるという、暴力的にそこを乗り越えていくという違いがありますね。

いずれにしても、桃源郷という言葉がいいかどうかはわからないですが、何か「建築って本当はこういうものなのじゃないかな」というような、現代の規制を超えた地点で夢を追い求める、「建築って自由なものなんだ」ということをやりたいわけですね。それによって、人に勇気を与えることができるのではないでしょうか。

建築は社会との関係でしか実現しないものですが、その自由度についてはいろいろな局面があっていいと思います。「台中国立歌劇院」は、われわれとしては現代社会において最大限自由度を追求できたと思っています。

― 藤森さんが言われた「日本でこれが出来ていたらな」というのは、すごく共感します。現代の日本の社会の中で、ここまで私たちがチャレンジすることはなかなか難しくなってしまっていると思うと、伊東さんの言葉を借りれば、それをぶち壊すというか、壁を壊したいですね。

今度の新国立競技場でも、安藤忠雄さんに日本の技術をもってすれば、ザハ・ハディドさんの案は実現できるというような言い方をしていますが、そういう実現への問題ではない。そこに立ちはだかっているもっと大きな壁があって、ザハさんはそれをぶち壊すことによってあの建築をつくろうとしているわけではなく、むしろその壁の手前側で何でもできてしまうという、そういうポジションに彼女は身を置いているような気がします。

「台中国立歌劇院」のようなものは、2年や3年にひとつできるものではなくて、さまざまな条件が重ならないとできないと思ってはいます。でも、希望はもち続けたいですね。

1. 個展「伊東豊雄 建築｜新しいリアル」2006年

"Home-for-All," for example, is being undertaken under utopian conditions, that is, outside the network of control called supervision. National Taichung Theater is different in that constructing it means possibly tearing down or knocking over the wall of supervision.

In any case, and I am not sure if Shangri-La is the right term to use, but I want to pursue a dream that transcends the regulations of today, something that is arguably the true essence of architecture, a vision of architecture as something free. I think doing that will encourage people.

Architecture can only be realized in relationship to society, but there can be many aspects to its freedom. I believe that in National Taichung Theater we have been able to pursue freedom to the greatest degree possible in contemporary society.

– I can sympathize with Mr. Fujimori when he says if only it were in Japan. When I think how difficult it is to take up such a challenge in Japanese society today, I would like to, as you put it, tear down the wall.

Mr. Tadao Ando says that Ms. Zaha Hadid's scheme for the New National Stadium is realizable with Japan's technology, but that is not the sort of problem we are talking about. There is a huge wall standing in our path, and Ms. Zaha is not proposing to tear that down in order to construct her structure. Her position is that she can stay on this side of the wall and still build whatever she wants.

Things like National Taichung Theater are not constructed once every two or three years. They require just the right set of conditions. Nonetheless, I wish to remain hopeful.

1. Solo exhibition Toyo Ito: The New "Real" in Architecture (2006)

## National Taichung Theater
台中国立歌劇院

建設中 under construction  台湾 台中  Taichung, Taiwan

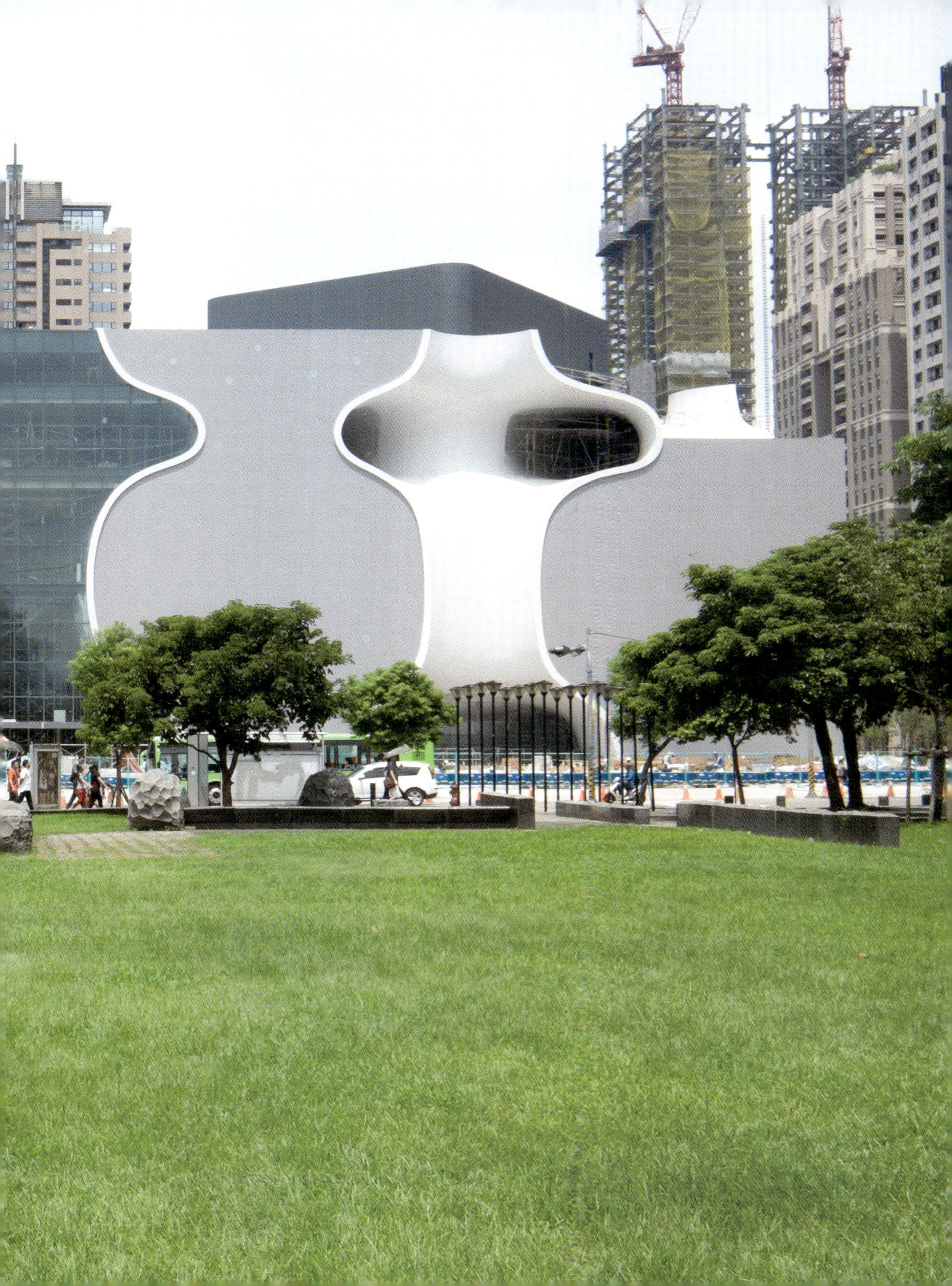

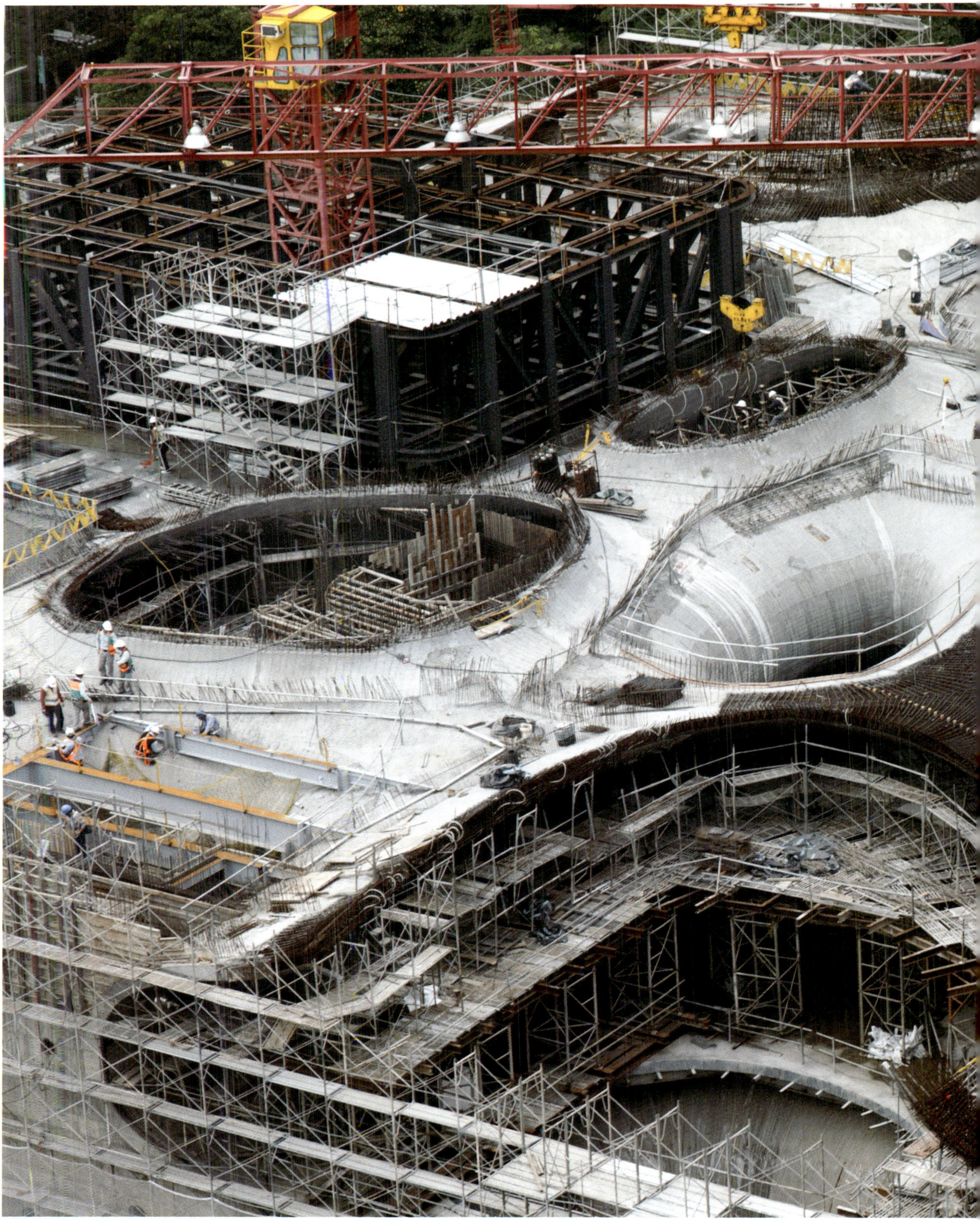

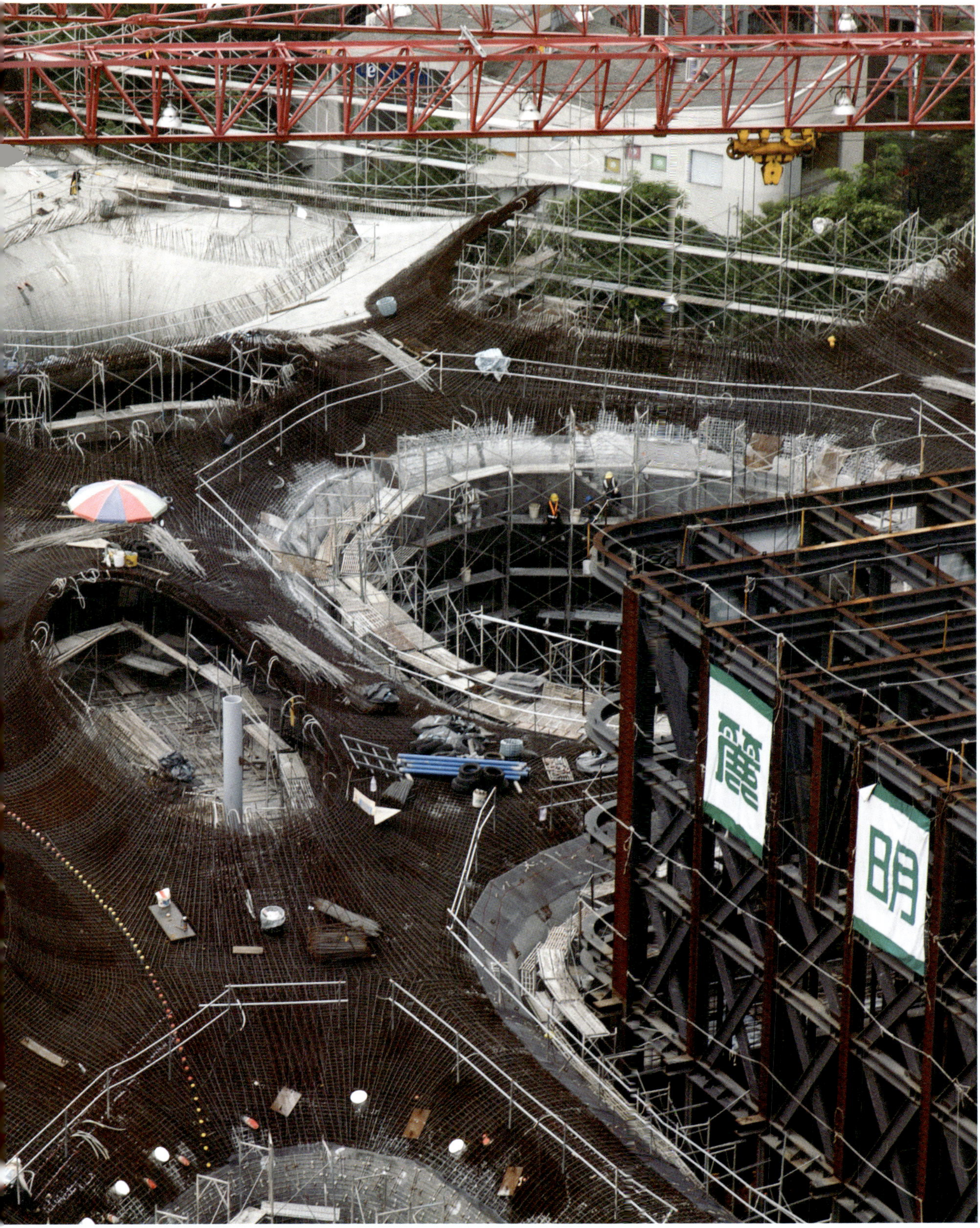
麗
明

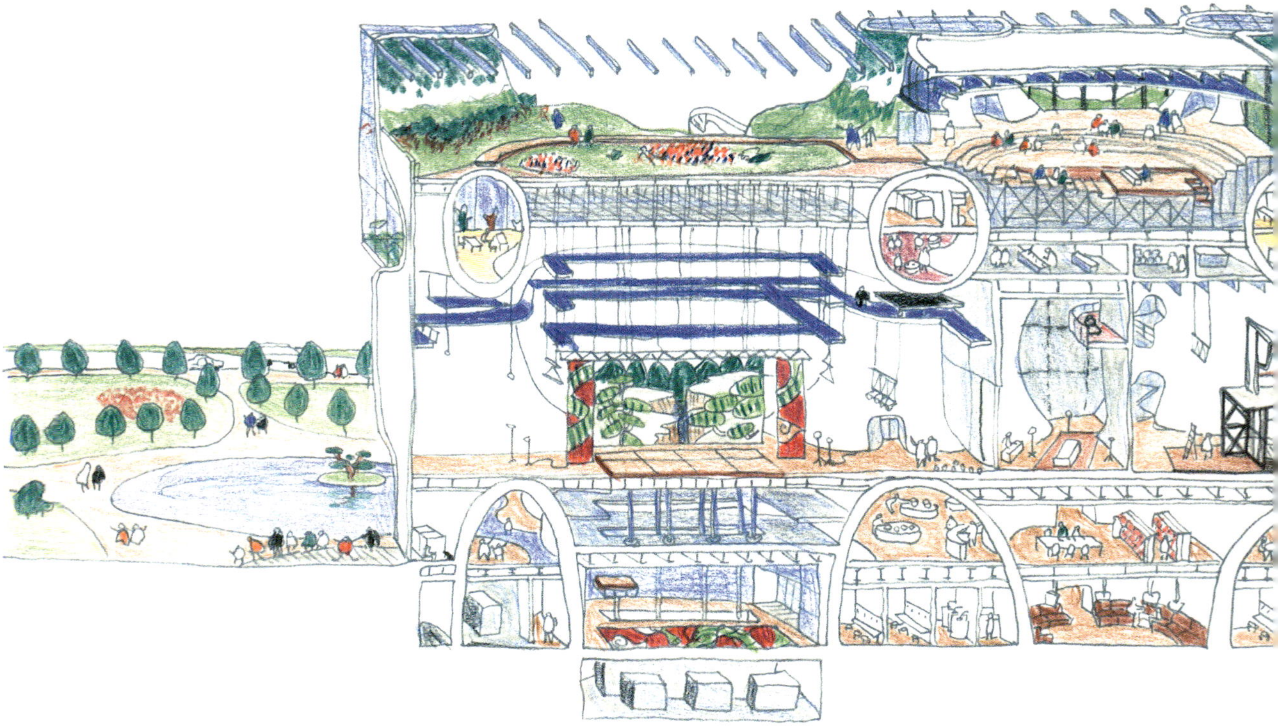

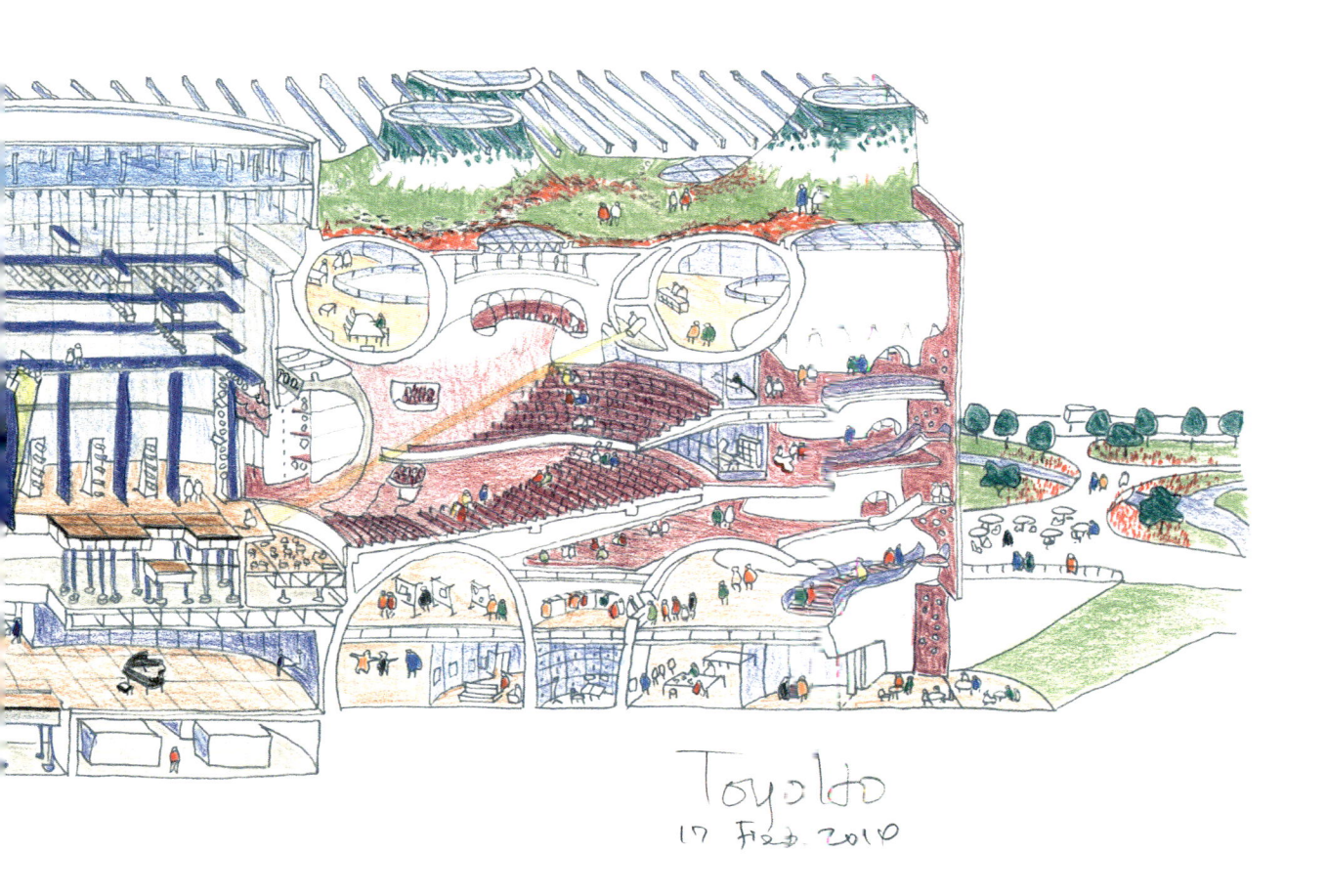

台中市の国際的なパフォーミング・アートの拠点となる3つのオペラ上演可能な劇場とリハーサル室、ショップ、レストラン、ルーフガーデンを含む複合施設。全体は、「カテノイド」と呼ぶ3次元曲面の構造体によって、縦横に連続するチューブ状空間が構成される。

Taking on the role as an international performing arts hub, the National Taichung Theater is a complex that houses three opera-compliant theatres, rehearsal rooms, shops, restaurant and a roof garden. The entire structure is made of a three-dimensional curved surface called "Catenoid", which is essentially vertically and horizontally interconnected tube-like spaces.

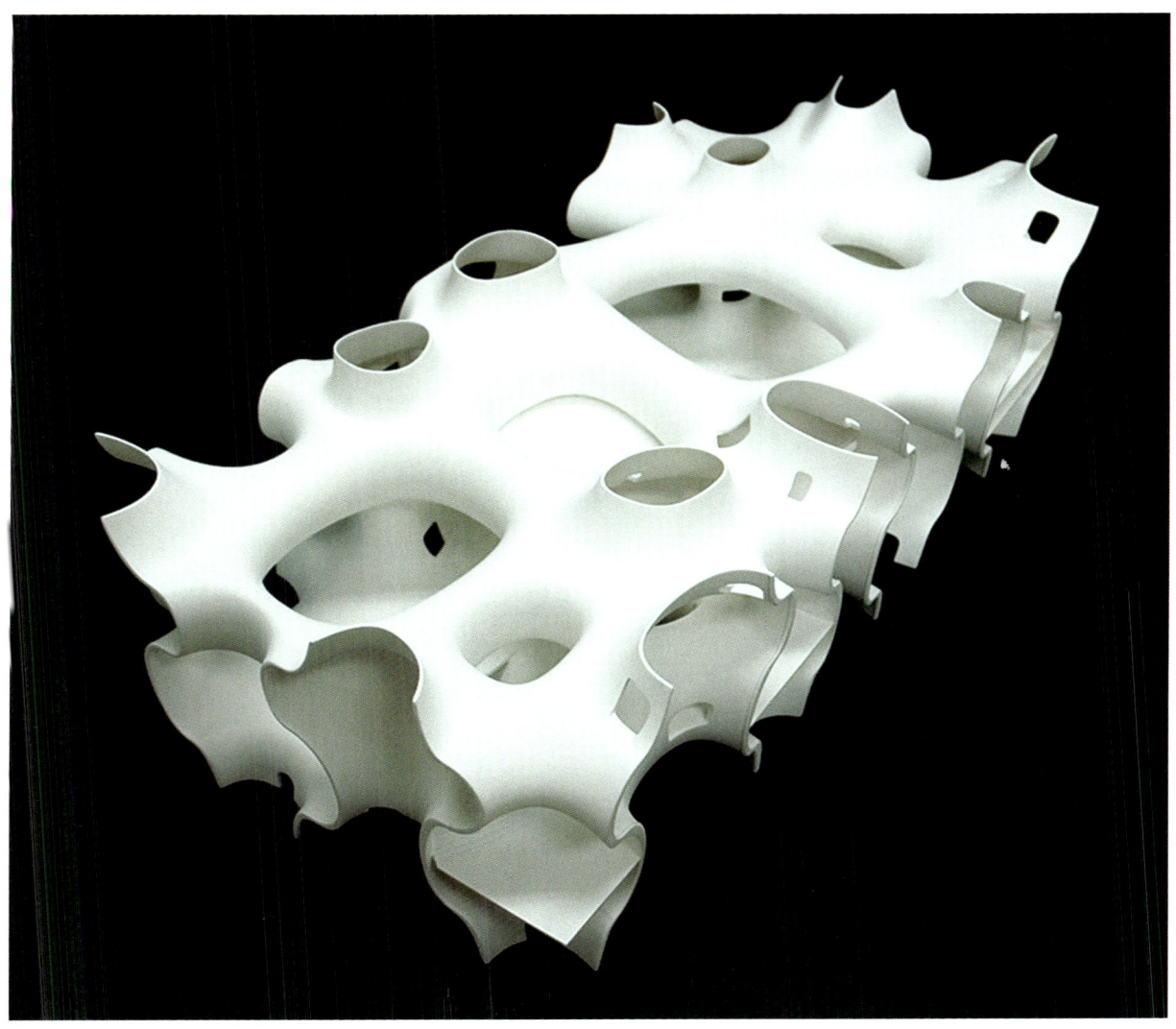

構造モデル
Structural model.

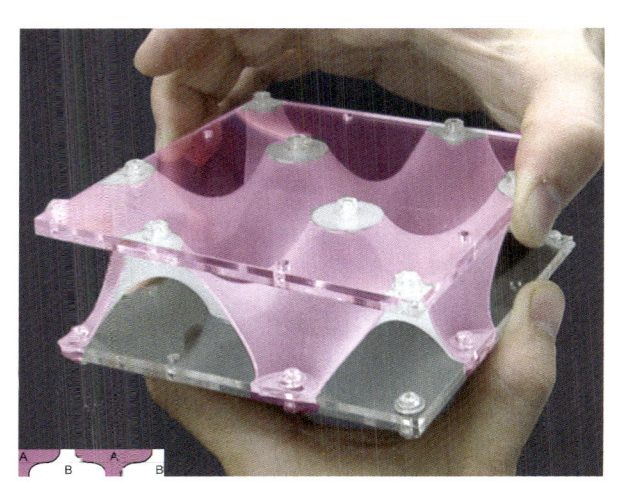

構造体の基本型。1枚の薄い膜でふたつのゾーンに分けられている
Prototype for the structure: Two separate zones are created with a thin membrane.

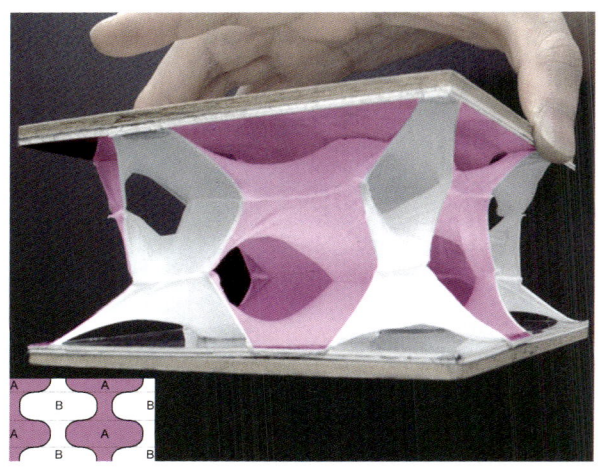

積層させることで縦横に連続したチューブ状空間が生まれる
By adding a succession of layers, the tubular space extends in both vertical and horizontal direction.

金属メッシュで作られた全体模型
Full model made of metal mesh.

金属メッシュによるスタディ模型
Study model made of metal mesh

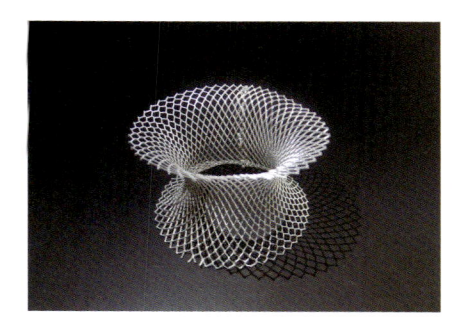

351

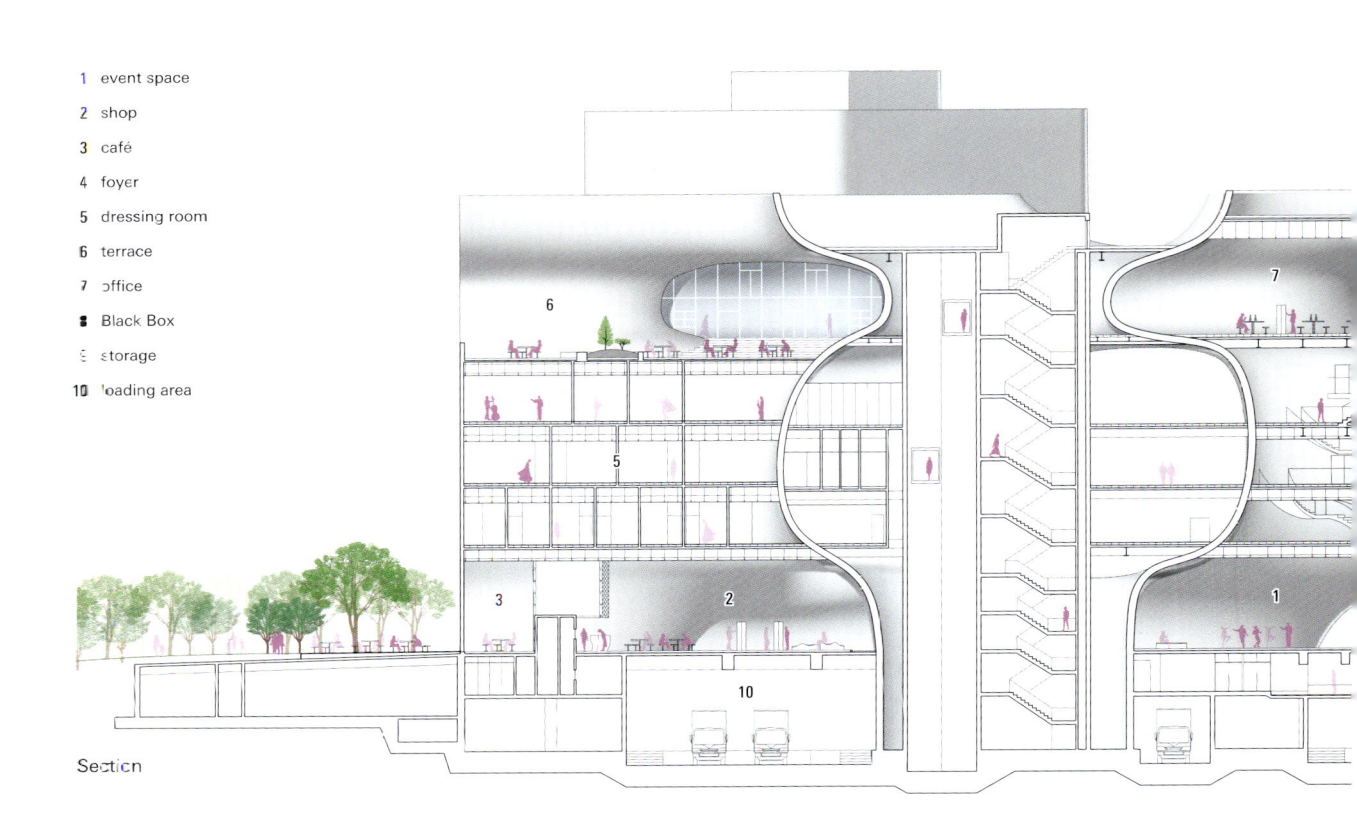

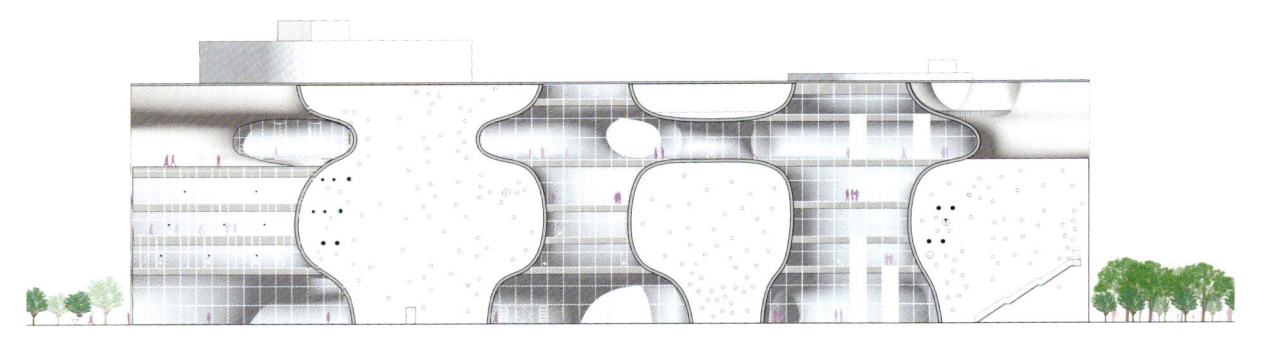

1 event space
2 shop
3 café
4 foyer
5 dressing room
6 terrace
7 office
8 Black Box
9 storage
10 loading area

Section

North-west elevation

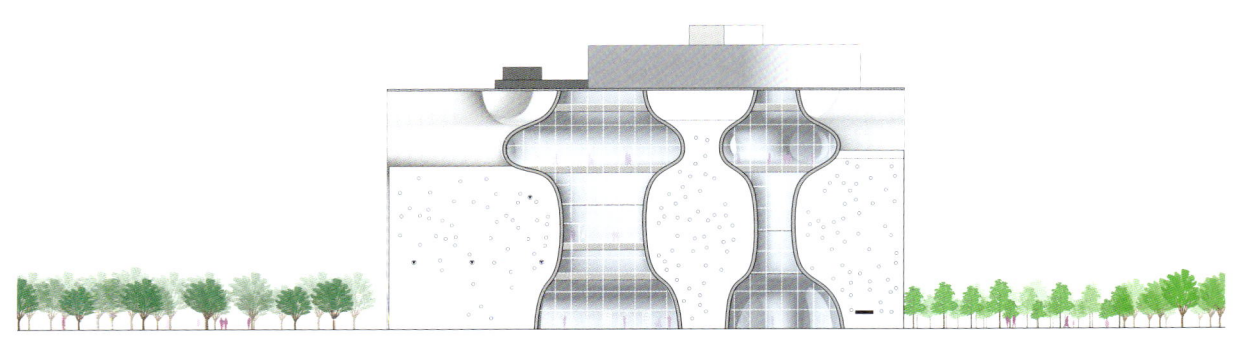

South-west elevation

352

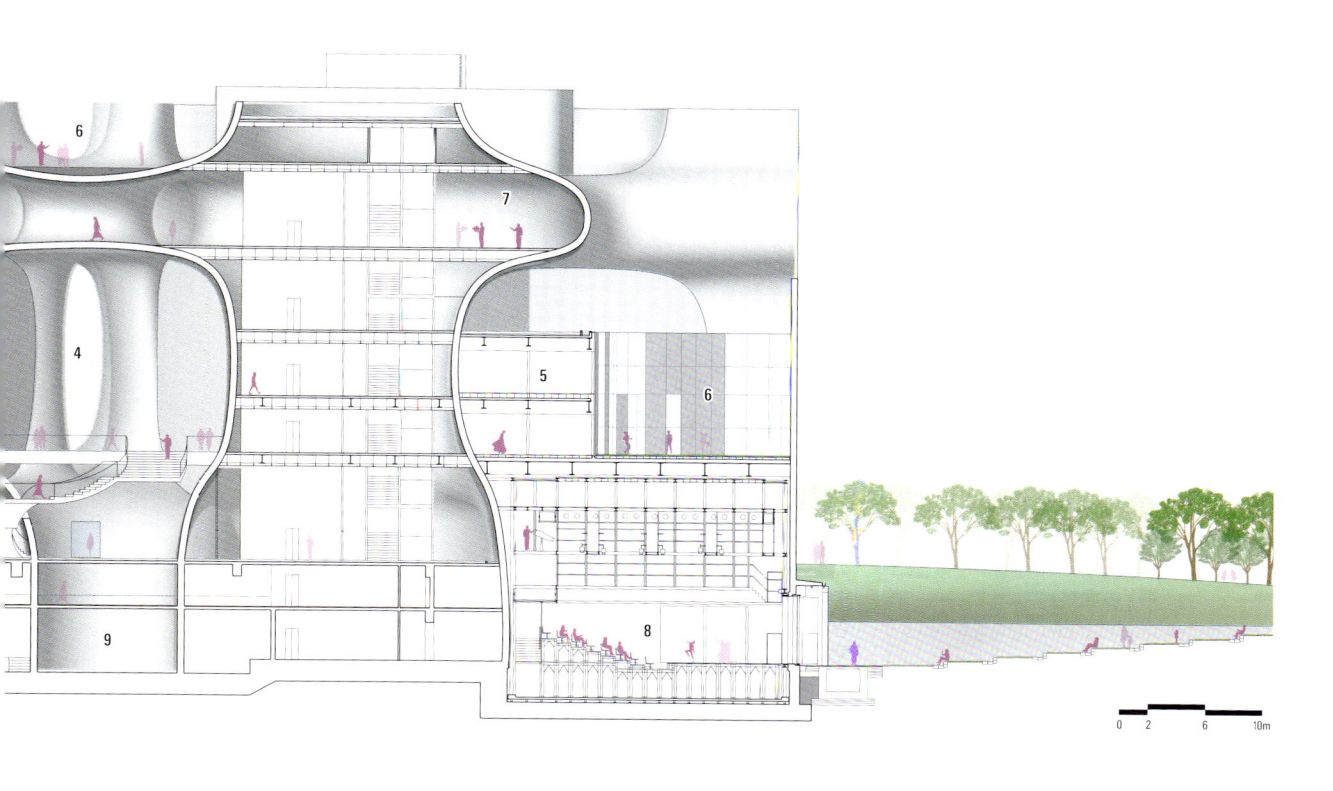

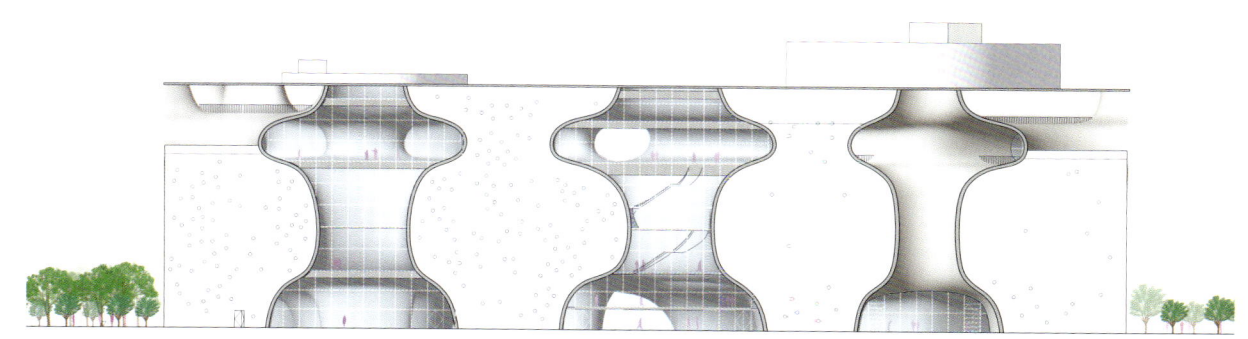

South-east elevation

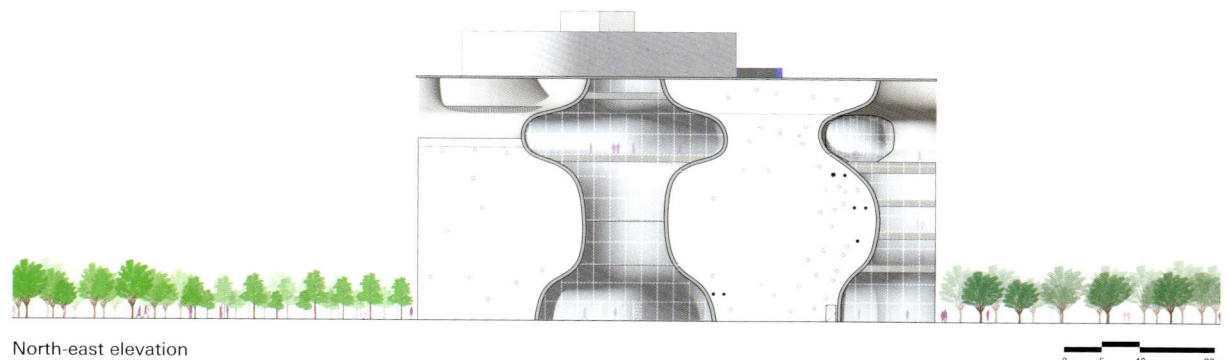

North-east elevation

353

公園の延長としての1Fエントランスホール
The first-floor entrance hall functions as an extension of the park.

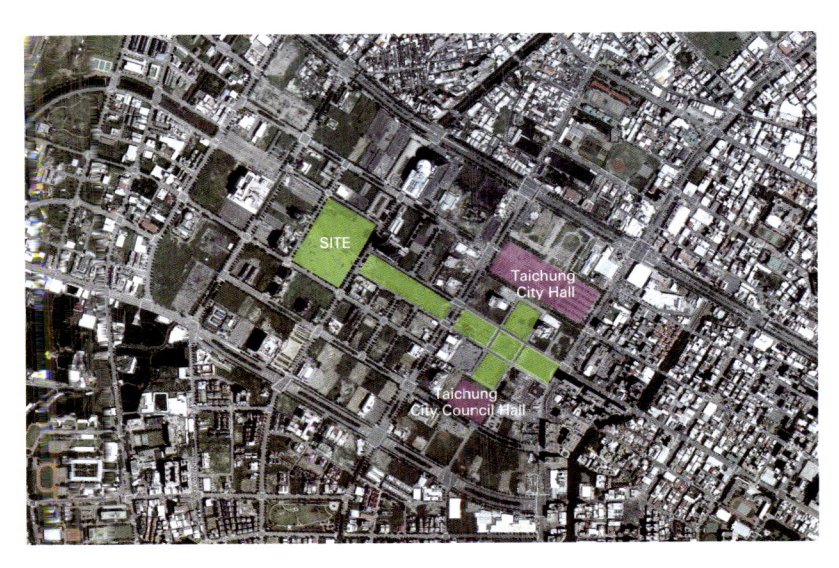

Site plan

1  main entrance
2  lobby
3  information counter
4  event space
5  coffee / snack shop
6  office
7  Grand Theater
8  foyer
9  Playhouse
10 terrace
11 green room
12 VIP room
13 restaurant
14 kitchen
15 assembly workshop
16 loading area
17 Black Box
18 rehearsal room
19 machine room
20 machine pit
21 studio

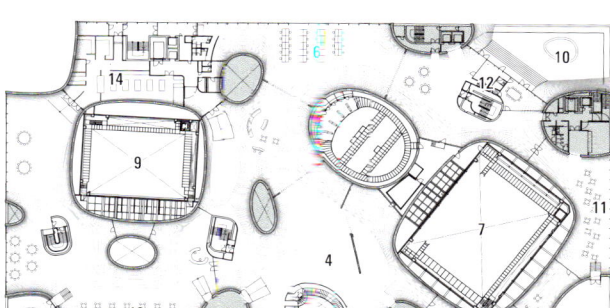

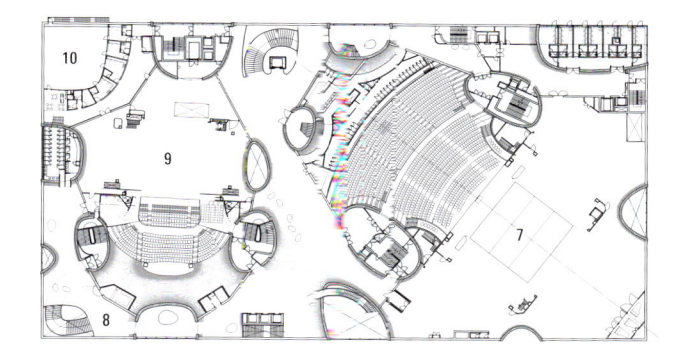

6F plan

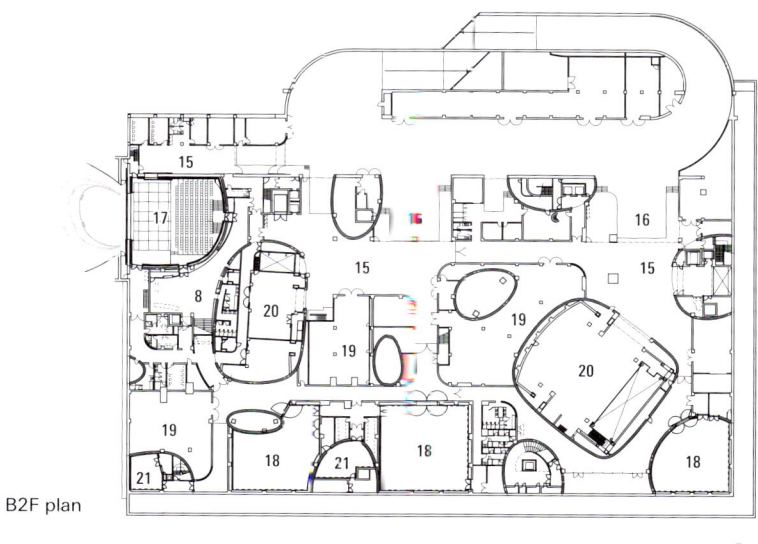

5F plan

2F plan

B2F plan

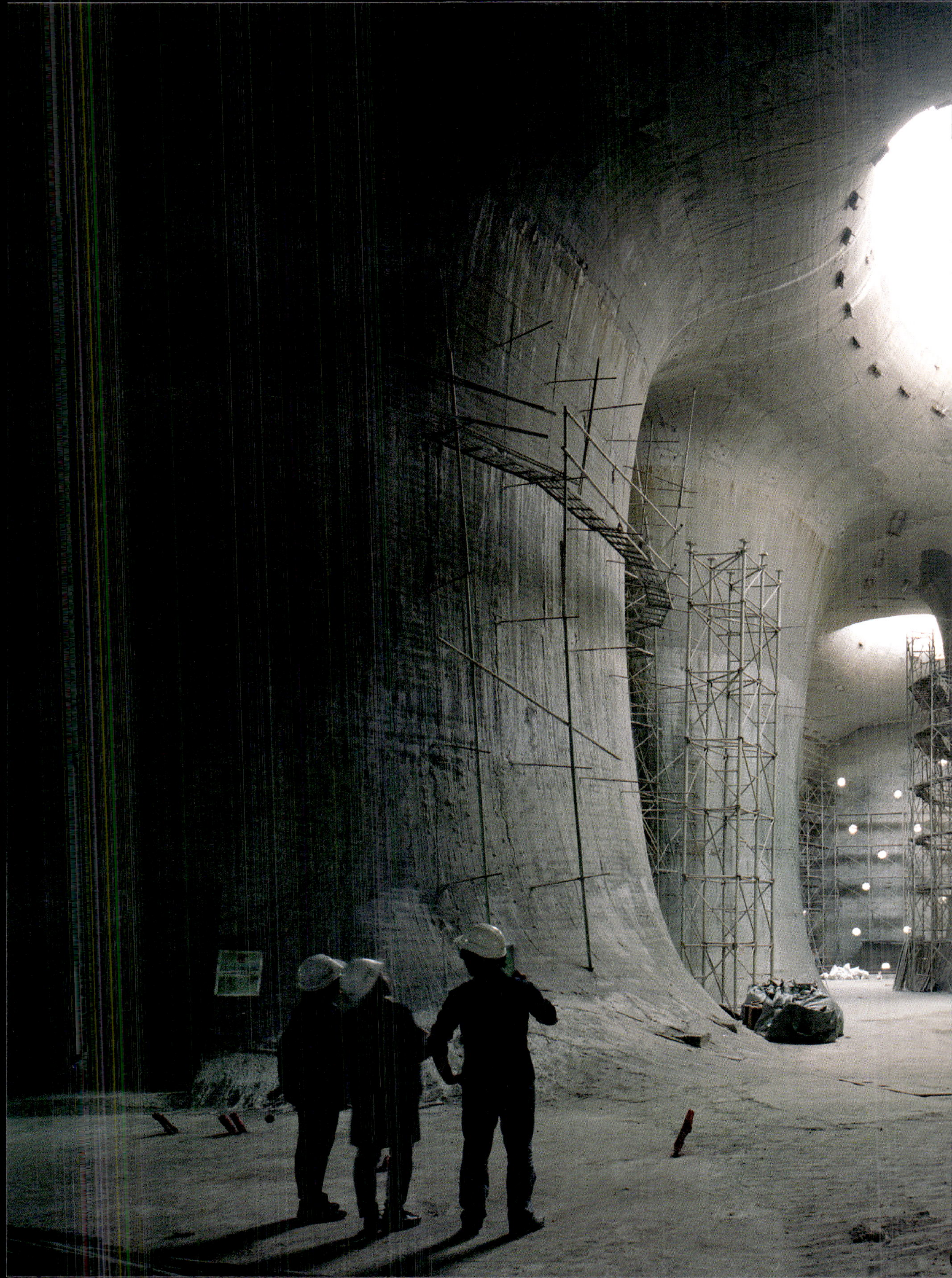

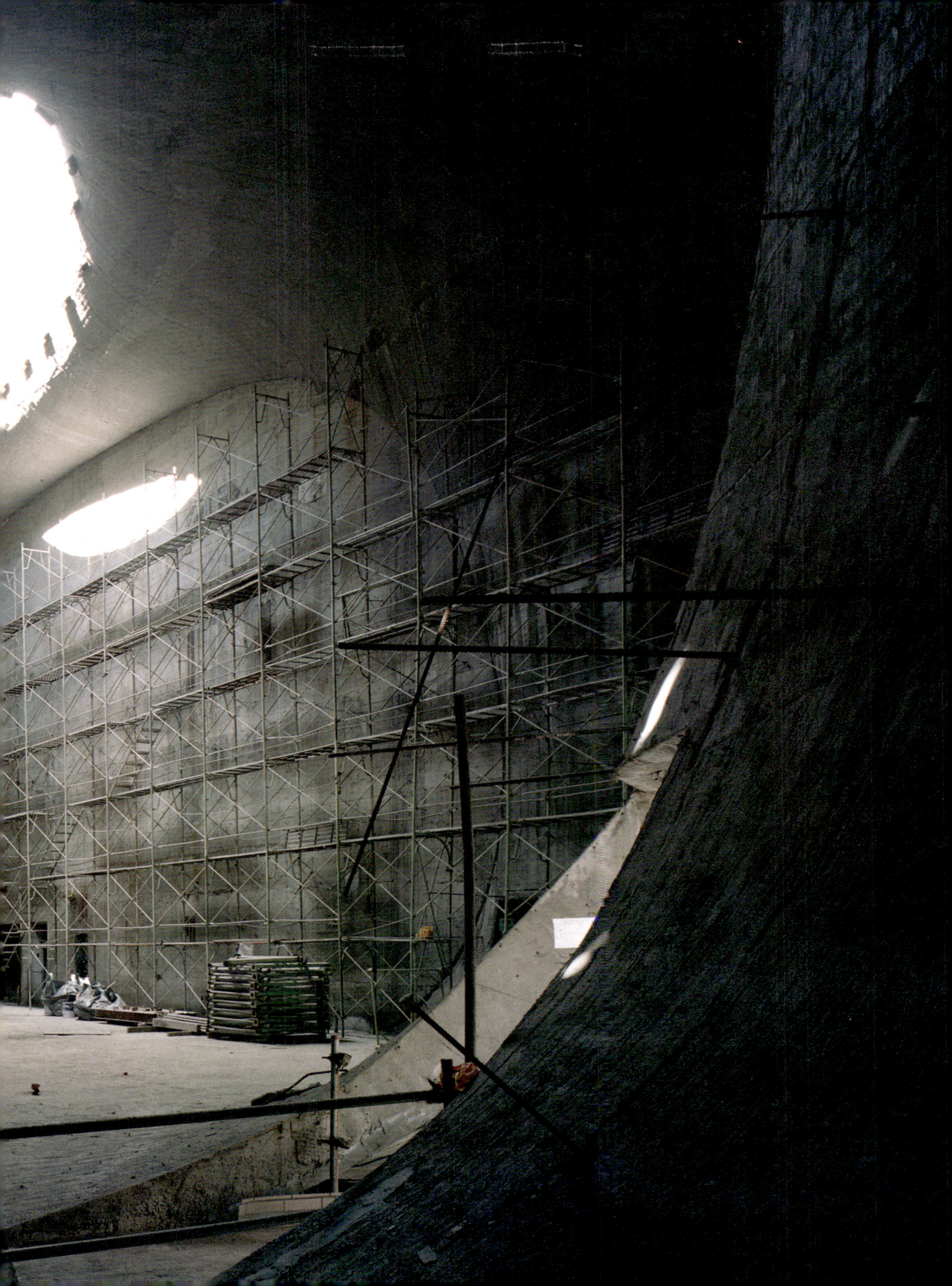

ルーフガーデン配筋
The reinforcement of the roof garden.

トラスウォール配筋図
Detail of truss-wall reinforcement.

カテノイドの構成ユニット
Catenoid construction unit.

1 Unit of Truss Walls

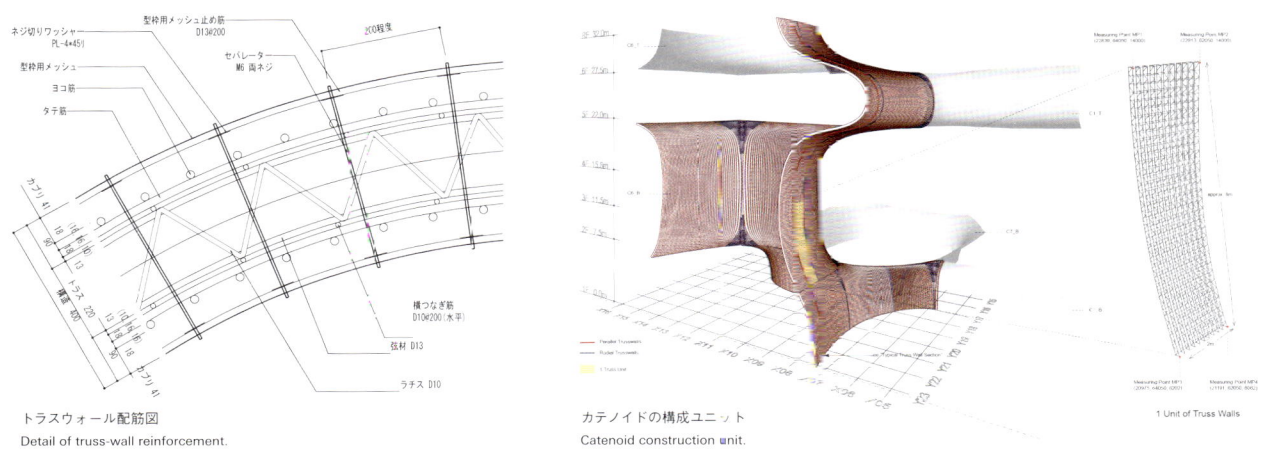

床に描かれた図に従って2次元トラスをつくる。トラスウォールの組立て
Creating a two-dimensional truss according to markings drawn on the floor and assembling the truss wall.

2次元トラスを水平に結んで3次元曲面のトラスをつくる
Creating a three-dimensional curved truss by connecting two-dimensional trusses horizontally.

完成したトラスユニット
Completed truss unit.

現場に設置され固定されている
Attaching and fixing the unit on the construction site.

構造体はトラスウォール工法と呼ばれるコンクリート造。現場内の工場で3次元トラスを組み上げ、現場で相互に結ばれた後、両サイドにメッシュを張ってコンクリートが流される。

The structure is made out of concrete using the truss-wall construction method. Assembling three-dimensional trusses in the on-site factory. After connecting them on site, a mesh is stretched across both sides and concrete is poured in.

工場で仮組立され、トラスウォールが製作される
After temporarily assembling them in the factory, the truss walls are assembled.

メッシュ型枠が張られ、コンクリートが打設される
A mesh mold is attached, and concrete is poured inside.

メッシュ型枠が外され、完成する
After the mesh mold is removed, the unit is complete.

洞窟のような空間内を光と音が伝播し、五感に訴える
Light and sound is diffused in various places in the cave-like space, appealing to the user's five senses.

(上) ブラックボックスのステージの背後が開くと野外劇場と連結する
(中) 1階ロビーイメージ
(左下) 劇場部分断面図
(右下) 3つの劇場の構成

(Above) When the back of the stage in Black Box is opened, it leads directly to the outdoor amphitheatre.
(Middle) Image of the first-floor lobby.
(Below left) Section diagram of the theatre area.
(Below right) Structure of the three theatres.

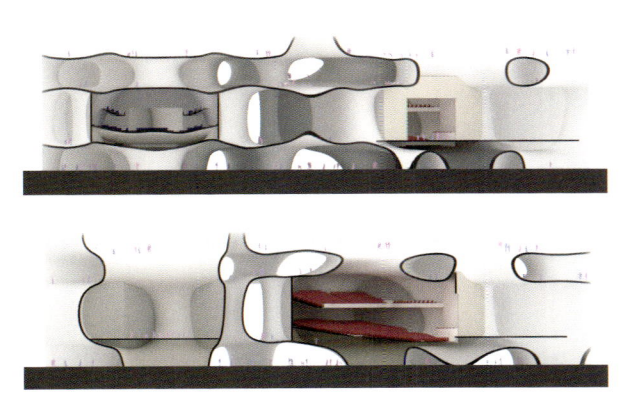

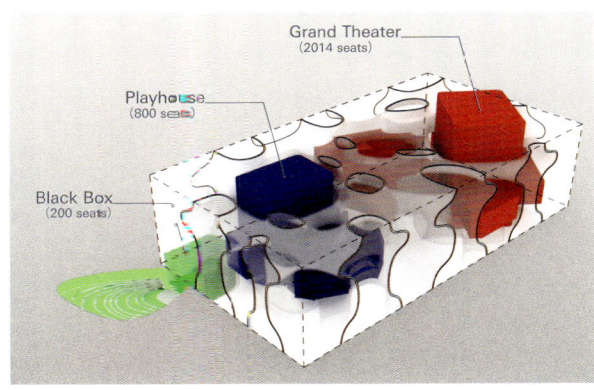

363

| | | |
|---|---|---|
| 1  event space | 5  rear stage | 8  rehearsal room |
| 2  shop | 6  terrace | 9  assembly workshop |
| 3  foyer | 7  office | 10  parking |
| 4  main stage | | |

Section (Drawing of Grand Theater)

2014席を有するグランドシアター、800席を有するプレイハウス。それらのホワイエは、アーティストの壁画で彩られる。

The Grand Theater contains 2,014 seats, and the Playhouse 800. The foyers of both theaters are decorated with murals by artists.

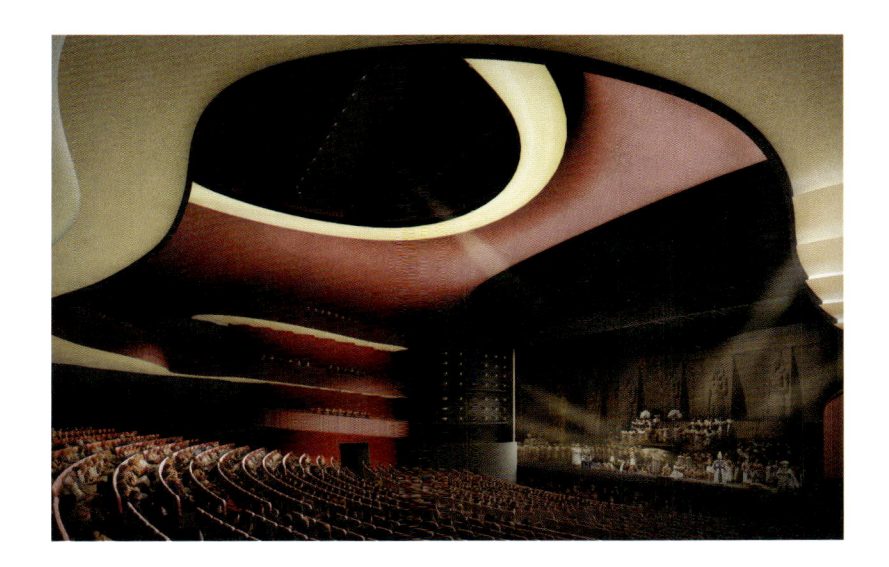

（上）グランドシアターのイメージ
（中）ホワイエ施工風景
（下）ホワイエのイメージ

(Above) Image of Grand Theater.
(Middle) Foyer in construction.
(Below) Image of foyer

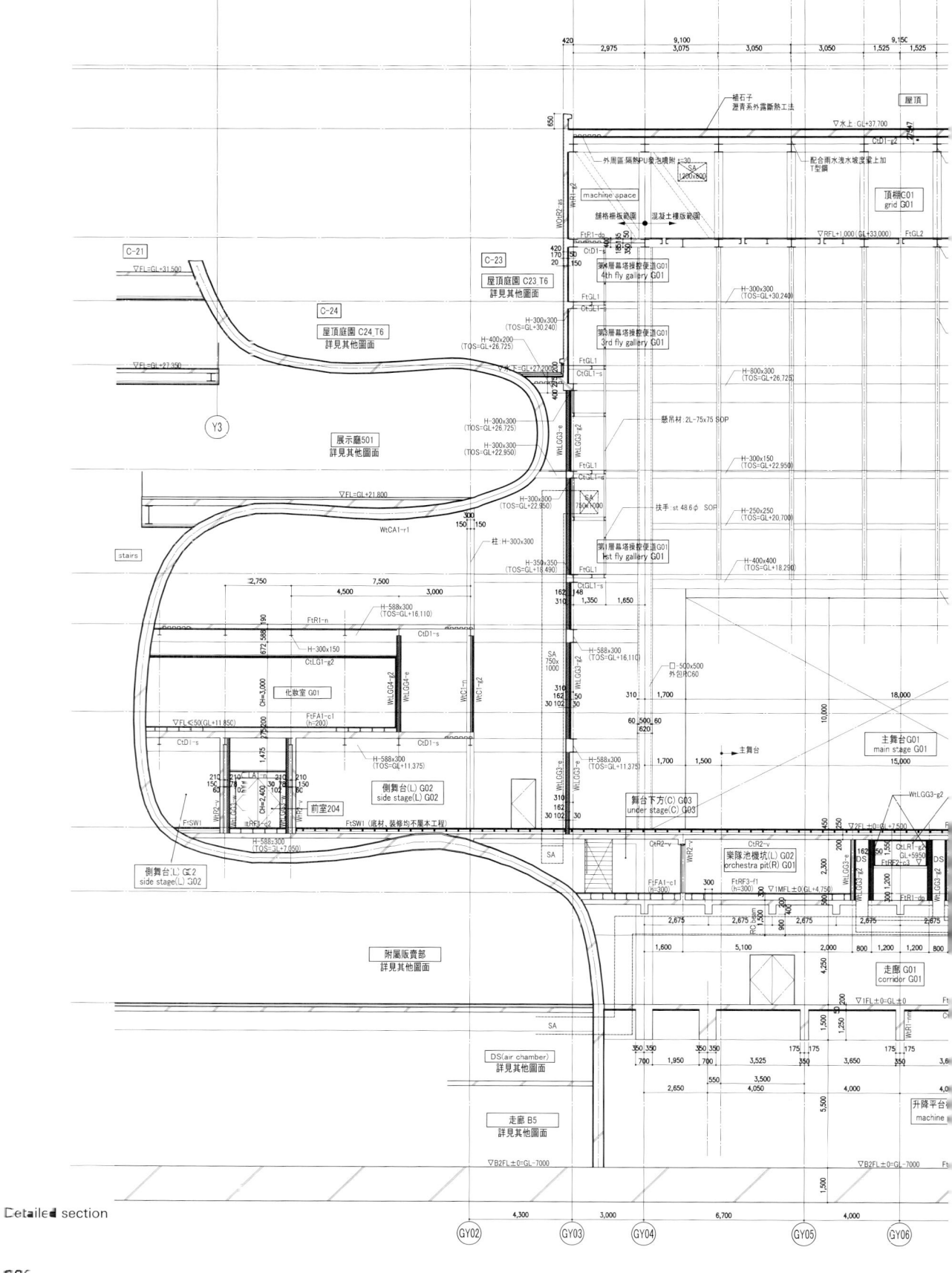

Detailed section

KEY PLAN 1:1000

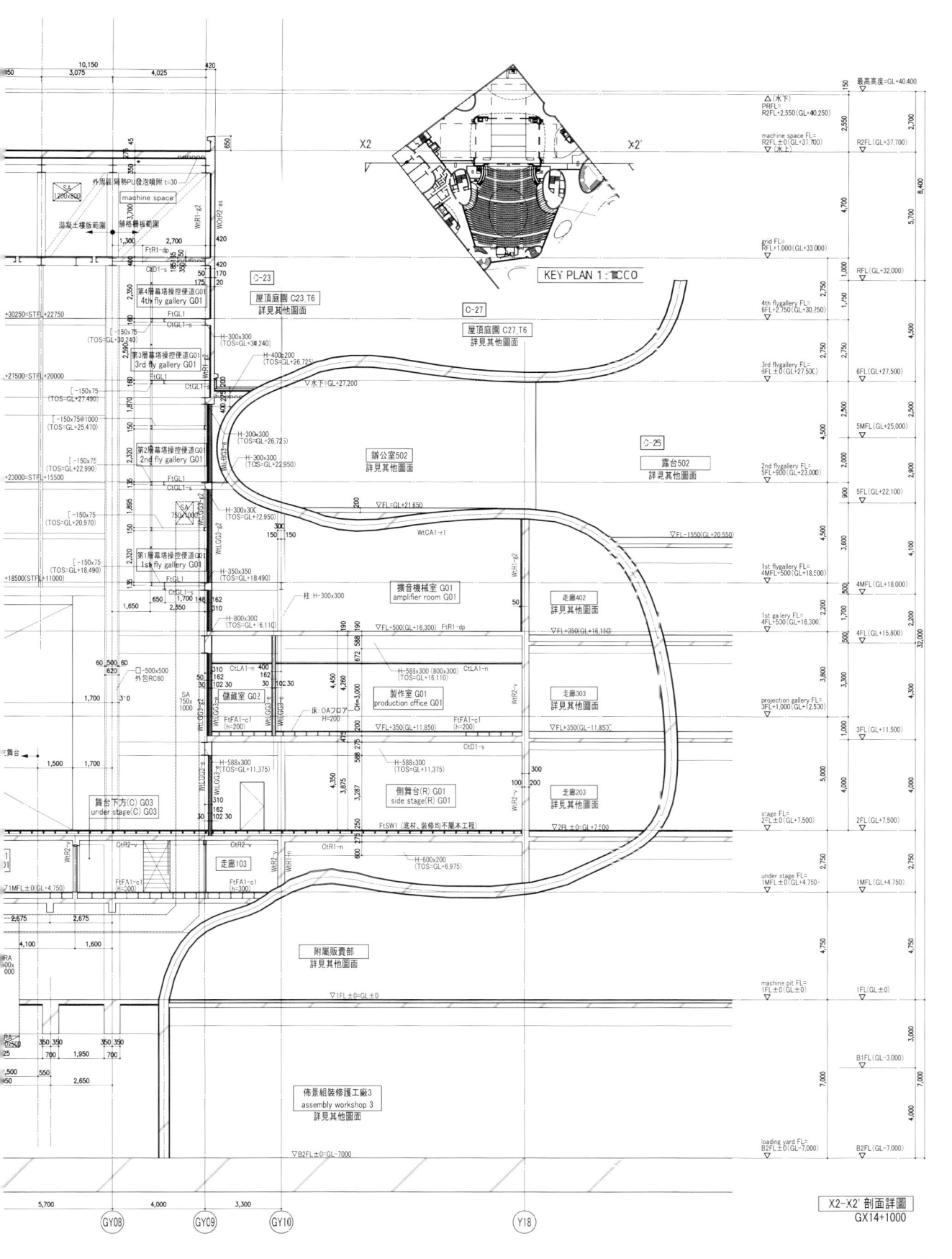

X2-X2' 剖面詳圖
GX14+1000

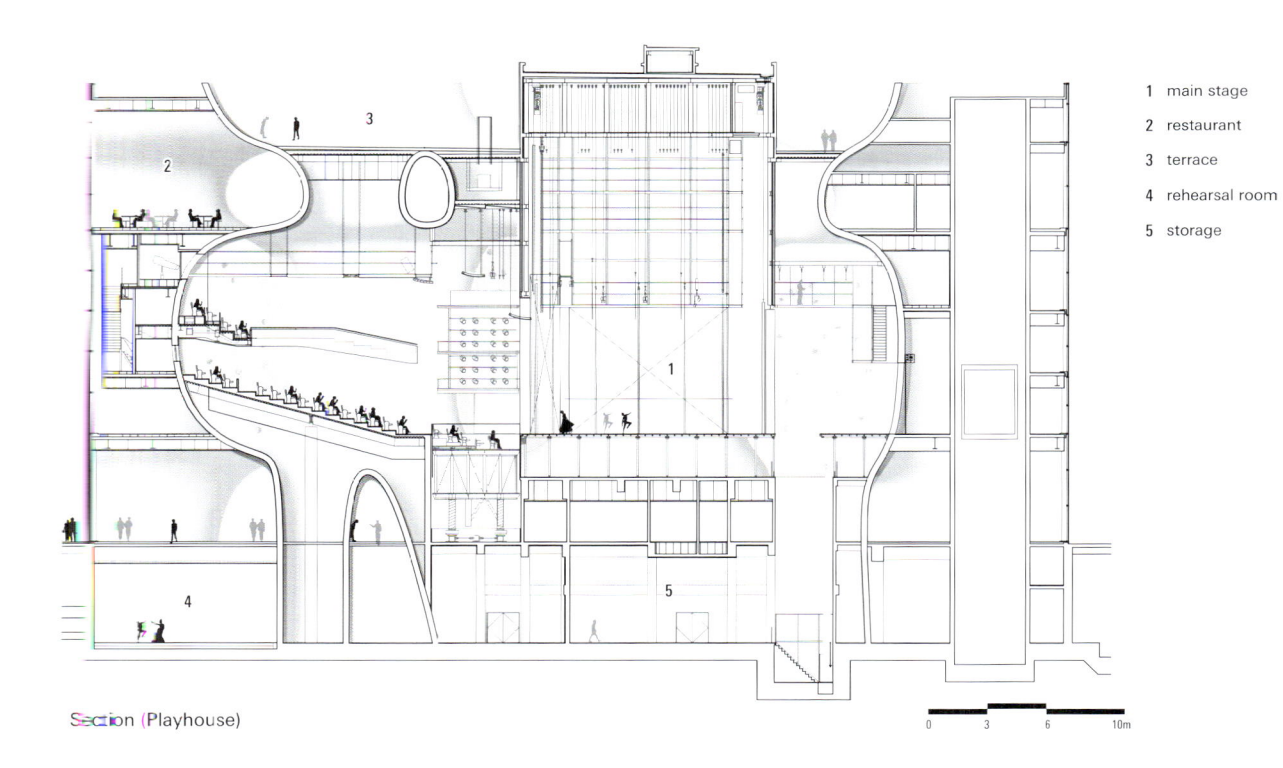

Section (Playhouse)

1 main stage
2 restaurant
3 terrace
4 rehearsal room
5 storage

プレイハウスのイメージ
Image of Playhouse.

## PLUG-IN

PLUG(Wall)

CATENOID

PLUG(Floor)

PLUG(Floor)

PLUG(Wall)

PLUG(Facade)

Floor level

Floor level +250UP

Floor level +500UP

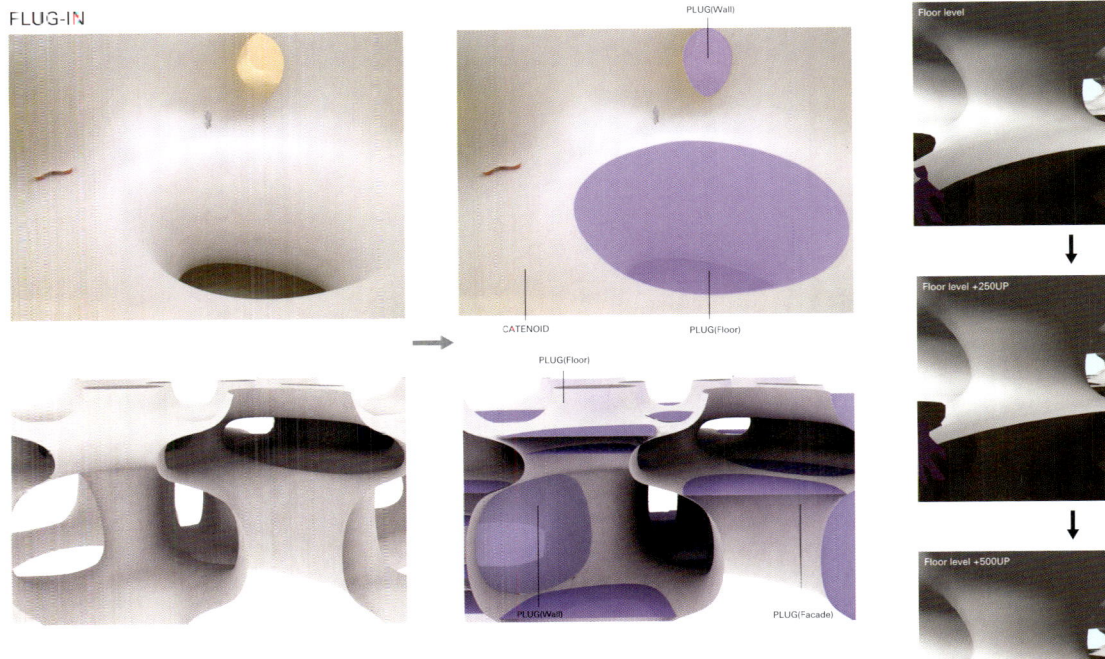

「プラグイン」の概念。穴に蓋をするように、水平・垂直な面を「プラグイン」することで、フロア・壁・ファサードが形成される。

The "Plug-In" concept is similar to covering a hole, which is possible to create floors, walls, and facades by plugging in vertical and horizontal surfaces.

洞窟状の空間によって切り取られた都市の風景
Urban landscape cropped by the cave-like space.

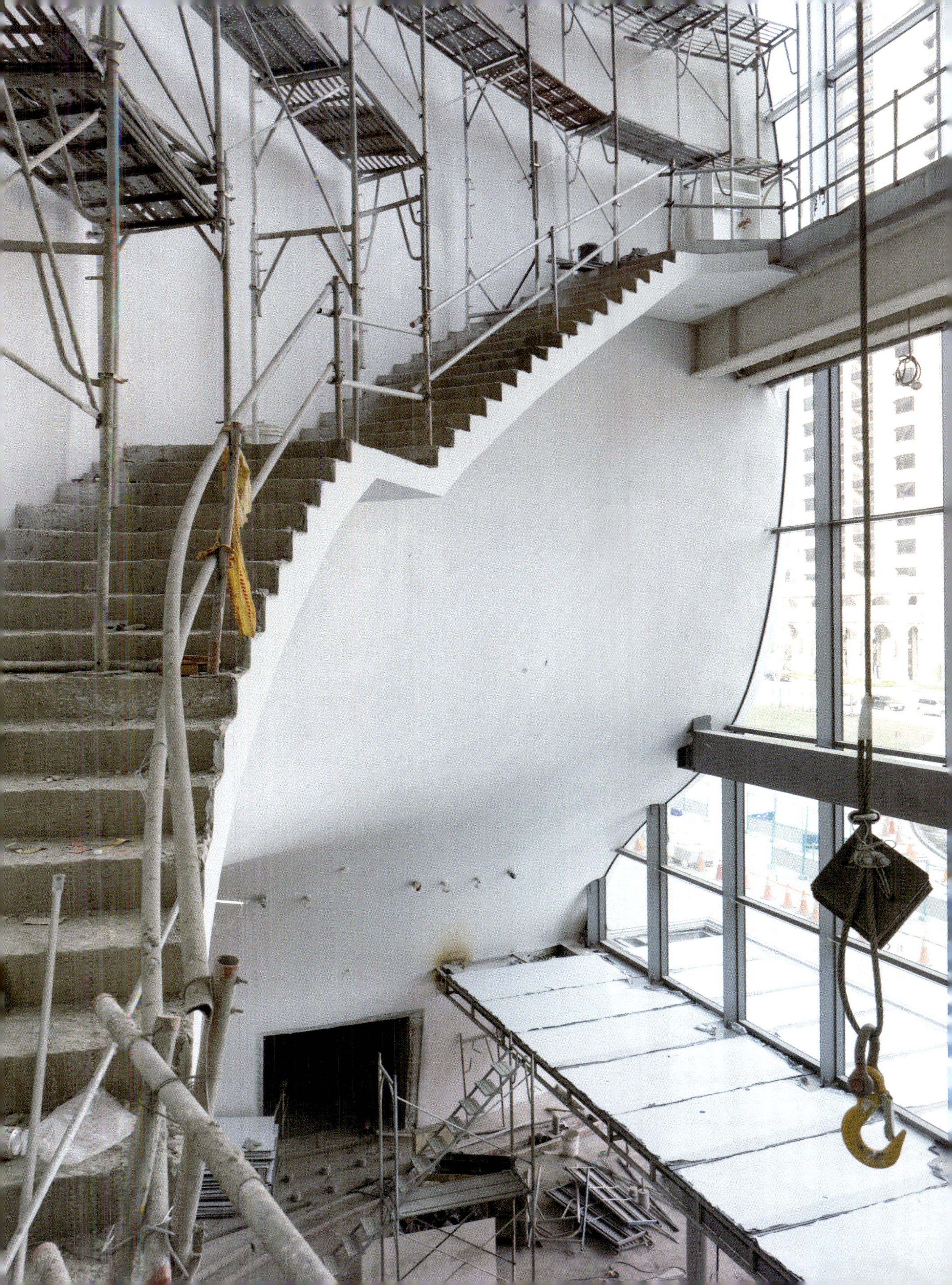

波打つルーフガーデン
The undulating roof garden.

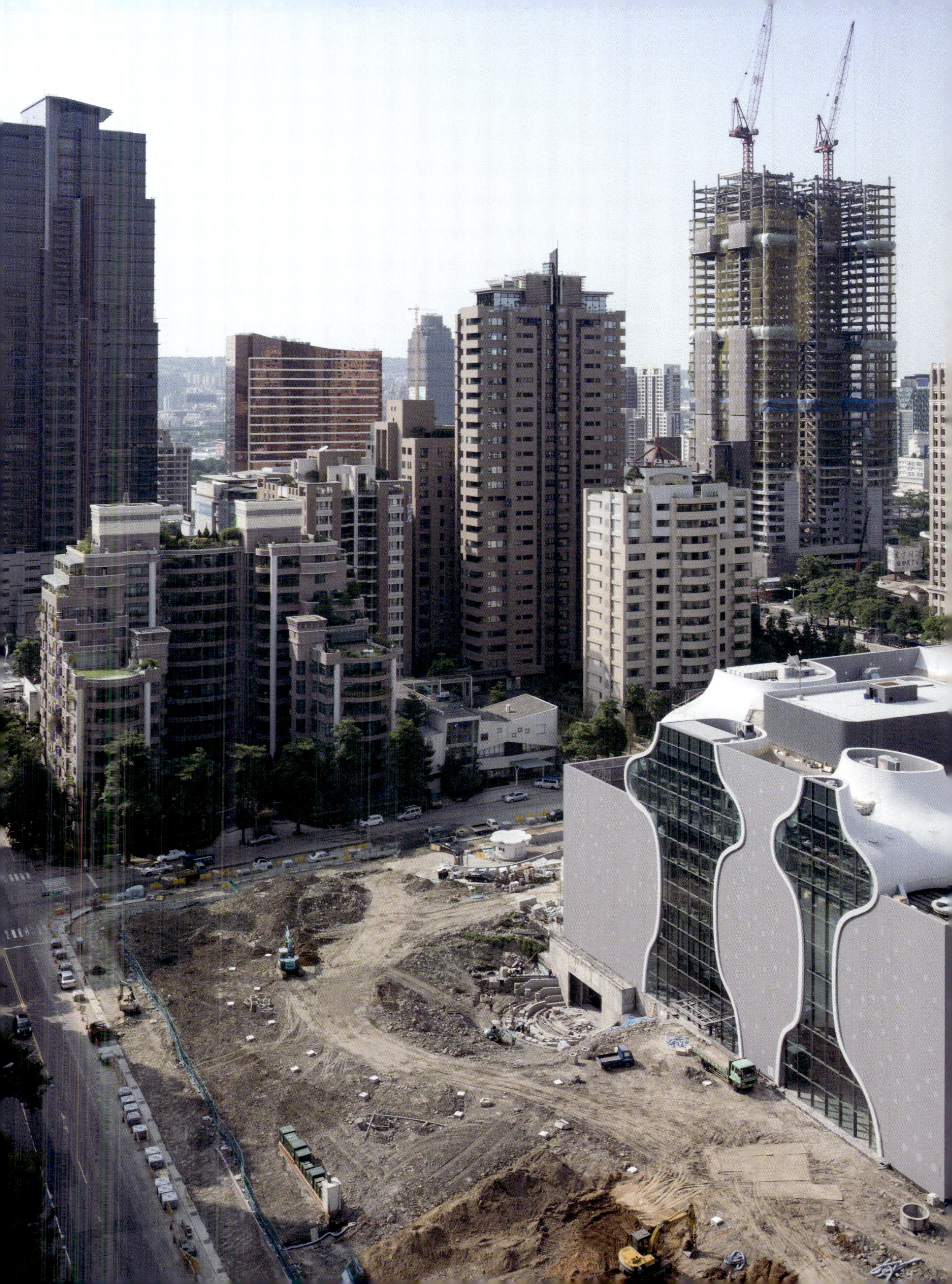

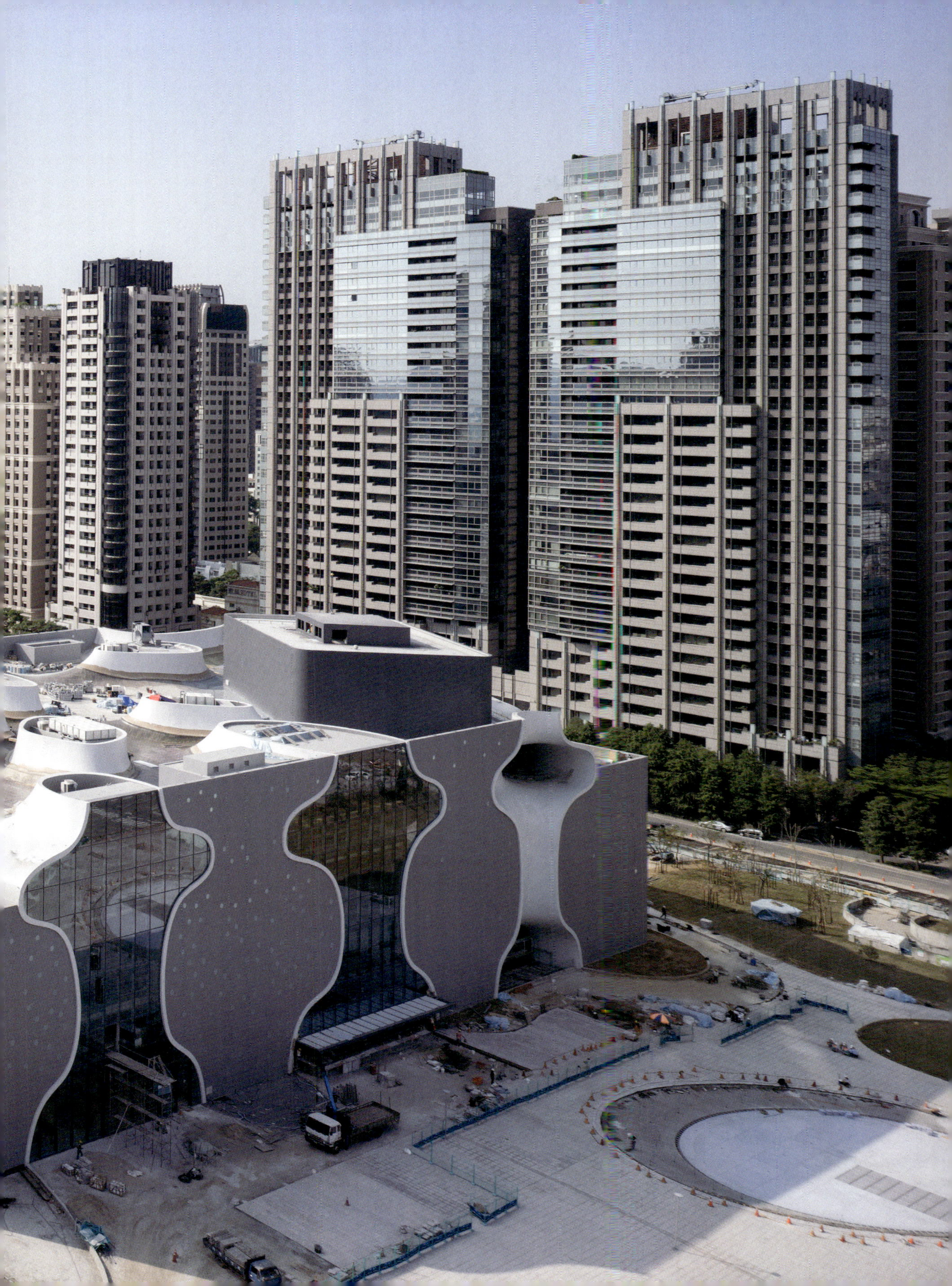

# Data on Works
## 作品データ

### 作品名
### Name of Work

1. 所在地／Location
2. 設計期間／Design period
3. 工事期間／Construction period
4. 会期／Term
5. 主要用途／Principal use
6. 共同設計／Joint design
7. 構造設計／Structural engineer
8. 設備設計／Facility engineer
9. その他設計・計画／〔外構・音響・照明・劇場・家具・オブジェ〕Other design / plans (exterior, acoustic, lighting, theatre, furniture, art objects, etc.)
10. 施工／Constructor
11. 設計、制作協力／Design / production assistance
12. 構造／Structure
13. 規模／Scale
14. 敷地面積／Site area
15. 建築面積／Building area
16. 延床面積／Total floor area

---

## ブルージュ・パヴィリオン
### Brugge Pavilion

1. ベルギー、ブルージュ／Bruges, Belgium
2. 2000.04-2001.10
3. 2001.11-2002.02
5. パヴィリオン／Pavilion
7. オーク構造設計／Structural Design Office Oak
12. アルミニウム／Aluminum Structure
13. 地上1階／1 story
15. 96.60㎡
16. 96.60㎡

## サーペンタイン・ギャラリー・パヴィリオン 2002
### Serpentine Gallery Pavilion 2002

1. イギリス、ロンドン／London, UK
2. 2002.01-2002.06
3. 2002.04-2002.07
4. 2002.07-2002.09
5. パヴィリオン／Pavilion
6. Cecil Balmond (Arup)
7. Arup
8. Arup
9. Ross Lovegrove（家具）
10. Sir Robert McAlpine
12. 鉄骨造／Steel Frame
13. 地上1階／1 story
15. 309.76㎡
16. 309.76㎡

## まつもと市民芸術館／「フィガロの結婚」舞台装置
### Matsumoto Performing Arts Centre / "LE NOZZE DI FIGARO" STAGE SET

1. 長野県松本市／Matsumoto, Nagano, Japan
2. 2001.11-2002.10
3. 2002.11-2004.03
5. 劇場／Theatre
7. 佐々木睦朗構造計画研究所／Sasaki Structural Consultants
8. 環境エンジニアリング／Kankyo Engineering
9. 石川幹子＋東京ランドスケープ研究所（外構）、永田音響設計（音響）、LIGHTDESIGN（照明）、小栗哲家（劇場舞台）、服部基（劇場照明）、市来邦比古（劇場音響）、建築都市ワークショップ＋マツダオフィス（サイン）／Mikiko Ishikawa + Tokyo Landscape Architects, Nagata Acoustics, LIGHTDESIGN, Tetsuya Oguri, Motoi Hattori, Kunihiko Ichiki, Workshop for architecture and urbanism + Matzda office
10. 竹中・戸田・松本土建JV／Takenaka Toda Matsumoto-doken JV
12. 鉄骨鉄筋コンクリート造、鉄筋コンクリート造、鉄骨造／Steel Reinforced Concrete, Reinforced Concrete, Steel Frame
13. 地上7階、地下2階／7 stories, 2 basements
14. 9,142.50㎡
15. 7,080.02㎡
16. 19,184.38㎡

## TOD'S 表参道ビル
### TOD'S Omotesando Building

1. 東京都渋谷区／Shibuya, Tokyo, Japan
2. 2002.04-2003.05
3. 2003.06-2004.11
5. 店舗、事務所／Shop, Office
7. オーク構造設計／Structural Design Office Oak
8. イーエスアソシエーツ／ES Associates
9. MODAR s.r.l.（家具）、GARDE U・S・P（家具什器）
10. 竹中工務店／Takenaka Corporation
12. 鉄筋コンクリート造、一部鉄骨造／Reinforced Concrete, Steel (partially)
13. 地上7階、地下1階／7 stories, 1 basement
14. 516.23㎡
15. 401.55㎡
16. 2,548.84㎡

## 福岡アイランドシティ中央公園 中核施設　ぐりんぐりん
### Island City Central Park "GRIN GRIN"

1. 福岡県福岡市／Fukuoka, Fukuoka, Japan
2. 2002.10-2003.11
3. 2004.03-2005.04
5. 温室／Exhibition Greenhouse
7. 佐々木睦朗構造計画研究所／Sasaki Structural Consultants
8. 環境エンジニアリング／Kankyo Engineering
9. 総合設計研究所（外構）、LPA（照明）／Sohgoh Landscape Planning Office, Lighting Planners Associates
10. 竹中・高松組JV／Takenaka Takamatsu JV
12. 鉄筋コンクリート造、一部鉄骨造／Reinforced Concrete, Steel (partially)
13. 地上1階／1 story
14. 129,170.00㎡
15. 5,162.07㎡
16. 5,033.47㎡

## 瞑想の森 市営斎場
Meiso no Mori Municipal Funeral Hall

1. 岐阜県各務原市／Kakamigahara, Gifu, Japan
2. 2004.05-2005.03
3. 2005.04-2006.05
5. 火葬場／Crematorium
7. 佐々木睦朗構造計画研究所／Sasaki Structural Consultants
8. 環境エンジニアリング／Kankyo Engineering
9. 慶應義塾大学教授　石川幹子（外構）、LIGHTDESIGN（照明）、安宅防災設計（防災）／Mikiko Ishikawa (Professor of Keio University), LIGHTDESIGN, Ataka Fire Safety Design Office
10. 戸田・市川・天龍JV／Toda Ichikawa Tenryu JV
12. 鉄筋コンクリート造、一部鉄骨造／Reinforced Concrete, Steel (partially)
13. 地上2階／2 stories
14. 6,695.97㎡
15. 2,269.66㎡
16. 2,264.57㎡

## 多摩美術大学図書館（八王子キャンパス）
Tama Art University Library (Hachioji campus)

1. 東京都八王子市／Hachioji, Tokyo, Japan
2. 2004.04-2005.10
3. 2005.11-2007.02
5. 図書館／Library
6. 鹿島建設／Kajima Design
7. 佐々木睦朗構造計画研究所、鹿島建設／Sasaki Structural Consultants, Kajima Design
8. 鹿島建設／Kajima Design
9. 建築都市ワークショップ（インタラクションデザイン）、藤江和子アトリエ（家具）、多摩美術大学八王子キャンパス設計室（キャンパスデザイン）、布（安東陽子）（カーテンデザイン）／Workshop for Architecture and Urbanism, Fujie Kazuko Atelier, Tama Art University Campus Project Team, Nuno Corporation (Yoko Ando)
10. 鹿島建設／Kajima Corporation
12. 鉄骨鉄筋コンクリート造、一部鉄筋コンクリート造／Steel Reinforced Concrete, Reinforced Concrete (partially)
13. 地上2階、地下1階／2 stories, 1 basement
14. 159,184.87㎡
15. 2,224.59㎡
16. 5,639.46㎡

## 座・高円寺
ZA-KOENJI Public Theatre

1. 東京都杉並区／Suginami, Tokyo, Japan
2. 2005.06-2006.08
3. 2006.12-2008.11
5. 劇場／Theatre
7. 佐々木睦朗構造計画研究所／Sasaki Structural Consultants
8. 環境エンジニアリング／Kankyo Engineering
9. 永田音響設計（音響）、LIGHTDESIGN（照明）、眞野純（劇場技術）、安宅防災設計（防災）、女子美術大学（佐藤真澄）（サイン）、布（安東陽子）（ファブリックデザイン）／Nagata Acoustics, LIGHTDESIGN, Jun Mano, Ataka Fire Safety Design Office, Joshibi University of Art and Design (Masumi Sato), Nuno Corporation (Yoko Ando)
10. 大成建設／Taisei Corporation
12. 鉄骨造、鉄筋コンクリート造／Steel Frame, Reinforced Concrete
13. 地上3階、地下3階／3 stories, 3 basements
14. 1,649.26㎡
15. 1,107.86㎡
16. 4,977.74㎡

## 2009高雄ワールドゲームズメインスタジアム
The Main Stadium for the World Games 2009 in Kaohsiung

1. 台湾、高雄／Kaohsiung, Taiwan
2. 2006.01-2007.03
3. 2006.09-2009.01
5. 競技場、公園／Stadium, Park
6. 竹中工務店、劉培森建築師事務所／Takenaka Corporation, Ricky Liu & Associates Architects+Planners
7. 竹中工務店、信業工程顧問有限公司／Takenaka Corporation, HSIN-YEH Engineering Consultants
8. 竹中工務店、泰迪工程顧問有限公司、玉堡冷凍空調工業技師事務所／Takenaka Corporation, Teddy & Associates Engineering Consultants, C.C.LEE & Associates Hvacr Consulting Engineers
9. 竹中工務店（外構・内装・防災）、中冶環境造形顧問有限公司（外構）、劉培森建築師事務所（内装）、台湾建築與都市防災顧問有限公司（防災）、多田脩二構造設計事務所（サインタワー）、信業工程顧問有限公司（サインタワー）、利道科技工程有限公司（3Dモデル）／Takenaka Corporation, Laboratory for Environment & Form, Ricky Liu & Associates Architects+Planners, Taiwan Fire Safety Consulting, Shutada Structural Consultant, HSIN-YEH Engineering Consultants, Lead Dao Technology and Engineering
10. 互助營造股份有限公司／Fu Tsu Construction
12. 鉄骨造、鉄筋コンクリート造／Steel Frame, Reinforced Concrete
13. 地上3階、地下2階／3 stories, 2 basements
14. 189,012.00㎡
15. 25,553.46㎡
16. 98,759.31㎡

## トーレス・ポルタ・フィラ
TORRES PORTA FIRA

1. スペイン、バルセロナ／Barcelona, Spain
2. 2004.06-2006.07
3. 2006.04-2010.01
5. ホテル、宴会場、貸オフィス、貸スペース／Hotel, Banquet Hall, Rental Offices, Retail Space
6. Fermín Vázquez - B720 arquitectos
7. IDOM Ingenieria Y Sistema
8. GRUPO JG
9. BET FIGUERAS（外構）、ARTEC（照明）、Identity design（サイン）
10. FCC Construccion
12. 鉄筋コンクリート造／Reinforced Concrete
13. （ホテル棟）塔屋1階、地上26階、地下2階／(Hotel) 1 penthouse, 26 stories, 2 basements
　（オフィス棟）塔屋1階、地上24階、地下3階／(Office) 1 penthouse, 24 stories, 3 basements
14. (Hotel) 5,755.55㎡　(Office) 4,801.55㎡
15. (Hotel) 4,810.08㎡　(Office) 4,049.73㎡
16. (Hotel) 34,688.10㎡　(Office) 45,419.59㎡

## バルセロナ見本市・グランビア会場拡張計画
Extension for the Fair of Barcelona Gran Via Venue

1. スペイン、バルセロナ／Barcelona, Spain
2. 2003.03-
3. 2003.10-
5. 見本市、コンベンションホール、オフィス、レストラン／Fair, Convention, Office, Restaurant
6. FIRA2000, IDOM Ingenieria Y Sistema
7. SAPS (Sasaki, and Partners), IDOM Ingenieria Y Sistema

8 環境エンジニアリング、IDOM Ingenieria Y Sistema／
Kankyo Engineering, IDOM Ingenieria Y Sistema

9 I.CON.（監理）、PAVLOV（サイン）、Identity Design, 三L（サイン）、J/T ARDÈVOL I ASSOCIATS（技術コンサルタント）／

10 （エントランスホール、パビリオン1）DRAGADOS、（セントラルアクシス）TIFERCA、（パビリオン8、セントラルアクシス）FCC CONSTRUCCION, S.A.+COMSA

12 鉄骨造、鉄骨鉄筋コンクリート造、鉄筋コンクリート造／
Steel Frame, Steel Reinforced Concrete, Reinforced Concrete

13 地上2階／2 stories

14 450,000㎡

15 60,800㎡（全施設完成後108,200㎡）

16 104,800㎡（全施設完成後185,300㎡）

※ The Fair for the Barcelona Gran Via Venue is operated by FAIR OF BARCELONA.

## 今治市伊東豊雄建築ミュージアム
Toyo Ito Museum of Architecture, Imabari

1 愛媛県今治市／Imabari, Ehime, Japan
16 6,295.06㎡
□ スティールハット／
Steel Hut – Exhibition Building
2 2008.07-2009.08
3 2010.08-2011.03
5 美術館／Museum
7 佐々木睦朗構造計画研究所／
Sasaki Structural Consultants
8 イーエスアソシエーツ、大瀧設備事務所／
ES Associates, Ohtaki E & M Consulting Office
9 廣村デザイン事務所（サイン）、イノウエインダストリィズ（家具）／
Hiromura Design Office, Inoue Industries
10 大成建設／Taisei Corporation
12 鉄骨造、一部鉄筋コンクリート造／
Steel Frame, Reinforced Concrete (partially)
13 地上2階／2 stories
14 194.42㎡
15 168.03㎡
□ シルバーハット／
Silver Hut – Archive/Workshop Building
(Rebuilding Toyo Ito's own house)
2 2009.04-2010.08
3 2010.09-2011.05
5 美術館／Museum
7 O.F.S.事務所／O.R.S. office
8 イーエスアソシエーツ、大瀧設備事務所／
ES Associates, Ohtaki E & M Consulting Office
9 廣村デザイン事務所（サイン）、イノウエインダストリィズ（家具）／
Hiromura Design Office, Inoue Industries
10 大成建設／Taisei Corporation
12 鉄筋コンクリート造、一部鉄骨造／
Reinforced Concrete, Steel (partially)
13 地上2階／2 stories
15 168.32㎡
16 188.32㎡

## 今治市岩田健母と子のミュージアム
Ken Iwata Mother and Child Museum, Imabari City

1 愛媛県今治市／Imabari, Ehime, Japan
2 2009.09-2010.03
3 2010.10-2011.05
5 美術館／Museum
7 佐々木睦朗構造計画研究所／
Sasaki Structural Consultants
8 イーエスアソシエーツ、大瀧設備事務所／
ES Associates, Ohtaki E & M Consulting Office
9 廣村デザイン事務所（サイン）／
Hiromura Design Office
10 大成建設、岡宮美術鋳造（彫刻鋳造・据付工事）／
Taisei Corporation, OKAMIYA Fine Art Foundry
12 鉄筋コンクリート造／
Reinforced Concrete
13 地上1階／1 story
14 1,912㎡
15 197.29㎡
16 197.29㎡

## 台湾大学社会科学部棟
National Taiwan University, College of Social Sciences

1 台湾、台北／Taipei, Taiwan
2 2006.11-2009.12
3 2010.03-2013.05
5 校舎／University Building
6 宗邁建築師事務所、A+B Design Group／
Fei & Cheng Associates, A+B Design Group
7 SAPS (Sasaki and Partners), Super tech Consultants International
8 竹中工務店、Shiunn-Maw Design & Engineering、Guan Yueun Electric Machinery Technicians Office、Technicians' Office（機械）／
Takenaka Corporation, Shiunn-Maw Design & Engineering, Guan Yueun Electric Machinery Technicians' Office, Technicians' Office
9 FID-TEK international Consultants（外構）
10 互助營造股份有限公司／
Fu Tsu Construction
12 鉄骨鉄筋コンクリート造、鉄筋コンクリート造／
Steel Reinforced Concrete, Reinforced Concrete
13 地上8階、地下2階／
8 stories, 2 basements
14 16,228㎡
15 6,776.9㎡
16 53,231.7㎡

## 松山 台北文創ビル
Songshan Taipei New Horizon Building

1 台湾、台北／Taipei, Taiwan
2 2008.10-2011.02
3 2011.07-2013.09
5 オフィス、商業、ホテル、コンサートホール、シネマ、イベントスペース／
Office, Hotel, Retail, Cultural space
6 大矩聯合建築師事務所／
Da-ju Architects & Associates
7 SAPS（Sasaki and Partners）、信業工程顧問／
Sasaki and Partners, Hsin-yeh Engineering Consultants
8 環境エンジニアリング、エービル、正弦工程顧問、林伸環控設計有限公司、萬泰工業技師事務所／
Kankyo Engineering, Alter Buildings Japan, Sine& associates. M/Elec Consultants & Engineers, T.S. Lin & Associates Consulting Engineers, Wang Tai Industrial Consultant Corp
9 永田音響設計（音響）、ジャトー株式会社（音響）、LIGHTDESIGN（照明）、ライティングカンパニーあかり組（照明）、廣村デザイン事務所（サイン）、安東陽子（ファブリックデザイン）／
Nagata Acoustics, JATO, LIGHTDESIGN, Lighting Company Akarigumi, Hiromura Design Office, Yoko Ando
10 （総括・建築）中鹿營造、（設備）東元電機、（文教エリア内装）匯僑設計、（舞台設備）宜盛科技／
Chung-lu Construction, TECO Electric & Machinery, Rich Honour International Design, IX Technology
12 鉄骨鉄筋コンクリート造、鉄骨造、鉄筋コンクリート造／
Steel Reinforced Concrete, Steel Frame, Reinforced Concrete
13 地上14階、地下5階／

14 stories, 5 basements
- [14] 12,000.00㎡
- [15] 6,378.30㎡
- [16] 105,742.55㎡

## みんなの森 ぎふメディアコスモス
### Minna no Mori Gifu Media Cosmos (tentative title)

- [1] 岐阜県岐阜市／Gifu, Gifu, Japan
- [2] 2011.02-
- [3] 2013.07-
- [5] 図書館、市民活動交流センター、展示ギャラリー／
  Library, Citizen's activity interchange center, Gallery
- [7] Arup
- [8] イーエスアソシエーツ、大瀧設備事務所／
  ES Associates, Ohtaki E&M Cunsulting Office
- [9] Arup(環境シミュレーション・防災)、東京大学石川幹子研究室(外構)、永田音響(音響)、LPA(照明)、安宅防災設計(防災)、藤江和子アトリエ(家具)、安東陽子デザイン(グローブファブリックデザイン)日本デザインセンター・原デザイン研究所(サイン)／
  Arup, University of Tokyo Mikiko Ishikawa lab, Nagata Acoustics, Lighting Planners Associates, Ataka Fire Safety Design Office, Fujie Kazuko Atelier, Yoko Ando Design, Nippon Design Center, HARA DESIGN INSTITUTE
- [10] 戸田建設・大日本土木・市川工務店・雛屋建設社特定建設工事共同企業体／
  Toba・Dainippon・Ichikawa・Hinaya JV
- [12] 1・M2階：鉄筋コンクリート造(一部鉄骨造)、2階：鉄骨造、木造(梁)／
  1F&M2F: Reinforced Concrete, Steel (partially), 2F: Steel Frame, Wood Frame
- [13] 地上2階、地下1階／
  2 stories, 1 basement
- [14] 14,725.39㎡
- [15] 7,294.642㎡
- [16] 15,225.836㎡

## CapitaGreen
### CapitaGreen

- [1] シンガポール、マーケットストリート／
  Market Street, Singapore
- [2] 2007.09-2008.10  2010.04-2012.12
- [3] 2012.02-
- [5] オフィス／Office
- [6] RSP Architects、竹中工務店／
  RSP Architects, Takenaka Corporation
- [7] SAPS (Sasaki and Partners)  RSP Architects
- [8] 環境エンジニアリング、Arup、Squire Mech Pte／
  Kankyo Engineering, Arup, Squire Mech Pte
- [9] Sitetectonix(外構)、三菱地所設計(内装)、LPA(照明)／
  Sitetectonix, Mitsubishi Jisho Sekkei, Lighting Planners Associates
- [10] 竹中工務店／Takenaka Corporation
- [12] 鉄筋コンクリート造、鉄骨鉄筋コンクリート造、鉄骨造／
  Reinforced Concrete, Steel Reinforced Concrete, Steel Frame
- [13] 地上40階、地下3階／
  40 stories, 3 basements
- [14] 5,479㎡
- [15] 2,847㎡
- [16] 82,371.13㎡

※ CapitaGreen is built by CapitaLand, CapitaCommercial Trust and Mitsubishi Estate Asia.

## (仮称)川口市火葬施設・赤山歴史自然公園
### Crematorium and Akayama Historic Nature Park in Kawaguchi (tentative title)

- [ ] (仮称)川口市火葬施設／
  Crematorium in Kawaguchi (tentative title)
- [1] 埼玉県川口市／
  Kawaguchi, Saitama, Japan
- [2] 2011.07-2014.04
- [3] 2014.12-(予定)
- [4] 火葬場／Crematorium
- [7] 佐々木睦朗構造計画研究所／
  Sasaki Structural Consultants
- [8] 総合設備計画／SOGO CONSULTANTS
- [9] 中央大学石川幹子研究室(外構)、LIGHT DESIGN(照明)、安宅防災設計(防災)／
  Chuo University Mikiko Ishikawa Lab., LIGHT DESIGN, Ataka Fire Safety Design Office
- [10] 未定
- [12] 鉄筋コンクリート造、鉄骨造／
  Reinforced Concrete, Steel Frame
- [13] 地上2階、地下1階／
  2 stories, 1 basement
- [14] 19,800.32㎡
- [15] 5,595.05㎡
- [16] 7,901.42㎡
- [ ] (仮称)歴史自然資料館／
  Historical natural information centre (tentative title)
- [5] 展示場／Exhibition Space
- [7] 鉄骨造／Steel  Frame
- [13] 地上1階／1 story
- [16] 491.51㎡
- [ ] (仮称)地域物産館／
  Regional products centre (tentative title)
- [5] 集会スペース、図書コーナー、カフェ、展示・販売スペース／
  Meeting Space, Library Corner, Cafe, Exhibition and Sale Corner
- [7] 鉄筋コンクリート造一部、鉄骨造／
  Reinforced Concrete (partially)
- [13] 地上1階／1 story
- [16] 416.70㎡

## バロックミュージアム・プエブラ
### Barroco Museo Internacional

- [1] メキシコ、プエブラ／Puebla, Mexico
- [2] 2012.10-2013.11
- [3] 2014.06-
- [4] 博物館／Museum
- [6] Estudio Arquitectura
- [7] SAPS (Sasaki and Partners)
- [8] AKF México
- [9] Artec 3(照明)、Identity Design(サイン)、藤江和子アトリエ(家具)／
  Artec 3, Identity Design, Fujie Kazuko Atelier
- [10] 未定
- [12] 鉄筋コンクリート造／
  Reinforced Concrete
- [13] 地上2階(＋中2階)／
  2 stories (+mezzanine)
- [14] 50,000㎡
- [15] 9,855㎡
- [16] 18,149㎡

## 台中国立歌劇院
### National Taichung Theater

- [1] 台湾、台中／Taichung, Taiwan
- [2] 2005.09-2009.11
- [3] 2009.12-
- [5] 劇場、店舗、レストラン、公園／
  Theatre, Shop, Restaurant, Park
- [6] 大矩聯合建築師事務所／
  Da-Ju Architects & Associates
- [7] Arup、永峻工程顧問股份有限公司／
  Arup, Evergreen Consulting Engineering, Inc.
- [8] 環境エンジニアリング(基本構想)、竹中工務店、林伸環控設計有限公司、漢達電機技師事務所／
  Kankyo Engineering (conceptual design), Takenaka Corporation, I.S. Lin & Associates Consulting Engineers, Handar Engineering & Construction Inc.
- [9] 老圃造園工程股份有限公司(外構)、永田

379

音響設計（音響・舞台音響設備）、國立台灣科技大學（音響）、岡安泉照明設計事務所（照明）、本杉省三（劇場）、ベアーズエンジニアリング（舞台機構設備）、ライティングカンパニーあかり組（舞台照明設備）、廣村デザイン事務所（サイン）、藤江和子アトリエ（家具）、安東陽子デザイン（ファブリックデザイン）、安宅防災設計（防災）、台湾建築與都市防災顧問有限公司（防災）、利道科技工程（3Dモデル製作）／
Old Farmer Landscape Architecture, Nagata Acoustics, National Taiwan University of Science and Technology, Izumi Okayasu Lighting Design, Shozo Motosugi, Bears Engineering, Lighting Company Akarigumi, Hiromura Design Office, Fujie Kazuko Atelier, Yoko Ando Design, Ataka Fire Safety Design Office, Taiwan Fire Safety Consulting Forerun Engineering Consultant, Lead Dao Technology and Engineering

[10] 麗明營造、金梭營造（舞台特殊設備施工）、台大丰實業（舞台特殊設備施工）／
Lee Ming Construction, Chin Shu Construction, Top Design Futurity International

[11] 旭ビルウォール、竹中工務店（モックアップ制作協力）／
Asahi Building-Wall, Takenaka Corporation

[12] 鉄筋コンクリート造、一部鉄骨造／
Reinforced Concrete, Steel (partially)

[13] 地上6階、地下2階／
6 stories, 2 basements

[14] 57,020.46㎡
[15] 8,228.76㎡
[16] 34,601.38㎡

※ National Taichung Theater is built by the Taichung City Government, Republic of China (Taiwan).

## 作品名
### Name of Work

[1] 所在地／Location
[2] 設計期間／Design period
[3] 工事期間／Construction period
[4] 施主／Client
[5] 主要用途／Principal use
[6] 建築設計／Architect
[7] 構造設計／Structural engineer
[8] 設備設計／Facility engineer
[9] その他設計、計画（外構・音響・照明・劇場・家具・オブジェ）／Other design / plans (exterior, acoustic, lighting, theater, furniture, art object, etc.)
[10] 施工／Contractor
[11] 設計、制作協力／Design/production assistance
[12] 構造／Structure
[13] 規模／Scale
[14] 敷地面積／Site area
[15] 建築面積／Building area
[16] 延床面積／Total floor area
[17] 協力者、提供者ほか

## くまもとアートポリス東北支援「みんなの家」
### "Home-for-All" by Kumamoto Artpolis Tohoku Support Group

[1] 宮城県仙台市宮城野区／Miyagino, Sendai, Miyagi, Japan
[2] 2011.06-2011.09
[3] 2011.09-2011.10
[4] くまもとアートポリス東北支援「みんなの家」建設推進委員会（熊本県、熊本県建築住宅センター、熊本県建築士事務所協会、熊本県建設業協会建築部会、熊本県木材協会連合会、熊本県建築士会）／
Kumamoto Artpolis Tohoku support group for "Home-for-All" (Kumamoto Prefecture, Building & Housing Center of Kumamoto, Kumamoto Association of Architectural Firms, Kumamoto Construction Association Building Branch, Kumamoto Association Of Wood Society, Kumamoto Association of Architects & Building Engineers)
[5] 集会所／Gathering place
[6] くまもとアートポリスコミッショナー／Kumamoto Artpolis Commissioner
伊東豊雄／Toyo Ito
同アドバイザー／Kumamoto Artpolis Advisers
桂英昭／Hideaki Katsura
末廣香織／Kaoru Suehiro
曽我部昌史／Masashi Sogabe
伊東豊雄建築設計事務所／Toyo Ito & Associates, Architects
熊本大学桂研究室／Katsura Laboratory in Kumamoto University
九州大学末廣研究室／Suehiro Laboratory in Kyushu University
神奈川大学曽我部研究室／Sogabe Laboratory in Kanagawa University
[7] 桃李舎／Torisha
[9] 花と緑の力で3.11プロジェクトみやぎ委員会（外構）、曽我部昌史（家具）、丸山美紀（マチデザイン）（家具）、イノウエインダストリーズ（既存集会所集会室家具）、安東陽子（座布団デザイン）／
Project 3.11 with Power of Flower and Green, Miyagi Committee, Masashi Sogabe, Miki Maruyama (matidesign), Inoue Industries Inc., Yoko Ando
[10] 熊谷組、熊田建業／Kumagai Gumi, Kumada Kengyo
[12] 木造／Wood frame
[13] 地上1階／1 story
[14] 16,094.55㎡
[15] 55.33㎡
[16] 38.88㎡

**17** 設計、製作協力
現地対応協力：小野田泰明（東北大学教授）、福屋粧子（東北工業大学専任講師）
仙台市側協力：仙台市宮城野区役所まちづくり推進課
**施工協力**
北本敏美、藤島大（原田木材）
熊本県公募ボランティア：田口太、津田純佳、佐藤友法
熊本大学桂研究室、九州大学末廣研究室、神奈川大学曽我部研究室、東北大学小野田研究室、東北工業大学福屋研究室及び東北工業大学工学部学生有志団体colors、花と緑の力で3.11プロジェクト、みやぎ委員会委員長、福田町南一丁目仮設住宅自治会の皆さん、安東陽子、伊東豊雄建築設計事務所、東北大学の関係者、東北工業大学の関係者
**協賛**
熊本県湯前町、熊本県水上村、熊本県い業生産販売振興協会、熊本建築、セントラル硝子本社、セントラル硝子東北、LIXIL、元旦ビューティ工業、東日本パワーファスニング、常松ガス、ヤマギワ
**ソファ提供**
Mike Campbell　Geoff Spiteri
**さまざまな協力**
福田町南一丁目仮設住宅自治会、せんだい演劇工房10-BOX、協同組合仙台卸商センター、せんだいメディアテーク

## 釜石市商店街「みんなの家・かだって」
"Home-for-All" for Kamaishi shopping street

**1** 岩手県釜石市只越町／
Tadakoe, Kamaishi, Iwate, Japan
**2** 2011.12-2012.03
**3** 2012.03-2012.06
**5** 事務所／Office
**6** 伊東豊雄建築設計事務所／
Toyo Ito & Associates, Architects
伊東建築塾／ITO JUKU
**7** 佐々木睦朗構造計画研究所／
Sasaki Structural Consultants
**9** イノウエインダストリィズ（家具）、矢内原充志（カーテンデザイン・製作）／
Inoue Industries, Mitsushi Yanaihara
**10** 熊谷組、堀間組／
Kumagai Gumi, Horimagumi
**12** 鉄骨造　一部木造／
Steel Frame, Wood (partially)
**13** 地上1階／1 story
**14** 167.52㎡
**15** 73.27㎡
**16** 67.55㎡（テラス18.7㎡含む）
**17** 施工協力
伊東建築塾、神戸芸術工科大学の関係者、釜石市ご関係の皆さん：新田国雄、磯田喜一、泉和子、菊池文子、齊藤雄一郎、土橋詩歩、伊藤芳美、瓦田尚、川野真緒
**協賛**
LIXIL、元旦ビューティ工業、大光電機、ヤマギワ、エーディーワールド、立川ブラインド工業、タキヤ
**草花提供**
エアー
**食器提供**
伊東豊雄
**現地協力**
嶋田賢和、川崎俊之、藤原佳奈子、岩間正行、三間妙子

## 陸前高田の「みんなの家」
"Home-for-All" in Rikuzentakata

**1** 岩手県陸前高田市高田町／
Takata, Rikuzentakata, Iwate, Japan
**2** 2011.11-2012.06
**3** 2012.07-2012.11
**5** 事務所／Office
**6** 伊東豊雄建築設計事務所／
Toyo Ito & Associates, Architects
乾久美子建築設計事務所／
office of kumiko inui
藤本壮介建築設計事務所／
Sou Fujimoto Architects
平田晃久建築設計事務所／
akihisa hirata architecture office
**7** 佐藤淳構造設計事務所／
Jun Sato Structural Engineers
**10** シェルター、千葉設備工業（衛生）、菅原電工（電気）／
Shelter, Chiba Setsubi Kogyo
Sugawara Denko
**12** 木造／Wood frame
**13** 地上2階／2 stories
**14** 901.71㎡
**15** 30.18㎡
**16** 29.96㎡
**17** 土地協力
中村正司
**山林協力**
菅野勝郎（丸枡材木店）
**撮影協力**
畠山直哉、畠山容平
**特別協力**
陸前高田市の皆様：菅野修吾、菊池満夫、吉田光昭、菅原みき子、中田英寿、他多数
**施工協力**
陸前高田市役所　農林課、銚子林業、雲原みき子、宮城大学中田千彦研究室、シェルター　畠山直哉、畠山容平、国際交流基金、東北大学、千葉武晴
**資金協力**
アーキテクツ・スタジオ・ジャパン、石橋財団、大光電機、田島ルーフィン、東工大建築さ39年卒有志の方々、Fashion Girls for Japan、Zoom Japon（＋募金いただいたフランスの方々）、JAPONAIDE、Corinne Quentin、芝崎佳代、相馬英子、富永伸平、陳飛翔、新沼桂子、オノデラマナブ、フジナキフキコ、N.Y.
**協賛**
荒川技研工業、安東陽子デザイン、岩岡、キャピタルペイント、ケイ・エス・シー、三陸木材高次加工協同組合、シェルター、大光電機、田島ルーフィング、チヨダウーテ、東工、日建総業、日進産業、日本エンバイロンケミカルズ、日本暖炉薪ストーブマイスターグループ［ぜいたく屋、小畠］、日本ペイント販売、ハーフェレジャパン　マグ　イゾベール、LIXIL

## 東松島「こどものみんなの家」
"Home-for-All" for children in Higashimatsushima

**1** 宮城県東松島市大塩／
Oshio, Higashimatushima, Miyagi, Japan
**2** 2012.07-2012.11
**3** 2012.11-2013.01
**4** Tポイント・ジャパン／Tpoint Japan
**5** 集会所／Gathering place
**6** 伊東豊雄建築設計事務所／
Toyo Ito & Associates, Architects
大西麻貴／o+h　Maki Onishi/o+h
**7** オーク構造設計／
Structural Design Office Oak
**9** イノウエインダストリィズ（家具）、安東陽子デザイン（カーテンデザイン）、コイズミ照明（照明計画）／
Inoue Industries, Yoko Ando Design,
KOIZUMI Lighting Technology
**10** シェルター／Shelter
**12** 木造　一部アルミ造／
Wood frame, Aluminum (partially)
**13** 地上1階／1 story
**14** 836.10㎡
**15** 31.04㎡
**16** 31.04㎡
**17** 施工協力
當眞嗣人、石黒萌子、菱沼健太、稲星裕史、吉沢周、宍戸優太、廣瀬晴香、諸星佑香、朴真珠、浜口篭博、犬塚恵介、熊谷祐紘、シェルター、Tポイント・ジャパン、大西麻貴＋百田有希／o+h、伊東豊雄建築設計事務所、グリーンタウンやもと応急仮設住宅住民の皆さん、髙橋工業、滋賀県立大学陶器浩一研究室、四duo製瓦工業所、グリーンタウンやもと応急仮設住宅地ひまわり集会所
**協賛**
YKK AP、チャネルオリジナル、TOTO、田島ルーフィング、田島応用化工、朝日ウッドテック、日進産業、イケダコーポレーション、マグ・イゾベール、ウエスト、日本暖炉薪ストーブマイスターグループ、オーシカ仙台営業所、グリーンハウザー大平営業所、相原木材、須藤製作所、コイズミ照明、シェルター
**家具・カーテン寄贈**
佐浦
**協力**
グリーンタウンやもと応急仮設住宅ひまわり集会所自治会、おがるスターズ、東松島市の関係者、東松島市復興協議会、矢本西サポートセンター

## 岩沼「みんなの家」
"Home-for-All" in Iwanuma

1. 宮城県岩沼市押分／Oshiwake, Iwanuma, Miyagi, Japan
2. 2012.12-2013.04
3. 2013.04-2013.07
4. インフォコム／INFOCOM
5. 事務所兼集会所／Office and Gathering place
6. 伊東豊雄建築設計事務所／Toyo Ito & Associates, Architects
7. 佐々木睦朗構造計画研究所／Sasaki Structural Consultants
8. エービル／Alter Buildings Japan
9. 安東陽子デザイン（カーテンデザイン・製作）、中央大学石川幹子研究室（外構）／Yoko Ando Design, Chuo University Mikiko Ishikawa Lab.
10. 今慶興産、熊谷組（施工監修）／Konkeikousan, Kumagai Gumi
12. 木造／Wood frame
13. 地上1階／1 story
14. 406.47㎡
15. 93.60㎡
16. 73.44㎡（テラス8.64㎡含む）
17. 施工協力
渋谷木材店、渡建、松建産業、青陽建築設計工房、ブルーベリーフィールズ紀伊國屋、ウォーテックヤオヤ、やさい工房八巻、丸富工業、村松建築設計事務所、茨城県建築士会、古積造園土木、大宮一弘、岩沼サポーターズ関係者、ロシナンテス、東北大学の関係者、東京大学の関係者、岩沼市金曜絆の会

協賛・協力
LIXIL、越井木材工業、チャネルオリジナル、大光電機、セントラル硝子、元旦ビューティ工業、Bb Wood Japan、田島応用化工、フジワラ化学、シンコー、タニタハウジングウェア、グローバル・リンク、三井化学産資、城東テクノ、YAMAGIWA、国代耐火工業所、サイレントグリス、富国物産、渋谷商事、住友林業緑化、ホンマ製作所、ユビレジ、池朋

庭石、樹木提供
フルール花の森：大泉淳子

ハーブ提供
エルフの森：岩佐和子

資金協力
菅沼家一同、ニュースト、アーキテクツ・スタジオ・ジャパン、宮城学院同窓会、RISTEX（社会技術研究開発センター）

企画
インフォコム

運営協力
がんばッと!!玉浦

特別協力
TAKE ACTION FOUNDATION

企画協力
エイトビー、エスピーアール、レコテック、和快

## 釜石漁師の「みんなの家」
"Home-for-All" for Fishermen in Kamaishi

1. 岩手県釜石市新浜町／Shinhama, Kamaishi, Iwate, Japan
2. 2013.04-2013.07
3. 2013.07-2013.10
4. ジャパン・ソサエティー東日本大震災復興基金／The Japan Society Tohoku Earthquake Relief Fund
5. 集会所／Gathering place
6. 伊東豊雄建築設計事務所／Toyo Ito & Associates, Architects
アトリエ・天工人／Atelier Tekuto
Ma 設計事務所／Ma Design office
7. 佐藤淳構造設計事務所／Jun Sato Structural Engineers
10. ホームビルダー（木工事）、熊谷組（仮設工事、基礎工事）、堀間組（仮設工事、基礎工事）、イズミ空調（衛生）、坂本電気（電気）／HOME BUILDER, Kumagai Gumi Horimagumi Izumi Kucho, Sakamoto Denki
12. 木造／Wood frame
13. 地上1階／1 story
14. 78.33㎡
15. 39.84㎡
16. 32.56㎡
17. 施工協力
田沢工務店、中部建設企業組合、渡辺建具／家具営業所、渋谷製作所、SAHI、新井建築板金、スーパーファクトリー

釜石市民の皆さん：岩間正行、君ヶ洞剛一、下村達志、伝藤聡、宮崎洋之、青木健一、齊藤雄一郎、岩間妙子、菊地圭介、大坂美和、阿部志穂、服部宗秋、平田附美子、西宗岳志、石津謙、金野義男、近江修
東北閣聖、遠野まごころネット
社会人ボランティア関係の皆さん：細田義裕、伊藤友紀、有松恵美、高橋千恵弥、佐藤あずさ、菅井牧子、佐藤美緒、日高光麻、森田喜晴、坂井聖美、山下海人、水上龍樹
愛知工業大学大学院の関係者、愛知淑徳大学の関係者、中東建築塾の関係者、鹿児島大学の関係者、北九州市立大学の関係者、九州大学の関係者、西南学院大学の関係者、筑波研究学園専門学校の関係者、東北大学の関係者、福岡大学の関係者、前橋工科大学の関係者、宮城大学の関係者、横浜国立大学の関係者、早稲田大学の関係者

協賛・協力
竹村工業、和以美、ポラテック東北、田島ルーフィング、セントラル硝子、有限会社 渋谷製作所、LIXIL、中西製作所 長野営業所、大光電機、釜石地方森林組合、釜石職業訓練協会、佐々忠建設、石村工業、SAHI、釜石ガス、小林石材工業、日新製鋼、カナメ、釜石砂利建設、堀商店、ロックストーン、三井化学産資、NHK、東京美工

現地協力
嶋田賢和、小友光晴、佐々木勝、川崎俊之、佐々木義友、藤原佳奈子、原田祐吉、菊地好広、藤原妙子、藤原綾子、菊地信平、鹿野順一、川原康信、横澤京子

## 釜石「みんなのひろば」
"Park-for-All" in Kamaishi

1. 岩手県釜石市鵜住居町／Unosumai, Kamaishi, Iwate, Japan
2. 2013.04-2013.09
3. 2013.10-2014.04
4. ナイキ（資金提供）、アーキテクチャー・フォー・ヒューマニティ（企画管理）、釜石市（寄贈先）／NIKE, Architecture for Humanity, Kamaishi-shi
5. クラブハウス／Clubhouse
6. 伊東豊雄建築設計事務所／Toyo Ito & Associates, Architects
7. 佐藤淳構造設計事務所／Jun Sato Structural Engineers
8. エービル／Alter Buildings Japan
10. 熊谷組／Kumagai Gumi
12. 鉄骨造／Steel frame
13. 地上2階／2 stories
14. 11,155.63㎡
15. 約121.99㎡
16. 約207.75㎡（2階ブルペン含む）
17. 設計協力
都市計画研究所

施工協力（2階ブルペン マウンド制作）
市立釜石東 中学校野球部保護者の皆様

協賛・協力
ウッドワン、エスケー化研、岡村製作所、角弘、三晃金属工業、スパンクリートコーポレーション、大光電機、日新工業、LIXIL

現地協力
釜石市、野田武則（市長）、嶋田賢和（前副市長）、小友光晴、正木隆司、川崎俊之、本間良春、金野尚史、村井大司、及川博
鵜住居復興まちづくり協議会、釜石市立釜石東中学校、釜石市立鵜住居小学校、鵜住居スポーツ少年団、日向ライナーズスポーツ少年団

# Toyo Ito Chronology
伊東豊雄年表

■ 実施案　realized plan
□ 計画案・未完　unrealized plan
● プロダクト　products

## 2002年　（所員数32人　studio staff size: 32）

- 京都大学工学部非常勤講師（-2007）
- 多摩美術大学美術学部客員教授（現在に至る）
- 2002年度建築業協会賞（BCS賞）（せんだいメディアテーク）
- ヴェネチア・ビエンナーレ「金獅子賞」（生涯業績部門）
- World Architecture Awards 2002 Best Building in East Asia（せんだいメディアテーク）
- ヴェネチア・ビエンナーレ-8. International Architecture Exhibition NEXT（イタリア）

このころから海外での仕事が急激に増えた。特にヨーロッパが多く、コンペティションのインタビュー、レクチャーを含めると、1、2カ月に1度は訪れることになる。

この年、ブルージュとロンドンで、ふたつの仮設パヴィリオンが完成した。前者はブルージュの欧州文化首都選定を記念して、まちの中央広場に1年間の仮設パヴィリオンをつくるという企画で、構造家の新谷眞人さんとアルミのストラクチャーでデザインした。2月20日のオープニングには国王夫妻も出席した。

後者はケンジントン公園のサーペンタイン・ギャラリーの前庭に夏の3カ月間だけ存在するパヴィリオンである。アラップの構造家、セシル・バルモンドさんとの協働により、楽しく実りの多いプロジェクトとなった。

- Visiting Lecturer in Faculty of Engineering, Kyoto University (-2007)
- Guest Professor in Faculty of Art and Design, Tama Art University
- Wins 2002 Japan Federation of Construction Contractors Awards (BCS Award) for Sendai Mediatheque
- Wins Golden Lion for Lifetime Achievement from the 8th International Architecture Exhibition "NEXT" at the Venice Biennale
- Wins World Architecture Awards 2002 Best Building in East Asia for Sendai Mediatheque
- "La Biennale di Venezia - 8. International Architecture Exhibition NEXT" (Venice, Italy)

Around this time there was a sharp increase in foreign jobs. Many of these were in Europe, so I began visiting the region once a month or once every other month to do things like interviews and lectures for competitions.

I finished two temporary pavilions in Bruges and London this year. The first was a project to create a temporary pavilion, which stood for a year in Bruges' central square to commemorate the city's designation as a European Capital of Culture. The aluminum structure was made with the structural designer Mr. Araya Masato. The King and Queen of Belgium attended the opening on February 20.

The second pavilion only stood for three months during the summer in the front garden of Serpentine Gallery in Kensington Park in London. This collaboration with Mr. Cecil Balmond, a structural designer at Arup, was an enjoyable and fruitful project.

■ ブルージュ・パヴィリオン（ベルギー、ブルージュ）
Brugge Pavilion, Bruges, Belgium (pp. 054-061)

■ サーペンタイン・ギャラリー・パヴィリオン2002（イギリス、ロンドン）
Serpentine Gallery Pavilion 2002, Kensington Gardens, London, UK (pp. 062-071)

□ オスロ・ウェストバーネン再開発計画コンペティション応募案
Architects Competition Vestbanen, Oslo, Norway (p. 04?)

## 2003年　（所員数38人　studio staff size: 38）

- 2003年度日本建築学会賞作品賞（せんだいメディアテーク）
- 『PLOT 03 伊東豊雄：建築のプロセス』（A.D.A. EDITA Tokyo）出版
- 『建築：非線形の出来事ー smtからユーロへ』（彰国社）出版

ますますヨーロッパ通いが激しくなった。2000年にコンペティションで勝ち取ったパリのホスピス「コニャック・ジェイ病院」のプロジェクトは、近隣住民の反対運動案もあって紆余曲折を経ながらも進む。しかしマニュエル・タルディッツさん（みかんぐみ）や柳澤潤さん（元スタッフ）らの協力もあってクライアントとの信頼関係はますます深まった。バルセロナの国際見本市会場「モンジュイック2」およびマドリードでの「ガヴィア公園」という息の長い大きなプロジェクトを手がけることが決まり、どっぷりとスペインに足を浸すことになった。

また秋にはシンガポール最大のショッピング・センターのプロジェクトを突然依頼され、慌ただしい1年となった。

- Wins 2003 Architectural Institute of Japan Prize for Sendai Mediatheque
- Publishes PLOT 03 Toyo Ito (A.D.A. EDITA Tokyo)
- Publishes Architecture: Non-linear Discoveries - From SMT to Europe (Shokokusha Publishing)

My commutes to Europe grew even more frequent. The Cognacq-Jay Hospital project, a competition which had won in 2000, began to move forward after a series of complications including an opposition movement by neighborhood residents. But with the cooperation of Mr. Manuel Tardits (Mikan Gumi) and Mr. Jun Yanagisawa (a former member of my staff), we were able to build a deeper relationship of trust. I also began to get involved with two large, long-term projects: the Montjuïc 2 international exposition site in Barcelona and Gavia Park in Madrid, so I immersed myself in Spain.

In the fall, I was also suddenly asked to oversee a project to create Singapore's largest shopping center. It was a hectic year.

■ 東雲キャナルコートCODAN2街区（東京都江東区）
Shinonome Canal Court, Block 2, Koto, Tokyo, Japan

■ みなとみらい線元町・中華街駅（神奈川県横浜市）
Motomachi Chukagai Station, Minatomirai Line, Yokohama, Kanagawa, Japan

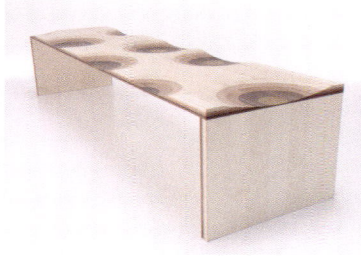

● Ripples（木製ベンチ）　Ripples, bench

## 2004年　（所員数44人　studio staff size: 44）

- 金のコンパス賞（Compasso d'oro ADI）（木製ベンチ "Ripples"）
- ヴェネチア・ビエンナーレ - 9. International Architecture Exhibition METAMORPH（イタリア）
- 『a＋u』404「特集：伊東豊雄／アンダー・コンストラクション」（エー・アンド・ユー）出版

なぜか劇場やコンサートホールの仕事が多い。この年の夏、松本市恒例の「サイトウ・キネン・フェスティバル松本」をこけら落とし公演として、「まつもと市民芸術館」がオープンした。大ホールでは小澤征爾さんの指揮によるアルバン・ベルクさんのオペラ「ヴォツェック」、小ホールでは館長、串田和美さん演出によるモリエール喜劇「スカパン」が上演された。コンペティション以来わずか4年で竣工したが、施工の良さもあって満足のいく出来栄えであった。

一方、アンドレア・ブランジさんらと組んで提案したベルギーの「ゲント市文化フォーラム」のコンペティションは、思い切り力を入れた自信作であったが、最終審査で惜敗した。慣習的なホールの形式にこだわらない提案だっただけに残念であった。

- Wins ADI Compasso d'Oro Award for Ripples (furniture design)
- La Biennale di Venezia - 9. International Architecture Exhibition Metamorph (Venice, Italy)
- Publishes a+u 404 Feature: Toyo Ito / Under Construction (A+U Publishing)

For some reason, I started doing lots of theatres and concert halls around this time. In the summer of this year, the opening performance of the Saito Kinen Festival Matsumoto, held as usual in the city of Matsumoto, took place at the new Matsumoto Performing Arts Centre. In the large hall, Mr. Seiji Ozawa conducted Alban Berg's opera Wozzeck, and Moliere's comedy Les Fourberies de Scapin, directed by the centre's director Mr. Kazuyoshi Kushida, was performed in the small hall. Though the building was completed only four years after

the competition, I was deeply satisfied with the results, including the excellent construction.
 On the other hand, I put a great deal of effort and was very confident about the plan, a collaborative effort with Mr. Andrea Branzi's office, I submitted for the competition for the Forum for Music, Dance, and Visual Culture, Ghent, Belgium, but I narrowly lost in the final round. This was unfortunate in that the proposal did not stick to the conventional hall format.

■まつもと市民芸術館（長野県松本市）
Matsumoto Performing Arts Centre, Matsumoto, Nagano, Japan (pp. 072-091)

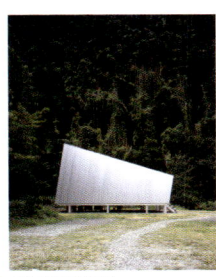

■アルミコテージ（山梨県南巨摩郡）
Aluminium Cottage, Minamikoma, Yamanashi, Japan

■TOD'S表参道ビル（東京都渋谷区）
TOD'S Omotesando Building, Shibuya, Tokyo, Japan (pp. 092-101)

□ゲント市文化フォーラム・コンペティション応募案
Forum for Music, Dance and Visual Culture, Ghent (p. 339)

□武蔵境新公共施設設計プロポーザル応募案　M project

□アミアンFRAC現代美術館　指名設計競技案
FRAC Contemporary Art Museum in Amiens

● Sendai 2005（展覧会の作品）　Sendai 2005

## 2005年 （所員数47人　studio staff size: 47）

・くまもとアートポリスコミッショナー就任（現在に至る）
・TOYO ITO made IN ITALY〈Museo Nacional Bellas Artes〔チリ〕、Ex Mercato ortofrutticol（イタリア）、Fontana Arredamenti（イタリア）、Design Museum（ベルギー）〉（-2006）
・『a+u』417『特集：伊東豊雄／イメージを超えて』（エーアンドユー）出版
・『みちの家』（子どもたちに伝えたい家の本08）（インデックス・コミュニケーションズ）出版
・El Croquis 123: Toyo Ito 2001-2005 – Beyond Modernism（Spain, El Croquis Editorial）出版
・Toyo Ito Conversaciones con estudiantes（Spain, GG, Editorial Gustavo Gili）出版

ここ数年間アルミ・ストラクチャーの建築に固執してきた。静岡に本社をもつSUSの石田社長のキャラクターもあって、新しい試みにきわめて意欲的である。この春、福島県須賀川市に、山本理顕さんによる「福島エコムスパビリオン」とわれわれの「SUS福島工場社員寮」が相次いで竣工した。アルミ・ストラクチャーの建築も数回の経験を経て、ようやくその可能性が見えてきた。それにしても石田社長の情熱には頭が下がる。

年末台湾でふたつのコンペティションに勝つことができた。ひとつは「2009高雄ワールドゲームズメインスタジアム」、もうひとつは「台中国立歌劇院」である。後者は前年コンペティションで敗れた「ゲント市文化フォーラム」と同じ構造システムを用いての再挑戦で、今後数年オフィスを挙げてのチャレンジングなプロジェクトとなるであろう。

・Commissioner of Kumamoto Artpolis
・Toyo Ito made in Italy (Museo Nacional Bellas Artes (Chile), Ex Mercato ortofrutticol (Italy), Fontana Arredamenti (Italy), Design Museum (Belgium)) (-2006)
・Publishes a+u 417 Feature: Toyo Ito / Beyond the Image (A+U Publishing)
・Publishes Michi no Ie (Index Communications)
・Publishes El Croquis 123: Toyo Ito 2001-2005 – Beyond Modernism (Spain, El Croquis Editorial)
・Publishes Toyo Ito Conversaciones con estudiantes (Spain, GG, Editorial Gustavo Gili)

For a few years around this period I was constantly involved with aluminum structures. This had to do Mr. Ishida's character, the CEO of SUS, headquartered in Shizuoka, and his extremely ambitious experiments. In the spring, Mr. Riken Yamamoto's Fukushima Ecoms Pavilion and our Dormitory for SUS Company Fukushima Branch were completed one after another in Sukagawa, Fukushima. After several experiences designing aluminum structures, I finally realized their true potential. Still, I have to salute Mr. Ishida for his unflagging passion.

 I won two competitions in Taiwan at the end of the year. One was for the Main Stadium for the World Games 2009 in Kaohsiung and the other for the National Taichung Theater. The latter, a renewed attempt to use a structural system like the one I had intended for Forum for Music, Dance, and Visual Culture, Ghent, Belgium, which had been defeated in the competition the year before. The National Taichung Theater presented the office with a series of challenges over the next few years.

■福岡アイランドシティ中央公園中核施設ぐりんぐりん（福岡県福岡市）
Island City Central Park "GRIN GRIN", Fukuoka, Fukuoka, Japan (sp. 102-115)

■「フィガロの結婚」舞台装置（長野県松本市）
"LE NOZZE DI FIGARO", STAGE SET, Matsumoto, Nagano, Japan (p. 030)

■フローニンゲン アルミブリック ハウジング（オランダ、フローニンゲン）
Aluminium Brick Housing in Groningen, Groningen, Netherlands

■オフィス・マーラー4・ブロック5（オランダ、アムステルダム）
MAHLER 4 Block 5, Amsterdam, Netherlands

■SUS福島工場社員寮（福島県須賀川市）
Dormitory for SUS Company Fukushima Branch, Sukagawa, Fukushima, Japan

■MIKIMOTO Ginza 2（東京都中央区）
MIKIMOTO Ginza 2, Chuo, Tokyo, Japan (p. 050)

● Kaeru（カップ＆ソーサー）　Kaeru, cup & saucer

## 2006年 （所員数48人　studio staff size: 48）

・65歳
・第10回公共建築賞 国土交通大臣表彰 文化施設部門（せんだいメディアテーク）
・2006年度建築業協会賞（BCS賞）（まつもと市民芸術館）
・王立英国建築家協会（RIBA）ロイヤルゴールドメダル
・個展「伊東豊雄　建築｜新しいリアル」〈東京オペラシティアートギャラリー（東京）、せんだいメディアテーク（宮城）、神奈川県立近代美術館葉山（神奈川）〉（-2007）

- 「東京－ベルリン／ベルリン－東京」展会場構成〈森美術館（東京）、国立新美術館（ベルリン）〉
- 『けんちく世界をめぐる10の冒険』（彰国社）出版

ヨーロッパのプロジェクトでは、日本では味わえない楽しさがある。総じてクライアントや市民たちが建築に大きな関心を寄せ、つくるプロセスを楽しんでいるからである。しかしいつ完成するのか、われわれにも分からないままに仕事をし続けなければならない。

そのひとつ、パリの病院が6年の歳月を経て、ようやくオープン間近である。先日オーナーと最後の現場視察を行った。彼は「ほとんどの部分にすごく気に入っている。でも1カ所だけ気になっている所がある」と言って中庭側のファサードの中央部へ私を連れていった。「ここのプロポーションが良くないと思う」と言われた。私も最初から気になっていたが、直しようのない部分だった。クライアントへの信頼は一層強まった。

- Turns 65
- Wins The 10th Public Building Award for Sendai Mediatheque
- Wins 2006 Japan Federation of Construction Contractors Awards (BCS Award) for Matsumoto Performing Arts Centre
- Wins Royal Gold Medal from The Royal Institute of British Architects
- Solo exhibition Toyo Ito: The New "Real" in Architecture 〈Tokyo Opera City Art Gallery (Tokyo), Sendai Mediatheque (Miyagi), The Museum of Modern Art, Hayama (Kanagawa)〉(-2007)
- Tokyo-Berlin / Berlin-Tokyo Exhibition configuration 〈Mori Art Museum (Tokyo), New National Gallery (Berlin)〉
- Publishes 10 Adventures in the Architectural World (Shokokusha Publishing)

My European projects provided me with a special kind of pleasure that I couldn't have enjoyed in Japan. This was because the clients and local residents took a great interest in architecture and enjoyed the process of making the buildings. But we also had to continue with the jobs without ever knowing for sure when they would be completed.

One project, a hospital in Paris was finally about to open after six years. A few days earlier I had conducted a final inspection of the site with the owner. He said, "I'm extremely happy with almost everything, but there's one part I'm a bit worried about," and led me over to the center of the facade on the courtyard side. He said, "I don't think these proportions are right." I had also been worried about this at the beginning, but then there wasn't anything I could do about it now. This experience strengthened my trust in the client.

■瞑想の森 市営斎場（岐阜県各務原市）
Meiso no mori Municipal Funeral Hall, Kakamigahara, Gifu, Japan (pp. 116-127)

■VivoCity（シンガポール、ハーバーフロント）
VivoCity, Harbour Front Walk, Singapore (p. 135)

■バルセロナ見本市・グランビア会場 セントラルアクシス・パヴィリオン8（スペイン、バルセロナ）
Extension for "The Fair of Barcelona Gran Via Venue" Central Axis, Pavilion 8, Barcelona, Spain (pp. 194-199)

●KL（カップ＆ソーサー）　KU, cup & saucer

●ストリート・ファーニチュア "Ripples"（東京都港区）
Street Furniture "Ripples", Minato, Tokyo, Japan

●Kaze（本棚）　Kaze, bookshelf

□レ・アール国際設計競技応募案　"Les Halles" Competition

## 2007年 （所員数45人　studio staff size: 45）

- 『つくる図書館をつくる』（鹿島出版会）出版

「多摩美術大学図書館（八王子キャンパス）」が竣工した。連続し、かつ湾曲するアーチの列を交差させた構造体である。この構造体は一見コンクリートの打ち放しのように見える。だがコンクリートにしては異常に薄く、アーチの足元も細い。構造家 佐々木睦朗さんの提案によってコンクリート壁の中央部にはすべて鉄板が入っているからである。こんな面倒な施工は日本以外ではまずできないだろう。日本のゼネコンの技術力の賜である。

またファサードのガラスも曲面で構成されている。見た目には曲面ガラスであることがわからないほど小さな曲率である。かくして私たちの作品の中でも最も精度の良い建築が出来上がった。日本の建築家はこのような施工技術に助けられることが多いのだが、その上に安住してはなるまい。

長年試行錯誤を繰り返していた照明器具のシリーズ「MAYUHANA」が発売された。その名の通り、繭のようにグラスファイバーを型に添わせて巻き付けて透明感のある球体が実現した。二重三重のレイヤーもあって、ぼんぼりのような和の趣も感じさせる。

- Publishes *Creating a Crative Library* (Kajima Institute Publishing)

The Tama Art University Library (Hachioji Campus) was completed. The structure consists of a sequence of linked, curved arches. At first glance, it looks like exposed concrete. But the concrete is extremely thin and the footing of the arches is also very narrow. This is because the structural designer Mr. Mutsuro Sasaki's proposal called for the center of the concrete walls to be made entirely of sheet iron. This type of arduous construction method would never have been possible outside of Japan. It is a product of the technical skills of Japanese general contractors.

The glass used in the facade also has a curved surface. But the curvature is so slight that it doesn't appear to be curved. This makes it possible for us to achieve the greatest precision in our work. Japanese architects are often aided by these construction techniques, but you can't rely on them completely.

After many years of trial and error, a series of lighting fixtures we made called MAYUHANA went on sale. As the name suggests (the word mayu means "cocoon"), glass fibers are wound around a mold to create a transparent sphere. With dual and triple layers, the lights convey a sense of Japanese elegance akin to a paper lantern.

■多摩美術大学図書館（八王子キャンパス）（東京都八王子市）
Tama Art University Library (Hachioji campus), Hachioji, Tokyo, Japan (pp. 140-155)

■バルセロナ見本市・グランビア会場／エントランスホール・パヴィリオン（スペイン、バルセロナ）
Extension for "The Fair of Barcelona Gran Via Venue" Entrance Hall, Pavilion 1, Barcelona, Spain (pp. 194-199)

■コニャック・ジェイ病院（フランス、パリ）
Hospital Cognacq Jay, Paris, France

●MAYUHANA I（照明）　MAYUHANA I, lighting／製作：YAMAGIWA
●Bo（美濃焼き カップ＆ソーサー）　Bo, cup & saucer

## 2008年 （所員数42人　studio staff size: 42）

- 2008年度建築業協会賞（BCS賞）（瞑想の森 市営斎場）
- 金のコンパス賞（Compasso d'oro ADI）（2005年ミラノサローネのHORM社のブースデザイン）
- 2008年度第6回オーストリア・フレデリック・キースラー建築芸術賞
- 生成する秩序〈台北市立美術館（台湾）〉
- 『伊東豊雄 最新プロジェクト』（A.D.A. EDITA Tokyo）出版

385

- 「伊東豊雄 建築論 文選 衍生的秩序」（田園城市、台湾）出版

東京都心に劇場「座・高円寺」がオープンした。200〜300席の劇場がふたつ、阿波踊りの練習ホールや大小リハーサル室などの組み合わされたコンパクトな建築である。東京の都心では、これまで「TOD'S表参道ビル」や「MIKIMOTO Ginza 2」などの商業ビルしか設計の機会がなく、初めての公共建築である。

杉並区には演劇関係者が多いこともあって、企画から運営に至るまで明確なポリシーに基づいていて、満足のいく設計が出来た。最大の英断は市民用、プロ仕様という同規模のふたつの劇場を設けたことである。杉並のような裕福な区だからこそ可能であったのだろうが、アマチュア、プロのいずれにも使いやすいホールが実現したように思う。

またリハーサル室を利用した演劇関係者養成のスクールや2階カフェを使っての子どもへの絵本の読み聞かせなど、将来の劇場運営の布石を打っている点で、これからの公共施設のモデルを示しているように見える。

- Wins 2008 Japan Federation of Construction Contractors Awards (BCS Award) for Meiso no Mori Municipal Funeral Hall
- Wins ADI Compasso d'Oro Award for the Stand Horm for Milan Salon 2005
- Wins 6th Austrian Frederick Kiesler Prize for Architecture and the Arts
- Toyo Ito: Generative Order (Taipei Fine Arts Museum, Taipei, Taiwan)
- Publishes Toyo Ito Recent Project (A.D.A. EDITA Tokyo)
- Publishes Toyo Ito: Generative Order (Taiwan, Garden City Publishers)

The ZA-KOENJI Public Theatre, located in the heart of Tokyo, opened. The compact building consists of two 200-to-300-seat theaters along with a practice hall for Awa dance and various sizes of rehearsal rooms. In the past, I only had the opportunity to design commercial facilities like TOD'S Omotesando Building and MIKIMOTO Ginza 2 in the center of the city; this was my first public building in the area.

There are lots of theatre people in Suginami Ward, and due to the clear-cut policy that extended from planning to operation, I was satisfied with the project. The most decisive step was to include two theaters of the same size, one for civic use and the other for professional use. This was possible in a wealthy ward like Suginami, and I think the hall can be easily used by amateurs and professionals alike.

In the sense that a school designed to cultivate theater people using the rehearsal rooms and a project to read picture books to children in the 2nd-floor cafe are strategic ways of continuing to operate the hall in the future, I think it will serve as a good model for other community facilities in the future.

■ SUMIKA パヴィリオン／SUMIKA Project by TOKYO GAS（栃木県宇都宮市）
SUMIKA PAVILION / SUMIKA PROJECT by TOKYO GAS, Utsunomiya, Tochigi, Japan

■ 座・高円寺（東京都杉並区）
ZA-KOENJI Public Theatre, Suginami, Tokyo, Japan (pp.156-169)

■ オカムラデザインスペースR 第6回企画展「風鈴」
The 6th OKAMURA Design Space R Exhibition: "Furin"

● Fin（ドアハンドル） Fin, door handle

## 2009年 （所員数47人 studio staff size: 47）

- 2009年度建築業協会賞（BCS賞）（多摩美術大学図書館（八王子キャンパス））
- マドリード美術協会（CBA）金メダル
- 『20XXの建築原理へ』（INAX出版）出版
- 『a+u』472 「特集：伊東豊雄／建築と場所」（エーアンドユー）出版
- EL Croquis 147: Toyo Ito 2005-2009 - Liquid Space（Spain, El Croquis Editorial）出版
- Toyo Ito（UK, Phaidon Press）出版

台湾で初めてのプロジェクト「2009高雄ワールドゲームズメインスタジアム」が竣工した。これは北京オリンピックに対抗して、台湾がワールドゲームを招致し、その主会場としてつくったものである。日本の竹中工務店、台湾の劉培森建築師事務所、互助営造のチームで設計施工のコンペティションに臨み、極めて短期間で完成した。特に互助営造の林総裁以下の真摯な取り組みに感激した。日本では既に失われた強い指導力の下に組織された建設会社の素晴らしさを久々に味わった。

この高雄でのプロジェクトが成功したことによって、その後台湾でいくつものプロジェクトを続けることになる。

また地球の裏側、チリでのウィークエンドハウス「White O」が完成して現地を訪れた。建て売りだが、オーナーのゴドイさんは家具の販売＋デベロッパーで個性豊かな魅力的なキャラクターの持ち主である。

住宅1軒の設計のために、地球の裏側からでも招待して建てようとするエネルギーと強い意志に感服する。「情熱」、この言葉こそ現在の日本に最も欠けているものではないか。

- Wins 2009 Japan Federation of Construction Contractors Awards (BCS Award) for Tama Art University Library (Hachioji campus)
- Wins Medalla de Oro from Circulo de Bellas Artes de Madrid
- Publishes Creating New Principles for 21st Century Architecture (INAX Publishing)
- Publishes a+u 472 Feature: Toyo Ito / Architecture and Place (A+U Publishing)
- Publishes EL Croquis 147: Toyo Ito 2005-2009 - Liquid Space (Spain, El Croquis Editorial)
- Publishes Toyo Ito (UK, Phaidon Press)

Our first project in Taiwan, the Main Stadium for the World Games 2009 in Kaohsiung, was completed. Taiwan staged the World Games in opposition to the Beijing Olympics, and this stadium was the main venue for the event. With the Japanese building contractor Takenaka and the Taiwanese firm Ricky Liu & Associates, Architects + Planners and Fu Tsu Construction we formed a joint venture for the design and construction competition, which enabled us to complete the project in an extremely short time. The earnest attitude of Mr. Ching-Po Lin, chairman of the Fu Tsu Construction Company, was particularly impressive. It had been a long time since I had experienced the wonderful character of a construction company founded on the strong leadership of a single individual – something that no longer exists in Japan.

Due to the success of this project in Kaohsiung, I was able to work on several other projects in Taiwan.

On the other side of the world, I also visited the site of the newly completed weekend house White O in Chile. The owner, Mr. Eduardo Godoy, is a very individualistic person with a charming character who works as a furniture seller and developer.

I was deeply impressed by his strong energy and will to invite someone from the other side of the world to design for a private residence. It seems to me this kind of "passion" is the thing that we lack the most in Japan today.

■ 2009高雄ワールドゲームズメインスタジアム（台湾、高雄）
The Main Stadium for the World Games 2009 in Kaohsiung, Kaohsiung, Taiwan (pp. 170-183)

■ スイーツアベニュー アパートホテル ファサードリノベーション（スペイン、バルセロナ）
Facade Renovation "Suites Avenue Aparthotel", Barcelona, Spain

■ White O（チリ、マルベリャ） White O, Marbella, Chile

□ オスロ市ダイクマン中央図書館 コンペティション応募案
The New Deichman Main Library Competition (p. 137)

□ 台北ポップミュージックセンター コンペティション応募案
Taipei Pop Music Center International Competition

■ カリフォルニア大学バークレー美術館／パシフィック・フィルム・アーカイブ 設計案（アメリカ、カリフォルニア州）
BAM / PFA University of California, Berkeley Art Museum and Pacific Film Archive, California, USA (p. 234)

## 2010年 （所員数47人　studio staff size: 47）

- 2009年度朝日賞
- 第22回高松宮殿下記念世界文化賞
- 建築はどこにあるの？　7つのインスタレーション〈東京国立近代美術館（東京）〉
- 『伊東豊雄』NA建築家シリーズ01（日経BP社）出版
- 『Pioneer Forever 建築家 伊東豊雄』（天下文化、台湾）出版

シンガポールの中心オーチャードロードの裏手にコンドミニアム「ベルビュー・レジデンシズ」が完成した。このプロジェクトのクライアント代表である、エドモンド・チェンさんは先のショッピングモール「VivoCity」のクライアントでもあった。彼の父親は中国から海を渡って香港に辿り着いた。エドモンドさんは香港で独立し、シンガポールに移住して成功した立志伝中の人物である。

「Vivo」の仕事を気に入ってくれて、以後東京を訪れるたびに食事に誘ってくれる。そのグルメぶりは半端でなく、毎回寿司のネタはすべて写真に収め、産地をすべてメモする。いったん友人として認めたら、徹底して尽くし、次々に設計を依頼してくれる。「人を信じる」ということを彼から心底教わった。

バルセロナで2002年以来続いている「FIRA 2000」メッセ・コンベンションセンターの一環である2本のタワー「トーレス・ポルタ・フィラ」も竣工した。ホテルとオフィスのツインタワーで、ねじれた円形のホテル棟に対し、四角い平面だがねじれたコアをもつオフィス棟によって2本を関係づけた。アースカラーの赤に塗装したパイプによってねじれのラインを強調したが、この赤はカタロニアの人びととの情熱を象徴したつもりである。

- Wins 2009 The Asahi Prize
- Wins The 22nd Praemium Imperiale in Honor of Prince Takamatsu
- Where is Architecture? Seven Installations by Japanese Architects (The National Museum of Modern Art, Tokyo)
- Publishes *Toyo Ito, NA Architect series 01* (Nikkei Business Publications)
- Publishes *Pioneer Forever: Architect Toyo Ito* (Taiwan, Bookzone)

The Belle Vue Residences, a group of condominiums located behind Orchard Road in Central Singapore, was completed. Mr. Edmund Cheng, who represented the client in this project, was also involved in the Vivo City shopping mall project I mentioned earlier. His father left China and sailed for Hong Kong. Edmund is a self-made man who became an independent businessman in Hong Kong and went on to even greater success after moving to Singapore.

After taking a liking to Vivo, he invited me to dinner every time he visited Tokyo. His devotion to gourmet dining is total – Cheng takes photos of all of the sushi materials and jots down memos about where each of them is from. Once he recognized me as a friend, he became completely devoted, inviting me to undertake one project after another. I learned the real meaning of "trust" from him.

The twin towers, TORRES PORTA FIRA, part of the FIRA 2000 Convention Center, a project we began in Barcelona in 2002, were completed. One tower serves as a hotel and the other an office building. While the former has a twisted circular shape, the latter is made up of square planes with a twisted core, creating a link between the two buildings. I accentuated the twisted lines with pipes that are painted a red earth tone. The color is meant to symbolize the passion of the Catalan people.

■ トーレス・ポルタ・フィラ（スペイン、バルセロナ）
TORRES PORTA FIRA, Barcelona, Spain (pp. 184-193)

■ ベルビュー・レジデンシズ（シンガポール、オクスリー・ウォーク）
Belle Vue Residences, Oxley walk, Singapore (p. 230)

■ ゲント市図書館及びニューメディアセンター　コンペティション応募案
Competition for WAALSE KROOK Master plan for the Waalse Krook Area and the Construction of a Library for the Future and Center for New Media in Ghent

■ ベガ・バハ博物館　コンペティション応募案
VEGA BAJA Museum Competition

## 2011年 （所員数48人　studio staff size: 48）

- 70歳
- 事務所設立40周年
- 東日本大震災
- 「みんなの家」第1号が仙台市宮城野区に竣工。その後2014年9月までに11軒が完成
- 釜石市復興プロジェクト会議顧問に就任、その後2012年に同市復興ディレクターに就任（現在に至る）
- 2011年度建築業協会賞（BCS賞）（座・高円寺）
- *Architecture Words 8: Tarzans in the Media Forest* (UK, AA Publications) 出版

3.11東日本大震災、私の建築人生、いや私の人生において最も衝撃的な年となった。2月には「みんなの森 ぎふメディアコスモス」のコンペティションに勝ち、事務所設立40周年のパーティーを「座・高円寺」で催した矢先の出来事だった。また年初めにはNPO法人「これからの建築を考える」を立ち上げて塾活動をスタートしようとしていた直前でもあった。

天井の一部が落下して閉館に追い込まれた「せんだいメディアテーク」に駆けつけた際、市の東側荒浜周辺を案内され、あまりの惨状に茫然とするばかりであった。

「みんなの家」に取り組んだのはこの訪問が契機であった。

- 批判をしない
- どんなに小さな活動でもできることからやる
- 個を超えた個を確立する

この3カ条を自らに課し、小さな活動としての「みんなの家」を始めた。5月半ば、くまもとアートポリスの会議でこの提案をし、協賛を請うた。蒲島知事の決断によってこの年10月には仙台市宮城野区の仮設住宅団地に「みんなの家」第1号が完成した。住

民の人びとをはじめとして、熊本県の役人、設計、施工の関係者が集まっての竣工式では、夜遅くまで酒を酌み交わし、住民手づくりの芋煮が振る舞われた。涙を流して喜んでくれた住民の姿は、いまも脳裡に焼きついている。

- Turns 70
- Ito's office celebrates 40th anniversary
- The Great East Japan Earthquake occurs
- Initiates the "Home-for-All" projects, completing the 3.11 Earthquake – Tsunami Disaster in North Eastern Japan. As of July 2014, 11 "Home-for-All" projects were completed with more underway
- Serves as adviser for the Kamaishi reconstruction conference (and becomes reconstruction director in 2012)
- Wins 2011 Japan Federation of Construction Contractors Awards (BCS Award) for ZA-KOENJI Public Theatre
- Publishes *Architecture Words 8: Tarzans in the Media Forest* (UK, AA Publications)

After the Great East Japan Earthquake occurred on March 11, this year became the most traumatic year in my life as an architect – or rather my life period. In Feburary, prior to the disaster, I won the Minna no Mori Gifu Media Cosmos competition and celebrated the 40th anniversary of my firm with a party at ZA-KOENJI. At the beginning of the year I also launched an NPO to consider the future of architecture and was getting ready to start a private school.

After dashing over to Sendai Mediatheque, where part of the ceiling had fallen in and the facility was forced to close, I was taken to the eastern coast of Sendai. I was simply dumbstruck by the miserable conditions I found there.

This experience led me to start Minna no Ie "Home-for-All." I set out to make it a small project and to impose the following three conditions on myself: 1. Refrain from judgment; 2. Do whatever possible no matter how small the job; and 3. Establish individual units that transcend themselves. In mid-May, at a meeting at Kumamoto Artpolis, I presented the proposal and received approval for the project. Based on Kumamoto Prefectural Governor Ikuo Kabashima's resolve, we completed "Home-for-All" No. 1 in a temporary housing area in Miyagino-ku, Sendai in October. At the completion ceremony, which, in addition to local residents was attended by Kumamoto prefectural administrators, and various people involved in the design and construction of the facility, alcohol flowed late into the night as homemade imoni soup was served. I will never forget the sight of the residents weeping with joy.

■ 今治市伊東豊雄建築ミュージアム（愛媛県今治市）
Toyo Ito Museum of Architecture, Imabari, Imabari, Ehime, Japan (pp. 200-217)

■ 今治市岩田健母と子のミュージアム（愛媛県今治市）
Ken Iwata Mother and Child Museum, Imabari City, Imabari, Ehime, Japan (pp. 218-225)

■ くまもとアートポリス東北支援「みんなの家」（宮城県仙台市）
"Home-for-All" by Kumamoto Artpolis Tohoku Support Group, Sendai, Miyagi, Japan (pp. 328-329)

■ 東京ガス 千住見学サイト　Ei-WALK CONCEPT ROOM（東京都荒川区）
TOKYO GAS Ei-WALK CONCEPT ROOM, Arakawa, Tokyo, Japan

■東京マザーズクリニック（東京都世田谷区）
Tokyo Mother's Clinic, Setagaya, Tokyo, Japan

## 2012年　（所員数47人　studio staff size: 47）

- 神戸芸術工科大学環境・デザイン学科客員教授（現在に至る）
- 第2回スペイン日本評議会賞
- ヴェネチア・ビエンナーレ「金獅子賞」（コミッショナーを務めた日本館が受賞）
- ヴェネチア・ビエンナーレ - 13. International Architecture Exhibition COMMON GROUND（イタリア）
- 『建築の大転換』中沢新一共著（筑摩書房）出版
- 『あの日からの建築』（集英社新書）出版
- Toyo Ito: Forces of Nature (Princeton Architecture Press, USA) 出版

「みんなの家」は妹島和世さんや山本理顕さん、アートポリスアドバイザーの桂英昭さん、末廣香織さん、曽我部昌史さんなどの協力もあって、今日までに東北で11軒、熊本県阿蘇で2軒が使われている。それぞれに受け皿も異なり、運営も独自に進められており、これらをネットワーク化したNPO法人「HOME-FOR-ALL」を起こして支援活動を始めつつある。

「陸前高田みんなの家」はヴェネチアでの建築ビエンナーレ日本館への出展を前提として計画された。建築家 乾久美子さん、藤本壮介さん、平田晃久さんの3氏と陸前高田出身の写真家 畠山直哉さんに私が加わってチームを構成し、現地で「みんなの家」を建てつつ、設計から建設に至るプロセスをヴェネチアで展示しようという試みである。

畠山さんの感動的なパノラマ写真をバックに、百数十点のスタディモデルが日本館を埋めた。極小の1軒の家に注がれた3人の建築家の労を惜しまないエネルギーが来館者に伝わり、金獅子パヴィリオン賞を得ることができた。

- Guest Professor in Department of Environmental Design, Kobe Design University
- Wins 2nd Edition of the Spain Japan Council Foundation Prizes
- Wins Golden Lion for Best National Participation for the Japan Pavilion in the 13th International Architecture Exhibition at the Venice Biennale (serves as Commissioner of Japan Pavilion)
- Exhibition La Biennale di Venezia - 13. International Architecture Exhibition – Common Ground (Venice, Italy)
- Publishes *Great Transformation of Architecture* (co-written with Shinichi Nakazawa; Chikumashobo)
- Publishes *Architecture ever since that day* (Shueisha Shinsho)
- Publishes *Toyo Ito: Forces of Nature* (USA, Princeton Architecture Press)

In the "Home-for-All" project, I received cooperation from Kazuyo Sejima and Riken Yamamoto, the Artpolis adviser Hideaki Katsura, Kaoru Suehiro, and Masashi Sogabe. At present, there are 11 houses in use in the Tohoku Region and two in the Aso area of Kumamoto Prefecture. Each is a different kind of receptacle, and each house is also managed in a different way. I also launched a networking NPO called HOME-FOR-ALL to provide support for the houses.

I designed "Home-for-All" in Rikuzentakata on the assumption that it would be shown in the Japan Pavilion at the Venice Architecture Biennale. With a team made up of the architects Ms. Kumiko Inui, Mr. Sou Fujimoto, and Mr. Akihisa Hirata, and the Rikuzentakata-born photographer Mr. Naoya Hatakeyama, I attempted to exhibit the entire process, from design to construction, as we created a house on site.

With Mr. Hatakeyama's stunning panoramic photographs in the background, we filled the pavilion with several hundred study models. The painstaking efforts and boundless energy of the three architects, minutely focused on this single house, was conveyed to visitors, leading us to win the Golden Lion for Best Pavilion in the Biennale.

■ヤオコー川越美術館（三栖右嗣記念館）（埼玉県川越市）
Yacko Kawagoe Museum (Yuji Misu Memorial Hall), Kawagoe, Saitama, Japan

■釜石市商店街「みんなの家・かだって」（岩手県釜石市）
"Home-for-All" in Kamaishi shopping street, Kamaishi, Iwate, Japan (pp. 330-331)

■陸前高田の「みんなの家」（岩手県陸前高田市）
"Home-for-All" for Rikuzentakata, Rikuzentakata, Iwate, Japan (pp. 332-333)

■東松島「こどものみんなの家」（宮城県東松島市）
"Home-for-All" for children in Higashimatsushima, Higashimatsushima, Miyagi, Japan (p. 333)

□新国立競技場国際デザイン・コンクール 応募案
New National Stadium Japan International Design Competition (p. 228)

## 2013年　（所員数46人　studio staff size: 46）

- 東京藝術大学美術学部建築科客員教授（現在に至る）
- プリツカー建築賞

毎年スイスのバーゼルで開催される時計のフェアのためのパヴィリオンを「エルメス」社のためにデザインした。広大なメッセ会場内の屋内パヴィリオンであるが、鉄骨の2層で構成され、1040㎡もある。木製の斜材を格子に組んでシェル状に湾曲するファサードをつくった。閉鎖的でどぎつい商業カラーに彩られたパヴィリオンの中にあって、エルメスのパヴィリオンだけは木の香りに包まれて暖かく、開放的な空間となった。

このデザインプロセスを通して私はエルメスの企業精神に深い感銘を受けた。特に代表のデュマさんのものづくりへの愛情は、現在のブランド万能の世界にあって異色と言ってよいだろう。そこにはファミリーによって継承された企業の、時代を超越した思想をうかがうことができた。

気仙沼における渡辺謙さんと安藤竜司さん両氏とのコラボレーションも実に爽やかであった。渡辺さんが自ら出資した「K-port」はイベントスペースを兼ねたカフェであるが、いまや地元の人びとの集まる公共空間的な性格を強くもち始めている。単に施設をつくれば人は集まるのではない。つくる人の想いの深さが人びとに伝わった時、人は集まるのだ。

- Guest Professor in Department of Architecture, Tokyo University of the Arts
- Wins Pritzker Architecture Prize

We designed a pavilion for the Hermes company at the annual watch fair held in Basel, Switzerland. The indoor pavilion, located inside the massive exhibition venue, was a 1,040-square-meter, two-floor, steel-frame structure. We created a shell-like curved facade with a lattice of diagonal wooden braces. In contrast to the other pavilions, which were closed and ornamented with garish, commercial touches, the Hermes Pavilion was a warm, open space shrouded in the fragrance of wood.

In the process of designing the pavilion, I was deeply impressed by Hermes' spirit of enterprise. I was particularly touched by CEO Mr. Alexis Dumas' love of manufacturing and what you might call his willingness to stand out in a world where everything has become a brand. From this, I sensed the timeless philosophy at the heart of the company which has been carried on by generations of the same family.

The collaborations I did with Mr. Ken Watanabe and Mr. Ryuji Ando in Kesennuma were also truly refreshing. K-port, an event space-cum-cafe that Mr. Watanabe created with his own money, has taken on a strong character as a public space for local people to gather. Merely creating a facility doesn't guarantee that people will assemble there. They only begin to gather when the depth of the creator's intentions is properly conveyed.

● MU（カトラリー）　MU, Cutlery

■岩沼「みんなの家」（宮城県岩沼市）
"Home-for-All" in Iwanuma, Iwanuma, Miyagi, Japan (pp. 334-335)

■エルメス パヴィリオン（スイス、バーゼル、バーゼルワールド）
Hermès Pavilion, Baselworld, Basel, Switzerland

□M+ Museum Kowloon Cultural District コンペティション応募案
Museum+ / West Kowloon Cultural District Conpetition

■磯谷水産港町一丁目店（宮城県気仙沼市）
Isoya Suisan Minatonmachi 1chome branch, Kesennuma, Miyagi, Japan

■伊東建築塾 恵比寿スタジオ（東京都渋谷区）
ITO JUKU Ebisu Studio, Shibuya, Tokyo, Japan (p. 241)

■葛飾にいじゅくみらい公園 パーゴラ（東京都葛飾区）
Katsushika niijukumirai Parks Pergolla, Katsushika, Tokyo, Japan (p. 045)

□ HOUSE VISION 2013 Tokyo Exhibition「住の先へ―懐かしい未来の家を考える」
HOUSE VISION "Beyond the Residence. Imagining a House for the Nostalgic Future"

■ 台湾大学社会科学部棟（台湾、台北）
National Taiwan University, College of Social Sciences, Taipei, Taiwan (pp.244-261)

■ 松山 台北文創ビル（台湾、台北）
Songshan Taipei New Horizon Building, Taipei, Taiwan (pp.262-273)

■ 釜石漁師の「みんなの家」（岩手県釜石市）
"Home-for-All" for Fishermen in Kamaishi, Kamaishi, Iwate, Japan (p. 336)

■ K-port（宮城県気仙沼市）　K-port, Kesennuma, Miyagi, Japan

## 2014年4月 （所員数46人 studio staff size: 46）

- 2014 Thomas Jefferson Foundation Medal in Architecture
- 『ArchiCreation/建築創作』No.176 伊東豊雄 2014 (Archicreation Journal、中国) 出版

1月に「台中国立歌劇院」の上棟式が行われた。市長以下市議会議員など市の要人も多数出席して上棟を祝った。

ここまで来るのは実に長い道のりであった。2005年末のコンペティション以来すでに9年目を迎えている。実現不可能と諦めかけた時も何度かあった。このプロジェクトの難しさはいろいろあるが、3次元曲面の連続する構造体をどのように施工できるかに集約される。

2次元の曲線をトラスでつくり、それらを組み合わせて3次元の曲面とするトラスウォール工法は、元は日本で開発された工法だが、これほど複雑かつ大規模に施工された例はない。試行錯誤を繰り返しながら一歩ずつ前へ進むしかない。地元の建設会社と日々厳しいやりとりをしながら、ようやくここまで到達できたことに、言葉では尽くせない感慨を味わった。

完成の日を未だに特定できない状況にはあるが、年内に大ホールの仮オープンは決定された。建物周辺の公園部分も一般に開放された。皆が抱き合って感涙を流す日はそう遠くないだろう。

海外でのビッグプロジェクト、台北の「台湾大学社会学部棟」は新学期から学生の使用が始まり、シンガポールでのオフィスタワー「CapitaGreen」や国内でも岐阜で進行中の「みんなの森 ぎふメディアコスモス」などが年内に竣工の予定である。私たちにとって、ここ数年の新しい試みが実現する年で胸踊る。

- Wins 2014 Thomas Jefferson Foundation Medal in Architecture
- Publishes *ArchiCreation No.176: Toyo Ito 2014* (Archicreation Journal, China)

In January, a framework-completion ceremony was held for the National Taichung Theater. The event was attended by countless people, including important officials from the city such as the mayor and members of the city council.

It was a long, hard climb to get to this point. This marks the ninth year since we won the competition in late 2005. There have been several times along the way when it seemed as if the facility would never be realized. There have been a variety of difficulties, but they are primarily related to the question of how to go about constructing a structure consisting of a series of three-dimensional curved surfaces.

Truss-wall construction, in which trusses made of two-dimensional curves are combined with three-dimensional curved surfaces, is a method that was developed in Japan, but it has never been used to make a building as complex and large as this one. After repeated trial and error, we have only been able to move forward one step at a time. And after engaging in strenuous daily exchanges with the local construction company, the fact that we have finally made it to this point fills me with unspeakable emotion.

Though it is still impossible to specify exactly when the structure will be completed, the large hall is scheduled to open temporarily before the year is out. The park that surrounds the building will also open to the public. The day when everyone hugs each other and sheds tears of gratitude is not far off.

College of Social Sciences in National Taiwan University, Taipei has officially opened and is being used by students for the new semester, and Capita Green office tower in Singapore is scheduled to be completed later this year, as is Minna no Mori Gifu Media Cosmos, which is currently underway in Gifu Prefecture. It is a truly heart-pounding year for us as a number of new challenges we have been working on for the last few years will at last be realized.

■ 釜石「みんなのひろば」（岩手県釜石市）
"Park-for-All" in Kamaishi, Kamaishi, Iwate, Japan (pp. 336-337)

進行中

□ 台中国立歌劇院（台湾、台中）
National Taichung Theater, Taichung, Taiwan (pp. 344-375)

□ CapitaGreen（シンガポール、マーケットストリート）
CapitaGreen, Market Street, Singapore (pp. 288-299)

□ バロックミュージアム・プエブラ（メキシコ、プエブラ）
Barroco Museo Internacional, Puebla, Mexico (pp.310-319)

□ みんなの森 ぎふメディアコスモス（岐阜県岐阜市）
Minna no Mori Gifu Media Cosmos (tentative title), Gifu, Gifu, Japan (pp. 274-287)

□ （仮称）新青森県総合運動公園陸上競技場（青森県青森市）
New Athletic Field and Sports Park in Aomori (tentative title), Aomori, Aomori, Japan

□ （仮称）川口市火葬施設・赤山歴史自然公園（埼玉県川口市）
Crematorium and Akayama Historic Nature Park in Kawaguchi (tentative title), Kawaguchi, Saitama, Japan (pp. 300-309)

□ （仮称）富邦人壽台中文心ビル（台湾、台中）
Fubon Life Insurances Taichung Wenxin Office Building (tentative title), Taichung, Taiwan

□ The Crest（シンガポールコンドミニアムプロジェクト）（シンガポール、プリンスチャールズクレセント）
The Crest [singapore condominium project], Prince Charles Crescent, Singapore (p. 231)

□ 富邦天空樹（台湾、台中）　Fubon Sky Tree, Taichung, Taiwan

□ （仮称）山梨学院大学国際リベラルアーツ学部（山梨県甲府市）
International College of Liberal Arts, Yamanashi Gakuin University (tentative title), Kofu, Yamanashi, Japan

□ 南洋理工大学学生寮計画（シンガポール、ナンヤン）
Residential Hall at Nanyang Drive for Nanyang Technological University, Nanyang, Singapore (p. 236)

# Staff List
スタッフリスト

## 現スタッフ
### Current Staff Members

伊東豊雄　Toyo Ito
泉 洋子　Yoko Izumi
古林豊彦　Toyohiko Kobayashi
伊藤 淳　Atsushi Ito
藤江 航　Wataru Fujie
大宮由紀子　Yukiko Omiya
澤村圭介　Keisuke Sawamura
水沼晴昭　Yasuaki Mizunuma
庵原義隆　Yoshitaka Ihara
● 矢部倫太郎　Rintaro Yabe
小針修一　Shuichi Kobari
佐野健太　Kenta Sano
大賀淳史　Junji Oga
■ 岡野道子　Michiko Okano
■ 樽谷 敦　Atsushi Tarutani
ニルス・ベッカー　Nils Becker
南 俊允　Toshimitsu Minami
近藤奈々子　Nanako Kondo
● 伊東美也　Miya Ito
● 磯田和明　Kazuaki Isoda
大原央行　Takayuki Ohara Martinez
竹内 啓　Kei Takeuchi
池田耕三　Kozo Ikeda
郷野正広　Masahiro Gouno
木下栄理子　Eriko Kinoshita
山田有彦　Yugo Yamada
● 井上智香子　Chikako Inoue
● 福田陽之輔　Yonosuke Fukuda
● 髙池葉子　Yoko Takaike
方 薇雅　Wei-ya Fang
ジュリア・リー・カ・イ　Julia Li Ka Yee
● 玉木浩太　Kota Tamaki
中村裕太　Yuta Nakamura
矢吹光代　Mitsuyo Yabuki
● 福西健太　Kenta Fukunishi
高橋真未　Mami Takahashi
● 長曽我部 亮　Ryo Chosokabe
● 高塚順旭　Nobuaki Takatsuka
● 山田明子　Meiko Yamada
中島成隆　Shigetaka Nakajima
● 林 盛　Sei Hayashi

青柳有依　Yui Aoyagi
太田由真　Yuma Ota
ルイ・イギェホン　Rui Igieon
井上裕之　Hiroyuki Inoue

## 旧スタッフ
### Former Staff Members

祖父江義郎　Yoshiro Sofue
柴田牧子　Makiko Shibata
石田敏明　Toshiaki Ishida
柴田いづみ　Izumi Shibata
片倉保夫　Yasuo Katakura
飯村和道　Kazumichi Iimura
妹島和世　Kazuyo Sejima
小宮 功　Isao Komiya
桑原立郎　Tatsuo Kuwahara
城戸崎和佐　Nagisa Kidosaki
二瓶 稔　Minoru Nihei
佐々木勉　Tsutomu Sasaki
佐藤光彦　Mitsuhiko Sato
小池ひろの　Hirono Koike
奥瀬公子　Kimiko Okuse
曽我部昌史　Masashi Sogabe
手塚義明　Yoshiaki Tezuka
徳永照久　Teruhisa Tokunaga
アストリッド・クライン　Astrid Klein
マーク・ダイサム　Mark Dytham
鈴木優子　Yuko Suzuki
横溝 真　Makoto Yokomizo
篠﨑健一　Kenichi Shinozaki
冨永 謙　Ken Tominaga
伊藤文子　Fumiko Ito
上條美枝　Yoshie Kamijo
佐藤京子　Kyoko Sato
石津麻里子　Mariko Ishizu
中村康造　Kozo Nakamura
ムーン・ギュー・チョイ　Moongyu Choi
柳澤 潤　Jun Yanagisawa
桜本まゆみ　Mayumi Sakuramoto
堀 達浩　Tatsuhiro Hori
竹内申一　Shinich Takeuchi
田畑美穂　Miho Tabata
福島加津也　Katsuya Fukushima

安田光男　Teruo Yasuda
奥矢 恵　Megumi Okuya
瀬尾拓広　Takuhiro Seo
高山正行　Masayuki Takayama
赤松純子　Junko Akamatsu
井上雅宏　Masahiro Inoue
高橋直子　Naoko Takahashi
荒木研一　Kenichi Araki
塚田修大　Nobuhiro Tsukada
久保田顕子　Akiko Kubota
関口惠津　Etsu Sekiguchi
松原弘典　Hironori Matsubara
平田晃久　Akihisa Hirata
式地香織　Kaori Shikichi
横田歴男　Leo Yokota
西村麻利子　Mariko Nishimura
細谷浩美　Hiromi Hosoya
中山英之　Hideyuki Nakayama
多羅尾 希　Nozomi Tarao
高塚章夫　Akio Takatsuka
金本智香子　Chikako Kanamoto
赤崎光基　Koki Akasaki
末光弘和　Hirokazu Suemitsu
三好隆之　Takayuki Miyoshi
青島琢治　Takuji Aoshima
横川雄一　Yuichi Yokokawa
中原英隆　Hidetaka Nakahara
白川 在　Zai Shirakawa
篠崎弘之　Hiroyuki Shinozaki
橋本朋子　Tomoko Hashimoto
クリストフ・セラリウス　Christoph Cellarius
アンドリュー・バーリー　Andrew Barrie
森畑孝幸　Takayuki Morihata
錦織真也　Maya Nishikori
平山高康　Takayasu Hirayama
足立 拓　Taku Adachi
木上理恵　Rie Kigami
秋山隆浩　Takahiro Akiyama
フロリアン・ブッシュ　Florian Busch
御手洗 龍　Ryu Mitarai
魚野美紀　Miki Uono
渡邊 弾　Dan Watanabe
鵜飼恵三子　Emiko Ukai
田邊 曜　Hikaru Tanabe
森山ちはる　Chiharu Moriyama

前田健太郎　Kentaro Maeda
福田 誠　Makoto Fukuda
星島美完　Minori Hoshijima
喜多 裕　Yutaka Kita
アンドレ・ギモンド　Andre Guimond
髙橋麻実　Asami Takahashi
百田有希　Yuki Hyakuda
花岡徳秋　Noriaki Hanaoka
林 俐廷　Lin Li-Ting
林 宜佩　Lin Yi Pei

※●は6〜10のインタビュアー
Numbers (6-10) indicate those who conducted the interviews in each of the five sections of the book.

# Credits
クレジット

## 写真 Photographs

Iwan Baan
p. 7, p. 250, p. 251 top, pp. 252-253, p. 362, p. 364, p. 365 middle, p. 368, p. 369 top, p. 371 bottom, p. 372, p. 373 bottom, pp. 374-375, p. 386 right row middle, and p. 388 right row upper

大橋富夫 Tomio Ohashi
p. 47 bottom, p. 48 top, p. 145 bottom, p. 151, pp. 154-155, and p. 383 middle row

CHRISTIAN GAHL
p. 52 bottom

ナカサ・アンド・パートナーズ Nacasa & Partners
pp. 54-55, pp. 64-65, p. 80 bottom, pp. 92-94, p. 98, and p. 100 top left, bottom left

Stefaan Ysenbrand
p. 57

上田宏 Hiroshi Ueda
pp. 84-85

坂口裕康 A to Z Hiroyasu Sakaguchi A to Z
p. 86 top, and p. 87

竹中工務店 Takenaka Corporation
pp. 102-103, p. 105, pp. 112-113, p. 114 top, and p. 115

福岡市 Fukuoka City
p. 110 bottom

阿野太一 Daici Ano
p. 136, p. 166, pp. 200-205, p. 214, pp. 216-219, p. 220 top, p. 222, pp. 224-225, and p. 388 middle row

石黒写真研究所 Ishiguro Photographic Institute
pp. 140-141, p. 142, p. 145 top, p. 148, p. 149 top, bottom left, p. 150, p. 152, and p. 153 bottom

提供：多摩美術大学 Courtesy of Tama Art University
写真：伊奈英次 Photo by Eiji Ina
p. 149 bottom right

港千尋 Chihiro Minato
p. 153 top

撮影：陳弘暐 David Chen
写真提供：互助營造 Fu Tsu Construction
pp. 170-174, pp. 176-177, and pp. 180-183

互助營造 Fu Tsu Construction
p. 256

中村絵 Kai Nakamura
p. 208 middle and, bottom, p. 209-210, pp. 212-213, p. 240 bottom, pp. 244-245, p. 247, p. 258, pp. 260-263, p. 265, p. 266 top, bottom left, p. 269, p. 270, pp. 272-273, p. 279, p. 281, p. 284, pp. 286-287, p. 336 left row fourth, pp. 346-347, pp. 356-359, and p. 388 left row

畠山直哉 Naoya Hatakeyama
p. 326 third row, p. 332 top, bottom right and p. 333 left row bottom

仙台市 Sendai City
p. 329 bottom left

インフォコム INFOCOM
p. 335

kentauros yasunaga (parade.inc)
p. 371 top

HORM
p. 383 right row second, p. 384 left row bottom, and p. 385 middle row upper, and second

アーキテクチャー・フォー・ヒューマニティ Architecture for Humanity
p. 336 right row top, third and bottom

浅田恒穂 Tsuneho Asada
p. 384 left row top

Wim te Brake
p. 384 right row top

Luuk Kramer
p. 384 right row second

小野祐次 Yuji Ono
p. 385 right row upper

提供：東京ガス Courtesy of TOKYO GAS
p. 387 right row

## 図版 Drawings

CG

kuramochi + oguma
p. 236 bottom, p. 288, p. 297 middle row, p. 298 bottom, p. 299, pp. 310-311, pp. 318-319, p. 363 top, p. 365 top and bottom, p. 369 bottom, p. 373 top, p. 386 right row bottom, p. 388 right row bottom, p. 389 middle row, and right row

ブロック・パーティー BROCK PARTY
p. 294, p. 306, and p. 307 bottom

Javier Cudazzo Trillo (Estudio-33)
pp. 316-317

解析図 Analysis

佐々木睦朗構造計画研究所 Sasaki Structural Consultants
p. 108, and p. 123 top

竹中工務店 Takenaka Corporation
p. 180 second and bottom

Arup
p. 285 bottom

上記以外は伊東豊雄建築設計事務所
Images / figures other than the above were provided by Toyo Ito & Associates, Architects.

＊数点に限り著作権が完全に判明しないものがありました。お心当たりの方は編集部までご連絡ください。
* The copyright holders could not be fully identified for several items. To provide this information, please contact our editorial department.

## 翻訳 Translations

英訳 Original English translation

渡辺洋 Hiroshi Watanabe
序文、対談、伊東豊雄との対話、カバー
Introduction, conversation with Toyo Ito and cover

Christopher Stephens
キャプション（1章〜8章、10章）、作品データ、年表
Caption (chapter 1-8, chapter 10 and data on works chronology)

伊東豊雄建築設計事務所
Toyo Ito & Associates, Architects
キャプション（9章） Caption (chapter 9)

英文文責
Responsible for the English wording and content of this publication

伊東豊雄建築設計事務所
Toyo Ito & Associates, Architects

## 編集協力 Editorial Cooperation

伊東豊雄建築設計事務所
Toyo Ito & Associates, Architects

南風舎 Nampoosha

伊東豊雄の建築 2 2002-2014

2014年10月29日 初版第1刷発行

著者：伊東豊雄
発行者：加藤徹
発行所：TOTO出版（TOTO株式会社）
　〒107-0062 東京都港区南青山1-24-3 TOTO乃木坂ビル2F
　［営業］TEL：03-3402-7138　FAX：03-3402-7187
　［編集］TEL：03-3497-1010
　URL：http://www.toto.co.jp/publishing/
アートディレクション＆デザイン：ASYL（佐藤直樹＋菊地昌隆）
印刷・製本：図書印刷株式会社

落丁本・乱丁本はお取り替えいたします。
本書の全部又は一部に対するコピー・スキャン・デジタル化等の無断複製行為は、著作権法上での例外を除き禁じます。本書を代行業者等の第三者に依頼してスキャンやデジタル化することは、たとえ個人や家庭内での利用であっても著作権法上認められておりません。
定価はカバーに表示してあります。

© 2014　Toyo Ito

Printed in Japan
ISBN978-4-88706-346-4

# TOYO ITO 2　2002-2014

First published in Japan on October 29, 2014

Author: Toyo Ito
Publisher: Toru Kato
TOTO Publishing (TOTO LTD.)
　TOTO Nogizaka Bldg., 2F,
　1-24-3 Minami-Aoyama, Minato-ku,
　Tokyo 107-0062, Japan
　[Sales] Telephone: +81-3-3402-7138　Facsimile: +81-3-3402-7187
　[Editorial] Telephone: +81-3-3497-1010
　URL: http://www.toto.co.jp/publishing/
Art Director and Designer: ASYL Naoki Sato + Masataka Kikuchi
Printer: Tosho Printing Co.,Ltd.

All rights reserved. No part of this book may be photocopied, scanned, digitized, or otherwise reproduced, aside from rare exceptions, as stipulated by copyright law. The scanning or digitizing of the book, even for personal or home use, by a third party is also strictly prohibited under copyright law.

ISBN978-4-88706-346-4